ZAGAT®

World's Top Hotels, Resorts & Spas

2007/08

EDITORS
Donna Marino Wilkins and David Downing

Published and distributed by
Zagat Survey, LLC
4 Columbus Circle
New York, NY 10019
T: 212.977.6000
E: travel@zagat.com
www.zagat.com

ACKNOWLEDGMENTS

We thank Steven Amsterdam, Tina Barseghian, Linda Burbank, Andy Collins, Constance Jones, Lori Midson, Mary Papenfuss, Sandra Ramani, John Rambow, Shelley Skiles Sawyer, Amy Serafin, Kerry Speckman and Alice Van Housen, as well as the following members of our staff: Josh Rogers (assistant editor), Sean Beachell, Maryanne Bertollo, Sandy Cheng, Reni Chin, Larry Cohn, Bill Corsello, Carol Diuguid, Caitlin Eichelberger, Victoria Elmacioglu, Jeff Freier, Caroline Hatchett, Roy Jacob, Natalie Lebert, Mike Liao, Dave Makulec, Emily Parsons, Andre Pilette, Becky Ruthenburg, Thomas Sheehan, Kilolo Strobert, Sharon Yates and Kyle Zolner.

We are especially appreciative to the American Society of Travel Agents, thanks to whose cooperation we have had the professional input of over 900 travel agents and meeting planners.

Contents

About This Survey

Here are the results of our **2007/08 World's Top Hotels, Resorts & Spas Survey,** covering 1,287 of the best places to stay in major cities and resort areas around the globe, including for the first time 147 of the best hotels in the U.S. Like all our guides, this one is based on the collective opinions of thousands of savvy consumers and is designed to help you make smart choices about where to spend your time and money.

HELPFUL LISTS: Whether you're traveling for business or planning the vacation of a lifetime, our lists can help you zero in on exactly the right place to stay. See Dialing Codes (page 9), Useful Web Sites & U.S. Toll-Free Numbers (page 10) and Top Ratings lists (pages 15–22). We've also provided 30 handy indexes (pages 315–396).

WHO PARTICIPATED: Input from 21,783 avid travelers and 1,626 travel agents and meeting planners forms the basis for the ratings and reviews in this guide (their comments are shown in quotation marks within the reviews). Of these surveyors, 51% are men, 49% women; the breakdown by age is 10% in their 20s; 28%, 30s; 23%, 40s; 23%, 50s; and 16%, 60s or above. They stayed at hotels an average of 36.9 nights per year, collectively bringing an annual total of roughly 803,000 nights worth of experience to this Survey. We sincerely thank each of these participants – this book is really "theirs." We're especially grateful to the American Society of Travel Agents, through whom we gained the participation of so many travel professionals. We are proud to have the benefit of their in-depth knowledge and expertise.

ABOUT ZAGAT: This marks our 28th year reporting on the shared experiences of consumers like you. What started in 1979 as a hobby involving 200 people rating NYC restaurants has come a long way. Today we have over 250,000 surveyors and now cover dining, entertaining, golf, hotels, movies, music, nightlife, resorts, shopping, spas, theater and tourist attractions worldwide.

MAKE YOUR OPINION COUNT: We invite you to join any of our upcoming surveys – just register at **zagat.com,** where you can rate and review establishments year-round. Each participant will receive a free copy of the resulting guide when published.

AVAILABILITY: Zagat guides are available in all major bookstores, by subscription at **zagat.com,** and for use on BlackBerry, Palm, Windows Mobile devices and mobile phones.

FEEDBACK: There is always room for improvement, thus we invite your comments and suggestions about any aspect of our performance. Just contact us at travel@zagat.com.

New York, NY
April 11, 2007

Nina and Tim Zagat

What's New

$ POCKETBOOKS TAKE A PUNCH: Consumers can expect to pay more across the board for both lodging and transportation this year. France, Germany, Italy and the U.K. have gotten more expensive, particularly for Americans watching the dollar drop against the euro. Better-priced choices include Spain and Portugal, and the new democracies of Eastern Europe. U.S. prices are heating up as well, yet one third of our surveyors report traveling more in the U.S. last year. To help meet their needs, we've added U.S. hotels to this guide, starting on page 276.

BALANCING THE BUDGET: With the upswing in prices, it's not surprising that 29% of our surveyors report an increase in their business travel budgets, and 43% report a rise in their leisure travel spending. In order to save money, 70% turned to the Internet to book their trips, with 95% purchasing airline tickets, 89% reserving hotel rooms and 71% making car rental reservations online. See "Useful Web Sites" on pages 10–12.

PAPER CHASE: While overall global travel has increased significantly since 2000, travel to the U.S. has not quite rebounded to pre-9/11 levels, and it gets a declining percentage of the world's visitors. Onerous visa regulations are contributing to this decline; some estimates put the loss of potential tourist spending at more than $90 billion since 9/11. Travelers from China, Eastern Europe, India, parts of Latin America and the Middle East especially complain about the difficulty of getting a U.S. visa. And in a survey conducted by Discover America Partnership, 39% of 2,000 international travelers said the U.S. has the world's worst entry process, citing long lines, unpleasant immigration officials and fears they'll be mistakenly detained. Meanwhile, about 71% of our surveyors are willing to undergo background checks and pay a yearly fee to speed up trips through security, i.e. use an 'Easy Pass' system. But such a system has yet to be implemented.

TERROR TOLL: Fears of terrorism centered on transport hubs or tourist sites in many countries continued, with 2006 bombing targets including an Egyptian resort and several trains in India. Meanwhile, America's global image has declined as a result of its policies around the world, according to a Pew Research Center study, which found that majorities in 10 major foreign countries believe the Iraq war has made the world more dangerous.

 STRENGTH IN FAVORITES: Even amid fears, the industry is strong in many areas. Switzerland, Austria and Germany are ranked the most attractive environments for travel, according to the World Economic Forum. Our surveyors' favorite international cities continue to be in Western Europe: 26% chose Paris, 19% London and 8% Rome. As for their favorites among U.S. cities, 25% chose New York, 20% Washington, DC, and 17% San Francisco.

SEASONS GREETINGS: Four Seasons continues to outshine its competitors around the globe. Four of the top 10 hotels

6

and six of the top 10 resorts in the world carry that well-trusted moniker. And it is opening lodgings at a fast clip, with two in the Maldives, another in Thailand, a re-branding in Lanai, Hawaii, and upcoming hotels in Dubai, Macau and Pudong, China.

BRANDING RIGHTS: About 16% of our respondents say brand recognition is the main factor in deciding where to stay. Well-known names, within and outside the industry, are drawing on this familiarity to launch new properties. Starwood Capital Group (Sheraton, W, Westin) has debuted a luxury brand called Crillon, after its Hôtel de Crillon in Paris. Starwood is also gearing up for the eco-friendly, five-star lodging, 1. Meanwhile Versace, Armani and Trump are all lending their names to new hotels.

AMENIT-EASE: From bed-sheet menus (four kinds at Mexico's Las Ventanas al Paraíso) to 15 soaps on offer at the Rome Cavalieri Hilton, there's no shortage of goodies at the world's top hotels. This suits our surveyors quite well, since 23% say the amenities offered – be they high-end bath products, digital devices or Internet connections – have the greatest impact on the hotel they choose.

 ALL HOOKED UP: Our surveyors' favorite in-room feature is the now ubiquitous WiFi access (66% of business travelers say it's most important), followed by the morning newspaper (46%). Plasma flat-screen TVs are at the top of the priority list for 20%. Marriott this year rolls out a plug-in panel so guests can connect laptops, video games, camcorders and other digital devices to flat-screen TVs. They'll also add stereo speakers for MP3 players.

PUFFLESS PATRONS: Lodging giants are just saying no – to smoking. And that's just fine with our surveyors, 71% of whom say it's the best innovation they've seen in hotel services. Marriott has banned it in the rooms and public spaces of its U.S. and Canadian hotels, including the Ritz-Carlton chain. Starwood has a similar policy in its Westin hotels in the U.S., Canada and the Caribbean, with penalties of up to $300.

LOOKING EAST: In anticipation of the 2008 Olympics, China is seeing an unprecedented level of development – and it's not just centered in Beijing where the Games take place. The big boom includes new hotels, restaurants and transportation – from the just-opened Shangri-La in Guangzhou and Le Royal Méridien in Shanghai to planned outposts from Kempinski in Wuxi and Huizhou, Mandarin Oriental on Hainan Island, Park Hyatt in Beijing and Ritz-Carlton in Beijing and Guangzhou. Tourism to China is expected to grow a whopping 10%, taking in more than $128 billion, in 2007. Reserve now.

New York, NY
April 11, 2007

Donna Marino Wilkins

Travel Tips

ASK AND YOU MAY RECEIVE: Although occupancies and room rates are on the rise, those consumers who ask for special rates can still find deals. But be sure to call the on-site hotel reservationist directly rather than the toll-free operator. Hoteliers often are ready to deal, especially if your dates are flexible or it's during an off-peak time. Remember, a hotel's "rack rates" are just a jumping-off point from which to negotiate, and don't forget to ask about special promotions, upgrades, etc.

 NET WORTH: The best bargains often reside on the Web, particularly for last-minute lodging. You can get marked-down excess inventory by booking online through individual hotels or via sites such as Expedia, Priceline and Travelocity. Fully 70% of our surveyors book their trips on the Internet, and 37% say Expedia is the best for booking travel (see "Useful Web Sites," pages 10–12).

HIDE-AND-SEEK COSTS: Sometimes a deal isn't a deal once you scratch the surface, so be leery of taxes and extra charges (such as 'resort fees,' valet parking, etc.). Hotel phone charges are especially exorbitant, so use your cell when possible.

LOYALTY PAYS: If you enroll in loyalty programs offered by hotel chains, airlines or affiliated credit cards you can earn free nights and upgrades at your favorite haunts. Many hotels are beefing up the amenities and personalized services they offer their most frequent guests. Take advantage of it.

BEYOND A ROOM WITH A VIEW: Make sure you know what you're getting when you book. There's a tremendous difference in room type, so ask where yours is located, what floor it's on, when it was last updated and what kind of view it has. Also inquire about renovations and any planned events that may disrupt your stay.

QUICK CHANGE: To speed your movement through airport security, wear outer clothing that's easily removable, and slip-on shoes that can be taken off and put back on quickly. If you're traveling with children, use a stroller you can open, close and lift onto a security belt with minimum effort.

HELPING HAND: Even sophisticated travelers rely on the expertise of others. A good travel agent can offer years of experience and contacts that are invaluable. Find one who understands your traveling tastes, and you'll save both time and money.

SPEAK UP: If you're dissatisfied by any aspect of your hotel, don't hesitate to let someone know. A good hotel does its best to rectify problems. If that doesn't work, send a letter to the hotel's general manager, with a copy to "Zagat Survey, Customer Satisfaction."

Dialing Codes

Country and Area Codes are included with each review.

(From the U.S., dial "011" and the country code. Countries marked by an asterisk only require dialing the prefix "1" before the code. To call the U.S. from abroad, dial "001" and the area code.)

COUNTRY	CODE	COUNTRY	CODE
Anguilla*	264	Kenya	254
Antigua*	268	Lebanon	961
Argentina	54	Malaysia	60
Aruba	297	Maldives	960
Australia	61	Mali	223
Austria	43	Mauritius	230
Bahamas*	242	Mexico	52
Barbados*	246	Monaco	377
Belgium	32	Morocco	212
Belize	501	Myanmar	95
Bermuda*	441	Nepal	977
Bhutan	975	Netherlands	31
Botswana	267	New Zealand	64
Brazil	55	Norway	47
BVI*	284	Oman	968
Cambodia	855	Panama	507
Canada*	area code	Peru	51
Cayman Islands*	345	Philippines	63
Chile	56	Poland	48
China	86	Portugal	351
China (Hong Kong)	852	Qatar	974
Colombia	57	Russia	7
Costa Rica	506	Saudi Arabia	966
Curaçao	599	Seychelles	248
Czech Republic	420	Singapore	65
Denmark	45	South Africa	27
Dominican Rep.*	809	South Korea	82
Ecuador	593	Spain	34
Egypt	20	St. Barts	590
Fiji	679	St. Kitts & Nevis*	869
Finland	358	St. Lucia*	758
France	33	St. Maarten	599
French Polynesia	689	St. Martin	590
Germany	49	Sweden	46
Greece	30	Switzerland	41
Grenada*	473	Taiwan	886
Grenadines*	784	Tanzania	255
Guatemala	502	Thailand	66
Hungary	36	Turkey	90
India	91	Turks & Caicos*	649
Indonesia	62	United Arab Emirates	971
Ireland	353	United Kingdom	44
Israel	972	Uruguay	598
Italy	39	Venezuela	58
Jamaica*	876	Vietnam	84
Japan	81	Zambia	260
Jordan	962	Zimbabwe	263

Useful Web Sites & U.S. Toll-Free Numbers

HOTEL CHAIN	WEB SITE	PHONE
Amanresorts	amanresorts.com	800-477-9180
Banyan Tree	banyantree.com	866-822-6926
Best Western	bestwestern.com	800-528-1234
Caesars	caesars.com	800-223-7277
Camino Real	caminoreal.com	800-722-6466
Concorde	concorde-hotels.com	800-888-4747
Conrad	conradhotels.com	800-445-8667
Crowne Plaza	crowneplaza.com	800-227-6963
Dan	danhotels.com	800-223-7773
Design Hotels	designhotels.com	800-337-4685
Fairmont	fairmont.com	800-441-1414
Four Seasons	fourseasons.com	800-332-3442
Hilton	hilton.com	800-445-8667
Holiday Inn	holiday-inn.com	800-465-4329
Hyatt	hyatt.com	800-233-1234
Ian Schrager	ianschragerhotels.com	800-334-3408
InterContinental	interconti.com	800-327-0200
Kempinski	kempinski.com	800-426-3135
Kimpton	kimptonhotels.com	800-546-7866
Leading Hotels	lhw.com	800-223-6800
Le Méridien	lemeridien.com	800-543-4300
Loews	loewshotels.com	800-235-6397
Luxury Collection	luxurycollection.com	800-325-3589
Mandarin Oriental	mandarin-oriental.com	866-526-6567
Marriott	marriott.com	800-228-9290
Millennium	millenniumhotels.com	866-866-6455
Nikko	jalhotels.com	800-645-5687
Oberoi	oberoihotels.com	800-562-3764
Omni	omnihotels.com	800-843-6664
Orient-Express	orient-express.com	800-524-2420
Pan Pacific	panpac.com	800-327-8585
Peninsula	peninsula.com	800-262-9467
Preferred Hotels	preferredhotels.com	800-323-7500
Prince	princehotelsjapan.com	800-542-8686
Radisson	radisson.com	800-333-3333
Raffles	raffles.com	800-637-9477
Regent Int'l	regenthotels.com	800-545-4000
Relais & Châteaux	relaischateaux.com	800-735-2478
Renaissance	renaissancehotels.com	800-468-3571
Ritz-Carlton	ritzcarlton.com	800-241-3333
Rosewood	rosewoodhotels.com	888-767-3966
Sandals	sandals.com	888-726-3257
Shangri-La	shangri-la.com	866-565-5050
Sheraton	sheraton.com	800-325-3535
Small Luxury Hotels	slh.com	800-525-4800
Sofitel	sofitel.com	800-763-4835
Sol Meliá	solmelia.com	888-336-3542
Sonesta	sonesta.com	800-766-3782
St. Regis	stregis.com	800-759-7550
Swissôtel	swissotel.com	888-737-9477

Taj	tajhotels.com	866-969-1825
Westin	westin.com	800-937-8461
W Hotels	whotels.com	877-946-8357
Wyndham	wyndham.com	800-822-4200

AIRLINE

Aer Lingus	aerlingus.com	800-474-7424
Aero Argentinas	aerolineas.com.ar	800-333-0276
Aeromexico	aeromexico.com	800-237-6639
Air Canada	aircanada.ca	888-247-2262
Air China	airchina.com.cn	800-982-8802
Air France	airfrance.com	800-237-2747
Air India	airindia.com	800-223-7776
Air Jamaica	airjamaica.com	800-523-5585
Air New Zealand	airnz.com	800-262-1234
Alitalia	alitalia.com	800-223-5730
American	aa.com	800-433-7300
ANA	fly-ana.com	800-235-9262
Asiana	asiana.co.kr	800-227-4262
Austrian	austrianair.com	800-843-0002
British Airways	britishairways.com	800-247-9297
Cathay Pacific	cathaypacific.com	800-233-2742
China Airlines	china-airlines.com	800-227-5118
Continental	continental.com	800-525-0280
Delta	delta.com	800-221-1212
EgyptAir	egyptair.com	800-334-6787
El Al	elal.co.il	800-223-6700
Emirates	emirates.com	800-777-3999
EVA Air	evaair.com	800-695-1188
Finnair	finnair.com	800-950-5000
Iberia	iberia.com	800-772-4642
Icelandair	icelandair.com	800-223-5500
JAL (Japan Airlines)	japanair.com	800-525-3663
JetBlue	jetblue.com	800-538-2583
KLM Royal Dutch	klm.com	800-225-2525
Korean Air	koreanair.com	800-438-5000
LAN	lanchile.com	866-435-9526
LOT Polish	lot.com	–
Lufthansa	lufthansa.com	800-645-3880
Malaysia Airlines	malaysiaairlines.com	800-552-9264
Malév	malev.com	800-223-6884
Mexicana	mexicana.com	800-531-7921
Northwest	nwa.com	800-225-2525
Olympic	olympicairlines.com	800-223-1226
Philippine Airlines	philippineairlines.com	800-435-9725
Qantas	qantas.com	800-227-4500
Royal Air Maroc	royalairmaroc.com	800-344-6726
SAS Scandinavian	scandinavian.net	800-221-2350
Singapore Airlines	singaporeair.com	800-742-3333
South African	flysaa.com	800-722-9675
Swiss	swiss.com	877-359-7947
TAP Air Portugal	flytap.com	800-221-7370
THAI	thaiair.com	800-426-5204
Turkish Airlines	turkishairlines.com	800-874-8875
United	united.com	800-241-6522
US Airways	usair.com	800-428-4322

| Varig Brasil | varig.com.br | 800-468-2744 |
| Virgin Atlantic | virgin-atlantic.com | 800-862-8621 |

CAR RENTAL

Alamo	alamo.com	800-327-9633
Auto Europe	autoeurope.com	888-223-5555
Avis	avis.com	800-230-4898
Budget	budget.com	800-527-0700
Dollar	dollar.com	800-800-4000
Enterprise	enterprise.com	800-736-8222
Europcar	europcar.com	877-940-6900
Europe by Car	europebycar.com	800-223-1516
Hertz	hertz.com	800-654-3131
Kemwel	kemwel.com	800-576-1590
National	nationalcar.com	800-227-7368
Payless	paylesscar.com	800-729-5377
Thrifty	thrifty.com	800-367-2277

RAILROAD

Orient Express	orient-expresstrains.com	800-524-2420
Rail Europe	raileurope.com	800-438-7245
VIA Rail Canada	viarail.ca	888-842-7245

WEB SITE/TRAVEL AGENCY

American Express	travel.americanexpress.com	800-297-2977
Carlson Wagonlit	carlsonwagonlit.com	800-335-8747
CheapTickets	cheaptickets.com	888-922-8849
11th Hour Vacations	11thhourvacations.com	888-740-1998
Expedia	expedia.com	800-397-3342
Hotels.com	hotels.com	800-219-4606
Hotwire	hotwire.com	877-468-9473
Liberty Travel	libertytravel.com	888-271-1584
Lowestfare	lowestfare.com	800-678-0998
OneTravel	onetravel.com	866-567-3594
Orbitz	orbitz.com	888-656-4546
Priceline	priceline.com	866-925-5373
Site 59	site59.com	800-845-0192
TravelNow	travelnow.com	877-524-7695
Travelocity	travelocity.com	800-249-4302
Travelweb	travelweb.com	800-818-0033
Uniglobe	uniglobetravel.com	800-999-8000
Virtuoso	virtuoso.com	800-401-4274

subscribe to zagat.com

Ratings & Symbols

Zagat Top Spot	Name	Symbols		Zagat Ratings				
				ROOMS	SERVICE	DINING	FACIL.	COST

Location, Contact, Room info	**Ⓩ Tim & Nina's** 👨‍👧 ▽ 18 | 5 | 14 | 22 | $110 Place de la Ville | (1-331) 977-6000 | fax 977-9760 | 800-977-9000 | www.zagat.com | 20 rooms, 2 suites
Review, surveyor comments in quotes	Despite "dazzling views" of the Seine and "lovely public spaces", this "minuscule", "mini-priced" Ile St. Louis boutique hotel splits surveyors; fans tout its "handy location", but critics knock "rooms too small to change your mind", dining at Chez Z that's "outshone by the corner cafe" and a staff "reminiscent of Inspector Javert in a bad mood."

Ratings	**Rooms, Service, Dining** and **Facilities** are rated on a scale of 0 to 30. Properties listed without ratings are **newcomers** or survey **write-ins.**

0	– 9	poor to fair
10	– 15	fair to good
16	– 19	good to very good
20	– 25	very good to excellent
26	– 30	extraordinary to perfection
▽		low response | less reliable

Cost reflects the hotel's high-season rack rate, i.e. its asking price for a standard double room. It does not reflect seasonal price changes or foreign exchange fluctuations.

Symbols	Ⓩ	Zagat Top Spot (highest ratings, popularity and importance)

👨‍👧	children's programs		⛳	18-hole golf course
✗	exceptional restaurant		Ⓢ	notable spa facilities
Ⓗ	historic interest		🎿	downhill skiing
🍳	kitchens		≈	swimming pools
🐾	allows pets		🎾	tennis
👀	views			

Hotel Chains	In the Hotel Chains section, cost in U.S. dollars is indicated as follows:

I	$149 and below
M	$150–$249
E	$250–$349
VE	$350 or more

Top Lists	Except where noted, the score listed is the average of the hotel's scores for Rooms, Service, Dining and Facilities.

Key Newcomers

New outposts by well-established veterans account for most of this year's crop of new hotels and resorts worldwide. Following are some of the most notable arrivals. For a full list of additions to this guide, see the Noteworthy Newcomers index on page 348.

Amanyara | *Turks & Caicos*

Cavas Wine Lodge | *Agrelo, Argentina*

Conrad | *Chicago*

Excellence Riviera | *Cancún*

Four Seasons Resort | *Koh Samui, Thailand*

Kempinski/Moika 22 | *St. Petersburg, Russia*

Le Royal Méridien | *Shanghai*

Le Méridien St. Julians | *Malta*

Mandarin Oriental | *Prague*

Pan Pacific | *Canadian Rockies*

Park Hyatt | *Buenos Aires*

Park Hyatt Saigon | *Ho Chi Minh City, Vietnam*

Shangri-La | *Guangzhou, China*

Sharq Village & Spa | *Doha, Qatar*

St. Regis | *Bora Bora, French Polynesia*

St. Regis | *San Francisco*

W Retreat & Spa | *Maldives*

Westin Bear Mtn. | *Victoria, Canada*

Westin Denarau | *Fiji*

Some noteworthy spots are actually reopenings after renovations or management changes. **The Four Seasons Resort Maldives at Kuda Huraa** finally completed its post-tsunami rebuilding, joining its new nearby sister at Landaa Giraavaru; similarly, **The Ritz-Carlton** in New Orleans debuted after a makeover following Hurricane Katrina. And the **Taj Boston** relaunched after a takeover of the venerable Ritz-Carlton.

Stylish boutiques continue to open, some with big names behind them. Bernard Arnault, chairman and CEO of luxury-goods giant LVMH, opened his first hotel, **Cheval Blanc,** in the ski resort of Courchevel, France. Another chic entrant in a snowy setting is the **Adara Hotel** in Whistler, Canada. And Denmark's **Copenhagen Island** borrows the sleek aesthetic of much smaller spots.

New lodgings on the horizon include lots of action in China with a **Park Hyatt** and a **Ritz-Carlton** to premiere in Beijing, a **Shangri-La** in Chengdu, a **Mandarin Oriental** on Hainan Island and two **Kempinski** hotels – one in Wuxi and another in Huizhou. Elsewhere, new spots will include a **Raffles** in Dubai, a **Peninsula** and a **Ritz-Carlton** in Tokyo and a **Rosewood** on Mexico's Riviera May.

Top Ratings

Overall ratings are shown to the left of hotel names, except where indicated. Excluding places with low voting.

TOP HOTEL CHAINS

29	Amanresorts (18)
28	Four Seasons (73)
27	Mandarin Oriental (21)
	Raffles (13)
	St. Regis (12)
	Ritz-Carlton (63)
	Rosewood (20)
	Orient-Express (38)
26	Oberoi (20)
	Shangri-La (43)
	Luxury Collection (59)
	Relais & Châteaux (377)
	Park Hyatt (25)
25	Leading Hotels/World (430)
	Small Luxury Hotels (400)
24	Kempinski (37)
	Fairmont (50)
	Conrad International (19)
	Preferred Hotels (152)
23	Loews (18)

The above list includes chains with a minimum of 10 hotels (in parentheses is the number of locations). In addition, we've listed prominent marketing groups such as Relais & Châteaux and Leading Hotels of the World. Although there are excellent values among our top-rated chains, many are expensive. The following list features midrange chains with the best bang for the buck.

CHAIN BEST VALUES

1. Camino Real
2. Renaissance
3. Westin
4. InterContinental
5. Marriott
6. Hyatt Regency
7. Hilton
8. Sheraton
9. Wyndham
10. Millennium

With 100 or more rooms, based on Overall score

28 Four Seasons George V | *Paris*
Peninsula | *Chicago*
Peninsula | *Bangkok*
Peninsula | *Hong Kong*
27 Oriental | *Bangkok*
Four Seasons | *Chicago*
Four Seasons | *Budapest*
Mandarin Oriental | *Miami*
Peninsula | *Los Angeles*
Four Seasons | *Las Vegas*
Four Seasons | *New York City*
Four Seasons | *Amman, Jordan*
Windsor Court | *New Orleans*
Mandarin Oriental | *New York City*
Four Seasons | *Philadelphia*
Four Seasons | *Hong Kong*
Mandarin Oriental | *Tokyo*
Four Seasons | *Miami*
de Paris | *Monte Carlo*
Four Seasons | *Mexico City*
Bellagio | *Las Vegas*
Four Seasons | *Boston*
Ritz-Carlton | *San Francisco*
Four Seasons | *Prague*
Ritz-Carlton Central Park | *New York City*
Four Seasons/Nile Plaza | *Cairo*
Four Seasons | *Milan*
26 Park Hyatt | *Tokyo*
Four Seasons | *San Francisco*
Cipriani | *Venice*
St. Regis | *San Francisco*
Ritz-Carlton | *Osaka, Japan*
Plaza Athénée | *Paris*
Ritz-Carlton | *Chicago*
Cape Grace | *Cape Town*
Ritz-Carlton Millenia | *Singapore*
Alvear Palace | *Buenos Aires*
St. Regis | *Shanghai*
Four Seasons Beverly Hills | *Los Angeles*
Wynn | *Las Vegas*
Sukhothai | *Bangkok*
du Cap-Eden-Roc | *Côte d'Azur*
St. Regis | *New York City*
Park Hyatt | *Chicago*
Four Seasons/Chinzan-so | *Tokyo*
Four Seasons | *Atlanta*
Brenner's Park | *Baden-Baden, Germany*
Ritz | *Paris*
Ritz-Carlton | *Santiago, Chile*
Four Seasons | *Buenos Aires*
Le Bristol | *Paris*
Beau-Rivage Palace | *Lausanne, Switzerland*

Westcliff | *Johannesburg, South Africa*
Island Shangri-La | *Hong Kong*
Ritz-Carlton | *Washington, DC*
Four Seasons | *Bangkok*
Çiragan Palace | *Istanbul*
Peninsula | *Beijing*
Four Seasons | *Lisbon*
Ritz-Carlton Battery Park | *New York City*
Mansion/Turtle Creek | *Dallas/Ft. Worth*
Four Seasons | *Shanghai*
Imperial | *Vienna*
25 Merrion | *Dublin*
Le Meurice | *Paris*
Arts | *Barcelona*
Mandarin Oriental/Landmark | *Hong Kong**
Setai | *Miami*
Beverly Hills Hotel | *Los Angeles*
Taj Mahal Palace | *Mumbai (Bombay)*
Raffles L'Ermitage | *Los Angeles*
Mandarin Oriental | *Washington, DC*
Adlon Kempinski | *Berlin*
Four Seasons | *Singapore*
Rome Cavalieri Hilton | *Rome*
Four Seasons | *Dublin*
Peninsula | *New York City*
Mandarin Oriental | *Hong Kong*
InterContinental | *Hong Kong*
Mandarin Oriental | *San Francisco*
Grand Hyatt | *Tokyo*
St. Regis | *Rome*
Table Bay | *Cape Town*
Ritz-Carlton | *Berlin*
Venetian | *Las Vegas*
Four Seasons | *Washington, DC*
Dromoland Castle | *Co. Clare, Ireland*
St. Regis | *Beijing*
Grand/Quisisana | *Amalfi Coast, Italy*
Baur au Lac | *Zurich*
Mandarin Oriental | *Kuala Lumpur, Malaysia*
Ritz-Carlton Huntington | *Los Angeles*
Sofitel Santa Clara | *Cartagena, Columbia*
Four Seasons | *Toronto*
Trump International | *New York City*
Raffles | *Singapore*
Four Seasons/First Residence | *Cairo*
Mount Nelson | *Cape Town*
Monasterio | *Cuzco, Peru*
Claridge's | *London*

---

* Indicates a tie with property above

TOP RESORTS

With 100 or more rooms, based on Overall score

29 Four Seasons/Hualalai | *Hawaii*
28 One & Only | *Baja Peninsula, Mexico*
Four Seasons Wailea | *Hawaii*
Four Seasons | *Canadian Rockies*
27 Burj Al Arab | *Dubai, United Arab Emirates*
Four Seasons Resort | *Guanacaste, Costa Rica*
Halekulani | *Hawaii*
Ritz-Carlton | *Cayman Islands*
Four Seasons Resort | *Provence*
Four Seasons | *Punta Mita, Mexico*
Four Seasons Jimbaran Bay | *Bali*
Ritz-Carlton | *Orlando*
Amarvilas Oberoi | *Agra, India*
Villa d'Este | *Lake Como Area, Italy*
Ritz-Carlton | *Cancún*
Lapa Palace | *Lisbon*
One & Only | *Bahamas*
Datai | *Langkawi, Malaysia*
Four Seasons | *Nevis, St. Kitts & Nevis*
Sandy Lane | *Barbados*
Four Seasons Resort | *Phoenix/Scottsdale*
26 Adare Manor | *Co. Limerick, Ireland*
One & Only | *Dubai, United Arab Emirates*
Fairmont Kea Lani | *Hawaii*
Four Seasons/Lanai | *Hawaii*
Phoenician | *Phoenix/Scottsdale*
Four Seasons | *Red Sea, Egypt*
Banyan Tree | *Phuket, Thailand*
Royal Palms | *Phoenix/Scottsdale*
Four Seasons | *Dallas/Ft. Worth*
Kahala | *Hawaii*
Gleneagles | *Perthshire, U.K. – Scot.*
Victoria-Jungfrau | *Interlaken, Switzerland*
Royal Hideaway | *Playa del Carmen, Mexico*
25 Boulders | *Phoenix/Scottsdale*
Ritz-Carlton | *Bali*
Carmel Forest Spa | *Haifa, Israel*
Grand Hyatt | *Hawaii*
Westin Turnberry | *Ayrshire, U.K. – Scot.*
Ritz-Carlton | *Las Vegas*
Cala di Volpe | *Sardinia, Italy*
Blue Palace Resort | *Crete, Greece*
Ritz-Carlton Kapalua | *Hawaii*
Hayman Island | *Great Barrier Reef, Australia*
Ritz-Carlton Key Biscayne | *Miami*
Sanctuary/Camelback Mtn. | *Phoenix/Scottsdale*
Rimrock | *Canadian Rockies*
Disney's Grand | *Orlando*
Princeville Resort | *Hawaii*
Grand Wailea Resort | *Hawaii*

TOP SMALL HOTELS

With less than 100 rooms, based on Overall score

29 Singita | *Kruger Area, South Africa*
Amanjiwo | *Borobudur, Indonesia*
28 Four Seasons Tented | *Golden Triangle, Thailand*
Como Shambala | *Bali*
Four Seasons | *Chiang Mai, Thailand*
Oberoi Udaivilas | *Rajasthan, India*
Amankila | *Bali*
Gidleigh Park | *Devon, U.K. – Eng.*
Four Seasons Sayan | *Bali*
Blanket Bay | *Queenstown, New Zealand*
Esperanza | *Baja Peninsula, Mexico*
Le Château/St-Martin | *Côte d'Azur**
Amanusa | *Bali*
Las Ventanas | *Baja Peninsula, Mexico*
Rajvilas Oberoi | *Rajasthan, India*
27 Kauri Cliffs | *Kerikeri, New Zealand*
Inn/Little Washington | *Washington, DC*
Kura Hulanda | *Curaçao*
La Casa Que Canta | *Zihuatanejo, Mexico*
Amansara | *Siem Reap, Cambodia*
Il San Pietro | *Amalfi Coast, Italy*
Amanpuri | *Phuket, Thailand*
Mombo Camp | *Okavango Delta, Botswana**
Mount Juliet Conrad | *Co. Kilkenny, Ireland*
Amandari | *Bali*
Londolozi | *Kruger Area, South Africa*
Bodysgallen Hall | *Llandudno, U.K. – Wales*
Bel-Air | *Los Angeles*
Wharekauhau | *Featherston, New Zealand*
Michel Bras | *Aveyron, France*
Four Seasons | *Carmelo, Uruguay*
Inverlochy Castle | *Fort William, U.K. – Scot.*
Amanjena | *Marrakech, Morocco*
Four Seasons | *Istanbul*
Le Taha'a | *Taha'a, French Polynesia*
Palazzo Sasso | *Amalfi Coast, Italy*
Le Toiny | *St. Barts*
Chateau/Crayeres | *Champagne, France*
Sheen Falls Lodge | *Co. Kerry, Ireland*
26 Domaine/Hauts de Loire | *Loire, France*
Hiiragiya Ryokan | *Kyoto*
Gora Kadan | *Hakone, Japan*
Amanpulo | *Cuyo Islands, Philippines*
Château de Bagnols | *Rhône, France*
Explora En Patagonia | *Patagonia, Chile*
Petit St. Vincent | *Petit St. Vincent, Grenadines**
Savute Elephant Camp | *Chobe Nat'l Park, Botswana**
Huka Lodge | *Taupo, New Zealand*
Malliouhana | *Anguilla*
Grand Cap-Ferrat | *Côte d'Azur*

TOP ROOMS

Based on Rooms score

29 Singita | *Kruger Area, South Africa*
Amanjiwo | *Borobudur, Indonesia*
Four Seasons/Hualalai | *Hawaii*
Amankila | *Bali*
Oberoi Udaivilas | *Rajasthan, India**
Rajvilas Oberoi | *Rajasthan, India*
Château de Bagnols | *Rhône, France*
Mandarin Oriental | *Tokyo*
Como Shambala | *Bali*
Four Seasons Resort | *Provence**
Kauri Cliffs | *Kerikeri, New Zealand**
Peninsula | *Chicago*
One & Only | *Baja Peninsula, Mexico*
Amanpulo | *Cuyo Islands, Philippines*
Amanjena | *Marrakech, Morocco*
Four Seasons | *Chiang Mai, Thailand*
Burj Al Arab | *Dubai, United Arab Emirates*
Four Seasons Tented | *Golden Triangle, Thailand*
Peninsula | *Bangkok*
Las Ventanas | *Baja Peninsula, Mexico*
Gora Kadan | *Hakone, Japan*
Le Château/St-Martin | *Côte d'Azur*
La Casa Que Canta | *Zihuatanejo, Mexico*
Mandarin Oriental | *Miami*
Four Seasons George V | *Paris*

TOP SERVICE

Based on Service score

29 Como Shambala | *Bali*
Amansara | *Siem Reap, Cambodia*
Four Seasons Tented | *Golden Triangle, Thailand*
Amanusa | *Bali*
Inn/Little Washington | *Washington, DC*
Le Château/St-Martin | *Côte d'Azur*
Amankila | *Bali*
MalaMala | *Kruger Area, South Africa**
Oriental | *Bangkok*
Seiyo Ginza | *Tokyo*
Singita | *Kruger Area, South Africa*
Amanjiwo | *Borobudur, Indonesia*
Gidleigh Park | *Devon, U.K. – Eng.*
Four Seasons Sayan | *Bali*
Oberoi Udaivilas | *Rajasthan, India*
Four Seasons/Hualalai | *Hawaii*
Amandari | *Bali*
Lapa Palace | *Lisbon*
Four Seasons | *Chiang Mai, Thailand*
Four Seasons | *Amman, Jordan*
Petit St. Vincent | *Petit St. Vincent, Grenadines*
Four Seasons | *Istanbul*
Four Seasons Wailea | *Hawaii*
Peninsula | *Hong Kong*
28 Halekulani | *Hawaii*

TOP DINING

Based on Dining score

29 La Maison Troisgros | *Loire, France*
Michel Bras | *Aveyron, France*
Inn/Little Washington | *Washington, DC*
L'Eau a la Bouche | *Montréal*
Hastings House | *Vancouver*
Singita | *Kruger Area, South Africa*

28 Chateau/Crayeres | *Champagne, France*
de Paris | *Monte Carlo*
Oustau Baumanière | *Provence*
Como Shambala | *Bali*
Gidleigh Park | *Devon, U.K. – Eng.**
Le Quartier Francais | *Franschhoek, South Africa**
Montpelier | *Nevis, St. Kitts & Nevis**
Four Seasons George V | *Paris*
Sharrow Bay | *Cumbria, U.K. – Eng.*
Bellagio | *Las Vegas*
Inn at Langley | *Seattle*
Le Manoir/Quat'Saisons | *Cotswolds, U.K. – Eng.*
Halekulani | *Hawaii*
Royal Palms | *Phoenix/Scottsdale*
Château/Chèvre D'Or | *Côte d'Azur*

27 Four Seasons | *Philadelphia*
Schloss. Bühlerhöhe | *Baden-Baden, Germany*
Las Mañanitas | *Cuernavaca, Mexico*
Hiiragiya Ryokan | *Kyoto*

TOP FACILITIES

Based on Facilities score

29 Amanjiwo | *Borobudur, Indonesia*
Singita | *Kruger Area, South Africa*
Oberoi Udaivilas | *Rajasthan, India*
Four Seasons/Hualalai | *Hawaii*
Blanket Bay | *Queenstown, New Zealand*
Four Seasons Resort | *Guanacaste, Costa Rica*
One & Only | *Baja Peninsula, Mexico*
Amankila | *Bali*
Four Seasons | *Chiang Mai, Thailand*

28 Carmel Forest Spa | *Haifa, Israel*
Four Seasons | *Carmelo, Uruguay**
Chiva-Som | *Hua Hin, Thailand*
Gleneagles | *Perthshire, U.K. – Scot.**
Ritz-Carlton | *Orlando*
Four Seasons | *Punta Mita, Mexico*
Grand Hyatt | *Hawaii*
Four Seasons | *Red Sea, Egypt*
Ritz-Carlton | *Cayman Islands*
Las Ventanas | *Baja Peninsula, Mexico*
Herods Vitalis Spa | *Eilat, Israel*
Kauri Cliffs | *Kerikeri, New Zealand**
Mount Juliet Conrad | *Co. Kilkenny, Ireland**
Four Seasons | *Canadian Rockies*
Burj Al Arab | *Dubai, United Arab Emirates*
Rajvilas Oberoi | *Rajasthan, India*

Based on Overall score

29 Four Seasons/Hualalai | *Hawaii*
28 Esperanza | *Baja Peninsula, Mexico*
Four Seasons Wailea | *Hawaii*
Las Ventanas | *Baja Peninsula, Mexico*
27 Four Seasons Jimbaran Bay | *Bali*
Amandari | *Bali*
Four Seasons | *Carmelo, Uruguay*
26 Phoenician | *Phoenix/Scottsdale*
Brenner's Park | *Baden-Baden, Germany*
Schloss. Bühlerhöhe | *Baden-Baden, Germany*
25 Carmel Forest Spa | *Haifa, Israel*
Chiva-Som | *Hua Hin, Thailand*
Herods Vitalis Spa | *Eilat, Israel*
Blue Palace Resort | *Crete, Greece*
Sanctuary/Camelback Mtn. | *Phoenix/Scottsdale*
Rancho La Puerta | *Baja Peninsula, Mexico*
Grand Wailea Resort | *Hawaii*
24 Park Hotel Kenmare | *Co. Kerry, Ireland*
Mizpe Hayamim | *Rosh Pinna, Israel*
Mandarin Oriental | *London*

HOTEL & RESORT CHAINS ALPHABETICAL DIRECTORY

	ROOMS	SERVICE	FACIL.	COST

☑ Amanresorts

| | 29 | 29 | 28 | VE |

800-477-9180 | www.amanresorts.com

"You'll never make a mistake" if you sleep in one of this "very expensive" chain's 20 locations situated in some of the world's most "stunning" locations, primarily Southeast Asia and the Pacific; voted the No. 1 Chain in our Survey, it consistently delivers "out-of-this-world experiences" via a staff that will "arrange anything and everything you need", "glorious" rooms, a feeling of "exclusivity" and outstanding spas; in sum, this "superlative product" is worth "taking out that second mortgage."

Banyan Tree

| | ▽ 28 | 28 | 26 | VE |

866-822-6926 | www.banyantree.com

"The Rolls-Royce of Asian resorts", these eight "magical" havens have a "delightful" "serenity" say surveyors who salute the "relaxing" hotel spas for which they are famous (home to Thai honey facials, mint footbaths, 'coffee exfoliator' body rubs and Hawaiian lomi lomi massage); staffers "pride themselves on offering guests every amenity", so "you'll never find a bad Banyan Tree" ("the Seychelles location is unparalleled") – but you'll also "never find a cheap one."

Camino Real

| | 23 | 21 | 22 | E |

800-722-6466 | www.caminoreal.com

"Typically very big", the 20 city and seaside properties of this "architecturally interesting" Mexico-based chain (rated the Best Value chain in our Survey) provide "luxury with local character", plus "helpful", "well-trained" staffs; the "always wonderful" facilities "allow the choice of an active or relaxing vacation" (resort revelry may even resemble a "frat party for adults"); however, reviewers report quality "varies" – most are "bright", but "older" ones are occasionally "just ok", with "not so helpful" service.

Conrad International

| | 26 | 23 | 24 | VE |

800-445-8667 | www.conradhotels.com

"At last, a bit of style" applaud aesthetes who approve of these 22 "excellent", "modern" hotels that are "the best Hilton has to offer"; they can be "lovely", especially in the East (Istanbul and Hong Kong earn particular praise), and fans find the food and service "above average", but a few simply label them "boring" yet "efficient" choices that "aren't firmly on the top tier."

Dan

| | ▽ 23 | 23 | 22 | E |

800-223-7773 | www.danhotels.com

It's a mixed bag for this "somewhat variable" Israeli chain whose flagship institution, the "superb" King David in Jerusalem, is "well worth the price", but other more "moderate" outposts "need refurbishing"; the dozen-strong brand appeals to kids with its Danyland children's program (playrooms and supervised activities), and courts the business crowd with "lots of amenities."

Design Hotels

| | - | - | - | E |

800-337-4685 | www.designhotels.com

More an international consortium of cutting-edge boutique hotels than a chain, these 135 "very hip" locations (including London's Metropolitan and Hamburg's 25hours) are "best when you want to be in a magazine spread"; they "emphasize decor", with "well-designed", "stylin'", "unconventional" rooms, but surveyors sigh "if only" the "minimal service" was "up to the level of coolness" – staffers may be "beautiful and well dressed", but could use an attitude adjustment.

Fairmont
24 | 24 | 24 | VE

800-441-1414 | www.fairmont.com

From "absolutely wonderful" resorts to "top-quality" city center hotels to "restored, grand, historic" properties, all imbued with "extra-special service", the 50 outposts in this group come "highly recommended"; "nothing beats the Gold floors for amenities" or the "perks for frequent guests", and though they're "definitely not hip", they are "lovely" enough that some loyalists go so far as to say "they give the Ritz-Carlton a run for its money."

☑ Four Seasons
28 | 28 | 28 | VE

800-332-3442 | www.fourseasons.com

"Still one of the best chains in the business", this "superb" group of 73 hotels aimed at "discriminating travelers" "always exceeds expectations"; expect "impeccable service and facilities that no others can match", "drop-dead locations in the world's best destinations", "exquisite food and wine" at "top-notch" restaurants and even "wonderful" children's services – "if you can afford it", you'll get "the best, period."

Grand Hyatt
22 | 21 | 23 | E

800-223-1234 | www.grand.hyatt.com

"There's a wide range" among the 30 worldwide outposts of this "business" chain – some, especially "outside the U.S.", are "outstanding" with "up-to-date" rooms and "well-maintained facilities", other "older" ones are "charmless" and "convention-overrun", with "rushed" service; still, you can usually expect grand public spaces, including large ballrooms for events, "central locations" and modern fitness centers, plus a Gold Passport frequent guest program that can yield free nights and special offers.

Hilton
19 | 18 | 19 | E

800-774-1500 | www.hilton.com

Being an "HHonors [frequent guest] member", with "terrific" perks like upgrades and room amenities, "makes a difference" at the "commuter train" of hotels, a "consistently reliable", if sometimes "average", choice for a "home away from home"; the 500 outposts may "lack character", but you can "count on them" for "decent value", "central locations", "accommodating service" and "extra effort in recent years."

Hyatt Regency
21 | 20 | 21 | E

800-223-1234 | www.hyatt.com

It's "always a pleasure" to visit one of the 159 locations in this group that boasts "reliably comfortable", "well-equipped" rooms, especially at the "beautiful" resort properties, along with "personal service" and "many amenities and activities"; "locations in some of the best places", "excellent concierges" and "value"-laden promotions that include free nights and breakfasts, plus a solid guest loyalty program, appeal to the convention crowd, but be warned the "food might leave something to be desired."

	ROOMS	SERVICE	FACIL.	COST

InterContinental

| 22 | 22 | 23 | E |

800-327-0200 | www.interconti.com

Sure, this business chain with more than 140 locations is "not as good as the best" out there, but it "continues to upgrade its properties", leading to some "excellent" spots; perfect for corporate types given the "generous-sized rooms" with "great pillows", "quiet halls" and "professional service", it often offers "discounts in some expensive markets" as well; excitement-seekers call these "generally boring", but most maintain "you know what to expect and you get it."

Kempinski

| 25 | 25 | 24 | VE |

800-426-3135 | www.kempinski.com

"An honored European name with a glorious tradition", this 37-strong chain is praised by those who've found its "traditional", "top-notch" properties in "far-flung locations" that include Mali, Bangkok and the United Arab Emirates; with "elegant" rooms, "superior service" and "excellent dining", they're often a "preferred", if "expensive", choice.

Kimpton Group

| 23 | 22 | 20 | E- |

800-546-7866 | www.kimptongroup.com

Each of the 41 U.S. and Canadian locations of this "quirky" boutique chain offers a "unique" spin – from dramatic striped upholstery to playful designs – and all of them are a world "apart from the cookie-cutter chains" (including the "always reliable" Monaco brand); fans flock for the "accommodating service", "impressive use of space", "complimentary happy hours", "luxurious bedding", "pet-friendly" rooms, "gay-friendly" attitude and "chic" scenes, finding "cute" concepts everywhere they look.

⚡ Leading Hotels of the World

| 26 | 25 | 24 | VE |

800-223-6800 | www.lhw.com

"A wonderful collection of gems, each with its own special personality" (e.g. Portofino's Grand Hotel Miramare, Seoul's Shilla), this 430-member worldwide marketing alliance is the stamp of approval that "guarantees a luxury" stay "without disappointment" say its fans; its members are almost "always amazing", from their "exceptional" facilities to their "excellent customer care" and "impressive" locations, but there is some "variability" in the high standards of each, so "pick and choose" wisely.

Le Méridien

| 23 | 22 | 21 | E |

800-543-4300 | www.lemeridien.com

"Breathtaking rooms", "flashy lobbies", "excellent service" and "French class" characterize the 120-plus outposts of this chain that offers "alternatives to the blah business stay"; the "modern" decor attracts a "savvy, suited" corporate crowd, but reasonable rates ("ask for an upgrade when you check-in") make it inviting for leisure lovers too; P.S. "now that it's part of Starwood", most expect them to "upgrade what they offer."

Loews

| 24 | 23 | 23 | E |

800-235-6397 | www.loewshotels.com

The "overlooked gems" of this "interesting collection" of 18 U.S. and Canadian hotels are "fabulous for business" as well as for "families with kids" (they treat children "like gold"); you'll most often find "accommodating staffers", "tasteful decor" and pet-friendly quarters, and if you "join their frequent guest program, you get great amenities" like welcome snacks, free fitness club access, airline miles and room upgrades; N.B. the health conscious like its new ban on all trans fats, right down to items in the minibars.

⊠ Luxury Collection, The
27 | 26 | 25 | VE

800-325-3589 | www.luxurycollection.com

The "best of the Starwood hotels", this upscale collection of 47 includes "always beautiful" resorts like Scottsdale's "enormous" Phoenician and Santorini's Vedema Resort, as well as "high-end" city spots such as Vienna's Hotel Bristol; the "plush" accommodations, service that "spoils" and "top-notch" facilities will require "deep pockets", but with such "incredible wow factors" and all those "upgrade benefits", it'll be worth it.

⊠ Mandarin Oriental
28 | 28 | 27 | VE

800-526-6566 | www.mandarinoriental.com

A "truly top-of-the-line" collection of "fashionable, upscale hotels", the 20 outposts of this Asia-based chain combine "amazing locations, gorgeous rooms", "outstanding service catering to your every whim", world-class, cutting-edge spas and some of the best dining in their respective cities; "exceptional attention to detail" includes high-tech electronics, "swanky" bath amenities and plush terry robes, but stepping into "another world" makes paying the bill in this one "very painful."

Marriott Hotels & Resorts
20 | 20 | 20 | E

800-228-9290 | www.marriott.com

"Never surprising, but never disappointing", the 482 members of this brand are hailed as "consistent no matter where you are", offering "modern rooms" with "delightful new beds", "decent fitness facilities", an "eager-to-help staff" and "all-around good value considering locations" (especially "on weekends"); even critics who cry foul over the "generic feel" say it "pays to be a Rewards Member" for the free breakfasts and other amenities, plus nonsmokers are smiling over the new smoke-free policy.

Millennium Hotels
17 | 18 | 17 | E

866-866-6455 | www.millenniumhotels.com

For a "serviceable", "reasonably priced" stay, head to one of the 101 hotels in this "business traveler's" chain; although there are some "nice city locations" and "helpful staffers", a lackluster loyalty program, "moderate" facilities and locations that need "face-lifts" mean they "aren't the favorite" of most.

Morgans Hotels
▽ 20 | 20 | 21 | VE

800-606-6090 | www.morganshotelgroup.com

These 10 "trendy" spots from the company originally founded by Ian Schrager, who practically invented the boutique concept, are "definitely worth a try" if you're into "funky, fun" small trendsters with the "best bars", "cool public spaces" and "pretentious service"; they get "low marks for tiny rooms" (witness London's St. Martins Lane), but the "great design" and see-and-be-seen scenes woo many a hipster.

	ROOMS	SERVICE	FACIL.	COST

Nikko
| | 23 | 25 | 22 | E |

800-645-5687 | www.jalhotels.com

"Japanese service" "always" come through, "no matter where" in the world you're staying with this "solid business" group of 63 "classy" hotels that is a subsidiary of Japan Airlines; some are pleased by "great lobbies" and restaurants "with Asian flair", but "disappointed" dime-counters say they're "too expensive for what they offer."

Oberoi
| | 25 | 28 | 25 | E |

800-562-3764 | www.oberoihotels.com

"These folks really have it together" in their 20 "exquisite" hotels that bring opulence to far-flung locales, especially their "oases of calm in India" where they're always *the* place to stay"; "they have spared no expense in providing for your needs" with "beautiful landscaping and lighting", spa facilities that astound and one of "the best staffs anywhere"; although they also offer outposts in Indonesia, Egypt, Australia and Saudi Arabia, it's too bad they haven't expanded farther afield.

Omni
| | 21 | 20 | 21 | E |

800-843-6664 | www.omnihotels.com

With "beautiful" lodgings "usually well-located in convenient downtown locations", this 37-member "solid performer" is a good bet if you want "better amenities" at a "price point comparable to the usual business chains"; they're "working hard to improve" their lodgings, which include resorts, landmark city locales and convention hotels, with features such as in-room exercise equipment, WiFi access and discounted rate promotions, but there's some disagreement over service (some say the staff "goes beyond its means to assist you", others that it "could be more attentive").

Z Orient-Express
| | 27 | 27 | 27 | VE |

800-524-2420 | www.orient-express.com

With 38 "crème de la crème" outposts, including Venice's Hotel Cipriani and Lisbon's Lapa Palace, plus six trains and two river cruisers, these "always tasteful and elegant" places are more like "stand-alone luxury resorts than part of a chain" since each "adorns itself with local color"; "giving Four Seasons a run for its money", these "exceptional" – and "exceptionally expensive" – gems target a "well-heeled traveler" looking for "outstanding" restaurants, service and facilities for a price.

Pan Pacific
| | 25 | 23 | 22 | E |

800-327-8585 | www.panpacific.com

The "contemporary luxury" of this Tokyo-based 21-member chain is spread too thin say fans of the "true first-class experiences" found at outposts like Tokyo's Cerulean Tower and a new spot in Chiang Mai, Thailand; highlights include "inviting service", high-quality restaurants, "exceptional rooms" with luxurious bathrooms and a special Pacific Floor with complimentary breakfasts, evening cocktails, butler service and express check-in/check-out.

Park Hyatt
| | 26 | 25 | 26 | VE |

800-233-1234 | www.park.hyatt.com

"Why can't all Hyatts be like this?" inquire impressed guests of this "top-of-the-line" brand that's a "real step up"; its 24 hotels "each have a unique personality" with "intimate" spaces, "a level of service that sets it apart", "up-to-date furnishings" and "high-tech" rooms that make "each and every stay consistent"; indeed, some "plan to live" at one if they "win the lottery."

☑ Peninsula Hotels

	ROOMS	SERVICE	FACIL.	COST
	28	28	28	VE

866-382-8388 | www.peninsula.com

"There really should be more" than only seven hotels in this "gold standard" that boasts especially "oustanding" experiences in Chicago, Bangkok and Hong Kong; loyalists have come to expect its "exceptionally trained" staff, "memorable restaurants", hotel bars with "the finest views" and "people-watching", and "luxurious" rooms with high-tech features like remote controls that operate all the electronics; maybe "paying this much money is ok" when you get a "seamless" experience.

Preferred Hotels & Resorts Worldwide

	ROOMS	SERVICE	FACIL.	COST
	25	23	23	E

800-323-7500 | www.preferredhotels.com

"Everything is exquisite" say fans of the 152 locations in this 40-year-old marketing confederation, "but at these price points they better be"; "typically very impressive" – e.g. Barbados' Sandy Lane, Crete's Porto Elounda – with "first-class service and rooms", the individual members "can vary", so just "check the hotel" to make it "worth every penny."

Raffles

	ROOMS	SERVICE	FACIL.	COST
	27	29	26	VE

800-637-9477 | www.raffles.com

It's not just luck that this "excellent" 13-member chain's "main hotel in Singapore" is "among Asia's best" – it's "loaded with history, intrigue and style"; the expanding outfit has "carved out a niche" in "wonderfully exotic" locations (Cambodia's Grand Hotel d'Angkor, Tahiti's Resort Taimana) with "amazing rooms" and "incredible service", including a "good computer system" that "tracks your likes from hotel to hotel"; N.B. the newest resort opens this year in Dubai.

Regent International

	ROOMS	SERVICE	FACIL.	COST
	▽ 27	27	25	VE

800-545-4000 | www.regenthotels.com

"The bath ritual is heavenly" when you're a guest at one of these 10 worldwide "impeccably appointed" hotels with some of the "largest" lavatories on offer throughout Asia and Europe; appealing to "anyone looking to be pampered" by a "gracious staff" in "excellent locations" (Beijing, Berlin, Kuala Lumpur), they offer a "grand" exerience for most; P.S. those who sigh "too bad they're not a larger chain" will be happy to note the openings of three more in 2007.

☑ Relais & Châteaux

	ROOMS	SERVICE	FACIL.	COST
	26	27	24	VE

800-735-2478 | www.relaischateaux.com

To find "simply the best" hotels and resorts in "stunning", sometimes "out-of-the-way locations" (e.g. Devon, England's Gidleigh Park, the Cote d'Azur's Le Château du Domain St-Martin) loyalists turn to this "highly selective" collection of 456 hotel and restaurant members worldwide that's "always worth trusting"; each "charming" lodging offers "unparalleled", "personable" service, "fabulous" restaurants made for "overindulging" and usually "romantic environments"; indeed, with such "high expectations met", even if you can't "charge it to your expense account", you'll still "never be disappointed."

	ROOMS	SERVICE	FACIL.	COST

Renaissance Hotels & Resorts

`22 | 22 | 22 | E`

800-468-3571 | www.renaissancehotels.com

With 137 "pretty consistent", "people-friendly" properties, this "notch above the regular Marriott" brand is a "pleasant surprise" that "usually treats guests very well" in stylish surroundings; "business" types appreciate the "comfortable beds", in-room work stations, "pleasant facilities" and "wonderful little extras", placing it at the "top of the middle" tier of lodgings.

☑ Ritz-Carlton

`27 | 27 | 27 | VE`

800-241-3333 | www.ritzcarlton.com

With a "well-earned reputation" for luxury, "top-notch" service ("your pleasure, is their pleaure"), "impeccably kept public areas" and "terrific rooms" with "outstanding beds" (especially on their "superb" club level floors), this chain of 63 hotels is where you "reliably turn when you want one of the best a city has to offer" (e.g. the ones in NYC, Osaka, Japan, and Santiago, Chile); even if "the rooms vary by property" and some of the older ones are a "little stuffy", most insist you really "can't go wrong" here.

☑ Rosewood

`28 | 26 | 26 | VE`

888-767-3966 | www.rosewoodhotels.com

The 15 hotels in this "elegant" collection – from Antigua's Jumby Bay to Mexico's Las Ventanas al Paraiso – are "some of the best places in the world" where "your every whim is catered to" and "the most beautiful" rooms can be had; "a rose by any name smells sweet", given their "spectacular settings" and "unique features", including a program that loans guests GPS navigators to more easily find their way around town.

Sandals

`▽ 16 | 21 | 21 | E`

888-726-3257 | www.sandals.com

These mostly "couples-only, all-inclusive resorts" make for "hassle-free" "honeymoons" with "a lot to do", like windsurfing, biking and snorkeling, in 12 Caribbean locations; still, the fun is lost on sophisticated sorts who say these "tired" spots are as "cheesy" as a "Carnival Cruise that never leaves the shore."

☑ Shangri-La

`26 | 27 | 25 | VE`

866-565-5050 | www.shangri-la.com

"Unusually gracious service" ensures a "very solid" stay with this "excellent upscale chain for business or tourism" that usually lives up to its name; reviewers single out the Island Shangri-La in Hong Kong, but appreciate all 44 of these "relaxing oases in stressful Asian cities" and not-so-stressful resort areas – with "lovely" rooms, "amazing restaurants" and "plenty of goodies thrown in"; they "make a person feel rich", though the "hefty bill" might have the opposite effect.

Sheraton

`18 | 18 | 18 | M`

800-325-3535 | www.sheraton.com

"Widely available" with 392 outposts, this Starwood brand draws patrons looking for "convenient locations" and keeps them with "extremely comfortable pillow-top beds" and generally "good service"; but with each spot "varying greatly" – some in dire need of an "upgrade" and others landing squarely in the "about average" category – there's "nothing to write home about here", except the ability to accumulate those "highly desirable" Starpoints.

☑ Small Luxury Hotels of the World | 26 | 26 | 22 | VE |
800-525-4800 | www.slh.com

This marketing alliance of "smaller properties" is so "reliable" you can choose from among its more than 400 members "with your eyes closed" and still be guaranteed an "outstanding experience" – from a staff that "really takes care of you" to "fabulous dining"; the "unique" spots (e.g. New Zealand's Blanket Bay, Paris' Hotel de Vendome) and rooms "vary tremendously", but each will "stay in your memory for years."

Sofitel | 22 | 21 | 20 | E |
800-763-4835 | www.sofitel.com

For a bit of "Euro cool", this "boutiquey" French chain with 200 locations offers a "quiet surprise" with "friendly service", "chic and crisp" rooms boasting their signature down feather beds and "peaceful" environs; "not all" of its outposts are "grand", yet you're more apt to have an "enjoyable" stay than not.

Sol Meliá | ▽ 20 | 19 | 20 | M |
888-336-3542 | www.solmelia.com

Whether seeking an "all-inclusive" resort or a city business hotel, "the sun always shines" for bargain-hunters with this Latin brand boasting 350 properties with "lots of amenities" for not a lot of money; "a reliable, middle-of-the-road choice" for "basic accommodations" and "views", they nevertheless "have a lot to learn about service."

☑ St. Regis | 27 | 27 | 26 | VE |
800-598-1863 | www.stregis.com

"A world of pleasure" awaits "for those who can afford" it say celebrants of this 12-member Starwood brand made up of "stupendous" properties defined by "impeccable" staffs that "treat you like royalty" (and include "fantastic personal butlers"), "tasteful, modern design", upscale spas and "always reliable" restaurants; all of the "understated class" and comfort leaves some who "splurge" on themselves wishing they could "stay more often without putting their retirement in jeopardy."

Swissôtel | 21 | 21 | 20 | E |
888-737-9477 | www.swissotel.com

"Oh-so-Swiss", i.e. "comfortable, clean and practical", this line of 24 "high-class" business hotels "tends to be more modern than others", with "high-tech furniture and gadgets"; some locations, such as Istanbul, come "highly recommended", but others are considered "boring" "has beens" – still, as a member of the Raffles group of properties, there's a similar luxe experience "at a fraction of the cost."

Taj Group | ▽ 24 | 26 | 22 | E |
800-223-6800 | www.tajhotels.com

Led by Ray Bickson, former general manager of The Mark in NYC, this chain with 71 hotels (most on or near the subcontinent) offers guests "the next best thing to being an India maharaja" with "all the creature comforts"; though most, such as the Taj Lake Palace in Udaipur, are super-luxurious and "restful", reviewers also say there "seems to be a variance in quality"; P.S. "if you can't stay there, eat there."

	ROOMS	SERVICE	FACIL.	COST

Westin

23	21	22	E

800-937-8461 | www.westin.com

Regulars of this "dependable" Starwood brand, with 128 U.S. locations, "love" the "sumptuous" Heavenly beds that are "close to heaven when stuck on a long business trip", "bath amenities are a step above their competitors'", fitness areas that let you "have a real workout", frequent-guest perks and the "gutsy" no-smoking policy in some locales; though a few have issues with service, and find "nothing special" at many, overall they're "usually a good value for the money."

W Hotels

22	21	21	E

877-946-8357 | www.whotels.com

"Built for hipsters and wannabes but surprisingly accommodating for business travelers too", this 21-member Starwood group (all but four are in the U.S.) defines itself in "trendy" terms, with "sexy" bars and restaurants, "top-notch Bliss bath products" (and on-site spas) and "luscious robes and linens" in its stylized, though often "infant-sized", rooms; sure, the service can be "cold" and there's often "too much hype and not enough substance", but "even a nerd can feel cool" for a while at one.

Wyndham

18	18	18	M

800-822-4200 | www.wyndham.com

They may "not be terribly unique", "but for the price, you can't beat the quality and accessibility" of this "friendly" group of 89 (and about a dozen under development); fans cite an "excellent frequent guest program" – Wyndham ByRequest – that gives you "personalized amenities that really make a difference" (like your favorite beverage and snack waiting for you when you arrive) plus a staff that "knows your needs"; some outposts are "great", "some not as good", but families love the resorts' kids' programs and all-inclusive packages.

HOTELS,
RESORTS & SPAS
ALPHABETICAL
DIRECTORY

Anguilla

Cap Juluca 🏕️ 🛁 ≈ ✎

| 28 | 26 | 24 | 26 | $825 |

Maundays Bay | (1-264) 497-6779 | fax 497-6340 | 888-858-5822 |
www.capjuluca.com | 35 rooms, 37 suites, 6 villas

"Leave your watch behind", as there's "not much to do" at this "stunning" resort but "roll out of bed" in your "fantastically sexy" room for a "perfect breakfast on the patio" above "your very private piece" of the "most picturesque spot on the planet"; "above and beyond in just about every respect", including "incredible service"and "fantastic food", it "will spoil you for anyplace else" – "no wonder the stars flock here."

CuisinArt Resort & Spa 🏕️ ✕ 🛁 Ⓢ ≈ ✎

| 25 | 23 | 23 | 25 | $685 |

Rendezvous Bay | (1-264) 498-2000 | fax 498-2010 | 800-943-3210 |
www.cuisinartresort.com | 11 rooms, 82 suites

As the name suggests, "the cuisine is the prize", especially given the "amazing" ingredients that come off the property's hydroponic farm; patrons profess the salads were the "best they've ever had", the cooking classes are "not to be missed", the spa facilities are "top-notch", the service is "unbelievable", the rooms are "spacious" – and it's all set on one of the "finest public beaches anywhere"; the only downside for a small majority is that there are "too many kids."

Malliouhana Hotel ✕ 🛁 Ⓢ ≈ ✎

| 26 | 27 | 26 | 26 | $720 |

Meads Bay | (1-264) 497-6111 | fax 497-6011 | 800-835-0796 |
www.malliouhana.com | 36 rooms, 19 suites

Sojourners "breathe a sigh of relief" at this "classy castle on the sea", comparing the bluff-top retreat to "paradise on earth" for its "incomparable" view, "super-friendly" staff, "out-of-this-world wonderful" spa and "quietly elegant" rooms, while extolling the "best wine cellar in the Carribean" and "delectable", "impeccable" dining; some "wish there were fewer children" at the family-friendly resort, but many more promise "you will never forget or regret" a stay here.

St. Regis Temenos Villas 🛏️ ≈ ✎

| ▽ 25 | 24 | 20 | 26 | $5714 |

Long Bay Village | (1-264) 222-9000 | fax 498-9050 | www.stregis.com |
3 villas

Loyalists "love" this small, "exquisite" by-the-week-only spot tucked into a cove on a white sand beach, where the well-heeled choose from three four-bedroom villas, each with Pratesi sheets, infinity pools (and Jacuzzis) and (need we mention?) ocean views and private beaches; other perks include a dedicated butler/chef/concierge, a Greg Norman–designed golf course and a lot of diving opportunities; N.B. above rates are per night based on a minimum weeklong stay.

Antigua

Carlisle Bay 🏕️ 🛁 Ⓢ ≈ ✎

| 26 | 23 | 23 | 26 | $990 |

St. Mary's | (1-268) 484-0000 | fax 484-0001 | 800-628-8929 |
www.carlisle-bay.com | 80 suites

Hotelier Gordon Campbell Gray (London's One Aldwych) is behind this "sleek" spot in the Antiguan rainforest whose "nicely understated" decor includes silk-draped suites with "vistas to die for"; there may be "nicer beaches elsewhere on the island" and service can be "a bit haphazard", but the "privacy", "wonderful food" and "relaxing" vibe are pefect for a "honeymoon"; N.B. the screening room is "a nice perk."

Curtain Bluff Hotel ✕ ♨ Ⓢ ≋ ☙ | 22 | 25 | 21 | 23 | $995 |

Morris Bay | (1-268) 462-8400 | fax 462-8409 | 888-289-9898 | www.curtainbluff.com | 24 rooms, 48 suites

"Like a country club in Connecticut", this "grand old place" on Antigua's southern tip embodies the "relaxing, low-key" "way the Caribbean used to be"; the pink-and-white plantation style is "not on the cutting edge" and the food service "needs attention", but the "local" staff is "attentive", "huge" rooms with beachfront balconies are "kept up to date in all important respects" and the wine list is "excellent."

Jumby Bay ♛ ✕ ♨ ≋ ☙ | 25 | 25 | 22 | 23 | $1150 |

Jumby Bay Island | (1-268) 462-6000 | fax 462-6020 | 888-767-3966 | www.rosewoodhotels.com | 40 rooms, 11 villas

You'll "love taking a walk around the whole island", pausing at "refreshment stops every few hundred feet" at this "wonderful" all-inclusive retreat, a 300-acre private island accessible only by boat with three "glorious" white-sand beaches; it has the "friendliest staff in the Caribbean", as well as "grand" rooms that are "nicely furnished", "amazing food" and "all the water sports equipment" you might ask for; N.B. there are private homes for rent.

Sandals Resort ♨ Ⓢ ≋ ☙ | 19 | 20 | 17 | 20 | $365 |

Dickenson Bay | (1-268) 462-0267 | fax 462-4135 | 800-726-3257 | www.sandals.com | 122 rooms, 71 suites

"Bright, airy and about as characterful as an all-inclusive can get", according to some, this Dickenson Bay spot with a "beautiful" but "crowded" beach draws mixed reviews for service and food that's alternately rated "top-notch" or "terrible", and for facilities that "should be better after renovations"; some fans of the chain call it "one of the nicer Sandals resorts", others say they'd "pass on this."

St. James's Club ♛ ☕ ♨ ≋ ☙ | 20 | 22 | 20 | 20 | $590 |

Mamora Bay | (1-268) 460-5000 | fax 460-3015 | 800-858-4618 | www.eliteislandresorts.com | 187 rooms, 72 villas

The "beautiful setting" on the Caribbean with two white-sand beaches is the draw at this "family-friendly" spot where spacious rooms make you "feel like a king" and the all-inclusive plan includes "brand-name alcohol and good food"; but spoilsports who are "not wowed" say there's "very little to do here" except gamble at a casino that could use a "face-lift."

Argentina

Agrelo

NEW Cavas Wine Lodge ✕ ♨ Ⓢ ≋ ▽ | 24 | 26 | 26 | 23 | $350 |

Costa Flores | (011-54-261) 410-6927 | fax 410-6927 | www.cavaswinelodge.com | 14 villas

Oenophiles find "paradise in a vineyard" at this "simply stunning" hotel "worth going to Mendoza for" that's "set in the midst" of 35 acres of grapevines; individual "peaceful" villas have "private plunge pools, outdoor showers" and patios facing the Andes, while the spa is set in the Spanish colonial main house and offers vinotherapy treatments; P.S. "be sure to have dinner" at the South American Cavas Wine Lounge.

Buenos Aires

[Z] Alvear Palace Hotel 🍴Ⓢ🏊

ROOMS	SERVICE	DINING	FACIL.	COST
27	28	25	25	$550

Ave. Alvear 1891 | (011-54-11) 4808-2100 | fax 4804-0034 | 800-4444-683 | www.alvearpalace.com | 110 rooms, 85 suites

"Feel like deposed royalty in this grand pile of gilt and marble", a "beautiful old classic" in Recoleta that's in a "pleasant time warp"; when you're in the city's "best neighborhood", "flanked by expensive" boutiques, a "super-posh" vibe comes naturally – from service that's "hard to beat" to "very comfortable" rooms, some with "outsize baths" and "plasma TVs" to dining so good you'll want to return "just to have dinner again"; all in all, most "don't want to leave this marvelous facility."

Caesar Park 🔭🏊

ROOMS	SERVICE	DINING	FACIL.	COST
23	22	20	20	$330

Posadas 1232 Capital Federal | (011-54-11) 4819-1100 | fax 4819-1121 | 877-223-7272 | www.caesar-park.com | 168 rooms, 4 suites

With a "*muy magnifico*" location right on Posadas Street in the city's most fashionable area, this chain tower offers "a nice option in Buenos Aires"; while it "has less character" and isn't as "glam" as its competitors, rooms are "clean and well kept", service is "hospitable" and there are five dining options, plus a pool with a fitness center; P.S. thrifty tippers tout the "frequent special rates."

Claridge 🔭Ⓢ🏊

ROOMS	SERVICE	DINING	FACIL.	COST
17	23	21	19	$350

Calle Tucumán 535 | (011-54-11) 4314-2020 | fax 4314-7700 | www.claridge.com.ar | 146 rooms, 6 suites

"You could imagine Cole Porter" crooning at this "quaint, British-type" property that's been holding its own near the Calle Florida shopping district since the 1940s; recent updates have added contemporary touches like gastronomic festivals, a full gym with "trainers" and a heated outdoor pool, and cell phones for guests (with free incoming calls); still, critics concur that despite "lots of personality", a "great old bar" and "service that matches the ambiance", "rooms need sprucing."

Four Seasons 🍴🔭🏊

ROOMS	SERVICE	DINING	FACIL.	COST
27	27	24	26	$310

Posadas 1086 | (011-54-11) 4321-1200 | fax 4321-1201 | www.fourseasons.com | 138 rooms, 27 suites

A "polite, well-trained staff" that "makes you feel like part of the family" leads loyalists to label this "gorgeous" hotel "better than home"; "modern rooms" are "spacious" and "luxurious", the location in Recoleta comes with "wonderful unobstructed views of the city" and is "perfect for shopping", the spa offers "oustanding massages" and the "superb" dining goes far beyond "the typical beef dinners"; N.B. next to the tower is a belle-epoque "château" that houses the highest-end rooms.

InterContinental Ⓢ🏊

ROOMS	SERVICE	DINING	FACIL.	COST
23	22	20	22	$180

809 Moreno St. | (011-54-11) 4340-7100 | fax 4340-7199 | 800-327-0200 | www.intercontinental.com | 299 rooms, 10 suites

A "solid business hotel" with "standards that remain high", this Gaslight District spot sports "large rooms" with satellite TVs, "delicious buffet breakfasts" and "superb service"; but a few sticklers suggest it's getting "a little worn around the edges" and the "location away from the city center" becomes "slightly dodgy at night."

[NEW] Park Hyatt 🫖🐕Ⓢ🏊

Rooms	Service	Dining	Facil.	Cost
25	25	22	24	$380

Ave. Alvear 1661 | (011-54-11) 5171-1234 | fax 5171-1235 | www.park.hyatt.com | 126 rooms, 39 suites

Partly set in a palace, this "minimalist" newcomer is "as good as they say" and fits right in with its "ritzy Recoleta" neighbors; expect "great character" in its "gorgeous" heavily "marbled lobby" with a Baccarat chandelier, along with "excellent meeting facilities", a 25-meter swimming pool, an "exquisite" art gallery and a "friendly", "impeccable" staff; the "up-to-the-second", high-tech quarters, decorated in soothing neutral tones, boast WiFi and flat-screen TVs, but the "dining room is still a work in progress."

Park Tower 🔭Ⓢ🏊🎾

Rooms	Service	Dining	Facil.	Cost
25	25	21	23	$410

Ave. Leandro N. Alem 1193 | (011-54-11) 4318-9100 | fax 4318-9150 | 800-325-3589 | www.luxurycollection.com | 164 rooms, 17 suites

Part of Starwood's Luxury Collection, this often "overlooked" "lovely hotel" close to Calle Florida and the train station is "the place to be" say devotees drawn to its "sumptuous" Biedermeier-influenced rooms boasting "great views" and Italianate baths with "the most romantic use of stone"; expect an "excellent breakfast buffet" and "first-class" service to match the "truly elegant surroundings" that include a tiled indoor pool and fitness center.

Patagonia

Llao Llao Hotel & Resort, Golf - Spa 👫🍴🔭⛳Ⓢ⛷🏊

Rooms	Service	Dining	Facil.	Cost
22	24	23	26	$395

Ave. Ezequiel Bustillo, Km. 25 | Bariloche | (011-54-2944) 448-530 | fax 445-781 | www.llaollao.com | 147 rooms, 11 suites, 1 cabin

With an "incomparable location" amid "lakes and snow-capped mountains", this grand log hotel with "extraordinary service" is "like a Swiss resort" "in the lap of Patagonia", featuring local stone and other "natural materials" throughout; you'll yodel with glee over the "breathtaking views" and enjoy "activities that suit every guest", including an 18-hole golf course and "excellent" spa services.

Aruba

Aruba Resort, Spa & Casino 👫🔭Ⓢ🏊🎾

Rooms	Service	Dining	Facil.	Cost
19	20	19	22	$399

Palm Beach | (011-297) 586-4466 | fax 586-0928 | 800-427-6144 | www.arubaresortspa.com | 402 rooms, 79 suites

The former "Windy Wyndham", now Westin, is notable for its "constant breeze" (it's like "sitting in a wind tunnel" when you're on the beach), but it still wins fans for its "beautiful free-form pool", "lots of interesting tropical birds" and a staff that goes "completely out of its way"; "pleasant enough" rooms and "so-so" dining are less impressive, but hopeful sorts "anticipate a vast improvement" under the new management.

	ROOMS	SERVICE	DINING	FACIL.	COST
Divi Aruba Beach Resort	17	18	16	18	$476
Hyatt Regency	22	23	23	26	$480
Marriott Resort & Stellaris Casino	23	22	20	25	$449
Marriott's Aruba Ocean Club	25	21	19	24	$580
Radisson Resort & Casino	22	22	21	25	$499
Renaissance Aruba Resort & Casino	19	20	19	21	$465

Divi Aruba Beach Resort 🔭Ⓢ🏊

J.E. Irausquin Blvd. 45 | Oranjestad | (011-297) 525-5200 | fax 525-5203 | 800-554-2008 | www.diviaruba.com | 203 rooms

Reviewers are divided over this "definitely not luxury" property with "no building higher than a palm tree" on the "best beach in Aruba"; while some insist it's "not bad for an all-inclusive" and "offers a lot for the price", others sigh over "just ok" rooms, "slightly cheesy entertainment" and "24-hour food" that gives guests "a big selection, but nothing worth selecting."

Hyatt Regency 👪🍴🔭⛳Ⓢ🏊🎾

Palm Beach | (011-297) 586-1234 | fax 586-5478 | 800-223-1234 | www.hyatt.com | 342 rooms, 18 suites

An "oasis" "covered with flowers, palm trees and tropical birds", this "excellent choice" "right in the middle of everything" offers "wonderful" service and "terrific dining" such as the "first-rate" Ruinas del Mar, where the "memorable" Sunday brunch is "worth a detour"; rooms are "small", but the renovated ones are "fantastic."

Marriott Resort & Stellaris Casino 👪🔭Ⓢ🏊🎾

L.G. Smith Blvd. 101 | Palm Beach | (011-297) 586-9000 | fax 586-0649 | 800-223-6388 | www.marriott.com | 378 rooms, 35 suites

A "beautiful location" "away from the crowded hotel strip", an "incredible" beach ("the best on the island"), a "fantastic" lagoon pool with a bar and a full-service Mandara spa win points for this "family-oriented" chain outpost; you'll also find a "smallish casino", "spacious rooms" and "polite and eager" service, but a handful maintain you "don't go for the food" since dining is "inconsistent."

Marriott's Aruba Ocean Club 👪🍳🔭Ⓢ🏊🎾

L.G. Smith Blvd. 99 | Palm Beach | (011-297) 586-9000 | fax 586-8000 | 800-223-6388 | www.marriott.com | 311 rooms

With its "beautiful location" at the north end of Eagle Beach, "spectacular pool" and access to the amenities of its nearby sister Marriott, this property with vacation ownership options is the "only place to stay" for luxury condos in Aruba; the staff is "sincerely cheerful" and the crowd includes a strong "family scene", but some say it's a little "generic."

Radisson Resort & Casino 👪🔭Ⓢ🏊

J.E. Irausquin Blvd. 81 | Palm Beach | (011-297) 586-6555 | fax 586-3260 | 800-333-3333 | www.radisson.com | 328 rooms, 25 suites

The grounds are "gorgeous" praise patrons partial to this "beautiful" resort set on 14 oceanfront acres, where the beach is "idyllic", the "great water facilities" include a "heavenly pool", the gardens are "lush" and there's a 16,000-sq.-ft. casino; "elegant" rooms are "spacious" enough for families, but some say the food is only "fair."

Renaissance Aruba Resort & Casino 👪Ⓢ🏊

Oranjestad | (011-297) 583-6000 | fax 583-4389 | 800-468-3571 | www.renaissancehotels.com | 290 rooms, 268 suites

It "feels more like Downtown Miami than a tropical paradise" at this property "just a stone's throw from the runway", but that means it's an "excellent location for business" and nightlife; the "free ferry" that shuttles guests to a private island brings it up a few notches ("provided the gnats aren't around"), but some still can't help asking "why would you go to a beautiful island to stay in the center of town?"

Australia

TOPS IN COUNTRY

26 Voyages Lizard Island | *Great Barrier Reef*
Bedarra Island | *Great Barrier Reef*
25 Hayman Island | *Great Barrier Reef*
24 Four Seasons | *Sydney*
Park Hyatt | *Sydney*
Westin | *Sydney*
23 Observatory | *Sydney*
Park Hyatt | *Melbourne*
Lilianfels Blue Mtns. | *Blue Mountains*
22 Daintree Eco Lodge | *Great Barrier Reef*

Adelaide

Hyatt Regency 🏊

ROOMS	SERVICE	DINING	FACIL.	COST
19	20	18	19	$275

North Terr. | (011-61-8) 8231-1234 | fax 8231-1120 | 800-223-1234 | www.adelaide.regency.hyatt.com | 346 rooms, 21 suites
With an unbeatably picturesque and "lovely" location on the River Torrens promenade and next to the Casino and Convention Centre, this "clean, comfortable" chainster with "beautiful views" is well-positioned for tourists embarking to wine country; three restaurants, a spa and fitness facilities are appreciated, although "nondescript" rooms have critics calling it a "basic conference hotel."

Ayers Rock

Sails in the Desert 🏋🏊

ROOMS	SERVICE	DINING	FACIL.	COST
19	19	20	21	$431

Yulara | (011-61-8) 8957-7888 | fax 8957-7474 | www.ayersrockresort.com.au | 224 rooms, 8 suites
"A welcome retreat in the Outback", this "wonderfully designed" "rose among the cacti" in the middle of the red desert offers "excellent views of Uluru" (Ayers Rock), a "delightful pool" and "accommodating service"; a few foes assail the food, saying there's "better on the flight over", and pooh-pooh the "plain" quarters.

Blue Mountains

Lilianfels Blue Mountains 🍴🏋💲🏊

ROOMS	SERVICE	DINING	FACIL.	COST
23	24	23	21	$492

Echo Point | Katoomba | (011-61-2) 4780-1200 | fax 4780-1300 | 800-524-2420 | www.lilianfels.com.au | 81 rooms, 4 suites
Across the road from the Three Sisters rock formation, this "divine" property furnishes "fantastic views" of the towering million-year-old rocks that are a highlight of the World Heritage–listed Blue Mountains National Park (about 60 miles west of Sydney); "getaway" groupies extol the "excellent" food, service that evokes the "good old days", "incredible spa treatments" and "spacious but cozy" rooms.

	ROOMS	SERVICE	DINING	FACIL.	COST

Gold Coast

Palazzo Versace ♒Ⓢ≋   ▽ 26 | 24 | 21 | 25 | $550

94 Sea World Dr. | (011-61-7) 5509-8000 | fax 5509-8888 |
www.palazzoversace.com | 151 rooms, 54 suites, 72 villas

Get instant "Versace overload" when you check into Donatella's gold-encrusted, Gold Coast landmark (about 50 miles south of Brisbane), where everything from the mosaic driveway to the lobby that "feels like a set" with its 1,500-pound chandelier to the "hot pink room key" to the "beach leading into the pool" has to be "seen to be believed"; there's an extensive spa and a busy marina as well, but sometimes the staff "acts as though life would be better if it wasn't for all these" guests.

Sheraton Mirage   20 | 21 | 17 | 22 | $499
Gold Coast ♔⌂♒Ⓢ≋ ✎

Sea World Dr. | (011-61-7) 5591-1488 | fax 5591-2299 | 800-325-3535 |
www.sheraton.com | 233 rooms, 6 suites, 54 villas

There's "no reason to leave the property" because "paradise is right here" praise proponents of this "fine resort" that boasts a "spectacular beach", "lovely grounds" and a health club "so good you could train for the Olympics"; though gourmands gripe the food's "generic" and find the rooms merely "fair" ("where's the gold?"), the "staff couldn't be nicer", so its fans say it's "still one of the best" of many hotels on Australia's Gold Coast.

Great Barrier Reef

Bedarra Island ♒Ⓢ≋ ✎   26 | 26 | 26 | 25 | $566

Bedarra Island | (011-61-7) 4068-8233 | fax 4068-8215 |
www.voyages.com.au | 16 villas

"Unrivalled" for "remote" "luxury", this "tranquil slice of paradise" on a private island tucked between a rainforest and Wedgerock Bay in North Queensland is a "totally isolated" escape; "romantics" relish the "unlimited supply of Louis Roederer champagne", while active sorts enjoy snorkeling, fishing, sailing and tennis at the facilities of Dunk Island; "heaven doesn't get much better", except maybe there aren't any jellyfish.

Daintree Eco Lodge & Spa ♒Ⓢ≋   23 | 24 | 21 | 21 | $385

20 Daintree Rd. | Daintree | (011-61-7) 4098-6100 | fax 4098-6200 |
www.daintree-ecolodge.com.au | 15 villas

The "focus is on 'eco'" at this "slightly rustic" but "oh-so-beautiful" nature-lovers' getaway in an "amazing location" in the heart of the world's oldest rainforest yet just 40 minutes from the Great Barrier Reef; the "surreal" cabins are set on stilts high in the trees, there's a "relaxing" spa (for unwinding after the crocodile cruise) and a restaurant that relies on local and Aboriginal ingredients; it's all a "wonderful wilderness" – just bring "lots of bug spray."

Dunk Island ♔♒Ⓢ≋ ✎   ▽ 21 | 21 | 20 | 24 | $164

Dunk Island | (011-61-7) 4068-8199 | fax 4068-8528 |
www.voyages.com.au | 88 rooms, 40 suites, 32 cabanas

Four kilometers off the North Queensland coast – or "way out in the middle of nowhere" as some sojourners say – this "low-key resort" offers

	ROOMS	SERVICE	DINING	FACIL.	COST

endless activities from hiking in the island's national park and diving the Great Barrier Reef, to playing tennis and golf, to "relaxing" in the cascade pools or the "comfortable rooms"; but a hardnosed handful harrumph it "leaves something to be desired", saying it has the "aura of a children's summer camp with the food to match."

☑ Hayman Island 🏕✕🎱⑤🏊🔍 | 26 | 24 | 23 | 27 | $488

Hayman Great Barrier Reef | Hayman Island | (011-61-2) 8272-7000 | fax 8272-7099 | www.hayman.com.au | 214 rooms, 20 suites, 1 villa, 9 penthouses

"Check-in takes place on the yacht" over to this "drop-dead gorgeous resort" on the Great Barrier Reef that's set around a pool you'll "never want to leave" and blends into the natural lush beauty of waterfalls and gardens; a "perfect place for a honeymoon", it offers "unobtrusive" service, "fantastic" dining and "luxurious" rooms with views of the "unmatched" beach and the Coral Sea; it's "like *Fantasy Island,* but better", since it's got "the greatest diving in the world."

Kewarra Beach Resort 🎱🏊 | 21 | 23 | 19 | 23 | $252

Kewarra Beach | Cairns | (011-61-7) 4057-6666 | fax 4057-7525 | www.kewarra.com | 61 rooms, 6 suites

"Removed from the touristy side of Cairns, but close enough for nights out" on the town, this resort sits in the middle of "magnificent, lush plantings" near a "gorgeous beach", and features "rustic" bungalows; it also boasts "great service" and "Aboriginal" decor, though water-logged vets warn "there's a reason they call it the 'rainforest.'"

Sebel Reef House & Spa ⑤🏊 | 21 | 21 | 20 | 18 | $350

99 Williams Esplanade | Palm Cove | (011-61-7) 4055-3633 | fax 4055-3305 | www.reefhouse.com.au | 63 rooms, 6 suites

Go to sleep to the "gentle sound of the surf" at this "gorgeous" Colonial-Mediterranean–style "secret" across from a "beautiful beach" with "romantic" rooms and two "killer pools"; a "knowledgeable staff", a 24-hour honor bar and a location that's "ideal for day tours of the reef and rainforest" are other reasons it's a veritable "Shangri-la."

Sheraton Mirage
Port Douglas 🎱⚓⑤🏊🔍 | 18 | 20 | 17 | 22 | $487

Davidson St. | Port Douglas | (011-61-7) 4099-5888 | fax 4099-4424 | 800-325-3535 | www.sheraton.com | 289 rooms, 100 villas, 3 suites

Situated on famous Four Mile Beach, and convenient to two World Heritage sites – the Great Barrier Reef and the Daintree Rainforest – this "venerable" "old lady" still has "a lot to offer", namely "attentive service", "wonderful lagoons", "loads of pools, tennis courts and sports" and a "pretty location"; but spoilsports snap there are "way too many families", the dining is "low-scale touristy" and the rooms are in "dire need of a face-lift" to rescue them from all that "faded '80s glory."

Voyages Lizard Island ✕🎱⑤🏊🔍 | 26 | 26 | 25 | 28 | $566

Lizard Island | (011-61-7) 4060-3999 | fax 4060-3991 | 800-225-9849 | www.lizardisland.com.au | 6 rooms, 18 suites, 15 villas, 1 pavilion

Even when full, this "romantic" all-inclusive Great Barrier Reef "escape" feels like it has "enough beaches for each couple to have their own"; the "beautiful and spacious" rooms come with "spectacular ocean views", the activities are "out of this world" and the food is

	ROOMS	SERVICE	DINING	FACIL.	COST

"amazing" – the "fantastic" staff will even pack a lunch of "wonderful treats" for your own private picnic; the whole "unspoiled paradise" is "heaven at hellish prices", but satisfied snorkellers swear it's "the most unique place in the world."

Wilson Island 🏨 Ⓢ

-	-	-	-	$502

Wilson Island | (011-61-2) 8296-8010 | fax 9299-2103 | www.voyages.com.au | 6 tents

Camp out in style when you stay at this tiny island outpost on the Great Barrier Reef where, at the right time of year, rare turtles lay their eggs and baby hatchlings emerge from shells (it's closed in February for seabird nesting season); the "place to go before you die" features permanent tents with reef and ocean views, raised wooden floors, king-size beds, dressing areas and daily housekeeping; guests converge at Longhouse for three-course dinners; N.B. no children under 15 permitted.

Melbourne

Adelphi, The ✕ 🏊

18	19	22	18	$440

187 Flinders Ln. | (011-61-3) 9650-7555 | fax 9650-2710 | www.adelphi.com.au | 30 rooms, 4 suites

Check out the "overhanging swimming pool" with a "clear glass bottom" that's perched "right over the city street" at this "cool, contemporary chic boutique"; arty guests appreciate the "angular materials, interesting textures and minimalist decor" while others love the "fusion food" at the on-site restaurant.

Grand Hyatt Ⓢ 🏊 ⚲

22	22	20	23	$285

123 Collins St. | (011-61-3) 9657-1234 | fax 9650-3491 | 800-223-1234 | www.grand.hyatt.com | 524 rooms, 24 suites

"Wait until you see the bathrooms" of this centrally located hotel: they're marble, "truly luxurious" and have a TV perched above the tub; "spacious" rooms boast "excellent decor" – some with great views, others with none – and "plenty of amenities" (especially in the "swank suites"); gym rats relish the "best" workout in the city and praise the hotel staff.

Langham 🏨 Ⓢ 🏊

▽ 24	24	19	21	$560

1 Southgate Ave. | (011-61-3) 8696-8888 | fax 9690-5889 | www.langhamhotels.com | 375 rooms, 12 suites

"Right where you want to be", this small riverside offering is a few minutes walk from the CBD, with its abundant galleries, cafes and parks; filled with "elegance and warmth", it has a "fantastic" spa, an "outstanding staff" and "wonderful views" from the corner rooms (a "real bargain"), plus the "extraordinary" breakfast buffet gets you off on the right foot.

Park Hyatt Ⓢ 🏊

25	24	21	23	$338

1 Parliament Sq. | (011-61-3) 9224-1234 | fax 9224-1200 | 800-223-1234 | www.park.hyatt.com | 216 rooms, 24 suites

Check into a "spacious" suite in this "stunning" art deco–esque beauty and check out the view of St. Patrick's Cathedral from the private terrace or relax in front of your fireplace; "elegant in every way", from the staff to the pampering spa to the "serene location", this chainster gets high marks, even though a few say the food is "marginal."

	ROOMS	SERVICE	DINING	FACIL.	COST

Rialto Hotel on Collins ≋

| | – | – | – | – | $317 |

495 Collins St. | (011-60-3) 9620-9111 | fax 9614-1219 | www.rialtohotel.com.au | 234 rooms, 10 suites

Business folks appreciate this InterContinental outpost's blue chip Collins Street address in the CBD (with close proximity to the stock exchange and the Melbourne Exhibition and Convention Centre); it features one of Australia's best examples of fin de siècle architecture, a rooftop heated swimming pool and spa, rooms with classic furnishings and satellite TVs and a chic European restaurant and outdoor bar.

Sofitel ✕ ⚇

| | ▽ 24 | 24 | 21 | 23 | $315 |

25 Collins St. | (011-61-3) 9653-0000 | fax 9650-4261 | 800-763-4835 | www.sofitel.com | 311 rooms, 52 suites

"Conveniently located" right Downtown and "situated high above Melbourne", this hotel offers a "great way to see the city", with "floor-to-ceiling windows" affording "incredible views"; "excellent concierge service", "good" food (try Cafe LA on the 35th floor) and proximity to the heart of town make it a solid choice.

Sunshine Coast

Hyatt Regency ☗⚇ㄴⓈ≋◜

| | ▽ 21 | 22 | 18 | 24 | $320 |

Warran Rd. | Coolum Beach | (011-61-7) 5446-1234 | fax 5446-2957 | 800-223-1234 | www.coolum.regency.hyatt.com | 156 village houses, 6 resort homes, 162 villas

This "overnight camp for adults" 90 minutes north of Brisbane on the Sunshine Coast is "fun for kids" and is known for its "well-kept grounds", golf course (home of the Australian PGA Championship), spa facilities and "miles of bike tracks."

Sydney

TOPS IN CITY

24	Four Seasons
	Park Hyatt
	Westin

Crowne Plaza Darling Harbour ⚇

| | ▽ 22 | 21 | 19 | 21 | $190 |

150 Day St. | (011-61-2) 9261-1188 | fax 9261-8766 | 877-227-6963 | www.crowneplaza.com | 322 rooms, 23 suites

Its location is the "best feature" of this chainster on the city side of Darling Harbour, within walking distance of the Sydney Convention Center, Harbourside complex and Sydney Aquarium; at times the public spaces feel "overwhelmed with tourists" complain critics, but comfortable rooms and a "helpful" staff are boons.

Four Seasons ✕⚇Ⓢ≋

| | 24 | 26 | 22 | 24 | $362 |

199 George St. | (011-61-2) 9238-0000 | fax 9251-2851 | 800-332-3442 | www.fourseasons.com | 410 rooms, 121 suites

"Make sure to upgrade to a premium view" "overlooking Sydney Harbour" and the Opera House at this luxury outpost in the Rocks since "there is no better urban vista in the world"; "typical for Four Seasons" means it has "the most responsive staff", "outstanding" fare and "location, location, location", but a handful are "disappointed", citing the "small" standard rooms and "bland pool."

	ROOMS	SERVICE	DINING	FACIL.	COST

InterContinental ✕🐾🏊♨ | 23 | 22 | 19 | 22 | $389

117 Macquarie St. | (011-61-2) 9253-9000 | fax 9240-1240 | 888-424-6835 | www.intercontinental.com | 481 rooms, 28 suites

"Drop-dead views of the Opera House and Harbour Bridge" are the chief "selling points" of this "oasis in the heart of Sydney" housed in the old Treasury Building, a "stunning mixture of old and new"; rooms are "elegant" (the "amazing" club level is a "great value"), the "friendly" staff is "superb" and there's a restaurant from up-and-coming chef Jeff Campbell; but a few reviewers find "nothing special" other than location.

Observatory Hotel, The 🏊♨♨🔍 | 25 | 24 | 21 | 23 | $625

89-113 Kent St. | (011-61-2) 9256-2222 | fax 9256-2233 | 800-524-2420 | www.orient-express.com | 78 rooms, 22 suites

"British elegance" plus "Aussie temperament" equals service that's "flawless" (including an "amazing concierge"), which is the hallmark of this "island of tranquility" located "within walking distance to the shopping and restaurants" of the Rocks District; surveyors single out the "posh" rooms, dining at Galileo, the "luxurious spa" and the "great pool."

Park Hyatt ✕🏊♨♨ | 26 | 24 | 22 | 24 | $740

7 Hickson Rd. | (011-61-2) 9241-1234 | fax 9256-1555 | 800-223-1234 | www.sydney.park.hyatt.com | 121 rooms, 9 suites

With a rooftop pool overlooking Sydney Harbour, this "exquisite property" at the water's edge in the Rocks, "right in the middle of tourist mayhem", makes "even hardened travelers swoon"; it "exudes style", from the "friendly staff" to the "hip bar", and if you "spend more" for a room you'll have "wonderful views" of the Opera House and Harbour Bridge; just a few, however, say the restaurant is a little "disappointing."

Shangri-La Hotel 🏊♨♨ | 23 | 22 | 21 | 19 | $371

176 Cumberland St. | (011-61-2) 9250-6000 | fax 9250-6250 | 800-942-5050 | www.shangri-la.com | 490 rooms, 73 suites

"Take-your-breath-away views" of the Harbour Bridge and Opera House (especially from the "fantastic" 36th floor bar and restaurant) and a massive renovation propel this Rocks District tower up a notch; the service is "very accommodating", the rooms are "spacious" and the location is "great for exploring the city on foot", but even those who like it say it "can't compete with the Shangri-La's in Asia"; N.B. the redo of all rooms and most public areas may outdate some of the above scores.

Sheraton on the Park 🏊♨♨ | 23 | 22 | 18 | 21 | $400

161 Elizabeth St. | (011-61-2) 9286-6000 | fax 9286-6686 | 800-325-3535 | www.sheraton.com | 509 rooms, 48 suites

Guests of this "attractive" Downtown hotel gush over the "lovely rooms" (some with "views of Hyde Park") featuring "fantastic marble-clad bathrooms", "beautiful public areas", "excellent rooftop pool" and an "overall polished atmosphere"; bonuses include "proximity to the Harbour and shopping" as well as a "special high tea."

Sir Stamford at Circular Quay 🏊♨ | ▽ 21 | 20 | 15 | 18 | $401

93 Macquarie St. | (011-61-2) 9252-4600 | fax 9252-4286 | www.stamford.com.au | 90 rooms, 15 suites

This "beautiful hotel" exudes "old-school charm" and "luxury" coupled with an "intimate atmosphere" in an "unbeatable location" just steps away from the Opera House; "wonderful service", "excellent food" and fairly "reasonable prices" make it a "home away from home" for aficionados who affirm "you can't go wrong here."

Westin 👪 🍴 [S] 🏊

ROOMS	SERVICE	DINING	FACIL.	COST
26	24	21	24	$450

1 Martin Pl. | (011-61-2) 8223-1111 | fax 8223-1222 | 800-937-8461 | www.westin.com | 393 rooms, 23 suites

An "attractive marriage of old and new", this "glitzy high-rise" in the Central Business District is grafted onto the 19th-century General Post Office, creating a "stellar" property that offers a choice of "modern", "stylish" accommodations with "chic" loos "partitioned by glass" or "charming" Heritage Wing rooms with soaring ceilings; city skyline views, a "friendly", "aim-to-please" staff, a "great bar and restaurant" and "fabulous" next-door health club make it a "world-class" perch.

Austria

Salzburg

Goldener Hirsch 🐕

ROOMS	SERVICE	DINING	FACIL.	COST
23	24	24	20	$687

Getreidegasse 37 | (011-43-662) 80840 | fax 843-349 | 888-625-5144 | www.goldenerhirsch.com | 65 rooms, 4 suites

For a taste of "quintessential Austria", this "beautiful, intimate" city hotel is a 15th-century "realization of elegant *gemütlichkeit*" in a "gorgeous location" where you can "open your window and breathe in Mozart"; "every desire is cared for graciously", and "excellent food" makes it "worth a detour", but even those who like the antique "rustic" rooms would "like to see some renovation."

Sacher Salzburg 🐕 🔭

	ROOMS	SERVICE	DINING	FACIL.	COST
▽	24	26	23	23	$463

Schwarzstrasse 5-7 | (011-43-662) 88977 | fax 88977-551 | www.sacher.com | 104 rooms, 12 suites

The "views are spectacular if you get a room on the Salzach River side" of this 19th-century "epitome of old-world grace and charm" in the heart of the city; fans look forward to "truffles upon arrival" as well as the "ubiquitous Sachertorte" that's "to die for", but a few find this "charming old lady" who "puts on airs" is "somewhat tired."

Schloss Fuschl [H] 🐕 🔭 [S] 🏊 🎾

ROOMS	SERVICE	DINING	FACIL.	COST
24	23	24	21	$661

Schloss Strasse 19, Hof bei Salzburg | (011-43-6229) 22530 | fax 22531-531 | 800-325-3535 | www.sheraton.com | 65 rooms, 39 suites, 6 cottages

Enjoy a "romantic escapade" at this 15th-century château on "crystal clear" Lake Fuschl outside Salzburg, where "exquisite, huge rooms", some with "breathtaking" lacustrine views, boast fine art and antiques, and the staff's "attention to detail" makes it all come together; expect "delicious" dining, decadent extras like tours in a vintage Rolls-Royce, a highly "recommended" spa and, finally, a "pricey" tab at the end.

Vienna

Grand Hotel Wien

ROOMS	SERVICE	DINING	FACIL.	COST
25	24	22	20	$529

Käerntner Ring 9 | (011-43-1) 515-800 | fax 515-1310 | www.grandhotelwien.com | 175 rooms, 30 suites

This belle epoque "favorite", originally built in 1870, offers "beautiful rooms and suites", "impeccable" "old European service" and a "per-

	ROOMS	SERVICE	DINING	FACIL.	COST

fect location" "in the heart of Vienna"; head to Le Ciel if you're in the mood for traditional Viennese and French cuisine or to the bar with outdoor seating on the Ringstrasse.

Hotel Bristol, A Westin Hotel ⚥ ⑪ ♨ | 24 | 23 | 21 | 20 | $694

Kärntner Ring 1 | (011-43-1) 515-160 | fax 515-16550 | 800-325-3589 | www.luxurycollection.com | 122 rooms, 18 suites

You'll "want to hire the decorator" of this "old-world" historic property in Innere Stadt that's "amazingly cozy" despite its "opulent decor"; each of the "incomparable" rooms and suites (think gold and grand) are "beautifully appointed" and come equipped with Biedermeier-style furnishings, fruit baskets and petit fours, and the "lovely dining room" (via chef Reinhard Gerer) serves up Austrian-French creations and "sparkles with all the glitter of the Hapsburg dynasty."

Imperial ♨♨ | 28 | 26 | 24 | 24 | $957

Kärntner Ring 16 | (011-43-1) 501-100 | fax 5011-0410 | 800-325-3589 | www.luxurycollection.com | 79 rooms, 59 suites

"The name aptly describes" this "gorgeous" "grande dame" opposite the Musikverein in central Vienna, an 1863 "period jewel" built for a prince; modern-day aristocrats (or those with "palatial" budgets) stay in "ornate rooms" where a riot of marble, silk and crystal boosts the "oooh factor" and "exquisite service" means "a concierge who can obtain any ticket"; P.S. "delicious" dining includes an imperial torte "to die for."

InterContinental ♨Ⓢ | 18 | 21 | 18 | 19 | $370

Johannesgasse 28 | (011-43-1) 711-220 | fax 713-4489 | 800-327-0200 | www.intercontinental.com | 392 rooms, 61 suites

A "pleasant alternative" to more expensive spots, this "modern chain" "across from the Stadtpark" is "good for business" and for "sightseers who like to walk"; while the rooms are "well appointed", some find them "a little tight" and short on character, summing it up as "not the best and not the worst."

Sacher Wien ♨♨Ⓢ | 24 | 26 | 25 | 21 | $551

Philharmonikerstrasse 4 | (011-43-1) 514-560 | fax 456-810 | www.sacher.com | 97 rooms, 55 suites

Home of the original Sachertorte, this Viennese "institution" recently revamped the rooms and public spaces; it boasts "superb concierge service" and a "great location" "perched at the beginning of an eye candy–filled shopping promenade" that's "less than a minute from the State Opera House"; best of all, you get the namesake dessert at turndown each night; N.B. new floors will open in early 2007.

Bahamas

Atlantis ⚥♨⌐Ⓢ≋✎ | 21 | 19 | 20 | 26 | $405

Casino Dr. | Paradise Island | (1-242) 363-3000 | fax 363-3524 | 800-285-2684 | www.atlantis.com | 2085 rooms, 215 suites

A "cruise ship meets Las Vegas" "on steroids" – this Paradise Island "tourist machine" may be "over the top", but the "gigantic", "adult Disney World" with "a zillion pools and waterslides" plus a subterranean aquarium is "something you have to see once"; just "don't stay too long" in this "too crowded" paradise since the service isn't up to

	ROOMS	SERVICE	DINING	FACIL.	COST

snuff and you'll have to withstand "very long waits" for "five-dollar sodas" and other "overpriced" fare.

Club Med Columbus Isle ⛎🏊🔍 ▽ | 19 | 21 | 21 | 24 | $180 |

San Salvador Island | (1-242) 331-2000 | fax 331-2458 | 800-258-2633 | www.clubmed.com | 200 rooms, 36 suites

"The bay is breathtaking" beam breathless fans of this chain's "highly recommended" outpost, where the "beautiful beach" and scuba excursions combine with a "very laid-back" vibe; others cite the "welcoming service" and food that's at least "on par with other all-inclusives", so they overlook "minimalist rooms."

Four Seasons ⛎🍴♨️▲①🏊🔍 | 26 | 23 | 20 | 25 | $495 |

Queen's Hwy., Emerald Bay | Great Exuma Island | (1-242) 336-6800 | fax 336-6801 | 800-332-3442 | www.fourseasons.com | 140 rooms, 42 suites, 1 villa

Whether they consider it "quiet and secluded" or "too far from anything else" on Great Exuma, participants say "even type A's can relax" at this resort's "to-die-for" beach, in its "lovely spa with unusual offerings" and on its "incredible" oceanfront Greg Norman–designed golf course; service is "professional and helpful", but some reviewers say "very ordinary" dining and rooms that are "quite a distance" from the water mean this one is "not on par with other Four Seasons."

Musha Cay 🖐🍴🏊🔍 | – | – | – | – | $24750 |

Mosstown | Great Exuma Island | (1-203) 602-0300 | fax 602-2265 | 877-889-1100 | www.mushacay.com | 5 villas

Very few guests hold the keys to this "one-of-a-kind", ultra-exclusive and expensive five-villa resort owned by illusionist David Copperfield set on a private out-island of the Exuma chain (85 miles southeast of Nassau), where ultra-luxurious English-colonial–style quarters range from a hilltop mansion to a thatched-roof beach cottage; highlights include seven private sand beaches, a lighted tennis court, bone-fishing, waterskiing, wind-surfing and scuba amid three uninhabited atolls; N.B. rates are per night for entire island for up to eight guests.

Ⓩ One & Only
Ocean Club ⛎🍴✕🖐♨️▲①🏊🔍 | 27 | 27 | 26 | 27 | $490 |

Casino Dr. | Paradise Island | (1-242) 363-2501 | fax 363-2424 | 800-321-3000 | www.oneandonlyoceanresort.com | 87 rooms, 14 suites, 3 villas, 2 cottages

"Splurge" with your one and only at this plantation-style "dream" resort that's "in a league by itself"; "astronomical" rates buy "impeccable", "very British" butler service, "luxurious accommodations" decorated with "beautiful local furniture", "divine" fare at Jean-Georges' Dune and "stunning" facilities that include a top-notch spa; it's the place where "the rich and famous (emphasize *rich*)" "chill", so you can do some "celeb spotting" before heading "for more action" next door at the Atlantis (guests share priviliges there).

Pink Sands 🖐🏊🔍 | 24 | 24 | 20 | 22 | $850 |

Chapel St. | Harbour Island | (1-242) 333-2030 | fax 333-2060 | www.pinksandsresort.com | 21 cottages, 4 duplexes

Sun worshipers say the "most beautiful beach on earth" ("it's really pink!") is the "highlight" of a stay in these "spacious and inviting" cot-

	ROOMS	SERVICE	DINING	FACIL.	COST

tages on "homey" Harbour Island, where the "nicely decorated" restaurant takes in an "unparalleled" view "compliments of mother nature"; even though it's "getting old" and the "food has slipped", the faithful assert that it's "still one of the best."

Rock House 🔭🏊 ▽ 26 | 24 | 24 | 23 | $300

Harbour Island | (1-242) 333-2053 | fax 333-3173 | www.rockhousebahamas.com | 8 rooms, 3 suites

Originally a bed-and-breakfast built in 1940, this "beautifully done" boutique hotel off the northern coast of Eleuthera was renovated and reopened by hotel designer J. Wallace Tutt III (who created Miami Beach's Hotel Impala); this "elegant" spot features rooms with king-size beds and 400-count linens, a "fabulous restaurant set around the pool" and lots of "models, pop stars and film actors."

Sandals Royal Bahamian 🔭[S]🏊🎾 21 | 22 | 19 | 23 | $400

Nassau | (1-242) 327-6400 | fax 327-6961 | 800-726-3257 | www.sandals.com | 248 rooms, 155 suites

Couples looking for a "romantic getaway" appreciate the "lovely atmosphere" and "friendly" staff at this Nassau outpost of the all-inclusive chain, where tons of activities keep them busy day and night; though some say "Baccarat gets two forks up" ("make reservations"), grumpy gourmands grouse the "international eateries here could improve."

Westin Our Lucaya Beach & Golf Resort 👪🔭⛳[S]🏊🎾 20 | 18 | 16 | 21 | $389

Royal Palm Way | Grand Bahama Island | (1-242) 373-1333 | fax 373-8804 | 866-716-8108 | www.westinourlucaya.com | 683 rooms, 57 suites

If you want a "gigantic facility that's extremely affordable", Lucaya lovers lead you to this "awesome compound", where you're "welcomed with delicious lemonade as you enter" and can enjoy a "beautiful day" by one of the infinity pools, on the beach or at the "world-class" spa; but a handful of the hungry harrumph over "mediocre fare."

Barbados

Cobblers Cove 👪🔭⛳[S]🏊🎾 22 | 23 | 23 | 19 | $820

Road View, Speightstown | St. Peter | (1-246) 422-2291 | fax 422-1460 | www.cobblerscove.com | 40 suites

"Secluded, even though it's just off the main road" near Speightstown, this "refined, elegant" English manor-style Relais & Châteaux boutique offers "low-key relaxation" via "impeccable service", "excellent" dining at the beachfront restaurant, tropical gardens, croquet courts and quaintly furnished quarters; while amenities addicts may find it a bit rustic (no AC, no TVs), at least the "roomy terraces catch those tropical breezes."

Coral Reef Club 👪🔭⛳🏊🎾 23 | 22 | 20 | 22 | $555

St. James | (1-246) 422-2372 | fax 422-1776 | 800-223-1108 | www.coralreefbarbados.com | 48 rooms, 40 suites

A "class act in every way", this colonial-style "haven" run by the "gracious" O'Hara family and its "attentive staff" comprises 12 acres of "beautiful grounds" featuring tennis courts, diving and boating facilities, and a health club with spa treatments; "tasteful" suites have "impeccable ocean views", while "refurbished cottages" boast plunge pools and wraparound terraces.

Crane, The 🏖🍴🏃🏊 | - | - | - | - | $550 |

St. Philip | (1-246) 423-6220 | fax 423-5243 | 800-223-9815 | www.thecrane.com | 126 rooms, 18 apartments, 2 penthouses

Originally built in the 19th century as Barbados' first resort, this historic spot on the Southeast coast fronts a half-mile of pink-sand beach and offers oceanfront accommodations with hardwood flors, full kitchens and wraparound balconies; ongoing major renovations are adding to the number of private residences available for interval ownership.

Lone Star | ▽ 23 | 22 | 24 | 18 | $850 |

St. James | (1-246) 419-0599 | fax 419-0597 | www.thelonestar.com | 4 suites, 1 villa

At this slicked up former auto-repair shop near Holetown, you can "watch locals playing cricket" on the beach or take "a swim with the turtles" steps from the four minimalist suites boasting baths with Philippe Starck fittings (there's also a separate Beach House that comes with butler, maid and chef); it's a "gem" of a boutique hotel, but the glitzy restaurant with "some of the best Asian fusion" is so pricey it prompts one reviewer to sigh "I'm glad I wasn't paying for the meal."

Sandpiper, The 🏖🏃⛱🏊⚲ | - | - | - | - | $745 |

Holetown | (1-246) 422-2251 | fax 422-0900 | 800-223-1108 | www.sandpiperbarbados.com | 37 rooms, 10 suites

The lush surroundings - flowering bougainvilleau, orchid and coconut trees - create a peaceful setting for this intimate property on the island's west coast, where rooms have views of the garden, pool or Caribbean and two suites offer four-poster beds, private pools and sundecks; facilities include two tennis courts, a pool, complimentary waterskiing, windsurfing, snorkeling, kayaking and Sunfish sailing, and a seasonal, supervised children's program.

☑ Sandy Lane 🎿✗🏃⛱Ⓢ🏊⚲ | 27 | 27 | 25 | 27 | $2800 |

St. James | (1-246) 444-2000 | fax 444-2222 | 866-444-4080 | www.sandylane.com | 96 rooms, 14 suites, 2 penthouses, 1 villa

Possibly the "most luxurious of the Caribbean resorts", this "venerable classic" in a gleaming white Palladian manor house has "all the boxes ticked" for the beach "vacation of your life": "gorgeous" rooms with "sumptuous fabrics", "outstanding" bathrooms, a "decadent" spa, multiple golf courses, a children's program and "unbeatable" "Barbados-style" service; even with "everything above expectations", some are shocked by the "top-dollar" prices, gasping "who pays these rates?"

Belgium

Brugges

Die Swaene 🍴🏃🏊 | 19 | 22 | 22 | 17 | $258 |

Steenhouwersdijk 1 | (011-32-50) 342-798 | fax 336-674 | www.dieswaene.com | 27 rooms, 3 suites

"Dripping with gold leaf" and "charm", this "well-situated" boutique hotel - actually three connected 18th-century residences - boasts a "grand" waterfront location at the heart of a beautifully preserved medieval UNESCO World Heritage Site; though some insist "only a grandmother would love" the "dated" rooms, insiders say just "get a canal view" and know that "breakfast makes up for it."

Heritage, Hotel 👥

-	-	-	-	$201

Niklaas Desparsstraat 11 | (011-32-50) 444-444 | fax 444-440 | www.hotel-heritage.com | 20 rooms, 4 suites

Once a private mansion, this 19th-century building just steps from the Market Square provides a central base for touring the city; rooms feature classic styling, Italian and French fabrics, WiFi access and baths with Hermès toiletries, and when it's time to relax from a day of sightseeing, weary souls can sip a drink in the fireplace lounge or have a soak in the Turkish steambath.

Brussels

Amigo, Hotel 👥🍴☕🛏

25	25	21	22	$756

(aka Hotel Rocco Forte Amigo)

Rue de l'Amigo 1-3 | (011-32-2) 547-4747 | fax 513-5277 | www.roccofortehotels.com | 156 rooms, 19 suites

Friends of this "intimate and elegant" property in Grand Place say it's "greatly improved" and sports "fantastic" contemporary and art deco rooms with Belgian linens, silk curtains and "interesting artwork" ("you'll even find slippers next to the bed"); the "attentive" staff includes an "amazing concierge" and the "location is perfect for exploring the city's main square."

Conrad International ☕🛏Ⓢ♨

25	22	20	24	$792

Ave. Louise 71 | (011-32-2) 542-4242 | fax 542-4200 | 800-445-8667 | www.conradbrussels.com | 230 rooms, 39 suites

It may be a "bit out of the way" but its location "at the top of the chic Avenue Louise" in Grand Sablon (within walking distance of Grand Place and the Royal Palace) along with its "blend of modern facilities and old-world charm" make this a "safe refuge"; it's got "aircraft hangar"–sized rooms, "excellent" (if sometimes "cool") service and "the best chocolate in the world at Pierre Marcolini's shop", but some aren't so smitten with the rest of the food.

Le Méridien 🛏

21	22	18	20	$614

Carrefour de l'Europe 3 | (011-32-2) 548-4211 | fax 548-4735 | 800-543-4300 | www.lemeridien.com | 198 rooms, 25 suites, 1 apartment

The "convenient" Grand Place location near the Central Station "minutes from everything", along with "comfortable" ("if average") rooms and "attentive" service make this a "reliable" find for business travelers who also appreciate the menu at L'Epicerie; but leisure loungers note a lack of luxury, lamenting it's all just "a bit too anonymous in style."

Métropole 🍴🛏

20	21	18	19	$435

Place de Brouckère 31 | (011-32-2) 217-2300 | fax 218-0220 | www.metropolehotel.com | 290 rooms, 15 suites

"Step back to a nicer era" of "old-fashioned grandeur" at this "belle epoque" "palace" known for its "accommodating service" and "fabulous" Downtown location where metropolitans "watch the city come to life" from the roof at night; though the newly renovated lobby draws kudos, some say the rooms and facilities are "starting to feel past their prime" – yet even they agree the accommodations are "huge" and "very comfortable."

Royal Windsor Hotel ⚴♨Ⓢ

| | 19 | 20 | 19 | 18 | $400 |

Rue Duquesnoy 5 | (011-32-2) 505-5555 | fax 505-5500 | 800-203-3232 | www.royalwindsorbrussels.com | 249 rooms, 17 suites

The 1970s-era brick facade may suggest it's "strictly for business", but this "friendly" family-run hotel's "perfect location" across the street from the Grand Casino Brussels and within "walking distance from all the tourist attractions" makes it a favorite base for sightseers and gamblers too; a few suggest the facilities "need to be upgraded" along with the "spartan rooms", but most find it hard to knock the "rock-bottom prices."

Belize

Dangriga

Kanantik Reef & Jungle Resort ♨≈

| | – | – | – | – | $285 |

Southern Hwy., mi. 18 | (011-501) 520-8048 | fax 520-8089 | 877-759-8834 | www.kanantik.com | 25 cabanas

Set on the southern coast of Belize, this ecologically designed seaside resort with modern Mayan huts sporting thatched roofs and netted, four-poster beds is an "amazing find"; located on 300 acres of mostly undeveloped lands perfect for rare bird-watching, game spotting, "superb diving" and relaxing (no children under 14 are allowed), it also offers "delicious" Creole-Med dining and a "welcoming", "hands-on" owner; just beware you'll sometimes encounter pesky "sand gnats."

Placencia

Turtle Inn ♙♨Ⓢ≈

| | 26 | 22 | 20 | 23 | $335 |

Placencia | (011-501) 523-3244 | fax 824-3878 | 800-746-3743 | www.blancaneaux.com | 1 pavilion, 18 cottages, 7 villas

Francis Ford Coppola's "beautiful and simple" "beachfront outpost" on the southern coast of Belize scores points for its "romantic" Balinese-inspired cabanas with "every amenity you could ever need" including "a wet bar, gorgeous high-vaulted ceilings" and "grand outdoor showers"; other highlights include an "open-air dining pavilion", a "phenomenal dive shop", a spa ("don't miss the Thai massage"), a "wonderful" white-sand beach and a "lovely" pool that's also "necessary", since "seagrass impedes" ocean swimming; P.S. "go now, before other tourists" "overrun the area."

San Ignacio

Blancaneaux Lodge ♙✕🅑♨Ⓢ≈

| | 28 | 27 | 23 | 24 | $250 |

Mountain Pine Ridge Forest Reserve | Cayo District | (011-501) 824-4913 | fax 824-3878 | 800-746-3743 | www.blancaneaux.com | 7 villas, 10 cabanas

A "fantasy" destination for a "memorable" vacation, this Francis Ford Coppola–owned resort just outside of San Ignacio and two hours from Belize City provides a "stunning", cinematic setting in a "beautiful forest" where "elegant bungalows overlook cascading waterfalls" and a "gurgling river", and hammocks are swayed by "fragrant" mountain breezes; the "superb" quarters feature "fantastic Japanese-style bathrooms", the Italian eatery offers Napa wines and the barkeeps "make a mean Latin cocktail."

Chaa Creek ☗ ☗ ⓢ

| 26 | 25 | 23 | 25 | $150 |

77 Burns Ave. | Cayo District | (011-501) 824-2037 | fax 824-2501 | www.chaacreek.com | 4 suites, 16 cottages, 2 villas

The "spacious suites" decorated with "local fabrics and accents" earn raves at this "spectacular" and "civilized" "jungle retreat" in the mountains of Belize that's "morphed into quite a resort over the years"; "idyllically" located along the Macal River and surrounded by "nature trails" and a Blue Morpho butterfly farm, it features an "incredibly accommodating" staff that helps arrange "excellent" expeditions to the Mayan Ruins, thatched-roof casitas and rustic cottages and a European-style spa, plus the chef serves up "gourmet dining" in the on-site restaurant.

San Pedro

Cayo Espanto ☀

| – | – | – | – | $1200 |

Cayo Espanto | (011-501) 220-5001 | fax 323-4272 | 888-666-4282 | www.cayoespanto.com | 5 villas

Only five private cabanas and a maximum of 14 guests – plus staff, of course – occupy this private island "paradise" located just off the coast of Belize; the "vacation of a lifetime" is "worth every penny" say fans of the private plunge pools, wraparound decks, hammocks and gourmet meals served on your private veranda, and "everyone is so friendly" to boot; for a fee, the marine lover's dream list of activities includes fly fishing, scuba diving, snorkeling and boating on the Caribbean Sea.

Bermuda

Ariel Sands ☗ ☗ ⓢ ☀ ☖

| 18 | 21 | 21 | 21 | $350 |

34 S. Shore Rd. | Hamilton | (1-441) 236-1010 | fax 236-0087 | 800-468-6610 | www.arielsands.com | 36 rooms, 3 suites, 4 cottages

This "peaceful" cottage colony co-owned by actor Michael Douglas wins applause for its "helpful", "willing" staff, rooms redone in "simple but attractive" fashion, oceanside salt-water pools that are "superb for children" and on-site moped rental; foes dis the memorabilia-festooned bar (a "shrine" to the Academy Award winner) and say the restaurant's contemporary fare is "boring."

Cambridge Beaches ☗ ☗ ⓢ ☀ ☖

| 24 | 24 | 23 | 23 | $430 |

30 Kings Point Rd. | Sandys | (1-441) 234-0331 | fax 234-3352 | 800-468-7300 | www.cambridgebeaches.com | 74 rooms, 21 suites, 3 cottages

Cambridge alums call this 1920s cottage-style resort "a true classic" citing "secluded beaches" and "wonderfully romantic" water views from every room; its position at a "remote, quiet end of the island" saddled between the Atlantic Ocean and Mangrove Bay may be "a bit far" from everything, but with a "fantastic" new inifinity edge pool, marina, comprehensive spa and "divine afternoon tea", there's simply "no reason to leave the property."

	ROOMS	SERVICE	DINING	FACIL.	COST
Elbow Beach 👪🔭[S]🏊🎾	21	23	21	24	$475

60 S. Shore Rd. | Paget | (1-441) 236-3535 | fax 236-3535 | 800-223-7434 | www.mandarinoriental.com | 142 rooms, 38 suites, 5 cottages

Since this nearly hundred-year-old enclave of "elegance" has been added to the Mandarin Oriental portfolio, "pampering" permeates the "beautiful rooms", "fab spa" and free-form pool (they "spritz you with water!"); while this hillside outpost is still "shabby genteel" in spots ("unless they can guarantee a renovated room, skip it") and the "food should be much better", romantics rave about the "gorgeous" half-mile of pink-sand beach and "lots of great coves to get lost in with your honey"; P.S. the main building will be renovated in 2007.

	ROOMS	SERVICE	DINING	FACIL.	COST
Fairmont Hamilton Princess, The 👪🏊	21	22	20	22	$519

76 Pittsbay Rd. | Hamilton | (1-441) 295-3000 | fax 295-1914 | 800-257-7544 | www.fairmont.com | 353 rooms, 57 suites

"Pink and picturesque" in the "center of Hamilton", the "business-minded brother" of the "relaxed Fairmont Southampton" has an "overwhelmingly helpful, knowledgeable and cheerful" staff, but the "shuttle to the beach is a hassle" and "frequent conventions" make it "less than ideal for a vacation getaway"; go for the Gold Floor's "higher service and top-notch amenities" and "avoid the annex", where you may be "surprised to find outdated decor and run-down fixings."

	ROOMS	SERVICE	DINING	FACIL.	COST
Fairmont Southampton 👪🔭⛳[S]🏊🎾	23	22	22	25	$519

101 S. Shore Rd. | Southampton | (1-441) 238-8000 | fax 239-6974 | www.fairmont.com | 558 rooms, 35 suites

"Way on top of a hill", with "beautiful" water views, this "large-scale" "queen" "towering over the south shore" is an "elegant respite" with "surprisingly good" food and rooms that "surpass" those of its sister, the Fairmont Hamilton Princess; "children are treated great", but the "good bone structure could use a new layer of makeup."

	ROOMS	SERVICE	DINING	FACIL.	COST
Horizons & Cottages 🍴[S]🏊🎾	21	24	24	23	$429

33 S. Shore Rd. | Paget | (1-441) 236-0048 | fax 236-1981 | 800-468-0022 | www.horizonscottages.com | 44 rooms, 4 suites

Built on a 1710 plantation, this 25-acre Relais & Châteaux hilltop refuge exudes "subdued class" and an "old Bermudian feel" via "great service", manicured gardens, a nine-hole golf course, access to the adjacent Coral Beach & Tennis Club (that has an on-site spa) and terrace dining that's "superb at sunrise" and "spectacular at sunset"; but a few fusspots fret that the effort "to be a hotel of days gone by" has left the rooms' "elegant charm" a bit "outdated."

	ROOMS	SERVICE	DINING	FACIL.	COST
Pink Beach Club & Cottages 🛏🔭🏊🎾	19	21	19	19	$600

Tucker's Town | (1-441) 293-1666 | fax 293-8935 | 800-355-6161 | www.pinkbeach.com | 62 rooms, 32 suites

This "well-heeled" all-inclusive on the "quieter side of the island" is "perfect for retreat seekers" or honeymooners who want "anonymity" in a setting of "British charm" without the stuffiness; renovated cottages have "wonderful European bathrooms", fireplaces and terraces, not to mention a "helpful, willing" staff that brings breakfast to your unit.

	ROOMS	SERVICE	DINING	FACIL.	COST

Reefs ✗⊙⚑🔍

| 22 | 26 | 26 | 23 | $512 |

56 S. Shore Rd. | Southampton | (1-441) 238-0222 | fax 238-8372 | 800-742-2008 | www.thereefs.com | 47 rooms, 18 suites

"A Greek villa on the Atlantic" is how guests describe this "gorgeous" all-inclusive "getaway" perched cliffside above the surf in Southampton; "personal service", "incredible seafood" and other "wonderful choices" at their three restaurants, plus "beautiful" ocean views "keep 'em coming back" (some "a few hundred times"); dinner on the "heavenly", if "small", private beach is "the ultimate romantic experience."

Waterloo House ✗✢🏨⚑

| 21 | 25 | 27 | 20 | $400 |

100 Pitts Bay Rd. | Hamilton | (1-441) 295-4480 | fax 295-2585 | 800-468-4100 | www.waterloohouse.com | 24 rooms, 6 suites

"Right on the harbor" a "convenient" "walking distance" from Hamilton's Front Street, this "formal", "intimate" boutique is "a place for stiff upper lips, stiff drinks" and "wonderful alfresco dining" proffered by "courteous and eager-to-please" staffers; "get a waterfront room" (it's "not on the beach"), but "do your homework before you book" because the "quirky charm" here includes quarters that "vary wildly."

Bhutan

Paro

Amankora 🏨⊙

| – | – | – | – | $1000 |

Paro | (011-975) 827-2333 | fax 827-2999 | 800-477-9180 | www.amanresorts.com | 56 suites

The first of six Aman resorts planned for Bhutan, this "wonderful" lodge is transforming the secluded Himalayan kingdom sandwiched between Tibet and India into *the* destination for South Asia–bound jet-setters looking for "remote" "comfort"; there are airy, wood-paneled suites that feature wood-burning stoves, "superb" Western- and Bhutanese-inspired fare, an on-site spa and "fabulous" service.

Uma Paro 🏨⊙⚑

| – | – | – | – | $280 |

Paro | (011-975) 827-1597 | fax 827-1513 | www.uma.como.bz | 18 rooms, 2 suites, 9 villas

This hilltop retreat in Paro has an unmistakably organic feel, from its on-site Shambhala spa that offers yoga, traditional herbal wrap therapies and Thai massages to its flower- and orchard-filled landscape; "big, comfortable" rooms, all of which have views of the region's varied topography, fuse modern and Bhutanese design (intricately carved wooden windows and doors, walls painted with religious motifs).

Botswana

Chobe National Park

Chobe Chilwero 🏨⚑

| 27 | 28 | 25 | 24 | $560 |

Chobe National Park | (011-27-11) 438-4650 | fax 787-7658 | www.sanctuarylodges.com | 15 bungalows

An "outstanding staff", "exceptional" food and a "magnificent" Chobe River setting ensure guests an "all-around awesome" time at this

	ROOMS	SERVICE	DINING	FACIL.	COST

"well-run" game resort; "huge" villas with "indoor-outdoor showers" add to the "luxurious" feel, and if a few insist its "crowded" national park location "detracts from the experience", others say the "proximity to the river" and "fantastic" wildlife make for a "fascinating" stay.

Chobe Game Lodge 🏊

	22	24	20	20	$630

Kasane | (011-267) 625-0340 | fax 625-0280 | www.chobegamelodge.com | 46 rooms, 4 suites

"One of the best lodges" in this remote African destination is this "not-to-be-missed experience" offering "grand game viewing" from "attractive" Moorish-style buildings; though the dining might not be on a par with the rest, its "beautiful location" overlooking the Chobe River and "wonderful suites with private pools" are great for "watching the elephants"; P.S. "Liz Taylor and Richard Burton honeymooned here."

Savute Elephant Camp 🏊

	27	27	24	27	$950

Chobe National Park | (011-27-11) 274-1800 | fax 481-6065 | 800-237-1236 | www.orient-express-safaris.co.za | 12 tents

Elephant enthusiasts say "don't miss" this "amazing" Orient Express-operated "tented-camp" property inside Chobe National Park, where you'll discover plentiful pachyderms "on parade" and "better animal sightings from your shower" than you'd experience at "most others from a jeep"; "wonderful" food, "sterling service" and "first-class" thatched-roof accommodations enhance the "great game viewing", making a stay "in the middle of the savanna" a "true adventure."

Okavango Delta

Abu Camp 🐘🏊

	-	-	-	-	$2252

Okavango Delta | (011-267) 686-1260 | fax 686-1005 | www.abucamp.com | 6 tents, 1 villa

Familiarizing guests with animals residing here - giraffes, zebras, antelopes, 500 species of birds and, most importantly, the majestic elephants - is the main focus at this "truly remarkable" luxury camp; guests (no more than 12 at a time) come for a three-night safari experience that includes game drives in 4x4s, rides atop the elephants (the memory of which will "stay with you the rest of your life") and guided nature walks, while tents feature hardwood floors, canopied beds and decks that yield unobstructed views.

Camp Okavango

	▽ 26	27	25	25	$630

Nxaragha Island | (011-27-11) 706-0861 | fax 424-1036 | www.desertdelta.co.za | 1 suite, 11 tents

Channel Adam and Eve at this "rugged", "magical" camp set on the remote African island of Nxaragha with a wetland ecosystem that's one of the "few remaining unspoiled plots on earth"; the "intimate" quarters - safari-style tents on raised teak platforms - are "well-integrated into the surroundings" and house only 24 adventurous guests.

Chief's Camp 🐘🏊

	25	28	22	25	$885

Chief's Island, Mombo Concession | Moremi Game Reserve | (011-27-11) 438-4650 | fax 787-7658 | www.sanctuarylodges.com | 12 pavilions

"Not much can beat" this remote luxury safari lodge set deep in the Mombo "wilderness" of the Moremi Game Reserve, where a dozen "fantastic" thatched-roof pavilions come with indoor and outdoor showers plus private verandas for candlelight dining overlooking the bush; the "awesome staff" includes "excellent guides" who facilitate the "outstanding game viewing" and spa therapists who adminster poolside massages; "if this is roughing it" say awestruck admirers, then they'd happily rough it "365 days a year", despite the "lack of air-conditioning."

Khwai River Lodge ≋

| 24 | 27 | 22 | 23 | $1692 |

Moremi Game Reserve | (011-27-11) 481-6052 | fax 424-1036 | 800-524-2420 | www.orient-express.com | 15 tents

One of Botswana's oldest safari lodges, this "low-key" venue offers "remarkable sights, sounds and wildlife" with a modern twist – i.e. you "soak in the pool while watching hippos soaking in the adjacent marsh"; its 15 "permanent" thatched-roof tents overlooking the Khwai River are "quite comfortable" and afford not only "great game viewing", but excellent bird-watching too.

❷ Mombo Camp ♙✕♟≋

| 28 | 28 | 25 | 28 | $1510 |

Mombo Island | Moremi Game Reserve | (011-267) 807-1800 | www.wilderness-safaris.com | 9 tents

Thrill to views of "lions before breakfast, lions after dinner and everything else in between" at this "ultra-luxurious" tent camp deep in the Okavango Delta's famed Moremi Game Reserve where the "amazing game viewing" ("elephants watch you shower" outside) is just part of the "first-rate" experience; with an "incredibly friendly staff" providing "the best service of your life" and "marvelous" cuisine prepared by an "innovative" chef, this may be the "gold standard" of safari lodgings.

Vumbura Plains ♙♟≋

| ▽ 26 | 29 | 25 | 29 | $1235 |

Okavango Delta | (011-27-31) 764-5075 | fax 764-6983 | www.wilderness-safaris.com | 14 tents

Be "treated like the King of the Jungle" at this "modern version of a bush camp", located "in the middle of the delta" on the edge of the Moremi Wildlife Reserve (expect panoramic views of the wildlife); raised above the ground on wooden platforms, each of the "large, exquisite" tented suites features multiple rooms and "private dipping pools", while "knowledgeable" guides and "impeccable" food help round out "one of the very best camps in Africa."

Brazil

Amazon

Tropical Manaus ♟≋🔍

| ▽ 17 | 17 | 14 | 20 | $129 |

Ponta Negra | Manaus | (011-55-92) 659-5000 | fax 658-5026 | 888-457-3266 | www.tropicalhotels.com.br | 589 rooms

At this "stunning resort" located on the edge of the rainforest, it's all about the "tropical beauty of the Amazon"; there's a "small zoo" on-site, a decent breakfast buffet and "large rooms" with "very charming decor" (some of them even have hammocks); but a few sullen spoilsports snipe about somewhat "slow" service and want more dining options.

	ROOMS	SERVICE	DINING	FACIL.	COST

Rio de Janeiro

Caesar Park Ipanema 🏃🏊

| 22 | 21 | 19 | 19 | $283 |

Ave. Vieira Souto 460, Ipanema | (011-55-21) 2525-2525 | fax 2521-6000 | www.caesarpark-rio.com | 201 rooms, 21 suites

"Looking out your window" at the "view of Ipanema beach" – "one of the most gorgeous stretches of sand anywhere" – will "put a samba in your step" when you stay at this "perfectly located" lodging; "try lounging by the rooftop pool drinking caipirinhas" and enjoying "attentive service", just don't expect much from "unremarkable rooms."

Copacabana Palace ✕🏃🏊🔍

| 24 | 25 | 24 | 25 | $420 |

Ave. Atlântica 1702, Copacabana | (011-55-21) 2548-7070 | fax 2235-7330 | 800-237-1236 | www.copacabanapalace.com.br | 108 rooms, 117 suites

Be part of the "sea-and-be-seen set" at this "grande dame" that still evokes Copa's "glory days", exuding "elegance" "perfect for impressing the unimpressible"; its "fantastic location" on the beach, "top-notch food", "service with a smile" and renovated "luxurious" rooms with "impeccable decoration" please most; P.S. there's an "exquisite" pool.

JW Marriott 🏃🏊

| 21 | 22 | 17 | 19 | $265 |

Ave. Atlântica 2600, Copacabana | (011-55-21) 2545-6500 | fax 2545-6555 | 800-703-1512 | www.marriott.com | 230 rooms, 15 suites

"From the front desk to the bartenders to the beach staff", they "work hard to please" at this chainster on the Copacabana strip that impresses both business and leisure travelers with its service; a few also mention the "interesting" breakfast buffet, but are less enamored by "small" "charmless" rooms and the iffy surrounding area.

Le Méridien Copacabana ✕🍴🏃🏊

| 19 | 21 | 20 | 18 | $300 |

Ave. Atlântica 1020, Copacabana | (011-55-21) 3873-8888 | fax 3873-8777 | 800-543-4300 | www.lemeridien.com | 442 rooms, 54 suites

One of "the best" restaurants in Rio, supervised by French chef Dominique Oudin, gives this "basic" Copacabana hotel an "edge on the competition"; it's in a "great location for those on business Downtown" and there are "incredible" views of the beach from the top floor, but crabby critics crank that it's in a "noisy" spot, so "while you can watch the world go by here, who wants to see the entire world on one corner?"

Sheraton Rio Hotel & Towers 👫🏃Ⓢ🏊🔍

| 19 | 17 | 16 | 20 | $300 |

Ave. Niemeyer 121 | (011-55-21) 2274-1122 | fax 2239-5643 | 800-325-3535 | www.sheraton-rio.com | 498 rooms, 61 suites

There's a mixed reaction to this "off-the-beaten-path" chainster in Leblon that requires taking a cab to the heart of the action: on the one hand you get a "great", "private beach" away from the "hubbub, hawkers and hookers" and can enjoy "spectacular" pools overlooking the ocean, but on the other, the rooms, while "comfortable and modern", are "tedious", the "service is mediocre at best" and the dining doesn't deliver.

Sofitel 🏃🏊

| ▽ 18 | 19 | 15 | 19 | $513 |

Ave. Atlântica 4240; Copacabana | (011-55-21) 2525-1232 | fax 2525-1200 | 800-763-4835 | www.sofitel.com | 355 rooms, 33 suites

This modern, "semiprecious jewel" with a "safe" beachside "location to die for" "between Copacabana and Ipanema" is "pretty good by Rio

	ROOMS	SERVICE	DINING	FACIL.	COST

standards"; the resort comes with "beautiful views" of the ocean and Sugarloaf Mountain and "two swimming pools", "one for the morning sun" and one for afternoon rays, plus the staff is "very helpful"; but the "spacious enough" rooms are in need of "serious updating and reno-vation" and the restaurants fall short.

São Paulo

Emiliano Ⓢ

| 26 | 25 | 23 | 23 | $395 |

Rua Oscar Freire 384 | (011-55-11) 3068-4399 | fax 3068-4398 | 800-223-6800 | www.emiliano.com.br | 19 suites, 38 apartments
In the heart of the Jardins district with its "excellent shops and restau-rants", this chic boutique "impresses" with such personal service that a half hour after arrival "everybody will be calling" you by name; you'll control much of the electronics in the "modern", "South Beach–like" rooms from a remote panel, and enjoy touch-screen telephones and down comforters.

Grand Hyatt Ⓢ ≋

| 26 | 23 | 22 | 24 | $240 |

Ave. Das Nações Unidas 13301 | (011-55-11) 6838-1234 | fax 6838-1235 | 800-223-1234 | www.saopaulo.grand.hyatt.com | 436 rooms, 34 suites
You won't want to leave your "luxurious", "take-your-breath-away" room at this "five-star hotel of the vintage sort", certainly "worthy of any traveler in need of an oasis in a busy town"; it's a "home away from home", with "outstanding" service, "excellent food" and "heart-of-the-city location"; P.S. "don't miss [jewelry designer] Antonio Bernardo's boutique near the concierge desk."

Gran Meliá ≋ ✎

| ▽ 23 | 21 | 17 | 20 | $200 |

Ave. Das Nações Unidas 12559 | (011-55-11) 3055-8000 | fax 3055-8002 | www.solmelia.com | 240 rooms, 60 suites
You'll enjoy "beautiful marble bathrooms" in "rock-star luxury" rooms at this business hotel that offers "friendly" service, "all the modern" in-room amenities and a breakfast buffet that some call "better than a dinner in Manhattan"; as for location, most say "it's fine if you don't need to be in São Paulo's Central Business District."

InterContinental ⬥⬥ ≋

| 20 | 20 | 17 | 17 | $250 |

Alameda Santos 1123 | (011-55-11) 3179-2600 | fax 3179-2666 | 888-424-6835 | www.intercontinental.com | 153 rooms, 36 suites
"Excellent service" from a "very friendly staff" that "anticipates your every need" is this "reliable" and "elegant" business hotel's best qual-ity; while rooms offer "every convenience" including "big desks and lots of work space", they vary from "cheery" to "tired and in need of freshening up"; at least the breakfast buffet pleases some, but a few "don't feel safe going out at night."

Unique, Hotel ⬥⬥ ≋

| 24 | 23 | 22 | 25 | $315 |

Ave. Brigadeiro Luis Antônio 4700 | (011-55-11) 3055-4710 | fax 3889-8100 | www.hotelunique.com.br | 85 rooms, 10 suites
A "must-see" for the "breathtaking design", this visual feast has rooms with hardwood floors that ascend into curved walls sporting plasma TVs, a "cool, trendy" lobby with soaring windows and a "de-licious" rooftop restaurant that overlooks a red-lit pool and draws a "late-night trendy crowd" – all packaged in a copper boatlike edifice

with porthole windows; seminal architect Ruy Ohtake offers so much to gawk at in this "striking" "cross between a nightclub, singles' bar and hotel" slicing across the São Paolo skyline in Jardim Paulista, that some "can't stop telling everyone about it" afterward.

British Virgin Islands

Peter Island

Peter Island Resort 👪 🍴 🛏 🔭 [S] 🏊 🎾

ROOMS	SERVICE	DINING	FACIL.	COST
24	25	23	25	$900

Peter Island | (1-284) 495-2000 | fax 495-2500 | 800-346-4451 | www.peterisland.com | 32 rooms, 20 suites, 2 villas

"Get in a hammock and never leave" or "find an isolated spot" on a "glorious stretch of sand" at this "tranquil" private-island "paradise" across the channel from Tortola with "amazing vistas" of the B.V.I. "no matter where you look"; "wonderful" staffers beckon with drinks at the beachfront bar, there's "fabulous" Caribbean fare at Tradewinds or you can get a "massage with your mate" at the "terrific spa", while beachfront suites are simply "paradiso"; P.S. a recent rebuild of a "noisy" generator may silence complaints from light sleepers in marina-side A-frames.

Tortola

Long Bay Resort 🛏 🔭 [S] 🏊 🎾

ROOMS	SERVICE	DINING	FACIL.	COST
18	16	14	19	$250

Long Bay | (1-284) 495-4252 | fax 495-4677 | 800-345-0356 | www.eliteislandresorts.com | 66 rooms, 11 suites, 36 villas, 5 houses

The best way to enjoy the "superb beach" at this "secluded" resort is to book a "wonderful" "cabana on the water" say sea-rebral sorts who also extol the "excellent facilities" (a "fun" pool, spa, tennis courts) and "great food"; "don't expect luxury", though, and the "steep hills" mean "you need to be in good shape."

Sugar Mill 🍴 🛏 🔭 🏊

ROOMS	SERVICE	DINING	FACIL.	COST
20	24	25	20	$325

Little Apple Bay | (1-284) 495-4355 | fax 495-4696 | 800-462-8834 | www.sugarmillhotel.com | 12 suites, 8 houses, 1 cottage, 1 villa

Known for its "outstanding restaurant" that rivals "top NYC" dining destinations, this "stylish" resort run by food writers Jinx and Jefferson Morgan serves "fabulous" regional fare in an "elegant", centuries-old setting; service is "impeccable" and the rooms, though "not luxurious", are "pleasant" (and feature special touches, like books); in fact, "the only bummer is that you have to cross the street" to reach the "postage stamp-size beach."

Virgin Gorda

Biras Creek Resort 🔭 [S] 🏊 🎾

ROOMS	SERVICE	DINING	FACIL.	COST
23	23	23	23	$980

North Sound | (1-284) 494-3555 | fax 494-3557 | 800-223-1108 | www.biras.com | 31 suites

A "world unto itself", this "romantic" Relais & Châteaux resort offers "secluded villas" where you can "listen to the waves all day"; groupies are also grateful for "great service", "outstanding food" and "many different activities" ("sitting on the beach works too"), and even if it's "tough to get to", it's "worth it."

	ROOMS	SERVICE	DINING	FACIL.	COST
Bitter End Yacht Club 👪🔭[S]🏊	19	20	17	23	$800

North Sound | (1-284) 494-2746 | fax 494-4756 | 800-872-2392 | www.beyc.com | 42 villas, 42 suites, 3 houses

Access to a fleet of wind- and motor-powered vessels (and every "water sport") keeps families occupied at this "boater's paradise" sprawled across a "picturesque harbor" at the tip of Virgin Gorda; "landlubbers" lub the "relaxed vibe" and "authentic rooms", but bitter-enders dub the food "so-so" and say it only "looks great if you've been at sea for weeks."

	ROOMS	SERVICE	DINING	FACIL.	COST
Guana Island 👪🏊🎾	▽ 21	27	25	26	$985

Guana Island | (1-914) 967-6050 | fax 967-8048 | 800-544-8262 | www.guana.com | 15 rooms, 1 cottage

Travelers who truly want to get away from it all will have no problem at this "secluded" tropical refuge where they can "really relax" since there are no phones or TVs in rooms; service is "extremely helpful", the "food is heavenly" (rates include all meals and most activities) and there's access to seven private beaches.

	ROOMS	SERVICE	DINING	FACIL.	COST
Little Dix Bay 👪🍴🔭[S]🏊🎾	24	24	23	26	$650

Little Dix Bay | (1-284) 495-5555 | fax 495-5661 | 888-767-3966 | www.rosewoodhotels.com | 92 rooms, 8 villas

"Blue bloods" sip "blue drinks" by the "blue sea" at this "luxurious" yet "laid-back" former Rockefeller property set on a "gorgeous sweeping bay" with white-sand beaches; "recreation options abound", and fans rave about "fabulous dining" and "impeccable service", but a few cite "monotony" in the former and "lapses" in the latter.

	ROOMS	SERVICE	DINING	FACIL.	COST
Necker Island 👪🍴🛁[S]🏊🎾	▽ 29	25	28	28	$3214

Necker Island | (1-203) 602-0300 | fax 732-473-9986 | 800-557-4255 | www.necker.com | 1 house, 4 cottages

Virginal is an apt descriptor for this "fabulous" ultra-exclusive and "very pricey" tropical retreat owned by airline magnate Richard Branson, considering its pristine sugary-white beaches, views of the turquoise Caribbean Sea and elegant, Bali-inspired, open-air cottages; with a "near perfect" staff and "exceptional" facilities (gourmet dining, world-class spa, swim-up sushi bar), there's "nothing like it in the world", so it's no surprise reported guests include Oprah Winfrey and Steven Spielberg; N.B. normally the entire island must be rented; above rates are per night based on a week stay during designated periods.

Cambodia

Phnom Penh

	ROOMS	SERVICE	DINING	FACIL.	COST
Raffles Hotel Le Royal [H]🔭[S]🏊	20	22	22	22	$260

92 Rukhak Vithei Daun Penh | (011-855-23) 981-888 | fax 981-168 | 800-637-9477 | www.raffles.com | 151 rooms, 20 suites

Glimpse the "lives of French aristocrats" in the colonial beauty of this 1929 restored "bit of calm" where you're "treated like royalty"; "exquisite" food is served in "lush extravagance", and an "inviting pool demands a dip at the end of a hot day"; in the center of a "fascinating city" with a "sad history", it "keeps the feeling of old Cambodia" as it "struggles to become part of the 21st century."

	ROOMS	SERVICE	DINING	FACIL.	COST

Siem Reap

☑ Amansara 🍴🏊

	28	29	26	25	$675

Road to Angkor | (011-855-63) 760-333 | fax 760-335 | 800-477-9180 | www.amanresorts.com | 24 suites

An "oasis of calm and serenity in the heat and beauty of Angkor" (the ruins are 10 minutes away), this former royal guesthouse boasts "magnificent" "modern" rooms, an on-site swimming pool, "warm service" and a "lovely" restaurant where "they'll prepare something to your liking" to combat "limited choices."

Raffles Grand Hotel D'Angkor ①🍳Ⓢ🏊🔍

	23	26	23	26	$310

1 Vithei Charles de Gaulle, Khum Svay Dang Kum | (011-855-63) 963-888 | fax 963-168 | 800-637-9477 | www.raffles.com | 119 rooms, 12 suites

"Minutes from the ruins" in Angkor, this step back into "British colonial times" "lives up to the Raffles name" with "class" and "old-world luxury" ("love the cage elevator"), a "helpful, discerning staff" and "beautiful" rooms furnished with local *objets*; the "gorgeous" grounds and "excellent amenities", including an "outstanding" pool and eight restaurants and bars, allow the Wat-weary to "relax after touring the temples."

Shinta Mani Ⓢ🏊

	–	–	–	–	$80

14th & Oum Khum Sts., Svay Dangkum Commune | (011-855-63) 761-998 | fax 761-999 | www.shintamani.com | 13 rooms, 5 suites

This "perfect boutique hotel" a short ride from Angkor Wat draws from an extensive menu of wellness options including master-in-residence workshops, where experts teach meditation and yoga; "don't expect luxury", but with "attentive" service, a "great" organic Asian restaurant and "bargain" rates, it's "more fun to stay here than those chain hotels."

Sofitel Royal Angkor 🐎Ⓢ🏊

	▽ 26	25	21	26	$272

Vithei Charles de Gaulle, Khum Svay Dang Kum | (011-855-63) 964-600 | fax 964-609 | 800-763-4835 | www.sofitel.com | 214 rooms, 24 suites

The "best rooms are poolside" say patrons of this "unbelievable" "real find" near the temples of Angkor, where "bike rentals offer the freedom to ride to the ruins" and an "unforgettable spa", "lush landscaping", a "large pool", an "outstanding staff" and "delicious" Asian and European meals make you glad to "come home after a hot day of sightseeing"; with so much "luxury", most find it a "super option" for Siem Reap.

Canada

TOPS IN COUNTRY

ROOMS	SERVICE	DINING	FACIL.	COST

Calgary

Fairmont Palliser, The 👪 Ⓗ 🐕 🏋 🔭 Ⓢ 🏊

ROOMS	SERVICE	DINING	FACIL.	COST
20	22	21	18	$285

133 Ninth Ave. SW | (1-403) 262-1234 | fax 260-1260 | 800-441-1414 | www.fairmont.com | 388 rooms, 17 suites

A "logical" choice for business, this "historic hotel" built in 1914 "in the heart of Calgary" is a "pleasant surprise", with service that's "every bit Fairmont" in a "well-run" way, but others find "nothing truly exceptional" and room quality that "varies."

Hyatt Regency Ⓢ 🏊

ROOMS	SERVICE	DINING	FACIL.	COST
21	19	20	20	$359

700 Centre St. | (1-403) 717-1234 | fax 537-4444 | 800-223-1234 | www.hyatt.com | 342 rooms, 13 suites

"Next to major restaurants and the Convention Center", this tower has a "perfect location", whether you're in town on business or "for the Stampede"; housed in a "remodeled historic building", some find its "modern" appearance "stark", but there's a "great" 18th-floor pool.

Westin 👪 🏋 🔭 🏊

ROOMS	SERVICE	DINING	FACIL.	COST
20	21	16	19	$355

320 Fourth Ave. SW | (1-403) 266-1611 | fax 265-7908 | 800-937-8461 | www.westin.com | 469 rooms, 56 suites

The service is the most appealing attribute of this central Calgary high-rise, a "functional business hotel" staffed by a "friendly" crew; most rooms are "hip-looking" with the chain's "signature Heavenly beds", though critics crab that others are "blah"; still, when you add a "rooftop pool" and all those corporate amenities, it becomes a "solid" selection.

Canadian Rockies

[NEW] Adara Hotel 🏋 🔭 🏊

ROOMS	SERVICE	DINING	FACIL.	COST
-	-	-	-	$216

4122 Village Green | Whistler | (1-604) 905-4009 | 866-502-3272 | www.adarahotel.com | 21 rooms, 20 suites

A modern, playful design with plenty of wood, stone and other natural ingredients is the highlight of this stylish boutique right near the Whistler and Blackcomb Mountain gondolas; rooms come with spa-like baths, 'floating' fireplaces and vibrant colors, while facilities include an outdoor heated pool (seasonal), a year-round hot tub with mountain views and a large lobby with fireplace.

Alive Health Resort Ⓢ

ROOMS	SERVICE	DINING	FACIL.	COST
-	-	-	-	$600

1708 Dolphin Ave. | Kelowna | (1-250) 763-4744 | fax 862-9101 | 888-763-4744 | www.aliveresort.com | 12 rooms

In an ideal setting in a valley amid British Columbia's Monashee Mountains, this serene, self-help-centric retreat offers a remote getaway dedicated to lifestyle improvements from diet to exercise to stress management; there's a staff of health professionals, an on-site Aveda spa and a restaurant with a menu of organic items.

Fairmont Banff Springs, The 👪 🏋 🔭 ⛳ Ⓢ ⛷ 🏊 🎾

ROOMS	SERVICE	DINING	FACIL.	COST
22	24	23	26	$333

405 Spray Ave. | Banff | (1-403) 762-2211 | fax 762-5755 | 800-441-1414 | www.fairmont.com | 683 rooms, 105 suites

An "enchanting" "palace" offering "baronial splendor in the Rockies", this "Canadian classic" is "like a castle out of *Harry Potter*", assuming the child-magician frequents fortresses with "must-do" golf courses, "to-die-for" buffets and "the most spectacular spa imaginable"; fans of the "surreal", "fairy-tale" experience say expect "some of the best service ever" – as well as "grazing elk", "strolling moose" and "ghosts in the hall" – even if skeptics swear it would take a wizard to transform "postage-stamp rooms."

Fairmont Chateau Lake Louise, The ♨♨♨♨♨♨

| 23 | 24 | 22 | 25 | $501 |

111 Lake Louise Dr. | Lake Louise | (1-403) 522-3511 | fax 522-3834 | 800-441-1414 | www.fairmont.com | 478 rooms, 72 suites

Nestled deep within Banff National Park, this "destination for all seasons" affords views of the "majestic" Rockies and "sparkling" Lake Louise that are so "breathtaking" they "seem unreal"; some find the rooms "on the small side" and "somewhat frumpy", but fans say the "courteous and helpful" staff makes for a "memorable" stay – unfortunately, so do the "hordes of tourists" in the lobby.

Fairmont Chateau Whistler, The ♨♨♨♨♨♨♨♨

| 24 | 25 | 22 | 26 | $233 |

4599 Chateau Blvd. | Whistler | (1-604) 938-8000 | fax 938-2291 | 800-441-1414 | www.fairmont.com | 493 rooms, 57 suites

The "only work you have to do" at this "fantastic" ski-in/ski-out resort "at the foot" of Blackcomb Mountain is shoosh down the slopes – "everything else is done for you" by an "affable", "impeccable" staff that goes "above and beyond" (they'll even "chase away the bears"); it's a "beautiful summer destination" too, since the "top-notch facilities" include a Robert Trent Jones Jr.-designed golf course, dining that "beats anything in town" and the "best bar."

Fairmont Jasper Park Lodge, The ♨♨♨♨♨♨♨♨♨

| 23 | 24 | 22 | 25 | $445 |

100 Old Lodge Rd. | Jasper | (1-780) 852-3301 | fax 852-5107 | 800-441-1414 | www.fairmont.com | 383 rooms, 60 suites, 10 cabins

With "elk at the door", "the setting alone" at this "spectacular secluded lodge" in the Canadian Rockies is "worth the price"; there's "so much to do", from golfing, hiking and canoeing, to ogling the wildlife and savoring the "stunning natural beauty"; the dining room serves "good", if "uninspired", "regional fare", but beware that it's "very spread out" and "more rustic" than other Fairmonts.

☑ Four Seasons ♨♨♨♨♨♨

| 28 | 28 | 25 | 28 | $429 |

4591 Blackcomb Way | Whistler | (1-604) 935-3400 | fax 935-3455 | 888-935-2460 | www.fourseasons.com | 183 rooms, 90 suites, 37 condos

The newest "champion of the region" is this three-year-old "incredibly posh" outpost of the venerable brand that may be a "little farther than other resorts from the lifts" but still "perfect for après ski" with its "cozy lobby" and "gorgeous" pool and hot tubs; reviewers swoon over the "ultramodern", "sleek" rooms with in-room fireplaces, the "excellent", though "exceedingly pricey", spa and the "innovative" restaurant, but it's probably the signature service from a "world-class", "pampering" staff (they'll "take your boots off for you") that makes this a truly "memorable experience."

NEW Pan Pacific Whistler Village Centre 🍳🐾Ⓢ⛷🏊

ROOMS	SERVICE	DINING	FACIL.	COST
26	22	19	24	$549

4229 Blackcomb Way | Whistler | (1-604) 966-5500 | fax 966-5501 | www.panpacific.com | 83 suites

In a "perfect location" in the middle of posh Whistler Village Resort, this "fabulous" boutique offers a "stylish" setting with "amazing" facilities that include "large" rooms with full kitchens, gas fireplaces and soaking tubs; a "stone's throw from all the action" with "everything you need for the ski trip of your dreams" (including "top-notch" service, a spa, outdoor hot tubs for soothing sore muscles and a "stick-to-the-ribs breakfast"), this one is "worth every penny."

Post Hotel 🍴🐾Ⓢ⛷🏊

ROOMS	SERVICE	DINING	FACIL.	COST
23	26	27	23	$290

200 Pipestone Rd. | Lake Louise | (1-403) 522-3989 | fax 522-3966 | 800-661-1586 | www.posthotel.com | 64 rooms, 28 suites, 4 cabins, 1 lodge

Even "serious foodies" are "flabbergasted" by the "exquisite" preparations and "huge selection of wines" (more than 2,000 labels) at this Relais & Châteaux "food central of the Rockies" that is "what every ski lodge should be"; "service with a smile", "riverside cabins with heated bathroom floors" and rooms with fireplaces prompt the question "what more could you want?"

Rimrock Resort 🍴🐾Ⓢ⛷🏊

ROOMS	SERVICE	DINING	FACIL.	COST
26	25	24	25	$405

300 Mountain Ave. | Banff | (1-403) 762-3356 | fax 762-4132 | 888-746-7625 | www.rimrockresort.com | 319 rooms, 27 suites

Given this "original, rustic" hotel's "stunning" location - "clinging to the side of a mountain" in the heart of the Canadian Rockies - "there isn't a bad view in the house"; loyalists laud the "luxurious and spacious" rooms, "superb" service and "fantastic" cuisine (including what some say is the best caribou and bison in the country), while outdoorsy types appreciate the "delightful" winter retreat's proximity to the Banff Gondola, Hot Springs and ski resorts.

Westin Resort & Spa 👪🍳🐕🐾⛳Ⓢ⛷🏊

ROOMS	SERVICE	DINING	FACIL.	COST
24	22	20	26	$690

4090 Whistler Way | Whistler | (1-604) 905-5000 | fax 905-5640 | www.westinwhistler.com | 419 suites

An all-suites example of "mountain-resort chic", this chainster "at the foot of the mountains" and"next to the lifts" and the "nightlife" boasts "beautifully appointed" quarters that are more like "fully equipped apartments" with the "best beds on the slopes", kitchenettes and "push-button fireplaces"; other highlights at this "family-friendly" retreat include a spa and health club with a pool, "complimentary shuttle service around Whistler Village" and a "friendly staff willing to accommodate" requests.

Cape Breton

Keltic Lodge 🐕🐾Ⓢ🏊

ROOMS	SERVICE	DINING	FACIL.	COST
18	23	22	24	$368

Ingonish Beach | (1-902) 285-2880 | fax 285-2859 | 800-565-0444 | www.signatureresorts.com | 72 rooms, 2 suites, 31 cottages

In a "magical" Nova Scotia "setting that you'll never forget", this "diamond in the rough" boasts "fabulous" Atlantic Ocean views and "su-

	ROOMS	SERVICE	DINING	FACIL.	COST

per facilities" that include a beach, hiking trails, an Aveda spa and access to Highland Links, one of Canada's top golf courses; although the rooms at this 1940 facility are just "basic" and the place can be a bit too popular with "bus tours", the "grand" service and truly "spectacular" location make it worthwhile.

Edmonton

Fairmont Hotel | 21 | 23 | 21 | 20 | $276 |
Macdonald, The 林✕⊕岩舶⑤衤≋

10065 100 St. | (1-780) 424-5181 | fax 429-6481 | 800-441-1414 | www.fairmont.com | 181 rooms, 18 suites
On a hill overlooking the city and the North Saskatchewan River Valley, this "beautifully redone" 1915 château may house the "best hotel in Edmonton"; admirers appreciate the stately "new-old" style, mixing traditional appointments and modern conveniences (including high-speed Internet, a saltwater pool and an on-site spa); the "professional staff" is "accommodating", and the Harvest Room restaurant, featuring Alberta beef, is among the area's tops.

Montebello

Fairmont Le Chateau | 18 | 21 | 21 | 24 | $250 |
Montebello 林岩舶⊥⑤≋🔍

392, rue Notre Dame | (1-819) 423-6341 | fax 423-5706 | 800-441-1414 | www.fairmont.com | 205 rooms, 6 suites
This "lovely secret" is a bit of "authentic Canadiana" - a "one-of-a-kind", "multistory, log cabin–style" "château" (with a towering fireplace) midway between Montréal and Ottawa; with "lots of activities" in winter or summer, this "rustic" resort can be a "wonderful enclave for families"; N.B. a new spa opened last year.

Montréal

Auberge du Vieux-Port 舶 | - | - | - | - | $160 |
97 rue de la Commune Est | (1-514) 876-0081 | fax 876-8923 | 888-660-7678 | www.aubergeduvieuxport.com | 27 rooms
With a picturesque setting on the riverfront in the heart of Old Montréal, this historic spot in an 1883 building draws loyalists for charming rooms that sport wood floors, original exposed-brick and stone walls, brass beds and views of the St-Lawrence River or historic St-Paul Street; other advantages include the on-site French eatery, Restaurant Les Remparts, a rooftop terrace and complimentary breakfasts and evening cocktails.

Fairmont | 20 | 22 | 21 | 21 | $224 |
The Queen Elizabeth 林岩舶≋

900, boul. Réne Lévesque Ouest | (1-514) 861-3511 | fax 954-2296 | 800-441-1414 | www.fairmont.com | 939 rooms, 100 suites
"Canadian tradition with a capital 'T'", this "grand" hotel is a "fine" choice with a "well-meaning", "pleasant" staff and an "extremely convenient" location for restaurants and shopping (its "best asset"); regulars recommend staying on the premium club floors and heading out for meals, since the dining is "nothing extraordinary."

Fairmont Tremblant 👪🔭Ⓢ⛷🏊 | 22 | 25 | 20 | 26 | $519

3045 Chemin de la Chapelle | Mont Tremblant | (1-819) 681-7000 | fax 681-7099 | 800-441-1414 | www.fairmont.com | 253 rooms, 61 suites

Schussers of all levels head to this "jewel in the crown" of Mont Tremblant village (a 90-minute drive from Montréal) for a "perfect ski-in/ski-out" vacation; an "obliging staff" welcomes you to the "inviting" mountain château at the foot of the Lauretian peaks, where "magnificent views", "massive" pools and spa and "lovely suites" await (though a few say "rooms are somewhat bland"); N.B. dining options are limited to a buffet restaurant, coffee shop and room service.

[Z] **L'Eau a la Bouche** | 18 | 21 | 29 | 17 | $502

3003 Blvd. Sainte-Adele | Sainte-Adéle | (1-450) 229-2991 | fax 229-7573 | 888-828-2991 | www.leaualabouche.com | 20 rooms, 1 suite

For the "best food north of Montreal" (43 miles away), head to this Relais & Châteaux country inn where chef Anne Desjardins creates "miracles" on the plate, turning out "simply superb" fare that "makes many NYC restaurants pale in comparison"; there's a "wonderful" staff and a "charming" setting with nearby hiking, biking and golfing, but it's mostly about the "fabulous" fare since the rooms are "nothing special."

Le Germain, Hotel | 27 | 26 | 18 | 21 | $475

2050, rue Mansfield | (1-514) 849-2050 | fax 849-1437 | 877-333-2050 | www.hotelgermain.com | 99 rooms, 2 suites

Ideal "for the van der Rohe set", this "chic, urban" boutique hotel with "industrial undertones" is an "oasis of calm and luxury" in the heart of Downtown and within "walking distance of everything"; "minimalist", "modern" rooms are "superbly designed" with "incredible bathrooms" and "terrific details" and fans also praise the "impeccable service" from a "staff in-the-know"; luckily there's "access to Montréal's many top-tier restaurants" so the "limited" dining is a "non-issue."

Le Westin Resort & Spa 🫖🐕🔭⛳Ⓢ⛷🏊🎾 | 23 | 21 | 19 | 22 | $300

100 Chemin Kandahar | Mont Tremblant | (1-819) 681-8000 | fax 681-8001 | 800-937-8461 | www.westin.com | 61 rooms, 65 suites

At this "high-tech" Mont Tremblant hotel located just "steps away from the ski lifts" and the village nightlife, the "sumptuous" rooms "rival the natural beauty of the mountain", the "heated outdoor pool" is bliss and the staff "tries hard."

Loews Hotel Vogue 👪🫖🐕 | 24 | 24 | 21 | 21 | $299

1425, rue de la Montagne | (1-514) 285-5555 | fax 849-8903 | 800-235-6397 | www.loewshotels.com | 126 rooms, 16 suites

The celeb clientele of this "splashy", "ritzy" lodging in the "heart of Downtown Montréal" make it a "good place for stargazing", plus it also has a "fantastic" "metrosexual" staff and "magnificent" rooms with "huge bathtubs" and "beds you can get lost in"; still, some critics aren't so keen on the "noisy" streetside units and the "average" Italian fare.

Omni Mont-Royal 👪🐕🔭Ⓢ🏊 | 22 | 22 | 19 | 21 | $328

1050, rue Sherbrooke Ouest | (1-514) 284-1110 | fax 845-3025 | 888-444-6664 | www.omnihotels.com | 271 rooms, 29 suites

"Massive rooms", "reasonable prices" and an "ideal location" across the street from McGill University are the lures at this "comfortable" hotel that's "perfect for business travelers"; while the "outdoor heated pool" and "gym are pluses", "dated furniture" have some concluding that it's "somewhere between a Best Western and the Ritz."

Ritz-Carlton, The ✕ⓗ

| 21 | 23 | 21 | 19 | $195 |

1228, rue Sherbrooke Ouest | (1-514) 842-4212 | fax 842-3383 | 800-241-3333 | www.ritzcarlton.com | 181 rooms, 48 suites

"If you can't be in Paris", this 1912 "grande dame" with "lots of character" in Montréal's Downtown "is the closest second", particularly if you dine alfresco at the hotel's Le Jardin du Ritz; "get a junior suite" advise admirers, and ignore what a minority calls the "faded glory."

St-Paul Hotel

| 24 | 23 | 24 | 19 | $229 |

355, rue McGill | (1-514) 380-2222 | fax 380-2200 | 866-380-2202 | www.hotelstpaul.com | 96 rooms, 24 suites

"The design is divine" at this "trendy" Montréal boutique that's so "sleek" and "chic" you expect to see celebs in the lobby at any moment; it's "well-situated" "on the edge of the old city and close to the port", with "loftlike" rooms, "über-modern" baths and a "killer bar", so if you "appreciate high style", "why would you stay anywhere else?"; N.B. a new restaurant opens in early 2007.

W Montreal ✗♨⑨

| 25 | 22 | 21 | 23 | $259 |

901 Sq. Victoria | (1-514) 395-3100 | fax 395-3150 | 514-395-3100 | www.whotels.com | 122 rooms, 30 rooms

"Very dark", "funky" and "flashy" – it's the standard W from the "trendy as trendy can be" entry to the "endlessly cool" lounges with "crowd-watching as fun as you can imagine"; but beyond that, it's "overpriced and poorly designed" say the disenchanted, with some of the "minimalist" quarters looking out on buildings full of "office drones at their desks" and others too close to a bar filled with "music well into the night", plus the staff can be both "confused" and "rude."

Niagara Falls

Embassy Suites Fallsview ♨≋

| 22 | 18 | 17 | 21 | $200 |

6700 Fallsview Blvd. | (1-905) 356-3600 | fax 374-5131 | 800-420-6980 | www.embassysuites.com | 512 suites

The "perfect location" "high on a cliff" just 100 yards from Niagara Falls means you can have "incredible views" from your "in-room hot tub" at this otherwise "ordinary" lodging; though the "huge rooms" and "free breakfast" are "great for a family trip", those who find "abrupt" service say the "only reason to stay" is the "close proximity" to those famous rushing waters.

Niagara Falls
Marriott Fallsview ♨⑨≋

| 25 | 20 | 18 | 22 | $247 |

6740 Fallsview Blvd. | (1-905) 357-7300 | fax 357-0490 | 888-501-8916 | www.niagarafallsmarriott.com | 347 rooms, 85 suites

Be sure to "ask for a Fallsview Room on a high floor" at this "highly recommended" tower since the "unbelievable" vistas make you "feel like you're standing right on top of the waterfalls" – indeed, some say you'll "never want to leave your room" since the view from here is "better" than being outside; when you do venture out, there's a spa, an on-site movie theater and a skywalk that connects to a casino.

	ROOMS	SERVICE	DINING	FACIL.	COST

Pillar and Post Inn ⊕Ⓢ
22 | 21 | 20 | 19 | $247

48 John St. | Niagara-on-the-Lake | (1-905) 468-2123 | fax 468-3551 | www.vintage-hotels.com | 109 rooms, 13 suites

A former canning factory, this hotel takes you "back to Victorian times" yet offers "all the modern indulgences" as well; "large" accommodations have "canopy beds laden with rose petals", a "wonderful" 13,000-sq.-ft. spa offers state-of-the-art treatments and "consistent fine dining" takes advantage of "several great Ontario wineries" that are nearby; while "impeccable service" is another plus, naysayers claim this lodging has "lost a bit of its polish and edge" in recent years.

Prince of Wales Hotel Ⓢ≋
23 | 23 | 22 | 22 | $256

6 Picton St. | Niagara-on-the-Lake | (1-905) 468-3246 | fax 468-5521 | 888-669-5566 | www.vintage-hotels.com | 90 rooms, 20 suites

"Such a beautiful town, such a grand old hotel" sigh those who love the "magnificent setting" and "in-the-middle-of-it-all" location of this "quaint" "best bet" within walking distance of "all the theaters" (great for the annual Shaw Festival); "attractively decorated" rooms offer "nice touches" like "faux fireplaces", and there's a "hearty Canadian breakfast" and "lovely afternoon tea", but the "awkward service" can be "dispiriting" for a few.

Sheraton on the Falls ⚼Ⓢ≋
22 | 18 | 14 | 19 | $199

5875 Falls Ave. | (1-905) 374-4445 | fax 371-0157 | www.sheraton.com | 667 rooms, 3 suites

A "room facing the Falls" with a "gorgeous view" is "the only way to stay" at this chainster adjacent to a huge casino-retail-entertainment complex, since aside from its "location, location, location" it doesn't inspire much praise; while reviewers say it's "not bad", others, citing "lackluster service" and "complacent dining", argue "there are better places to stay."

Ottawa

Arc The.Hotel
21 | 22 | 19 | 18 | $226

140 Slater St. | (1-613) 238-2888 | fax 238-8421 | 800-699-2516 | www.arcthehotel.com | 110 rooms, 2 suites

Bringing a "hip" choice to the nation's capital, this "cute little boutique" in Downtown Ottawa boasts "modern, elegant", though "tiny", rooms, a library with complimentary Starbucks and Tazo teas, a "discreet" staff and a "wonderful" bar "for a romantic drink" (check out the 'Mood Booth' where the colors change constantly); if you avoid the "very noisy" quarters that face the street, this one is a "unique" and "welcome change from the boring hotels" in town.

Fairmont Chateau Laurier ⊕⚲⚼≋
21 | 23 | 20 | 22 | $346

1 Rideau St. | (1-613) 241-1414 | fax 562-7030 | 800-441-1414 | www.fairmont.com | 389 rooms, 40 suites

"You can feel the history" at this "elegant" "old-school" "classic" just "a hockey puck's throw from Parliament" where you can "view the political intrigues of Ottawa"; "from the copper roof to the sensational" "grand lobby" to the "amiable service", it exudes "importance", even if its rooms are "variable."

Québec City

Auberge Saint Antoine ⚏♨

| 25 | 25 | 24 | 23 | $193 |

8, rue Saint-Antoine | (1-418) 692-2211 | fax 692-1177 | 888-692-2211 | www.saint-antoine.com | 82 rooms, 12 suites

This "modern" "gem" of a boutique "right in the Old City" "beats the pants off" its competition with "fabulous views" of the St. Lawrence River and "hip yet comfy decor" "infused with creativity" (there are "cool architectural artifacts" on display); the "friendly, young" staff is "attentive", plus the "romantic" "gourmet" French restaurant with "stone walls" and "lofted ceilings" serves "ambitious" food "to die for."

Dominion 1912

| 27 | 28 | 21 | 22 | $365 |

126, rue Saint-Pierre | (1-418) 692-2224 | fax 692-4403 | 888-833-5253 | www.hoteldominion.com | 60 rooms

A "fabulous little find" in the "trendy part" of Vieux Québec, this "chic" boutique is set in a "glorious, old stone building" from 1912; the deft blending of "historic charm" (there's a "huge lobby fireplace"), "modern" touches (rooms have Bose radios) and "outstanding personal service" have some guests swearing they "could move in and never leave"; the "lovely" buffet breakfast seals the deal.

Fairmont Le Château Frontenac ♛⊛⚏♨≋

| 22 | 24 | 23 | 23 | $432 |

1, rue des Carrieres | (1-418) 692-3861 | fax 692-1751 | 800-441-1414 | www.fairmont.com | 585 rooms, 33 suites

Set in a "perfect location" atop a plateau overlooking the St. Lawrence River, this "regal" "urban castle" "captures the magic of Old Québec" with its "imposing" exterior, "spectacular views from the lounge" and "enormous" interior that "doesn't seem crowded" despite "hordes of conventioneers"; while it also gets smiles for the "warm" and "courteous staff" and the overall "grand" setting, a critical contingent complain the rooms and food are "a little disappointing."

Fairmont Le Manoir Richelieu ♛⚏♨▲☉≋

| 23 | 23 | 21 | 25 | $181 |

181, rue Richlieu | La Malbaie | (1-418) 665-3703 | fax 665-8131 | 800-441-1414 | www.fairmont.com | 385 rooms, 20 suites

"Sit and watch the St. Lawrence" at this riverside "retreat", designed like a French castle in the Charlevoix region an hour-and-a-half from Québec City; it's "a superb getaway" for golfing (on a Herbert Strong-designed course), swimming and relaxing (a spa completes the picture); the handful of surveyors who've sampled its charms conclude "it lives up to the Fairmont name."

Ice Hotel ☉

| - | - | - | - | $599 |

Sainte-Catherine-de-la-Jacques-Cartier | (1-418) 875-4522 | fax 875-2833 | 877-505-0423 | www.icehotel-canada.com | 36 rooms, 10 suites

Take a holiday on ice at this "once-in-a-lifetime experience", a "unique" "igloo" complex (including exhibition halls, a wedding chapel and bar) that's rebuilt yearly out of ice and snow, and thus only open January to early April; outdoor activities include dogsledding, snowmobiling and ice fishing, while indoors you'll hibernate in an insulated sleeping bag on a bed piled high with deer pelts.

La Pinsonnière ⛳🏋Ⓢ🏊🎾 ▽ 24 | 25 | 28 | 19 | $290

124, rue St-Raphael | La Malbaie | (1-418) 665-4431 | fax 665-7156 | 800-387-4431 | www.lapinsonniere.com | 16 rooms, 1 suite

"Homey" yet "refined", this "wonderful" Relais & Châteaux hotel set on a bluff with "killer views of the St. Lawrence River" earns high praise for its French restaurant, which serves "some of the best food in Canada" plus "dynamite vodka martinis"; about 90 miles from Québec City, it's a "truly glorious" spot to "get away from it all", with "lovely" service and cushy digs with bathrooms you "want to take home."

St. Andrews

Fairmont Algonquin, The 👪🐕⛳🏋⛵Ⓢ🏊🎾 ▽ 21 | 23 | 23 | 24 | $207

184 Adolphus St. | (1-506) 529-8823 | fax 529-4194 | 800-441-1414 | www.fairmont.com | 221 rooms, 13 suites

Staying at this "classy dowager" in the "wonderful little town" of St. Andrews is a "treat" thanks to "friendly" service, "beautiful" grounds and a well-regarded golf course with "spectacular views" of the Bay of Fundy; although "pleased" patrons find it all "grand", disappointed guests say it's "clear this place is from another era."

Kingsbrae Arms ✕Ⓗ⛳🏋🏊 - | - | - | - | $411

219 King St. | (1-506) 529-1897 | 800-735-2478 | www.kingsbrae.com | 2 rooms, 8 suites

Popular with golfers headed for the McBroom-designed course nearby, this "elegant", pet-friendly Relais & Châteaux 19th-century country house in the seaside resort of St. Andrews (on the border between Maine and the province of New Brunswick) is furnished with antiques, a grand piano and lots of books; the bed-and-breakfast-style rooms include cast-iron bathtubs, handmade four-poster feather beds, satellite TV and kitchens, but it's "worth the visit" mostly for the elegant, French-influenced restaurant that offers an impressive wine list.

St. John's

Fairmont Newfoundland ⛳🏋⛷🏊 ▽ 20 | 22 | 21 | 21 | $181

115 Cavendish Sq. | (1-709) 726-4980 | fax 726-2025 | 800-441-1414 | www.fairmont.com | 301 rooms, 14 suites

A massive hotel right on St. John's Harbor and within walking distance of major shopping and offices, this chainster "fits in well in a hip young town"; you'll enjoy some "good" local seafood at Cabot Club restaurant, and, if you "stay on the concierge floor", you'll get "professional pampering" and "breathtaking sunsets"; those who find an "old-fashioned" look, deem it only an "adequate hotel in a great city."

Toronto

Fairmont Royal York, The Ⓗ⛳🏋Ⓢ⛷🏊 19 | 22 | 20 | 21 | $294

100 Front St. W. | (1-416) 368-2511 | fax 368-9040 | 800-441-1414 | www.fairmont.com | 1174 rooms, 191 suites

For a "solid choice" in Downtown Toronto's Financial District, many turn to this "wonderful example of Fairmont hospitality", an "elegant", "ornate" 1843 "monument to Victorian style" where the "extremely helpful bellmen and concierge" win fans; while most reviewers applaud this railway hotel's "atmospheric public" areas and "old-world grace", skeptics say the "tired" "tiny" rooms "need remodeling."

Four Seasons ✕ 🛏 🐕 🔭 🏊

Rooms	Service	Dining	Facil.	Cost
24	26	25	24	$294

21 Avenue Rd. | (1-416) 964-0411 | fax 964-8699 | 800-332-3442 | www.fourseasons.com | 342 rooms, 38 suites

The "flawless" staff "fulfills all requests" at this "chic" Four Seasons flagship "perfectly located in Yorkville" near Bloor Street; the "exceptional" dining at Truffles, courtesy of chef Lynn Crawford, and an "amazing lobby bar" where you can "hobnob with stars" are the standout features, but seasoned travelers who believe this "old broad" is "showing her age" say the planned new property nearby "will be a welcome replacement."

Langdon Hall Country House Hotel & Spa ✕ 🐕 🔭 Ⓢ 🏊 🎾

Rooms	Service	Dining	Facil.	Cost
25	24	26	23	$285

1 Langdon Dr. | Cambridge | (1-519) 740-2100 | fax 740-8161 | 800-268-1898 | www.langdonhall.ca | 39 rooms, 13 suites

Guests report feeling "like a country squire" at this "peaceful, tranquil" and "remote" Relais & Châteaux inn, built in 1898 on 200 acres of gardens an hour from Toronto; the royal treatment at this "quintessential romantic getaway" includes "service above reproach", "a first-class kitchen", a traditional afternoon tea overlooking the grounds and "perfect Anglophile rooms" with antiques and feather beds; N.B. it's a good base for the summer Stratford Shakespeare Festival.

Le Royal Méridien King Edward 🐕 🔭 Ⓢ

Rooms	Service	Dining	Facil.	Cost
21	22	19	19	$368

37 King St. E. | (1-416) 863-9700 | fax 863-4102 | 800-543-4300 | www.lemeridien.com | 248 rooms, 48 suites

"Pretend you're a royal relation" at this "refurbished landmark" in the business district, "a gorgeous bit of Edwardian splendor" known as the "King Eddie to its friends"; guests gush over the "flawless service from check-in to check-out", but some sniff that this "vintage" property (just over 100 years old) is getting "a little dowdy."

Metropolitan Hotel ✕ 🔭 🏊

Rooms	Service	Dining	Facil.	Cost
19	20	19	17	$133

108 Chestnut St. | (1-416) 977-5000 | fax 977-9513 | www.metropolitan.com | 362 rooms, 60 suites

The "free morning limousine service will make co-workers jealous" advise road warriors who appreciate this "boutique"-style business hotel with a decent Cantonese restaurant, Lai Wah Heen ("go for the dim sum"); just beware that the lovely "minimalist decor" means "microscopic rooms."

Park Hyatt 🛏 🔭 Ⓢ

Rooms	Service	Dining	Facil.	Cost
24	24	21	23	$499

4 Avenue Rd. | (1-416) 925-1234 | fax 924-4933 | 800-223-1234 | www.parkhyatttoronto.com | 301 rooms, 45 suites

"To work or play" in Toronto's "chic" Yorkville area, reviewers recommend this "well-located and well-run property", a "classy", "modern" hotel "in the heart of the city"; the "know-your-name service" makes this an "oasis" "for business travelers", and you can't beat the "spacious rooms" or the "great views" from the "terrific rooftop bar"; P.S. "be sure to book a massage" at the "fabulous spa."

| | ROOMS | SERVICE | DINING | FACIL. | COST |

Soho Metropolitan Hotel ✕ · 27 · 22 · 22 · 23 · $333

318 Wellington St. W. | (1-416) 599-8800 | fax 599-8801 | 866-764-6638 | www.metropolitan.com | 75 rooms, 17 suites

The "beautiful", "modern" rooms are the standout feature of this Downtown "avant-garde" boutique that's not one bit short on "style – or expense"; enjoy "cozy down duvets, remote-control curtains", Frette linens, floor-to-ceiling windows that open and "stunning bathrooms" with German-crafted Dornbracht fixtures, "incredible" Molton Brown amenities and "heated floors"; the location is equally "great", near "many hip restaurants on King Street" and "shopping on Queen Street", and the "friendly" service and "memorable" dining at Senses also score points.

Westin Harbor Castle · 21 · 19 · 17 · 21 · $250

1 Harbour Sq. | (1-416) 869-1600 | fax 869-0573 | 800-937-8461 | www.westin.com | 970 rooms, 7 suites

"Always request a harbour view" at this "big conference" favorite, where the "breathtaking" vistas of Lake Ontario make stays "worth every penny"; "renovated rooms breath new life" into "previously dated decor" with "flat-screen TVs, great bathrooms", top-notch amenities and that famous 'Heavenly bed'; while fans find that the "terrific staff" goes "beyond the basics", naysayers caution that "service is uneven" and the "revolving restaurant is for tourists only."

Windsor Arms · 23 · 23 · 22 · 21 · $295

18 St. Thomas St. | (1-416) 971-9666 | fax 921-9121 | 800-525-4800 | www.windsorarmshotel.com | 2 rooms, 26 suites

"Celebrities who want to stay unnoticed" hide out at this 1927 landmark turned "elegant" boutique hotel, an "intimate" property that's full of "thoughtful amenities" (like "fluffy comforters" and a "lovely spa"); the location is prime for "upscale shopping", and you can revive yourself afterwards with the "scrumptious high tea" in the "spectacular dining room"; if a few critics cry "pretentious", supporters say it "gets our vote."

Vancouver

Fairmont Hotel Vancouver, The ✕ · 21 · 24 · 21 · 22 · $259

900 W. Georgia St. | (1-604) 684-3131 | fax 662-1907 | 800-441-1414 | www.fairmont.com | 520 rooms, 36 suites

Emanating "old-world elegance" from the "grand lobby" to the "traditional" "English-style rooms", this 1939 "landmark" is "perfectly situated to get the most out of the city", particularly if you're on "a shopaholics holiday"; the "cordial" staff "spoils you in the best possible ways", and "power diners" devour steak and seafood at 900 West Lounge; "like an old lady trying to keep up", however, this "dowager" works hard for her "charms."

Fairmont Vancouver Airport · 27 · 25 · 22 · 24 · $233

3111 Grant McConachie Way | (1-604) 207-5200 | fax 248-3219 | 800-441-1414 | www.fairmont.com | 390 rooms, 2 suites

"If only all airport hotels were this nice" sigh sojouners smiling over this "utterly sybaritic" spot where the "vast", "whisper-quiet" rooms are

	ROOMS	SERVICE	DINING	FACIL.	COST

"surprisingly contemporary" (bathrooms are a "sea of beige marble") and you can "plane-watch from the floor-to-ceiling windows"; there's "nothing like a Jacuzzi and a visit to the excellent spa to while-away a stopover" say some who are so impressed by the "cool pool" and "wonderful service" that they'd "spend a week here" if they could.

Fairmont Waterfront, The ⑪ ✿ ♨ 🐕 ≋ | 25 | 24 | 21 | 24 | $354 |

900 Canada Place Way | (1-604) 691-1991 | fax 691-1999 | 800-441-1414 | www.fairmont.com | 459 rooms, 30 suites

Morgan, "the resident mutt", "welcomes" guests to this "modern" cruise-shipper favorite, "conveniently" located directly across from the "huge" Downtown port; "spectacular views" of the bay, mountains, city and Stanley Park distinguish the "spacious and well-appointed" (if "unimaginative") rooms, and help "set this apart from Fairmont's other" local offerings; the "quiet and near-perfect" service –"particularly" on the "Gold Level" – also draws raves, as does the "elevated pool."

Four Seasons ✕ ✿ ♨ ≋ | 23 | 26 | 23 | 23 | $303 |

791 W. Georgia St. | (1-604) 689-9333 | fax 844-6744 | www.fourseasons.com | 306 rooms, 70 suites

"Not once will you hear a 'no'" from the "superb" staff that's "up to the chain's usual exemplary standards" at this "lovely" lodging in a "terrific location" with "easy access to Vancouver's Downtown core"; though a few find it's "not the jewel" in the Four Seasons crown, citing a need to "remodel" the "tired" rooms (a renovation is planned for early 2007), others praise the "fantastic" Chartwell restaurant and insist it "still ranks among the best" in town.

Z Hastings House ✕ ♨ Ⓢ | 24 | 27 | 29 | 20 | $420 |

160 Upper Ganges Rd. | Salt Spring Island | (1-250) 537-2362 | fax 537-5333 | 800-661-9255 | www.hastingshouse.com | 16 suites, 2 cottages

Experience "sinful comfort" at this "tranquil" Relais & Châteaux lodging situated in "one of the most magical places on the planet", a few hours from Vancouver on Salt Spring Island; accommodations are in hillside suites or a cozy 1938 manor house and there are "spectacular" water views, lush gardens and a "friendly" staff that pays "almost too much attention" to guests, but it's the "outstanding food" that "alone is worth the trip"; P.S. "bring a titanium credit card."

Listel ▽ 22 | 25 | 20 | 20 | $189 |

1300 Robson St. | (1-604) 684-8461 | fax 684-7092 | 800-663-5491 | www.listel-vancouver.com | 119 rooms, 10 suites

"Conveniently" located near "the best shopping and eating in town", this "intimate" "low-rise" with an "art theme" is a "pleasant change"; "minimalist" rooms are stocked with "excellent amenities" and, thanks to partnerships with galleries and UBC's Museum of Anthropology, are decorated with "original art"; the gym with "coed whirlpool", the restaurant's "fantastic selection of wine" and a "highly attentive and helpful" staff help make this "a treat on Robson."

Metropolitan Hotel ✕ 🐕 ≋ | 21 | 24 | 24 | 18 | $229 |

645 Howe St. | (1-604) 687-1122 | fax 689-7044 | 800-667-2300 | www.metropolitan.com | 179 rooms, 18 suites

"The design is state-of-the-art, but the staff exudes old-fashioned hospitality" at this "efficient" business travelers' boutique hotel that radiates a "simple elegance" in the middle of "vibrant", bustling Vancouver; impressed foodies praise Diva's "top-drawer" "innovative cuisine", but a minority says that "rooms could use a bit of freshening."

Opus Hotel 🍴🐕🔭

Rooms	Service	Dining	Facil.	Cost
24	26	21	21	$285

322 Davie St. | (1-604) 642-6787 | fax 642-6780 | 866-642-6787 | www.opushotel.com | 84 rooms, 12 suites

"Put the blinds down in the W/C" since there are some "street-facing bathrooms" at this "one-of-a-kind" boutique hotel in "trendy" Yaletown - "the place in Vancouver to see and be seen"; from the "refreshingly" "hip" rooms, done in a rainbow of "funky", vibrant hues, to the "hot" lobby bar where you're apt to "run into movie stars" to the classic French brasserie, Elixir's, the scene is "sexy and modern."

Pacific Palisades 🫖🐕🔭Ⓢ🏊

	Rooms	Service	Dining	Facil.	Cost
▽	20	21	15	20	$161

1277 Robson St. | (1-604) 688-0461 | fax 688-4374 | 800-663-1815 | www.pacificpalisadeshotel.com | 233 suites

Fans of the Miami "retro look" go gaga for the "quirky decor" and "bold colors" at this "fun" spot, where the "spacious suites" - like "furnished apartments" - are "very comfortable, especially for longer stays" and you'll have "terrific views of the Vancouver skyline" if your room is high enough; run by a "helpful staff", it's a "true value" just off "the best shopping street in town."

Pan Pacific 🔭Ⓢ🏊

Rooms	Service	Dining	Facil.	Cost
25	24	23	25	$511

300-999 Canada Pl. | (1-604) 662-8111 | fax 685-8690 | 800-937-1515 | www.panpac.com | 465 rooms, 39 suites

With an "incredible location" on "Vancouver's waterfront", "right at the back door" of the docks, this favorite of "conventions" and "the cruise-ship crowd" is best loved for its "spectacular views" of the harbour and Stanley Park; inside, "modern" rooms, a stellar spa and gym and "first-rate service" make this one of the most "consistently high-quality" spots in town; fans recommend "booking directly", as they can be "very generous with upgrades" for those "not part of a big group."

Sutton Place Hotel 🐕🔭Ⓢ🏊

Rooms	Service	Dining	Facil.	Cost
24	25	23	22	$257

845 Burrard St. | (1-604) 682-5511 | fax 682-5513 | 866-378-8866 | www.suttonplace.com | 350 rooms, 47 suites

"Canadian hospitality at its finest" distinguishes this "lively, upscale" Downtowner, which drew surveyor raves for its "fabulous", "attitude-less" staff and concierge and - thanks to its popularity with "Hollywood North" - the "star-sightings galore"; near the "active lobby", the Fleuri restaurant serves "fine food" and "a chocolate-lover's buffet to die for", while upstairs, "immaculate" rooms have a "European feel."

Wedgewood Ⓢ

Rooms	Service	Dining	Facil.	Cost
24	26	24	22	$228

845 Hornby St. | (1-604) 689-7777 | fax 608-5348 | 800-663-0666 | www.wedgewoodhotel.com | 41 rooms, 42 suites

"A little bit of Europe" "in the heart of Vancouver", this "charming" boutique "favorite" makes you feel like you're "staying with a wealthy socialite aunt" who knows just how to make the "mixed crowd" "feel comfortable"; many of the "understated, lovely" rooms feature jetted tubs, while the four Penthouse suites recently underwent a million-dollar renovation; add in the "exceptional staff", "decent spa", "fabu-

	ROOMS	SERVICE	DINING	FACIL.	COST

lous bar and restaurant" – where dinner "is not to be missed" – and "yummy cookies" "at turndown", and there's "no need to leave."

Westin Bayshore ✎♨≈ | 23 | 23 | 19 | 22 | $420 |

1601 Bayshore Dr. | (1-604) 682-3377 | fax 687-3102 | 888-219-2157 | www.westin.com | 511 rooms

"Jog out the back door" to the seawall for an "exceptional" workout, when you stay at this sprawling property on Coal Harbor, just "a stone's throw from Stanley Park"; it has "beautiful views of the marina and the mountains", "well-appointed rooms" and business-friendly service, as well as "great conference facilities"; just beware that there are "virtually negligible dining options."

Westin Grand ♯✎♨♨⊙≈ | 24 | 20 | 17 | 21 | $373 |

433 Robson St. | (1-604) 602-1999 | fax 647-2502 | 800-937-8461 | www.westingrandvancouver.com | 207 suites

You might not realize that this "chic" "all-suite hotel" is "shaped like a grand piano", but you will notice it's got a "clever design", including "practical" mini-kitchens tucked into the walls; athletic types "love the fitness facilities and outdoor pool", and the city center location is "excellent for business"; N.B. a spa was recently added.

Victoria

Aerie Resort ✗♨⊙✎ | 25 | 26 | 24 | 24 | $295 |

600 Ebedora Ln. | Malahat | (1-250) 743-7115 | fax 743-4766 | 800-518-1933 | www.aerie.bc.ca | 9 rooms, 26 suites

"Divine location, views and dining" sums up this "beautiful" Relais & Châteaux "haven on Vancouver Island", an "out-of-the-way" retreat just 30 minutes from Victoria; proponents praise the "impeccable service" and "lovely rooms with balconies overlooking the forest", advising "get a suite with a sunken tub."

Delta Victoria Ocean Pointe Resort & Spa ♯✎♨⊙≈✎ | 23 | 20 | 18 | 20 | $199 |

45 Songhees Rd. | (1-250) 360-2999 | fax 360-1041 | 800-667-4677 | www.deltahotels.com | 235 rooms, 5 suites

"Striking" views of Victoria's Inner and Outer Harbour and Parliament buildings "make up for" this spot's somewhat removed perch "about a 10-minute walk" or short water taxi ride from the city center; those water vistas also help elevate what a few detractors deem "somewhat dated" rooms", though most enjoy the complimentary breakfast and spa facilities.

Fairmont Empress, The ♯✎♨↥⊙≈ | 21 | 25 | 23 | 24 | $302 |

721 Government St. | (1-250) 384-8111 | fax 381-4334 | 800-257-7544 | www.fairmont.com | 441 rooms, 36 suites

You'll "step back in time" as you enter this "incredibly beautiful" British "landmark" with "gorgeous" Inner Harbour views, a "postcard-perfect" setting ("everything is within walking distance") and a "can-do" staff; it takes "plenty of walking" to "get anywhere" inside this "rambling" hotel, but find your way to the "best high tea" ("you must try it before you're dead") and the "lovely blue tile pool"; even if some complain the "grand lady" is "stuffy" and "needs a revamp", she's still the "queen of hotels in B.C." and "not just a tourist destination."

	ROOMS	SERVICE	DINING	FACIL.	COST
Grand Pacific, Hotel 🐕👪Ⓢ🏊	▽ 24	25	21	22	$285

463 Belleville St. | (1-250) 386-0450 | fax 380-4475 | 800-663-7550 | www.hotelgrandpacific.com | 258 rooms, 46 suites

"A saving grace in Victoria", this imposing, pink-tinged lodging with châteaulike gables is blessed with an "excellent location on the Inner Harbour" as well as "service that's eager to please"; all rooms and suites have balconies, and other amenities include extensive banquet and meeting rooms, a spa and a health club with a pool, though some say the on-site dining "isn't quite up to the hotel's overall standards."

	ROOMS	SERVICE	DINING	FACIL.	COST
Laurel Point Inn 🐕👪🏊	▽ 20	19	15	17	$207

680 Montreal St. | (1-250) 386-8721 | fax 386-9547 | 800-663-7667 | www.laurelpoint.com | 135 rooms, 65 suites

From the most "amazing Japanese garden" to the "large deck" overlooking the water, this "airy" "contemporary" building has a simply "beautiful setting" at the entrance to busy Victoria Harbour; guests gush about the "spectacular views from the south wing" and consider the rooms overall to be "well appointed" (particularly the "luxurious bathrooms"); although the stylish sniff "pedestrian", at least it's a "good value."

	ROOMS	SERVICE	DINING	FACIL.	COST
Sooke Harbour House 🐕👪	25	26	27	21	$337

1528 Whiffen Spit Rd. | Sooke | (1-250) 642-3421 | fax 642-6988 | www.sookeharbourhouse.com | 11 rooms, 17 suites

Surrounded by the Pacific Ocean and colorful gardens, this "serene and sophisticated" inn on Vancouver Island, 45 minutes from Victoria, gets the nod for "unobstructed views of the harbor" and "outstanding gourmet cuisine" that incorporates local seafood; "cozy" quarters are "individual works of art" with antiques, rock fireplaces, a bottle of port and several pairs of rainboots to encourage exploration of the extensive grounds, and the "welcoming staff" creates a "restful" environment.

	ROOMS	SERVICE	DINING	FACIL.	COST
[NEW] **Westin Bear Mountain Victoria Golf Resort & Spa, The** ⛳🖥🐕👪🎾Ⓢ🏊	-	-	-	-	$449

1999 Country Club Way | (1-250) 391-7160 | fax 391-3792 | 888-533-2327 | www.bearmountain.ca | 86 rooms, 70 suites

Duffers are the target audience of this resort set on the fairways of the Bear Mountain Golf and Country Club, co-designed by Jack and Steve Nicklaus; rooms have views of the course and of Mount Finlayson, and feature deap-soaking tubs, natural slate flooring and balconies or terraces; other amenities include a pool, a spa and a fitness center; N.B. there are plans to open a second course and a Nicklaus Academy in 2008.

	ROOMS	SERVICE	DINING	FACIL.	COST
Wickaninnish Inn ⛳🐕👪Ⓢ	27	26	26	26	$381

500 Osprey Ln. | Tofino | (1-250) 725-3100 | fax 725-3110 | 800-333-4604 | www.wickinn.com | 63 rooms, 12 suites

"When you really want to get away" come to this "truly spectacular" Relais & Châteaux "dream of a place" on the rugged coast of Vancouver Island with "delightful" rooms where you can "lay in bed looking out" at the "fabulous views over the Pacific"; the "first-class" staff's "attention to detail is astounding", and the "excellent" food extends to an all-you-can-eat "crab cookout on the beach that's not to be missed" - it's "wild", "wonderful" and definitely "worth the trek."

	ROOMS	SERVICE	DINING	FACIL.	COST

Cayman Islands

Hyatt Regency 🏃🛏️🖥️Ⓢ🏊🌊🏌️   22 | 22 | 21 | 23 | $650

Seven Mile Beach | Grand Cayman | (1-345) 949-1234 | fax 949-8528 |
800-223-1234 | www.hyatt.com | 53 suites

This "wonderful" resort has "come back" from a hurricane several
years ago, "doing it right" with an "excellent" staff that "makes you
feel like an old friend", a "beautiful" Jack Nicklaus–designed golf
course, two "great" swimming pools, a spa, "suites that are excellent
for families" and decent enough dining; although some are annoyed
they have to "trek" to the "crowded" Seven Mile Beach, others say "it's
close enough to not be an issue", plus there are "spectacular sunsets."

Z Ritz-Carlton, The 🏃🏌️🎾🛏️Ⓢ🏊🌊🏌️   28 | 27 | 26 | 28 | $749

Seven Mile Beach | Grand Cayman | (1-345) 943-9000 | fax 943-9001 |
800-241-3333 | www.ritzcarlton.com | 341 rooms, 24 suites

Have "one of the best vacations you've ever taken" at this beachfront
hotel with "the best spa in the world" and one of the best restaurants
as well – superstar chef Eric Ripert's Blue; it's a "no-brainer" say its
fans, citing the "service-oriented" spirit, the "fantastic" rooms, the
tennis center with Nick Bollettieri–designed courts and the "incredible
views" – just "don't get sticker-shocked" on the way out.

Chile

Atacama

Explora En Atacama,   - | - | - | - | $515
Hotel de Larache Ⓢ🌊

Ayllu de Larache | (011-56-2) 206-6060 | fax 228-4655 | 866-750-6699 |
www.explora.com | 50 rooms

Located about 18 miles from the oasis town of San Pedro de Atacama at
the foot of the Andes, this low-key "rustic" yet luxe desert resort in an
"amazing setting" sits ripe for exploration; "super" guides lead half- or
full-day excursions that explore the natural surroundings and "leave
you completely wiped out at day's end"; spectacular design, in keeping with local traditions, includes rooms with tile accents, unique linens and custom furnishings, plus there are four swimming pools and
"high-quality" dining featuring wines from an on-site vineyard.

Patagonia

Explora En Patagonia,   26 | 27 | 25 | 27 | $525
Hotel Salto Chico 🛏️🌊

Torres del Paine National Park | (011-56-2) 206-6060 | fax 228-4655 |
866-750-6699 | www.explora.com | 44 rooms, 6 suites

Inside the Torres del Paine National Park and a five-hour drive from the
airport, this "gem in the boonies" that feels like an "upscale summer
camp" is "worth the effort"; the clapboard lodge "takes advantage of
its spectacular setting" with "stupendous views" and "helpful guides"
that are "well-trained for the treks"; rooms are "comfortable rather
than luxurious", but overall it's the "most elegant way to visit the Chilean
side of Patagonia"; N.B. the minimum stay is four nights.

ROOMS | SERVICE | DINING | FACIL. | COST

Santiago

Grand Hyatt 🖥🏋Ⓢ🏊🎾 26 | 24 | 23 | 25 | $315

4601 Avenida Kennedy | (011-56-2) 950-1234 | fax 950-3155 | 800-223-1234 | www.santiago.grand.hyatt.com | 287 rooms, 23 suites

All stone and glass, this "very glossy", "airy" chain outpost may be "a bit out of the way", but it's "worth the effort" to get here; "split-level" rooms are "suitelike", the service is "ready to satisfy" and the "awesome gym" and "beautiful" lagoon-style pool surrounded by fountains and gardens are perfect places to unwind.

Ritz-Carlton, The 🏋Ⓢ🏊 27 | 26 | 24 | 26 | $340

Calle El Alcalde 15, Las Condes | (011-56-2) 470-8500 | fax 470-8501 | 800-241-3333 | www.ritzcarlton.com | 189 rooms, 16 suites

The "generously sized" rooms with "top-flight" beds and "to-die-for baths" have "every amenity imaginable" at this "modern" outpost that has all "you'd expect" from a Ritz; there's a "good residential location" in El Golf that's within walking distance of equally ritzy boutiques, a "wonderful" glass-domed rooftop swimming pool, "fantastic dining" that includes a "chocolate buffet for dessert" and a bar that offers 365 Chilean wines; no wonder fans say "you don't want to leave this place."

San Cristobal Tower 👪🏋Ⓢ🏊🎾 24 | 23 | 20 | 23 | $315

Josefina Edwards de Ferari 0100 | (011-56-2) 707-1000 | fax 707-1010 | 800-325-3589 | www.sancristobaltower.cl | 127 rooms, 12 suites

The staff "remembers you by name" at this modern high-rise at the foot of San Cristobal Hill, minutes from the business district, where some of the "wonderfully appointed" rooms have "outstanding views" of the Andes; other features include indoor and outdoor pools, a fitness center, a lighted tennis court and a 21st-floor restaurant.

Sheraton Miramar 🏋🏊 ▽ 23 | 20 | 18 | 25 | $269

Avenida Marina 15 | Viña del Mar | (011-56-32) 2388-600 | fax 388-799 | www.sheraton.com | 92 rooms, 50 suites

Set in Viña del Mar, one of Chile's premier summertime destinations and casino districts, this "modern", curved structure sits in front of rocky Caleta Abarca Beach just west of Santiago and takes full advantage of its prime seaside locale - "all rooms have balconies literally over the Pacific"; there's a "gorgeous pool overlooking the water" and an on-site spa, plus "friendly" service brings it all together.

China

TOPS IN COUNTRY

28 Peninsula | *Hong Kong*
27 Four Seasons | *Hong Kong*
26 St. Regis | *Shanghai*
Island Shangri-La | *Hong Kong*
Peninsula | *Beijing*
Four Seasons | *Shanghai*
25 Mandarin Oriental/Landmark | *Hong Kong*
Mandarin Oriental | *Hong Kong*
InterContinental | *Hong Kong*
St. Regis | *Beijing*

Beijing

China World Hotel 🏊 🔍

No. 1 Jianguomenwai Ave. | (011-86-10) 6505-2266 | fax 6505-0828 |
866-565-5050 | www.shangri-la.com | 660 rooms, 56 suites
Frequent fliers find this "modern" business hotel, managed by the
Shangri-La company, "great for meetings" and just "a short ride from
Tiananmen Square"; it features "comfortable", "Western"-style
rooms and first-rate massages, but nitpickers note this onetime lead-
ing light has been "surpassed by many competitors"; N.B. the Horizon
Club offers 24-hour butler service.

Grand Hyatt 🏋 🏊

1 E. Chang An Ave. | (011-86-10) 8518-1234 | fax 8518-0000 |
800-522-1100 | www.beijing.grand.hyatt.com | 773 rooms, 52 suites
"Within spitting distance of the Forbidden City", this "glossy", "power
scene"-heavy "business hotel for the Western traveler" is connected
to a shopping mall and thereby a "destination unto itself"; the "spectacular" underground swimming pool with an "ever-changing artificial
sky" "makes you feel like you're on a tropical island", and the "fantastic"
gym earns praise as well; less grand are rooms "a bit on the small side",
service that's a bit "full of itself" and food that's so-so unless you're enjoying the "superb" Peking duck or the "over-the-top" breakfast buffet.

Kempinski Hotel Beijing
Lufthansa Center 🎿 🏊 🔍

50 Liangmaqiao Rd. | (011-86-10) 6465-3388 | fax 6465-3366 |
800-650-0362 | www.kempinski.com | 487 rooms, 39 suites
"In a good location" near the embassies and "just a cheap taxi ride to
many destinations", this marble-heavy "monster" earns mixed reviews;
most praise the "very friendly staff" and the "lovely" swimming pool,
but others are not so keen on the "tired" rooms and "nothing special"
vibe; at least you can "take advantage of shopping" and a wide variety
of restaurants and cuisines at the "adjoining Lufthansa Center" mall.

Kerry Centre Hotel, The 🏊 🔍

1 Guang Hua Rd. | (011-86-10) 6561-8833 | fax 6561-2626 |
866-565-5050 | www.shangri-la.com | 466 rooms, 23 suites
A "hip hotel" (at least "by Beijing standards"), this "modern" high-rise
with a "high-tech lobby" is part of the Shangri-La chain, offering "stylish", "well-equipped" rooms and a "terrific staff" that "anticipates every need"; it's a "fine" option for business, and when work is done,
choose between the fitness center, indoor pool, billiards room, tennis
courts and outdoor jogging track.

Peninsula, The 🛏 Ⓢ 🏊
(fka Peninsula Palace, The)

8 Goldfish Ln. | (011-86-10) 8516-2888 | fax 6510-6311 | 866-382-8388 |
www.peninsula.com | 468 rooms, 57 suites
After an "excellent" five-year rehab, this "impeccable hotel" is an even
more "fabulous escape from the noise" of the city, "as long as you
don't mind not having Asian flavor"; "within easy walking distance of
the Forbidden City", it offers "exceptional staffers" (they "bring towels
and water while you're on the treadmill"), "five-star–quality" rooms

with "bedside remote controls", a "glitzy", "acres-of-marble" lobby and an upscale shopping arcade; N.B. be sure to try the Cantonese restaurant, Huang Ting.

Raffles Hotel 🏊 — - | - | - | - | $180

33 E. Chang An Ave. | (011-86-10) 6526-3388 | fax 6526-3838 | www.beijing.raffles.com | 151 rooms, 20 suites

Step into the past at this newly renovated venue that sits in the historic building of the former Grand Hotel de Peking just a few minutes from the Forbidden City and Tiananmen Square; the site of significant political and cultural affairs over the years and now run by Raffles International, it boasts rooms with a mix of Asian and French accents and high-tech amenities, 'Personality Suites' that pay homage to luminaries who've stayed here over the years (George Bernard Shaw, Sun Yat Sen) and facilities that include an indoor swimming pool and four restaurants.

St. Regis 🛏 🔭 Ⓢ 🏊 — 26 | 26 | 22 | 26 | $327

21 Jian Guo Men Wai Ave. | (011-86-10) 6460-6688 | fax 6460-3299 | 877-787-3447 | www.stregis.com | 205 rooms, 68 suites

Fans "love the butler" concierge and the "service fit for a king" at this gleaming, "truly Western" Beijing skyscraper "near the embassies", where "great" guestrooms feature calming bronze-toned interiors and Chinese quilts and artwork; the expansive breakfast buffet "overwhelms any stomach", but you can work it off at "one of the grandest" gyms in Asia or at the eight-lane bowling alley.

Guangzhou

[NEW] **Shangri-La Hotel** 🔭 🏊 — - | - | - | - | $113

1 Hui Zhan Dong Lu, Hai Zhu District | (011-86-20) 8917-8888 | www.shangri-la.com | 641 rooms, 63 suites, 26 apartments

The newest China outpost for this luxury chain boasts a convenient corporate location adjacent to the Guangzhou International Convention Centre with impressive views of the Pearl River and landscaped gardens; eight restaurants and bars, rooms with flat-panel TVs and WiFi access, indoor and outdoor swimming pools and a putting green round out the offerings; N.B. CHI spa opens in 2007.

White Swan Hotel 🛏 🔭 🏊 🎾 — 20 | 20 | 18 | 20 | $189

Shamian Island | (011-86-20) 8188-6968 | fax 8186-1188 | www.whiteswanhotel.com | 737 rooms, 106 suites

Nicknamed "the White Stork because of all the adoptive parents who stay here", this "tourist hotel" on Shamian Island has "been around for a while"; it still offers elements of "luxury", with "hanging gardens" and "sumptuous rooms", though non-nostalgics note "it must be sentiment, not sensibility", that appeals to fans of this "faded" facility.

Hong Kong

TOPS IN CITY

28 Peninsula
27 Four Seasons
26 Island Shangri-La
25 Mandarin Oriental/Landmark
Mandarin Oriental

	ROOMS	SERVICE	DINING	FACIL.	COST
Conrad International 🔭🏊	24	25	23	24	$407

Pacific Pl., 88 Queensway | (011-852) 2521-3838 | fax 2521-3888 | 800-445-8667 | www.conradhotels.com | 467 rooms, 46 suites

"Ah! being picked up by a red Conrad Bentley at the airport is just the beginning" at this "gorgeous" (and "convenient") Central Business District choice; the staff is "extremely helpful", rooms are "pure luxury" (particularly if you opt for one with "magnificent" "views of Victoria Peak and the harbor") and "good business facilities" mean it's "reliable all the way around"; though a few detractors decry the rather "bland", "Westernized" ambiance, most like it that way.

	ROOMS	SERVICE	DINING	FACIL.	COST
[Z] **Four Seasons** 👪🐕🔭Ⓢ🏊	28	27	25	27	$489

8 Finance St. | (011-852) 3196-8888 | fax 3196-8899 | www.fourseasons.com | 345 rooms, 54 suites

Seasoned travelers say Hong Kong is "another tough market that Four Seasons has captured in the best possible way" with this sleek tower full of "stone and marble", "impeccable restaurants" (so popular they may be hard even for "guests to secure reservations") and "spacious" rooms with "amazing views"; the "warm staff can't do enough to help you" and the "extraordinary pool area" takes full advantage of the "breathtaking location" "six stories up overlooking Victoria Harbor" - it's "as close to perfect as possible" proclaim patrons.

	ROOMS	SERVICE	DINING	FACIL.	COST
Grand Hyatt 🔭Ⓢ🏊🎾	24	25	24	25	$398

1 Harbour Rd. | (011-852) 2588-1234 | fax 2802-0677 | 800-223-1234 | www.grand.hyatt.com | 500 rooms, 49 suites

Consider springing for the "wonderful Harbor view" option at this tower block - you'll get "an unobstructed vista of one of the most famous scenes in Hong Kong"; but even if you don't get the vista, you'll get "beautifully designed" interiors with "modern yet Asian touches" and "lots of marble in baths", plus an overall "grand" experience from the "opulent lobby" to the "classy service" to the "excellent dining" and "spectacular" 80,000-sq.-ft. Plateau spa that's a "destination in itself."

	ROOMS	SERVICE	DINING	FACIL.	COST
InterContinental 🍴🔭Ⓢ🏊	26	25	25	25	$600

18 Salisbury Rd., Tsim Sha Tsui, Kowloon | (011-852) 2721-1211 | fax 2739-4546 | 800-327-0200 | www.intercontinental.com | 403 rooms, 92 suites

"You're in the midst of the hustle and bustle of Hong Kong", but "feel like you're in an island resort" at this "ultramodern and super-luxurious" Kowloon contender with "outstanding service", where the views from the "amazing" harbor-side rooms are "worth the price of admission" and "blinds can be opened by pushing a button near the bed"; an "illusionist couldn't do better" than the experience of "relaxing in a glass-sided" pool that "visually spills over into" the water below, plus Alain Ducasse's Spoon restaurant is "one of the best" in town.

	ROOMS	SERVICE	DINING	FACIL.	COST
Island Shangri-La 🍴🔭🏊	26	26	25	26	$386

Supreme Court Rd. | (011-852) 2877-3838 | fax 2521-8742 | 800-942-5050 | www.shangri-la.com | 531 rooms, 34 suites

"This really is Shangri-La" swear smitten sojourners of this "island of tranquility and beauty", where the "doting" staff "knows what you want before you do" and the "very modern", "spacious" rooms are "oh-so-nice" ("heavenly" harbor views are "worth the extra $$$"); the

	ROOMS	SERVICE	DINING	FACIL.	COST

"busy staff" still manages to be "amazing", and the location in the Central Financial District above the Pacific Place Mall means there's "easy access to shopping."

Jia 🖉🏍 | - | - | - | - | $206 |

1-5 Irving St. | (011-852) 3196-2004 | fax 3196-9001 | www.jiahongkong.com | 24 suites, 2 penthouses, 28 studios

Designer Philippe Starck (along with John Hitchcox) are behind the first boutique apartment-style hotel for "hipsters" in Hong Kong – this "trendy" spot in the Causeway Bay area; "ultramod design that includes teak floors, white-curtained walls, eclectic chandeliers and African artifacts, and accommodations that range from studios to two-bedroom duplex penthouses with marble kitchens and baths (featuring Kiehl's toiletries), flat-screen TVs and home-theater systems "set it apart from the standard" in this city.

JW Marriott 🏍🏊 | 24 | 24 | 22 | 23 | $436 |

Pacific Pl., 88 Queensway | (011-852) 2810-8366 | fax 2845-5808 | 800-228-9290 | www.marriott.com | 577 rooms, 25 suites

"Well located" in the Pacific Place Central Financial District, this "tried-and-true" choice mixes "luxury" with a "friendly" staff and offers a "great place to network" in the "concierge lounge" as well as the club level ("worth the extra cost"); there's an "excellent" 24-hour health club and spa and rooms with "huge marble bathrooms" and "wonderful harbor views", though a few find them "a little too Western."

Kempinski Hotel Shenzhen 🏊🔍 | - | - | - | - | $229 |

1110 Nanshan Rd., Nanshan District | Shenzhen | (011-86-755) 2652-3344 | fax 2652-8437 | www.kempinski.com | 351 rooms, 39 suites

Meeting the exploding demand of business travelers to China, this hotel, located across the bridge from Hong Kong in Nanshan District, provides the signature Kempinski service along with a state-of-the-art conference facility, a wellness center with indoor pool and a variety of restaurants and cafes, including a Chinese eatery with private dining areas; rooms have WiFi access and baths with TVs and rainshower fixtures.

Kowloon Shangri-La 🖉🏍🏊 | 24 | 25 | 23 | 22 | $370 |

64 Mody Rd., Kowloon | (011-852) 2721-2111 | fax 2723-8686 | 800-942-5050 | www.shangri-la.com | 670 rooms, 30 suites

A "Kowloon classic" with "outstanding interior design and architecture", this hotel is the "favorite place" for those who find a staff that goes "way, way out of its way to make your stay unbelievably easy", plus "marvelous buffets" and a "happening lobby bar"; it's "worth the extra money" to get a room overlooking the Harbor and watch the "nonstop action" (you "can't beat the view"), but a few are "disappointed" overall in this "slightly dated", "touristy" choice.

Le Méridien Cyberport 🏍🏊 | ▽ 24 | 17 | 16 | 19 | $346 |

100 Cyberport Rd. | (011-852) 2980-7788 | fax 2980-7888 | 800-543-4300 | www.lemeridien.com | 169 rooms, 4 suites

"Oozing a high-tech feel perfect for its location" in the Cyberport complex (aka 'Digital City') on Hong Kong's south side, this "cool" hotel sports "innovative", ultramod rooms (heavy on glass and chrome) and wireless services that allow guests to take calls, check in and surf the Internet from anywhere within the property; a few are bothered by an address far from the city center that "isn't ideal for either business or pleasure", but the "relaxed service", on-site wine bar and knockout view of the Lamma Channel make up for it.

Mandarin Oriental ✕🏖⊛≋

| 24 | 28 | 26 | 24 | $463 |

5 Connaught Rd. | (011-852) 2522-0111 | fax 2810-6190 | www.mandarinoriental.com | 430 rooms, 72 suites

"Effortless" service is the hallmark of this "ritzy" veteran with the "right address" (in the Central Business District) when you're on the corporate dime; while a masssive renovation completed last year added a spa and gussied up the "opulent" rooms, it's still filled with tons of "old-world style" and a "wonderful air of history", "especially in the bar"; the "unforgettable experience" includes "exquisite" dining.

Mandarin Oriental The Landmark 🏖🏖⊛≋

| 27 | 26 | 24 | 24 | $515 |

15 Queen's Road Central | (011-852) 2132-0188 | fax 2132-0199 | 800-526-6566 | www.mandarinoriental.com | 101 rooms, 12 suites

With a "hip central location" in the premier commercial and shopping district, this "fabulous" hotel has some of the "most spacious", "spectacular" rooms in this city, with cutting-edge entertainment systems, 400-thread-count linens and a design so stunning "you'll take pictures so you can renovate your own when you go home"; other highlights include "warm" service, a "state-of-the-art gym" and chef Richard Ekkebus' "outrageously priced" modern European haute cuisine at Amber, with an interior designed by Adam Tihany.

☑ Peninsula, The ✕🏖⊛≋

| 28 | 29 | 27 | 27 | $470 |

Salisbury Rd., Tsim Sha Tsui, Kowloon | (011-852) 2366-6251 | fax 2722-4170 | 866-382-8388 | www.peninsula.com | 246 rooms, 54 suites

"Heaven, I'm in heaven" sigh smitten sojourners who say "it doesn't get much finer" than inside this "grande dame of the Far East" in Kowloon where truly "amazingly spacious", high-tech rooms, an indoor pool with "mesmerizing views of the harbor", "second-to-none" service and the "best" dining at the Philippe Starck–designed Felix restaurant make you "feel like a rich king"; indeed, you'll need to raid the royal treasury to pay off the "eye-popping" bill, but "when you need a sure thing – and can pay for it", there's no other choice.

Ritz-Carlton, The 🏖✕🏖≋

| 23 | 27 | 23 | 22 | $526 |

3 Connaught Rd. | (011-852) 2877-6666 | fax 2877-6778 | 800-241-3333 | www.ritzcarlton.com | 190 rooms, 26 suites

"You can't go wrong" at this "paradise for stressed business travelers" that's "an oasis for tourists" too; located in the Central Business District, it "does everything a Ritz-Carlton ought to do"– the staff makes you feel "as important as the person staying in the presidential suite" (afternoon tea is "served in white-gloved perfection"), Toscana restaurant is "wonderful" and the "killer views" impress; but just a handful are surprised that the "roms are in need of renovation."

Shangri-La Hotel Zhongshan 🏖≋

| – | – | – | – | $116 |

16 Qi Wan Rd. N, Eastern Area | Zhongshan | (011-86-760) 838-6888 | fax 838-6666 | www.shangri-la.com | 423 rooms, 40 suites

Zhongshan's government-designated title of 'National Clean City' (a quick ferry ride from Hong Kong) also aptly applies to this tidy chainster with "top-notch service" and bright rooms offering all the expected business necessities; it's "well worth" "paying for the upgrade" to the Horizon Club level for free buffet breakfasts in the lounge, morning delivery of tropical fruits, an international newspaper and complimentary suit pressings and shoe shines; among the cuisine choices are Cantonese, Japanese and a noodle and soup station.

Macau

Mandarin Oriental 🏃🚣🔍Ⓢ🌊🔍 ▽ | 16 | 20 | 19 | 19 | $250
(aka MOMFM)

956-1110 Ave. da Amizade | (011-853) 2856-7888 | fax 2859-4589 | 866-526-6567 | www.mandarinoriental.com | 407 rooms, 28 suites

Facing the harbor, within "very convenient" walking distance of the ferry terminal, this "outstanding" resort-style complex, built around gardens and a waterfall, appeals to athletic types with a heated pool, tennis and squash courts and a rock climbing wall; for corporate travelers, there are state-of-the-art facilities, and for sybarites, a "wonderful" spa, a 24-hour "high-stakes" casino and restaurants serving up everything from Italian to Thai to Chinese fare.

Shanghai

88 Xintiandi 🚣🔍Ⓢ🌊 | 21 | 20 | - | 16 | $288

380 Huangpi Nan Lu | (011-86-21) 5383-8833 | fax 5383-8877 | www.88xintiandi.com | 42 rooms, 11 suites

The "perfect boutique" is how fans describe this hotel in buzzing Xintiandi; besides the "heart-of-the-city" location, it boasts service-apartment-type quarters with mini-kitchens and stylish Chinese-Southeast Asian furnishings that are a "fantastic" change from "cookie-cutter" decor (deluxe rooms also have a "nice" lake view); there's no on-site restaurant, but the executive lounge serves breakfast and beverages, and guests can work off calories in the adjoining Alexander Center gym and A-Spa; N.B. patrons receive temporary membership to nearby Villa du Lac, a private club.

Four Seasons ✕🔍Ⓢ🌊 | 27 | 27 | 23 | 26 | $418

500 Weihai Lu | (011-86-21) 6256-8888 | fax 6256-5678 | www.fourseasons.com | 360 rooms, 79 suites

It's no surprise that "you're treated like royalty" at this modern Jing An high-rise since service is the hallmark of this "winning" brand; with an "immaculate", "unbelievably plush" interior, "extravagant suites" and "ample facilities" including an "outrageously wonderful spa", "impressive fitness area" and "fantastic pool", it's "about as good as it gets in Shanghai"; just a few sophisticated Seasonites are "not particularly inspired" by the "sub-optimal location" and the on-site dining.

Grand Hyatt 🚣🔍Ⓢ🌊 | 26 | 24 | 22 | 26 | $475

Jin Mao Tower, 88 Century Blvd./Shiji Da Dao | (011-86-21) 5049-1234 | fax 5049-1111 | 800-223-1234 | www.shanghai.grand.hyatt.com | 310 rooms, 45 suites

Sporting a "space-age", *Blade Runner*-esque look, this "impressive" "landmark" that's "cool even by Shanghai standards" floats "high in the clouds" on the 53rd to 87th floors of this Pudong tower; rooms are "ultramodern", some with "beautiful views of the Bund" from "floor-to-ceiling" windows in the "generously sized" bathrooms, while the "pool overlooking the Harbor" and a "superior" staff further help it stand out; the "expensive" dining has "good and bad moments", however.

Grand Pacific Suites 🐾Ⓢ

| - | - | - | - | $107 |

288 Shaanxi Bei Lu | (011-86-21) 3218-4555 | fax 3218-4556 | 866-652-2041 | www.sinohotel.com | 300 suites

The first China venture for Australian suite-hotel chain Pacific International occupies floors 10 to 29 of a renovated office across from Jing An's Plaza 66 shopping complex; the apartment-style quarters blend Asian hardwoods and Western furnishings and include a kitchenette, washer/dryer, massage showers and lots of windows.

Hilton ✕♨Ⓢ≋✎

| 20 | 22 | 20 | 22 | $175 |

250 Huashan Lu | (011-86-21) 6248-0000 | fax 6248-3868 | 800-445-8667 | www.hilton.com | 696 rooms, 24 suites

"Centrally located" in Jing An, this 43-story tower was "the grande dame of Shanghai in the 1980s" and is still considered a "very nice" choice, especially for "businesspeople", thanks to its "excellent" service, "not-to-be-missed spa", gym and indoor pool, as well as its multiple restaurants and 39th-floor penthouse bar; still, up-to-the-minute types say it's feeling "a bit worn-out" despite undergoing a major renovation two years ago.

JC Mandarin ♨Ⓢ≋✎

| 18 | 20 | 18 | 18 | $194 |

1225 Nanjing Xi Lu | (011-86-21) 6279-1888 | fax 6279-1822 | www.jcmandarin.com | 476 rooms, 35 suites

Regulars recommend this "modern business hotel" managed by the Meritus chain for its "great views of the city skyline", "wonderful service" and a "convenient shopping area" location in Jing An; foes who find "nothing special" may be glad to hear there's a new fitness center and Carita spa.

JW Marriott Hotel Shanghai at Tomorrow Square ✕♨Ⓢ≋

| 27 | 26 | 22 | 25 | $432 |

399 Nanjing Xi Lu | (011-86-21) 5359-4969 | fax 6375-5988 | 800-228-9290 | www.marriotthotels.com | 264 rooms, 78 suites

"Not your typical Marriott", the chain's China flagship is a shiny 60-story tower that's "fantastically central" – next to People's Park, opposite the Shanghai Art Museum and "within walking distance of just about everywhere"; in addition to "amazing views" (including a 360-degree city panorama from the "sky-high" 38th-floor lobby), this "home away from home" has "classy", "wonderfully decorated" rooms, "excellent service" and an exceptional "gym, pool and spa"; the only downside is the "so-so" food.

Le Méridien She Shan ♨Ⓢ≋✎

| - | - | - | - | $321 |

1288 Linyin Xin Lu | (011-86-21) 5779-9999 | fax 5779-8999 | 800-543-4300 | www.lemeridien.com | 313 rooms, 12 suites

Fronting a partially man-made lake in the Shanghai area, and within the expansive grounds of the National Tourist Resort in the northern part of Songjiang district, this hotel draws some for a Sunday day trip to "gorge on brunch"; it features views of its "bucolic" grounds from the large, airy lobby as well as all its guest quarters, which boast floor-to-ceiling windows and balconies; other highlights are a full-service spa, indoor and outdoor swimming pools and a tennis court.

[NEW] Le Royal Méridien 🛁 [S] 🏊 — - | - | - | - | $407

789 Nanjing Lu E. | (011-86-21) 3318-9999 | fax 6361-3388 | www.starwoodhotels.com | 655 rooms, 115 suites

One of the tallest buildings in the city, this ultramodern newcomer, opposite People's Square and overlooking the Shanghai Museum (the Bund is a 20-minute walk away), appeals to both leisure and business travelers; watch the mesmerizing city and river views from the room's floor-to-ceiling windows or just watch the 42-inch plasma TVs instead, then choose from 10 restaurants and bars, before heading to the indoor heated pool and fitness center

Marriott Hongqiao 🔭 🏊 🎾 — - | - | - | - | $247

2270 Hongqiao Lu | (011-86-21) 6237-6000 | fax 6237-6222 | 800-228-9290 | www.marriott.com | 187 rooms, 126 suites

A location that's right on the highway and "very convenient" to the domestic airport is a plus for business travelers, though it's a "long (but inexpensive) cab ride" to the center of town from this "pleasant", "very Western" hotel; praise goes to its "good facilities", including a health club, pool and dining options ranging from a U.S.-style steakhouse to Chinese cuisine; N.B. it supposedly pioneered the local trend of using chemically preserved palm trees in the lobby.

Okura Garden Hotel 🍴 [H] 🏊 🎾 — ▽ 25 | 24 | 23 | 21 | $230

58 Maoming Nan Lu | (011-86-21) 6415-1111 | fax 6415-8866 | 800-223-6800 | www.gardenhotelshanghai.com | 478 rooms, 22 suites

"Modern facilities" meet "old-world charm" and "history" at this "unique" hotel comprising a 33-story tower fronted by a baroque 1920s French mansion set in tranquil gardens between bustling Huaihai Lu and Nanjing Lu; "elegant" and "comfortable without being ostentatious", it accommodates business as well as leisure travelers thanks to its "central location", "wonderful service (as one would expect from the Okura group)" and "good value"; assets include a business center, gym, pool, tennis and Japanese dining at Yamazato.

Portman Ritz-Carlton 🛁 🏊 🎾 — 23 | 25 | 22 | 24 | $326

Shanghai Ctr., 1376 Nanjing Xi Lu | (011-86-21) 6279-8888 | fax 6279-8800 | 800-241-3333 | www.ritzcarlton.com | 510 rooms, 88 suites

"If you want to feel pampered in Shanghai, stay at the Ritz" advise admirers of this "top-drawer" property that's an excellent choice "if you're looking for luxury"; the "spacious" rooms are "extremely comfortable", and the "lavish" public spaces feel "intimate"; set in Nanjing Lu's Shanghai Centre Complex, it's "in the best area for shopping" plus the "spectacular" service satisfies all.

Pudong Shangri-La 🛁 🔭 [S] 🏊 🎾 — 23 | 24 | 22 | 23 | $323

33 Fucheng Lu | (011-86-21) 6882-8888 | fax 6882-6688 | 800-942-5050 | www.shangri-la.com | 917 rooms, 64 suites

"East meets West" at this "excellent business hotel", where the "generous rooms" have "spectacular views" of the Bund, the river and Pudong's "incredible" new buildings that have turned the district into a "contest for the world's architects"; there's an "incredible array" of restaurants - Yi Café, Nadaman and Jade on 36 - and road warriors

	ROOMS	SERVICE	DINING	FACIL.	COST

recommend the "well-equipped Horizon Club" rooms (with separate check-in and a lounge with breakfast buffet and other amenities); other highlights include "fabulous service", a "nice indoor pool" and the country's first outlet of Shangri-La's Chi spa.

Regent, The 🐕🏧⊗🏊🔍 | - | - | - | - | $169 |

1116 Yan'an Xi Lu | (011-86-21) 6115-9988 | fax 6115-9977 | 800-545-4000 | www.regenthotels.com | 419 rooms, 92 suites

The famous luxury chain's first hotel in China is located on the 27th to 53rd floors of a Changning high-rise, with rooms that yield spectacular city views and boast 42-inch plasma TVs and high-design bathrooms; three themed restaurants keep guests sated, and for business travelers, the CO_2 Cigar Club is the hot spot; others might prefer a swim in the glass-roofed indoor pool, a workout with a fitness instructor in a state-of-the-art health club or a sauna soak in the high-end Guerlain spa.

Renaissance Pudong 🏊 | - | - | - | - | $286 |

100 Changliu Lu | (011-86-21) 3871-4888 | fax 6854-0888 | 800-260-0600 | www.renaissancehotels.com | 357 rooms, 13 suites

This "very good" business-oriented hotel on the southeast edge of Pudong is "convenient to the Expo Center" but "a little out of town" in relation to some major tourist sites; expect contemporary-meets-traditional decor (the back lobby Shanghai Bar is particularly funky), dining options including a Western buffet and Cantonese-Shanghainese restaurant, a health club, pool and full array of business facilities.

Sheraton Grand Hotel 🏊 | ∇ 23 | 20 | 22 | 20 | $315 |

5 Zunyi Nan Lu | (011-86-21) 6275-8888 | fax 6275-5420 | 800-325-3535 | www.sheratongrand-shanghai.com | 406 rooms, 90 suites

Most say this Hongqiao hotel provides "dependable lodging for business travel", with "comfortable", "thoroughly renovated" rooms and a staff that "tries hard"; dining options range from Japanese to Italian and there's a health club, indoor pool and business facilities, but it's "far from the action" of the city's center and some are disappointed in both service and dining.

Sofitel Hyland | ∇ 19 | 21 | 19 | 19 | $189 |

505 Nanjing Dong Lu | (011-86-21) 6351-5888 | fax 6341-7466 | 800-763-4835 | www.sofitel.com | 340 rooms, 61 suites

This soaring glass tower boasts a "convenient" location five blocks from the Bund and overlooking the "exciting" walking-street strip of shop-filled Nanjing Lu; fans praise its "upscale but relaxed" feel, "spacious" rooms and "management that goes beyond 100 percent", but a few critics cry it "lacks" the chain's "usual charm"; N.B. there's a business center, health club and French brasserie.

❑ St. Regis 🐕🏧⊗🏊🔍 | 28 | 28 | 23 | 26 | $290 |

889 Dongfang Lu | (011-86-21) 5050-4567 | fax 6875-6789 | 877-787-3447 | www.stregis.com | 274 rooms, 44 suites

It's "absolutely fabulous" from "soup to nuts" at this corporate-friendly hotel that's a "quiet place for the harried business traveler to rest"; even though you're "30 minutes into the middle of nowhere in Pudong", you'll enjoy the "stunning entryways", "impeccable service" that includes a "personal butler" who "brews your tea" and "ginormous", glitzy-gold rooms whose "bathrooms and bathtubs" are "easy to get lost in."

	ROOMS	SERVICE	DINING	FACIL.	COST
Westin ✗[S]🏊	26	24	23	25	$400

Bund Ctr., 88 Henan Zhong Lu | (011-86-21) 6335-1888 | fax 6335-2888 | 800-937-8461 | www.westin.com | 320 rooms, 250 suites

If you stay at this "glitzy" chainster you can "walk to the Bund", "just minutes away", while "guests of other hotels are stuck in traffic", but you may never want to leave given the "wonderful" Banyan Tree spa, "music in the atrium" (dig the neon-lit glass stairs) and "comfortable, inviting" bar; other reasons your stay may be "so easy to enjoy" include the "deep-soaking tubs" in the "stylish" rooms, an "always obliging" staff and a buffet that's "among the most extravagant."

Yunnan Province

Banyan Tree 🔭[S]	-	-	-	-	$400

Hong Po Village | Jian Tang | (011-86-887) 828-8822 | fax 828-8911 | www.banyantree.com | 21 suites, 11 lodges

True to its Shangri-la setting, this resort, surrounded by rugged mountains, reflects its culture in every detail; the lodges are replicas of Tibetan farmhouses, with fireplaces, local tapestries, wood carvings and wooden hot tubs, and the famous Banyan Tree spa incorporates native Himalayan ingredients; two restaurants and a teahouse serve regional cuisine, and organized tours take visitors on unique adventures to nearby pottery villages, the Yangtze and Gonjo rivers and farmhouses to taste homemade yak butter tea.

Colombia

Bogotá

Casa Medina	23	26	22	20	$176

69A-22 Carrera 7 | (011-57-1) 312-0299 | fax 312-3769 | 800-735-2478 | www.hoteles-charleston.com | 32 rooms, 25 suites, 1 apartment

The "great" financial district location and "fantastic rooms" with "gorgeous bathrooms" and "lovely amenities" as well as "excellent service" make it "a delight" to stay at this historic "oasis of tranquility" in a "harsh city"; hand-carved wood ceilings, stone walls, "delightful restaurants" and "lots of little touches" make it "one of the top hotels in Bogotá."

Cartagena

Sofitel Santa Clara, Hotel 🛁🔭🏊	25	25	25	25	$257

Calle del Torno | (011-57-5) 664-6070 | fax 664-8040 | 800-763-4835 | www.hotelsantaclara.com | 96 rooms, 19 suites

Within the walled, ancient city of Cartagena, this "tranquil", "converted convent" is a welcome "respite from the boisterous" town outside, and "despite its age" is "still beautiful"; the "gorgeous interior courtyard" gives way to "very good service", crisply furnished rooms with WiFi and flat-screen TVs and food that some say they "love", and divers appreciate that the hotel's private island is a 45-minute speedboat ride away; N.B. an 8,600-sq.-ft. spa is opening in 2007.

Costa Rica

Arenal

Tabacón Grand Spa Thermal Resort 🔭Ⓢ🏊

ROOMS	SERVICE	DINING	FACIL.	COST
20	21	18	25	$215

La Fortuna | (011-506) 519-1900 | fax 519-1940 | 877-277-8291 | www.tabacon.com | 103 rooms, 11 suites

This "unique", "rustic" resort garners the biggest raves for its "amazing" view of Arenal Volcano ("pray for clear skies"), its "blissful" hot springs and a "serene" spa with plenty of hydrotherapy and volcanic mud treatments; even though some say the "no-frills" rooms are "overpriced" and the food "mediocre", they still believe there's "nothing like drinking a beer" while "soaking in the natural mineral" waters and "waiting for an eruption."

Guanacaste

[Z] Four Seasons Resort 👪🔭⛳Ⓢ🏊🎾

ROOMS	SERVICE	DINING	FACIL.	COST
29	27	25	29	$545

Peninsula Papagayo | (011-506) 696-0000 | fax 696-0500 | 800-332-3442 | www.fourseasons.com | 120 rooms, 35 suites

Four Seasons chose the slender Peninsula Papagayo near Palo Verde National Park – "in the middle of nowhere" say some intrepid trekkers – to set up this "elegant but low-key" resort that boasts "beaches on both sides"; the "gorgeous" accommodations employ "native wood" and other "indigenous materials", while outside your door you'll discover "amazing pools", a "magnificent" spa with "treatments to die for", "hiking, yoga, Pilates" and "faultless service"; meanwhile, duffers are delighted by the "most magnificent" golf course, designed by Arnold Palmer, that gets its fair share of both monkeys and "spectacular sunsets."

Paradisus Playa Conchal 👪🐕🔭⛳Ⓢ🏊🎾

ROOMS	SERVICE	DINING	FACIL.	COST
25	23	19	24	$464

Playa Conchal | (011-506) 654-4501 | fax 654-4181 | 800-336-3542 | www.solmelia.com | 308 suites

The "magnificent, split-level rooms with sitting areas" are the best part of this "vast, elegant" resort "cut into the jungle", where "colorful long-tailed parrots" perch on branches and monkeys swing in trees overlooking the pool; even though it's "remote from other sights", strollers say the beach "covered in sea shells" is a "must-visit", there's a "great" Robert Trent Jones Jr.-designed golf course and the "service is outstanding."

Punta Islita, Hotel 🍴🐕🔭Ⓢ🏊🎾

ROOMS	SERVICE	DINING	FACIL.	COST
25	25	23	25	$218

Coyote Beach | Islita | (011-506) 231-6122 | fax 231-0715 | www.hotelpuntaislita.com | 17 villas, 8 suites, 8 casitas, 14 rooms

"One of the finest and most hidden resorts on earth" is how awed surveyors of this "tranquil heaven for lovers" describe this "stunning" destination; it's so remote, you must either ride in "a jeep over a river" – a "difficult" though "adventurous" drive – or take a plane (guests advise the latter), but once there "splurge for one of the junior suites with plunge pools" and the bonfire dinner on the "incredible black sand beach."

	ROOMS	SERVICE	DINING	FACIL.	COST

Osa Peninsula

Aguila de Osa 👬

| - | - | - | - | $613 |

Drake Bay | (011-506) 296-2190 | fax 232-7722 | 866-924-8452 |
www.aguiladeosa.com | 11 rooms, 2 suites

Make like the king or queen of the jungle at this "peaceful" resort accessible only by boat on Drake Bay; the adventurous find luxury amid handcrafted furnishings, cathedral ceilings, Italian marble, local hardwoods and "delicious" outdoor gourmet "meals that are fun at communal tables"; regulars recommend cocktails overlooking the Aguilas River to take the edge off a hike through Corcovado National Park.

La Paloma Lodge 👫👬🏊

| - | - | - | - | $1050 |

San Antonio de Belén | Drake Bay | (011-506) 293-7502 | fax 239-0954 |
www.lapalomalodge.com | 4 rooms, 7 bungalows

It's a barrelful of monkeys at this "enchanting" "remote jungle lodge" on Drake Bay where the white-faced capuchines peer down from the branches and howlers boom in the canopy; after a scuba, dolphin-watching, horseback or hiking trip, the "friendly staff" helps create a "great atmosphere" while you take drinks in the clubhouse or relax in a hammock on your open-air porch with a view of Caño Island.

Puntarenas

La Mariposa 🐾👬🏊

| 22 | 21 | 19 | 22 | $195 |

Manuel Antonio | Quepos | (011-506) 777-0355 | fax 777-0050 |
800-416-2747 | www.lamariposa.com | 27 rooms, 30 suites

Aptly named 'the butterfly' – "the grounds are covered in them" – this "pretty" boutique next to Manuel Antonio National Park provides plenty of outdoor pleasures; you can "hang out with iguanas" at the "airy mountaintop restaurant", take in the "killer" sunset over the ocean from the infinity pool or shower outside "with the frogs"; with its "large", "luxurious" rooms, "friendly", "low-key" service and tropical gardens, "you can't not relax" at this "relatively child-free" property.

Los Sueños Marriott Ocean & Golf Resort 👫👬📖☺🏊🔍

| 24 | 24 | 22 | 25 | $319 |

Playa Herradura | (011-506) 630-9000 | fax 630-9090 | 800-228-9290 |
www.marriott.com | 191 rooms, 10 suites

Fans of this massive colonial-style resort point to the charming "old-world furniture", exposed beams and floors covered with tile, as well as a "friendly, smiling staff" (just "remember to adopt the local attitude toward timeliness") and "wonderful fishing charters out of the marina" as the highlights here; rooms are "nicely appointed" and have "views of the beach", but there isn't much of one (some call it a "major disappointment"), so the "enormous", "fantastic" pool will have to do.

San José

Costa Rica Marriott 📖☺🏊🔍

| 22 | 24 | 22 | 24 | $229 |

700 meters west of Firestone | (011-506) 298-0000 | fax 298-0011 |
800-228-9290 | www.marriott.com | 238 rooms, 6 suites

This "superb colonial-style building" resembling an "old Spanish hacienda", "nestled in the middle of a coffee plantation", offers patrons a plethora of "lovely" attributes: "gorgeous" grounds that include an infinity pool and "wonderful spa", "reasonable prices", "over-the-top service", "great rooms that are not your typical Marriott" style and "delicious dining options."

Finca Rosa Blanca Country Inn 🥾🏊

	21	25	25	22	$185

Central Valley | (011-506) 269-9392 | fax 269-9555 |
www.fincarosablanca.com | 3 rooms, 4 suites, 2 villas

"Everything clicks" at this "small but beautiful" "Gaudí-esque" "work of art" above the Central Valley amid 10 acres of trees and flowers; from the "unusual" design to "genuinely warm" service to "communal dining" to rooms that have private decks, handmade furniture and unique artwork, it's a true "hilltop oasis"; when it's time to venture out, a "day of sightseeing" and personalized tours, including horseback rides up the slopes of Barva Volcano, can be arranged by the hotel staff.

Pura Vida Retreat & Spa

	-	-	-	-	$150

Apartado 1112 | Alajuela | 678-388-9564 | fax 483-0041 |
www.puravidaspa.com | 35 rooms, 14 tents, 1 house

At this "heavenly" 12-acre mountaintop yoga retreat surrounded by coffee plantations 20 minutes from the airport, downward-facing dogs are the least of it – five halls are available for daily classes (many yogis arrive as a group, with their own teacher in tow) and accommodations include low-key rooms, permanent tents and a freestanding villa; when all those positions and meditation get old, there are gourmet vegetarian meals, nature hikes through beautiful gardens, beach trips and white-water rafting available.

Curaçao

Avila Beach Hotel 🐾🥾🛎Ⓢ

	ROOMS	SERVICE	DINING	FACIL.	COST
▽	19	16	19	17	$270

130 Penstraat | Willemstad | (011-599-9) 461-4377 | fax 461-1493 |
800-747-8162 | www.avilahotel.com | 108 rooms, 10 suites

Curaçao's oldest hotel in continuous operation, this "very convenient" family-run beachsider benefits from plenty of historic charm, a staff that "bends over backwards to accommodate guests" and owners with a real "vision of hospitality"; the multiple room options include those in the original Dutch colonial mansion, ones with terraces overlooking a private beach in the Blues Wing and new quarters with modern touches in the Octagon Wing.

Z Kura Hulanda 🏊

	28	28	27	26	$290

Langesraat 8 | Willemstad | (011-599-9) 434-7700 | fax 434-7701 |
www.kurahulanda.com | 58 rooms, 22 suites

"Less like going to a hotel than visiting a friend in a quaint town", this "charming and welcoming" "small gem" with "well-restored" Dutch colonial buildings contains "extremely beautiful grounds and views" as well as "breathtakingly elegant rooms" filled with antiques and handmade fabrics; "praiseworthy food" at the Continental Astrolab Observatory restaurant makes dining "especially worthwhile", plus a shuttle runs to the Lodge Kura Hulanda, its "sister resort on the beach."

	ROOMS	SERVICE	DINING	FACIL.	COST

Marriott Beach Resort &
Emerald Casino ♨ⓢ⚓🏊

| 21 | 22 | 19 | 22 | $274 |

Piscadera Bay | (011-599-9) 736-8800 | fax 462-7502 | 800-228-9290 |
www.marriott.com | 237 rooms, 10 suites

"Marriott strikes again" with this "well-maintained", "beautiful re-sort", complete with a 5,000-sq.-ft. casino, an "incredible", albeit "man-made", beachfront with waiter service and a "convenient" on-site dive shop with a "low-key" staff; the pool with its swim-up bar is "inviting" too, though some snipe that the "simple" rooms overlooking it can be "quite noisy from all the kids."

Cyprus

Paphos

Almyra ♨♨⚓🏊

| – | – | – | – | $280 |

Poseidonos Ave. | (011-357-26) 888-700 | fax 942-888 |
www.thanoshotels.com | 121 rooms, 37 suites

Laid-back luxury is on tap at this renovated, sleek seaside resort set on eight acres of picturesque grounds; a reimagining of the former Paphos Beach Hotel, it has kept its '70s-inspired facade, but now sports a contemporary Japanese- and Mediterranean-style interior with custom-designed furnishings; other features include a sea sports center, four restaurants and a children's program with a dedicated kids' pool.

Polis

Anassa Hotel ♨ⓢ⚓🏊

| – | – | – | – | $640 |

Baths of Aphrodite Rd. | (011-357-26) 888-000 | fax 322-900 |
www.thanoshotels.com | 142 rooms, 35 suites

Designed to resemble a small village on the coast at Polis, this "amazing" property abutting a national park has rooms with marble floors and balconies offering sweeping Mediterranean views (some with private plunge pools), four restaurants, a thalassotherapy spa with an indoor pool, a kids' club and a private beach; the name is ancient Greek for 'queen', and surveyors say it is indeed "grand", if just a bit "impersonal."

Czech Republic

Karlovy Vary

Grand Hotel Pupp ⓗ♨ⓢ

| ∇ 21 | 19 | 18 | 19 | $280 |

Mírové námestí 2 | (011-420-35) 310-9172 | fax 322-4032 | www.pupp.cz |
77 rooms, 28 suites, 7 apartments

It's "breathtakingly beautiful country" in the spa town of Karlovy Vary, and this 305-year-old "delightful architectural confection", drenched in "old European ambiance", makes quite a "sumptuous" base from which to take it in; perched on a hill, it has "simply spectacular views" of the surrounding area and boasts in-house Roman baths and a full spa.

subscribe to zagat.com

	ROOMS	SERVICE	DINING	FACIL.	COST

Prague

🛂 Four Seasons 🕴✕🏖🎎 | 27 | 27 | 26 | 26 | $436

Veleslavínova 2a/1098 | (011-420-2) 2142-7000 | fax 2142-6000 |
www.fourseasons.com | 141 rooms, 20 suites

"Prague Castle makes a terrific nightlight" for those who splurge on a "plush" premier room or "gorgeous" suite "overlooking the water" at this "island of opulence" with a "phenomenal" Vlatva-side location; "exquisite" service, "stylish" decor, chef Vito Mollica's Italian restaurant oft touted as the "best in the city" (it was voted No. 1 for Food in Prague in our *Europe's Top Restaurants* Survey) and "first-class" extras like a "Mercedes pickup at the airport" cause believers to crow "it just doesn't get any better than this."

Hoffmeister ⓢ | 21 | 23 | 23 | 18 | $291

Pod Bruskou 7 | (011-420-2) 5101-7111 | fax 5101-7120 |
www.hoffmeister.cz | 28 rooms, 8 apartments

This "quiet", "charming" family-run former residence near Prague Castle is a tribute to the owner's father, artist Adolf Hoffmeister, and the "hallways are lined" with his work; its "nice-size" accommodations are a quirky mix – art deco here, Gothic there – but surveyors praise the "don't-miss" 15th-century "stone cave" of steam in the spa, "enthusiastic service" and "unexpectedly fantastic" French fare.

InterContinental 🕴🏖🎎ⓢ⛲ | 19 | 21 | 18 | 20 | $342

Namesti Curieovych 43-5 | (011-420-2) 9663-1111 | fax 2481-1216 |
888-424-6835 | www.intercontinental.com | 283 rooms, 89 suites

Don't be put off by its "dour" exterior, because within this stalwart in the heart of the old city is a "surprisingly" "luxurious" and "up-to-date facility"; "efficient" service wins near-unanimous praise, as does the "fantastic pool" and "wonderful" ninth-floor Czech-International restaurant with panoramic vistas; but the rooms strike some as "impersonal."

NEW Mandarin Oriental ⓤ🎎ⓢ | - | - | - | - | $463
(aka Karmelitska Hotel)

Nebovidska 459/1 | (011-420-2) 3308-8888 | fax 3308-8668 |
www.mandarinoriental.com | 77 rooms, 22 suites

There's nothing monastic about a retreat to this newly opened hotel, set in a restored 14th-century abbey in the Mala Strana; the inspired renovation of its historical architecture is sure to intrigue: there are baroque arches and Oriental silks in rooms, vaulted ceilings in a sophisticated EurAsian restaurant, afternoon tea service among the columns of a cloister corridor and sinfully divine spa treatments on the site of a Renaissance chapel.

Paris, Hotel ⓤ🏖ⓢ | 24 | 22 | 22 | 19 | $423

U Obecniho Domu 1 | (011-420-2) 2219-5195 | fax 2422-5475 |
800-888-4747 | www.hotel-pariz.cz | 73 rooms, 10 suites, 3 apartments

This "gorgeous art nouveau" "grande dame" in a "prime" spot near the Old Town Square is just over 100 years old, and its "old-world" ambiance remains as "charming" as ever; however, while its lobby, dining room and other public areas are filled with "fabulous art and antiques", some find it all a little bit "dog-eared."

	ROOMS	SERVICE	DINING	FACIL.	COST

Savoy, Hotel ⚐

| 20 | 23 | 19 | 17 | $482 |

Keplerova 6 | (011-420-2) 2430-2430 | fax 2430-2128 | 800-223-6800 | www.hotel-savoy.cz | 55 rooms, 6 suites

The "good news" is that this "wonderful place to stay" 20 minutes from the Prague Castle is "away from the hustle and bustle" – but "that's also the bad news" (it's "a hike from the other sights"); "efficient", top-drawer service makes for quite a "fine experience" overall, but some say the rooms "need a bit of attention."

Denmark

Copenhagen

Admiral Hotel Ⓗ🐾

| 17 | 20 | 18 | 17 | $240 |

Toldbodgade 24-28 | (011-45) 3374-1414 | fax 3374-1416 | www.admiralhotel.dk | 314 rooms, 52 suites

Housed in a former warehouse dating from 1787 and replete with "historic charm", this Copenhagen hotel may make you "feel like you're on a big ship" given its "perfect location", affording "great harbor views" as well as convenience to the city's shops and restaurants; though most patrons "love the rustic feel", other visitors complain it can be "dark"; P.S. don't miss the "gorgeous" bar and eatery designed by the Terence Conran group.

NEW Copenhagen Island 🐾

| – | – | – | – | $290 |

Kalvebod Brygge 53 | (011-45) 3338-9600 | fax 3338-9601 | www.copenhagenisland.dk | 324 rooms, 4 suites

Danish design disciples dig this "charming" new hotel "on the harbor" where the cool white-and-glass decor with funky touches of color has a distinct "feel of Scandinavia"; many of the "small" rooms and conference facilities offer water views, as does the contemporary restaurant, but urban explorers complain it's a little "far away from the tourist sites."

D'Angleterre Ⓗ🐾Ⓢ♨

| 19 | 21 | 19 | 19 | $447 |

Kongens Nytorv 34 | (011-45) 3312-0095 | fax 3312-1118 | 800-223-6800 | www.remmen.dk | 110 rooms, 13 suites

"On the doorstep of Copenhagen's pedestrian shopping" district and other attractions, this "beautiful" "old-world" "palace" built in 1755 "retains a spirit of sophistication" due to its "elegant" good looks and "formal, hospitable service"; fans praise the "huge" quarters, "state-of-the-art spa", Arndal, and New French dining, but hint that the "dated" "grande dame" might "need a face-lift."

Skt. Petri Hotel ⚐

| 24 | 22 | 21 | 21 | $425 |

Krystalgade 22 | (011-45) 3345-9100 | fax 3345-9110 | www.hotelsktpetri.com | 244 rooms, 24 suites

The escalators start "moving as you approach" and the "night tables glow" at this "avant-garde" "place to be in Copenhagen", set in a remodeled department store that screams "Scandinavian chic" (right down to the designer dog baskets); it's no surprise, there's a "beautiful staff" ("nobody over 30"), "hip" cocktail bar that's spawned its own CD, a sixth-floor sundeck and an overall "vibrant atmosphere", so who cares if the rooms are "tiny" and the dining "below par"?

	ROOMS	SERVICE	DINING	FACIL.	COST
Sønderho Kro Ⓗ	-	-	-	-	$195

Kropladsen 11 | (011-45) 7516-4009 | fax 7516-4385 | www.sonderhokro.dk | 14 rooms

It's a ferry ride to the oldest inn in Denmark, this "very quaint" Relais & Châteaux spot in the small village of Sønderho on the North Sea island of Fanø, where two adjoining thatched-roof dwelling built in 1722 house charming rooms named after local ships; guests can enjoy beachfront horseback riding, fishing, sailing and kayaking, or just savor the herring smoked on-site while sipping a glass of herb-infused *kryddersnaps.*

Dominican Republic

Casa de Campo 👪 ✕ 🏇 ⛵ Ⓢ 🏊 🎾	22	23	21	26	$390

La Romana | (1-809) 523-3333 | fax 523-8698 | 800-877-3643 | www.casadcampo.com | 300 rooms, 150 villas

With three "phenomenal" Pete Dye courses, including the Teeth of the Dog, this "wonderful" lodging is a "paradise" for golfers, but even non-swingers are swayed by the "stunning villas" with "mahogany colonial beds" and "plantation shutters" that "keep out the blinding sun", as well as by the "exceptional facilities" - 13 tennis courts, 18 pools, a marina and a man-made beach; just a few say "dining could improve."

Excellence Punta Cana 🏇 🏊 🎾	25	23	22	25	$150

Playa Uvero Alto | Punta Cana | (1-809) 685-9880 | fax 689-6343 | www.excellence-resorts.com | 446 suites

This "adults-only" resort ranks "far above the usual" all-inclusives because of "nice luxury touches", including "coconut drinks, poolside beds with curtains" and afternoon "dessert served in the lobby"; when idleness begins to pall, there's horseback riding, scuba diving, kayaking and many other diversions; P.S. the beach is "rough", so you "may find yourself sitting by the pool most of the time."

Punta Cana Beach Resort 👪 🏇 ⛵ Ⓢ 🏊 🎾	20	21	18	22	$100

Punta Cana | (1-809) 959-2262 | fax 959-3951 | 888-442-2262 | www.puntacana.com | 420 rooms, 37 villas

White-sand "beaches to die for" plus a "gorgeous swimming pool and surrounding garden" have sun-seekers sighing that this developing area is the "Caribbean of your dreams"; there are "loads of activities on-site" including golfing, a full-service marina and a spa, but there's "boring" food; N.B. Tom Fazio will design a sister course to open in 2008.

Ecuador

Quito

La Mirage Garden Hotel & Spa Ⓢ 🏊 🎾	▽ 26	29	28	26	$280

Cotacachi | (011-593-6) 291-5237 | fax 291-5065 | 800-327-3573 | www.mirage.com.ec | 8 rooms, 15 suites

Sensualists sigh over this "secret" Relais & Châteaux charmer that's 90 minutes north of Quito, a "little oasis" where the staff's "signature touches" include placing "hot-water bottles under the sheets" and "lighting fireplaces" in your "gorgeous room" at night; there are "romantic candlelight dinners" that feature "excellent menus" along with "outstanding facilities" (a spa among them), so some ask "who wouldn't spend a night here?"

Swissôtel Ⓢ🏊🎾

ROOMS	SERVICE	DINING	FACIL.	COST
23	22	18	21	$215

Ave. 12 de Octubre 1820 y Luis Cordero | (011-593-2) 256-7600 | fax 256-8079 | 800-637-9477 | www.swissotel.com | 173 rooms, 104 suites

This "large modern complex" is appreciated in a city that sometimes "lacks dependable accommodations"; "well-located in the new" section of town, it offers "several dining options", "fresh roses everywhere", "junglelike showers" and a "world-class spa."

Egypt

Aswan

Sofitel Old Cataract 🔭🏊🎾

ROOMS	SERVICE	DINING	FACIL.	COST
20	20	18	23	$200

Abtal El Tahrir St. | (011-20-97) 231-6000 | fax 231-6011 | 800-763-4835 | www.sofitel.com | 123 rooms, 8 suites

Note the "strong whiff of Agatha Christie" that permeates this "faded" but "not-to-be-missed" Aswan "dowager" that's "right out of the colonial era" (*Death on the Nile* was filmed here); nothing beats "siping a Pimm's" cocktail or mint tea while "watching feluccas float by" under a "beautiful sunset" from the hotel's riverside grand terrace, but, alas, this "tired old lady photographs better than she plays" - service is sometimes "lacking" and the rooms could use "some updating."

Cairo

Cairo Marriott Hotel & Omar Khayyam Casino Ⓗ🫖🐕🔭Ⓢ🏊🎾

ROOMS	SERVICE	DINING	FACIL.	COST
18	19	17	22	$190

16 Saray El Gezira St. | (011-20-2) 735-8888 | fax 735-6667 | www.marriott.com | 1138 rooms, 112 suites

There's a certain "old-school glamour in this palace-turned-hotel" on the Nile where you can take an "evening stroll" amid the six acres of "lovely gardens" and "fantastic grounds" before heading to the "exclusive shops of Zamalek"; the good news is that the "tired" rooms and facilities are undergoing a multimillion-dollar makeover to be completed in 2007 (possibly outdating some of the above scores), while "excellent service" offsets the "average food" and "big crowds."

Conrad 🔭🏊

ROOMS	SERVICE	DINING	FACIL.	COST
▽ 22	22	17	23	$250

1191 Corniche El Nil | (011-20-2) 580-8000 | fax 580-8080 | 800-445-8667 | www.conradhotels.com | 565 rooms, 52 suites

While no one disputes the "exquisite views of the Nile and Cairo" that can be had from this business hotel adjacent to the World Trade Center, surveyors tend to split on the rest: fans find "fabulous" service and "gorgeous" accommodations that feature "outstanding bathrooms", while the less impressed deem it just "decent" "for an overnight stay" if you avoid dining that's considered "on par with a Midwestern Holiday Inn."

	ROOMS	SERVICE	DINING	FACIL.	COST

Four Seasons at First Residence ♨Ⓢ≋

27 | 26 | 23 | 24 | $270

35 Giza St. | (011-20-2) 570-1212 | fax 570-4939 | www.fourseasons.com | 226 rooms, 43 suites

They "do it right" at this "faultless", "uncontested king of Cairo hotels", which enjoys an enviable location overlooking the Nile in Giza; many of the "palatial" rooms face the Great Pyramids, and all are outfitted with "superior Egyptian cotton linens", plus the "young" "accommodating staff" creates a "really personalized" experience; with a "wide selection of dining" that includes some "fantastic" fare, a relaxing riverside spa and other truly "impeccable" facilities, most "can't wait to go back" despite the "expense."

⊘ Four Seasons Hotel Cairo at Nile Plaza ☕♨Ⓢ≋

27 | 27 | 25 | 27 | $310

1089 Corniche El Nil | (011-20-2) 791-7000 | fax 791-6900 | www.fourseasons.com | 288 rooms, 77 suites

Guests gush over the second "not as stuffy" Four Seasons outpost in Cairo, "the perfect place for business or leisure" given its "efficient, friendly" staff ("nothing is too much" for them), "delicious" food and "exceptional" Nile views; you can bliss-out beside the "fantastic" rooftop pool or at the full-service spa when you're not in your "large" plush room, happy in the knowledge you're staying at "the best hotel in Egypt."

InterContinental Semiramis ≋

20 | 20 | 13 | 18 | $240

Corniche El Nil | (011-20-2) 795-7171 | fax 796-3020 | 888-424-6835 | www.intercontinental.com | 660 rooms, 79 suites

"Big", "busy" and "well run", this Nile-fronter "full of Saudi and Oman" businessmen boasts "spacious rooms", "stunning views" and a "convenient" location, but some patrons say the "mediocre" quarters are "getting old" and are "disappointed" in the "awful dining" and "lackluster service."

Mena House Oberoi ✕⊕☕♨⊾≋⚲

19 | 21 | 21 | 22 | $160

Pyramids' Rd. | (011-20-2) 377-3222 | fax 376-7777 | 800-562-3764 | www.oberoihotels.com | 510 rooms, 13 suites

"Floating in the swimming pool looking up at the pyramids" – there's "nothing better" muse mavens of this more-than-100-year-old Giza former "royal hunting palace", whose "beautiful" 40-acre grounds adjoin a golf course watched over by the Sphinx; more exacting travelers tsk over guest quarters that are "a little worn", but the majority shrugs "with a view like that, who cares?" (just "be sure" to "ask for a room overlooking" the main attraction); P.S. check out the "excellent" Indian eatery.

Nile Hilton ☕⚶♨≋⚲

19 | 20 | 17 | 20 | $155

1113 Corniche El Nil | (011-20-2) 578-0444 | fax 578-6475 | 800-445-8667 | www.hilton.com | 377 rooms, 54 suites

"If you like being in the center of things", you "just can't beat the location" of this longtime Cairo "luxury" hotel that's right on the Nile, and "around the corner from the Egyptian Museum"; other pluses are the "excellent swimming pool", casino, nearby "great shopping mall" and "breathtaking view", but critics claim it's an "aging paradise."

	ROOMS	SERVICE	DINING	FACIL.	COST

Luxor

Sheraton Luxor Resort ♨≋🔍 ▽ | 17 | 19 | 18 | 18 | $100
Khaled Ben Walid St. | (011-20-95) 273-4544 | fax 237-4941 |
800-325-3535 | www.sheraton.com | 284 rooms, 6 suites
Ideal for "washing the dust off after your walking tours", this Luxor resort on the east bank of the Nile is a "convenient" base "from which to explore" the local sights, many of which are "within walking distance"; "simple but very cozy atmosphere", "high-quality service" and "enjoyable dining" options, plus outdoor tennis courts and a nearby golf course, make it a good value.

Red Sea

Ⓩ Four Seasons 👫✕🍴♨Ⓢ≋🔍 | 26 | 28 | 22 | 28 | $400
1 Four Seasons Blvd. | Sharm El Sheikh | (011-20-69) 360-3555 |
fax 360-3550 | 800-332-3442 | www.fourseasons.com | 109 rooms, 91 suites
There's "no other place on earth" like this "fantastic" resort that clings to a "desert hillside that drops steeply" into the Red Sea, where you'll find a stunning white-sand beach and a coral reef offering "incredible scuba diving"; as befits the luxury chain, there's a "highly attentive staff" ("need your sunglasses polished?" – "with pleasure"), "tastefully furnished" rooms and "beautifully landscaped gardens"; it's only the food that "can be better" given such high expectations.

Oberoi Sahl Hasheesh 👫♨Ⓢ≋🔍 | - | - | - | - | $320
Red Sea | Hurghada | (011-20-65) 344-0777 | fax 344-0788 |
800-562-3764 | www.oberoihotels.com | 102 suites
Set on the Red Sea, this "excellent" all-suite resort has a contemporary Arabic design of domed pavilions, marbled colonnades, open-air atriums and galleried courtyards; "very spacy" suites have "private pools", the Banyan Tree spa offers holistic therapies and the staff "can't do enough" for you; some say it's the "only place to consider staying when in Hurghada."

Ritz-Carlton, The 👫🍴Ⓢ≋ ▽ | 25 | 26 | 21 | 26 | $280
Sharm El Sheikh | (011-20-69) 366-1919 | fax 366-1920 | 800-241-3333 |
www.ritzcarlton.com | 286 rooms, 35 suites
"Hide away and enjoy pure luxury" at this "dream" of a resort on the Red Sea in Sharm El Sheikh, where the "fantastic" facilities include a "wow" "set of pools", not to mention an on-site spa whose treatments take place under an open-air Arabian tent; a few restaurants and a "fantastic" staff capable of "instantly guessing your every need" ensure it "lives up to the Ritz-Carlton reputation."

Estonia

Tallinn

Three Sisters Hotel Ⓗ | 23 | 21 | 19 | 18 | $449
Pikk 71/Tolli 2 | (011-372) 6306-300 | fax 6306-301 |
www.threesistershotel.com | 23 rooms
This trio of "lovely" ladies consists of adjacent Tallinn merchant houses from 1362, joined and "beautifully restored" to create a "fairy-

tale setting" mixing "old-world charm" with "21st-century amenities", in a "perfect location" inside the medieval walls of the city; each of the rooms is different, with details like exposed beams, spiral staircases, curtained beds or a rare Estonian piano, but the old girls also surprise with plasma TVs, free Internet and Bulgari bath accessories.

Fiji

Shangri-La's Fijian Resort & Spa ✻ ♨ⓢ ≈ ✎

	ROOMS	SERVICE	DINING	FACIL.	COST
▽	20	21	16	20	$324

Viti-Levu | Yanuca | (011-679) 652-0155 | fax 650-0402 | 866-565-5050 | www.shangri-la.com | 420 rooms, 12 suites, 4 villas

Conveniently connected to the mainland by bridge, this "comfortable, leisurely" chain property sits on a private island of white-sand beaches; fans find a "friendly staff", recently refurbished, though "not glitzy", rooms boasting "earthy colors" and five dining options, while families fall for the "fabulous" camp program, canoeing, biking and nature walks.

Sheraton Denarau Villas ✻ ♨ⓢ ≈

ROOMS	SERVICE	DINING	FACIL.	COST
-	-	-	-	$157

Denarau Island | (011-679) 675-0777 | 800-325-3535 | www.starwoodhotels.com | 164 rooms

Part of a larger resort complex with which it shares facilities, this lodging 20 minutes from Nadi International Airport boasts individual villas with fully equipped kitchens, dining and living areas, as well as an on-site spa, a lagoon pool, golf and kids' programs; dining can be taken in one of 17 outlets within the complex, including beachside grills, a steakhouse and a Japanese eatery, while activities run the gamut from tennis to windsurfing.

Sheraton Fiji Resort ✻ ♨ ▴ ⓢ ≈ ✎

	ROOMS	SERVICE	DINING	FACIL.	COST
▽	19	22	20	20	$300

Denarau Island | (011-679) 675-0777 | fax 675-0818 | 800-325-3535 | www.sheraton.com | 291 rooms, 1 suite

"Warm service from a wonderful staff" and a "great location" "minutes from the airport" give this resort an edge according to its admirers who also extol the "excellent" food and "to-die-for golf course"; detractors, though, warn the rooms, while "comfortable", lack "personality" and suggest it's "nothing special."

Turtle Island Resort ✗

ROOMS	SERVICE	DINING	FACIL.	COST
25	26	25	24	$1632

Turtle Island | (011-679) 672-2780 | fax 672-0007 | 800-255-4347 | www.turtlefiji.com | 14 villas

"The snootiest of patrons should be smitten" by this "spectacular", "highly recommended", eco-friendly all-inclusive perched between rainforest and the original *Blue Lagoon*; seclusion-seekers savor "rustic", thatched cottages with 21-ft. ceilings and verandas and the "private (and I mean private) beach picnics", while the "five-star" communal dining is a "welcome respite from the delicious isolation"; everyone give kudos to the staff that makes you "feel like a long-lost family member coming home."

Vatulele Island Resort ≈ ✎

	ROOMS	SERVICE	DINING	FACIL.	COST
▽	26	28	24	27	$1386

Vatulele | (011-679) 672-0300 | fax 672-0060 | www.vatulele.com | 19 villas

It's all just "absolutely amazing" at this "stunning" South Pacific "paradise" gush giddy guests, who come to this private island resort for

	ROOMS	SERVICE	DINING	FACIL.	COST

the "best vacation" they've ever had; there are no TVs, newspapers or phones, and an air of unspoken privilege pervades throughout the dozen individual villas (or *bures*), each with private terraces; N.B. patrons post a flag in the sand for immediate service.

Wakaya Club, The ✕ Ⓢ ✎ | ▽ 29 | 29 | 29 | 28 | $1900

Wakaya Island | (011-679) 344-8128 | fax 344-8406 | 800-828-3454 | www.wakaya.com | 9 cottages

"There aren't enough words to describe this fabulous place", but "it starts with the staff" that provides "undreamed-of comforts", continuing to the "amazing" setting and onto the "great lodging" (nine *bures* for a maximum of 18 guests) and rounded out by "exquisite food"; throw in "lots of fun things to do" as well as "serene relaxation" and it's no wonder partisans proclaim "if we were Bill Gates, we'd live here."

NEW Westin Denarau Island Resort & Spa 🕴🛁⌐Ⓢ🏊 | ▽ 24 | 16 | 18 | 21 | $397

Denarau Island | (011-679) 675-0000 | fax 675-0259 | www.westin.com | 265 rooms, 8 suites

On 30 acres of beachfront property, this secluded resort features rooms with private verandas and balconies, flat-screen TVs and traditional Fijian crafts and artwork, while facilities include an 18-hole golf course, a two-tier pool, a beachfront Jacuzzi and a full-service spa with a large meditation garden; four restaurants and a poolside lounge round out the relaxing picture.

Finland

Helsinki

Kämp, Hotel 🛁Ⓢ | 26 | 25 | 21 | 24 | $542

Pohjoisesplanadi 29 | (011-358-9) 576-111 | fax 576-1122 | 800-325-3589 | www.luxurycollection.com | 164 rooms, 15 suites

"Who would believe one of the best European business hotels could be found in Helsinki?" marvel mavens of this "glorious old classic", a 19th-century "writer and artist hangout" that has been "beautifully updated" and restored for the 21st century; overall it's voted a "star" by most surveyors thanks to its "spacious" rooms and "impeccable" staff.

France

TOPS IN COUNTRY

28	Four Seasons | *Paris*
	Le Château/St-Martin | *Côte d'Azur*
27	Four Seasons Resort | *Provence*
	Michel Bras | *Aveyron*
	Chateau Crayeres | *Champagne*
26	Domaine/Hauts de Loire | *Loire*
	Château de Bagnols | *Rhône*
	Plaza Athénée | *Paris*
	Grand Cap-Ferrat | *Côte d'Azur*
	du Cap-Eden-Roc | *Côte d'Azur*

	ROOMS	SERVICE	DINING	FACIL.	COST

Aveyron

Z Michel Bras 🐾🏃 | 26 | 28 | 29 | 24 | $284 |

Rte. de L'Aubrac | (011-33-5) 65-51-18-20 | fax 65-48-47-02 |
800-735-2478 | www.michel-bras.com | 15 rooms

"People from all over the world come" to "the middle of nowhere" just
"to taste Michel Bras' remarkable cuisine" at this modernist Relais &
Châteaux lodging that has "no pretensions"; it juts out of the Aubrac
plateau, with picture windows offering "spectacular views" of green
rolling hills, wildflowers and grazing cattle, and the "bright" rooms
boast lots of "up-to-date amenities" – but it's really the very
sophisticated cooking that's "worth the drive" to Aveyron; N.B. it's
closed November–March.

Biarritz

du Palais, Hôtel 🏊🏃🕐🌊   ▽ | 26 | 26 | 24 | 25 | $562 |

1, av de L'Impératrice | (011-33-5) 59-41-64-00 |
fax 59-41-67-99 | 800-223-6800 | www.hotel-du-palais.com |
124 rooms, 30 suites

"A sense of royal leisure pervades" this "elegant" "classic" commanding "spectacular views" of the Basque coastline; everything is "sure to
please" including impeccable ("yet non-stuffy") service, a "grand dining room", "luxuriously appointed" Second Empire sleeping chambers
and "exquisitely designed" public facilities like the new Spa Impérial,
which visitors "love"; the price may be "high" – but remember: "it *was*
Napoleon's" summer palace.

Bidarray

Ostapé 🏊🏃🌊 | - | - | - | - | $429 |

Domaine de Chahatoa | (011-33-5) 59-37-91-91 | fax 59-37-91-92 |
www.ostape.com | 19 rooms, 3 suites

Well-known chef Alain Ducasse opened this Basque country inn
45 minutes from Biarritz, set in a converted 18th-century manor
house and five farmhouses turned into villas with antique furnishings
and balconies or terraces; there's a heated outdoor pool and a top-
notch Navarrian restaurant overseen by chef Alain Souliac that utilizes
fresh regional farm ingredients, but fans of the renowned owner will
want to visit his nearby restaurant Iparla.

Burgundy

Bernard Loiseau ✕🏊🏃🕐🌊 | 26 | 26 | 27 | 22 | $394 |

Saulieu | (011-33-3) 80-90-53-53 | fax 80-64-08-92 | 800-735-2478 |
www.bernard-loiseau.com | 23 rooms, 9 apartments

It's the "food at Côte D'Or that remains the real draw" of this "superb"
Relais & Châteaux "gem", despite the "tragic death of Bernard
Loiseau" a few years ago; veteran chef Patrick Bertron prepares "exquisite food" at the "front edge of innovative French cuisine" and the
staff is "keeping up standards"; rooms are "charming", some with
"views of the lovely gardens", others with a "turret that's straight out
of a storybook", so while you might "go for the dining", you'll stay for
the "top-notch" everything else.

	ROOMS	SERVICE	DINING	FACIL.	COST

Château de Gilly 👫 ☆ 🏊 🔍 | 20 | 22 | 23 | 19 | $179

Gilly-les-Cîteaux | (011-33-3) 80-62-89-98 | fax 80-62-82-34 |
www.chateau-gilly.com | 36 rooms, 12 apartments

This "magical" "château in the middle of vineyards" between Dijon
and Beaune is a "wonderful spot for an intimate, wine-tasting honeymoon" in the Burgundy region; there are "fabulous gardens", an
"outdoor veranda", "unique cellar restaurant" and "medieval"
atmosphere, but the rooms can "vary widely" – some are "a bit funky"
with "matching floral print wallpaper, chairs and bedspread"
creating a "dizzying" experience, while others are "luxurious"
and "well appointed."

Le Cep ☆ | 19 | 23 | 22 | 17 | $248

27, rue Maufoux | Beaune | (011-33-3) 80-22-35-48 | fax 80-22-76-80 |
800-525-4800 | www.slh.com | 40 rooms, 22 suites

It's a good "value in the heart of beautiful Beaune", say wallet-
watchers of this "delightful hotel", where the "helpful" staff is "knowledgeable about the surrounding region", the "wonderful" restaurant
offers a "festival of flavors" and the "classic" vineyard-named rooms
are "filled with antiques"; although the size of the accommodations
varies from "huge, even by American standards", to the size of a
"shoebox with a tiny window", it's mostly "charm" that keeps
guests "going back."

Carcassonne

de la Cité, Hôtel 👫 ⑪ 🛁 🏊 | 24 | 23 | 25 | 21 | $463

Place de l'Eglise | (011-33-4) 68-71-98-71 | fax 68-71-50-15 |
800-524-2420 | www.orient-express.com | 40 rooms, 21 suites

This sprawling, castlelike pile is just as "magical" as its "unsurpassed
setting" – a medieval walled city "directly out of a fairy tale" that "becomes yours from early evening to late morning" when day-trippers
thin out; "old-world elegance" is evident in everything from the
"lovely" suites to the beautiful gardens and pool to the three "excellent" on-site restaurants crowned by La Barbacane with its "exceptional" French fare; N.B. closed for much of the winter.

Domaine D'Auriac ✕ ☆ 🏊 🔍 | ▽ 23 | 24 | 27 | 22 | $250

Rte. de Saint-Hilaire | (011-33-4) 68-25-72-22 | fax 68-47-35-54 |
800-735-2478 | www.domaine-d-auriac.com | 20 rooms, 4 apartments

Try the "foie gras prepared three ways", an "amazing" dish in the "excellent dining room" of this "beautiful château" right next to the
Carcassonne that's "away from the crowds" but still "convenient"; admirers adore the "gorgeous rooms", the "friendly staff" and the "gracious owners", and have "only good things to say" about this "lovely
Relais & Châteaux" member; N.B. closed five weeks each winter.

Champagne

Chateau Les Crayeres ☆ 🔍 | 27 | 28 | 28 | 23 | $370

64, bd Henry Vasnier | Reims | (011-33-3) 26-82-80-80 | fax 26-82-65-52 |
800-735-2478 | www.lescrayeres.com | 20 rooms

It's "as good as it gets in France" swear supporters of this "storybook"
Relais & Châteaux castle in Reims, a century-old building with "mag-

nificent grounds" and "palatial" accommodations that are "like sleeping inside Versailles"; "bend-over-backwards service" earns raves, as does the "opulent" dining room where chef (and Alain Ducasse protégé) Didier Elena creates haute cuisine that "you'll never forget"; yes, it's "extraordinarily expensive", but worth popping the cork for a "fabulous indulgence"; N.B. it's closed from Christmas week through mid-January.

Chartres

Château d'Esclimont 🌾🏛♨🔍 | 26 | 25 | 24 | 22 | $175 |

St. Symphorien le Château | (011-33-2) 37-31-15-15 | fax 37-31-57-91 | 800-525-4800 | www.esclimont.com | 52 rooms

When you "simply have to get away from Paris", hop on a "short train ride" "back in time" to this "picture-perfect romantic" Relais & Châteaux "getaway" set in a "gorgeous castle"; the "elegant dining room" pleases some, while the "lovely" grounds and "large" rooms win over others, but leisure types lament it "seems more inclined to seminars than guests" and it's a bit "too far off the beaten path."

Côte d'Azur

Byblos ✕🌾🏛☺♨ | 21 | 23 | 22 | 22 | $542 |

Avenue Paul Signac | St. Tropez | (011-33-4) 94-56-68-00 | fax 94-56-68-01 | 800-223-6800 | www.byblos.com | 44 rooms, 55 suites

"Go for the see-and-be-seen scene and the late-night club", Les Caves du Roy, "where celebs and diplomats let loose" at this "chic" and "ultratrendy" "mythic" hot spot that "soaks up the atmosphere of St. Tropez"; famed chef Alain Ducasse's Spoons restaurant pleases, as do the "renovated rooms", but some find it "more for posing" among "shiny, happy people" than for anything else, so it's probably "hype over substance" and "overpriced" as a result; N.B. the resort is closed in winter.

Château de la Chèvre D'Or ✕🏛♨ | 24 | 24 | 28 | 24 | $347 |

Rue de Barri | Eze | (011-33-4) 92-10-66-66 | fax 93-41-06-72 | 800-735-2478 | www.chevredor.com | 24 rooms, 9 suites

"Perched high over the Mediterranean", this medieval hotel "carved into the mountainside" serves up "super food" in its "fabulous" Relais Gourmand restaurant "on par with anything in France, including Ducasse"; "be prepared to duck at each doorway" as you enter period-decorated rooms with "luxurious bathrooms" and "spectacular" views of the "incredibly blue waters"; N.B. closed from November to February.

Château Eza ✕🌾🏛 | 24 | 25 | 27 | 22 | $402 |

Rue de la Pise | Eze | (011-33-4) 93-41-12-24 | fax 93-41-16-64 | 800-525-4800 | www.chateaueza.com | 6 rooms, 4 suites

Set on a clifftop 1,300 feet above the Mediterranean Sea, this "charming" medieval castle "requires a difficult walk up a steep hill" that's worth it for "absolutely breathtaking views"; a former home to the Prince of Sweden, it has "impeccable service and food", as well as "individually decorated rooms" where you can enjoy a "croissant and *jus d'orange* on your balcony."

	ROOMS	SERVICE	DINING	FACIL.	COST

Château Hotel de la Messardière 🏨🛏🌊

| ▽ 24 | 23 | 23 | 24 | $640 |

Rte. de Tahiti | St. Tropez | (011-33-4) 94-56-76-00 | fax 94-56-76-01 | www.messardiere.com | 78 rooms, 37 suites

You'll "feel like you've been taken to a different (much better) planet" when you arrive at this "extraordinary" seasonal hotel, perched over the hillside of St. Tropez "away from the hustle and bustle of Downtown" yet just a five-minute hotel-provided shuttle bus from town; the views from the pool overlooking the vineyards below are "spectacular", the service is "impeccable" and the dining experience is "outstanding", especially from the "terrace at sunset" when the trees take on a "pink glow."

de Mougins, Hotel ✕🛏🌊🔍

| 19 | 23 | 26 | 18 | $344 |

205, av du Golf | Mougins | (011-33-4) 92-92-17-07 | fax 92-92-17-08 | www.hotel-de-mougins.com | 50 rooms, 1 suite

Even if you pick it because there's a "Lamborghini parked outside", you'll be happy with your choice at this unique property 10 minutes from Cannes, consisting of four Provençal farmhouses with balconied rooms overlooking a "fantastic pool and gardens" of lavender, rosemary, mimosa and fig trees; the locally inspired cuisine at Côté Jardins gets raves, especially when taken outside under the shade of an old ash tree, while "excellent service" rounds out the package.

🇿 du Cap-Eden-Roc, Hotel 🛏🌊🔍

| 27 | 25 | 25 | 27 | $930 |

Boulevard J.F. Kennedy | Cap d'Antibes | (011-33-4) 93-61-39-01 | fax 93-67-13-83 | www.edenroc-hotel.fr | 110 rooms, 20 suites

"The über-rich play and stay" at this "retreat" that "feels like a private, palatial villa" with "one of the most beautiful views on the French Riviera"; "gorgeous rooms" and "sublime" service match "out-of-this-world" extras, including a seaside restaurant, five clay tennis courts, a pier for visiting yachts and a "spectacular" infinity pool where "stars and supermodels" frolic; N.B. now ("finally") accepting credit cards; closed mid-October to mid-April.

Grand-Hotel du Cap-Ferrat 🛏🌊🔍

| 26 | 26 | 26 | 26 | $439 |

71, bd Général de Gaulle | St-Jean-Cap-Ferrat | (011-33-4) 93-76-50-50 | fax 93-76-04-52 | 800-525-4800 | www.grand-hotel-cap-ferrat.com | 44 rooms, 9 suites

"Romance blooms" among the palms at this "Riviera favorite" that's attracted stars and royalty in search of "privacy" since 1908; a sun-drenched "old Hollywood–style resort" with a "magical location" at the end of a peninsula between Monaco and Nice, it boasts guestrooms decorated with exotic woods and rare marbles, "impeccable service", an infinity pool "to die for" and "picture-perfect cuisine" on a "beautiful" terrace overlooking the Mediterranean; grand it is, and "insanely expensive" too, but all agree it's "one of a kind."

InterContinental Carlton Cannes 🏨🛏Ⓢ

| 24 | 24 | 23 | 22 | $595 |

58, La Croisette | Cannes | (011-33-4) 93-06-40-06 | fax 93-06-40-25 | 888-424-6835 | www.intercontinental.com | 302 rooms, 36 suites

"You'll feel like a celebrity yourself" when you stay at this "lovely landmark, evocative of the fin de siècle French Riviera" that some say is "the only place to stay in Cannes"; "this hotel is good for your soul" sigh some, who awake to "a perfect view of the Mediterranean", an "amazingly beautiful environment", "spacious rooms with all the conceivable amenities" and "luscious breakfasts"; but disloyal detractors dis this "grande dame" as "a mediocre convention beehive, a once handsome disappointment."

La Colombe d'Or ☲

20	23	25	21	$363

Place des Gaulles | St-Paul-de-Vence | (011-33-4) 93-32-80-02 | fax 93-32-27-78 | www.la-colombe-dor.com | 16 rooms, 10 apartments

"Dining on the patio at lunch" is "what it's all about" gourmands gush of this "secluded oasis" – a "mixture of the ancient past with the modern cuisine of France", "perched at the top of a hill and a short walk" from everything; but art lovers contend the paintings and other works "alone are worth the trip", with "masterpieces by Chagall, Picasso", Miró and Matisse, among others; add to that a "beautiful" pool and gardens and "quaint" rooms, and it's absolutely "*charmant.*"

La Réserve de Beaulieu ☲☲☉☲

24	25	26	24	$655

5, bd du Général Leclerc | Beaulieu-sur-Mer | (011-33-4) 93-01-00-01 | fax 93-01-28-99 | 800-735-2478 | www.reservebeaulieu.com | 28 rooms, 9 suites, 1 pavilion, 1 villa

This "beautiful" Italianate "gem" typifies "what people come to the French Riviera for": a "pretty setting" and ample opportunities for relaxation whether in lush gardens, the full-service spa with *hammam* or the seaside saltwater pool; diners praise the "excellent" Mediterranean preparations of chef Olivier Brulard and suggest taking "lunch poolside"; expect a "wonderful" staff that knows how to "make you feel important" but remember, they also "know how to charge."

La Voile d'Or ☲☲

23	26	25	22	$547

7, av Jean Mermoz | St-Jean-Cap-Ferrat | (011-33-4) 93-01-13-13 | fax 93-76-11-17 | 800-888-4747 | www.lavoiledor.fr | 41 rooms, 4 suites

You could "get used to this kind of living" where you "don't have to move your pinkie" to be served and your "buttery French vanilla" rooms "shift to yellow and orange as the sun streams through the windows" (there's even one in the marble bathroom); then there are those "views from the chaise on the pool deck overlooking the Mediterranean" and the "complete privacy" of the peninsula setting; yes, life is "wonderful" at this "understated" Riviera hotel between Nice and Monaco.

☑ Le Château du Domaine St-Martin ☲☲☍

29	29	26	27	$650

Avenue des Templiers | Vence | (011-33-4) 93-58-02-02 | fax 93-24-08-91 | 800-735-2478 | www.chateau-st-martin.com | 38 suites, 6 cottages, 3 rooms

"Away from the hustle and bustle" of the Côte d'Azur (and "sans the chichi set"), this "serene" Relais & Châteaux hotel perched "high over the sea" offers "the ultimate Provence experience" in all its "casual luxury"; "exceptional" accommodations with terraces or balconies give "incomparable" views of the Med, "spacious grounds" feature a "lovely" overflowing mirror pool, a "superb" restaurant serves refined regional cuisine and "*déjeuner* in the outside olive garden is a must-do"; N.B. closed mid-November to mid-March.

Le Palais de la Mediterranée 🔭🏊

ROOMS	SERVICE	DINING	FACIL.	COST
20	19	21	21	$475

13, Promenade des Anglais | Nice | (011-33-4) 92-14-77-00 | fax 92-14-77-14 | 800-223-6800 | www.lepalaisdelamediterranee.com | 176 rooms, 12 suites

Originally built in 1929, this property in a "magnificent setting" on the Promenade des Anglais has much of its belle epoque spirit still intact (the original art deco facade was left untouched and the interior underwent a "magnificent renovation"); you'll find a "unique layout" that creates a "condo feeling", "roomy" quarters with modern, Scandinavian decor, an "accommodating staff", an on-site casino and contemporary Med fare.

Le Saint Paul 🐕

ROOMS	SERVICE	DINING	FACIL.	COST
22	26	25	22	$285

86, rue Grande | St-Paul-de-Vence | (011-33-4) 93-32-65-25 | fax 93-32-52-94 | 800-735-2478 | www.lesaintpaul.com | 11 rooms, 8 suites

Several 16th-century residences comprise this "tiny", "romantic" Relais & Châteaux property "in the center" of St-Paul-de-Vence, a "touristy but special" walled medieval town; top-shelf service draws surveyor kudos, as does "superb" seasonal French cuisine, especially when enjoyed on the "beautiful terrace"; rooms are "petite" yet "charming", but insiders say be sure to ask for one "overlooking the valley" or it may "feel as if the tourists are walking through it."

Majestic Barrière 👪🐕🔭Ⓢ🏊🎾

ROOMS	SERVICE	DINING	FACIL.	COST
20	21	24	21	$540

10, La Croisette | Cannes | (011-33-4) 92-98-77-00 | fax 93-38-97-90 | www.lucienbarriere.com | 282 rooms, 23 suites

"The grande dame of La Croisette" "is still the place to be seen" and to take in "outstanding views of the Mediterranean" from the "lovely pool" and private beach; fans say it lives up to "the first word of its name", particularly the "extraordinary" tasting menu at La Villa des Lys, "one of the best restaurants in Cannes"; still, others suggest her majesty looks a "bit tired around the edges."

Martinez 👪🐕🔭Ⓢ🏊

ROOMS	SERVICE	DINING	FACIL.	COST
21	22	23	22	$568

73, La Croisette | Cannes | (011-33-4) 92-98-73-00 | fax 93-39-67-82 | 800-888-4747 | www.hotel-martinez.com | 392 rooms, 23 suites

"Vegas meets the Côte d'Azur" at this "art deco gem-by-the-sea" where "you can pretend you're at the film festival" amid all the "glitz and glamour"; "get a room overlooking La Croisette" - the view is matched by the room's "mod, luxurious" look that's "straight out of a swanky French movie" - then head to the Givenchy spa; although you have to pay to use the "wonderful" beach, riding the "old-fashioned elevators" is free.

Negresco, Hotel 🔭

ROOMS	SERVICE	DINING	FACIL.	COST
23	24	24	22	$335

37, Promenade des Anglais | Nice | (011-33-4) 93-16-64-00 | fax 93-88-35-68 | 800-223-6800 | www.hotel-negresco-nice.com | 121 rooms, 24 suites

Chef Bruno Turbot brings a new menu to The Chantecler restaurant, one of the highlights of this venerable "living museum" where the "eclectic" belle epoque decor "full of swagger and decadence" along with "views of the Promenade Des Anglais" prompt thoughts of the "sumptuous Nice of bygone days"; only a few spoilsports snap that "Liberace" or "my grandmother" must be in charge of the design.

	ROOMS	SERVICE	DINING	FACIL.	COST

Résidence de la Pinède 🍴🛏⛱

▽ 25 | 25 | 25 | 24 | $1006

Plage de la Bouillabaisse | St. Tropez | (011-33-4) 94-55-91-00 | fax 94-97-73-64 | 800-735-2478 | www.residencepinede.com | 35 rooms, 4 suites

Fans of this Relais & Châteaux "beach paradise" that's "close to town but far enough to get some peace and quiet" "wish they could be there tomorrow" amid the "elegance and grace"; though it's quite "expensive", "everything about this hotel is perfect", from the dining room that serves "excellent" "breakfast on your balcony overlooking the water" to the "super service."

Royal Riviera 🚹🍴🛏Ⓢ⛱

23 | 24 | 25 | 26 | $426

3, av Jean Monnet | St-Jean-Cap-Ferrat | (011-33-4) 93-76-31-00 | fax 93-01-23-07 | 800-223-6800 | www.royal-riviera.com | 89 rooms, 7 suites

Thanks to Grace Leo-Andrieu's "signature style", which threads through all of the "beautiful common areas" and "charming rooms", this sister to Paris' Hotel Lancaster is a "chic" "alternative" to the other grand Côte d'Azur institutions; it also boasts a "world-class" restaurant, Le Panorama, a "gorgeous" private beach (though it's tempting to "spend all day in the swimming pool with occasional trips to the gourmet lunch buffet" instead) and a spa with alfresco treatments under the palm trees; the normally "gracious" staff loses points for "snootiness", however.

Courchevel

NEW Cheval Blanc 🍴🛏Ⓢ🎿⛱

- | - | - | - | $1321

Le Jardin Alpin | (011-33-4) 79-00-50-50 | fax 79-00-50-51 | www.chevalblanc.com | 23 rooms, 10 suites, 1 apartment, 1 chalet

The chairman and CEO of luxury-goods maker LVMH, Bernard Arnault, has opened his first hotel – a haute ski resort in the French Alps on the Jardin Alpin slope; the intimate and exclusive spot features luxury suites with contemporary furnishings, two private chalets, a Givenchy spa, a pool, two restaurants and the requisite Louis Vuitton boutique.

Dordogne

Le Moulin de L'Abbaye ✕⊕🍴

▽ 22 | 22 | 17 | 22 | $244

1, rte. de Bourdeilles | Brantôme-en-Périgord | (011-33-5) 53-05-80-22 | fax 53-05-75-27 | 800-735-2478 | www.moulin-abbaye.com | 16 rooms, 3 suites

"If the monks lived here, they couldn't have been that pious" joke worshipers of this Relais & Châteaux "fine old" 12th-century inn with an "incomparable setting on the river" in the "cute Dordogne village" of Brantôme; fans say the "imaginative regional" cuisine comprised of "wonderful local" ingredients is "outstanding", especially taken on the waterside terrace, and the "attentive service" makes many mourn that they're not "staying longer" to explore the prehistoric grottos; N.B. closed from the end of October to the start of May.

Le Vieux Logis ✕⊕🍴🛏⛱

24 | 25 | 26 | 24 | $190

Trémolat | (011-33-5) 53-22-80-06 | fax 53-22-84-89 | 800-735-2478 | www.vieux-logis.com | 17 rooms, 8 suites

You'll have a "fairy-tale experience" at this "wonderful, family-run auberge", a member of Relais & Châteaux located in the "very quiet

| | ROOMS | SERVICE | DINING | FACIL. | COST |

town" of Trémolat near the Dordogne River; a limestone swimming pool, Linden trees and gardens create the "beautiful surroundings", while the "excellent cuisine" at chef Vincent Arnould's Vieux Logis is "the best one can imagine"; "elegant" rooms contain original furnishings from four centuries ago, so even if the "floors squeak" it's all part of the "charm."

Haute-Loire

Les Deux Abbesses ✕ⓗ≋

ROOMS	SERVICE	DINING	FACIL.	COST
-	-	-	-	$555

43300 Saint Arcons d'Allier | (011-33-4) 71-74-03-08 | fax 90-65-62-86 | www.lesdeuxabbesses.com | 4 rooms, 8 cottages
Twelve medieval-style buildings comprise this "quirky but fun" Relais & Châteaux masterpiece that spans a large part of a tiny village; each "original" room is wildly different in its high-concept design – from a cottage set in an 18th-century barn with a four-poster bed of birch tree trunks to a unit with a bath fashioned from a block of lava stone set against an illuminated rock cascading with water; walkways paved with river stones wind around elaborate gardens, and musical chimes indicate dinner, which highlights the produce grown on-site.

Haute-Savoie

Évian Royal Palace ♀♂⛄⌧Ⓢ🏊≋🎾

ROOMS	SERVICE	DINING	FACIL.	COST
-	-	-	-	$172

South Bank of Lake Geneva | Evian-les-Bains | (011-33-4) 50-26-85-00 | fax 50-75-61-00 | 800-223-6800 | www.evianroyalresort.com | 82 rooms, 8 suites
Since 1909 weary bodies have sprung to this "enchanting landmark" to soak in the thermal baths and drink in "mesmerizing views" of Lake Léman from "large", "classic" rooms and a belle epoque restaurant; today guests take the waters in the "spacious" spa and romp in the resort, a vast park with swimming pools, tennis, the "outstanding" Evian Masters Golf Club, a free kids' club and ski slopes nearby; N.B. the less-swanky Ermitage hotel shares the same property and facilities.

Les Fermes de Marie ♀♂🍴⛄Ⓢ🏊≋

ROOMS	SERVICE	DINING	FACIL.	COST
∇ 21	26	24	25	$302

Megeve | (011-33-4) 50-93-03-10 | fax 50-93-09-84 | www.fermesdemarie.com | 71 rooms, 8 chalets
Tucked away in Megeve village in the French Alps, this "elegantly rustic hotel with beautiful views and grounds" is "not to be missed"; "charming" rooms are decorated with traditional French fabrics and furniture, the food wins praise and the cozy library draws fans for tea or an après-ski drink.

Île de Ré

L'Hotel de Toiras ⓗ

ROOMS	SERVICE	DINING	FACIL.	COST
-	-	-	-	$291

1, quai Job-Foran | Saint-Martin-de-Re | (011-33-5) 46-35-40-32 | fax 46-35-64-59 | www.hotel-de-toiras.com | 10 rooms, 7 suites
For four centuries this harborside former residence attracted sailors who came into the port of Saint Martin de Ré, and for the past two it's operated as a "charming" hotel (now a member of Relais & Châteaux), boasting "luxurious" rooms dedicated to historical figures from the region and decorated with antiques and fine fabrics; set on the tiny island of Île de Ré, it offers a great base for exploring the area's picturesque little towns by bicycle on 60 miles of paths.

Loire

Château de Marçay ☒♨≋☌

▽ 21 | 21 | 25 | 21 | $195

Chinon | (011-33-2) 47-93-03-47 | fax 47-93-45-33 | 800-735-2478 |
www.chateaudemarcay.com | 30 rooms, 3 suites

This "country hotel in the Loire Valley" has a "*très romantique!*" setting;
rooms "vary greatly" from "cute" to "large with eclectic decor" to "motel-
ish, except for the private outdoor seating area", but there's no arguing
that some of the bathrooms are "like personal spas"; picky patrons
pout "what's the fuss about?"; N.B. closed mid-January to early March.

Château de Noirieux ☓☒≋☌

- | - | - | - | $315

26, rte. du Moulin | Briollay | (011-33-2) 41-42-50-05 | fax 41-37-91-00 |
800-735-2478 | www.chateaudenoirieux.com | 18 rooms, 1 suite

Fans of this Relais & Châteaux hotel are drawn to chef Gérard Côme's
"world-class" dining as well as the "exquisite", "serene" surroundings;
you'll find "some of the finest roms" and "impeccable service" as well,
so even if it's out of the way, it's a "lovely stop in the Loire Valley."

Château de Noizay ☒≋☌

22 | 22 | 22 | 20 | $178

Rte. de Chançay | (011-33-2) 47-52-11-01 | fax 47-52-04-64 |
www.chateaudenoizay.com | 19 rooms

Loire-lovers looking for their own royal chamber hail this "lovely", "romantic" 16th-century Relais & Châteaux castle that's "wonderfully
situated" in the Valley; a "suit of armor" points the way to "quaint" rooms
with period furnishings, the French gardens shelter a heated swimming
pool and tennis courts and the restaurant alone is "worth the trip."

Domaine des Hauts de Loire ☓≋☌

27 | 27 | 26 | 26 | $271

Rte. de Herbault | Onzain | (011-33-2) 54-20-72-57 | fax 54-20-77-32 |
800-735-2478 | www.domainehautsloire.com | 23 rooms, 10 suites

"Enter a fairy tale" "complete with swans floating in the pond" at this
"secluded" Relais & Châteaux "joy", a "great base for touring the
Loire" and nearby castles; the vine-covered 1860 hunting lodge offers
spacious, "well-appointed" rooms decorated with antiques and toile
de Jouy, the restaurant serves "exceptional" regional cuisine and the
"sublime" "woody estate" offers "hiking and biking trails" and a "gorgeous pool"; N.B. closed late November to mid February.

Grand Hôtel du Lion d'Or ☓

▽ 24 | 24 | 27 | 20 | $218

69, rue Georges Clemenceau | Romorantin-Lanthenay |
(011-33-2) 54-94-15-15 | fax 54-88-24-87 | 800-735-2478 |
www.hotel-liondor.fr | 10 rooms, 6 suites

"Is there a better stay and restaurant in France?" ask foodies who savor
the "best frogs' legs in the world" courtesy of chef Didier Clement, at this
"charming" Relais & Châteaux Renaissance-period manor house two
hours south of Paris; the answer is "not when you consider its elements":
"luxurious rooms", a staff that believes "your wish is their command"
and a "romantic" setting; N.B. closed mid-February to the end of March.

Jean Bardet Château Belmont ☓≋

23 | 24 | 27 | 19 | $185

57, rue Groison | Tours | (011-33-2) 47-41-41-11 | fax 47-51-68-72 |
800-735-2478 | www.jeanbardet.com | 16 rooms, 5 suites

"Go for the superb food" and feast upon "fantastic" fare, much of it from
the on-site vegetable gardens, at this 17th-century property; ok, "you

	ROOMS	SERVICE	DINING	FACIL.	COST

might as well stay" too, and be surrounded by "flowers everywhere" and a staff that "really means to please" ("even helping you with a little French"); it's just the rooms that a few aren't sure of, with opinions varying between "phenomenal" and "in need of a little sprucing up."

☑ La Maison Troisgros ✕ ⚒

	24	28	29	18	$463

Place Jean Troisgros | Roanne | (011-33-4) 77-71-66-97 | fax 77-70-39-77 | 800-735-2478 | www.troisgros.com | 13 rooms, 5 suites

It's "worth a visit" to this charming Relais & Châteaux hotel "just for the superlative dinner" prepared in the "superb kitchen" of chef Michel Troisgros and served by an "outstanding staff" that brings a certain "rhythm and serenity" to the culinary experience; it's no surprise that this one was voted the top hotel for Dining in the world in this Survey, but it also offers "wonderful rooms" done in "exquisite simplicity", with appreciated touches like "cedar closets" and "beautiful flowers."

Le Chateau d'Artigny ✕ ⓗⓢ ⚒ 🔍

	25	25	26	25	$211

Rte. d'Azay-le-Rideau | Montbazon | (011-33-2) 47-34-30-30 | fax 47-34-30-39 | www.grandesetapes.fr | 45 rooms, 11 suites, 1 apartment

"Sumptuous luxury" has been the raison d'être of this "stunning château" since 1929 when a perfume creator built it in lavish 18th-century style about 10 miles from Tours in the Loire Valley; the air still smells sweet in this "exceptional lodging" with "classic" French decor, a "splendid" park where guests can swim or practice their golf putt and a restaurant that garners mostly "excellent" reviews; tipplers can take part in monthly wine tastings or splurge on a glass of century-old Armagnac at the bar.

Mercuès

Château de Mercuès ⚒ ⚒ 🔍

	23	19	24	18	$238

Mercuès | (011-33-5) 65-20-00-01 | fax 65-20-05-72 | www.chateaudemercues.com | 24 rooms, 6 apartments

"It's the view" and "unique" location that dazzle at this 13th-century Relais & Châteaux hotel perched on a cliff overlooking the Lot Valley, not to mention the "history" of counts, bishops and other notable former habitués; gourmets gush over the stellar cuisine and "wine from its own vineyard", but while the imposing, turreted structure is "beautiful" on the outside, the simply furnished rooms strike some as slightly "medieval" and in need of "freshening up."

Paris

TOPS IN CITY

28	Four Seasons
26	Plaza Athénée
	Ritz
	Le Bristol
25	Le Meurice
	de Crillon
	Park Hyatt
23	Saint James
	Lancaster
22	Hyatt Reg./Madeleine

Astor Saint-Honore, Hotel 🍴

ROOMS	SERVICE	DINING	FACIL.	COST
23	22	21	19	$502

11, rue d'Astorg, 8th | (011-33-1) 53-05-05-05 | fax 53-05-05-30 | www.astorsainthonore.com | 125 rooms, 2 suites

A credit card's throw from shopping on the Faubourg St-Honoré, this "charming" "boutique-type" "pearl" is "tucked away on a quiet street" in the "central Right Bank"; surveyors applaud the "helpful staff", "excellent rooms" and "luxurious touches" including 19th-century moldings, WiFi, a fitness center and library, along with a sophisticated bar and restaurant offering creative French haute cuisine.

Champs-Elysées Plaza, Hotel 🔭

ROOMS	SERVICE	DINING	FACIL.	COST
22	23	19	21	$648

35, rue de Berri, 8th | (011-33-1) 53-53-20-20 | fax 53-53-20-21 | www.champselyseesplaza.com | 20 rooms, 13 suites

Built as an apartment in the era of Baron von Haussman (the 19th-century prefect who redesigned the city), this "cute" boutique that sits in a "fantastic location" near the City of Light's eternal monuments and swank shopping addresses reflects the elegance of its environs; there's a lot of charm even after you get past the property's 19th-century facade, such as the ornately detailed rooms and suites that feature enough modern amenities to keep most satisfied.

Costes Ⓢ🏊

ROOMS	SERVICE	DINING	FACIL.	COST
20	17	23	20	$598

239, rue Saint-Honore, 1st | (011-33-1) 42-44-50-00 | fax 42-44-50-01 | 82 rooms, 6 suites, 1 apartment

"There's nothing like sitting in a club room at 2 AM sipping $400 bubbly" at this "epicenter of hip" that's "still the coolest hotel in Paris", with "sexy" brothel-inspired decor (even the rooms are "dark"), a "fab courtyard" and a location "perfect for a retail-therapy frenzy"; "beautiful people are everywhere", right down to the servers that "look like models" but ooze "attitude" - which some say makes it feel "that much more rock 'n' roll."

de Crillon, Hôtel 👪Ⓗ🐕🔭

ROOMS	SERVICE	DINING	FACIL.	COST
25	25	26	23	$918

10, pl de la Concorde, 8th | (011-33-1) 44-71-15-00 | fax 44-71-15-03 | 800-888-4747 | www.crillon.com | 103 rooms, 44 suites, 3 apartments

Notables from the Dalai Lama to Madonna have bedded at this "oasis of luxe" overlooking Place de la Concorde, a "*magnifique*" former palace with "gilded extravagance" throughout, New French dining via chef Jean-François Piège that "competes with the best in Paris" and a "polite, professional staff" that ensures "every whim is accommodated" ("they changed the color of the roses in the room daily upon request"); in short, it's "heaven", with "astronomical" prices to match; N.B. major renovations are scheduled for late 2007.

de Vendôme, Hôtel 🐕

ROOMS	SERVICE	DINING	FACIL.	COST
21	20	17	18	$868

1, pl Vendôme, 1st | (011-33-1) 55-04-55-00 | fax 49-27-97-89 | 800-525-4800 | www.hoteldevendome.com | 19 rooms, 10 suites

A "Fabergé egg of a hotel", this boutique with "wonderful, luxurious decor" and a "nice sense of privacy" is "perfectly located near the Louvre and the Metro"; the staff is "incredibly helpful", and though it's "expensive" and sometimes "the a/c is out and nothing can be done until the next day", its "small size" can be a "great alternative" to the larger hotels nearby.

du Petit Moulin, Hotel

-	-	-	-	$238

29-31, rue du Poitou, 3rd | (011-33-1) 42-74-10-10 |
www.hoteldupetitmoulin.com | 17 rooms

"It's all about style" at this *petit* hideout for design devotees, a 17th-century building and former bakery in the historic Marais district done up in a profusion of colors and styles by Christian Lacroix; the "interesting" rooms are "tony but tiny" and all individually decorated, from classic (toile de Jouy) to retro kitsch (polka dot rugs) or even bordello chic, with blood-red tiles and heart-shaped mirrors.

☑ Four Seasons Hotel George V

29	28	28	28	$910

31, av George V, 8th | (011-33-1) 49-52-70-00 | fax 49-52-70-10 |
800-332-3442 | www.fourseasons.com | 186 rooms, 59 suites

"Those who want only the best" say "gorgeous George", the No. 1–rated Hotel in our Survey, is "the crème de la crème", from the "spectacular" floral arrangements in the lobby to the "crystal chandeliers" and "stunning" city views in the rooms; Le Cinq, its Haute Cuisine restaurant, is rated "among the best in the world" and the "seamless, understated service" includes a concierge capable of arranging a wedding in one day "complete with a serenading boys' choir"; you'll experience "the way life should be", but as far as the cost, well, "if you have to ask . . ."

Hyatt Regency Paris-Charles de Gaulle

21	20	17	21	$394

351, av du Bois de la Pie, 12th | (011-33-1) 48-17-12-34 | fax 48-17-17-17 |
800-223-1234 | www.hyatt.com | 376 rooms, 12 suites

"What a surprise!" rave runway reviewers who disembark on this "modern American chain hotel" near the airport that boasts art deco "rooms free of jet rumbles" and full of paned glass, an "eatery that won't make you wish you're spending your last night in Paris" and a "nice gym"; it has "all the amenities for business travelers", so it's *the* choice when "you've missed your flight."

Hyatt Regency Paris-Madeleine

24	23	20	21	$418

24, bd Malesherbes, 8th | (011-33-1) 55-27-12-34 | fax 55-27-12-35 |
800-223-1234 | www.paris.madeleine.hyatt.com | 82 rooms, 4 suites

This "discrete hotel" located in a "charming" neighborhood is "not what you'd expect from an American chain" and proves that "good things come in small packages"; from the entrance on the tree-lined street to the "staff that knows you on a first-name basis" to the "contemporary, clean and comfortable" rooms with down comforters that feel "as light as feathers" to the "cozy bar", this could well be one of the "best-kept secrets in Paris."

InterContinental Le Grand Paris

23	21	21	22	$833

2, rue Scribe, 9th | (011-33-1) 40-07-32-32 | fax 42-66-12-51 |
888-4246835 | www.intercontinental.com | 400 rooms, 70 suites

The "rooms are much better since the renovation" of this "grande dame", a "large and busy hotel" that boasts "sparkling everything"; request quarters "with a view" of the Garnier Opera, recommend regulars, as "it's a sight to behold first thing in the morning and at night"; other than that, the "beautiful marble floors in the atrium" get a nod, but the service "is still only fair."

	ROOMS	SERVICE	DINING	FACIL.	COST

Lancaster ⚑
	25	27	19	20	$588

7, rue de Berri, 8th | (011-33-1) 40-76-40-76 | fax 40-76-40-00 |
800-223-6800 | www.hotel-lancaster.fr | 49 rooms, 11 suites
Good enough for Marlene Dietrich, who lived here for three years, this
"beautifully appointed" boutique hotel "in the heart of Paris" is
"heaven" for those who care that "the flowers go with the wallpaper";
formerly a 19th-century private townhouse, it still displays "timeless
elegance" and "real antiques", plus "impeccable service", a "charming" Asian-inspired courtyard garden and "adventurous dining" in a
Michel "Troisgros restaurant to die for."

Le Bristol ⚑⚑✕Ⓢ≋
	26	27	26	24	$850

112, rue du Faubourg Saint-Honoré, 8th | (011-33-1) 53-43-43-00 |
fax 53-43-43-01 | 800-223-6800 | www.lebristolparis.com |
89 rooms, 73 suites
As befits its enviable address on the Faubourg St-Honoré, this "sedate" hotel in an 18th-century mansion offers "the epitome of luxury",
from the "huge" guest quarters with "rich fabrics" and "elegant antiques" to the "lovely" pool featuring "a view of *les toits de Paris*";
"splurge" on chef Eric Frechon's "inventive" Haute Cuisine served in
an "extraordinary" winter dining room (or in the garden "oasis" during
summertime); N.B. it's expanding in autumn 2007 with additional
rooms and an informal restaurant.

Le Meurice ⚑⚑✕♨Ⓢ
	27	26	25	24	$800

228, rue de Rivoli, 1st | (011-33-1) 44-58-10-10 | fax 44-58-10-15 |
800-223-6800 | www.lemeurice.com | 121 rooms, 39 suites
Fans fall for this "forever fabulous" landmark hotel in the first arrondissement with a "superb" location across from the Tuileries
Gardens and "incredible" views of the city, a "chic atmosphere" with
"luxurious" decor of gilt, crystal and mosaics, chef Yannick Alléno's
"fancifully extravagant" Haute Cuisine table and service so "wonderful" that some clients wish they could "bring the staff home"; in short,
it's "a dream", but patrons wake up when the bill arrives – it's "breathtakingly expensive even by Parisian standards."

Le Parc Sofitel, Demeure
	22	22	22	20	$529

55-57, av Raymond Poincarè, 16th | (011-33-1) 44-05-66-66 |
fax 44-05-66-00 | 800-763-4835 | www.sofitel.com | 116 rooms
For a "quaint" city hotel in the 16th with a "wonderful garden" for taking meals, "who wouldn't want to stay here?" say pragmatic patrons
praising this practical property with "friendly" service and rooms that
"vary from tiny to spacious" with "lovely furnishings"; some aren't
sure if they "love this place because it's beautiful or just because it's
in Paris", but either way it comes out "pleasant enough with affordable
prices and a great location."

L'Hotel ⑪Ⓢ
	19	20	16	17	$319

13, rue des Beaux Arts, 6th | (011-33-1) 44-41-99-00 | fax 43-25-64-81 |
800-525-4800 | www.l-hotel.com | 11 rooms, 8 suites, 1 apartment
"Paris' most unique" boutique hotel is "filled with history" and reflects
it with "chic", "over-the-top" decor in each one of its "differently
styled", though "incredibly small", accommodations – Victorian in
#16, where Oscar Wilde spent his last days, art deco in Mistinguett's

former digs; and while it's "wonderfully located near antiques shops and art galleries", a few find the rooms "need to be freshened" and service can be "snooty."

Montalembert, Hôtel [H] 🐕 🔭 — 17 | 20 | 17 | 16 | $470

3, rue de Montalembert, 7th | (011-33-1) 45-49-68-68 | fax 45-49-69-49 | 800-323-7500 | www.montalembert.com | 56 rooms, 7 suites

"Raise your personal chic quotient" by checking into this "stylish" Left Bank boutique hotel frequented by "fabulous people", with a "wonderful location" "between the Seine and Boulevard Saint-Germain" (the Atelier of chef "Joël Robuchon is next door"); aesthetes admire the modern, "minimalistic" decor in "distinctive dark blue and naturals" and "useful" amenities like WiFi and flat-screen TVs, but if the rooms are "exquisite" they're also so "teeny" - "even by Parisian standards" - that residents report "I kept running into myself."

Murano Urban Resort 🐕 🏊 — - | - | - | - | $350

13, bd du Temple, 3rd | (011-33-1) 42-71-20-00 | fax 42-71-21-01 | www.muranoresort.com | 43 rooms, 9 suites

Straight out of *2001: A Space Odyssey,* this "über-cool, chic and sleek" hotel at the edge of the Marais district is decorated with crisp, white linens and floors set against "stark furnishings", bright flowered patterns and whimsical artwork, and some suites boast their own swimming pools or outdoor terraces; "flawless service" and "fabulous food" in a "happening restaurant" boost this "trendster" up a notch, and a new spa with its own *hammam,* will open this year.

Park Hyatt Paris-Vendôme [S] — 25 | 25 | 24 | 24 | $773

5, rue de la Paix, 2nd | (011-33-1) 58-71-12-34 | fax 58-71-12-35 | 800-223-1234 | www.paris.vendome.hyatt.com | 143 rooms, 35 suites

"Ooh-la-la" exclaim enthusiasts of this "sexy" spot they dub "the coolest of Paris' top hotels", with "a choice location near Place Vendôme", an "excellent" staff and a "contemporary" interior by designer Ed Tuttle that's totally "glam": "custom-made brass sculptures" serve as door handles and sconces, marble bathrooms "as large as a house" contain "amazing" amenities and the lighting is "a work of art"; the place even "smells divine", though you'll "pay through the nose" at check-out time.

Pavillon de la Reine 🐕 🔭 — 23 | 25 | - | 19 | $530

28, pl des Vosges, 3rd | (011-33-1) 40-29-19-19 | fax 40-29-19-20 | 800-525-4800 | www.pavillon-de-la-reine.com | 31 rooms, 25 suites

"The best part about" this "charming small hotel" "is the location" "right on the Place des Vosges" in the Marais district, "surrounded by small shops" and an easy walk to the Picasso museum, not to mention a "lovely" park; other attributes include an "inviting front sitting room with its honesty bar", a "beautiful French ambiance" and a "nonintrusive", "extremely accommodating" staff; ok, so there's no on-site restaurant and "you might have to turn down some older rooms before they show you the new ones", but once you "settle in", you'll likely "love it."

[Z] **Plaza Athénée** ✕ 🐕 🔭 — 26 | 27 | 27 | 25 | $879

25, av Montaigne, 8th | (011-33-1) 53-67-66-65 | fax 53-67-66-66 | 866-732-1106 | www.plaza-athenee-paris.com | 145 rooms, 43 suites

This "simply perfect" "palace" in the 8th is "everything it's cracked up to be", with "sophisticated" style, "immaculate service" and a "personalized feel" that includes a choice of art deco or classic rooms (some with an Eiffel Tower view) and a six-selection pillow menu; fashionistas insist "no shopper could pick a better location", "beautiful people" adore the "hip bar scene", foodies fawn over "dining chez Ducasse" and lovebirds coo "no wonder Carrie Bradshaw chose it for her romantic escapade" on *Sex and the City*.

Prince de Galles 🔭 — 22 | 23 | 21 | 20 | $806

33, av George V, 8th | (011-33-1) 53-23-77-77 | fax 53-23-78-78 | 800-325-3589 | www.luxurycollection.com | 138 rooms, 30 suites

Right Bankers rhapsodize about the "ideal location" of this "Starwood stalwart" in the Golden Triangle, and the "elegant" art deco facade and "stunning lobby" bestow a certain "glamour" to the place; the staff is "gracious" and the rooms done up in toile de Jouy are "comfortable", if "a little tired"; but sour subjects sigh, even if this Prince has "charm", he's "not aging well" and destined to be "second tier royalty" hosting the "wannastays" who can't get into the George V next door.

Raphael, Hôtel 🔭 — 24 | 24 | 19 | 19 | $425

17, av Kléber, 16th | (011-33-1) 53-64-32-00 | fax 53-64-32-01 | 800-223-6800 | www.raphael-hotel.com | 36 rooms, 50 suites

Just down the road from the Arc de Triomphe is this "lovely, small hotel" that achieves "the perfect mix between a certain Paris style and the modern world"; guests advise, "spring for the junior suite!" and "enjoy Paris at its most romantic", or sink into the "huge" tubs in rooms "tastefully furnished" in Louis XV and XVI antiques (there's also satellite TV and wireless Internet access); the staff is "wonderful", the "British bar is charming" and even if food can be "a bit common", it's "nice to try" as well.

Relais Christine 🏠 🔭 Ⓢ 🏊 — 22 | 23 | 17 | 19 | $412

3, rue Christine, 6th | (011-33-1) 40-51-60-80 | fax 40-51-60-81 | 800-525-4800 | www.relais-christine.com | 32 rooms, 19 suites

It's the "dedicated staff" at this "classy small hotel" on the Left Bank as well as a "wonderful ambiance" combining "history, charm and lovely" surroundings and a spa set under 13th-century stone walls that "make the stay memorable"; but unfortunately, rooms can be "a real crap shoot" - "some are lovely, but many are way too small and inconvenient for the price" forcing "a choice between your luggage and yourself."

Relais Saint-Germain 🏠 — 21 | 22 | 21 | 17 | $363

9, carrefour de l'Odéon, 6th | (011-33-1) 43-29-12-05 | fax 46-33-45-30 | www.hotel-paris-relais-saint-germain.com | 18 rooms, 4 suites

"It's all about" the "marvelous restaurant", Le Comptoir, which fronts this "small" 17th-century townhouse in the 6th run by chef Yves Camdeborde (formerly at La Régalade); sure, patrons praise the "perfect Rive Gauche location", the "lovely" "traditional" decor that manages to be both "hip" and "homey" and the "friendly" reception, but foremost they realize staying here is the "easiest way to get dinner reservations."

Ritz Paris 🍴 🔭 Ⓢ 🏊 — 26 | 26 | 26 | 26 | $888

15, pl Vendôme, 1st | (011-33-1) 43-16-30-70 | fax 43-16-36-68 | 800-223-6800 | www.ritzparis.com | 107 rooms, 55 suites

"You walk in wanting to apologize that you're not a princess" but soon "feel like royalty" at this "quintessential Paris" "legend" replete with "crystal, gold leaf and marble", where chef Michel Roth's Classic French restaurant, L'Espadon, is "glorious", the pool "gorgeous" and the ambiance as sinfully "snooty as you'd expect it to be"; critics caution that rooms "range from opulent to closet-sized" and some need a "face-lift", but loyalists love how this one "doesn't change" - it's "still without peer."

Saint James Paris 🐕 — 23 | 25 | 22 | 23 | $451

43, av Bugeaud, 16th | (011-33-1) 44-05-81-81 | fax 44-05-81-82 | 800-525-4800 | www.saint-james-paris.com | 18 rooms, 30 suites

Visitors say they "feel like a local" in this "small, intimate" spot, a 19th-century mansion with its own garden, located in a "quiet" part of the "upscale, residential" 16th arrondissement; since it's also a private club, guests mingle with members in the exclusive restaurant, "relax" in the library bar with live jazz on Fridays and have access to meeting rooms, a gym and "all the amenities of a top luxury" hotel in a setting that's the "epitome of charming."

Trémoille, Hotel de la 🐕Ⓢ — 23 | 22 | 17 | 19 | $527

14, rue de la Trémoille, 8th | (011-33-1) 56-52-14-00 | fax 40-70-01-08 | 800-323-7500 | www.hotel-tremoille.com | 88 rooms, 5 suites

"The fashion crowd" flips over this "secret treasure" "steps from the Champs Elysées", "a perfect blend of an old-world building" with "whimsical" yet "chic" decor; the "awesome" accommodations feature mohair curtains, fake fur bedspreads, walls in "funky" patterns and "modern amenities" such as a "fabulous" private room service system using individual hatches; the spa is equally cool, as are the meeting rooms and contemporary restaurant decorated by British designer Sir Terence Conran.

Provence

Auberge de Noves 🍴🏊🎾 — 23 | 24 | 26 | 22 | $291

Rte. de Châteaurenard | Noves en Provence | (011-33-4) 90-24-28-28 | fax 90-24-28-00 | 800-735-2478 | www.aubergedenoves.com | 19 rooms, 4 suites, 2 apartments

The "wonderful cuisine" and 60,000-bottle wine list clearly stand out at this Relais & Châteaux "lovely little hideaway" located in a "sylvan setting" a few minutes from Avignon where it's "hard to beat a meal in the beautiful garden"; though there's a "romantic and peaceful ambiance" and "big rooms", a few say they may "need to be refurbished", so go for the fare and the "warm welcome"; N.B. closed in November and for two weeks in December.

d'Europe, Hôtel Ⓗ🐕 — 22 | 23 | 25 | 18 | $161

12, pl Crillon | Avignon | (011-33-4) 90-14-76-76 | fax 90-14-76-71 | www.heurope.com | 41 rooms, 3 suites

If you look carefully, you just "might see a ghost or two from the legions of legends who've stayed here over the centuries" say smitten souls who alight at this 16th-century "piece of history" "steps from the Palais des Papes"; the "elegant architecture" includes rooms with "marble-ous bathrooms", a "courtyard for cocktails" ("watch out for pigeons") and an "excellent restaurant" via chef Bruno D'Angelis; most find the service "gracious", though a portion feel it's "chilly."

	ROOMS	SERVICE	DINING	FACIL.	COST

☑ Four Seasons Resort Provence at Terre Blanche 🏌️🏖️🍴🛎️⛰️☉🏊‍♀️🔍

| 29 | 28 | 24 | 28 | $859 |

Domaine de Terre Blanche | Tourrettes | (011-33-4) 94-39-90-00 |
fax 94-39-90-01 | 800-332-3442 | www.fourseasons.com | 96 suites, 10 villas
Surveyors say this Provençal "piece of heaven", a "stunning" resort with a "remote" location "in the hills north of Cannes", offers "Four Seasons polish" in "spacious" villas and "secluded, sunny" suites with modern furnishings; two "magnificent" 18-hole golf courses, a "dreamy" pool (like "swimming in the mountains") and "fabulous" restaurants elicit raves, as does the "kid-friendly" policy and extra "pampering"; N.B. a spa is scheduled to open in spring 2007.

Hostellerie de Crillon le Brave ✕🛎️🏊

| 22 | 22 | 23 | 21 | $190 |

Place de l'Eglise | Crillon-le-Brave | (011-33-4) 90-65-61-61 |
fax 90-65-62-86 | www.crillonlebrave.com | 24 rooms, 8 suites
Winding paths surround "quiet", "postcard"-perfect landscaped gardens and a heated pool in this 16th-century countryside "getaway", an assemblage of seven ancient stone buildings that used to comprise an entire village; each of the "simple" rooms is "unique", but most feature French country decor and stone floors, claw-foot tubs and "spectacular" views of the surrounding vineyards and Mont Ventoux; the "amazing" classic Provençal fare is prepared by chef Philippe Monti (formerly of Chewton Glen) and served alfresco on summer evenings, complemented by local wines.

La Bastide de Moustiers ✕🛎️🏊

| 25 | 26 | 26 | 21 | $238 |

Chemin de Quinson | Moustiers-Sainte-Marie | (011-33-4) 92-70-47-47 |
fax 92-70-47-48 | www.bastide-moustiers.com | 11 rooms, 1 suite
"What can you say about an Alain Ducasse inn in the south of France", other than it's a "gourmet's paradise retreat", where the "vegetables and herbs are picked in the morning and savored under the setting sun over dinner" created by "one of France's best-known chefs"; apart from that, the "staff goes out of its way to make you feel at home", and the surroundings are "sublime"; rooms can be "quirky", but in the end, you've "come for the cuisine."

La Mirande ✕🍴🛎️

| 23 | 24 | 26 | 22 | $484 |

4, pl de la Mirande | Avignon | (011-33-4) 90-14-20-20 | fax 90-86-26-85 |
www.la-mirande.fr | 19 rooms, 1 suite, 1 apartment
"Hidden away" in an "awesome location" on the "quiet side of the Palais des Papes", but an "easy walk to almost everything", this "jewel box" that "takes you back 300 years" has gourmands gushing over "exquisite dining" at Restaurant La Mirande (there are also "excellent cooking classes taught by local chefs"); "gorgeous rooms" excite, as do the "serene" gardens "far away from the hustle and bustle", so "book early" to nab your place.

Le Petit Nice Passedat 🍴🛎️🏊

| ▽ 20 | 23 | 27 | 22 | $510 |

Corniche J.F. Kennedy | Marseille | (011-33-4) 91-59-25-92 |
fax 91-59-28-08 | 800-735-2478 | www.passedat.com | 13 rooms, 3 suites
A "most wonderful" restaurant with "fabulous" food and wine is the highlight of this "delightful" Relais & Châteaux hotel in an "amazing setting" "overlooking the Mediterranean" where the cuisine goes "beyond expectation"; "get a room with a terrace" and a sea view, recom-

	ROOMS	SERVICE	DINING	FACIL.	COST

mend regulars, just keep in mind that each one has "different decor" and some "could use a freshening", which is just what they'll get in 2007.

Le Prieuré ⊕✦≋✎

| 21 | 23 | 23 | 20 | $191 |

7, pl du Chapitre | Villeneuve-Les-Avignon | (011-33-4) 90-15-90-15 | fax 90-25-45-39 | 800-735-2478 | www.leprieure.fr | 25 rooms, 11 apartments

At this "lovely" Relais & Châteaux spot, you'll be greeted by "charming hosts", roam "magnificent gardens" and eat in a "beautiful dining room" that serves "wonderful" food (some say "the best meal of their trip"); a restoration of a wonderful 600-year-old priory, it "couldn't be better located for village exploring"; N.B. it has recently been sold to new owners who will turn it into a year-round hotel after renovations at year's end.

Oustau de Baumanière ✕✦Ⓢ≋

| 23 | 25 | 28 | 25 | $313 |

Les-Baux-de-Provence | (011-33-4) 90-54-33-07 | fax 90-54-40-46 | 800-735-2478 | www.oustaudebaumaniere.com | 17 rooms, 13 suites

To partake of chef-owner Jean-André Charial's "spectacularly delicious" regional cuisine (and "fabulous wine list") on the terrace of this Relais & Châteaux "gastronomic delight in the heart of Provence" "is one of life's great moments" gush gourmands; its "breathtaking location" "below the rocky remains of Les Baux" is "magical", and "stunning gardens", a "large, pretty lap pool" and a staff that's "always there to serve" make this "small, tucked away" seasonal inn "absolutely worth the effort to get there"; N.B. a spa opens in spring 2007.

Villa Gallici ✦♨≋✎

| 26 | 26 | 24 | 24 | $400 |

Avenue de la Violette | Aix-en-Provence | (011-33-4) 42-23-29-23 | fax 42-96-30-45 | 800-735-2478 | www.villagallici.com | 18 rooms, 4 suites

You'll find yourself in a "designer's showcase" of French country decor, with "antiques, Provençal fabric" and "tassels on fringe on ruffles on lace" in the "detached private rooms" of this "charming" Relais & Châteaux restored villa on a hill overlooking Aix en Provence; the service is "wonderful", the grounds are "beautifully landscaped" and the "aroma of lavender" "welcomes you before you enter"; N.B. closed for one month annually beginning in early January.

Rhône

Château de Bagnols ⊕✦♨≋

| 29 | 26 | 27 | 23 | $526 |

Le Bourg | Bagnols | (011-33-4) 74-71-40-00 | fax 74-71-40-49 | 800-223-6800 | www.roccofortehotels.com | 8 rooms, 12 suites, 1 apartment

A drawbridge leads to this "fantastically restored" 13th-century "castle" overlooking Beaujolais Valley vineyards outside Lyon, where "luxurious" rooms "out of another millennium" (some with "turret bathrooms") feature antiques and "21st-century amenities" like flatscreen TVs; surveyors give high marks to regional fare and to the "devoted staff" that makes them feel "like a king or queen for a day"; N.B. closed January through March

Cour des Loges ✦≋

| 24 | 23 | 22 | 18 | $318 |

2-8, rue du Boeuf | Lyon | (011-33-4) 72-77-44-44 | fax 72-40-93-61 | www.courdesloges.com | 52 rooms, 10 suites

Four Renaissance-era residences comprise this "small paradise" in an "extraordinary" Vieux Lyon location, where Florentine arches, stone spiral staircases and rooftop gardens contrast with "high-tech" design (such as Philippe Starck bathroom fixtures, "glass walls" and "tubs in the middle of the rooms"); the concierge garners raves, and if a few find the food just "ok", they're quick to point out the "many great bistros" nearby.

Villa Florentine 🐕 👪 [S] 🏊 26 | 25 | 26 | 23 | $179

25-27, Montee St-Barthelemy | Lyon | (011-33-4) 72-56-56-56 | fax 72-50-90-56 | 800-735-2478 | www.villaflorentine.com | 12 rooms, 16 suites

Check out "beautiful views" from the admittedly "small" but "excellent rooms" when you stay at this "lovely" Relais & Châteaux former convent in the hills above Lyon that's a "fairly easy walk to the main sights", but far enough to "make you forget you're in a busy city"; reviewers cite the "friendly and helpful service" and "excellent", if "expensive", fare.

Versailles

Sofitel Château de Versailles [H] 🐕 ▽ 21 | 20 | 19 | 19 | $522

2 bis, av de Paris | (011-33-1) 39-07-46-46 | fax 39-07-46-47 | 800-763-4835 | www.sofitel.com | 146 rooms, 6 suites

Fans of this "gorgeous" spot near the Château de Versailles find it a "wonderful retreat from Paris" with "unbelievable restaurants"; its stunning entrance is designated a historic monument, while inside, the rooms and fitness center have modern amenities.

Trianon Palace [H] 🐕 [S] 🏊 🎾 25 | 24 | 24 | 25 | $460

1, bd de la Reine | (011-33-1) 30-84-50-00 | fax 30-84-50-01 | 800-937-8461 | www.westin.com | 166 rooms, 26 suites

"No wonder there was a French Revolution" exclaim subjects struck by the royal treatment at this "magnificent" Westin hotel "in the gardens of Versailles", "right next to the palace", with "exquisite" rooms that are "fit for a king" ("make sure to book into the historic section" and "pay extra for a view of the park"); admirers also approve of the "superb" spa, indoor pool and the Haute Cuisine restaurant.

French Polynesia

Bora Bora

Bora Bora, Hotel 🎾 26 | 24 | 22 | 24 | $700

Point Raititi | (011-689) 604-460 | fax 604-466 | 800-477-9180 | www.amanresorts.com | 54 bungalows

"The stress of the outside world melts away" at this "exceptional hotel" providing the "ultimate in luxury" from the "the overwater villas" to the "amazing tropical fish" and "surreal sunsets"; "top-class" service, "impeccable" food and "unbelievable snorkeling outside your back door" are other reasons "you'll cry when you leave."

Bora Bora Lagoon Resort & Spa 👪 [S] 🏊 🎾 28 | 23 | 20 | 26 | $621

Motu Toopua | (011-689) 604-000 | fax 604-001 | 800-524-2420 | www.boraboralagoon.com | 3 suites, 71 bungalows, 2 villas

It's the "spectacular" overwater bungalows with private decks that most impress fans of this "honeymooner's paradise" on a "lovely secluded island" with "breathtaking views" and "amazing sunsets"; other pluses include a "friendly staff" with a "'Don't Worry, Be Happy'" attitude and the Banyan-perched spa overlooking the lagoon, but dining options are "limited" and fairly "average", leading some to stiffen at the "top-dollar prices."

Bora Bora Pearl Beach Resort 🛁Ⓢ≋🔍

| 26 | 23 | 17 | 25 | $570 |

Motu Tevairoa | (011-689) 605-200 | fax 605-222 | 800-657-3217 | www.pearlresorts.com | 30 suites, 50 bungalows

With views of Mount Otemanu and just 10 minutes by boat from Bora Bora, this "breathtaking" secluded resort offers garden suites with personal pools, beach suites with private Jacuzzis and "absolutely incredible" overwater bungalows with glass coffee tables that slide out so you can feed the tropical fish; while the professional staff is "extremely helpful", culinary critics don't find much luster to this pearl's "ordinary" dining.

Le Méridien 👫🛁≋

| 27 | 26 | 21 | 25 | $748 |

Motu Tape | (011-689) 605-151 | fax 605-152 | 800-905-552 | www.lemeridien.com | 99 bungalows

There's "loads to do including nothing at all" at this "gorgeous property" with a "quite helpful" staff and "incredible surrounding views"; swim with sea turtles, feed reef sharks or relax in "fantastic", "romantic" overwater bungalows with glass-bottom floors and "sleek, contemporary design", but don't expect much from the "lackluster" dining.

NEW St. Regis Resort 👫✕🛁Ⓢ≋

| ▽ 29 | 28 | 27 | 29 | $998 |

Motu Ome'e | (011-689) 607-888 | fax 607-889 | 888-625-5144 | www.starwoodhotels.com | 92 villas

You might want to "jump through the [glass] coffee table" in your "budget-busting" overwater bungalow and "swim with the fish" at this new "ultimate honeymoon destination" where "the diving is unmatched", the dining comes courtey of renowned chef Jean-Georges Vongerichten in a space suspended over the water with views of Mount Otemanu and there's a world-class spa on its own private island; add in multiple pools (one with private daybed cabanas, another filled with saltwater and sea creatures), and this posh spot is poised to "become number one" in the Pacific.

Moorea

InterContinental Resort & Spa Moorea 👫🛁Ⓢ≋🔍

| 24 | 20 | 18 | 23 | $475 |

Papetoai | (011-689) 551-919 | fax 551-955 | 888-424-6835 | www.intercontinental.com | 48 rooms, 95 suites

This solid choice for a "honeymoon" or a family vacation boasts an "awesome setting" and "fantastic" overwater bungalows allowing for "great sunrise and sunset views" along with a boat-delivered breakfast; there are "plenty of activities" and excursions to suit children as well (the "fantastic" "dolphin encounter is worth the price"), but service that's on the "slow" side and unimpressive dining take the shine off this one.

Taha'a

Le Taha'a Private Island & Spa ♨ 🔭 🏊 🎾

28 | 27 | 24 | 27 | $1053

Taha'a | (011-689) 608-400 | fax 608-401 | www.letahaa.com | 48 bungalows, 12 villas

A "little piece of magic" just a 15-minute flight from Bora Bora, this "very secluded" and "exclusive" Relais & Châteaux resort is "probably the most romantic place on earth, hands down" say seasoned travelers; "immaculately decorated" quarters, on the beach or overwater ("the fish swim under your bed!" and "some of the world's best snorkeling is right outside your door"), along with "excellent cusine", "massages on the beach" and a staff that's "ahead of every whim" (they'll place "flower petals in a drawn bath") make it "absolute heaven" for most.

Tahiti

InterContinental Resort Tahiti 🔭 🏊 🎾

21 | 20 | 17 | 23 | $366

Point Tahiti | (011-689) 865-110 | fax 865-130 | 800-327-0200 | www.intercontinental.com | 230 rooms, 32 bungalows, 1 suites

"Incredible views of Moorea" from the "amazing" sand-bottom pool and "lovely" drinks at the swim-up bar are par for the course at this "pleasant" hotel with "marvelous" overwater bungalows and "quaint rooms"; guests disagree on the cuisine ("creative" vs. "average") and nix the "annoying noise" from the nearby airport.

Le Méridien 🔭 🏊 🎾

▽ 19 | 19 | 18 | 20 | $481

Tamanu | (011-689) 470-707 | fax 470-708 | 800-905-552 | www.lemeridien.com | 130 rooms, 8 suites, 12 bungalows

Well-situated near the Gauguin Museum and the Caves of Maraa, but perhaps "too close to the airport", this "pricey" luxury chain boasts the largest sand-bottomed pool in the South Pacific; in a region rich with overwater bungalows, the ones at this "heavily French speaking" property still get raves, though some say "the common areas are a touch run-down" and it could use "more choices in dining."

Germany

TOPS IN COUNTRY

26 Brenner's Park | *Baden-Baden*
Schloss. Bühlerhöhe | *Baden-Baden*
25 Adlon Kempinski | *Berlin*
Ritz-Carlton | *Berlin*
Schloss. Kronberg | *Kronberg*

Baden-Baden

Brenner's Park Hotel & Spa 👪 ♨ [S] 🏊

27 | 27 | 24 | 27 | $350

Schillerstrasse 4-6 | (011-49-72) 219-000 | fax 213-8772 | 800-223-6800 | www.brenners-park.de | 68 rooms, 32 suites

Guests "feel like an aristo" (and often run into the real thing) at this 170-year-old "palace" in "charming" Baden-Baden, a "luxurious, restful spot" with a "polished" "old-world" feel; expect "outstanding" spa

| | ROOMS | SERVICE | DINING | FACIL. | COST |

facilities (both beauty and medical), an "excellent" staff that "jumps to attention" and "wonderful" rooms; P.S. a "parkside" perch is a "must" to view the "lovely gardens."

Schlosshotel Bühlerhöhe 𝄞 Ⓢ 🏊 ≋ ◔   25 | 26 | 27 | 26 | $407

Schwarzwaldhochstrasse 1 | Bühl | (011-49-72) 26550 | fax 265-5777 | 800-223-6800 | www.buehlerhoehe.de | 75 rooms, 15 suites
This baroque "fairy-tale castle", built as a convalescent home for Prussian generals in the early 20th century, has "secluded grounds" and an "idyllic setting" "on the slopes of the Black Forest", along with "breathtaking" views of the mountains from "gorgeous rooms" and a "spectacular terrace"; cure-seekers make the pilgrimage to the resort's "impeccable" spa for La Prairie treatments and a springwater pool, and note it's near Baden-Baden "without the bustle of being in town."

Berlin

Adlon Kempinski, Hotel 🐾Ⓢ≋   27 | 26 | 23 | 25 | $483

Unter den Linden 77 | (011-49-30) 22610 | fax 2261-2222 | 800-426-3135 | www.hotel-adlon.de | 328 rooms, 66 suites
"A phoenix has risen from the ashes" at this "mythic" spot that was one of the city's most glamorous addresses in Mitte, once frequented by maharajahs and movie stars and now "superbly restored" to its former glory to the delight of "dignitaries" and other discerning patrons; "elegant" rooms and public spaces are "a visual treat", "exemplary service" provides "every convenience at one's fingertips" and Sunday brunch is "a forte" (as is most of the classic French dining at Lorenz Adlon), but the awesome "view of the Brandenburg Gate trumps it all."

Grand Hyatt 🐾Ⓢ≋   26 | 25 | 23 | 25 | $400

Marlene-Dietrich-Platz 2 | (011-49-30) 2553-1234 | fax 2553-1235 | 800-223-1234 | www.berlin.grand.hyatt.com | 323 rooms, 19 suites
Despite its "perfect location" at Potsdamer Platz "where all the action is", tech-loving travelers "hardly leave" this "very cool, high-design" hotel where the "sleek, modern" accommodations feature Internet access and PlayStation sets; "high-quality" dining includes fusion fare at the "trendy" eatery Vox, and the rooftop boasts a "fabulous" spa and pool with amazing views of Berlin; in sum, it's a state-of-the-art "city oasis", right down to the "excellent" service – "they even have a technology concierge."

InterContinental 🐾Ⓢ≋   20 | 22 | 20 | 23 | $198

Budapester Strasse 2 | (011-49-30) 26020 | fax 2602-2600 | 800-327-0200 | www.intercontinental.com | 530 rooms, 54 suites
The briefcase brigade finds "everything you could ask for as a business traveler" at this former Hilton in Charlottenburg that boasts "hip and modern rooms" (though a bit "cold and stark" for classic types) and a "perfect location"; eat at Hugos "on top of the hotel" recommend regulars, then consult the "great concierge staff" when it's time to go out; even if it's "large" and "impersonal", you should still watch the rates because "sometimes it can be a bargain."

	ROOMS	SERVICE	DINING	FACIL.	COST

Kempinski Hotel Bristol 🎾🏊🔍 | 20 | 22 | 22 | 20 | $239

Kurfürstendamm 27 | (011-49-30) 884-340 | fax 884-34-878 |
800-426-3135 | www.kempinski.com | 248 rooms, 53 suites

Known to insiders as the 'Kempi', this "grande dame" was built in 1952 on the famous Kurfürstendamm shopping boulevard; "rooms are lofty and extremely well appointed" in a "comfortable" "classic" style (though some say they could use "a bit of a spruce up"), the staff is "A+" and the "cute" pool area with mosaics and palms was the first inside a Berlin hotel; but while Westsiders say the "location is unbeatable", dissenters declare "East is the way to go now."

Regent, The 🎾🍽🏊🎾 | ▽ 28 | 28 | 23 | 25 | $410

Charlottenstrasse 49 | (011-49-30) 20338 | fax 2033-6119 |
www.theregentberlin.com | 156 rooms, 39 suites

"Service sets this property apart" say surveyors seduced by the "responsive" reception and special touches like VIP treatment for kids offering DVDs and a back-of-the-house tour (upon advance request); this "opulent" hotel has "lovely, spacious rooms" with marble baths and antique desks, a formal seafood restaurant and a "desirable" location overlooking historic Gendarmenmarkt Square; though it's far from cheap, it's "not as expensive as one might expect."

Ritz-Carlton, The 🎾Ⓢ🏊 | 26 | 26 | 25 | 25 | $258

Potsdamer Platz 3 | (011-49-30) 337-777 | fax 337-775-555 |
800-241-3333 | www.ritzcarlton.com | 302 rooms, 38 suites

"Top hats" would not be out of place in this three-year-old "beautifully gaudy" hotel featuring a marble stairway in the lobby, "gorgeous" "cherry wood accents" in guestrooms and a La Prairie spa where the ceiling over the pool twinkles with a constellation of crystals; it's a "fantastic" interpretation of "old-world luxury in postmodern Berlin", and "ritzy" residents say it's worth "splurging for the club floor" to get "exceptional" service and panoramic views over Potsdamer Platz and Tiergarten Park.

Schlosshotel im Grunewald ✕Ⓗ🎾🎾Ⓢ🏊 | ▽ 28 | 28 | 23 | 24 | $265

Brahmsstrasse 10 | (011-49-30) 895-840 | fax 8958-4800 | 800-223-6800 |
www.schlosshotelberlin.com | 42 rooms, 12 suites

Built in 1914 as a private palace, this "aristocratic hideaway" was opened to guests in 1994 after a complete reinvention by designer Karl Lagerfeld; set "away from hordes of tourists" in the "wonderful, quiet" Grunewald residential neighborhood, the "affordable" rooms and suites "feel timeless", but feature modern amenities like in-room WiFi, fax machines and heated marble bathrooms; the gourmet Vivaldi Restaurant, open-air Catalina Bar, and full spa and fitness facilities with pool add to the luxury.

Cologne

Hyatt Regency 🎾🎾Ⓢ🏊 | 22 | 23 | 22 | 21 | $197

Kennedy-Ufer 2A | (011-49-221) 828-1234 | fax 828-1370 | 800-223-1234 |
www.cologne.regency.hyatt.com | 288 rooms, 18 suites

"Breathtaking views of the Dom" and the Rhine make a glamorous backdrop for meetings and dinners at this waterfront business hotel

| | ROOMS | SERVICE | DINING | FACIL. | COST |

with a modern design and striking glass atrium lobby, "comfortable" and soberly decorated rooms, "great" Asian-German fusion cuisine, a spa and fitness club, and a staff that's both "friendly" and "knowledgeable"; the only downside is that the spectacular vista comes at a price – it's "clearly on the wrong side of the river."

Dresden

Taschenbergpalais Kempinski, Hotel ⓗⓟ☂✿♠Ⓢ≋

| ▽ 26 | 24 | 23 | 25 | $289 |

Taschenberg 3 | (011-49-351) 49120 | fax 491-2812 | 800-426-3135 | www.kempinski.com | 182 rooms, 32 suites

Destroyed in 1945 and "rebuilt superbly", this "palace" "right on the square" ("an easy walk" from "all the historic sites") "shines" as it did when a Saxon ruler erected it three centuries ago; guests "feel like the Kaiser" in "opulently appointed" rooms, where the heated floors in the bathrooms are "most appreciated", and further swoon over "efficient, attentive German service" and a "sensational indoor pool."

Frankfurt

Kempinski Hotel Gravenbruch Frankfurt ⓗ

| ▽ 23 | 21 | 18 | 23 | $404 |

1 Graf zu Ysenburg und Buedingen Platz | (011-49-69) 389-88-744 | fax 389-88-911 | www.kempinski.com | 317 rooms, 30 suites

A contrast to the city's glass-and-steel skyline, this former hunting mansion in a "wonderful parklike setting" overlooking a lake is "one of the few buildings in Frankfurt to reflect the pre-war days", offering a large selection of individually decorated rooms and suites, a "fantastic" indoor pool, a spa and tennis courts; though a little "far from the dining/business district", there are numerous conference rooms and a cigar smokers' lounge for wheeling and dealing around the humidor.

Steigenberger Frankfurter Hof ⓗ✿Ⓢ

| 23 | 22 | 21 | 20 | $532 |

Am Kaiserplatz | (011-49-69) 21502 | fax 215-900 | www.frankfurter-hof.steigenberger.de | 180 rooms, 41 suites

This "elegant" 130-year-old landmark on the Kaiserplatz was a favorite hangout of the philosopher Schopenhauer, and now business travelers frequent the hotel for its "large" rooms and numerous meeting facilities, "attentive" staff (though critics claim "the service is not as good as they think"), an upgraded New French restaurant and an after-hours stogy in the exclusive Havana Lounge; but while some find "charm", the frank assessment of others is that it's "over the hill."

Steigenberger Hotel Metropolitan

| – | – | – | – | $501 |

Poststrasse 6 | (011-49-69) 506-0700 | www.metropolitan.steigenberger.de | 127 rooms, 4 suites

Corporate commuters can bank on a quite "liveable" stay at this recently opened hotel close to the 'Mainhattan' financial district, where the staff is "helpful" and a historic sandstone facade contrasts with the modern interior; rooms are decorated in earthy tones and have granite bathtubs, and guests do business in five conference rooms, work out at the state-of-the-art gym and dine in one of two restaurants or an English-style bar.

	ROOMS	SERVICE	DINING	FACIL.	COST

Hamburg

Kempinski Hotel Atlantic ⓘ🅿️🍴♨️Ⓢ🏊
| 23 | 24 | 22 | 21 | $345 |

(aka Atlantic or White Castle on Lake Alster)

An der Alster 72-79 | (011-49-40) 28880 | fax 247-129 | 800-426-3135 | www.kempinski.com | 58 suites, 194 rooms

Fondly called the 'White Castle on the Alster', this "gorgeous old" hotel, built in 1909, offers "great views" of Hamburg's Outer Alster Lake, a "stylish" clientele and a convenient location for a "walk to museums and shopping"; it "lives up to the Kempinski reputation" for service and luxury in many respects, but a couple of critics cringe over "surprisingly small rooms needing refurbishment" (there's a planned renovation in 2007).

Louis C. Jacob, Hotel ✕♨️
| - | - | - | - | $308 |

Elbchaussee 401-403 | (011-49-40) 8225-5405 | fax 8225-59405 | www.hotel-jacob.de | 66 rooms, 19 suites

This historic riverside mansion in a "lovely location" in Nienstedten takes its name from its founder (who fled France at the time of the Revolution); the "superlative" rooms virtually hang over the Elbe, offering vistas from floor-to-ceiling windows, while at the on-site French-Mediterranean restaurant, Jacobs, chef Thomas Martin creates "great" meals paired with a choice of 50,000 bottles of wine.

Park Hyatt Ⓢ🏊
| ▽ 26 | 25 | 23 | 25 | $219 |

Bugenhagenstrasse 8 | (011-49-40) 3332-1234 | fax 3332-1235 | 800-223-1234 | www.hamburg.park.hyatt.com | 232 rooms, 21 suites, 30 apartments

"A restored warehouse" is the site of this "stylish and distinctive" hotel that many travelers call their "preferred place in Hamburg", thanks to a convenient location "near the central shopping district", "attentive service", "a modern European ambiance" and "sleek" rooms with "rainforest showerheads" in marble baths; devotees' only reservations might be the restaurant – it's "good" but "could be better" – while spa buffs are tickled pink to find "one of the best health clubs in all of Europe."

Raffles Hotel Vier Jahreszeiten ✕♨️Ⓢ
| ▽ 25 | 25 | 25 | 22 | $330 |

Neuer Jungfernstieg 9-14 | (011-49-40) 34940 | fax 3494-2600 | 800-637-9477 | www.raffles.com | 143 rooms, 14 suites

Located in the city center with a "nice view" of Alster Lake, this Neustadt "gem" practically "defines good service" and is "worth the expense" to experience it "at least once in your life"; reviewers give many accolades to the staff, and also find "superb" antiques-filled rooms, "lovely" French-Mediterranean cuisine at chef Christoph Rüffer's Haerlin (voted No. 1 for Food in Hamburg in our *Europe's Top Restaurants* Survey) and a fun hot spot at Doc Cheng's.

Side 🅿️♨️Ⓢ🏊
| - | - | - | - | $218 |

Drehbahn 49 | (011-49-40) 309-990 | fax 3099-9399 | 800-337-4685 | www.side-hamburg.de | 168 rooms, 10 suites

Another "cool and chic" boutique, this spot in central Hamburg's Neustadt neighborhood boasts a futurist, ultramodern look via architect

Jan Störmer, with plenty of glass and stone, an "impressive" eight-story atrium and an underground pool with Technicolored cabanas; the "well-designed", minimalist rooms boast windowed walls, prompting some to "take notes for their own house"; but the staff, like the property, can be a "little cool", marring an otherwise grand experience.

–	–	–	–	$133

25hours Hotel
Paul-Dessau-Strasse 2 | (011-49-40) 855-070 | fax 8550-7100 | 800-337-4685 | www.25hours-hotel.com | 92 rooms, 5 studios

The style-conscious crowd is heading to this hip spot in the Western Business District, created by well-known Hamburg hotelier Kai Hollmann; creative types from the publishing and advertising industries gravitate to its exclusive lounge, then cocoon in small rooms with high ceilings, exposed brick, plastic furnishings and psychedelic wallpaper.

Kronberg

	ROOMS	SERVICE	DINING	FACIL.	COST
Schlosshotel Kronberg ✕ ⊕	25	25	25	25	$380

Schlosshotel Kronberg ✕ ⊕
Hainstrasse 25 | (011-49-61) 737-0101 | fax 7370-1267 | 800-223-6800 | www.schlosshotel-kronberg.de | 51 rooms, 7 suites

"Ooh-la-la, very impressive!" exclaim enthusiasts enamored by this "magnificent castle", once the home of Queen Victoria's daughter, Empress Frederick, where, assisted by a staff that moves seamlessly through the "well-run" operation, "you can pretend to be royal" yourself; loyalists love the "charming" rooms that overlook "beautiful" grounds, duffers delight in the on-site golf and prissy patrons appreciate the "formal" feeling, saying it's "not a place you'd feel comfortable in shorts."

Munich

	ROOMS	SERVICE	DINING	FACIL.	COST
Bayerischer Hof ⊕ ⬚ ♠ ⓢ ≋	21	22	21	22	$348

Bayerischer Hof ⊕ ⬚ ♠ ⓢ ≋
Promenadeplatz 2-6 | (011-49-89) 21200 | fax 212-0906 | 800-223-6800 | www.bayerischerhof.de | 335 rooms, 60 suites

Privately owned for four generations, this "grande dame" mixes "old-world charm" "with elite services and modern updates", making it popular with both the "mink coat" and "Bavarian bling bling" sets; pluses include "responsive" service, a "breathtaking" rooftop spa and pool, "amazing" "champagne breakfast" and a "very central" location; less rave-worthy are the rooms, which, despite scattered renovations and plush "feather beds", range from "luxe" to "shoebox" and "badly in need of work" – be sure to request an updated one.

	ROOMS	SERVICE	DINING	FACIL.	COST
Kempinski Vier Jahreszeiten, Hotel ⊕ ⓢ ≋	21	22	20	20	$469

Kempinski Vier Jahreszeiten, Hotel ⊕ ⓢ ≋
Maximilianstrasse 17 | (011-49-89) 21250 | fax 2125-2000 | 800-426-3135 | www.kempinski.com | 246 rooms, 62 suites

"Within an easy walk" of the Downtown shopping district, and situated on the "Oktoberfest parade" route, this Munich "must-stay" is still a "celebrity hangout" and "classic Kempinski", despite being "a little frayed around the edges"; "first-rate" concierges, a "breakfast to die for" and a new Mediterranean-German restaurant win over some friends, but rooms, generally in "need of renovating", are described as "modern closets."

	ROOMS	SERVICE	DINING	FACIL.	COST

Königshof ⌘

| | 20 | 25 | 25 | 19 | $376 |

Karlsplatz 25 | (011-49-89) 551-360 | fax 5513-6113 |
www.geisel-privathotels.de | 74 rooms, 13 suites

One of the highlights of this "understated jewel" on the Stachus Plaza
is the "excellent" New French–International menu of chef Martin
Fauster that's served in an elegant room with live piano music and dramatic views of Innenstadt's Karlsplatz ("quite the experience"); even
if the rooms are "a bit small", the service is "outstanding."

Le Méridien ⌘♨Ⓢ≋

| | 22 | 21 | 18 | 21 | $522 |

Bayerstrasse 41 | (011-49-89) 24220 | fax 2422-1111 | 800-543-4300 |
www.lemeridien.com | 352 rooms, 29 suites

The "high-tech" rooms are the standout feature of this "sleek", "contemporary" Maxvorstadt property across from the main train station
and within close proximity of "just about everything" (including the
Bavarian State Opera and the Hofbrauhaus); rooms feature "wall-
mounted" plasma flat-screen TVs with satellite channels, Internet access and electronic minibars, and "everything looks modern"; a few
like the Classic French restaurant and the bar, but this "diamond in the
rough" can be "sterile" for others.

Mandarin Oriental ⌘Ⓢ≋

| | 26 | 26 | 25 | 23 | $648 |

Neuturmstrasse 1 | (011-49-89) 290-980 | fax 222-539 |
www.mandarinoriental.com | 53 rooms, 20 suites

Mandarin mavens marvel at this "very upscale", "intimate" "real gem"
in the Altstadt section of Innenstadt near the opera and beer gardens;
its "large" rooms feature "well-appointed" high-tech touches and
"heated marble bathroom floors" for those "cold Munich winters", the
staff "takes care of every need" and the "inspired" Med-International
cuisine of chef Mario Corti completes the "purely elegant" picture.

Rothenburg

Eisenhut, Hotel ⊕⌘♨

| | 19 | 25 | 22 | 17 | $145 |

Herrngasse 3-5/7 | (011-49-98) 617-050 | fax 617-0545 |
www.eisenhut.com | 76 rooms, 2 suites

"Charm goes a long way" at this historic spot, set "smack dab in the
middle" of a "storybook town" in four houses that date back to the
15th and 16th centuries; "outstanding" and "very professional" services manifests in details like "a feast" delivered to the room "on gorgeous trays" for those requiring a pre-breakfast check-out and "your
name on a porcelain plate to hold" your dinner reservation; although
rooms have "outdated furniture", most also have "breathtaking views"
"over the valley" and enough of "a luxurious feel" that it's "like living in
the Middle Ages with 21st-century amenities."

Wiesbaden

Nassauer Hof ♨Ⓢ≋

| | ▽ 26 | 25 | 24 | 25 | $286 |

Kaiser-Friedrich-Platz 3-4 | (011-49) 611-1330 | fax 611-133632 |
www.nassauer-hof.de | 139 rooms, 30 suites

Live "like a king" at this "fun and first-rate" "old-world classic", a favorite of real-life royalty – and tourists, businessmen and wellness-
seekers – since 1819; the past and present meet in details like marble

bathrooms, antique furnishings and in-room WiFi, while the gourmet restaurant, Ente , Estee Lauder Beauty Center and vast pool filled with thermal spring water help keep the vibe "plush in every way"; even detractors who claim it's "not what it used to be" admit it's "still the one to go to in Wiesbaden."

Wolfsburg

Ritz-Carlton, The 🛁Ⓢ

-	-	-	-	$403

StadtBrücke | (011-49-5361) 607-000 | fax 608-000 | 800-241-3333 | www.ritzcarlton.com | 153 rooms, 21 suites

You'll get what you bargained for if you want a "very different experience" when visiting this luxury hotel in the Autostadt, a theme park devoted to automobiles; the "very elegant" design "impacts the area", "sleek rooms" boast all heated marble bathroom floors, there's dining at Aqua and The Grill and art lovers appreciate the collection of more than 600 original works; although casual critics carp it's a "little stuffy", more maintain it's "amazing."

Greece

Athens

Astir Palace Vouliagemni 👫🛁🏖🔍

20	21	21	25	$300

40 Apollonos St. | (011-30-210) 890-2000 | fax 896-0758 | www.astir-palace.com | 294 rooms, 27 suites, 76 bungalows

This "magnificent, secluded hotel" about 15 miles from Athens in the "exclusive" Vouliagemni neighborhood is comprised of three hotels overlooking the bay; there are "amazing outdoor pools" and "the best sunset views", and "now that it's managed by Starwood" (one is a Westin, the other a Luxury Collection and the third to reopen as a W in 2008), reviewers predict service "should improve."

Atheneum InterContinental 🛁🏖

21	20	20	21	$260

89-93 Syngrou Ave. | (011-30-210) 920-6000 | fax 920-6500 | 800-327-0200 | www.ichotelsgroup.com | 483 rooms, 60 suites

"Ask for a room with a view" and you may be lucky enough to get one of the two with "vistas of the Acropolis" at this "well-situated" "Athens oasis" "geared to business travelers" and in close proximity to many sights and financial destinations; some find it rather "workmanlike", with "clean, nice rooms", "efficient service" and "standard fare that's good, not outstanding", but most insist that "if big chains are your thing, you can't go wrong here"; P.S. head up to the rooftop restaurant for a "drink at sunset and the best photo ops in the city."

Grande Bretagne 🛁Ⓢ🏖

26	24	23	25	$383

Constitution Sq. | (011-30-210) 333-0000 | fax 322-8034 | 800-325-3589 | www.grandebretagne.gr | 262 rooms, 59 suites

A "massive" renovation several years ago for the Olympics made this "historic and elegant" "sanctuary" in the "center of the action" in Athens "unbeatable"; "brocade, chintz and dark-wood" "rooms that really work" (although they're "smallish by today's standards"), an "incredible spa", a "pretty roof deck" pool-bar-restaurant with "stunning" views of the Acropolis and an "attentive" staff make this a "true winner"; just "be sure to book a room with a view" to see it like the "gods of Olympus."

King George Palace 🏊 — - | - | - | - | $700

3 Vas. Georgiou A' St. | (011-30-210) 322-2210 | fax 210-325-0504 | www.lhw.com | 78 rooms, 24 suites

After a head-to-toe renovation, this hotel set in a historic landmark has gained a new luster in fully soundproofed rooms boasting handcrafted armoires, custom raw silk fabrics and marble baths with deep-soaking tubs; other highlights include a state-of-the-art health club and spa offering personal training, an Alain Ducasse-inspired restaurant and a seventh-floor cocktail lounge with views of the Acropolis.

Crete

[Z] Blue Palace Resort & Spa 👪 👀 Ⓢ 🏊 🎾 — 27 | 24 | 23 | 26 | $611

Elounda | (011-30-28410) 65500 | fax 89712 | www.bluepalace.gr | 14 rooms, 183 bungalows, 51 suites, 4 villas

"Nothing on the island compares" to this "magical" resort "built up a hillside" facing the Mediterranean and Spinalonga; the "romantic rooms" have "everything you want" and most have "saltwater pools and verandas" that allow for "the ultimate in private sunbathing" (request one "away from the funicular"); there's a "spa with superb thalassotherapy" and a "great staff", but a few find this resort that's almost an hour from the airport "somewhat remote"; N.B. closed May-October.

Elounda Beach Hotel 👪 🐕 👀 Ⓢ 🏊 🎾 — 27 | 24 | 23 | 24 | $462

Elounda | (011-30-28410) 63000 | fax 41373 | 800-223-6800 | www.eloundabeach.gr | 150 rooms, 93 suites

Blessed with a "beautiful setting", this outpost of "glamour by the sea", where "rockers" and other high-profile types "get away from it all", offers "everything and more" - "pools, tennis, boating and sightseeing tours all at your fingertips" ("and oh, what a beach"); there are "stellar rooms" and "delightful waterfront villas", plus "a ton of dining options", so sit back and "gaze at the stars" (both the "celeb" and celestial sorts).

Elounda Mare 👀 Ⓢ 🏊 🎾 — 27 | 27 | 22 | 26 | $522

Elounda | (011-30-28410) 41512 | fax 41307 | 800-735-2478 | www.eloundamare.com | 30 rooms, 37 bungalows, 13 suites

"A relaxed holiday" awaits at this Relais & Châteaux resort in a "quiet location" on an otherwise "touristy island"; in addition to "beautiful grounds", a "great beach", "excellent service" and "quite good dining", it boasts "amazing common rooms" that "integrate antique finds" and "Cretan fabrics and weavings" "into the design", and some of its "little cottages" have their own "spectacular private pools"; with such "excellence all the way", it's the place to Crete yourself right.

Mykonos

Grecotel Mykonos Blu 👀 Ⓢ 🏊 — ▽ 26 | 27 | 25 | 23 | $548

Plati Yalos | (011-30-22890) 27900 | fax 27783 | 800-736-5717 | www.grecotel.gr | 102 bungalows

"The views are wonderful" from this hotel and spa "on top of a hill" where all of the sleek, "tastefully done" bungalows have "very modern" baths and terraces and the "private beach is a real plus"; high-lights include an outdoor seawater pool, supervised kids' programs in the summer and an Elemis spa, but there are "a lot of steps" to the beach, so "if you have problems climbing" you might reconsider.

22	20	19	23	$621

Santa Marina
Resort & Villas 🏝🅢🌊🔍

Ornos Bay | (011-30-22890) 23220 | fax 23412 | 800-325-3589 | www.santamarinahotel.com | 60 rooms, 21 suites, 9 villas

This "quiet" property on a private peninsula with a "gorgeous rocky beach" and "amazing" views of the "crystal-clear waters" of Ornos Bay offers "attractive rooms", a "stunning pool", a "friendly" staff and lots of "island delicacies to linger over"; it's a "perfect place to get away" from it all, until you want to enjoy the "all-night bacchanal" in nearby Mykonos town; N.B. open May through October.

Santorini

Katikies 🏝🌊

26	26	25	26	$614

Oia | (011-30-22860) 71401 | fax 71129 | 800-525-4800 | www.katikies.com | 6 rooms, 19 suites

Some surveyors insist it's "what heaven must look like", others that "heaven cannot compare" to this "very pampered, very private" resort "hanging over a caldera" – but all agree it's a "perfect honeymoon destination" (no children under 13 permitted) that offers "the thrill of a lifetime"; the "fantastic views, rooms and service" – from the "excellent food" at the open-air rooftop restaurant to the "charming staff" to the "authentic atmosphere" – are "worth every penny", so "transport yourself to decadence."

Vedema Resort 🅔🍴🏝🅢🌊

24	26	26	25	$648

Megalohori | (011-30-22860) 81796 | fax 81798 | 800-325-3589 | www.vedema.gr | 34 apartments, 11 villas

Despite an "off-the-beaten-path" location about "10 minutes from town", this "tucked-away" seasonal Santorini "masterpiece" entices with "exquisite dining" on "the picture-perfect patio", "its own winery in the basement" offering "famous" "tastings" and service that's "above and beyond"; what rooms lack in the area's requisite "caldera view" they make up for with "great decor" and an "amazing presentation" for the in-room breakfast; P.S. renting a car is recommended since "the infrequent bus to the beach and town can be frustrating."

Grenadines

Canouan Island

Raffles Resort 🎿🅔⛱🅢🌊🔍

▽	25	25	27	28	$750

Canouan Island | (1-784) 458-8000 | fax 458-8885 | www.raffles.com | 156 villas

No wonder this 300-acre "tropical paradise" is a "playground for the rich and famous" – it's remote, quiet and "you'll need to take out a mortgage to pay for it"; "gorgeous" rooms, situated around a protected bay, are spacious (no less than 560 sq. ft.) with "magnificent" views, and four gourmet restaurants, a golf course, "stunning"

	ROOMS	SERVICE	DINING	FACIL.	COST

European-style casino and star treatment from an "above-level staff" ("there's nothing but service, service, service") make this resort "so amazing, it's ridiculous."

Mustique

Cotton House ✕🔭[S]🏊🎾 ▽ 24 | 22 | 20 | 22 | $700

Endeavour Bay | (1-784) 456-4777 | fax 456-5887 | 888-452-8380 | www.cottonhouse.net | 8 rooms, 7 suites, 3 cottages, 1 villa

You can "rent the rock star life" at this "ultimate hideaway" surrounded by "estates of the rich and famous" where you'll have "miles of beaches" "virtually all to yourself" (though "you might see Mick Jagger") and can retreat to "flawless" rooms with "casual" decor; you'll get satisfaction from "personal service", "excellent food", "great drinks" and a luxury spa - but it comes at "insane prices."

Petit St. Vincent

Petit St. Vincent Resort 🔭🎾 26 | 29 | 25 | 26 | $740

Petit St. Vincent Island | (1-954) 963-7401 | fax 963-7402 | 800-654-9326 | www.psvresort.com | 22 cottages

"Bring a good book or your lover" to this "very quiet" "paradise that's tucked away from distractions and disruptions"; each of the stone cottages "has its own charm" - "some are directly on the beach, others are atop a hill (but with ocean access)" and "you choose" how much "pampering" you want by raising a flag to attract the "genuinely friendly" service; the fine dining can include "lobster with every meal" to boot, so those "returning for the fifth time" deem it "the best in the Caribbean."

Guatemala

Antigua

Antigua, Hotel 👪[H]🏊 ▽ 23 | 24 | 21 | 21 | $150

8a Calle Poniente 1 | (011-502) 7832-2801 | fax 7832-0807 | www.portahotels.com | 73 rooms, 5 suites

Full of "colonial charm", this gem (open since 1955) is ideally situated for exploring both the "quaint" World Heritage town of Antigua and nearby Guatemala City; modern facilities, a swimming pool, a kids' club, two restaurants and the Bar El Conquistador - overlooking the famed rose gardens - help create an experience that fans rave is "like no other."

Casa Santo Domingo [H]🏊 ▽ 24 | 25 | 24 | 27 | $170

3a Calle Oriente 28A | (011-502) 7820-1222 | fax 7832-4155 | www.casasantodomingo.com.gt | 105 rooms, 20 suites

More than a "lovely hotel in a charming" colonial city, this centuries-old converted monstery draws fervent worshipers for its "authentic" taste of "Guatemalan culture" from the "luxurious and unique" rooms with "nice antiques" to the "romantic" vibe created by candles floating in pools of water throughout to the "top-of-the-line service" and "sumptuous" food; it all combines to be one of the "nicest" "landmarks" in Antigua.

	ROOMS	SERVICE	DINING	FACIL.	COST

Guatemala City

Westin Camino Real ≋ ☜ | 23 | 22 | 18 | 22 | $120

Ave. Reforma y 14 Calle | (011-502) 2333-3000 | fax 2337-4313 |
800-937-8461 | www.westin.com | 255 rooms, 16 suites

A "beautiful entryway" and an "attentive staff" welcome guests to this
"centrally located" city resort that recently completed three years of
renovations; "large, comfortable rooms" with European decor, an "excellent" spa and multiple outdoor pools attract the vacation crowd,
while a "good" "business center" and meeting/conference facilities
assist those on the clock; still, a few find "nothing special here."

Panajachel

Atitlán, Hotel ♨Ⓢ≋☜ | 22 | 24 | 21 | 21 | $120

Finca San Buenaventura | Lake Atitlán | (011-502) 7762-1441 |
fax 7762-0048 | www.hotelatitlan.com | 53 rooms, 7 suites

With its "spectacular setting" on the shores of Lake Atitlán, this "gem
in the middle of nowhere" offers "breathtaking views of one of the
most beautiful places in the world"; the rooms, surrounded by "wonderful gardens, people and birds" (note: the peacocks can be "noisy at
night"), flaunt "creative decor" that includes hand-carved wooden furniture and ceramic tiles, while the restaurant and bar feature a fireplace and mahogany-and-gold-leaf tables; to get up close with the
area's "south of France" feel, "don't miss the nature walk."

Hungary

Budapest

Danubius Hotel Gellért ⊕♨Ⓢ≋ | 15 | 18 | 15 | 22 | $225

Szent Gellért tér 1 | (011-36-1) 889-5500 | fax 889-5505 |
www.danubiusgroup.com | 221 rooms, 13 suites

On the right bank of the Danube near the Liberty Bridge, this "fascinating" "trip back to the glory days of the Austro-Hungarian empire" (it
opened in 1918) is "showing a bit of wear" in "furnishings and facilities stuck in a Communist time warp" but "you gotta love" the adjacent Geller Bath that's "like no other" with its "marble-columned pool"
and "old-style steam and massage"; overall, this is "not Budapest's
best" (the "service needs to be friendlier" and the rooms cry for "refurbishment"), but those "fantastic" waters hold a lot of charm.

Z Four Seasons Hotel | 28 | 28 | 27 | 28 | $422
Gresham Palace ♯⊕♨Ⓢ≋

Roosevelt tér 5-6 | (011-36-1) 268-6000 | fax 268-5000 | 800-332-3442 |
www.fourseasons.com | 165 rooms, 14 suites

Surveyors repeatedly call this "stunningly restored" 1906 art nouveau
palace in "a perfect location for touring Budapest" "one of the best hotels in the world"; "exquisite inside and out", with a lobby that "makes
you feel like royalty" and a "spectacular view overlooking the
Danube's Chain Bridge", it boasts the "city's best restaurant by a long
shot" (Páva), "service in a class by itself" and "large, wonderful
rooms" – no wonder many "want to stay forever."

InterContinental 🔭🏊

ROOMS	SERVICE	DINING	FACIL.	COST
22	21	20	21	$180

Apaczai Csere J.U. 12-14 | (011-36-1) 327-6333 | fax 327-6357 | 800-327-0200 | www.intercontinental.com | 380 rooms, 18 suites

The location of this American hotel "right on the Danube" affords "amazing views" that have some "staying awake each night to watch the lights on the castle get switched off"; there are "more than comfortable" accommodations, "delicious food" at the Hungarian-Mediterranean restaurant, Corso, and "first-class hospitality"; while a few fusspots find "nothing about its decor and service elevates it above a standard four-star chainster", most say if you have a river vista, it's a "memorable" stay.

Kempinski Hotel Corvinus 👪💼🐕🔭[S]🏊

ROOMS	SERVICE	DINING	FACIL.	COST
24	23	22	24	$471

Erzsébet tér 7-8 | (011-36-1) 429-3777 | fax 429-4777 | 800-426-3135 | www.kempinski.com | 345 rooms, 21 suites

It's "clearly the best and most Westernized hotel in Budapest" applaud admirers of the "outstanding rooms" with "gorgeous baths" that are "elegant without being stuffy", the "sharp" interior design and the "efficient service" at this hotel with a "perfect location"; chef Rudolf van Nunen's "fine" Hungarian-International fare at Bistro Jardin further cement it as "the place to stay for business."

Le Méridien 👪🔭🏊

ROOMS	SERVICE	DINING	FACIL.	COST
26	23	23	22	$399

Erzsébet tér 9-10 | (011-36-1) 429-5500 | fax 429-5555 | 800-543-4300 | www.lemeridien.com | 192 rooms, 26 suites

This "outstanding" spot is winning fans who say it gives the nearby Kempinski some stiff competition; "sinfully" comfy rooms have "air-conditioning that functions perfectly in spite of the heat", while the "tasteful" decor, "attentive", "knowledgeable" service and "convenient location" make it an "excellent value for the price"; just a few say it "lacks the views over the Danube that some other" properties have.

India

TOPS IN COUNTRY

28 Oberoi Udaivilas | *Rajasthan*
Rajvilas Oberoi | *Rajasthan*
27 Amarvilas Oberoi | *Agra*
25 Taj Mahal Palace | *Mumbai (Bombay)*
Rambagh Palace | *Rajasthan*

Agra

[Z] **Amarvilas Oberoi** 🎾🔭[S]🏊

ROOMS	SERVICE	DINING	FACIL.	COST
28	28	25	27	$600

Taj E. Gate Rd. | (011-91-562) 223-1515 | fax 223-1516 | 800-562-3764 | www.oberoihotels.com | 95 rooms, 7 suites

Step into a "picture-perfect setting" at this "outstanding", "dream-like" resort, where "rooms are subtly, yet richly decorated to give full emphasis to their amazing view of the Taj Mahal", the spa is "to-die-for", the pool area is "gorgeous" and the service is "amazing"; with the famous monument just a few thousand feet away, "everyone should stay here once – it's defintely worth the price"; P.S. try to come during "a full moon, and pray for clear skies" for the best views.

Calcutta

Oberoi Grand 🛁Ⓢ≋

| | 25 | 25 | 24 | 22 | $270 |

15 Jawaharlal Nehru Rd. | (011-91-33) 2249-2323 | fax 2249-1217 | 800-562-3764 | www.oberoihotels.com | 204 rooms, 9 suites

The "grand old lady of Calcutta" provides an "oasis" with its "luxurious", "elegant" rooms and "superb service" ("management does a stellar job of maintaining the highest standards"); its "central location", "good restaurant featuring local specialties" and "great gym" are other reasons many maintain it's the "best."

Goa

Leela Goa 🛖🛁Ⓢ≋🔍

| | 26 | 27 | 23 | 26 | $200 |

Mobor | (011-91-832) 287-1234 | fax 287-1352 | 800-417-4168 | www.theleela.com | 54 rooms, 94 suites, 4 villas

With a "beautiful beach setting" that includes 75 acres of gardens and lagoons as well as a 12-hole golf course, this "isolated and quiet" resort by the Arabian Sea makes each guest feel like a "prince or princess"; bright, coolly decorated rooms and villas, some with plunge pools, a holistic spa, "stunning food" and lots of water sports create fans who "never want to go home."

Mumbai (Bombay)

Oberoi 🛁Ⓢ≋

| | 23 | 25 | 25 | 23 | $350 |

Nariman Point | Mumbai | (011-91-22) 6632-5757 | fax 6632-4142 | 800-562-3764 | www.oberoihotels.com | 312 rooms, 21 suites

"Unrivaled" service ("just ring the butler button and they'll be at your door in a minute") and "excellent" restaurants make this a "top choice" for some discerning travelers, who also love the "views" of the Indian Ocean, the "tasteful decor" and the "great shopping"; unfortunately, the rooms are "a bit small" and "tired" say a few who deem it best for "business."

Taj Lands End 🛁Ⓢ≋

| | 22 | 24 | 24 | 24 | $250 |

Bandstand, Bandra | Mumbai | (011-91-22) 5668-1234 | fax 5699-4488 | 800-223-6800 | www.tajhotels.com | 353 rooms, 15 suites

Perhaps the "best location of all the suburban hotels" in Mumbai for business travelers, this "modern oasis" near the financial district offers "solid" rooms, "gorgeous" views of the Arabian Sea and a "pleasant" ambiance; "service has improved since Taj took over", and the spa, health center and new executive club provide "lovely" diversions.

Taj Mahal Palace & Tower Ⓢ≋

| | 25 | 26 | 26 | 25 | $325 |

Apollo Bunder | Mumbai | (011-91-22) 5665-3366 | fax 5665-0323 | 866-969-1825 | www.tajhotels.com | 565 rooms, 46 suites

With a "commanding view of the Gateway of India and the harbor", this turreted and domed "gem" "in the heart of" Mumbai with an "overattentive staff" "makes you feel like you're in the India of old"; travelers agree that "rooms in the tower wing could use an upgrade", so head to the "simply charming" palace wing for "larger", Victorian-era rooms that "continue to dazzle" with bathrooms boasting a "quarry's worth of marble"; P.S. don't miss the "outstanding" restaurant.

New Delhi

Hyatt Regency ♀️🎒💲🏊

| 21 | 21 | 20 | 21 | $220 |

Bhikaji Cama Pl. | (011-91-11) 2679-1234 | fax 2679-1122 | 800-223-1234 | www.delhi.hyatt.com | 508 rooms, 28 suites

A "beautiful oasis in a dusty city", this "luxury hotel" in the business district offers "every imaginable comfort", including "great restaurants" (one serving "delicious Italian fare") and a "modern" health club; a few renegades rue the "small rooms" and "haphazard service", but a majority reports a "good value."

Imperial Hotel ✕ 🏊

| 25 | 26 | 24 | 23 | $425 |

Janpath Rd. | (011-91-11) 2334-1234 | fax 2334-2255 | www.theimperialindia.com | 188 rooms, 43 suites

"Set on immaculate grounds" and "gorgeously refurbished" to emphasize its "style straight out of the late colonial period", this "well located" 1936 product of the Raj manages to remain "steeped in history" – "from the mustachioed, turbaned doorman to the Victorian pictures and furniture" – "without sacrificing function", plus "the facilities sparkle"; rooms are "expansive", the service "discreet" and the restaurants, especially Spice Route, are "excellent."

ITC Hotel Maurya Sheraton & Towers ✕ 🎒 🏊 🔍

| 23 | 23 | 25 | 21 | $400 |

Sardar Patel Marg | (011-91-11) 2611-2233 | fax 2611-3333 | 800-325-3535 | www.sheraton.com | 320 rooms, 120 suites

"Diplomats abound" at this "beautiful" New Delhi "embassy section" chain link "close to the airport" that gets raves for its "good value" yet "impeccable" rooms, many recently renovated; though some find the setting "remote", its "gorgeous grounds", "refreshing" pool and gardens and "state-of-the-art" health club create "an oasis", as does the "delectable" Bukhara restaurant, whose "affable staff" serves up "some of the best Indian in the city."

Oberoi 💲 🏊

| 24 | 25 | 24 | 23 | $350 |

Dr. Zakir Hussain Marg | (011-91-11) 2436-3030 | fax 2436-0484 | 800-562-3764 | www.oberoihotels.com | 279 rooms, 29 suites

The "attention to detail" from the "excellent" staff, along with rooms that overlook a nearby 18-hole golf course, a "beautiful swimming pool" and "exceptional dining choices" from Continental to Pan-Indian to Thai make this resort a "safe haven after a long flight"; though a few say it might be a "bit sterile", others find a "good mix of character and luxury."

Shangri-La Hotel 🎒 👥 🏊

| ▽ 25 | 23 | 20 | 23 | $199 |

19 Ashoka Rd., Connaught Pl. | (011-91-11) 5119-1919 | fax 4119-1988 | www.shangri-la.com | 287 rooms, 36 suites

All of a business traveler's creature comforts are found in this centrally located hotel where "high-tech" rooms come equipped with Internet access, flat-screen TVs and electronic safes, and Horizon Club guests get a complimentary breakfast buffet, as well as daily fruit and newspaper deliveries; "service is outstanding" and dining includes restaurants serving Indian, Continental and Mediterranean fare, and a fitness center features Ayurvedic massages and herbal baths.

	ROOMS	SERVICE	DINING	FACIL.	COST

Taj Mahal Hotel ✕ⓈՁ   23 | 24 | 23 | 23 | $325

1 Mansingh Rd. | (011-91-11) 2302-6162 | fax 2302-6070 |
800-223-6800 | www.tajhotels.com | 269 rooms, 27 suites
You'll "never want to leave" this "large, striking" "haven" that combines "gracious", "high-end service" with a boutique setting; it has
"comfortable" quarters with "state-of-the-art" touches, "fabulous
food" ("the House of Ming is a must-try"), "fantastic Ayurvedic massages" in the spa and "excellent" facilities.

Taj Palace Ⓢ   21 | 26 | 22 | 22 | $375

Sardar Patel Marg | (011-91-11) 2611-0202 | fax 2611-0808 |
866-969-1825 | www.tajhotels.com | 382 rooms, 40 suites
"Big" and "upscale" yet possessing a "great deal of warmth", this
"comfortable, convenient" "resort-style" property near the airport
shines thanks to its "hospitable", "well-trained" staff's "wonderful attention to detail"; though "some rooms are more modern than others",
"excellent" public facilities draw raves, as does the "fine" fare at the
"recently revamped" Masala Art restaurant.

Rajasthan

Amanbagh Ⓢ   - | - | - | - | $600

Ajabgarh, Alwar | (011-91-14) 652-2333 | fax 5223-335 |
www.amanresorts.com | 24 rooms, 16 suites
Like a "palace landed from outer space", this "extraordinarily fantastic" Rajasthan property is set dramatically in the Aravalli hills within a
walled resort that mimics the region's Mughal architecture, with
plenty of columns, marble and sweeping staircases; rooms are in separate courtyard, garden or terrace units, or in a pavilion area with its
own private swimming pool, while meals can be eaten at an informal
poolside eatery, in a dramatic double-height room or on the outdoor
rooftop terrace; it's "worth a trip" to India "just to experience it";
N.B. there's also a full-service spa, a shopping boutique and a library.

Aman-i-Khás Ⓢ   - | - | - | - | $750

Sawai Madhopur | (011-91-74) 6225-2052 | fax 6225-5178 |
800-477-9180 | www.amanresorts.com | 10 tents
The newest jewel in the Amanresorts crown, located at the edge of
Ranthambore National Park, comprises just 10 tents (plus three for
dining, lounging and spa treatments) and is only open October
through April; it affords a memorable experience for tiger-watchers
who like a little luxe with their wildlife – the canvas quarters are cooled
by air-conditioning and feature king-size beds.

Le Méridien Jaipur ⚐ ⚑Ⓢ Ձ ✎   - | - | - | - | $200

1 Riico Kukas | Jaipur | (011-91-141) 511-4455 | fax 511-4466 |
800-543-4300 | www.lemeridien.com | 94 rooms, 20 villas, 2 suites
Spread over 25 "beautiful" acres in Jaipur, this outpost from Le
Méridien offers a mix of traditional Indian and modern design; rooms
have wooden floors, local artwork and satellite TVs, while on-site
dining options include a poolside eatery with regional cuisine and an
International restaurant with a breakfast buffet; there's also a nightclub, bar, fully equipped fitness center, putting green and swimming
pools for adults and kids.

	ROOMS	SERVICE	DINING	FACIL.	COST
[Z] **Oberoi Udaivilas** 👪 🔭 [S] 🏊 🎾	29	29	25	29	$630

Haridasji Ki Magri | Udaipur | (011-91-294) 243-3300 | fax 243-3200 | 800-562-3764 | www.oberoihotels.com | 82 rooms, 5 suites

"Nothing was spared in designing" this "opulent" "fantasy" that's "fit for a raja" and "no rating can capture the real magic" either gush guests smitten by the "palatial grandeur"; "overlooking Lake Pichola" with a "royal hunting lodge" and a 20-acre "wildlife preserve on the premises", it also offers "exquisite rooms" with baths that are "the most divine in the world", the "utmost in service" and "delicious Indian food"; P.S. book a suite with infinity pool - it's "sublime" and "worth every penny."

	ROOMS	SERVICE	DINING	FACIL.	COST
[Z] **Rajvilas Oberoi** 🍴 ⛳ [S] 🏊 🎾	29	28	25	28	$530

Goner Rd. | Jaipur | (011-91-141) 268-0101 | fax 268-0202 | 800-562-3764 | www.oberoihotels.com | 54 rooms, 14 tents, 3 villas

At this "fantasyland of elegance and comfort" 20 minutes outside of Jaipur, everything is a "feast for the eyes", from the "dazzling tile and water gardens to the use of folk art as design elements"; the "unique", "luxurious" tents are "magical" (and air-conditioned), but even the standard rooms are "spacious", and the "attention to detail" includes a "pigeon chaser" to "scare away the birds when you're dining alfresco"; indeed, former President "Clinton stayed here for a reason."

	ROOMS	SERVICE	DINING	FACIL.	COST
Rambagh Palace [H] 🏊	25	27	23	25	$515

Bhawani Singh Rd. | Jaipur | (011-91-141) 221-1919 | fax 238-5098 | 800-223-6800 | www.tajhotels.com | 71 rooms, 14 suites

"You can feel the history in the walls" of this "beautiful converted palace" with "unique" rooms, "gorgeous gardens with roaming peacocks", "atmospheric bar" and "fabulous indoor pool"; a few rabble rousers roar it's "touristy" and "down on its heels", but more appreciate the "excellent service" and "fascinating architecture."

	ROOMS	SERVICE	DINING	FACIL.	COST
Taj Lake Palace [H] 🔭 [S] 🏊	25	26	23	24	$550

Lake Pichola | Udaipur | (011-91-294) 252-8800 | fax 252-8700 | 800-223-6800 | www.tajhotels.com | 83 rooms, 17 suites

"Talk about spectacular" - this "unique" "fairy-tale" resort in the middle of Lake Pichola can be approached only by "gliding" across in a boat, but when you reach it the "service makes you feel like royalty" and the "setting is not to be believed"; further reasons to love this 250-year-old "dream palace" are the the "superlative" dining, "magical" views and the fact it was used in the film *Octopussy* ("James Bond should have stayed longer"); P.S. "ask if there is water in the lake before you go", since levels have fluctuated in recent years.

Shimla

	ROOMS	SERVICE	DINING	FACIL.	COST
Oberoi Cecil, The 👪 [H] 🐎 🔭 [S] 🏊	-	-	-	-	$240

Chaura Maidan, Himachil Pradesh | (011-91-177) 280-4848 | fax 281-1024 | 800-562-3764 | www.oberoihotels.com | 27 rooms, 22 suites, 22 pavilions, 5 penthouses

Located 7,000 feet up into the Himalayas, this "very unique" century-old building (renovated and opened 10 years ago) has understandably impressive views of mountains and cedar forests; within walking distance of ancient monasteries and the Vice Regal Lodge (former summer residence of the Viceroy of India), it also has elegant interiors that recall the days of the Raj, a children's activity center, a spa, "gorgeous" rooms with DVD players and "excellent, attentive" service.

Wildflower Hall 🏨⚓Ⓢ🏊🔍 | – | – | – | – | $390

Chharabra | (011-91-177) 264-8585 | fax 264-8686 | www.oberoihotels.com | 81 rooms, 4 suites

You don't have to hire a sherpa to enjoy jaw-dropping views of the Himalayas if you stay at this 23-acre Oberoi mountaintop resort (45 minutes from Shimla) encircled by forests at a dizzying 8,250 feet; onetime home of the British Commander-in-Chief, Lord Kitchener, it offers epic vistas of snowcapped peaks and cedar forests in every teak-floored room and from the spa with outdoor Jacuzzis; other activities include billiards, river rafting, trekking and horseback riding.

Indonesia

Bali

TOP·S IN AREA

28 Como Shambala
Amankila
Four Seasons Sayan
Amanusa
27 Four Seasons

Z Amandari ✕🍴🏨Ⓢ🏊🔍 | 28 | 29 | 25 | 27 | $675

Ubud | (011-62-361) 975-333 | fax 975-335 | 800-477-9180 | www.amanresorts.com | 30 suites, 1 villa

All "hotels should be like this" declare denizens of this "exceptional" resort above the "mystical" Ayung River gorge where "incredible" villas with private pools are serviced by "legendary" "ghost" staffers who keep it "impeccable 24 hours a day" but are rarely seen; you'll enter "another world" here where you're "immersed in the Balinese culture", from "special touches" like "handwritten notes, sarongs and baskets" on arrival to the "best meals you've ever had in Bali"; indeed, "if you can pay" the steep price, you'll experience "one of the nicest places to stay in the world."

Z Amankila ✕🏨Ⓢ🏊 | 29 | 29 | 25 | 29 | $675

Manggis | (011-62-363) 41333 | fax 41555 | 800-477-9180 | www.amanresorts.com | 34 suites

Awed "Amanjunkies" admire this "secluded" "beach paradise" and "Garden of Eden" that's the best of this super-luxury chain's three Bali entries – "which is saying a lot"; "so beautiful, so restful" and so "remote from the tourist areas", it impresses with its "magnificent setting", a three-tiered infinity pool you'll "never forget", thatched-roof "villas on stilts" and truly unrivaled service – "even your grandmother couldn't make you feel this special."

Z Amanusa ✕🏨Ⓢ🏊🔍 | 28 | 29 | 26 | 27 | $675

Nusa Dua | (011-62-361) 772-333 | fax 772-335 | 800-477-9180 | www.amanresorts.com | 35 suites

It's "like living in a Balinese village" at this "luxurious hideaway" – one with "sumptuous architecture", "gorgeous wood carvings" and suites containing four-poster beds; the "fabulous" offerings also include a "romantic and amazing" Italian restaurant that's "sooo magical", the "best views in Nusa Dua" and proximity to wonderful golf (it's located just above the Bali Golf and Country Club); once again, loyalists declare "you simply can't go wrong with this chain."

☑ Como Shambala Estate ✕ ⊟ ♨ ≋ | 29 | 29 | 28 | 26 | $495
(fka Begawan Giri Estate)

Ubud | (011-62-361) 978-888 | fax 978-889 | 800-225-4255 |
www.begawan-giri.com | 22 suites, 7 villas

In this "gorgeous" "dreamland" with a "stunning" forest setting, every detail reflects the area: teak-wood paneling, thatched roofs, open-air walkways, hand-carved doors, Asian antiques and artifacts and "Balinese hospitality at its best" (it was voted the world's No. 1 for Service); the "very private" suites are "huge" and clustered in groups of four or five, set with their own pool, a concierge that seems able to "read minds" and "every imaginable amenity"; although you'll pay "a tidy sum", you'll "feel like royalty the entire time."

☑ Four Seasons | 28 | 28 | 25 | 28 | $585
Jimbaran Bay 👫 ✕ ♨ ⑤ ≋ ⚲

Jimbaran Bay | (011-62-361) 701-010 | fax 701-020 | 800-332-3442 |
www.fourseasons.com | 147 villas

The "stunning individual villas" resemble "mini-Balinese homes", each with a plunge pool and a "private porch" that's "blissful in the morning", at this "always amazing" resort that manages to "exceed even Four Seasons' own exceptionally high standards"; there's "service, service, service" ("everyone, and I mean everyone, knows your name"), "absolutely the best kids' club in Asia", "gorgeous scenery" and a wonderful "dining area in front of the beach" ("you'll be talking about the food for days"); the only downside is a location a little too close to the airport.

Four Seasons Sayan 👫 ✕ ♨ ⑤ ≋ | 29 | 29 | 26 | 28 | $460

Sayan-Ubud | (011-62-361) 977-577 | fax 977-588 | 800-332-3442 |
www.fourseasons.com | 18 suites, 42 villas

"Sybaritic splendor amid a lush" "paradise" is how some describe this "dreamlike" resort built "inside a rainforest" along the Ayung River; its "mysterious", "organic" and "architecturally stunning" design makes it "blend into the surrounding jungle and rice paddies", with "peaceful and spacious" rooms sporting handmade fabrics and local furnishings and a pool featuring cascading waterfalls; the chain's signature "genuinely caring staff", "wonderful dining" and a "sublime spa" are further reasons most "have to be pried away" from this one.

Grand Hyatt 👫 ≋ ⚲ | 23 | 24 | 22 | 25 | $225

Nusa Dua | (011-62-361) 771-234 | fax 772-038 | 800-223-1234 |
www.grand.hyatt.com | 607 rooms, 39 suites, 2 villas

"Heaven couldn't be nicer than the facilities" at this sprawling "mega-resort", where "gambalin music fills the air" and "real Balinese temples" are on the premises; the "wonderful, large rooms" come with "outdoor patios" and there's a private beach, five pools and five restaurants (including a "nice Italian" one "on the beach"); budget-minded family folk consider it a "better value and more child-friendly than the other hotels on the island."

	ROOMS	SERVICE	DINING	FACIL.	COST
InterContinental Resort Bali 👫🔭Ⓢ🏊🎾	▽ 26	24	21	24	$280

Jalan Uluwatu 45 | Jimbaran Bay | (011-62-361) 701-888 | fax 701-777 | www.ichotelsgroup.com | 399 rooms, 26 suites

Set on 35 acres that includes an "idyllic beach", this "magic" retreat is blessed with "warm, gracious" and "helpful" service, plus "well-priced" rooms furnished with handcrafted pieces and locally made textiles ("paying a premium for the club level is worth it for snacks and drinks throughout the day"); there are also nine swimming pools, a 24-hour gym and a children's center, but a few deem the food "not that great."

	ROOMS	SERVICE	DINING	FACIL.	COST
Laguna Resort & Spa Nusa Dua, The 🔭Ⓢ🏊🎾	22	24	19	23	$258

Nusa Dua | (011-62-361) 771-327 | fax 771-326 | 800-325-3535 | www.luxurycollection.com | 252 rooms, 18 suites

The "super butler service" and a concierge that "takes care of everything" propels the service scores up at this "lovely resort" with "immaculate grounds" and an on-site spa; detractors dis the "cozy" but "not fabulous" rooms and the "so-so" dining ("best done off property"), but the "gorgeous swimming pool" and location win back a few complainers.

	ROOMS	SERVICE	DINING	FACIL.	COST
Legian, The 👫🍴🔭Ⓢ🏊	24	26	24	25	$450

Seminyak Beach | (011-62-361) 730-622 | fax 730-623 | 800-223-6800 | www.ghmhotels.com | 67 suites, 1 house

An all-suite escape "from the craziness", this "elegant", "understated" spot near Seminyak Beach boasts "spacious suites" with views of the Indian Ocean, a staff that "can't help you enough" and a setting that provides lots of "magical moments"; you "can lounge all day reading or sipping cocktails" in peace, yet be "close enough to the center of Bali's nightlife", and if you can afford the more exclusive Club at the Legian, you'll have an even more "outstanding" time.

	ROOMS	SERVICE	DINING	FACIL.	COST
Le Méridien Nirwana Golf & Spa Resort 🔭⛳Ⓢ🏊🎾	▽ 25	24	21	28	$220

Jalan Raya Tanah Lot | Kediri | (011-62-361) 815-900 | fax 815-901 | 800-543-4300 | www.lemeridien.com | 252 rooms, 12 villas, 14 suites

The "secluded, spectacular" location of this oceanfront resort might be a little "out of the way", but it's the "most beautiful" brag those who've found this somewhat "undiscovered" place; the lobby has a hand-thatched ceiling, there are "gorgeous" views of the Tanah Lot sea temple and it's the only hotel in the city with a Greg Norman-designed golf course (hackers hail it as "spectacular"); it also boasts multiple swimming pools that "must be seen to be believed", a "wonderful spa" with "reasonable prices" and "amazing" villas featuring outdoor showers and plunge pools.

	ROOMS	SERVICE	DINING	FACIL.	COST
Nusa Dua Beach Hotel & Spa 👫🔭Ⓢ🏊🎾	▽ 23	26	22	24	$229

Nusa Dua | (011-62-361) 771-210 | fax 772-617 | 800-745-8883 | www.nusaduahotel.com | 352 rooms, 29 suites

It's all about the "extraordinary spa experience" for some pampered patrons of this spot, who enjoy exotic body scrubs that blend native herbs and spices; one of the older luxury properties in Bali, it can "still compete" with its younger brethren, since it's got "solid service" and "lovely rooms"; romantic types should be warned, it's "not the place for couples to escape", but with two children's pools, a playground, a variety of water sports and activities including Balinese dance and wall climbing, it can be "great for families."

Puri Wulandari Boutique Resort & Spa 🔭 [S] 🏊 — - | - | - | - | $715

Ubud | Canggu Beach | (011-62-361) 980-252 | fax 980-253 | www.puriwulandari.net | 34 villas

Traditional Balinese style greets guests at this resort above the Ayung River, where rooms are individual, air-conditioned villas with four-poster beds, 29-inch flat-screen TVs, sunken tubs, outdoor showers, private infinity pools and butler service; the Lila Ulangun spa offers traditional treatments like the Javanese lulur (a massage, scrub and bath using herbs and yogurt), and the on-site restaurant features Eurasian cuisine.

[Z] **Ritz-Carlton, The** 👪 🍴 🔭 ⛳ [S] 🏊 🎾 — 25 | 27 | 24 | 26 | $205

Jimbaran Bay | (011-62-361) 702-222 | fax 702-455 | 800-241-3333 | www.ritzcarlton.com | 275 rooms, 85 villas, 15 suites

Come to this "wonderful resort" "for the [bluffside] views, but stay for the service" provided by a "clairvoyant" staff that "anticipates your every need" (it's the "best on the island, bar none") insist its many admirers; most are smitten by the "spectacular cliff villas" ("splurge" for one), the "amazing" "infinity pool over the Indian Ocean" and the "excellent spa", although a few fume that rooms in the main hotel are "not entirely in keeping with the local flavor."

Viceroy Bali 🍴 🐕 🔭 [S] 🏊 — - | - | - | - | $640

Jalan Lanyahan, Br. Nagi | Ubud | (011-62-361) 971-777 | fax 970-777 | www.theviceroybali.com | 8 villas, 2 suites, 1 villa

Private infinity-edge pools dangling over a forest ridge, Balinese figures hand-carved into marble walls, an indoor waterfall and terraces overlooking the Lembah River Gorge are just the beginning of the story at this luxury villa resort; next comes the spa with traditional Balinese treatments and then the top-shelf restaurant, CasCades, headed by French chef David Sosson, serving wine from around the world.

Bintan

Banyan Tree 👪 🔭 ⛳ [S] 🏊 🎾 — - | - | - | - | $590

Jalan Teluk Berembang Laguna Bintan | Tanjong Said | (011-62-770) 693-100 | fax 693-200 | 866-822-6926 | www.banyantree.com | 70 villas

"Get away from it all" at this "wonderful escape" just a boat ride from Singapore, where "private villas" are "set among the trees" with "views out to the sea" and the "excellent" service caters to your whims; there's a Greg Norman–designed golf course and a spa, but some say the "main pool is small."

Borobudur

[Z] **Amanjiwo** 👪 [H] 🔭 🏊 🎾 — 29 | 29 | 27 | 29 | $650

Central Java | (011-62-293) 788-333 | fax 788-355 | 800-477-9180 | www.amanresorts.com | 36 suites

"Everyone knows your name" and "whatever you want is never too much to ask for" at this "gorgeous" resort in Central Java with "architecture like a holy shrine", inspired by the largest Buddhist sanctuary in the world, located nearby; guests have "private access" to the ruins at sunrise and "the elephant ride back is a memory to treasure", but so is just about everything else here, including facilities that were rated No. 1 in this Survey, "out-of-this-world" accommodations and "fantastic food"; it's no wonder some find "no words can describe" "one of the best hotels in the world"; P.S. "don't miss taking a hike on the volcano."

Jakarta

Dharmawangsa, The 🫖🐕Ⓢ🏊🎾 ▽ 26 | 28 | 23 | 25 | $300

Jalan Brawijaya Raya 26 | (011-62-21) 725-8181 | fax 725-8383 | 800-745-8883 | www.the-dharmawangsa.com | 64 rooms, 36 suites

Handcrafted tapestries, each one designed to reflect a different Indonesian region, hang in the rooms of this "very good" hotel - one of "the best in Jakarta" according to a few reviewers; other standouts that make it a "favorite" include "unsurpassed" service, an "incredible spa" offering exotic seaweed treatments and the local specialties at the on-site Sriwijaya restaurant.

Four Seasons 🔭Ⓢ🏊🎾 ▽ 27 | 24 | 23 | 23 | $140

Jalan H.R. Rasuna Said | (011-62-21) 252-3456 | fax 252-4480 | 800-332-3442 | www.fourseasons.com | 321 rooms, 44 suites

Situated amid six acres of landscaped gardens, this "low-profile luxury hotel" in Jakarta's Golden Triangle stands out with its "serene" modern design, "huge", "glorious" rooms - all with private balconies and opulent touches like marble soaking tubs - and its "spectacular" service ("à la Four Seasons"); other pluses include an "impressive spa" and health club, tennis courts and a "superb" steak-and-seafood restaurant.

Grand Hyatt Ⓢ🏊🎾 ▽ 25 | 24 | 23 | 26 | $185

Jalan M.H. Thamrin | (011-62-21) 390-1234 | fax 3193-4321 | 800-223-1234 | www.jakarta.grand.hyatt.com | 391 rooms, 22 suites, 15 apartments

It's "over-the-top luxury" at this "oasis in a maddening city" where the "huge mall attached" is "a bonus for shopping addicts" and the "central location can't be beat" for business folks; it's "the place to be seen" (you may spot a local celebrity), and the "ever-smiling service" is "always good without being too much"; even the food is "well prepared", so despite what a few say is a "lack of style", many maintain they could "actually live here without ever leaving."

Mandarin Oriental 🫖🏊 ▽ 19 | 24 | 24 | 22 | $200

Jalan M.H. Thamrin | (011-62-21) 3983-8888 | fax 3983-8889 | 800-526-6566 | www.mandarinoriental.com | 348 rooms, 19 suites, 37 apartments

In the heart of Jakarta's financial district, this outpost of the luxury chain group is a boon to working travelers with its extensive business center, "superior service" that includes translation and secretarial assistance and "comfortable" rooms with high-speed Internet access, telephones with voicemail and daily newspapers; it may be "ordinary for Mandarin" regulars, but gym rats relish the fitness center with state-of-the-art equipment and diners appreciate two bars, four restaurants and a cigar specialty shop.

	ROOMS	SERVICE	DINING	FACIL.	COST

Ritz-Carlton, The ♥ ⚐ ≈ `-  -  -  -  $120`

Jalan Lingkar Mega Kuningan Kav E. 1.1 No. 1 | (011-62-21) 2551-8888 |
fax 2551-8889 | 800-241-3333 | www.ritzcarlton.com | 296 rooms, 37 suites
Leave it to Ritz-Carlton to provide such a "shining star" in the midst of
this hectic city; "well-appointed" rooms feature 42-inch plasma TVs,
sunken marble tubs and featherbeds, "service is clued-in", the spa offers
a steam room, sauna and pool, and the "huge array of dining" includes
the Italian restaurant Portvenere, the Prime Steak House or Airlangga,
serving Asian-based cuisines; after dinner, you can sing your heart out
at Mistere, "one of the best" nightclubs, with 15 karaoke rooms.

Surabaya

Mandarin Oriental
Hotel Majapahit ⓘ ♨ Ⓢ ≈ ☍ `-  -  -  -  $170`

65 Jalan Tunjungan | (011-62-31) 545-4333 | fax 545-4111 |
www.mandarinoriental.com | 44 rooms, 99 suites
You "feel as if you're no longer in the present" when you stay at this
"enjoyable" "historic" property; "it beats everything else" in Surabaya
say the handful of reviewers who've stayed here, boasting the largest
rooms in the city, Euro-Asian and Chinese restaurants, an outdoor
pool and tennis courts and a comprehensive spa offering exotic treatments utilizing Asian healing traditions; road warriors appreciate the
full lineup of business facilities and "every modern amenity."

Ireland

TOPS IN COUNTRY

27 Mount Juliet Conrad | *Co. Kilkenny*
Sheen Falls Lodge | *Co. Kerry*
26 Adare Manor | *Co. Limerick*
K Club | *Co. Kildare*
25 Merrion | *Dublin*

County Clare

Dromoland Castle ⓘ ☕ ♨ ≛ Ⓢ ⚐ ≈ ☍ `25  26  24  25  $566`

Newmarket-on-Fergus | (011-353-61) 368-144 | fax 363-355 |
www.dromoland.ie | 94 rooms, 6 suites
You may "feel like you've stepped back in time" amid the "haunted"
towers and "magnificent grounds" of this 16th-century "fairy-tale castle"
with a staff as "warm and welcoming as Ireland itself"; a golf course, spa
and "excellent" fishing guides are "great for the sporting set" and the
location near Shannon is "convenient for day trips", but rooms "vary
widely in size and quality" – "new rooms" are "substantially nicer."

County Kerry

Park Hotel Kenmare ♨ Ⓢ ≈ ☍ `24  26  24  24  $338`

Kenmare | (011-353-64) 41200 | fax 41402 | www.parkkenmare.com |
26 rooms, 9 suites
There's plenty of "Irish hospitality" and "impeccable" service at this
1897 hotel overlooking Kenmare Bay that boasts Ireland's first desti-

nation spa, a "great" facility with rooms that open to a private garden, couples' private treatment suites, a tai-chi pavilion and 'experience showers' (aka the 'Irish Mist' is cold with a hint of mint); expect a "country cool" vibe, with "squeaky floorboards", "antique furniture", "gorgeous views" and a "superb" restaurant with "wonderful" local food.

Sheen Falls Lodge ✕ⓗ♨ⓢ⚡≋🔍 | 27 | 27 | 26 | 26 | $566 |

Sheen Falls Estate | Kenmare | (011-353-64) 41600 | fax 41386 | 800-735-2478 | www.sheenfallslodge.ie | 46 rooms, 20 suites, 3 cottages

This "world-class", 17th-century Relais & Châteaux hunting lodge in "gorgeous surroundings" beside Kenmare Bay and Sheen Falls puts "every conceivable luxury at your fingertips", plus "lots to do", including on-site spa treatments and nearby golfing, horseback riding and fly fishing; "wonderful" dinners of "fresh-caught trout or salmon" are accompanied by "romantic piano music" (although "you'll pay big-time" for your meal), and if you get one of the "stunning" rooms "within sight (and sound) of the waterfalls", "two days here are as relaxing as two weeks anywhere else."

County Kildare

K Club ⚲ⓢ≋ | 27 | 26 | 24 | 28 | $687 |

Straffan | (011-353-1) 601-7200 | fax 601-7297 | www.kclub.ie | 69 rooms, 23 apartments

A "golfer's dream", this "posh" "rural" 1830 estate with two "world-class" Arnold Palmer–designed courses is an "easy escape from Dublin" for "Ireland's movers and shakers"; along with the "unrivaled" play, there are "impeccably detailed" rooms and "delicious" dining, but it's the "sincere service" "without a smidgen of pretention" that has some folks saying the "K should stand for king because that's how they make you feel."

County Kilkenny

☒ Mount Juliet Conrad ⚲ⓢ≋🔍 | 27 | 27 | 26 | 28 | $344 |

Thomastown | (011-353-56) 777-3000 | fax 777-3009 | 800-445-8667 | www.conradhotels.com | 40 rooms, 10 lodges

"Classic luxury" and a "forgotten sense of style" survive at this "beautifully restored" 1758 manor house in an "idyllic setting" on 1,500 acres in County Kilkenny where the "gracious" staff makes guests feel at home in the "glorious" original house ("the bathrooms are the clincher") and in lodges that are "perfect for traveling families"; three-time home of the Irish Open, the "absolutely lovely" Jack Nicklaus-designed golf course is "the main attraction", but there's also an equestrian center, skeet shooting, archery and fishing.

County Limerick

☒ Adare Manor ⓗ♨⚲ⓢ≋ | 27 | 27 | 25 | 27 | $330 |

Adare | (011-353-61) 396-566 | fax 396-124 | 800-462-3273 | www.adaremanor.com | 63 rooms, 25 townhouses, 5 suites, 40 villas

The staff "actually lines up" in a "fantastic welcoming reception" that makes any guest "feel like a lord" at this "stately", "gorgeous old manor" near a "quaint thatched-roof village"; highlights include "ter-

	ROOMS	SERVICE	DINING	FACIL.	COST

rific" Irish breakfasts, "stunning rooms", the "fun-to-play" Robert Trent Jones Sr.-designed golf course where you "tee off near a ruined abbey" and "exquisite" dining "in a medieval hall" (try the high tea); overall, most "love" this "very posh" place.

County Mayo

Ashford Castle ⓗⓈ✎

| 24 | 25 | 25 | 26 | $568 |

Cong | (011-353-94) 954-6003 | fax 954-6260 | 800-346-7007 | www.ashford.ie | 72 rooms, 11 suites

From the "amazing gardens" to the "school of falconry", you can "live like a king" at this 13th-century Relais & Châteaux "old Irish" castle, once the estate of the Guinness family, that's been a hotel since the 1930s; "enter through the ancient gate" and be greeted by a staff that "goes out of its way to assist you" and "don't miss" the "wonderful pub"; the rooms may be "small" and the "dining options limited", but most find this "sumptuous" spot truly "enchanting."

County Waterford

Waterford Castle Hotel ⵌ✎

| 25 | 24 | 25 | 26 | $502 |

The Island | Ballinakill | (011-353-51) 878-203 | fax 879-316 | www.waterfordcastle.com | 14 rooms, 5 suites

It's crystal clear for some critics: this "fairy-tale" island castle on the River Suir ("you take a ferry over") is "among the finer establishments" in the area, with "impeccable" service, "one of the best golf courses" and "grand" and "gorgeous" rooms; take time to "enjoy the grounds" and the "spectacular restaurant", and maybe you'll have the "most romantic night of your life."

Dublin

Clarence, The ⵌ✕⯑

| 24 | 23 | 24 | 22 | $449 |

6-8 Wellington Quay | (011-353-1) 407-0800 | fax 407-0820 | www.theclarence.ie | 43 rooms, 5 suites, 1 penthouse

"Come for the rock 'n' roll" connection at this "hip" sanctuary in the middle of the Temple Bar district, owned by U2 front man Bono and lead guitarist Edge; "very much a place to be seen", it's "what a boutique is all about" say some, with "wonderful design", a bar (the Octagon) that "draws celebrities", the "modern" Irish-International Tea Room with 20-ft. ceilings and a "youthful", if "clueless" staff; with all this buzz, who cares if the rooms are "a bit cramped", most think they're "comfortable" enough.

Conrad

| 20 | 19 | 18 | 19 | $304 |

Earlsfort Terr. | (011-353-1) 602-8900 | fax 676-5424 | 800-445-8667 | www.conradhotels.com | 176 rooms, 16 suites

"Conveniently located" off Dublin's "beautiful" St. Stephen's Green, this "serviceable" hotel that just spent a few pots of gold on a complete renovation garners praise for its "amazing" beds and rooms that are "bigger than many competitors'"; there are no complaints about the business and fitness centers, restaurant and bars or close proximity to Grafton Street's fashionable stores, but the less-impressed shrug it "could be better."

IRELAND – DUBLIN

Fitzwilliam ✻🏃

| 22 | 23 | 20 | 19 | $449 |

St. Stephen's Green | (011-353-1) 478-7000 | fax 478-7878 |
www.fitzwilliamhotel.com | 138 rooms, 1 penthouse

"Ask for a room overlooking St. Stephen's Green" at this "chic opera-tion" that has a hip, contemporary look via designer Terence Conran; there's also rather "amazing" service, a "perfect location within walking distance of the high streets of Dublin" and top-shelf French-International dining at chef Kevin Thornton's on-site, though indepen-dent, Thornton's (voted No. 1 for Food in Dublin in our *Europe's Top Restaurants* Survey); but snippy sorts say they're not too satisfied with the "small" rooms.

Four Seasons 🖉✻🏃ⓈṨ

| 26 | 27 | 23 | 25 | $648 |

Simmonscourt Rd. | (011-353-1) 665-4000 | fax 665-4099 |
www.fourseasons.com | 156 rooms, 40 suites

You can expect the "quintessentially reliable" Four Seasons service and amenities at this "lovely", "quiet" property in suburban Ballsbridge, "a short cab ride" or "a long walk" away from Dublin's city center; the hotel is "elegant without being ostentatious", the accom-modations are "beautiful" and the Irish-European cuisine is "excel-lent", but some reviewers say decor that's "barren of charm" "does not feel like Ireland."

Merrion ✕⊕🏃ⓈṨ

| 26 | 26 | 25 | 24 | $542 |

Upper Merrion St. | (011-353-1) 603-0600 | fax 603-0700 | 800-223-6800 |
www.merrionhotel.com | 122 rooms, 20 suites, 1 penthouse

The "smell of peat burning in the parlor fireplace" "makes you think you could write *Ulysses*" at this "treat in the heart of Dublin" created from four 18th-century Georgian townhouses; surveyors find "bliss" in two "lovely internal courtyards", "outstanding service", "extra-large" rooms (some with 15-ft. ceilings) and the "delightful" afternoon tea, as well as in the "fancy and pricey" French fare at Patrick Gilbaud; P.S. for both "the best people-watching" and "the best fish 'n' chips" head to Cellar pub.

Morgan, The

| ▽ 25 | 24 | 20 | 18 | $304 |

10 Fleet St. | (011-353-1) 679-3939 | fax 679-3946 | www.themorgan.com |
65 rooms, 55 suites

On Fleet Street in a "raucous" Temple Bar location, this boutique hotel features uncluttered, "modern", "stylish" accommodations and a "friendly" and knowledgable staff; but it may be best for night owls since it's "central to the drinking establishments" and can get "a little loud on weekends."

Morrison 🏃Ⓢ

| 20 | 22 | 19 | 17 | $423 |

Lower Ormond Quay | (011-353-1) 887-2400 | fax 878-3185 |
www.morrisonhotel.ie | 138 rooms

"Wonderfully located" on Dublin's "hip" if "down at the heels" North Side, this "still trendy but a bit worn" boutique has "sufficiently cool" rooms with a "minimalist", "dark" mood (created by designer Douglas Wallace and fashion guru John Roche) and fine fare at chef Jean-Michel Poulot's Halo; still, it's not enough to offset a "surly", "condescending" staff and an overall scene that some say "peaked about four years ago."

	ROOMS	SERVICE	DINING	FACIL.	COST

Israel

TOPS IN COUNTRY

25 Carmel Forest Spa | *Haifa*
Herods Vitalis Spa | *Eilat*
24 King David | *Jerusalem*
Mizpe Hayamim | *Rosh Pinna*
Eilat Princess | *Eilat*

Dead Sea

	ROOMS	SERVICE	DINING	FACIL.	COST
Le Méridien Dead Sea Hotel & Spa 🔭Ⓢ🏊🎾	22	20	18	23	$220

Ein Bokek | (011-972-8) 659-1234 | fax 659-1235 | 800-543-4300 | www.deadsea.lemeridien.com | 562 rooms, 38 suites
"Visit the Dead Sea in comfort" at this "getaway" located just "steps away" from that famous body of water; "spa services are divine" ("don't miss the mud wrap"), the "disco is a hoot" and the staff is "very knowledgeable", if a little "abrupt"; rooms, however, "need updating" and "food is average at best", causing some surveyors to find the experience "disappointing" and the hotel not "up to the Le Méridien name."

Eilat

	ROOMS	SERVICE	DINING	FACIL.	COST
Dan Eilat 🏊	25	21	22	25	$414

North Beach | (011-972-8) 636-2222 | fax 636-2333 | 800-223-7773 | www.danhotels.com | 329 rooms, 49 suites
A "wonderful holiday destination" that both "Israelis and European tourists love" to visit year-round, this grand-scale Red Sea resort serves as a "beautiful" gateway to the area's desert and tropical marine life; the "first-rate" property boasts an outdoor pool with direct access to the beach, a shopping arcade, conference and banquet facilities, a children's recreation area and a colorful "*Jetsons*"-esque "futuristic design" that's a "radical departure from the typical Dan hotel."

	ROOMS	SERVICE	DINING	FACIL.	COST
Eilat Princess 🔭Ⓢ🏊🎾	25	22	22	25	$320

Taba Beach | (011-972-8) 636-5555 | fax 637-6333 | www.eilatprincess.com | 355 rooms, 65 suites
Set into the side of a mountain on the shores of the Red Sea, this "gorgeous" glass-and-marble hotel is appreciated for its "spectacular", "huge lobby", "gorgeous pool" (complete with "slides, coves and a swim-up bar") and other "top-notch" amenities that make for "wonderful, Riviera-type holidays"; if the location's a tad "far from the center" of things, most don't mind venturing off the strip for this "desert oasis."

	ROOMS	SERVICE	DINING	FACIL.	COST
Herods Vitalis Spa 🔭Ⓢ🏊	27	25	21	28	$590

North Beach | (011-972-8) 638-0000 | fax 638-0010 | 800-325-3589 | www.luxurycollection.com | 49 rooms, 4 suites
Boasting a "breathtaking" Red Sea and desert mountain backdrop, this resort in Eilat offers "terrific service", the "best spa in Israel" with an "amazing" array of treatments (think "mud wrap overlooking the sea") and suites with "huge balconies"; even if some say it's a bit "over the top", most experience a "great" vacation; N.B. children under 18 not permitted in the spa.

	ROOMS	SERVICE	DINING	FACIL.	COST

Haifa

[Z] Carmel Forest Spa Resort 🍴🔭[S]🏊🎾

	ROOMS	SERVICE	DINING	FACIL.	COST
Carmel Forest Spa Resort	23	26	24	28	$446

Carmel Forest | (011-972-4) 830-7888 | fax 830-7886 | www.isrotel.co.il | 110 rooms, 16 suites

"Extraordinarily beautiful grounds" and a "gorgeous" remote location on 15 acres of private woodlands in the middle of the Carmel Forest outside Haifa have gaga guests calling this "world-class facility" "the best hotel in Israel"; it's also celebrated for a "terrific" spa (the largest in the country), "excellent organic food", "knowledgeable and friendly" staffers and rooms that have "views of the forest", garden or sea; N.B. no kids under 16 and no cell phones.

Dan Carmel 👪🔭🏊

	ROOMS	SERVICE	DINING	FACIL.	COST
Dan Carmel	21	21	19	20	$226

85-87 Hanassi Ave. | (011-972-4) 830-3030 | fax 830-3040 | 800-223-7773 | www.danhotels.com | 200 rooms, 22 suites

On top of Mount Carmel, commanding a "fantastic" "panoramic view" "over Haifa and its harbor", this "grande dame" enjoys a "can't-be-beat" location and a "lovely" atmosphere; the staff's "congenial assistance" and decor that captures "the feel and color of the beach" also win wide approval, plus a renovation last year upgraded what some call "a tired look."

Jerusalem

American Colony Hotel 🐕🏊

	ROOMS	SERVICE	DINING	FACIL.	COST
American Colony Hotel	23	25	23	22	$325

23 Nablus Rd. | (011-972-2) 627-9777 | fax 627-9779 | 800-735-2478 | www.americancolony.com | 73 rooms, 11 suites

Visitors to this 19th-century "wonderfully evocative" Relais & Châteaux "slice of history" near the Old City might feel like they're "being transported back in time", were it not for "all the diplomats" and "world-renowned journalists and newscasters" here; the rooms (both in the old and new wings) and "can't-be-beat" dining lead lauders to suggest "if you're staying in East Jerusalem", "this is a must."

Inbal [S]🏊

	ROOMS	SERVICE	DINING	FACIL.	COST
Inbal	22	23	20	23	$245

Liberty Bell Park | (011-972-2) 675-6666 | fax 675-6777 | www.inbal-hotel.co.il | 278 rooms, 16 suites

Touters of this "busy-all-the-time" Jerusalem property say it's still "tops", boasting "upscale", "modern", "light-filled" facilities (including a full spa and pool), "pleasant" rooms wrapped around a central courtyard and a "superb location" about a 30-minute walk to the Old City, plus, it doesn't hurt that "hospitality is a strong suit here"; P.S. "breakfast buffets in Israel are always fabulous, but this one ranks among the best."

King David Hotel 👪🏊🎾

	ROOMS	SERVICE	DINING	FACIL.	COST
King David Hotel	25	25	23	24	$300

23 King David St. | (011-972-2) 620-8888 | fax 620-8882 | 800-223-7773 | www.danhotels.com | 200 rooms, 37 suites

"History and politics combine in this venerable hotel" that's literally "fit for a king" (royalty and other international dignitaries often bunk here) and set in a prime location where you can practically "reach out and touch the Old City"; disciples praise the "first-class dining", especially the "out-of-this-world breakfast", "helpful" staff and "superb" rooms.

		ROOMS	SERVICE	DINING	FACIL.	COST
Regency 🔭Ⓢ🏊🎾	▽	22	22	23	23	$186

32 Lehi St. | (011-972-2) 533-1234 | fax 581-5947 | 800-223-1234 | www.regency.co.il | 450 rooms, 55 suites
Given its "exhilarating" (if somewhat "out-of-the-way") location on Mount Scopus overlooking the Old City, it's no wonder the views from this Jerusalem hotel are positively "gorgeous", especially at sunset; its "beautiful grounds" also win wows, but keep in mind that "once inside, you could be in Pittsburgh" - "if you need to feel a little bit of America while traveling, this is the place."

Rosh Pinna

Mizpe Hayamim Ⓢ🏊🎾	23	23	25	25	$295

Rosh Pinna | (011-972-4) 699-4555 | fax 699-9555 | www.mizpe-hayamim.com | 65 rooms, 33 suites
High above the Sea of Galilee with "beautiful" views of the Hula Valley and Golan Heights, this "lovely" Relais & Châteaux health spa surrounded by herb and floral gardens is a "haven for vegans" and veggie lovers thanks to its "self-contained farm" that provides the organic ingredients for its restaurants; further enhancing the "special" experience is the wide range of "great" spa treatments.

Tel Aviv

Carlton 🔭🏊	▽	21	18	20	20	$154

10 Eliezer Peri St. | (011-972-3) 520-1818 | fax 527-1043 | 800-888-4747 | www.carlton.co.il | 274 rooms, 6 suites
The location "right on the beach" may be the biggest asset of this "lovely hotel", which boasts "excellent views" over the Mediterranean and an address within walking distance of Tel Aviv's tourist and cultural attractions; "aim-to-please" staffers who "look after you nicely" compensate for rooms and public areas that are modern and "serviceable" but "a little dull."

Dan 🏊	20	21	19	20	$250

99 Hayarkon St. | (011-972-3) 520-2525 | fax 524-9755 | 800-223-7773 | www.danhotels.com | 250 rooms, 36 suites
One of the "old-line luxury hotels" along "Tev Aviv's famous beach", this more-than-50-year-old high-rise is "still reliable" and popular with "upper-echelon" travelers, business and otherwise; "stunning" Mediterranean Sea views, the "nicest staff", "terrific" on-site dining and a "great location" not far from the city center are the secret to its continued appeal.

Hilton 🔭Ⓢ🏊	21	21	20	22	$270

Independence Park | (011-972-3) 520-2222 | fax 527-2711 | 800-445-8667 | www.hilton.com | 500 rooms, 82 suites
"A perfect choice when touring Tel Aviv", this "solid" chain link on the Mediterranean shore is your "home away from home" when you really want to "feel like an American"; prized for its "beautiful beach location", "pool area and balconies overlooking the sea", it's also "the place where everyone meets" (the "lobby's a scene" packed with businessmen and "tourists from all over the world"); P.S. insiders suggest "stay on the club floor."

ISRAEL – TEL AVIV

Sheraton Hotel & Towers 🏨⛵

20	19	17	20	$338

115 Hayarkon St. | (011-972-3) 521-1111 | fax 523-3322 |
800-325-3535 | www.sheraton.com | 327 rooms, 16 suites

"If you love the beach and the boardwalk", this tower with a "very pretty setting" overlooking the Mediterranean, yacht marina and promenade may be your "place to stay in Tel Aviv"; it offers "modern rooms", two "beautiful" outdoor pools, bars, kosher restaurants and up-to-date business facilities, not to mention a "helpful staff"; still, some sigh this "mediocre" spot is "nothing special."

Italy

TOPS IN COUNTRY

27 Il San Pietro | *Amalfi Coast*
Villa d'Este | *Lake Como Area*
Palazzo Sasso | *Amalfi Coast*
Four Seasons | *Milan*

26 Cipriani | *Venice*
Splendido | *Portofino*
Villa La Massa | *Florence*
Il Pellicano | *Porto Ercole*
L'Albereta | *Erbusco*
Villa San Michele | *Florence*

Amalfi Coast

Buca di Bacco 🍴🏨

21	24	24	19	$289

Via Rampa Teglia 4 | Positano | (011-39-089) 875-699 | fax 875-731 |
www.bucadibacco.it | 47 rooms

"*Molto bene!*" cheer devotees of this intimate Positano hillsider esteemed for its "fabulous" namesake restaurant's prime Amalfi Coast views and its individually appointed rooms (the majority sporting sea-facing terraces) situated just "steps to the beach"; "fantastic service" overseen by owner-operators who've had it in the family for over a century has many calling it a model of "Italian charm and gentility."

Caesar Augustus 🏨⛵

21	20	21	21	$529

Via G. Orlandi 4 | Capri | (011-39-081) 837-3395 | fax 837-1444 |
www.caesar-augustus.com | 38 rooms, 14 suites

"Away from the tourist hordes in town", this Relais & Châteaux hotel boasts a "spectacular setting" on the cliffs of Capri a thousand feet above the sea; the experience is made "lovely" by "fabulous views" and "beautiful sunsets" from the infinity pool, alfresco terrace restaurant and private balconies in each of the whitewashed rooms; but a few say the "hardware is much better than the software", citing "somewhat indifferent" service; N.B. closed November to mid-April.

Capri Palace Hotel & Spa 🏨Ⓢ⛵

22	23	24	26	$555

Via Capodimonte 2b | Capri | (011-39-081) 978-0111 | fax 837-3191 |
www.capripalace.com | 65 rooms, 15 suites

"White furnishings surrounded by colorful tropical plants" and "limestone everywhere" set a certain "elegant", Med style at this "lush oasis of tranquility" that's "fantastic" in an "understated way"; rooms

ROOMS | SERVICE | DINING | FACIL. | COST

have "beautiful views", and there's "pampering galore", a "wonderful" spa and "excellent food."

Caruso, Hotel 🔭🏊 — 24 | 24 | 23 | 24 | $803

Piazza San Giovanni Del Toro 2 | Ravello | (011-39-01) 852-67890 | fax 852-67895 | 800-223-6800 | www.hotelcaruso.com | 28 rooms, 24 suites

Set around an 11th-century cathedral on the Sorrento Peninsula with "spectacular" views of the stunning Amalfi Coast, this "amazing" Orient-Express "oasis" in Ravello was once the palace of the Marquis d'Afflitto and "will soon be the leading hotel on the coast" according to its early fans; "perfect for romance", it offers a "genial staff", "large rooms" with balconies and "magnificent" ocean vistas, a "beautiful pool area", three restaurants and a cocktail lounge.

Eden Roc 🔭🏊 — 25 | 26 | 21 | 21 | $365

Via G. Marconi 110 | Positano | (011-39-089) 875-844 | fax 875-552 | www.edenroc.it | 7 rooms, 15 suites, 3 suites

"Nothing is too much trouble" for the "extremely friendly staff" of this "little" Amalfi Coast "gem" "right in the heart of Positano", where all of the "well-maintained", antiques-filled rooms have "balconies overlooking the azure sea"; a pool, solarium, easy access to the beach and private Jacuzzis in some suites make this "memorable" sleeper both "family-friendly" and "perfect for romance."

Grand Hotel Excelsior Vittoria 🐤🔭[S]🏊 — 22 | 24 | 23 | 23 | $500

Piazza Tasso 34 | Sorrento | (011-39-081) 877-7111 | fax 877-1206 | www.exvitt.it | 78 rooms, 20 suites

Head down a "flowered walkway" into the five lovely acres of gardens and lemon groves, at this cliffside hotel that boasts views of the Bay of Naples and Mount Vesuvius; the "knowledgeable" staff features a "very helpful concierge", and "superb dining" includes a "wonderful breakfast buffet"; but design gurus groan it "needs to redecorate a bit."

Grand Hotel Quisisana 🔭[S]🏊🎾 — 25 | 25 | 24 | 26 | $436

Via Camerelle 2 | Capri | (011-39-081) 837-0788 | fax 837-6080 | 800-223-6800 | www.quisi.it | 150 rooms, 7 suites

"The place to be" "in the heart of Capri" for the "happening crowd", this "romantic" "bit of heaven" boasts "beautiful rooms" with "stunning views" and the "hugest bathrooms" around; "fabulous dining" (including a "wonderful" poolside lunch), a "pampering" spa and "pleasant, sophisticated service" have fans enthusing "the grande dame still rules"; N.B. it's open March to November only.

[Z] **Il San Pietro, Hotel** 🍴🐤🔭[S]🏊🎾 — 27 | 27 | 27 | 28 | $529

Via Laurito 2 | Positano | (011-39-089) 875-455 | fax 875-089 | www.ilsanpietro.it | 40 rooms, 22 suites

"The only bad thing is leaving" promise patrons who laud this "dramatic" Relais & Châteaux hotel "built into the side of a mountain" as "the ultimate in romance"; "whimsical" "clifftop" rooms feature balconies and "perfect views" and the "spectacular beachside elevator" whisks you down to the private beach and back up again to "truly gourmet meals with fresh local produce" on the terrace; add "caring" "service that couldn't be better" and it's "as close to perfection as it gets."

	ROOMS	SERVICE	DINING	FACIL.	COST

La Scalinatella 👭🎐

| | 24 | 26 | 23 | 23 | $661 |

Via Tragara 8 | Capri | (011-39-081) 837-0633 | fax 837-8291 |
www.scalinatella.com | 30 rooms

This "hideaway" (open early April to early November) makes a "design statement" with its "serene and sophisticated" look and "big, bright rooms that open to the sea"; they've got the "best poolside lunches" laud loyalists, and some of the "best service anywhere" as well, but the price-conscious quibble that it's "terribly expensive."

Le Sirenuse ✗⊕👭🎐

| | 26 | 26 | 25 | 26 | $687 |

Via Crisioforo Colombo 30 | Positano | (011-39-089) 875-066 |
fax 811-798 | www.sirenuse.it | 54 rooms, 9 suites

"The favorite haven for A-listers" on the Amalfi coast, this "family-run" hotel is "the place to go on your honeymoon" or to "celebrate an anniversary"; doze in "spacious" "antiques-filled rooms" with "handcrafted white tile floors" and "mesmerizing beach views", float in the "lovely" rooftop pool, revel in the staff's "rock star treatment" or "enjoy sedate outdoor dining" at "excellent" La Sponda – "what more could you want?"; N.B. closed from December through February.

Palazzo Murat ⊕🏵👭

| | 23 | 23 | 24 | 23 | $337 |

Via dei Mulini 23 | Positano | (011-39-089) 875-177 | fax 811-419 |
www.palazzomurat.it | 30 rooms

"Make sure to hit the restaurant for wonderful gourmet Italian" and "have cocktails at sunset in the courtyard" at this "calm and cool" 18th-century baroque hotel with "beautiful gardens in a most picturesque setting"; "fantastic" complementary sailing excursions make up for the lack of a pool, and the "helpful staff" keeps it all running smoothly, so this one's "a great find in Positano."

Palazzo Sasso ✗⊕👭Ⓢ🎐

| | 26 | 28 | 27 | 26 | $600 |

Via San Giovanni del Toro 28 | Ravello | (011-39-089) 818-181 |
fax 858-900 | www.palazzosasso.com | 32 rooms, 11 suites

"If heaven is as good as a week here, I will never sin again" pledge innamorati of this "opulent" 12th-century villa a thousand feet above the sea; from its "seamless, superlative service" ("they serve you amuse-bouche" at the "sumptuous pool area") to "incredible food" that's "some of the best dining on the Amalfi coast" to "exquisite rooms", some with "beyond-belief views", it's "fabulous in all respects"; N.B. closed from November to mid-March.

Palumbo ✗⊕🏵👭🎐

| | ▽ 19 | 23 | 23 | 19 | $529 |

Via San Giovanni del Toro 16 | Ravello | (011-39-089) 857-244 |
fax 858-133 | www.hotel-palumbo.it | 17 rooms, 3 suites

A "place of tranquility in a wonderful setting" overlooking the Amalfi coast, this 12th-century palace is all "faded elegance with the most spectacular view on earth", "halfway between sky and sea"; if you "reserve a suite, you'll never want to leave" unless it's to eat an "outstanding" "dinner on the roof" of this truly "romantic" "charmer."

Poseidon 🏵👭Ⓢ🎐

| | 21 | 23 | 21 | 24 | $361 |

Via Pasitea 148 | Positano | (011-39-089) 811-111 | fax 875-833 |
www.hotelposeidonpositano.it | 48 rooms, 4 suites

It's a "small jewel" of a family-run hotel with "warm service" and the "most spectacular views imaginable" rave regulars relishing this "wonderful" seasonal adventure; maybe it's also the "simply marvel-ous" staff, the "refreshing pool", the on-site spa or just the "inexpensive" rates compared to nearby properties – but whatever it is, you'll keep "coming back again and again"; N.B. open early April to early December.

Santa Caterina ✕ 🏧 Ⓢ ≋ | 24 | 26 | 24 | 25 | $509 |

S.S. Amalfitana 9 | Amalfi | (011-39-089) 871-012 | fax 871-351 | 800-223-6800 | www.hotelsantacaterina.it | 42 rooms, 20 suites

The location of this "jewel on the Amalfi coast" built into the side of a cliff "can't be beat" say saints who don't mind the drive to this "perfect hideaway" "overlooking the glimmering Mediterranean"; from the "amazing" outdoor "glass elevator that goes down to the seawater pool" to the "wonderful food" on the lunch balcony to the "caring ser-vice", this "alternative to the too-hot spots" "whispers charm and grace"; though a few complain "rooms could be nicer", with such "to-die-for" views, they're fine for most.

Bologna

Grand Hotel Baglioni Ⓗ ⛄ | 23 | 22 | 22 | 20 | $514 |

Via Indipendenza 8 | (011-39-051) 225-445 | fax 234-840 | 800-223-6800 | www.baglionihotels.com | 113 rooms, 11 suites

This 17th-century palace is in an "ideal location for shopping, sight-seeing and eating" with an "attentive" staff, "spacious" rooms, "hall-ways wider than your house" and frescoes dating to the 15th century; though some are "disappointed" by a "tired look" and "standard" quarters, others say it's "the only place to stay in Bologna."

Castiglione della Pescaia

L'Andana ✕ Ⓗ 🏧 Ⓢ ≋ | – | – | – | – | $773 |

Localita Badiola | (011-39-0564) 944-800 | fax 944-577 | www.andana.it | 20 rooms, 13 suites

Acres of vineyards and olive trees surround this "absolutely magical" old-world property, the former home of the Duke of Tuscany and the perfect setting for an Alain Ducasse restaurant since many of his Tuscan recipes use the wine and oil made here; foodies have "the best meal of their vacation", while "wonderful" rooms feature decorative fireplaces, hardwood floors, antique furnishings and bathrooms with marble or claw-foot tubs; there's a mosaic-tile swimming pool and a spa on-site, and a nine-hole golf course is under construction.

Erbusco

L'Albereta ✕ 🏧 Ⓢ ≋ | 26 | 25 | 27 | 25 | $291 |

Via Vittorio Emanuele 11 | (011-39-030) 776-0550 | fax 776-0573 | www.albereta.it | 36 rooms, 21 suites

A "gourmand's dream come true", this "magnificent" family-owned 19th-century manor house between the Alps and Lake Iseo has the "best restaurant in Italy" thanks to chef Gualtiero Marchesi, who cooks up such a "divine dining experience" that "people drive for hours" just to eat here; there are also "sublime" surroundings and "comfortable rooms", but it's mostly the "eventful" cuisine at this "re-fined" Relais & Châteaux resort that keeps them returning.

Florence

TOPS IN CITY

26	Villa La Massa
	Villa San Michele
25	Westin Excelsior

Astoria � 🛏

| 23 | 21 | 23 | 21 | $330 |

Via del Giglio 9 | (011-39-055) 239-8095 | fax 214-632 |
www.boscolohotels.com | 92 rooms, 6 suites

The "central yet quiet location" in the heart of Florence "near the Duomo" is the highlight of this hotel, especially if you "get a room with a view of the Cupola"; there are "real showers" in the "big rooms" and a "friendly staff", so even though you probably "won't be overwhelmed" (it's "not exactly bare-bones, but not out-of-this-world either"), it offers a touch of "home."

Beacci Tornabuoni, Hotel ⚡🛏

| 21 | 24 | 18 | 20 | $216 |

Via Tornabuoni 3 | (011-39-055) 212-645 | fax 283-594 |
www.tornabuonihotels.com | 38 rooms, 2 suites

There's "soul and character" to spare at this "charming boutique hotel" where the "staff has heart" and some rooms have frescoes and vaulted ceilings; it's "not the most hip of hotels" admit style-conscious *signore*, but there's a "rooftop terrace with lovely views" and a "fabulous" location for museumgoers and "well-heeled fashionistas", so it's a "great value" all the same.

Bernini Palace ⓗ⚡

| 23 | 22 | 20 | 19 | $370 |

Piazza di San Firenze 9 | (011-39-055) 288-621 | fax 268-272 |
www.baglionihotels.com | 66 rooms, 8 suites

"Just steps away" from the Uffizi and "all of the major Florence sites", this converted 15th-century palazzo garners praise for its "fantastic central location", "architecture and ambiance"; "comfortable" rooms feature richly colored wallpaper and crystal chandeliers, "service has the warmth you expect in Italy" and the "fabulous bar" is the place to unwind after sightseeing.

Gallery Hotel Art 🛏

| 23 | 22 | 20 | 19 | $494 |

Vicolo dell'Oro 5 | (011-39-055) 27263 | fax 268-557 | 800-337-4685 |
www.lungarnohotels.com | 65 rooms, 9 suites

It's no wonder this "modern boutique" is so "chic and classy" – the Salvatore Ferragamo fashion group created the "wonderfully minimalist" look; design divas determine it's "definitely the cool place to stay", thanks to the "subtle, low-key service", alternating art exhibits and "lively local nightlife" at Fusion Bar; although it's "not your usual Florentine experience" (more like a "mini-Manhattan" one), the "incredibly foamy cappuccino" at breakfast surely reminds you where you are.

Grand Hotel ⓗ⚡🛏

| 25 | 25 | 22 | 23 | $1024 |

Piazza Ognissanti 1 | (011-39-055) 27161 | fax 217-400 | 800-325-3589 |
www.luxurycollection.com | 94 rooms, 13 suites

"The most gorgeous" "frescoed" rooms "you've ever seen" is the grandiose description of some guests who say "no two are the same" at this "ritzy" hotel in an 18th-century palazzo; better yet, request a suite "with a balcony overlooking the piazza and the Arno" River, and enjoy the "perfect location" and "friendly" service; a few find the dining "just so-so", but overall it's got that "palpable sense of history."

Grand Hotel Villa Medici ⚅♨ | 25 | 24 | 19 | 20 | $555 |

Via il Prato 42 | (011-39-055) 238-1331 | fax 238-1336 | 800-223-6800 | www.villamedicihotel.com | 88 rooms, 15 suites

A former 18th-century palace, this Florence spot surrounded by "peaceful gardens" pleases some with its "great location within walking distance to all the major areas" and "attentive service"; but more discriminating visitors are vexed that it's "not up to par with other four- and five-star properties" in the city and it "needs updating", so they find "nothing exceptional" here.

Helvetia & Bristol ⚅ | 24 | 25 | 20 | 21 | $502 |

Via dei Pescioni 2 | (011-39-055) 26651 | fax 288-353 | www.hotelhelvetiabristolfirenze.it | 46 rooms, 21 suites

Serene sorts savor the serenity of this "boutique" "jewel", originally a 19th-century townhouse, that's "very quiet despite the city center rumble"; the "central location" means you can "walk to almost all you want to see", and with "excellent rooms" and "great Florentine hospitality", it's "easy to feel like a celebrity" – if you're not brought down by the "gloomy colors."

Lungarno, Hotel ⚅♨ | 24 | 23 | 21 | 22 | $463 |

Borgo San Jacopo 14 | (011-39-055) 27261 | fax 268-437 | www.lungarnohotels.com | 61 rooms, 12 suites

Part of the Salvatore Ferragamo group, this "stunning boutique hotel" "nails it" with "simple, rich, chic" design that includes "beautifully decorated rooms" with "killer fabrics", antiques and original paintings (be sure to "demand a river view with balcony"); the "wonderful" "service with a smile" is as "terrific" as the location, though some say they can "hear Vespas running all night"; N.B. the separate Lungarno Suites apartment-style property is part of the same hotel group.

Regency, Hotel ⚅ | ▽ 24 | 25 | 23 | 20 | $523 |

Piazza Massimo D'Azeglio 3 | (011-39-055) 245-247 | fax 234-6735 | 800-223-6800 | www.regency-hotel.com | 33 rooms, 2 suites

A onetime 19th-century villa for government officials, this "small", "friendly" spot in a "quiet residential neighborhood with a park at its front door" is "just enough out of the way for a needed respite" yet close enough to "stroll to attractions"; no two rooms are alike, but all are "uniquely decorated" in a "very homelike" style with tapestries and Carrara marble, and you can enjoy a "romantic morning breakfast in the garden"; just a portion of patrons take potshots at decor that "needs an update."

Savoy, Hotel ⚔⚅ | 24 | 24 | 21 | 23 | $859 |

Piazza della Repubblica 7 | (011-39-055) 27351 | fax 273-5888 | 800-745-8883 | www.roccofortehotels.com | 88 rooms, 14 suites

This "sleek", "lively and modern" Rocco Forte hotel with a "perfect", "central location" provides a "welcome change" for the "jet-set crowd" on classic-art overload; some of the "minimalist" and "well-appointed" rooms have "breathtaking" views, though nitpickers grouse they're "so small" the "luggage wouldn't fit"; good thing the "discreet" staff "bends over backwards" to help, and if you opt against the "cozy tables and candlelight" at L'Incontro, the concierge "knows every restaurant in the city."

Villa La Massa ✕⊕🍴🏊Ⓢ≋

| 27 | 27 | 25 | 24 | $648 |

Via della Massa 24 | (011-39-055) 62611 | fax 633-102 | www.villalamassa.it | 19 rooms, 18 suites

Situated south of the city, this "special" 16th-century Medici river-sider offers all the "glory of Florence" with easy access to other areas in Tuscany; in a "picturesque setting", guests savor "wonderful" food and "beautiful", distinctly decorated rooms, while concierges who "care that you have a great experience" arrange nearby activities like biking, horseback riding, tennis, golf and shopping on the Ponte Vecchio (there are complimentary shuttles to and from, but you "better have a reservation").

Villa San Michele ✕⊕🍴🏊≋

| 25 | 26 | 26 | 25 | $1093 |

Via Doccia 4 | Fiesole | (011-39-055) 567-8200 | fax 567-8250 | 800-524-2420 | www.villasanmichele.com | 21 rooms, 25 suites

"Take out a second mortgage", then "stay here, eat here, live here" command converts who find "part of heaven on earth" at this converted 15th-century former monastery "perched in the Fiesole hills" six miles from Florence; part of the Orient-Express chain, this seasonal spot has "magnificent", "original" rooms, "impeccable service", "the most romantic setting you've ever seen" and an "unforgettable", "mouthwatering" Italian restaurant where you'll want to "eat every meal for a week"; N.B. it also runs the unique Capannelle lodging, located in a nearby working vineyard.

Westin Excelsior 🏃🍴🏊

| 26 | 25 | 23 | 25 | $922 |

Piazza Ognissanti 3 | (011-39-055) 264-201 | fax 210-278 | 800-937-8461 | www.westin.com | 136 rooms, 16 suites

Pampered patrons proclaim one "highlight is the staff", which aims to please with "truly outstanding service" and dishes out "excellent breakfast buffets" in the "beautiful stained-glass dining room" of this "classic" chain outpost; "right on the river", it's "close to everything, yet a little apart", and boasts "beautifully appointed", "oversized, plush rooms", some with "dreamlike views" "overlooking the Arno and the Tuscan hills" – just "get a quiet room on an upper floor" to avoid all that street noise.

Lake Como Area

Grand Hotel Villa Serbelloni 🍴🏊Ⓢ≋🔍

| 24 | 25 | 24 | 24 | $535 |

Via Roma 1 | Bellagio | (011-39-031) 950-216 | fax 951-529 | www.villaserbelloni.it | 61 rooms, 20 suites, 13 apartments

"Nothing is left to chance" at this "spectacular" spot that simply "oozes with class"; the "most helpful concierge" and "can't-be-beat" staff make you "feel like Rockefeller", while the views of Lake Como and the mountains are "stunning", especially while enjoying "melt-in-your-mouth" cuisine or "coffee served with chocolate sprinkled in the shape of a heart"; the "cushy" rooms ("reserve one with a balcony") are "replete with romance"; N.B. open November–March.

	ROOMS	SERVICE	DINING	FACIL.	COST

⚡ Villa d'Este ✕ ♨ ⓢ ≋ ⚲
| | 26 | 27 | 27 | 28 | $793 |

Via Regina 40 | Cernobbio | (011-39-031) 3481 | fax 348-844 |
800-223-6800 | www.villadeste.it | 83 rooms, 70 suites, 2 villas

This "magnificent palace" "has it all": a "fairy-tale" Italian Alps setting
on "impossibly serene Lake Como", "opulent" rooms "exuding old-
world charm" and "unparalleled" dining options ("happily, jacket and
tie are still required for dinner"); indeed, "you'll think you're royalty"
since "no request seems too outrageous" for the "perfect staff", and
whether strolling the "dreamy" grounds or "sunning at the floating
pool", guests swear it's "as good as it gets"; N.B. open March–
mid-November only.

Milan

TOPS IN CITY

27 Four Seasons
25 Bulgari Milan
24 Park Hyatt

Bulgari Milan ♨ ⓢ ≋
| | 27 | 24 | 23 | 25 | $823 |

Via Privata Fratelli Gabba 7b | (011-39-02) 805-8051 | fax 805-222 |
800-628-5427 | www.bulgarihotels.com | 44 rooms, 14 suites

Expanding its brand name to the high-end hospitality business, the
well-known jeweler has partnered with the Ritz-Carlton group to
unveil this "very chic and secluded" red-hot address in Milan's glamorous shopping district; expect extremely "cool" interiors with clean
lines and monochromes, with accents of teak here and black
Zimbabwe marble there, along with service that some say "could be a
little more congenial and a little less hip"; style-savvy guests dine on
"authentic" Italian at the on-site eatery or just go "for a cocktail
to people-watch."

⚡ Four Seasons ♙ ✕ 🖉 🍴 ♨
| | 28 | 27 | 25 | 26 | $674 |

Via Gesù 6/8 | (011-39-02) 77088 | fax 7708-5007 | 800-332-3442 |
www.fourseasons.com | 77 rooms, 41 suites

Devoted followers "feel like saying a prayer of thanks" for this "peaceful" "converted convent" that's a respite from the "crowded, noisy"
city yet mere "steps away from the Duomo and Prada"; whether clois-
tered in "state-of-the-art" "modern Euro-sleek rooms", breaking
bread at chef Sergio Mei's "superb" Il Teatro or praising "attentive",
"friendly" service, guests profess it's "between heaven and earth", or
at least "the only choice in Milan."

Grand Hotel et de Milan ⑪♨
| | 22 | 22 | 21 | 20 | $633 |

Via Manzoni 29 | (011-39-02) 723-141 | fax 8646-0861 |
800-223-6800 | www.grandhoteletdemilan.it | 45 rooms, 27 rooms,
15 suites, 8 suites

Even if you don't book them, "try to see Verdi's rooms" or Maria
Callas' suite at this "elegant, refined" Milanese classic in an "unbeatable" central location; even the regular rooms are filled with "old-
world charm" (though some report they "vary distressingly in size"),
but it maintains an up-to-date reputation thanks to its "accommodating, friendly" staff, "surprisingly well-equipped" gym and "marvelous"
Don Carlos restaurant, where meals are deemed "delicious and
worth every euro."

	ROOMS	SERVICE	DINING	FACIL.	COST

Grand Hotel Tremezzo ♋Ⓢ⚑🔍 ▽ 21 | 22 | 23 | 22 | $429
Via Regina 8 | Tremezzo | (011-39-34) 442-491 | fax 440-201 |
www.grandhoteltremezzo.com | 98 rooms, 2 suites
Enjoy "awesome views of the lake and Bellagio" at this "grand hotel"
that's 30 miles north of Milan, so it's "a favorite way to end a trip and
avoid the tensions" of the city; with three pools, including one "floating
on the lake", a spa, gardens and a tennis court, it offers "resort-style
relaxed comfort", "old-fashioned" (if "variable") rooms "with modern,
elegant conveniences" and an "efficient staff."

Il Sole Di Ranco ✕♋⚑ ▽ 24 | 27 | 28 | 23 | $272
Piazza Venezia 5 | Varese | (011-39-331) 976-507 | fax 976-6-20 |
www.ilsolediranco.it | 10 suites, 4 rooms
Expect "an especially warm greeting from the family" that's run this
Relais & Châteaux "country house" 34 miles north of Milan for more
than 150 years along with its "wonderful staff"; "the rooms are large
and the views a delight", and guests enjoy the gardens, pool and "gorgeous lakefront setting" on Lago Maggiore; meanwhile, gourmands
are drawn to the "superb" meals prepared by chefs Carlo and Davide
Brovelli at the restaurant The Cookery, which also hosts cooking courses
every autumn; N.B. closed in December and January.

Le Méridien Gallia ▽ 21 | 21 | 19 | 19 | $337
Piazza Duca d'Aosta 9 | (011-39-02) 67851 | fax 6671-3239 |
800-543-4300 | www.lemeridien.com | 223 rooms, 14 suites
If you're looking for "spacious" rooms with "artwork that alone is
worth the visit", board this "first-class hotel" right across from the
train station in the Piazza Duca d'Aosta; the superior rooms have mirror
designs, a mix of modern and classic furniture and embossed frescoes, but sourpusses pout over the "less than desirable location" of
this veteran that's "showing its age."

Park Hyatt ♥♒Ⓢ 26 | 24 | 22 | 23 | $516
Via Tommaso Grossi 1 | (011-39-02) 8821-1234 | fax 8821-1235 |
800-223-1234 | www.milan.park.hyatt.com | 97 rooms, 20 suites
Set in a circa-1870 building with interior design by Ed Tuttle of Paris-
Vendôme fame, this "wonderful addition to the city" "incorporates local touches" in its "gorgeous" modern rooms and interiors sporting
high ceilings, muted colors, luxury fabrics and travertine stone; a
"perfect location a stone's throw from the Piazza del Duomo and
the best shopping", "impeccable service from a designer-clad" staff
and a "top-notch" Italian-Mediterranean restaurant draw both the leisure and "biz crowds."

Principe di Savoia ♥🖼♒♋Ⓢ⚑ 25 | 23 | 21 | 23 | $872
Piazza della Repubblica 17 | (011-39-02) 62301 | fax 659-5838 |
www.hotelprincipedisavoia.com | 269 rooms, 132 suites
"If Signore Armani's got a full house while you're in town for fittings",
then send your Vuittons to this "palatial" Milanese "favorite"; it has a
staff that "knows your name after the first day" and "divine accommodations" (opulently outfitted in Venetian, Florentine or Neo-Classical
style) offering "all the comforts of home" – and if you have a
"Donatella Versace sighting", ask her to join you in a free limo to the
shopping area, because it's "a bit of a walk."

		ROOMS	SERVICE	DINING	FACIL.	COST
Straf 🏛🔭	▽	21	22	16	18	$436

Via San Raffaele 3 | (011-39-02) 805-081 | fax 8909-5294 | www.straf.it | 61 rooms, 3 suites

"Stay here and save your money for shopping" say thrifty sorts keen on this "plenty fashionable" "bargain" boutique, just steps from the Piazza del Duomo that's "artistic to its core"; the "beautiful-to-look-at" high design includes unique elements like gauze between panes of glass and lots of burnished brass, black stone and iron, plus there's a "lively bar at happy hour."

	ROOMS	SERVICE	DINING	FACIL.	COST
Westin Palace	22	20	20	20	$915

Piazza della Repubblica 20 | (011-39-02) 63361 | fax 654-485 | 800-937-8461 | www.westin.com | 215 rooms, 13 suites

"Gorgeous" rooms earn points among demanding business travelers who like the location and amenities of this American chain link; but views are decidedly mixed on the rest: service is "efficient" to some, but others find "no one has time", and puzzled patrons "can't understand why things have to be so overpriced."

Naples

	ROOMS	SERVICE	DINING	FACIL.	COST
Grand Hotel Vesuvio 🏛🔭Ⓢ🏊	22	21	21	21	$555

Via Partenope 45 | (011-39-08) 1764-0044 | fax 1764-4483 | 800-223-6800 | www.vesuvio.it | 144 rooms, 16 suites

Admirers appreciate this hotel's "harbor view rooms", "magnificent" spa and "beautiful rooftop restaurant" (named after former patron Enrico Caruso) that sports panoramic "views of Capri and Vesuvius"; but opinions diverge over the "uneven" service, "not great" food and "historic" location that's "too touristy."

Perugia

	ROOMS	SERVICE	DINING	FACIL.	COST
Brufani Palace, Hotel Ⓗ🔭🏊	21	27	22	20	$313

12 Piazza Italia | (011-39-075) 573-2541 | fax 572-0210 | www.sinahotels.com | 59 rooms, 35 suites

Join urbane Perugini in the "afternoon *passeggiata*" along Corso Vanucci, just outside the door of this "excellent palace hotel", whose "superb" hilltop perch affords "fantastic" views of the valley and Assisi from the "wonderful restaurant" and from some of the "lovely" rooms (some "could use a touch-up"); the indoor "glass-floored pool with lighted Etruscan ruins underneath" and the "eager-to-please staff" both win notice, but a few find the "noisy groups" annoying.

Porto Ercole

	ROOMS	SERVICE	DINING	FACIL.	COST
Il Pellicano 🍴🔭Ⓢ🏊	25	26	26	26	$679

Cala dei Santi | (011-39-0564) 858-111 | fax 833-418 | www.pellicanohotel.com | 32 rooms, 19 suites

"The most romantic place in the world" sigh visitors smitten by the "phenomenal sea views" and "quiet privacy" of this "magical" Relais & Châteaux villa nestled on the terraced Tuscan coast, whose "wonderful staff" is "beyond remarkable"; even those who "typically shy away from hotel restaurants" pronounce chef Antonio Guida's cuisine "exquisite", but some recoil at the "frightful prices"; N.B. open April to October.

	ROOMS	SERVICE	DINING	FACIL.	COST

Portofino

Excelsior Palace Hotel ⚲♨⚙≋ | 23 | 25 | 23 | 23 | $225 |

Via San Michele di Pagana 8 | Rapallo | (011-39-0185) 230-666 |
fax 230-214 | www.excelsiorpalace.thi.it | 114 rooms, 17 suites

Overlooking the bay of Rapallo and a few minutes' drive from
Portofino, this "lovely hotel" provides a "convenient location" for exploring the Italian Riviera, if you can pull yourself away from the "spectacular" setting of the Beach Club and the "helpful staff" that "caters
to your every whim"; rooms are "ornate yet functional and comfortable",
and "breakfast on the terrace is worth the entire price of the room."

Grand Hotel Miramare ⚲♨⚙≋ | 23 | 23 | 19 | 22 | $415 |

Via Milite Ignoto 30 | Santa Margherita Ligure | (011-39-0185) 287-013 |
fax 284-651 | 800-223-6800 | www.grandhotelmiramare.it | 75 rooms,
5 suites, 4 suites

"Save money and stay outside Portofino" at this "peaceful" property in
Santa Margherita Ligure that brings to mind a giant "wedding cake";
after enjoying "fabulous" views of the Mediterranean during "breakfast
on the portico", have a swim in its "pretty" seawater pool or go to the
"private beach club", then ask the "helpful concierge" to schedule a
service in the "lovely" spa before napping in your "spacious suite."

Splendido, Hotel ✕⚲♨⚙≋⚲ | 25 | 26 | 27 | 26 | $1328 |

Viale Baratta 16 | (011-39-0185) 267-801 | fax 267-806 | 800-524-2420 |
www.hotelsplendido.com | 31 rooms, 34 suites

Loyalists laud this Orient-Express "hideaway" with "impeccable service"
that consists of sister properties separated by a "steep walk" or courtesy shuttle; from its "sublime setting" "perched over Portofino" to La
Terrazza's "excellent" "alfresco dining at sunset" to the "spectacular
views" from the "stunning infinity pool" – it's "breathtaking in every
way, including the price"; N.B. closed mid-November to mid-March.

Rome

TOPS IN CITY

25   Rome Cavalieri Hilton
      La Posta Vecchia
      St. Regis

Aldrovandi Palace ≋ | 22 | 22 | 23 | 22 | $570 |

Via Ulisse Aldrovandi 15 | (011-39-06) 322-3993 | fax 322-1435 |
800-223-6800 | www.aldrovandi.com | 105 rooms, 15 suites

It's "a haven in a maelstrom" insist fans of this "elegant" hotel by the
Villa Borghese gardens "away from noisy Downtown Rome" that's
prized for its "terrific" "rare" pool in the city and "spacious rooms";
contrarians grumble it's "too far out of the way to be of interest", despite the free "hourly shuttle to the center", but have no such reservations about the "memorably good" Neapolitan-Med restaurant, Baby.

de Russie, Hotel ⚙≋ | 26 | 26 | 23 | 25 | $814 |

Via del Babuino 9 | (011-39-06) 328-881 | fax 3288-8888 |
www.roccofortehotels.com | 94 rooms, 31 suites

"Magnifico" exclaim guests of this "Rocco Forte masterpiece" that
feels "like a trendy hotel in LA" ("only the most chic stay" here), yet

provides the "quintessential Roman experience" with its "superb location" between the Spanish Steps and Piazza del Popolo and "extraordinary service" from a "friendly" staff; "luxurious rooms" feature "funky but elegant decor", and the "delightful terraced gardens" of Le Jardin de Russie restaurant provide the setting for "exquisite alfresco dining" that's "the perfect end to a hectic day."

Eden, Hotel 🍴🏋️

23	25	24	22	$991

Via Ludovisi 49 | (011-39-06) 478-121 | fax 482-1584 | 800-543-4300 | www.lemeridien.com | 100 rooms, 13 suites, 8 studios

"Be sure to enjoy a cocktail" at the rooftop bar or feast at the "exceptional" restaurant, La Terrazza ("oh! those breakfasts"), and soak up "bountiful views" of Rome and perhaps a celebrity or two at this "elegant" hotel with an "excellent location" near the Via Veneto; the "super-friendly" "staff makes you feel at home", and though most think rooms are "luxurious", cheapskates chirp they're "small" and "your wallet gets lighter by the minute."

Grand Hotel de la Minerve 🍴

▽ 24	23	22	21	$588

Piazza della Minerva 69 | (011-39-06) 695-201 | fax 679-4165 | www.grandhoteldelaminerve.com | 118 rooms, 17 suites

A "very kind and courteous staff" presides over this "absolutely beautiful" "total gem" in "the best location because you can walk to everything"; "you'll love rooms that face the Piazza Minerva" and the "high level of comfort and ease", especially when dining in the romantic restaurant or enjoying the roof garden.

Grand Hotel Palace 🍴🏋️Ⓢ♨

24	24	22	22	$480

Via Vittorio Veneto 70 | (011-39-06) 478-719 | fax 4787-1800 | www.boscolohotels.com | 88 rooms, 6 suites

Guestrooms and suites "fit for a king and queen" are just the beginning of la dolce vita offered at this "palace" occupying an "excellent" spot on Via Veneto ("within walking distance" to the Spanish Steps and many museums); the public spaces are laden with frescoes depicting '30s Roman high society, and the service and amenities are just as upper-crust, from the "staff that makes you feel valued" to the glamorous spa.

Hassler ✕Ⓗ🏋️Ⓢ

24	27	24	23	$766

Piazza Trinità dei Monti 6 | (011-39-06) 699-340 | fax 678-9991 | 800-233-6800 | www.hotelhassler.com | 85 rooms, 13 suites

"Old-world charm" and "swellegance" reign at this "classic" "grand hotel" whose "stunning" newly refurbished rooftop restaurant, Imàgo, provides both the "best view in town" and a venue "to see and be seen" over "the imperative drink" or an "exquisite" meal; rooms can be "small" and "pricey for what you get" unless you "have a view over the Spanish Steps", in which case they're "worth every euro", and depending on who you ask, service is "marvelous" or "snooty."

Inn at the Spanish Steps 🍴🏋️

21	20	19	18	$925

Via dei Condotti 85 | (011-39-06) 6992-5657 | fax 678-6470 | www.atspanishsteps.com | 28 rooms

If you can brave the "overwhelming crowds outside", this "lovely" boutique hotel in a national monument building with a "fantastic" Via Condotti location next to Prada and Gucci (and at the foot of the Spanish

Steps) is "peaceful and romantic inside"; the "warm staff" "welcomes" you to comfortable rooms (some with fireplaces and frescoed ceilings), and there's an "amazing roof deck where breakfast is served"; N.B. don't miss the historic Caffe Greco coffeehouse next door, where the likes of Byron, Wagner, Liszt and Goethe once drank.

InterContinental De La Ville 🏨

| 20 | 21 | 19 | 18 | $354 |

Via Sistina 67/69 | (011-39-06) 67331 | fax 678-4213 | 888-424-6835 | www.intercontinental.com | 169 rooms, 23 suites

It's all about the "wonderful" location right at the top of the Spanish steps at this "small hotel" with "character", since "some rooms are definitely better than others" and the public areas feel "dated"; but with a "terrific concierge" and a "wonderful inside terrace sheltered from the street noise", it's a "convenient" "bargain" spot.

La Posta Vecchia 🏨ⓢ🏊

| 26 | 25 | 25 | 25 | $780 |

Palo Laziale | Ladispoli | (011-39-069) 949-501 | fax 949-507 | 800-735-2478 | www.lapostavecchia.com | 11 rooms, 8 suites

"Keep it a secret" plead patrons who treasure this "real find" "close to the airport" that's "the most charming place" to start or end your Roman holiday; the "incredible former Paul Getty villa" is now a Relais & Châteaux hotel that's "a dream", from the "beautiful outdoor dining terrace overlooking" the Tyrrhenian Sea to the staff that "goes out of its way to please" to the rooms (go for a "suite on the lower floors").

Lord Byron 🏨

| 21 | 22 | 19 | 18 | $383 |

Via Giuseppe de Notaris 5 | (011-39-06) 322-0404 | fax 322-0405 | www.lordbyronhotel.com | 20 rooms, 12 suites

A "quiet" boutique bordering the "beautiful" Borghese Gardens north of the center of Rome, this "romantic hideaway" is the right choice when you want to be "off the beaten path" (there's a free shuttle to Via Veneto, but, if you walk, "add 15 minutes"); an award-winning wine cellar makes the Italian-seafood restaurant "worth it", and while some find the "smallish" art deco rooms "cozy", others "can't warm up" to it.

Raphaël 🏨

| 22 | 23 | 21 | 22 | $555 |

Largo Febo 2 | (011-39-06) 682-831 | fax 687-8993 | www.raphaelhotel.com | 36 rooms, 20 suites

"Tucked away and always discreet, this hotel is a perfect pied-a-terre in Rome" with an "incredible location on Piazza Navona" and a "friendly and efficient staff"; its "wonderful" rooftop restaurant earns kudos for the view and romance factor, but the "decor could use a dust-up", especially in the "old-fashioned" "cramped" rooms (get a "modern and stylish" renovated one instead).

Rome Cavalieri Hilton ⚑🏨ⓢ🏊🔍

| 26 | 25 | 25 | 26 | $423 |

Via Alberto Cadlolo 101 | (011-39-06) 35091 | fax 3509-2241 | 800-445-8667 | www.hilton.com | 347 rooms, 25 suites

Set "atop of one of the hills of Rome", this modern resort boasts "gorgeous" gardens, "fantastic pool facilities" and "rich, comfortable rooms" with "unparalleled" "views of St. Peter's"; stalwarts enthuse over a staff that "prides itself on personal service", and chef Heinz Beck's restaurant, La Pergola, is "one of the finest" in the city (so "reserve when you book your room"); "the only drawback" is the "remote location", but there's a "handy shuttle into the heart" of the city.

	ROOMS	SERVICE	DINING	FACIL.	COST
St. Regis Grand 🍴Ⓗ🐕🔭	27	26	24	24	$991

Via Vittorio Emanuele Orlando 3 | (011-39-06) 47091 | fax 474-7307 | 877-787-3447 | www.starwoodhotels.com | 136 rooms, 25 suites

As "grand as grand gets", a stay in this "top-notch old-world" hotel is "like living in a villa", albeit an "outrageously decadent" one with luxe touches like "frescoed rooms", "seemingly million-thread-count sheets and Hermès toiletries" in the "huge bathrooms"; add "outstanding cuisine" at the "not-to-be-missed" restaurant, Vivendo (it was voted No. 1 for Food in Rome in our *Europe's Top Restaurants* Survey), and "superlative service" from "obliging" staffers ("you can't beat" the private 24-hour butler service), and it's "close to perfection."

	ROOMS	SERVICE	DINING	FACIL.	COST
Westin Excelsior 🐕🔭Ⓢ🏊	25	23	21	22	$1083

Via Vittorio Veneto 125 | (011-39-06) 47081 | fax 482-6205 | 800-937-8461 | www.westin.com | 287 rooms, 32 suites

Next to the American Embassy on the Via Veneto, "the spiritual home of la dolce vita", this bastion of "grandeur and comfort" is "right out of a Fellini movie"; habitués appreciate the "enormous", "beautifully redone rooms" ("old-world charm meets Internet and plasma TVs"), "incredible" marble bathrooms and "top-notch" spa, but contrarians criticize "tired" rooms and service that's "not obliging."

Sardinia

	ROOMS	SERVICE	DINING	FACIL.	COST
[Z] **Cala di Volpe** 🔭⛳🏊🎾	24	25	25	26	$2470

Costa Smeralda | (011-39-0789) 976-111 | fax 976-617 | 800-325-3589 | www.luxurycollection.com | 107 rooms, 16 suites

"Deities do exist" declare well-heeled travelers "blown away" by the "otherworldly beauty" of this resort near "chic" Porto Cervo; it's "so much more than just location", with "stunning Sardinian-style", "fabulously unique" rooms and a "gigantic seawater pool", plus "impeccable service" and "extravagant" lunch buffets; it might "delay your retirement by 10 years", but "it's worth every penny"; N.B. closed October–April.

	ROOMS	SERVICE	DINING	FACIL.	COST
Pitrizza, Hotel 🔭⛳🏊	▽ 27	26	25	26	$2920

Costa Smeralda | (011-39-0789) 930-111 | fax 930-611 | 800-325-3589 | www.luxurycollection.com | 33 rooms, 19 suites, 3 villas

Set on Costa Smeralda, one of the "most amazing places on earth", this "chic", "intimate" retreat is "pure romance", albeit of the "rather expensive" variety; "it may not look like much when you first arrive, but each moment is like being in a dream" suggest sleepwalkers who savor "incredible service", "endless food" ("they'll prepare anything you wish") and proximity to Roman and Carthaginian ruins; N.B. closed from early October to early May.

	ROOMS	SERVICE	DINING	FACIL.	COST
Romazzino, Hotel 👪🔭🏊🎾	-	-	-	-	$2030

Costa Smeralda | Porto Cervo | (011-39-0789) 977-111 | fax 977-614 | www.luxurycollection.com | 78 rooms, 16 suites

Perched above its private sandy beach on the Costa Smeralda, this "relaxing" resort resembles a village, with its whitewashed, typically Sardinian buildings accented with curving archways; rooms continue the theme, with artisan-designed mosaic tilework and private ocean-view balconies plus modern luxe touches like plasma TVs; with "outstanding" dining in the hotel, beachside and by the pool and

| | ROOMS | SERVICE | DINING | FACIL. | COST |

"personable and genuinely accommodating" service, "you'll feel like a king"; N.B. closed October to mid-May.

Sicily

Grand Hotel Timeo 🏨🏊

| 24 | 24 | 22 | 24 | $529 |

Via Teatro Greco 59 | Taormina | (011-39-0942) 23801 | fax 628-501 | www.framonhotels.com | 89 rooms, 16 suites

The first hotel in Taormina (built it 1873) is the "place to splurge" say Sicilian sojourners since the "killer views" from the terrace are "perfect" for "watching the sunset over Mt. Etna, Campari in hand", and "you're treated like a celebrity" with "delightful service and wonderful attention to detail"; "amazing" gardens impress floral fans, and even though "rooms vary", they all come with outdoor spaces and period furnishings.

San Domenico Palace ⊕🏨🏊

| 25 | 26 | 22 | 26 | $502 |

Piazza San Domenico 5 | Taormina | (011-39-0942) 613-111 | fax 625-506 | www.thi.it | 86 rooms, 16 villas

Cherish the "delightful sense of peace and quiet" at this "15th-century monastery meets 21st-century luxury" graced with "dramatic views" of Mt. Aetna and the bay of Taormina from some of its "beautifully decorated, immaculate rooms"; "seclusion is the greatest pleasure", but leave the cloisters for the "stunning public rooms" and "gardens filled with oranges", or for a "lovely lunch on the patio", attended by an "extremely helpful, attentive and, of course, impeccably dressed" staff.

Villa Igiea Hilton Palermo ⊕🍽🏨🏊🔍

| 22 | 22 | 20 | 23 | $379 |

Salita Belmonte 43 | Palermo | (011-39-091) 631-2111 | fax 547-654 | www.hilton.com | 96 rooms, 13 suites

Hallways filled with "pictures of royalty and celebrity guests" and "gorgeous" art nouveau appointments set a "charming" scene at this petite "Liberty-style" Palermo castle, where a "pretty covered terrace" provides "wonderful" views of the sea and of the "luxuriant grounds"; with "understated, elegant" service and "grand dining spaces", no one seems to mind this landmark's "remove" from "frenetic" Downtown – of course, it helps that "the free shuttle makes touring a breeze."

Siena

Certosa di Maggiano, Hotel ✕⊕🏊🔍

| ▽ 21 | 23 | 23 | 19 | $300 |

Strada di Certosa 82 | (011-39-0577) 288-180 | fax 288-189 | 800-735-2478 | www.certosadimaggiano.com | 9 rooms, 8 suites

Another "unique, beautiful former monastery with great charm in the hills", this *perfetto* example of how "reliably excellent" the Relais & Châteaux hotels can be delights most with "elegant" rooms and an "amazingly romantic" setting amid olive groves and vineyards; it's also easily a "gourmet mecca", and has an "attentive staff", so even if it also has a lot of 692-year-old "quirkiness", it's "everything you'd expect."

Locanda dell'Amorosa 🏨🏊

| 25 | 25 | 27 | 24 | $322 |

Localita l'Amorosa | (011-39-0577) 677-211 | fax 632-001 | www.amorosa.it | 17 rooms, 8 suites

"Welcome to medieval Italy" and get ready for a "romantic experience bar none" in this "idyllic Tuscan setting"; the "amazing" grounds that feel like "your own private village" include a "beautiful interior courtyard" and a "great swimming pool with views of the countryside", while accommodations with antique furnishings and paintings are "spacious and elegant"; add in an "outstanding" Mediterranean restaurant and "welcoming service" and this solid, though "isolated", spot is "unforgettable."

Relais Borgo San Felice, Hotel ⓤ⌖♨♒�🌊🔍

21 | 24 | 25 | 23 | $396

Castelnuovo Berardenga | San Felice | (011-39-0577) 3964 | fax 359-089 | www.borgosanfelice.it | 28 rooms, 15 suites
An "exceptionally friendly and accommodating" staff that offers "charming personal service" is the standout at this "lovely" Relais & Châteaux "hamlet" in a "peaceful" setting 10 miles from Siena where you can "rent one of the villas if you have a week" and "dine alfresco on a summer evening overlooking the vineyards"; city sorts say it's "too far from civilization" and "sterile" like "a country club in Connecticut", but others "think of Borgo" when they think of Tuscany.

Relais Il Falconiere ✕ⓤ♨♒🌊

21 | 23 | 24 | 23 | $357

Localita San Martino 370 | Cortona | (011-39-0575) 612-679 | fax 612-927 | www.ilfalconiere.com | 13 rooms, 8 suites
Foodies flock to "one of the best country restaurants in Italy" at this Relais & Châteaux "beauty" (one hour from Siena), where the "unique", "creative" cuisine is as captivating as "the sunsets over the terrace"; it's "just like having your own Italian villa" in "bungalow-style rooms and suites" "that make you want to stay forever", while the staff helps it all "shine"; it's "ostentatious" to some, but most find it the "ultimate Tuscan experience"; N.B. a new spa opened in early 2007.

Relais La Suvera ⓤⓢ🌊

23 | 22 | 22 | 23 | $509

Pievescola | (011-39-0577) 960-300 | fax 960-220 | 800-525-4800 | www.lasuvera.it | 19 rooms, 13 suites
"The ultimate romantic getaway" reminisce guests still dreaming of "the delicate scent of olive oil, lavender and lemons" floating through this "magnificent former papal palace" in the Tuscan countryside, 17 miles from Siena; with "centuries-old tapestries" on the walls and "antiques-filled" rooms, it's "regal without being fussy", and "like living in a museum" but with the modern conveniences of a pool, spa and "nimble staff" to fulfill requests "at lightning speed"; N.B. closed from mid-November to mid-April.

Venice

TOPS IN CITY

26 | Cipriani
25 | Gritti Palace
24 | Villa Cipriani

Bauer, Hotel ♒

25 | 24 | 22 | 22 | $795

San Marco 1459 | (011-39-041) 520-7022 | fax 520-7557 | 800-223-6800 | www.bauervenezia.com | 91 rooms, 18 suites
This "fabulous hotel" actually has two sections: a 19th-century, "really palatial Il Palazzo wing" with "rooms straight out of a Merchant Ivory film" boasting Murano fixtures and classic furnishings, as well as a more

modern "1950s chic" portion in "deco drag" (actually added in 1945); the outside dining at De Pisis has "the best view in town", and guests enjoy hearing the "gondoliers sing to their passengers"; though most find service "excellent", a minority says they're "too sure of themselves."

Ca'Pisani Hotel ⑪🛏🏌♨

| 23 | 25 | 17 | 20 | $548 |

Dorsoduro 979/a | (011-39-041) 240-1411 | fax 277-1061 | 800-337-4685 | www.capisanihotel.it | 23 rooms, 4 suites, 2 studios

"A modern twist on Venice seems oxymoronic", but it works for many at this "high-tech" spot near the Grand Canal and "next to Peggy Guggenheim's museum"; "dark woods, exposed beams and spiral staircases", along with rooms that have "incredible black-out curtains", and jetted tubs, it's "new meets old" with a crowd that veers safely away from the fanny-pack folks; but mature mavens mumble, it's got that "tragically hip" "boutique syndrome – a cool vibe, but lousy service."

☑ Cipriani, Hotel ✕⑪🍴🏌♨ⓢ♒🔍

| 26 | 27 | 26 | 27 | $1123 |

Giudecca 10 | (011-39-041) 520-7744 | fax 520-3930 | 800-524-2420 | www.hotelcipriani.com | 46 rooms, 58 suites

Soak up "luxury across the lagoon from Piazza San Marco" at this "lush retreat" that's "hotel to the stars"; "they wrote the book" on "seamless attention to detail", from "unmatched" dining at Fortuny and Cip's Club to the "sparkling saltwater pool", plus "tremendous personal service" includes "private boats" to whisk guests to "the action on the Grand Canal"; if you land a room with views, you'll agree "magnificence, thy name is Cipriani"; N.B. it's closed November–early April and the adjoining Palazzo Vendramin is closed early January–mid-March.

Danieli, Hotel ✕⑪🏌🛏

| 23 | 23 | 22 | 22 | $1016 |

Castello 4196 | (011-39-041) 522-6480 | fax 520-0208 | 800-325-3589 | www.luxurycollection.com | 222 rooms, 11 suites

"Everyone who is anyone for the past 500 years" has stayed at this "fabled hotel next to the Doge's Palace" for its "ambiance beyond compare", from the "glittering marble lobby" to the "visually thrilling" rooftop restaurant with "breathtaking views"; admirers purr over "dark and exotic" accommodations "with fabulous touches" and a "helpful staff", but "trapped tourists" snap over "tired rooms" and "reluctant service", advising "if you can't get a view, skip it."

Des Bains 🏌🛏♒🔍

| 21 | 22 | 20 | 24 | $875 |

Lungomare Marconi 17 | Lido | (011-39-041) 526-5921 | fax 526-0113 | 800-325-3535 | www.sheraton.com | 173 rooms, 18 suites

Hop on the "free boat to San Marco" in the morning, then "get away from the crowds" and spend the afternoon "relaxing on the beach" at this Lido "turn-of-the-century jewel" that offers "old-world grandeur" (like "lovely" rooms with belle epoque flourishes); while most revel in the fact that it "looks like it hasn't changed in 100 years", some suggest it "needs a major update"; N.B. closed from late-October to mid-March.

Gritti Palace ✕🏌🛏

| 26 | 26 | 24 | 24 | $1193 |

Campo Santa Maria del Giglio 2467 | (011-39-041) 794-611 | fax 520-0942 | 800-325-3589 | www.luxurycollection.com | 82 rooms, 9 suites

"If your wallet can take it", this "dream" of a boutique hotel right on the Grand Canal is worth digging out the euro, especially if you "splurge for a room overlooking" the famed waterway; you can sip a "Bellini on the terrace" before dining on Venetian-Med fare at Club del Doge and then retiring to "high-ceilinged" accommodations with "glorious linens" and "marvelous marble tubs", all the while appreciating "stellar service"; it's "out of this world", though critics cringe when the staff seems to "turn up its noses" breathing in this "rarified" air.

Londra Palace, Hotel ✕ ⊕ ♨   23 | 23 | 22 | 20 | $357

Riva Degli Schiavoni 4171 | (011-39-041) 520-0533 | fax 522-5032 | www.hotellondra.it | 36 rooms, 17 suites

"Fall madly in love" with this hotel where Tchaikovsky composed his Fourth Symphony overlooking the lagoon across to San Giorgio; there's a "beautiful" Italian neoclassical design, with mosaic floors and "fabulous fabrics"; "if it's possible, get a balcony" with "to-die-for" "views of the gondolas docked off St. Mark's", enjoy service from a "kind" and "attentive" staff, then eat "superb" fare at Do Leoni.

Luna Hotel Baglioni ♨   24 | 24 | 21 | 22 | $834

San Marco 1243 | (011-39-041) 528-9840 | fax 528-7160 | www.baglionihotels.com | 69 rooms, 35 suites

Even after 10 centuries in the same "*perfetto* location" "steps from St. Mark's Square", Venice's oldest hotel is still an "unexpected gem", with "decadent" "antique decoration" in "huge" rooms (some with balconies that feel "larger than most quarters at other properties in town") and service that "exceeds expectations"; adding to the "pleasantly old-fashioned" ambiance are the breakfast buffets served amid "breathtaking frescoes" in the Salone Marco Polo.

Monaco & Grand Canal, Hotel ⊕ ♨   22 | 21 | 21 | 20 | $370

San Marco 1332 | (011-39-041) 520-0211 | fax 520-0501 | www.hotelmonaco.it | 114 rooms, 17 suites

Step into a Merchant-Ivory film set, complete with marble pillars, frescoed ceilings and stone floors, at this "intimate and lovely" property with the "best location" fronting the Grand Canal; beginning in 1638, the building served as the home of a wealthy family and was rumored to be the setting for Casanova's many conquests, but a restoration has created "glamorous" rooms with "fabulous" city views, a Venetian restaurant offering "oustanding" outside dining with the water "at your feet" and furnishings that reflect the grandeur of its past.

San Clemente Palace ⊕ ♨ ☄ ⚲   25 | 22 | 20 | 24 | $683

Isola di San Clemente 1 | (011-39-041) 244-5001 | fax 244-3800 | www.sanclemente.thi.it | 117 rooms, 83 suites

Early reports rave about this "stunningly beautiful" hotel in a 17th-century monastery on a 17-acre private island in the Venetian lagoon complete with pool, golf and tennis; those who've been say it's more than "worth considering", especially if you're looking to escape "a city overloaded with people" (it's a short boat ride from both St. Mark's Square and the Lido), and it offers "spectacular" service, a spa that "makes you feel like a princess" and "some of the best food in Venice."

Villa Cipriani, Hotel ⊕ ♨ ♨   24 | 27 | 24 | 23 | $510

Via Canova 298 | Asolo | (011-39-0423) 523-411 | fax 952-095 | 800-325-3535 | www.sheraton.com | 31 rooms

In the hills of Asolo about an hour from Venice, this "elegant" hotel appeals to literary lodgers, since the 16th-century building was once home to famous authors Robert and Elizabeth Barrett Browning; it impresses most others as well, with its "luscious" countryside views, "great location" in "one of the prettiest villages" and rooms sporting beautiful vistas of surrounding "gorgeous" gardens; though a few say the quarters need "freshening", most are so "enchanted" they plead "please don't tell anyone else" about this one.

Westin Europa & Regina ⛱♨🔍   `24 | 24 | 22 | 22 | $930`

San Marco 2159 | (011-39-041) 240-001 | fax 523-1533 | 800-937-8461 | www.westin.com | 167 rooms, 18 suites

A "quiet" property on the Grand Canal consisting of five 17th-, 18th- and 19th-century houses near Piazza San Marco, this "charmer" offers a "grand interior", "beautifully appointed" accommodations, "impressively professional service" and a "very good" Venetian-International restaurant; but dissenters diverge, saying despite a "lovely location", "don't expect a view of the canal from your room unless you pay a fortune"; N.B. moviegoers recognize this hotel's balcony from the movie *The Talented Mr. Ripley*.

Westin Excelsior 👫⛱♨🌊🔍   `24 | 22 | 21 | 24 | $1043`

Lungomare Marconi 41 | Lido | (011-39-041) 526-0201 | fax 526-7276 | 800-937-8461 | www.westin.com | 179 rooms, 18 suites

Outfitted to look like a "Moorish palace", this "storybook" Lido resort provides the "perfect antidote to the heat and hustle" of the Venetian summer with a pool, beach, "spacious, welcoming" workout facilities, "scrumptious food" in the Tropicana restaurant and an easy jaunt to and from St. Mark's via free, "luxurious" "high-speed motor boats"; though a few nitpick it's "long past its 'best before' date", most contend the "glamour endures"; N.B. closed November to March.

Jamaica

Kingston

Strawberry Hill ☕♨⑤🌊   `26 | 26 | 25 | 25 | $590`

St. Andrew | (1-876) 944-8400 | fax 944-8408 | www.islandoutpost.com | 12 cottages

"Nestled in the cooler hills" 20 minutes outside Kingston, this mountainside property offers an "idyllic place" that's "great for a laid-back spa weekend" (there's an Aveda Concept Spa on-site) and a "respite from the heat and bustle"; you "can't help but fall in love with the view and the food" or the acres of gardens where the "world below melts away"; rooms are rich with mahogany, and nearby excursions include deep-sea fishing and diving.

Montego Bay

Grand Lido Braco ♨⑤🌊🔍   `20 | 23 | 20 | 24 | $387`

Trelawney | (1-876) 954-0000 | fax 954-0020 | 877-467-8737 | www.superclubs.com | 170 rooms, 56 suites

Besotted beachgoers believe a visit to this adults-only, all-inclusive is "like going home" because the "friendly staff" pays such close "attention to guests" and the extensive facilities (including a faux Jamaican village peopled with artisans) and "excellent food" guarantee "there's no need to leave the property"; birthday-suiters call the *"au naturel"* section a "great experience" ("I've never been this relaxed in my life"), but critics condemn rooms that "could have been nicer."

Half Moon Montego Bay ⚒✕🏋️⬆️Ⓢ♨️🗡️

22	21	19	24	$355

(1-876) 953-2211 | fax 953-2731 | 800-626-0592 | www.halfmoon.com | 34 rooms, 164 suites, 200 villas

This eco-friendly resort's 400-acre "sprawling" campuslike layout "never feels too crowded" yet it's filled with "awesome facilities": numerous tennis courts and pools, an equestrian center and a Robert Trent Jones Sr. golf course (plus a dolphin lagoon and a "fantastic" children's center make it "kid-friendly without being kid-centric"); the "diverse" dining options are "not spectacular", but folks are more than half moony over the "fantastic" staff and the "fabulous" Hibiscus Suites "right on the beach"; N.B. the spa should transition into a brand-new facility by March 2007.

Ritz-Carlton Golf & Spa Resort, Rose Hall ⚒🏋️⬆️Ⓢ♨️🗡️

26	25	23	25	$399

1 Ritz-Carlton Dr. | St. James | (1-876) 953-2800 | fax 953-2501 | 800-241-3333 | www.ritzcarlton.com | 375 rooms, 52 suites

"Absolute bliss" is how fans describe this "unsurpassed" tropical haven where the "relaxing" vibe extends to a staff that "doesn't have the word 'no' in its vocabulary" and to the "large" "wonderful" rooms with ocean or garden views; a "stunning golf course" delights duffers, a "great kids' club" appeals to tots and the "excellent" though "pricey" fare finds foodie fans; the only downside say a few is the "small and crowded" beach and pool.

Rose Hall Resort & Country Club ⚒🏋️⬆️Ⓢ♨️🗡️

17	19	19	19	$259

(1-876) 953-2650 | fax 953-2617 | 866-831-1313 | www.rosehallresort.com | 475 rooms, 13 suites

Brace yourself for "a lot of goofy fun" shooting down the 280-ft. slide in the "mini water park" at this family-oriented playground on Montego Bay; adults find "good value" in the "bountiful food and drink" (some at swim-up bars), "wonderful" golf course and staff that "makes you feel special", but a few are soured by legions of "loud little kids" ("brats"); N.B. a post-Survey renovation of this former Wyndham addressed rooms in need of "serious updating", possibly outdating the above Rooms score.

Round Hill Hotel & Villas ⚒🏋️Ⓢ♨️🗡️

24	24	20	23	$590

Round Hill Bluff | (1-876) 956-7050 | fax 956-7505 | 800-972-2159 | www.roundhilljamaica.com | 36 rooms, 74 suites, 27 villas

You'll "feel like John and Jackie on their honeymoon" at this "secluded 1950s-style getaway" for famous folks and "beautiful people" that, "despite the potential for snobbery", offers "unpretentious", "attentive" service and a "relaxed, low-key" atmosphere; loyalists "never want to leave" the "terrific" villas with private pools, unless it's for the "amazing" spa hidden in an 18th-century plantation house, the "fantastic", though "small" beach or the "surprisingly good food"; it's all "the perfect mix of comfort and glamour."

ROOMS | SERVICE | DINING | FACIL. | COST

Sandals Montego Bay 🔭Ⓢ🏊🎾 — 18 | 21 | 17 | 19 | $300

(1-876) 952-5510 | fax 952-0816 | 800-726-3257 | www.sandals.com | 251 rooms

Even if the original is "not the best of the Sandals" all-inclusives, supporters say it's "one of the most fun", a "great place" for couples with "lots of activities to keep you busy" or an expansive beach for "relaxing", adding up to a "good resort for not very much money"; detractors disagree, deeming the five eateries "so-so" while wryly noting that the "convenient" location "close to the airport" entails lots of "jets roaring past, shaking the windows and waking you."

Tryall Club 👫🫖🔭⛳Ⓢ🏊🎾 — 21 | 23 | 18 | 20 | $440

Sandy Bay Main Rd. | (1-876) 956-5660 | fax 956-5673 | 800-238-5290 | www.tryallclub.com | 78 villas

"From a bright Jamaican 'good morning'" to "tasty tropical drinks" delivered to your room, staffers "take care of every need" allowing vacationers to focus on the "calming lull of the ocean and warm sun" at this secluded resort with "one of the best golf courses on the island"; but some surveyors are not keen on the rest, from rooms that "vary greatly from villa to villa", to food that's not the best "quality" (though "nicely presented") to a lack of activities "in the immediate area."

Negril

Couples Swept Away 🔭🏊🎾 — 24 | 24 | 20 | 25 | $620

(1-876) 957-4061 | fax 957-4060 | 800-268-7537 | www.couples.com | 312 suites

This "sports-centric" all-inclusive is a "perfect place for the health-minded" with its extensive exercise space, tennis courts and water activities, though many choose to just "lay on" the "pristine" beach all day "doing nothing at all" (or "rekindling a romantic flame"); the "helpful staff that treats you like family" and the "adults-only" policy create a "relaxing" vibe at this "peaceful" "secret" oasis in "mostly-tacky" Negril, so it's only the food that "leaves" something "to be desired."

Grand Lido Negril 🔭Ⓢ🏊🎾 — 22 | 24 | 20 | 23 | $522

Manley Blvd. | (1-876) 957-5010 | fax 518-5147 | 800-467-8737 | www.grandlidonegril.com | 210 suites

"Caring" hosts "provide for all your needs" at this "totally relaxed" all-inclusive on a "beautiful" stretch of Seven Mile Beach; unlimited booze from nine bars, meals at five restaurants, beach volleyball, tennis, greens fees at Negril Hill Golf Club, shuttles to and from the airport and even "to-die-for sunsets" are part of the package, so even if the "food could be a little better" and the whole place is "a bit mass market", "it's still worth every cent"; N.B. no children 16 and younger.

Sandals Negril Beach Resort & Spa 🏊🎾 — ▽ 18 | 22 | 15 | 19 | $350

(1-876) 957-5216 | fax 957-5338 | 800-726-3257 | www.sandals.com | 137 rooms, 86 suites

"The beach is like velvet" coo contented congregators at this eco-friendly, couples-only resort "located in a gorgeous area of Negril" that's "simply paradise", where "pleasant" staffers provide "everything you want, when you want it"; the all-inclusive's activities feature

| | ROOMS | SERVICE | DINING | FACIL. | COST |

tennis, racquetball and squash along with the usual water sports and spa treatments, but a few foes fuss about "problems with the rooms" and figure "you can do better" for the money elsewhere.

Ocho Rios

Beaches Boscobel Resort & Golf Club ♀♠⚕⬆⚙⛵⚲

| 20 | 20 | 18 | 22 | $325 |

(1-876) 975-7777 | fax 975-7622 | 888-232-2437 | www.beaches.com | 223 rooms

With a "pleasant" 22-acre setting on the island's northern shore, this family-oriented all-inclusive is "great for children" who "love the pools", waterslides, day-camp programs, video arcade, petting zoo and beach; "unfortunately, that's not enough for adults" gripe grown-ups who "aren't all that impressed" with the rooms, the "mediocre" food and the "subpar" golf.

Couples Sans Souci ♠⚙⛵⚲

| 20 | 21 | 20 | 20 | $420 |

(1-876) 994-1206 | fax 994-1544 | 800-268-7537 | www.couples.com | 148 suites

This all-inclusive, couples-only resort "with a European flavor" is tagged a "top value" by tourists, "the place to go for the perfect blend of luxury and rustic charm"; four pools, mineral springs housing a resident sea turtle and a sizable slate of sports and spa amenities accompany "amazing service" and a "beautiful setting"; a few detractors, however, dislike the dining and counted on more lavish rooms.

Jamaica Inn ♠⚙⛵

| - | - | - | - | $500 |

876-974-2514 | fax 974-2449 | 800-837-4608 | www.jamaicainn.com | 47 suites, 4 cottages

If it's peaceful relaxation you're after, this small elegant inn with no TVs or radios, a cliffside holistic spa and rooms with balconies or verandas overlooking the water may be an appropriate choice; the romantic alfresco restaurant has views of the Bay and features live music, while onsite activities include croquet, snorkeling, kayaking, sailing and diving.

Sandals Dunn's River Golf Resort & Spa ♠⚙⛵⚲

| 22 | 23 | 21 | 24 | $350 |

(1-876) 972-1610 | fax 972-1611 | 800-726-3257 | www.sandals.com | 234 rooms, 16 suites

Recently "redone" and "very Venetian"-looking, this couples-only resort is "bellissimo" sigh sun worshipers who find "fantastic" facilities, particularly the massive outdoor pool/patio complex with waterfall and swim-up bars ("watch inebriated patrons flounder"); with "so many dining choices", spa treatments and Sandal's golf club half an hour away by shuttle, there's almost "too much to do for one trip"; P.S. if you can't "splurge and book an oceanfront suite", no worries: all rooms come with a private balcony or terrace.

Sandals Grande Ocho Rios ☞♠⚙⛵⚲

| 19 | 21 | 17 | 20 | $390 |

(1-876) 974-5691 | fax 974-5700 | 800-726-3257 | www.sandals.com | 520 rooms, 9 villas

Built right on a mountainside, this "charming" all-inclusive couples' "hideaway" features water sports, gym, spa, many pools and "even a

	ROOMS	SERVICE	DINING	FACIL.	COST

nightclub", so visitors can do "as much or as little as they want" without leaving the resort; "no request is too small or too large" for the "friendly" staff to fulfill, but foes fret about "waiting for a minibus to drive" them to the "painfully small" public beach, where the "number of guests far surpasses the number of chairs."

Japan

TOPS IN COUNTRY

Hakone

Gora Kadan ✗ ⊕ 🎎 Ⓢ ≈

| 29 | 26 | 25 | 25 | $448 |

1300 Gora | (011-48-1) 602-3331 | fax 602-3334 | www.gorakadan.com | 24 rooms, 13 suites

You'll find "ultimate luxury, Japanese-style" at this Relais & Châteaux hotel in hot-spring–rich Hakone, near Mount Fuji; part traditional ryokan, part slick spa, this spot appeals to sybarites who soak up the "discrete, flawless service" (your own maid), "classic cuisine" and healing waters in the indoor and outdoor pools.

Kyoto

Hiiragiya Ryokan ✗ 🎎

| 26 | 28 | 27 | 24 | $281 |

Nakahakusancho, Fuyacho Anekoji | Nakagyo-ku | (011-81-75) 221-1136 | fax 221-1139 | www.hiiragiya.co.jp | 28 rooms

"Be prepared to go back in time" at this "incredible" ryokan close to the entertainment district where traditional rooms have tatami mats, shoji screens and "super"-personalized service; "you can only stay like this in Japan" and "reservations are not easy to come by", so revel in the "phenomenal" landscaped gardens while enjoying "exquisite" Kyoto-style kaiseki meals on local ceramic and lacquerware.

Tawaraya Ryokan 🎎

| ▽ | 29 | 29 | 29 | 26 | $363 |

Fuyacho Anekoji | Nakagyo-ku | (011-81-75) 211-5566 | fax 211-2204 | www.ryokan.or.jp | 6 rooms, 12 suites

The "true decadence" of "Japan the way it used to be" thrives at this "quaint", nearly 300-year-old Kyoto inn, where the "delightful pampering" comes via a staff that treats guests "like queens and kings", overseeing everything from the in-room meal service (dinner and breakfast are included) to providing guests with a clean *yakuta* (robe) after their baths to spreading the futon over the tatami at bedtime; surveyors say it's the "real deal", providing a "most restful" stay.

Westin Miyako 🎎 ≈ ✎

| 22 | 23 | 21 | 22 | $280 |

Sanjo, Keage | Higashiyama-ku | (011-81-75) 771-7111 | fax 751-2490 | 800-937-8461 | www.westin.com | 488 rooms, 14 suites

The Western-style quarters are "comfortable" at this "good alternative" "in the midst of temples and shrines", but the "best-kept secret" is the

	ROOMS	SERVICE	DINING	FACIL.	COST

Japanese guesthouse, with traditional rooms that are "truly memorable"; the "amazing" staff is "helpful" and "solicitous", and its location makes it a "wonderful spot from which to explore a historic city."

Osaka

Hyatt Regency ⑤⩩ ▽ 26 | 22 | 24 | 24 | $272

1-13-11 Nanko-kita | Suminoe-ku | (011-81-6) 6612-1234 | fax 6614-7800 | www.osaka.regency.hyatt.com | 439 rooms, 48 suites

The "peacefully appointed rooms" get solid support from sojourners sweet on this "super" spot, located on the bay at Cosmo Square and adjacent to INTEX Osaka; a true "city resort" that "knows how to make Westerners feel welcome", its highlights include indoor and outdoor pools, a fully equipped business center and a 28th-floor Chinese restaurant with views of Osaka Bay.

Imperial Hotel ⩍⩩⚲ ▽ 26 | 26 | 25 | 23 | $272

1-8-50 Temmabashi | Kita-ku | (011-81-6) 6881-1111 | fax 6881-4111 | www.imperialhotel.co.jp | 370 rooms, 17 suites

Fans are fond of this "beautiful" hotel with a "great" central location that affords "views of the Okawa River"; the restaurants are "fabulous", the rooms are "comfortable" yet "luxurious" and public spaces, designed to evoke the original Frank Lloyd Wright interiors of its sister property in Tokyo, are "elegantly simple."

Nikko-Bayside, Hotel ⩍⑤ - | - | - | - | $295

6-2-45 Shimaya | Konohana-ku | (011-81-6) 6460-3111 | fax 6460-3115 | www.hotelnikkobaysideosaka.com | 637 rooms, 4 suites

This skyline landmark, part of the JAL Hotel chain, is just two minutes from Universal Studios Japan, and offers low-key, modern facilities with luxurious touches like panoramic windows; cinematically minded surveyors are satiated by the Californian cuisine at Top of Hollywood, while sybarites savor the treatments at SkySpa, with its traditional onsen that brings hot spring waters from half-a-mile underground up to the 31st floor.

☒ Ritz-Carlton, The ✕⩍⑤⩩ 27 | 28 | 25 | 25 | $248

2-5-25 Umeda | Kita-ku | (011-81-6) 6343-7000 | fax 6343-7001 | 800-241-3333 | www.ritzcarlton.com | 262 rooms, 30 suites

It "doesn't get much better" rave reviewers of this "lovely" skyscraper in Umeda where "huge", "immaculate" rooms (with "superb" linens) that some call "a bargain by Japanese standards" start on the 24th floor, offering "amazing" panoramic views; surveyors also praise the spa and dining options as well as the "incredible" service – in short, it's "exactly what you'd expect from a Ritz."

Westin ⩩ 23 | 25 | 19 | 22 | $370

1-1-20 Oyodo Naka | Kita-ku | (011-81-6) 6440-1111 | fax 6440-1100 | 800-937-8461 | www.westin.com | 256 rooms, 48 suites

"Large", "reliable" accommodations with "marble bathrooms and all the amenities" for business and leisure plus "excellent" service from a staff that tries to "make your stay perfect" are the draws at this "quiet oasis"; the "only downsides" are its "pricey" restaurants and "slightly off-the-beaten-track" location, but there are "convenient and free bus shuttles" to the train station.

Tokyo

TOPS IN CITY

27 Mandarin Oriental
26 Park Hyatt
Four Seasons/Chinzan-so
Four Seasons/Marunouchi
Seiyo Ginza

Cerulean Tower 🔭🏊 22 | 22 | 20 | 22 | $180

26 Sakuragaoka-cho | Shibuya-ku | (011-81-3) 3476-3000 | fax 3476-3001 | 800-888-4747 | www.ceruleantower-hotel.com | 409 rooms, 5 suites

"Big thumbs-up" for the "spacious rooms" and "huge views" at this "excellent value" "business hotel" in the "literal center of the universe of Shibuya"; the "perfect place for a Westerner" offers an international array of dining options, a pool and spa "worth visiting" and "personal, accommodating service" - all of which create a "classy", "tranquil oasis."

Four Seasons at Chinzan-so 🍴🔭Ⓢ🏊 25 | 27 | 25 | 27 | $453

2-10-8 Sekiguchi | Bunkyo-ku | (011-81-3) 3943-2222 | fax 3943-2300 | 800-332-3442 | www.fourseasons.com | 232 rooms, 51 suites

Tucked into the "spectacular" and historic 17-acre Chinzan-so Gardens, this "luxurious" yet "low-key" hotel combines "typical Four Seasons" "impeccable service" with something atypical in Tokyo: "gigantic rooms"; "well-prepared" food and the newly refurbished Japanese onsen and spa draw raves as well, and while some find the location "inconvenient", others feel the "slightly out-of-the-way" setting makes for a perfect "romantic" "getaway."

Four Seasons at Marunouchi 🔭 28 | 28 | 23 | 24 | $520

1-11-1 Marunouchi | Chiyoda-ku | (011-81-3) 5222-7222 | fax 5222-1255 | 800-332-3442 | www.fourseasons.com | 48 rooms, 9 suites

"Intimacy and understated elegance" render this "amazing boutique hotel" in the "perfectly located" business district a "peaceful haven" where "flawless service" and "fantastically equipped rooms" make fans "feel like Japanese royalty"; "fabulous dining", "stunning interior design" and an "excellent" gym and spa please as well, and though it's pricey, the well-heeled say anyplace where "even the laundry is gift-wrapped" is "worth every yen."

Grand Hyatt Ⓢ🏊 26 | 25 | 25 | 25 | $439

6-10-3 Roppongi | Minato-ku | (011-81-3) 4333-1234 | fax 4333-8123 | 800-223-1234 | www.grand.hyatt.com | 368 rooms, 21 suites

"No expense was spared" on what fawning fans call "the nicest Grand Hyatt" where high-tech (yet "smallish") rooms with "subtle Asian" accents feature flat-screen TVs, "motorized blinds" and bathrooms with "to-die-for" "rainstorm showers"; "awe-inspiring views" of "bustling Roppongi", "extraordinary service", a "serene" spa and seven restaurants earn kudos too.

Imperial Hotel Ⓢ🏊 22 | 26 | 23 | 22 | $332

1-1-1 Uchisaiwai-cho | Chiyoda-ku | (011-81-3) 3504-1111 | fax 3581-9146 | www.imperialhotel.co.jp | 960 rooms, 60 suites

"The entire world seems to pass through the lobby" of this "classic" known for "legendary", "personal" service ("charming elevator la-

ROOMS SERVICE DINING FACIL. COST

dies") and a "prime location"; "rock stars, princes and heads of state" appreciate the proximity to the Imperial Palace as well as "comfortable rooms", though a few mere mortals malign the "generic" quarters; P.S. "don't miss the bar" that features relics from the original Frank Lloyd Wright–designed building.

Z Mandarin Oriental 🐾Ⓢ   29 26 25 27 $555

2-1-1 Nihonbashi Muromachi | Chuo-ku | (011-81-3) 3270-8950 | fax 3270-8886 | www.mandarinoriental.com | 157 rooms, 22 suites
"Clearly the 'it' hotel in Tokyo", this "superb" spot "raises the bar" with "insane" rooms ("they thought of everything") and "stunning" views of the city and "Mount Fuji on a clear day"; the "über-cool" "adult" atmosphere is supported by "exceptional service", top-notch dining at eight eateries and a high-tech spa on the 36th floor; says one smitten surveyor, "if you have the money, this is the best."

New Otani, Hotel Ⓢ 🏖   19 23 21 22 $213

4-1 Kioi-cho | Chiyoda-ku | (011-81-3) 3265-1111 | fax 3221-2619 | www.newotani.com | 1467 rooms, 66 suites
"Breathtaking gardens and grounds" make it hard to "believe you're in the center of Tokyo" at this "huge" but "comfortable" hotel, and the "top-notch" service and "well-appointed rooms" make it a "reliable" choice; though accommodations are "on the small side" and the large size equals "no warmth" for some, most report a "pleasant" experience and enjoy "food from around the world."

Nikko, Hotel 🐾Ⓢ 🏖   ▽ 23 23 20 20 $328

1-9-1 Daiba | Minato-ku | (011-81-3) 5500-5500 | fax 5500-2525 | 800-645-5687 | www.jalhotels.com | 435 rooms, 18 suites
A bit of "peace in bustling Tokyo", this "waterfront" property offers "skyline views" (the "excellent" heated swimming pool overlooks the bay and all the "surrounding amusements"); the "decent-sized rooms" feature balconies, there's "amazing concierge service" and the Zen spa furnishes an array of treatments.

Okura, Hotel ✕🐾Ⓢ 🏖   20 26 23 20 $313

2-10-4 Toranomon | Minato-ku | (011-81-3) 3582-0111 | fax 3582-3707 | www.okura.com | 744 rooms, 90 suites
Located across the street from the American Embassy, this "dignified and reserved" Tokyo "grande dame" has a reputation of "catering to U.S. businesspeople" with amenities like a gym, pool and tea ceremony room, as well as a "mind-boggling" array of "wonderful" restaurants and bars; staffers "thoroughly dedicated to meeting everyone's needs" "make up for" rooms on the "small" side, but some surveyors can't get beyond the public spaces' "retro" decor, asking "what decade is this?"

Palace Hotel   18 23 18 17 $281

1-1-1 Marunouchi | Chiyoda-ku | (011-81-3) 3211-5211 | fax 3211-6987 | www.palacehotel.co.jp | 384 rooms, 5 suites
A "wonderful location by the Imperial Palace and train station" along with "outrageously great service" are lauded by loyal subjects of this "convenient" hotel; some of the "comfortable" (if "small") rooms have "glorious views", and considering the "reasonable" prices, fans contend it "couldn't be better."

	ROOMS	SERVICE	DINING	FACIL.	COST
[Z] **Park Hyatt** 🍴🔭Ⓢ🏊	27	27	25	26	$460

3-7-1-2 Nishi Shinjuku | Shinjuku-ku | (011-81-3) 5322-1234 | fax 5322-1288 | 800-223-1234 | www.park.hyatt.com | 154 rooms, 23 suites

"When you're tired of normal hotels", stay in a celebrity one - this star of the film *Lost in Translation* offers a "perfect experience" with "drop-dead views" from Shinjuku's "forest of skyscrapers" to Mt. Fuji; rooms are "classy with substance", "impeccable service meets every real and imagined need without intrusiveness" and the "amazing restaurants", "way cool" lobby bar and extensive health club are further draws; while a few say it's "too expensive" and there's "nothing especially Japanese about it", most believe it's "worth every single yen."

	ROOMS	SERVICE	DINING	FACIL.	COST
Seiyo Ginza, Hotel 🍴🔭	27	29	24	23	$387

1-11-2 Ginza | Chuo-ku | (011-81-3) 3535-1111 | fax 3535-1110 | 888-767-3966 | www.seiyo-ginza.com | 52 rooms, 25 suites

The "polite" staff "sets the standard" at this "intimate" "jewel" in Ginza, with "world-class concierge service" that "caters to your every wish"; the "unequaled" rooms feature "big, luxurious" bathrooms, the restaurants are "fantastic" and the "location is excellent."

	ROOMS	SERVICE	DINING	FACIL.	COST
Westin	25	24	21	23	$500

1-4-1 Mita | Meguro-ku | (011-81-3) 5423-7000 | fax 5423-7600 | 800-937-8461 | www.westin.com | 418 rooms, 20 suites

"Spacious", "comfortable" rooms with "huge bathtubs" and "great amenities" are the hallmark of this "simply dreamy" chain, and this "fabulous" Tokyo link is no exception; it's known for "fantastic", "personalized" service, an "excellent location" in Yebisu Garden Place and a "variety of dining options" from Chinese to Continental to Japanese.

Jordan

Amman

	ROOMS	SERVICE	DINING	FACIL.	COST
[Z] **Four Seasons** 👪🛏🐕🔭Ⓢ🏊🎾	28	29	24	27	$434

Al-Kindi St., 5th Circle | (011-962-6) 550-5555 | fax 550-5556 | 800-819-5053 | www.fourseasons.com | 163 rooms, 29 suites

Bring your crowns and tiaras since everyone is treated like "royalty" at this hilltop "oasis of calm" where everything is "in keeping" with this chains' expected "standards and style"; it's considered "one of the best in the Middle East", given the "stunning infinity pool on a terrace overlooking the city", the "modern, sleek and authentic restaurant", little touches like fruit kebabs served poolside and "ohhh . . . the rooms" - "luxurious" and amenity-laden; indeed, most "love every moment" of their "totally elegant" stay.

Petra

	ROOMS	SERVICE	DINING	FACIL.	COST
Mövenpick Resort & Spa 🍴🏊	23	24	23	25	$120

Wadi Mousa | (011-962-3) 215-7111 | fax 215-7112 | www.movenpick-hotels.com | 179 rooms, 4 suites

An "amazing" resort on the Dead Sea and near "the entrance of Petra", this "exotic little haven" is a world unto itself; with "lush" rooms, a "spa that makes you feel you've died and gone to heaven", "beautifully terraced pools, "excellent facilities and service" (it's even "kid-friendly) and a "really good restaurant", there's "no better way to enjoy" the area.

Kenya

Amboseli Game Reserve

Amboseli Serena Safari Lodge 👫 🏊 | 18 | 23 | 17 | 20 | $275

Amboseli | (011-254-45) 622-361 | fax 622-430 | www.serenahotels.com | 96 rooms

With its "view of Mt. Kilimanjaro as backdrop" and "little huts that blend into the landscape", this "fine member of a reliable chain" provides an "unbelievable" experience according to safari surfers who also support the "wonderful staff"; a few fusspots fume over "small rooms" and "nothing-special" fare, but the "beautiful setting" and nearby "watering hole with roaming animals" (occasionally including "monkeys who steal your breakfast") have many more "loving every minute" of it.

Masai Mara Game Reserve

Governor's Camp 👫👫 🛥 Ⓢ | 22 | 24 | 21 | 22 | $394

Masai Mara | (011-254-2) 273-4000 | fax 273-4023 | www.governorscamp.com | 37 tents

A "solid safari camp surrounded by some of the best game viewing", this "legendary" spot on the Mara River boasts "knowledgeable guides", a "rustic, colonial feel" with its luxury tents and "excellent" dining that includes a "pleasing" afternoon tea; some say it's "not as intimate as its smaller" sibling, but it's "worth the price."

Kichwa Tembo Tented Camp 👫👫 | 23 | 26 | 21 | 24 | $350

Masai Mara | 1-305-221-2906 | fax 221-3223 | 888-882-3742 | www.ccafrica.com | 40 tents

For a "wonderful" tent experience on the Mara, this "magical place" features an "awesome" and "friendly" staff, "well-outfitted" quarters with private decks and "some of the best food in East Africa"; the "amazing setting" near a spot where a scene from *Out of Africa was filmed*" is "surely Eden", and activities include "great game drives", bird-watching and guided walking tours.

Little Governor's Camp 👫👫 🛥 Ⓢ | ▽ 25 | 29 | 28 | 27 | $431

Masai Mara | (011-254-2) 273-4000 | fax 273-4023 | www.governorscamp.com | 17 tents

"Truly an African experience" awaits at this small, "lovely" tented camp, a little brother to nearby Governor's Camp, "in the middle of lion country"; "everything is wonderful" from the "delicious food" to the "absolutely exciting and eye-filling" safaris to quarters with "all the comforts of a hotel room" (and the "added excitement of night-visiting hippos"); most "would go every year if they could afford it."

Mara Serena Safari Lodge 👫 🏊 | 22 | 26 | 21 | 23 | $220

Masai Mara | (011-254-50) 22253 | fax 271-8100 | www.serenahotels.com | 72 rooms, 1 suite

"Incredible hospitality" is the attraction at this "authentic but luxurious" lodge, a "good value" "right in the thick of things" where an "outstanding" staff "attentively caters to your needs" and the pool "overlooks the vast plain of the Masai Mara"; "each comfortable cottage is well appointed", and the "well-staffed dining room" serves "delicious meals."

Nairobi

Giraffe Manor 👪 [H] 🔭

▽ 23 | 26 | 23 | 23 | $298

Gogo Falls Rd. | (011-254-20) 891-078 | fax 890-949 | www.giraffemanor.com | 5 rooms

"Like nowhere else" in the world, this hotel set in a "1930s English country" mansion near Nairobi is a kind of "safari halfway house", as it's home to several Rothschild giraffes, an endangered species sheltered here since 1974; though there are "only a few rooms", it's an "amazing" experience, since the namesake creatures routinely "stick their heads through the windows"; P.S. "*White Mischief* was filmed here."

Nairobi Serena 🔭 ⛳ [S] 🏊

21 | 22 | 20 | 21 | $340

Kenyatta Ave. | (011-254-20) 282-2000 | fax 272-5184 | www.serenahotels.com | 168 rooms, 16 suites

A "superb" place "to start or finish your Kenyan travels", this "peaceful haven" in the middle of Nairobi has "lovely" and "luxurious" rooms, "unsurpassed hospitality" from a "fabulous staff", a "nice spa featuring incredible massages" and an "oasis"-like pool; the "fantastic" Mandhari restaurant and "in-room Internet" service are other "civilized" touches.

Norfolk Hotel, The 👪 [H] 🔭 🏊

18 | 20 | 19 | 19 | $290

Harry Thuku Rd. | (011-254-2) 216-940 | fax 216-796 | 800-845-3692 | www.lonrhohotels.com | 140 rooms, 28 suites

"Start your safari where Teddy Roosevelt did" at this "legendary" century-old "charmer" known for its "beautiful grounds and gardens" (the porch alone is "worth the visit"), "impeccable", "personal" service, "luxurious, comfortable accommodations" and "exquisite breakfasts" that can be eaten alfresco; finicky folks feel it's "tired", but most are enamored of the "traditional" style, calling it a "must-stay in Nairobi."

Treetops 🔭

16 | 22 | 17 | 19 | $300

Aberdare National Park | (011-254-2) 445-2095-9 | fax 445-2102 | www.aberdaresafarihotels.com | 48 rooms, 2 suites

If it's wild animals you came to see, "this is where you'll get them" say fans who "get woken up in the middle of the night" by creatures "right outside" their rooms; there's a "palpable sense of history" (Queen Elizabeth II ascended the throne when the king died while she was here in 1952) so even if the accommodations are "spartan", "you spend little time in them" during your "ultimate safari", enjoying "stunning views" instead; P.S. there's "communal dining."

Windsor Golf & Country Club 🔭 ⛳ 🏊 🎾

▽ 21 | 17 | 17 | 23 | $168

Ridgeways Rd. | (011-254-20) 856-2300 | fax 856-0160 | www.windsorgolfresort.com | 95 rooms, 20 suites, 15 cottages

A "wonderful" "surprise" 10 miles outside Nairobi, this "relaxing" "escape from the city" features "elegant rooms", "beautiful gardens" and a "great" golf course (watch for "baboons on the fairways" and "monkeys on the back nine"); though it's "not bad after a couple of weeks in the bush", unfortunately, the food ranges from "good" to "airport"-quality.

ROOMS | SERVICE | DINING | FACIL. | COST

Nanyuki

Mount Kenya Safari Club 24 | 25 | 22 | 25 | $430
Nanyuki | (011-254-6) 230-000 | fax 231-316 | www.fairmont.com |
35 rooms, 63 cottages, 10 villas, 8 suites
You'll feel like a "British colonialist" at this "exclusive" lodge that's set
on a mountainside overlooking Mt. Kilimanjaro and was founded by
William Holden in 1959; expect "perfect pampering" from the staff,
"delightful" accommodations with "fires made for you each night" and
outstanding bird- and game-watching; there are "no safari drives
here" and a handful believe it's "living off its reputation" with "uninspired" cuisine and rooms that "need renovation", but many love the
adjacent animal rescue facility.

Lebanon

Beirut

Albergo, Hotel ▽ 25 | 21 | 22 | 19 | $250
137, rue Abdel Wahab El Inglizi | (011-961-1) 339-797 | fax 339-999 |
www.albergobeirut.com | 33 suites
Tourists may not be flocking to Beirut just yet, but this "romantic"
Relais & Châteaux "hideaway" with "hospitable service" could draw
them back for a "rendezvous" in a "superb" boutique setting; the rooftop
bar, terrace and pool are "amazing", "transporting you anywhere your
imagination takes you", and the nearby area has "lots of nightlife";
suites come in different themes (Mediterranean, Colonial, European,
etc.), and working stiffs say it's "safe for business foreigners."

Luxembourg

Le Royal, Hotel ▽ 18 | 19 | 19 | 17 | $476
12, bl Royal | (011-352) 241-6161 | fax 225-948 |
www.leroyalluxembourg.com | 190 rooms, 20 suites
Just 10 minutes from the airport and with an "ideal location for meetings" "steps from the city center", this veteran is dubbed "a place for
business only"; though there's a "very professional staff", "spacious
rooms" with flat-screen TVs and a fitness center and spa with *hammam*,
a few find the quarters "a bit tired" and the food "subpar."

Malaysia

Kuala Lumpur

Mandarin Oriental 26 | 26 | 24 | 25 | $203
City Centre | (011-60-3) 2380-8888 | fax 2380-3388 |
www.mandarinoriental.com | 551 rooms, 41 suites, 51 apartments
The "welcome is genuine" at this "top-notch" "business-oriented" hotel
in a "brilliant Midtown location" next to the Petronas Towers and the
Convention Center and close to "excellent" shopping "and people-
watching"; expect "fabulous rooms" with "amazing bathrooms", a
"superb" Chinese restaurant and a "stunning" gym with a "wonderful"

infinity pool overlooking a park; though a few sniff it's "not up to Mandarin standards", most agree it's "the place to be in KL."

Regent, The 🔭Ⓢ🏊

ROOMS	SERVICE	DINING	FACIL.	COST
22	23	20	20	$75

160 Jalan Bukit Bintang | (011-60-3) 2117-4888 | fax 2141-1441 | 800-545-4000 | www.regenthotels.com | 437 rooms, 31 suites

Loyalists like this business hotel for "longer stays", praising the "gracious" service, "great location across from Bukit Bintang" for shopping, a 10,000-sq.-ft. state-of-the-art health club and rooms that feature high-speed Internet access; but grumpy guests say it's "getting a little tired."

Ritz-Carlton, The 🔭Ⓢ🏊

ROOMS	SERVICE	DINING	FACIL.	COST
23	23	18	22	$245

168 Jalan Imbi | (011-60-3) 2142-8000 | fax 2143-8080 | 800-241-3333 | www.ritzcarlton.com | 219 rooms, 29 suites

"A great hotel in a city that is woefully short of great hotels", this "boutique"-style property panders to business folks with an "excellent location" near Bintang Walk, a "staff that couldn't be nicer" and club level rooms with "your own private butler"; "afternoon tea is great", the rest of the food is "fantastic" and the "nice" fitness center and spa is an added benefit; but a few regulars report "it's not at the same standards as the RCs in other locales."

Shangri-La Hotel Ⓢ🏊🎾

ROOMS	SERVICE	DINING	FACIL.	COST
22	24	23	23	$122

11 Jalan Sultan Ismail | (011-60-3) 2032-2388 | fax 2070-1514 | 866-565-5050 | www.shangri-la.com | 648 rooms, 53 suites

Visitors voice mixed views on the KL outpost of this "fantastic chain": while most maintain "the service and attention could not be better" and the "breakfast buffet is the most diverse" they've ever seen, a few others find "it's not the best from Shangri-La", though the rooms are "well appointed" and "the lobby looks a lot better after the renovation."

Langkawi

[Z] **Datai, The** 🔭⛳Ⓢ🏊🎾

ROOMS	SERVICE	DINING	FACIL.	COST
27	28	26	25	$455

Jalan Teluk Datai | (011-60-4) 959-2500 | fax 959-2600 | www.ghmhotels.com | 54 rooms, 18 suites, 40 villas

Expect "the best of both worlds - luxury and untouched nature" - at this "breathtaking" island "paradise"-cum-über-chic" golf resort nestled between a "lush" rainforest and a private white-sand cove on the Andaman Sea; rapturous reviews roll in for "spacious" "villas on stilts", a "wonderful" "multinational staff" that "makes it all happen", "unbelievable", "exotic" Pan-Asian fare and, of course, all the "simian visitors" you could hope for; the less loquacious simply call it "heaven on earth."

Four Seasons Resort Langkawi 👪🛏🐾🔭⛳🏊🎾

	ROOMS	SERVICE	DINING	FACIL.	COST
∇	29	25	23	27	$450

Jalan Tanjung Rhu | (011-60-4) 950-8888 | fax 950-8899 | 800-332-3442 | www.fourseasons.com | 68 rooms, 23 villas

"Spacious bungalows with wraparound balconies, huge bathrooms" and a "very private feel" make this "incredible" spot, set between the Andaman Sea and the tropical rainforest, "one of the top resort hotels in Southeast Asia"; other winning attributes include the "stylish" design, service that's "better than in heaven" and "impressive grounds" that include a mile of white-sand beach and "incredibly landscaped" pavilions and pools.

Pangkor Laut Resort 🫖🔭Ⓢ🏊🎾 — ▽ 22 | 23 | 19 | 20 | $245

Pangkor Laut Island | (011-60-5) 699-1100 | fax 699-1200 | www.pangkorlautresort.com | 145 villas, 3 suites

Three miles from the mainlaind in the Straits of Malacca lies an "unbelievably romantic" private island where Malaysian-style villas (rainforest and overwater) and a "to-die-for" spa win over some fans; but others say the "large tour groups" make it all "not so peaceful" at certain times, while the food is "not up to the standard one would expect."

Penang

Tanjong Jara Resort 🔭Ⓢ🏊🎾 — - | - | - | - | $390

Batu 8, off Jalan Dungun, Terengganu | (011-60-9) 845-1100 | fax 845-1200 | www.tanjongjararesort.com | 98 rooms

Starting with architecture based on the palaces of sultans, this recently refurbished honeymooner's resort on the South China Sea offers an upscale Malay experience; rooms are finished with local timber, restaurants utilize regional ingredients and spa treatments feature galanga and nutmeg, plus a traditional *gamelan* orchestra plays every night.

Maldives

Banyan Tree 🔭Ⓢ — ▽ 27 | 26 | 25 | 26 | $720

Vabbinfaru Island | North Malé Atoll | (011-960) 664-3147 | fax 664-3843 | 866-822-6926 | www.banyantree.com | 48 villas

Admirers "appreciate the supreme experience" of a stay at this "remote" atoll "paradise" of thatched-roof villas, "pure white-sand beaches" and turquoise water views; it's "astonishingly swish" (great after such a long flight) yet "low-key" due to the "unobtrusive service" and "romantically secluded" location; there's a "soothing" spa that boasts a RainMist room and traditional Balinese treatments that "truly rejuvenate", as well as "excellent" cuisine; all in all, it's a "wonderfully relaxing retreat."

Four Seasons Resort Maldives at Kuda Huraa 🍴🔭Ⓢ🏊 — - | - | - | - | $900

North Malé Atoll | (011-960) 664-4888 | fax (960) 664-4800 | 800-332-3442 | www.fourseasons.com | 64 bungalows, 25 villas, 7 suites

Reopened after a rebuilding following the devastating tsunami several years back, this posh resort on a private coral island features stylish beachside and overwater palm-thatched bungalows and villas constructed by local craftsmen using indigenous materials; other highlights include a spa with Asian-based treatments, a children's program, plenty of complimentary watersports and access to the facilities of the new Four Seasons at Landaa Giraavaru; N.B. a three-deck catamaran takes guests island-hopping, stargazing and diving.

[NEW] Four Seasons Resort Maldives at Landaa Giraavaru 👪Ⓢ🏊🎾 — - | - | - | - | $990

Baa Atoll | (011-960) 660-0888 | fax 660-0800 | www.fourseasons.com | 29 rooms, 5 suites, 68 villas

Hop on a seaplane to the beach-fringed coral island where this newcomer resides, the latest of two over-the-top Four Seasons resorts in the Maldives; expect thatched-roof beach and water villas, some sporting

	ROOMS	SERVICE	DINING	FACIL.	COST

private plunge pools, outdoor showers, four-poster beds with mosquito netting and glassed living areas with views; a spa features Ayurvedic treatments, and the on-site restaurant appears to float above the water.

One & Only Kanuhura 🐾Ⓢ

▽ 28	29	28	29	$620

Lhaviyani Atoll, 2/1 Neelo Faru Magu | Kanuhura | (011-960) 662-0044 | fax 662-0033 | 866-552-0001 | www.oneandonlyresorts.com | 5 suites, 95 villas

"Four hundred 'good mornings'" from the "smiling" staff is a "wonderful way to start the day" at this "lover's" "getaway" on a private atoll that has "everything you can imagine"; "if you can afford it and don't mind the flight" (you'll arrive by seaplane), it's "ideal for a honeymoon" given the "private butler service", "spectacular" overwater bungalows and beach villas, and dining so good you'll "gain weight."

Soneva Fushi Resort & Spa Ⓢ🔍

▽ 28	28	25	26	$530

Kunfunadhoo Island | (011-960) 660-0304 | fax 660-0374 | www.six-senses.com | 65 villas

"Time stops" at this secluded, "died-and-went-to-heaven" resort, where you might experience "the best vacation you've ever had", as long as you remember that the "no news/no shoes policy is more agreeable than it may seem at first"; guests luxuriate in "spacious" bungalows (some over the water), each with its own outdoor shower and water garden, while being "discreetly assisted by a surprisingly professional staff"; meals too are "wonderful", as are the "fantastic" holistic spa treatments.

Taj Exotica Resort & Spa 🏨Ⓢ🌊

-	-	-	-	$850

Emboodhu Finolhu Island | South Malé Atoll | (011-960) 664-2200 | fax 664-2211 | 866-969-1825 | www.tajhotels.com | 60 villas, 2 suites

With crystal blue water in every direction you look, overwater palm-thatched huts with sun decks and 15-ft. private plunge pools, and gourmet cuisine, this resort in one of the largest lagoons in the Maldives is about as exotica as it gets; so light up the in-room candles, flick on the provided MP3 player and take it easy until it's time to muster the energy for a treatment in the Indian-themed Jiva Grande Spa.

NEW W Retreat & Spa 🏨Ⓢ🌊

-	-	-	-	$1250

North Ari Atoll | Fesdu Island | (011-960) 666-2222 | fax 666-2200 | www.whotels.com | 74 rooms, 4 suites

Amid a wealth of rich dive sites in the North Ari Atoll, this posh newcomer amps up the tropical indulgence; high-design villas – complete with plasma TVs and Bose stereos – blend into the lush flora or look out over the ocean fauna, while tempting distractions include an array of dining options, indulgent spa treatments and transparent kayaks.

Mali

Bamako

Kempinski Hôtel El Farouk 🏨🌊

-	-	-	-	$144

Quartier du Fleuve | (011-223) 222-3030 | fax 222-6161 | 800-426-3135 | www.kempinski.com | 80 rooms, 10 suites

The first Kempinski in this West African nation, this hotel in a dramatic setting on the banks of the Niger River offers rooms with satellite TVs

MAURITIUS

ROOMS
SERVICE
DINING
FACIL.
COST

and direct-dial telephones (some units have water views); other facilities include two on-site restaurants, a bar and an outdoor pool.

Malta

NEW Le Méridien ⎯ | ⎯ | ⎯ | ⎯ | $345
St. Julians 🏌️♂️ 🛁 Ⓢ 🏊

39 Main St., Balluta Bay | Valletta | (011-356) 2311-0000 | fax 2311-0001 | www.starwoodhotels.com | 243 rooms, 33 suites

With a seafront location overlooking Balluta Bay, this newcomer offers contemporary rooms with impressive water views from the balconies; other features include a spa and fitness center, a squash court, a casino, a rooftop pool and bar, restaurants offering local and French fare and an alfresco lounge with striking sunset vistas.

Mauritius

Le Prince Maurice 🏌️♂️ 🛁 Ⓢ 🏊 🔍 ⎯ | ⎯ | ⎯ | ⎯ | $1686

Choisy Rd. | Pointe de Flacq | (011-230) 413-9100 | fax 413-9129 | www.princemaurice.com | 89 suites

"Fit for a king", this "enchanting" Relais & Châteaux "secluded paradise" enjoys a "dream location" "on a remote peninsula" about 22 miles from the capital city of Port-Louis; "wood and stone" suites with "thatched roofs and enormous bathrooms" "are wonderfully spacious and romantic", "public areas are stunning, particularly at night", and the "discreet" staff provides "unbelievable" service, including setting up "private, lantern-lit" dinners "on the beach"; P.S. surveyors recommend "the half-board option", since "there are few places to eat nearby."

Le Saint Géran 🏌️♂️ ✕ 🛁 Ⓢ 🏊 🔍 ▽ 24 | 25 | 22 | 26 | $2464

Pointe de Flacq | (011-230) 401-1688 | fax 401-1668 | 866-552-0001 | www.oneandonlyresorts.com | 162 suites, 1 villa

"Heaven on earth" is yours at this "personification of paradise" on Mauritius' Belle Mare peninsula, where "you don't have to worry about anything" thanks to its "regal service", "unbeatable beach", "luxurious" suites done in colonial style and an "exquisite", Alain Ducasse restaurant (Spoon des Iles); all this "luxury" can add up to "preposterous prices", but many still rate it one of the "best places to be pampered."

Le Touessrok 🏌️♂️ 🛁 Ⓢ 🏊 🔍 ▽ 28 | 25 | 23 | 28 | $1956

Trou d'Eau Douce | (011-230) 402-7400 | fax 402-7500 | 866-522-0001 | www.oneandonlyresorts.com | 68 rooms, 132 suites, 3 villas

An "amazing" complex on the east coast of Mauritius, this renovated favorite boasts rooms and recreation spread out over three private islands, one connected to the mainland by a bridge and the others reachable by water taxi; its buildings are "gorgeous", the "sea isn't nicer anywhere" and the staff makes you "feel like you're the only client."

Oberoi 🛁 Ⓢ 🏊 ▽ 26 | 25 | 25 | 27 | $913

Pointe aux Piments | Baie aux Tortues | (011-230) 204-3600 | fax 204-3625 | 800-562-3764 | www.oberoihotels.com | 48 pavilions, 24 villas

"Everything you could wish for" – starting with that "magnificent setting" on Mauritius' northwest coast – can be found at this "stunning" resort complete with "amazing dining" and a "fabulous" Banyan Tree spa; granted, it's "expensive", but the pleasures include "beautiful rooms", a variety of activities and a staff that "seems to materialize out of thin air."

Taj Exotica Resort & Spa 👪 🔭 Ⓢ 🏊 🎾 - | - | - | - | $1189

Wolmar | Flic en Flac | (011-230) 403-1500 | fax 453-5555 | 866-969-1825 | www.tajhotels.com | 65 villas

You know you're in for a treat when your room not only offers flat-screen TVs with surround sound and a private outdoor dining area, but butler service as well; located on 27 acres overlooking Tamarin Bay with architecture that blends African and Arabic with French Colonial, this "peaceful oasis" is "the best" some have seen, with "fantastic", "unpretentious" service and facilities that include a lighted tennis court, a sports center, authentic Indian fare at Cilantro, cocktails at the Breakers Bar and several infinity pools.

Mexico

TOPS IN COUNTRY

28 One & Only | *Baja Peninsula*
Esperanza | *Baja Peninsula*
Las Ventanas | *Baja Peninsula*
27 Four Seasons | *Punta Mita*
La Casa Que Canta | *Zihuatanejo*
Ritz-Carlton | *Cancún*
Four Seasons | *Mexico City*
26 Las Mañanitas | *Cuernavaca*
Royal Hideaway | *Playa del Carmen*
25 Villa del Sol | *Zihuatanejo*

Acapulco

Fairmont Acapulco Princess, The 👪 🔭 ⛳ Ⓢ 🏊 🎾 22 | 22 | 20 | 25 | $289

Playa Revolcadero | (011-52-744) 469-1000 | fax 469-1016 | 800-441-1414 | www.fairmont.com | 923 rooms, 94 suites

"At a distance from the center of Acapulco" is a fairly "nice hotel" "frequently used by large cruise groups"; its pools and "fantastic water-slide" are "great" for the kids, while adults can be "transported" by the "lovely grounds" and the spa's "unusual treatments"; still, this "dinosaur" "has not aged gracefully" and may be in need of a "makeover."

Fairmont Pierre Marques, The 👪 🔭 ⛳ 🏊 🎾 22 | 24 | 23 | 24 | $289

Playa Revolcadero | (011-52-744) 435-2600 | fax 466-1046 | 800-441-1414 | www.fairmont.com | 295 rooms, 40 suites

Nestled in a "gorgeous location" "away from the action" of Acapulco, this "more exclusive sibling to the Fairmont Princess" was once the private getaway of J. Paul Getty, and still maintains a vibe that's both "wonderfully romantic" and "great for family vacations"; "discreet" pools, an "incredible beach", a solid golf course and a relaxing spa are pluses, as are the "refurbished" rooms and gourmet restaurants offering "fresh seafood and a beautiful view."

	ROOMS	SERVICE	DINING	FACIL.	COST

Las Brisas 🏨⊙⛱🔍
| | 25 | 25 | 21 | 25 | $500 |

Carretera Escénica 5255 | (011-52-744) 469-6900 | fax 446-5328 | 800-223-6800 | www.brisas.com.mx | 228 casitas, 35 suites

Longevity is one reason this "charming" 1950s hotel, perched on a hilltop on the Bay of Acapulco, is a local landmark, but there are many others: "spectacular views", "solitude and privacy", "can't-be-beat casitas" surrounded by 40 acres of hibiscus gardens, "elegant dining" and "old-time excellent" service; even nitpickers who note it's "starting to show signs of age" that warrant a "reevaluation" can't help being "endeared" by the "romance" of it all.

Baja Peninsula

Casa Del Mar Beach Golf & Spa Resort 🏨⊥⊙⛱🔍
| | 21 | 22 | 19 | 24 | $619 |

Carretera Transpeninsular, Km. 19,5 | Cabo San Lucas | (011-52-624) 145-7700 | fax 144-0034 | 888-227-9621 | www.casadelmarmexico.com | 33 suites

Guests at this "pristine", intimate Cabo San Lucas resort are *mucho relaxed*" thanks to its "lovely rooms" sporting Jacuzzis and "unparalleled" views of the "gorgeous beach" and surrounding championship golf course, spa, six "super pools" and other "excellent amenities"; "personalized service" from an "engaging staff" impresses, and though the "average" dining may not, given its location "close to terrific restaurants in town", "who cares?"; N.B. a post-Survey redo may outdate the above scores.

Casa Natalia ✕🏨⛱
| | 23 | 24 | 26 | 22 | $295 |

Blvd. Mijares 4 | San José del Cabo | (011-52-624) 142-5100 | fax 142-5110 | 888-277-3814 | www.casanatalia.com | 14 rooms, 2 suites

Away from the touristy Cabo crowds sits a "wonderfully charming" boutique hotel amid palm trees, waterfalls and bougainvillea; the European-Mexican Mi Cocina restaurant is "worth visiting even if you're not staying here", and the "eye-catching" rooms, with handmade furniture, local artwork and private terraces also earn praise, plus the adults-only Beach Club is a free shuttle ride away; N.B. no kids under 13.

Dreams Los Cabos Suites Golf Resort & Spa 👫🐾⛱
| | 22 | 19 | 21 | 23 | $270 |

Carretera Transpeninsular, Km. 18.5 | Los Cabos | (011-52-624) 144-0202 | fax 144-0217 | www.dreamsresorts.com | 144 rooms, 63 suites

"A *sueño* come true" for guests seeking a "good deal", this all-inclusive, all-suites resort suits both families and couples; active types enjoy the variety of land-based activities and water sports, foodies find something to like among its five restaurants and loafers laud it as a "wonderfully relaxing place to do nothing"; it's just the "usually unswimmable" surf and a staff that "needs more training" that mar the experience.

⧉ Esperanza ✕🍴🏨⊙⛱🔍
| | 28 | 28 | 26 | 28 | $575 |

Carretera Transpeninsular, Km. 7 | Cabo San Lucas | (011-52-624) 145-6400 | fax 145-6499 | 866-311-2226 | www.esperanzaresort.com | 50 casitas, 6 villas

"Celebrity spotting is as common as fresh margaritas" at this "charming, intimate" and expensive hideaway, where Gwynnie, Goldie and Sir

Paul have all reportedly slumbered; non-A-listers, too, are "pampered beyond belief" by a "caring and attentive – but not hovering" staff in "gorgeous" rooms with "huge" terraces and hammocks overlooking the Pacific; with "world-class" dining complemented by "to-die-for" views (sometimes of migrating whales) thrown into the mix, "you get what you pay for", which is a "steep" sum indeed; P.S. children under 16 are "not welcome" except in villas.

Fiesta Americana Grand Los Cabos 👫🔭⛳Ⓢ🏊🎾

ROOMS	SERVICE	DINING	FACIL.	COST
22	21	21	24	$389

Carretera Transpeninsular, Km. 10.3 | Los Cabos | (011-52-624) 145-6200 | fax 145-6265 | 800-343-7821 | www.fiestaamericana.com | 231 rooms, 19 suites

This "minimalist" "wonder" in Los Cabos sits next to "one of the world's great" golfing destinations – the Jack Nicklaus-designed Ocean Course – and putters posit "that should be enough" to merit a stay; off the links, guests cozy up in "lovely" contemporary Mexican-style rooms after hitting the "amazing infinity pools" overlooking the surf or the "terrific" buffets (which can make the rest of the culinary offerings seem "uninspired"); admirers award the staff an A for "attentive", but the "disappointed" say the service "could be better."

Finisterra, Hotel 🔭🏊🎾

ROOMS	SERVICE	DINING	FACIL.	COST
20	21	18	22	$229

Cabo San Lucas | (011-52-624) 143-3333 | fax 143-0590 | 800-347-2252 | www.finisterra.com | 183 rooms, 4 suites

The "setting is exceptional" at this "charming" "older hotel" perched on a cliff and reminiscent of "old Mexico with lots of Talavera accents"; guests grumble about being in Cabo San Lucas and not being able to swim in the ocean since it's "too rough", but the "endless" pool and swim-up bar allow for great whale watching; just beware: the "old rooms are not as nice."

[Z] Las Ventanas al Paraíso 🍴🔭Ⓢ🏊🎾

ROOMS	SERVICE	DINING	FACIL.	COST
29	28	26	28	$650

Carretera Transpeninsular, Km. 19.5 | San José del Cabo | (011-52-624) 144-2800 | fax 144-2801 | 888-767-3966 | www.lasventanas.com | 71 suites

As the name implies, these "windows to paradise" open onto a "divine" "land of their own" filled with "spectacular" views of the Sea of Cortez, "stunning" architecture and "the most amazing service on the planet"; "gorgeous" suites feature adobe fireplaces, personal telescopes and "rain showers as wonderful as the soaps and lotions" provided, plus there's "one of the best options for dining in Cabo"; just try to ignore the pesos that "disappear before your eyes" at this "ultimate resort."

[Z] One & Only Palmilla 👫🐕🔭Ⓢ🏊🎾

ROOMS	SERVICE	DINING	FACIL.	COST
29	28	26	29	$575

Carretera Transpeninsular, Km. 7.5 | San José del Cabo | (011-52-624) 146-7000 | fax 146-7001 | 866-829-2977 | www.lhw.com | 61 rooms, 111 suites

Prospective guests should pack a thesaurus since "gorgeous" and "exquisite" don't do this "alluring", "blissful" and "idyllic" resort justice (it's the top spot in Mexico in this Survey); despite its out-of-the-way location, it's "in a class by itself" with "lush" grounds "landscaped within an inch of Eden" and "scenery that screams 'paradise'"; rooms are "spacious" and have terrace daybeds and personal telescopes, service is "impeccable", especially the "addictive" round-the-clock butlering, and dining, which includes Charlie Trotter's C restaurant, is "world-class."

Rancho La Puerta 🛁 🔭 [S] 🏊 🎾 — 23 | 25 | 23 | 28 | $481

Tecate | (011-52-665) 654-9155 | fax 654-1108 | 800-443-7565 | www.rancholapuerta.com | 44 haciendas, 32 studios, 9 villas

Since 1940, fitness fiends and soul-searchers looking to "recharge their batteries" have flocked to this destination spa at the foot of Mount Kuchumaa, where they "relish in healthy diversions" like sunrise hikes, yoga and "the best rabbit food imaginable" (meals are modified vegetarian); in keeping with the "adult summer camp" experience, there are no phones or TVs and no luxurious accommodations, but there is an "attentive" staff, an abundance of "camaraderie" and activities that just may "change your life."

Twin Dolphin, Hotel 🐕 🔭 🏊 🎾 — 22 | 23 | 22 | 23 | $395

Cabo San Lucas | (011-52-624) 145-8191 | fax 145-8196 | 800-421-8925 | www.twindolphin.com | 34 rooms, 16 suites

"Get disconnected from civilization" "with no phones or TVs", just plenty of nature and "Zen tranquility" amid "whitewashed rooms scattered around the rocks" far "away from town"; "the rooms are pretty bare", but "minimal" trappings mean maximum "relaxation" where the boob tube is swapped for whale sightings in the "Pacific crashing below your balcony"; even if it is "a little frayed at the edges", this "small, luxury" spot remains "great after all these years."

Westin Resort & Spa Los Cabos 👪 🔭 [S] 🏊 🎾 — 23 | 22 | 21 | 25 | $359

Carretera Transpeninsular, Km. 22.5 | San José del Cabo | (011-52-624) 142-9000 | fax 142-9050 | 800-228-3000 | www.westin.com | 229 rooms, 14 suites

"Candyland meets Frank Lloyd Wright" at this "colorful" and "exciting architectural gem" that "blends into" its surroundings on the tip of the peninsula; a "refreshingly clean resort" "good for families", it impresses with seven "tremendous" pools leading down to a "beautiful" beach (though the ocean is not swimmable), "large, bright and comfortable" rooms, a staff "devoted to making you feel welcome", "world-class golf" and varied, if somewhat "expensive", dining options; P.S. "angled balconies" offer an uninterrupted panorama of the Sea of Cortez from inside the rooms.

Cancún

TOPS IN CITY

- 27 Ritz-Carlton
- 25 Maroma
- JW Marriott
- 23 Iberostar
- Hilton Beach

Aventura Spa Palace Resort [S] 🏊 🎾 — 22 | 24 | 20 | 25 | $400

Carretera Cancún-Tulum, Km. 72 | (011-52-984) 875-1100 | fax 875-1101 | 877-505-5515 | www.spa-palace-resorts.com | 1224 rooms, 42 suites

"Detail-oriented" staffers "make you feel welcome" at this "big", "tranquil" adults-only resort appreciated for its "exquisite" seaside grounds featuring "myriad pools", "amazing" spa and numerous activities from yoga and tennis to climbing and water sports (plus "access to other Palace resorts" via "free shuttle"); "comfy" rooms and a variety of restaurants have most touting it as a "good value", though gourmands grumble that the food, while "good for an all-inclusive", tends toward the "basic and repetitive."

CasaMagna Marriott Resort 👪 🔭 Ⓢ 🏊 — 21 | 21 | 20 | 23 | $309

Blvd. Kukulcán, Retorno Chac L-41 | (011-52-998) 881-2000 | fax 881-2085 | 800-228-9290 | www.marriott.com | 401 rooms, 31 suites

At this "gorgeous" beachside lodge, families enjoy the "central" Hotel Zone location ("a little removed" from "noisy" party-centric Downtown), while lovebirds gravitate to its "very good spa" and enjoy "intimate romantic dinners" overlooking the "beautiful" beach and pool; "typical Marriott" hallmarks like "comfortable rooms" and "consistent service" are appreciated, but a "disappointed" contingent claims the Spanish-themed surroundings are starting to feel a little "worn out."

Dreams Resort & Spa 👪 🛁 🔭 Ⓢ 🏊 — 19 | 20 | 20 | 20 | $355

Punta Cancún | (011-52-998) 848-7000 | fax 848-7001 | 866-237-3267 | www.dreamsresorts.com | 363 rooms, 18 suites

"You can ignore" Cancún when "ensconced" in this "sprawling" all-inclusive with a "lovely setting" that includes a "gorgeous pool", "delicious" white-sand beach and "amazing views"; but those who aren't dreaming say the "restaurants leave a lot to be desired" and this "'70s pyramid" "is showing its age."

[NEW] Excellence Riviera 🔭 Ⓢ 🏊 🎾 — ▽ 27 | 27 | 26 | 28 | $820

Carretera Federal 307 | (011-52-998) 872-8500 | fax 872-8501 | www.excellence-resorts.com | 440 suites

With a deluge of dining options – namely eight restaurants and 10 bars – and an abundance of activities, including yoga, hiking, snorkeling and Spanish lessons, guests at this all-inclusive, all-suites resort on the Riviera Maya feel like they're "part of the rich and famous" on "a cruise without the ship"; rooms that feature furnished patios and whirlpool tubs, as well as the "excellent" service, live up to the resort's name; N.B. no children under 18.

Fiesta Americana Grand Coral Beach 👪 🔭 Ⓢ 🏊 🎾 — 23 | 22 | 21 | 25 | $322

Blvd. Kukulcán, Km. 9.5 | (011-52-998) 881-3200 | fax 881-3288 | 800-343-7821 | www.fiestaamericana.com | 602 suites

Feel "filthy rich" at this "classy", "contemporary" central Cancún behemoth, whose public spaces gleam as if "they polished the marble with toothbrushes" and are manned by a "top-notch" staff; given its "surprisingly large" all-suites rooms, "excellent" spa and "fully equipped gym", tennis center, "incredible" pool and "amazing" (if "narrow") beach, it's no wonder devotees keep returning.

Gran Meliá 👪 🔭 Ⓢ 🏊 🎾 — 21 | 21 | 19 | 22 | $245

Blvd. Kukulcán, Km. 16.5 | (011-52-998) 881-1100 | fax 881-1740 | 888-956-3542 | www.solmelia.com | 640 rooms, 38 suites

As "aesthetically appealing on the outside as they come" shout spring breakers of this Mayan temple-style resort with a "glass atrium in the lobby" featuring "lots of plants"; there's a cool pool where they "can sun all day with a view of the ocean" and stay till "happy hour", then "swim right up to the bar", but a few say it's "not as good as it's hyped to be."

Hilton Beach & Golf Resort 👪 🔭 ⛳ [S] 🏊 🎾

Rooms	Service	Dining	Facil.	Cost
24	23	20	25	$299

Blvd. Kukulcán, Km. 17 | (011-52-998) 881-8000 | fax 881-8080 | 800-445-8667 | www.hilton.com | 321 rooms, 23 suites, 82 villas

With contemporary Mexican decor and architecture inspired by ancient Mayan pyramids, this "well-maintained" resort "on the crystal blue sea" caters to families seeking a "lively" international experience without "the frat party antics"; fans praise the "attentive" service, "spacious" pool complex and "well-appointed" rooms (with villas that are "worth the upgrade"), but some surveyors find the dining disappointing - "luckily, lots of good inexpensive options are easily accessible."

Hyatt Caribe Villas & Resort 🏊

Rooms	Service	Dining	Facil.	Cost
21	18	19	21	$219

Blvd. Kukulcán, Km. 10.5 | (011-52-998) 848-7800 | fax 883-2715 | 800-223-1234 | www.cancun.caribe.hyatt.com | 233 rooms, 55 villas

For a vacation that's as "good for kids" as it is for parents, this "family place" keeps everyone busy in the day with "lots of activities" like sailing, snorkeling and scuba diving, and at night with a jazz club and "memorable" "oceanfront dining"; even after a major renovation that "freshened and lightened" the rooms and the "worth-the-price" beachside villas, the overall look still strikes some as a bit on the "plain" side.

Iberostar Paraiso Lindo 👪 🔭 ⛳ [S] 🏊 🎾

Rooms	Service	Dining	Facil.	Cost
23	23	20	26	$191

Carretera Chetumal Puerto Juarez, Km. 309 | Riviera Maya | (011-52-984) 877-2800 | fax 877-2849 | www.iberostar.com | 382 rooms, 64 suites

"All-inclusive" has a double meaning here since this sprawling "family-oriented" resort on the Playa Paraiso encompasses just about everything: 12 restaurants, 14 bars, five "outstanding" pools (including a wave pool and lazy river), a salon, a golf course and a supermarket; understandably, "there are a lot of activities going on", so some say you'll need to "subscribe to the theory that bigger is always better" to truly enjoy it, though a staff who "can't do enough for you" helps it run smoothly.

JW Marriott Resort & Spa 👪 🔭 [S] 🏊 🎾

Rooms	Service	Dining	Facil.	Cost
25	24	22	26	$529

Blvd. Kukulcán, Km. 14.5 | (011-52-998) 848-9600 | fax 848-9601 | 800-228-9290 | www.marriott.com | 374 rooms, 74 suites

Top-to-bottom renovations have advanced this once just-plain resort into a "stellar" "slice of paradise"; refurbished rooms are "elegant" with "high-end bathrooms large enough to live in" and upgrades like flat-screen TVs and "comfy plush beds"; other comforts include a "top-notch" spa, "incredible" pools, 24-hour room service, WiFi access (even on the beach) and employees who "fall over each other to assist you."

Le Méridien Cancún Resort & Spa 🐕 🔭 [S] 🏊 🎾

Rooms	Service	Dining	Facil.	Cost
24	24	21	23	$325

Retorno del Rey, Km. 14 | (011-52-998) 881-2200 | fax 881-2201 | 800-543-4300 | www.lemeridien.com | 187 rooms, 26 suites

Visitors to this "boutique-style" surfside hotel call it *muy* "classy for Cancún", citing its "off-the-beaten-craziness" tranquility as well as its "beautiful", "super-clean, comfy rooms" and "casually friendly yet professional" service; the bi-level pool's a "highlight", as are the popular fitness center and European spa ("makes this resort really special"), but the restaurants elicit mixed reactions ("great" vs. "dine elsewhere!").

Maroma Resort & Spa 🛏🏋Ⓢ🏊🎾 25 | 25 | 24 | 25 | $570

Carretera Cancún-Tulum, Km. 51 | Riviera Maya | (011-52-998) 872-8200 | fax 872-8220 | 866-454-9351 | www.maromahotel.com | 47 rooms, 18 suites

Find "old Mexico at her most romantic" via this "idyllic hideaway" in the Yucatán jungle 20 miles outside Cancún, where a "beautifully trained staff" guides guests to "exceptional", authentically rustic rooms that open onto lush gardens or the "top-notch, swimmable beach"; the "excellent" food's "expensive", as is most "everything extra", but fans say "you pay, but you're happy"; N.B. no kids under 12 or 16, depending on the time of year.

Omni Hotel & Villas 👪🏋Ⓢ🏊🎾 ▽ 18 | 19 | 17 | 21 | $395

Blvd. Kukulcán, Km. 16.5 | (011-52-998) 881-0600 | fax 885-0059 | 800-843-6664 | www.omnihotels.com | 273 rooms, 60 suites, 20 villas

"Totally lovely" enthuse wallet-watchers who find this recently renovated resort a "relatively affordable" all-inclusive option when they want to just "relax" in a beachfront mega Jacuzzi or beside "beautiful" tropical-garden-trimmed pools and "swim-up bars"; but the quality of dining and rooms are open to debate - some find the quarters "very nice", others "below average."

[Z] Ritz-Carlton, The 👪🍴🏋Ⓢ🏊🎾 27 | 28 | 25 | 27 | $649

Retorno del Rey, Km. 36 | (011-52-998) 881-0808 | fax 881-0815 | 800-241-3333 | www.ritzcarlton.com | 315 rooms, 50 suites

"Impeccable" service, "gorgeous surroundings" and "exceptionally well-appointed" rooms (gourmet coffee makers, flat-screen TVs, rainforest showerheads) have admirers calling this "glorious Yucatán escape" "far away from the tourist crush and kitsch" of the city "the best hotel in Cancún"; other highlights include a "spectacular and very private" beach, "to-die-for" dining and "over-the-top" details like chilled towels in the fitness center and bath butlers who draw aromatherapy soaks for guests.

Secreto, Hotel 🏋🏊 - | - | - | - | $185

Punta Norte | Isla Mujeres | (011-52-998) 877-1039 | fax 877-1048 | www.hotelsecreto.com | 9 rooms

A "great little hideaway" in the Mexican fishing village of Isla Mujeres, this "charming" little spot won't stay a secret for long, since "one glance at the infinity pool overlooking Halfmoon Beach and you'll be hooked"; there's a "good mix of international guests and locals", and the "modern" high design includes rooms with private terraces, canopy beds, floor-to-ceiling windows, stone floors and original artwork, plus service is "personal and unaffected."

Secrets Capri Riviera Cancun 🏋Ⓢ🏊🎾 ▽ 26 | 25 | 24 | 25 | $408

Carretera Federal 387, Km. 299 | Riviera Maya | (011-52-984) 873-4880 | fax 873-4881 | www.secretsresorts.com | 186 rooms, 104 suites

Located on the Mexican Riviera, just minutes from ancient Mayan ruins and one of the world's longest barrier reefs, this "subdued" adults-only "top-level" all-inclusive is a "great place to get away from your kids and just chill"; it gets high marks for the "amazing" spa, "excellent cuisine" and in-room amenities including Jacuzzis, minibars, Internet access and 24-hour room service, though you "must" get one "with a full ocean view" to best appreciate the surroundings; N.B. no guests under 18.

Villa Rolandi Gourmet & Beach Club 👬🏖

| ∇ 22 | 26 | 28 | 21 | $380 |

Isla Mujeres | (011-52-998) 877-0500 | fax 877-0100 | 800-525-4800 | www.villarolandi.com | 28 suites

"Mellow, gorgeous and private", this "adorable" little spot accessible via yacht from the mainland is a "must-stay" on Isla Mujeres; "great" nightly Italian "meals by the sea" win applause as does the service and the "very transparent" ocean waters (though some prefer the "divine" pool, since the beach can get crowded with "day-trippers"); suites boast Jacuzzis and high-speed Internet, while a thalassotherapy spa is slated for 2007.

Westin Resort & Spa 👬🍴👬☺🏖⚓

| 21 | 21 | 18 | 20 | $469 |

Blvd. Kukulcán, Km. 20 | (011-52-998) 848-7400 | fax 885-0779 | 800-228-3000 | www.westin.com | 360 rooms, 19 suites

"Spectacular views" and sleek, "comfortable" rooms enhance the "truly relaxing" stays at this resort "at the very end of hotel row", where a "choice of pools" ensures "peace and quiet" even "when children invade"; before heading to the "rocking" spa or superior snorkeling amid the off-shore reefs, make sure you fill up on the "great breakfast" – some say the rest of the "plentiful food" is "nothing to write home about."

Cuernavaca

Las Mañanitas ✕👬🏖

| 25 | 27 | 27 | 24 | $210 |

Ricardo Linares 107 | (011-52-777) 314-1466 | fax 318-3672 | 888-413-9199 | www.lasmananitas.com.mx | 28 suites

"Enchanting" and "intimate" is how infatuated surveyors describe this Relais & Châteaux "heaven on earth" "where peacocks roam and palm trees sway" and the staff is "laid-back" yet "attentive"; the hotel's colonial elegance, accented by an impressive art collection, makes for "truly special" rooms, and the "outstanding" Mexican-International restaurant is considered among the most famous in the world – it might just be the "ultimate", "romantic" spot "for a getaway with your lover."

Guadalajara

Camino Real 👬👬🏖⚓

| 22 | 23 | 22 | 22 | $275 |

Ave. Vallarta 5005 | (011-52-333) 134-2424 | fax 134-2404 | 800-722-6466 | www.caminoreal.com | 198 rooms, 7 suites

In this "nice enough hotel", known as a "reliable chain" link, renovated rooms are "large", there are "lovely surroundings and grounds" with four swimming pools and a kids' play area, and the "breakfast buffet" is "amazing"; though some conclude it's merely "fine", others say it's "the place" where you'll want to stay.

Ixtapa

Las Brisas 👫🏨🏊🎾

| 21 | 22 | 19 | 24 | $411 |

Playa Vistahermosa | (011-52-755) 553-2121 | fax 553-1038 |
888-559-4329 | www.brisas.com.mx | 390 rooms, 26 suites

"Why go home" when "every room faces the ocean" and boasts a "balcony complete with lounge chairs and hammock"? reflect regulars who are content to stay at this "architecturally magnificent hotel, built on the side of a mountain, overlooking its own large private beach"; instead, they'll just lounge in the four swimming pools, applaud "the sunset from the lobby bar" and revel in all the "Mexican style."

Manzanillo

Las Alamandas 👫🏨🏊🎾

| - | - | - | - | $360 |

Carvetera Federal 200, Km. 83 | (011-52-322) 285-5500 | fax 285-5027 |
888-882-9616 | www.alamandas.com | 14 suites

"Get away from the world" at this "secluded", "great-for-honeymoons" "classic", located "in the middle of nowhere" between Puerto Vallarta and Manzanillo; set in a "beautiful" 1,500-acre property with three "private beaches" and its own landing strip, the luxury suites are done up with bright colors and Mexican folk art; personalized service, gourmet cuisine, spa services and amenities like complimentary one-hour horseback rides help ensure that "guests are treated right."

Las Hadas
Golf Resort & Marina 👫🏨⛳🏊🎾

| 23 | 22 | 20 | 23 | $248 |

Ave. Vista Hermosa | (011-52-314) 331-0101 | fax 331-0121 |
888-559-4329 | www.brisas.com.mx | 204 rooms, 30 suites

An "architectural wonder" "reminiscent of an old Moorish castle" that "overlooks the marina and the town", this "true getaway" has singles saying they made a mistake by going alone since it's clearly "honeymoon central"; it may be "still living off its prominent role in the [1979] movie *10*", since some say "the beach is only so-so" and the food "average", but others find a "wonderful spot to relax and do some fishing."

Mexico City

Camino Real 👫✕🏊🎾

| 22 | 23 | 23 | 23 | $280 |

Mariano Escobedo 700 | (011-52-55) 5263-8888 | fax 5263-8889 |
800-722-6466 | www.caminoreal.com | 667 rooms, 45 suites

This "boutique" "visual masterpiece" is designed in "beautiful" Nouveau Mexican architecture with "cool geometric styling" featuring "20th-century masterpieces", gardens and "large rooms" that "vary depending on the section" they're in; with "some of the best dinner spots in Mexico City" – China Grill and Le Cirque – and a "great" location in Polanco, many would "come back" again.

🅩 Four Seasons 👫✕🍽🛎🏨🕐🏊

| 28 | 28 | 25 | 26 | $345 |

Paseo de la Reforma 500 | (011-52-55) 5230-1818 | fax 5230-1808 |
800-906-7500 | www.fourseasons.com | 200 rooms, 40 suites

The "fabulous" architecture "feels like Mexico" but everything else about this "truly exceptional" "oasis" on the Reforma is quintessential Four Seasons, from the "huge rooms that open into a lush interior courtyard" to "fantastic service" that's a "benchmark in Latin America" to "sophisticated dining" "with imaginative menus", not to mention "divine margaritas"; it's all "so lovely" that you "shouldn't stay anywhere else."

Habitá Hotel 🔭Ⓢ🏊 — 22 | 19 | 20 | 20 | $265

Ave. Presidente Masaryk 201 | (011-52-55) 5282-3100 | fax 5282-3101 | www.hotelhabita.com | 32 rooms, 4 suites

From the get-go, you can tell this former 1950s apartment building encased in blue-green sandblasted glass isn't the warm and fuzzy type; rather, the "über-chic" boutique in the "trendy" Polanco district caters to the "young and hip" with "ultramodern" decor, including Eames chairs, flat-screen TVs and stainless-steel accents in the "small, sparse rooms"; the "effective" but "slightly arrogant" staff is par for the course, but the "fabulous" rooftop terrace bar and pool deck with "magnificent views" are nice surprises.

JW Marriott Ⓢ🏊 — 25 | 25 | 21 | 23 | $399

Andres Bello 29 | (011-52-55) 5999-0000 | fax 5999-0001 | 800-228-9290 | www.marriott.com | 283 rooms, 28 suites

Situated "in the best part of Mexico City", the fashionable Polanco district, this "surprisingly nice" hotel features "great modern Mexican architecture", a pool on the seventh floor, and "large rooms" that boast "generally good views" and "Mexican amenities such as Talavera pottery in every bathroom"; with its "attentive staff" that is "friendly yet formal" and "fabulous food at reasonable prices", it's a solid option, especially for business travelers.

Marquis Reforma 🔭Ⓢ🏊 — ∇ 20 | 21 | 18 | 20 | $350

Paseo de la Reforma 465 | (011-52-55) 5229-1200 | fax 5229-1250 | 800-235-2387 | www.marquisreforma.com | 125 rooms, 84 suites

A fully equipped business center and "really sweet" gym make this executive hotel a "solid" choice for expense-accounters, while lower weekend rates ensure that pleasure-seekers have plenty of extra pesos for the fab shopping of nearby Zona Rosa; adding to the "nice ambiance" is an "expensive"-looking art deco design, a pleasant staff and a "good location" in the heart of the Financial District.

Nikko, Hotel 🔭🏊🎾 — 22 | 23 | 22 | 23 | $300

Campos Eliseos 204 | (011-52-55) 5283-8700 | fax 5280-9191 | www.hotelnikkomexico.com.mx | 728 rooms, 24 suites

White-collar travelers find "every detail is carefully attended" to at this "safe, clean and centralized" Financial District tower boasting a 24-hour biz center and health club with tennis courts, spa services and a practice golf range; "Asian-influenced" modernity and "great views" from the "technically advanced" rooms make staying inside a pleasure, and "sooo good" Japanese fare from the "excellent" restaurants adds to a fine night out.

W Mexico City 🐕🔭Ⓢ🏊 — 22 | 20 | 19 | 22 | $369

Campos Eliseos 252 | (011-52-55) 9138-1800 | fax 9138-1899 | 877-946-8357 | www.whotels.com | 214 rooms, 23 suites

"The fiesta never stops" at the W's first foray into Mexico; for starters, there are those "hot and sexy" guestrooms, decked out in cherry red and ebony, and bathrooms with soak tubs, hammocks and "killer views", then there's the "extremely friendly" staff that includes "cute" bell boys who will "flirt you peso dry" and the "hopping" "madhouse" of a lobby bar; party-poopers maintain the "ultrahip" vibe is so much "style over substance."

Monterrey

Quinta Real Monterrey

▽ 25 | 25 | 23 | 24 | $300

Diego Rivera 500, Oriente | (011-52-81) 8368-1000 | fax 8368-1070 | 866-621-9288 | www.quintareal.com | 165 suites

Located on the edge of the Sierra Madre Oriental mountain range 15 minutes from Downtown Monterrey, this all-suites hotel embraces both tourists and corporate travelers with its colonial-style decor, modern amenities and "excellent business facilities"; "large" "beautifully decorated" rooms feature a sitting area or separate living room with work space, minibar, TV and Hermès toiletries, and the "amazing" "power" bar also wins praise; N.B. a new pool and spa will open in 2007.

Oaxaca

Camino Real 🔭🏊

23 | 24 | 22 | 23 | $270

Calle 5 de Mayo 300 | (011-52-951) 501-6100 | fax 516-0732 | 800-722-6466 | www.caminoreal.com | 85 rooms, 6 suites

This is an "oasis of calm and civility", in a "centuries-old building that was, in previous times, a prison as well as a convent" before undergoing a "stunning renovation"; "remnants of ancient frescoes adorn the walls", and while "some rooms are small and others have no outward facing windows", each has its own unique "personality and charm"; "wonderful grounds", "beautiful tile work" and "lovely, poolside gardens" make this "star in Oaxaca" shine brightly as a "base for further exploring."

Playa del Carmen

Deseo Hotel & Lounge 🔭🏊

22 | 19 | 18 | 21 | $148

5a Ave. y Calle 12 | (011-52-984) 879-3620 | fax 879-3621 | 800-337-4685 | www.hoteldeseo.com | 12 rooms, 3 suites

This "sleek, modern" property brings "Miami chic" to "an old-fashioned beach resort" with "lots of wood and white stucco", "stylish" rooms hung in flowing curtains and hammocks and a "great party scene" around the "raging swim-up bar" at a "pool with lights that change colors"; "don't stay here" for "peace and quiet", but for grooving to "techno" on an outdoor lounge bed amid "beautiful" "twentysomething" "hipsters."

Ikal del Mar 🔭Ⓢ🏊

▽ 28 | 27 | 28 | 26 | $625

Riviera Maya | (011-52-984) 877-3000 | fax 877-3009 | 888-230-7330 | www.ikaldelmar.com | 30 villas

"It's like visiting Bali without the 24-hour flight" say fans of this eco-resort deep in the Mayan jungle, where the separate thatched-roof "villas with private plunge pools", outdoor showers and terraces featuring chaise lounges and "crocheted hammocks" make this an "absolutely amazing" location for a "romantic getaway", espcially since there are no motorized vehicles or cell phones allowed and no artificial lighting (just torches) in the public areas; don't miss the "night massage near the beach" or the Mediterranean-Mexican and Mayan cuisine at Azul; P.S. "bring your platinum card!"

	ROOMS	SERVICE	DINING	FACIL.	COST

☑ Royal Hideaway Playacar ✕ ♨Ⓢ☼🍸

| 25 | 27 | 25 | 26 | $689 |

Lote Hotelero 6 | (011-52-984) 873-4500 | fax 873-4506 | 800-999-9182 | www.royalhideaway.com | 192 rooms, 8 suites

"Gorgeous rooms", "impeccable service" and "immaculate grounds" are only a few reasons admirers say this beachfront "paradise" surrounded by 13 acres of tropical foliage is "five-star all the way"; foodies praise the "varied", "divine" cuisine as the "finest dining at an all-inclusive anywhere", while the spa and signature mango margaritas both add, in their own ways, to the "relaxing" vibe; just be warned, you may "check out with a zero bank balance"; N.B. no children under 13 allowed.

Puerto Vallarta

CasaMagna Marriott Resort ♟♨☼🍸

| 21 | 23 | 20 | 25 | $319 |

Paseo de la Marina 5, Marina Vallarta | (011-52-322) 226-0000 | fax 226-0063 | 800-228-2290 | www.marriott.com | 404 rooms, 29 suites

Although "lotsa kids" have the run of this "huge" but "elegant" bayside resort, grown-ups still say it's "relaxing" and boasts most "everything you could want": "extensive" gardens, "nicely appointed" interiors and a "helpful staff"; those who say the "rocky" beach is "uninviting" allow that the "pool with swim-up bar more than makes up for it", while foodies who find the cuisine "generic" recommend "eating out Downtown" or at the marina (a "short walk" away).

Dreams Resort & Spa ♟♨Ⓢ☼🍸

| ▽ 24 | 23 | 22 | 26 | $330 |

Playa las Estacas | (011-52-322) 226-5000 | fax 221-6000 | 866-237-3267 | www.dreamsresorts.com | 326 rooms, 11 suites

With a "secluded location" on one of "the most beautiful" beaches in Puerto Vallarta, this "private" all-inclusive is a "relaxing" respite that's also "close to town"; there's an "experienced, friendly" staff, club rooms with hot tubs, a spa and plenty of *palapas* for everyone.

La Jolla de Mismaloya ♟♨☼🍸

| 19 | 19 | 15 | 21 | $182 |

Zona Hotelera, Km. 11.5 | (011-52-322) 226-0660 | fax 228-0500 | 877-868-6124 | www.barcelo.com | 304 suites

Like a "movie fantasy" of tropical "isolation" at all-inclusive "budget" prices, this "lovely" all-suiter is considered a "wonderful deal"; whether it's taking advantage of "great excursions" like hiking and fishing or just sipping "large, delicious drinks" by the "gorgeous" pool, there's plenty of "fun" to be had for families and honeymooners alike, though a few grumble about the dining options (the food "gets a little tiring") and location "a ways out of town."

NH Krystal ☼🍸

| ▽ 16 | 20 | 17 | 19 | $120 |

Ave. de las Garzas | (011-52-322) 224-0202 | fax 224-0222 | 888-726-0528 | www.nh-hotels.com | 379 rooms, 11 suites, 12 villas

"Say *hola* to a great deal" at this "tranquil retreat" in a "perfect location" close to town; it's "built horizontally" hacienda-style, so "if the tram isn't available, you need good shoes to walk" to the "three large pools" or "cozy breakfast courtyard" from your "spacious suite" or "comfortable, no-frills room"; don't sweat the heat, though – "just grab a towel and head" to the "fabulous beach" where "*palapas* provide shade."

ROOMS | SERVICE | DINING | FACIL. | COST

Westin Resort & Spa 👪 🏋 Ⓢ 🏊 🎾 — 22 | 21 | 18 | 24 | $559

Paseo de la Marina 205 | (011-52-322) 226-1100 | fax 226-1131 | 800-228-3000 | www.westin.com | 266 rooms, 14 suites

A "showy" set of "interlinked", "almost sculptural" pools are the highlight of this "overall beautiful" property in a destination resort town with "plenty of activities for everyone" (including a kids' club); the "staff is warm and efficient", and balconied rooms have many sitting pretty (for the best view, ask for "an upper floor"), though some remain iffy, citing an "Americanized" marina setting and "minimal character."

Punta Mita

[Z] **Four Seasons** 👪 🍴 🛎 🏋 ⛳ Ⓢ 🏊 🎾 — 28 | 28 | 25 | 28 | $545

Bahia de Banderas | (011-52-329) 291-6000 | fax 291-6015 | 800-332-3442 | www.fourseasons.com | 114 rooms, 26 suites

The staff must be "clairvoyant" at this "oasis of elegance" since "it seems to know what you want before you ask"; in a "gorgeous", "isolated setting" an hour from Puerta Vallarta, it "defines tropical luxury" with "awesome facilities" including beach hammocks and personal *palapas,* a free-form infinity pool serving hourly amenities, a "magnificent" Jack Nicklaus-designed golf course and an "amazing" spa; "bring money" because the "food, drink" and room rates "will cost you", but most "love it" regardless; N.B. a new beach restaurant opens in 2007.

San Miguel de Allende

Antigua Villa Santa Mónica Ⓗ 🏋 🏊 — ▽ 22 | 25 | 21 | 24 | $185

Baeza 22 | (011-52-415) 152-0427 | fax 152-0518 | www.antiguavillasantamonica.com | 14 suites

A "gem" of a colonial hotel in a historic setting, this tiny, "arty" inn "away from the hustle and bustle of Zocalo" dates from the 17th century; it was purchased in 1930 by opera singer Jose Mojica, and offers some rooms with balconies and a "lovely" outside patio for dining; a few find this secret "paradise" their "favorite" in the area.

Casa de Sierra Nevada 🍴 🏋 🏊 — 24 | 26 | 24 | 22 | $279

Hospicio 35 | (011-52-415) 152-7040 | fax 152-1436 | 800-701-1561 | www.casadesierranevada.com | 17 rooms, 16 suites

A "cool, quiet" retreat awaits at this Orient-Express hotel in the heart of a historic mountain town, where each "unique" room is "furnished with local handicrafts" and "transports you to Spanish colonial times" (the hotel is comprised of renovated colonial houses); no kids under 16 allowed, which makes it easier to enjoy the fireplaces that several rooms feature - just get up in time for breakfast at the "divine restaurant."

Tulum

Maya Tulum Wellness Retreat & Spa 🏋 Ⓢ — ▽ 21 | 22 | 17 | 25 | $145

Carretera Boca Paila Punta Allen, Km. 7 | (011-52-984) 877-8638 | fax 770-785-9260 | 888-515-4580 | www.mayatulum.com | 41 rooms, 2 suites

"Get away from it all" at this "laid-back" health-focused hideaway, located on the Yucatán Peninsula near the Tulum ruins; rebuilt in late

2005 after Hurricanes Wilma and Emily, the "pretty basic", electricity-free thatched-roof cabanas feature open showers, sitting areas and views of the ocean, gardens or "endless", "gorgeous" beach; all-inclusive packages, such as the Mind-Body-Spirit deal, include "wonderful" yoga classes, "excellent" vegetarian (plus seafood) cuisine and Mayan-inspired treatments at the extensive spa.

Zihuatanejo

[Z] La Casa Que Canta ✗🔭🏊 29 | 28 | 26 | 26 | $415

Camino Escénico a Playa la Ropa SN | (011-52-755) 555-7030 | fax 554-7900 | 888-523-5050 | www.casaquecanta.com | 25 suites, 2 resort homes

If a house *could* sing, as this "enchanting" property's name suggests, the tune here would be "pure understated luxury"; infatuated guests gush that the "cliffside marvel" overlooking Zihuatanejo Bay is "spectacular in every way" from a "sweet and efficient" staff to "out-of-this-world" cuisine, but it's the "romantic" details like flower petal arrangements on the beds at turndown and the fact that no two rooms are alike that make it "a dream come true."

Villa del Sol, Hotel 👪🔭[S]🏊🎾 26 | 26 | 24 | 24 | $430

Playa la Ropa | (011-52-755) 555-5500 | fax 554-2758 | 888-389-2645 | www.hotelvilladelsol.com | 35 rooms, 36 suites

Pampered patrons appreciate a staff that is "always there but never there", adding to the "peace and tranquility" that pervades this "excellent little gem" in the Zihuatanejo area; indeed, the "beautiful" garden-laden grounds, complete with four pools (including an infinity-edger that visually spills onto the beach), and a range of "incredible" accommodations, will leave you with "little need to leave the resort", so "relax, read, walk on the beach, drink margaritas" and feast on "delicious" food.

Monaco

Monte Carlo

Columbus Monaco 👪🔭🏊 ▽ 22 | 23 | 23 | 22 | $350

23 ave. des Papalins | (011-377) 9205-9000 | fax 9205-2386 | www.columbushotels.com | 153 rooms, 28 suites

A "super-cool" sleek, minimalist design and a "fun location" make this boutique hotel a haven for hipsters and others who appreciate its high style; rooms have dark woods, French deco decor and garden or water views, while an on-site, state-of-the-art gym and restaurant are further draws; dubbed "a W hotel with better lighting" by one reviewer, it's definitely for those who've "had enough of old-world charm" and want the "modern" thing.

[Z] de Paris, Hôtel [H]👪🔭[S]🏊🎾 26 | 26 | 28 | 26 | $792

Place du Casino | (011-377) 9806-3016 | fax 9806-3850 | 800-595-0898 | www.montecarloresort.com | 112 rooms, 75 suites

"It doesn't get better" than this "elegant" 1864 "high French" "grande dame", a "world-class" palace located a dice roll from the Monte Carlo Casino in the "heart of Monaco"; "lovely", "traditional" rooms offer "amazing" harbor or town views, and staffers make "guests feel like royalty"; lose yourself in the luxe 66,000-sq.-ft. Thermes Marins spa or savor some of the "best dining in Europe" at Alain Ducasse's "phenomenal" Louis XV restaurant – just be sure to "bring your wallet."

Fairmont Monte Carlo 🍴🏋💰🏊

| 20 | 20 | 18 | 18 | $461 |

12 ave. des Spélugues | (011-377) 9350-6500 | fax 9330-0157 |
800-257-7544 | www.montecarlograndhotel.com | 579 rooms, 40 suites

"Be sure to get a room facing the Mediterranean" for "unimaginable" views at this convention resort known as Monte Carlo's "fantastic value"; a "great location" and private balconies in all accommodations please guests, as do solid service and six bars and restaurants; the rooftop pool is "exceptionally noteworthy" too, but for the jackpot-jazzed it's the in-house Sun Casino that gets the "ahhhhhhs."

Hermitage, Hôtel 🍴🛎💰🏊

| 25 | 26 | 24 | 25 | $654 |

Sq. Beaumarchais | (011-377) 9806-4812 | fax 9806-3852 | 800-595-0898 |
www.montecarloresort.com | 226 rooms, 46 suites, 8 apartments

"Quiet, professional" and "luxurious", this "stylish" belle epoque choice is a "delightful respite from the buzz of Monaco"; "extra-large" rooms "decorated with taste" offer "beautiful" harbor vistas, and the "impeccable" service is "friendly" too; for a "memorable experience" enjoy breakfast or a "romantic" dinner at its "excellent" Le Vistamar restaurant, or hit the pool at the "great" Thermes Marins – it's the "spot to relax", but Yanks be warned: "topless is de rigueur."

Metropole, Hotel 🍴✕💰🏊

| ▽ 22 | 22 | 23 | 24 | $700 |

4, ave. de la Madone | (011-377) 9315-1515 | fax 9324-2444 |
800-223-6800 | www.metropole.mc | 82 rooms, 59 suites, 5 apartments

Fit for a queen (or someone with a similar purse and aesthetic), this "terrific" old-school hotel has emerged from a "nice renovation" that pairs classic European styling with modern amenities; the elegant French eats at Joël Robuchon are nearly matched by the stunning views of Monte Carlo and the new "magical" ESPA spa.

Morocco

Casablanca

Le Royal Mansour Méridien 🛎

| ▽ 23 | 21 | 21 | 21 | $391 |

27, ave. de l'Armée Royale | (011-212-2) 231-3011 | fax 229-5508 |
800-543-4300 | www.lemeridien.com | 159 rooms, 22 suites

This longtime (circa 1952) Casablancan hotel offers a "convenient location" opposite the Hassan II mosque in the business district, near the old quarter; though some find it "respectable, but nothing extraordinary", others call it a "top-notch" indulgence.

Essaouira

Dar Loulema 🛎

| - | - | - | - | $126 |

2, rue Souss | (011-212-24) 475-346 | fax 475-348 | www.darloulema.com |
7 suites

Not many have yet discovered this tiny, family-run hotel that combines dramatic Moorish details in a design that utilizes rich fabrics and handcrafted furnishings; apartment-size quarters boast living rooms and intricately tiled baths, and meals can be taken by a fireplace in one of the living rooms, on the patio by a central fountain or on one of the terraces.

Fès

Sofitel Palais Jamai [H] 🐕 👪 [S] 🏊 🎾 — 23 | 22 | 22 | 22 | $300

Bab Guissa | (011-212-35) 634-331 | fax 635-096 | 800-763-4835 | www.sofitel.com | 123 rooms, 19 suites

Take a "journey back in time" at this "converted royal residence" in Fès that "still makes you feel like a king" with its "excellent service" and "soul-stirring view of the Medina"; although "location sells this hotel" (namely its "proximity to the souk"), repeat visitors suggest you "stay in the original" part of the building.

High Atlas

Kasbah du Toubkal, The 🛁 👪 🏊 — ▽ 21 | 25 | 21 | 24 | $198

Imlil | (011-212-24) 485-611 | www.kasbahdutoubkal.com | 11 rooms, 3 suites

Nestled at the foot of Jbel Toubkal, North Africa's highest peak, this secluded High Atlas mountain retreat with views of three major valleys an hour and a half from the airport offers a "once-in-a-lifetime" experience; the "staff will do anything to please", the "rustic rooms" are full of "character" and the overall operation is "sensitive to local culture"; "factor in" everything, say its fans, and then "dare to have one critical thing to say about this very special place."

Marrakech

Amanjena 👪 [S] 🏊 🎾 — 29 | 27 | 25 | 26 | $850

Rte. de Ouarzazate, Km. 12 | (011-212-24) 403-353 | fax 403-477 | 800-477-9180 | www.amanresorts.com | 6 maisons, 32 pavilions, 1 suites

This "staggeringly fantastic" resort "turns you into an Aman junkie" say awestruck admirers who claim this hotel group "always gets it right" and this outpost in the outskirts of Marrakech is no exception; from the "managers who greet you at check-in" to the "wonderful" guest pavilions and two-story *maisons* to the "idyllic" olive-tree-shaded grounds, you'll leave saying "if there's a more luxurious hotel, I haven't seen it."

Ksar Char-Bagh 👪 🏊 🎾 — - | - | - | - | $727

Palmeraie de Marrakech | (011-212-24) 329-244 | fax 329-214 | 800-735-2478 | www.ksarcharbagh.com | 11 rooms, 1 suite, 1 apartment

You'll feel like a Moor when you settle into a *harim* (suite) with its own private garden at this "fabulous" Relais & Châteaux "desert oasis" surrounded by the Atlas Mountains; expect "exotic" grounds embellished with crisscrossing streams, a tennis court set amid century-old olive trees, an extensive library and a traditional Turkish *hammam.*

La Maison Arabe 🐕 [S] 🏊 — 26 | 25 | 25 | 24 | $225

1, Derb Assehbé | (011-212-24) 387-010 | fax 387-221 | www.lamaisonarabe.com | 9 rooms, 8 suites

To experience "something special" "don't bother staying in the big hotels in town" since this "small" spot is "sooo much better" boast bullish boosters of this "elegant" property full of "character"; rooms with balconies are "lovely", there's "good dining", "wonderful cooking courses" and a "friendly" staff; it could be "the closest thing to living a Moroccan life" in the "middle of the Medina."

Palmeraie Golf Palace ⚥♨⟂Ⓢ≋🔍 ▽ | 25 | 21 | 18 | 23 | $343 |

Les Jardins de la Palmeraie, Circuit de la Palmeraie | (011-212-24) 301-010 | fax 302-020 | 800-323-7500 | www.pgpmarrakech.com | 286 rooms, 28 suites

Boasting more than just "incredible" links, this "quiet, remote" and sporty Marrakech "gem" also offers horseback riding, tennis, bowling and five "amazing" pools, set in a "beautiful" spread filled with palm trees and "picturesque mosaics"; "pure luxury" and relaxation can be found in its "spacious rooms" done up in a rich North African style.

Taroudant

La Gazelle d'Or ♨Ⓢ≋🔍 | 26 | 26 | 23 | 22 | $589 |

Taroudant | (011-212-28) 852-039 | fax 852-737 | www.gazelledor.com | 6 rooms, 24 suites

"Escape from reality" at this "exquisite" resort on the "last stop to the middle of nowhere", i.e. "outside the walled town" of Taroudant on the "desert's edge"; the "staff knows what you desire before you do", plus you'll "want to redo your home" after you see the "gorgeous" tiling.

Myanmar

Yangon

Governor's Residence ≋ | - | - | - | - | $190 |

35 Taw Win Rd., Dagon Township | (011-95-1) 229-860 | fax (011-95-1) 228 260 | www.governorsresidence.com | 45 rooms, 3 suites

Housed in a teak mansion from the 1920s, this Orient-Express hotel in the Embassy Quarter, 10 minutes from Yangon's city center, is surrounded by lotus ponds; the previous residence of the Kaya state governor, it features rooms with teak furnishings, freeform bathtubs and satellite TVs, while the restaurants serves Asian and European fare.

Strand, The Ⓗ♨ | 21 | 23 | 18 | 17 | $475 |

92 Strand Rd. | (011-95-1) 243-377 | fax 243-393 | www.ghmhotels.com | 32 suites

Built in 1901 across from the Yangon River, this colonial landmark offers "old-world charm" to spare; sure, it "could be better", but with "true hospitality" that includes 24-hour butler service, a "delightful afternoon tea" and suites with high ceilings, teak floors and antiques, it's unlike other options in this "faded capital."

Namibia

Ongava Game Reserve

Little Ongava Lodge ♨≋ | - | - | - | - | $830 |

Ongava Game Reserve | (011-264-61) 274-500 | fax 239-455 | www.wilderness-safaris.com | 3 suites

"Live with the animals" (including the elusive white rhino) without sacrificing "comforts and luxuries" at this "outstanding" safari spot on the western edge of Etosha National Park; a "thoroughly professional staff" watches over guests of the three tented suites, which each boast private infinity pools, outdoor showers and "native materials" that are "deftly incorporated into" the decor; patrons often combine stays with time at two nearby sister lodges.

Nepal

Kathmandu

Le Méridien Kathmandu Gokarna Forest [H] 🔭 ⛳ [S] 🏊

Rooms	Service	Dining	Facil.	Cost
-	-	-	-	$180

Rajnikunj Gokarna, Thali | (011-977-1) 445-1212 | fax 445-0002 | 800-543-4300 | www.lemeridien.com | 52 rooms, 3 suites

It's hard to believe this property in the shadow of Mount Everest is just a half-hour from the center of Kathmandu; set on a serene ridge on 470 acres of Gokarna Forest that were once hunting grounds for Nepalese kings, it is home to deer, monkeys and hundreds of bird varieties that roam freely alongside the 18-hole golf course; when it's time to relax after any number of adventure excursions (mountain biking through the forest, perhaps?), you can head to the Harmony Spa.

Yak & Yeti, Hotel [H] 🔭 [S] 🏊 🎾

Rooms	Service	Dining	Facil.	Cost
▽ 20	22	18	19	$185

Durbar Marg | (011-977-1) 424-8999 | fax 422-7882 | www.yakandyeti.com | 253 rooms, 17 suites

"An exotic hotel in an exotic country" - just "saying that you stayed at the Yak puts you in-the-know" boast intrepid travelers who find this is "much nicer than its name infers" with "fabulous architecture", "very pleasing" gardens and "first-class service"; indeed, it's a "quiet refuge" of "luxury."

Netherlands

Amsterdam

Ambassade [H] 🔭 [S]

Rooms	Service	Dining	Facil.	Cost
22	23	17	18	$297

Herengracht 341 | (011-31-20) 555-0222 | fax 555-0277 | www.ambassade-hotel.nl | 51 rooms, 7 suites, 1 apartment

"Cobbled together" from 10 17th-century canal houses, this "pleasant venue" in a "great location" in Centrum along the Herengracht Canal has "adorable rooms, each one different", that are "hidden up and down tiny winding stairs"; while service is "very friendly", watch out for food that's "a joke."

Amstel InterContinental [H] 🔭 🏊 (aka Amstel Hotel)

Rooms	Service	Dining	Facil.	Cost
26	25	23	24	$786

Professor Tulpplein 1 | (011-31-20) 622-6060 | fax 622-5808 | 888-424-6835 | www.intercontinental.com | 55 rooms, 24 suites

For a "divine experience in the heart" of Centrum, head to this "world-class" property that's "magnificent in every respect" from the "generously sized" rooms (some sporting "blue silk swag drapes") oozing "turn-of-the-century charm" to "unpretentious" service; the fare at chef Edwin Kats' French-Med restaurant, La Rive, is "fabulous" as are the "picture-perfect" waterfont views.

	ROOMS	SERVICE	DINING	FACIL.	COST
de l'Europe, Hotel [H] 🐕 🔭 🏊	23	23	21	19	$390

Nieuwe Doelenstraat 2-8 | (011-31-20) 531-1777 | fax 531-1778 | 800-888-4747 | www.leurope.nl | 77 rooms, 23 suites

You can arrive by water taxi to this 1896 Renaissance-style "antique gem" overlooking a river in Centrum where "European charm" means "plush rooms", "warm service", the wonderful French Excelsior restaurant under chef Jean-Jacques Menanteau and a location that's "terrific for tourists"; but a few finicky fusspots fume over an "unimpressive" lobby and a certain "shabbiness" that makes it seem "well past its sell date."

	ROOMS	SERVICE	DINING	FACIL.	COST
Dylan [H] 🔭	25	22	24	20	$357

Keizersgracht 384 | (011-31-20) 530-2010 | fax 530-2030 | 800-525-4800 | www.dylanamsterdam.com | 27 rooms, 14 suites

"Amazing dining, amazing rooms, amazing attitude" gush guests of this boutique hotel created by London hotelier and designer Anouska Hempel in a "fantastic location" on Amsterdam's Keizersgracht canal; "creative", "trendy decor" shares accolades with one of the city's "best tables", featuring French-North African cuisine; the "pretty", "eclectic" rooms are individually designed and theme-based so travelers can go green in the Garden Room or try Manhattan hip.

	ROOMS	SERVICE	DINING	FACIL.	COST
Grand Sofitel Demeure [H] 🔭 🏊	21	23	21	19	$581

Oudezijds Voorburgwal 197 | (011-31-20) 555-3111 | fax 555-3222 | 800-763-4835 | www.thegrand.nl | 131 rooms, 35 suites, 16 apartments

A "perfect" location in the city's historic center close to great restaurants and shops draws devotees to this chain hotel housed in a 14th-century building with a "courtyard that's beautiful", a restaurant with an "excellent wine list" and "well-appointed" rooms; but a few others find this one "a bit sterile" rather than grand, with service that tends toward the "snooty."

	ROOMS	SERVICE	DINING	FACIL.	COST
Okura, Hotel 🔭 [S] 🏊	20	22	23	19	$500

Ferdinand Bolstraat 333 | (011-31-20) 678-7111 | fax 671-2344 | 800-223-6800 | www.okura.nl | 243 rooms, 72 suites

Sojourners single out the sushi and other "good Japanese" fare at Yamazato and the New French dishes at Ciel Bleu as well as the "very receptive" staff at this business hotel in Pijp that offers all the corporate in-room amenities like fax machines, Internet access and satellite television as well as an on-site sports facility with a Turkish bath; but it's a "little bit out of the way" for some who find "nothing to write home about."

	ROOMS	SERVICE	DINING	FACIL.	COST
Pulitzer, Hotel 🛏 🐕 🔭	22	22	19	20	$470

Prinsengracht 315-331 | (011-31-20) 523-5235 | fax 627-6753 | 800-325-3589 | www.pulitzer.nl | 223 rooms, 7 suites

"What fun to get lost" wandering through passageways in this "fairytale" "maze" of 25 restored and connected 17th-century canal houses in the Jordaan that "captures the flavor" of old Amsterdam; "each room is unique" and so "cozy" it "feels like home", with service that's both "friendly and efficient"; the "hip bar" and "incredibly convenient" location for shopping and visiting the Anne Frank Museum are draws, but the "merely average" dining detracts.

	ROOMS	SERVICE	DINING	FACIL.	COST

Seven One Seven, Hotel ⓗ ✠ 🏃 — 25 | 25 | 16 | 17 | $415

Prinsengracht 717 | (011-31-20) 427-0717 | fax 423-0717 |
www.717hotel.nl | 2 rooms, 6 suites

Set in a "very private" 19th-century guesthouse, this stylish boutique in Centrum overlooks the Prinsengracht Canal and is within easy walking distance of museums, galleries and the famous Spiegerstraat; "individually decorated rooms" offer handmade brass beds, Bang & Olufsen DVD sets and CD players, and "fabulous service" makes it all come together; though there's no restaurant and it's "not ideal for a long stay due to the lack of many amenities", rates include "made-to-order breakfast" that can be taken on the charming back patio.

The Hague

Le Méridien Hotel Des Indes ⓗ 🏃 🌊 — 25 | 24 | 21 | 23 | $324

Lange Voorhout 54-56 | (011-31-70) 361-2345 | fax 361-2350 |
800-543-4300 | www.lemeridien.com | 79 rooms, 13 suites

It's not unusual to see "prime ministers loitering in the lobby" of this "historic" manor located in a leafy square in the center of The Hague; impressed guests marvel at how "well conceived and executed" everything is, from the "discreet", "amiable" service and "beautiful presentation of food" in the formal restaurant (which also serves a "lovely afternoon tea") to the "grand, imposing public areas" and "enormous" accommodations sporting "period furnishings", elaborate draperies and "plush bathrooms."

New Zealand

Auckland

Hilton 🖉 🏃 🌊 — 23 | 22 | 22 | 21 | $369

Prince's Wharf, 147 Quay St. | (011-64-9) 978-2000 | fax 978-2001 |
800-445-8667 | www.hilton.com | 158 rooms, 8 suites,
31 apartments

"Is it really a Hilton?" marvel impressed guests of this "fabulous contemporary addition to the Kiwi scene", which must be "one of the funkiest hotels" in this American chain; "perfectly perched" at the end of Prince's Wharf "like a luxury ship", its "sleek", "modern" rooms offer "stunning views" of Auckland Harbor as well as "huge balconies" from which to savor them; but there are whispers that beyond its "architecturally impressive" design, it's "nothing very special"; P.S. don't miss the "very cool" dining room, White.

Hyatt Regency 🖉 🏃 Ⓢ 🌊 — 22 | 23 | 20 | 22 | $95

Princes St. | (011-64-9) 355-1234 | fax 302-2932 | 800-223-1234 |
www.auckland.regency.hyatt.com | 232 rooms, 144 suites,
4 penthouses

A $45-million renovation added a spa, fitness center, more rooms and a 17-story residence tower to this "beauty" boasting "excellent views" of Auckland Harbor, a "friendly" staff and a "terrific", "convenient" location; "as long as you don't mind the hike back up the hill", it's a "great place for business travelers and tourists alike" – "everything you expect a good hotel to be."

Christchurch

George, The 🍴🔭

ROOMS	SERVICE	DINING	FACIL.	COST
22	25	23	20	$231

50 Park Terr. | (011-64-3) 379-4560 | fax 366-6747 | 800-525-4800 | www.thegeorge.com | 47 rooms, 8 suites

"A quaint, quiet hotel in a quaint, quiet city", this "stylish" boutique is best known for its "outstanding service" (the staff's almost "pathologically nice") and two restaurants that reviewers rate among the "best in New Zealand"; its location near Hagley Park means it's well situated "for exploring", and it also serves as a convenient point for "transition travel to other parts" of the country.

Featherston

[Z] Wharekauhau 🔭Ⓢ🏊🎾

ROOMS	SERVICE	DINING	FACIL.	COST
28	26	26	27	$421

Western Lake Rd. | (011-64-6) 307-7581 | fax 307-7799 | www.wharekauhau.co.nz | 10 cottages, 9 rooms

Loyalists love this "absolute heaven on earth" modeled after an Edwardian country mansion with a "spectacular" 5,000-acre setting on the southeast coast of the North Island; there are "few faults" here, from the "wonderful" accommodations in free-standing cottages with pebble mosaics, clay tiling and ocean views to the "outstanding" (though often "lengthy") dining; add in a cellar stocked with wonderful wines from the nearby Martinborough region and an endless list of activities from hiking in a private reserve to clay trap shooting, and some have "seldom been as impressed."

Kerikeri

[Z] Kauri Cliffs 🔭⛳Ⓢ🏊🎾

ROOMS	SERVICE	DINING	FACIL.	COST
29	27	26	28	$540

Matauri Bay | (011-64-9) 407-0010 | fax 407-0061 | 800-735-2478 | www.kauricliffs.com | 22 suites

"A long way from civilization", this "golfer's paradise" and member of Relais & Châteaux on the cliffs of the North Island offers "impeccable", "unpretentious" service with a "country club" feel, not to mention what some say is "the prettiest course in the world"; with spacious cottages, all with Pacific views, private porches and fireplaces, along with "superb food" and access to local activities - diving, kayaking, gamefishing and hunting for boar - it's no wonder new fans keep finding this once "hidden gem."

Queenstown

[Z] Blanket Bay 🔭⛷🏊

ROOMS	SERVICE	DINING	FACIL.	COST
28	27	26	29	$891

Glenorchy | (011-64-3) 442-9442 | fax 442-9441 | 800-525-4800 | www.blanketbay.com | 5 rooms, 3 suites, 4 chalets

"Don't miss this place!" exclaim enthusiasts of this remote, ultradeluxe resort near Glenorchy, whose "fantastic" location at the north end of Lake Wakatipu enjoys an epic Humboldt Mountain backdrop; guests choose among rooms and suites in the main lodge, crafted from local timber and stone, or private chalets, all of which offer picture-window views and crackling log fires, plus the "very hospitable staff" can arrange any number of adventurous activities, from fly fishing and helicopter fishing to heli-skiing, horseback riding, rafting or bungee jumping.

	ROOMS	SERVICE	DINING	FACIL.	COST

Millbrook ⊕🐾🐴⚓Ⓢ🏊🔍   ▽ 23 | 21 | 21 | 25 | $269

Malaghans Rd., Arrowtown | (011-64-3) 441-7000 | fax 441-7007 |
www.millbrook.co.nz | 51 rooms, 70 suites, 12 villas, 36 cottages

The "fantastic" golf is the center of attention at this hotel where the long summer days mean you can play "until 10 PM"; there are views of the surrounding mountains, "hearty breakfasts" and "beautiful grounds", plus it's close to the historic gold-mining village of Arrowtown, but a few warn that it's "a bit of a drive to Queenstown."

Taupo

Huka Lodge ✕🐾🐴🏊🔍   26 | 27 | 26 | 25 | $1187

Huka Falls Rd. | (011-64-7) 378-5791 | fax 378-0427 | 800-223-6800 |
www.hukalodge.com | 20 suites, 1 cottage

The Queen of England stays at this "exquisite" lodge on the North Island's Lake Taupo, but everyone is "treated like royalty, minus the pomp" say commoners further contented by the "superb accommodations", easy access to fishing in the "mesmerizing" lake and "unbelievable meals" enjoyed by the fireplace or at your own table under the stars; all this "privacy" in such a "spectacular setting" makes you feel "a million miles away", but it's so "worth the effort to get there."

Wellington

InterContinental 🐴Ⓢ🏊   24 | 24 | 19 | 23 | $216

2 Grey St. | (011-64-4) 472-2722 | fax 472-4724 | 888-424-6835 |
www.intercontinental.com | 224 rooms, 7 suites

The "superior location" near top sights and the waterfront plus "corner rooms with lots of light and views" place this chainster a cut above some of its sister hotels; a renovated fitness center and solid service also please, but the "average food choices" are a downer.

Norway

Oslo

Continental, Hotel ⊕🐴   19 | 19 | 19 | 15 | $506

Stortingsgaten 24-26 | (011-47) 2282-4040 | fax 2242-9689 |
800-223-6800 | www.hotel-continental.no | 131 rooms, 23 suites

"Get a junior suite with a view of the park" when visiting this "charming" family-run hotel located across from the National Theatre "in the heart of Oslo"; the dramatic Theatercaféen restaurant gets a round of applause, as does the "terrific breakfast with Norwegian specialties", but critics note that the "beautiful" building may "need a face-lift."

Grand Hotel, The ⊕💇🐴Ⓢ🏊   19 | 19 | 17 | 17 | $315

Karl Johansgate 31 | (011-47) 2321-2000 | fax 2321-2100 |
www.grand.no | 238 rooms, 51 suites

Fans of this Louis XVI revival–style business hotel that opened its doors in 1874 find it a "real treat" with a "wonderful staff" and a "central location"; there's an "amazing view" from the indoor pool and "great" though "simple" food, but a handful finds it more like a "conservative old aunt" – "grand by name but dated by nature."

	ROOMS	SERVICE	DINING	FACIL.	COST

Oman

Muscat

**Shangri-La's Barr Al Jissah
Resort & Spa** ✻✗⊘🛁☉⛱🔍

| | – | – | – | – | $340 |

Bay at Barr Al Jissah | (011-968) 24-776666 | fax 24-776677 |
www.shangri-la.com | 302 rooms, 198 suites, 180 penthouses
It's all about the numbers at this "large" seaside "Disney World"-like
palace on the Gulf of Oman – three hotel buildings, 124 acres of manicured gardens, 19 restaurants and bars, four tennis courts and three
private beaches; the service is "top quality", and there's an on-site
children's program, spa and dive center, but food is somewhat "average."

Palau

Koror

**Palau Royal Resort
(Nikko Hotels)** 🛁☉⛱🔍

| | – | – | – | – | $275 |

Malakal Island | (011-680) 488-2000 | fax 488-6688 |
www.palau-royal-resort.com | 151 rooms, 6 suites
"A bit far removed" on the eastern coast of Malakal Island, this six-story
chainster has become the epicenter for Palau-bound dive enthusiasts –
in fact, some say "the only reason to stay is as a jump-off point for
world-class scuba"; but even non-submergers find perks, including an
array of treatments at the Mandara Spa and "great" service.

Panama

Gamboa

**Gamboa
Rainforest Resort** ⊘🛁☉⛱🔍

| | ▽ 20 | 20 | 19 | 22 | $150 |

Soberania National Park | (011-507) 314-9000 | fax 314-9020 |
877-800-1690 | www.gamboaresort.com | 107 rooms, 38 villas
"Escape from the city madness" to this resort near the Panama Canal
that's in the "untouched" Soberania National Park; the views afforded
by its "striking setting" "make you feel like you've entered the jungle
without having to brave the mosquitoes, snakes and alligators", though
adventurous visitors avail themselves of ecotours, boating, fishing
and cycling; P.S. "don't miss the tram ride to the rainforest canopy!"

Peru

Cuzco

Machu Picchu Sanctuary Lodge ⑪🛁

| | 19 | 22 | 19 | 20 | $715 |

Monumento Arqueológico de Machu Picchu | (011-51) 1242-3428 |
fax 211-053 | 800-237-1236 | www.orient-express.com | 29 rooms, 2 suites
"The grandeur of Machu Picchu" is the "over-the-top setting" of this
"unique" venue, "the only hotel up at the ruins" of the ancient Inca cit-

adel; the "staff is capable", the "rustic" but "clean" facilities are "quite adequate", "the food is delicious" and the "heavenly" location means guests have the privilege of experiencing the "magic" while "avoiding the lines" who trek up the hill daily; you'll "need to pay big bucks", but "if you can afford it", it's "a must."

Monasterio, Hotel 👪 [H] 🔭 — 25 | 26 | 24 | 25 | $470

Calle Palacio 136, Plazoleta Nazarenas | (011-51-84) 241-777 | fax 246-983 | 800-237-1236 | www.monasterio.orient-express.com | 108 rooms, 18 suites

It's sort of "like living in a museum" at this "astonishing" and "welcoming" medieval monastery 10,000 feet above sea level where the "haunting Gregorian chants", hallways lined with "art and antiques" and "lovely" 'Cuzco Baroque' style (Spanish colonial blended with Peruvian) creates a unique "sanctuary"; even though most find "suprising luxury", a few fault rooms that are a little *too* authentic ("stark" and "cell-like") and food that's "nothing to write home about"; P.S. to help prevent "wheezing" from the altitude, you can pay for extra "oxygen forced into them at night."

Lima

Country Club Lima Hotel [H] ⛳ [S] 🏊 — 26 | 25 | 22 | 24 | $295

Los Eucaliptos 590 | (011-51-1) 611-9000 | fax 611-9002 | www.hotelcountry.com | 75 suites

An "excellent restoration" of a 1927 landmark building, this all-suite "luxurious retreat" in the city's "upscale" San Isidro district offers "wonderful" accommodations filled with Peruvian colonial artworks and facilities that "cater more to businesspeople than tourists"; there's convenient access to the exclusive Lima Golf Club across the street, an on-site restaurant, "beautiful" public spaces showcasing art from Museo de Osma and a "professional staff"; just a few find fault with "unimpressive" food, but suggest stopping for a Pisco Sour in the English bar.

Miraflores Park 🔭 [S] 🏊 — 25 | 26 | 23 | 24 | $365

Ave. Malecón de la Reserva 1035 | (011-51-1) 242-3000 | fax 242-3393 | 800-237-1236 | www.mira-park.com | 72 rooms, 10 suites

"Newly remodeled", this "amazing" Orient-Express boutique high-rise in the affluent Miraflores section of Lima is "top-notch in all aspects"; staffers "go the extra mile", "beautiful" rooms have "huge and luxurious" baths and the "terrific" "views of the ocean are unobstructed"; add in a rooftop pool, decent food and a "welcoming" lounge and bar, and this may be the "nicest hotel" in town.

Swissôtel 🫖 🐕 🔭 [S] 🏊 🎾 — 24 | 24 | 20 | 21 | $215

Via Central 150 | (011-51-1) 611-4400 | fax 611-4401 | 800-637-9477 | www.swissotel.com | 223 rooms, 21 suites

If you need an "oasis" in Lima, "this is the place" proclaim patrons pleased by the "modern comforts" at this "fine", "high-quality" hotel situated in San Isidro, a "lovely, quiet area" of the city; "rooms are modern and luxurious", the "efficient" staff offers "impeccable service", the health spa is "great" and the Peruvian, Mediterranean and Swiss cuisine at its trio of restaurants is "excellent"; N.B. armchair archaeologists should visit the nearby Huaca Huallamarca, a pre-Inca pyramid with an on-site museum.

Philippines

Cebu

Shangri-La's Mactan Island Resort & Spa 👪 🐕 🔭 Ⓢ 🏊 🎾

▽ 23 | 25 | 21 | 23 | $206

Punta Engan Rd., Lapu-Lapu City | (011-63-32) 231-0288 | fax 231-1688 | 866-565-5050 | www.shangri-la.com | 504 rooms, 43 suites

"You don't need to go anywhere else in Cebu" when you settle into this "secluded" resort that has everything "you'd expect from a Shangri-La anywhere in the world": "beautiful grounds", "extremely attentive" service, rooms with water views and a "cozy" feeling; ocean lovers get their fix with a "good dive shop" and options like fishing, scuba, snorkeling, waterskiing, windsurfing, jet skiing and parasailing, while landlubbers love the on-site Chi spa.

Cuyo Islands

Amanpulo 👪 🐕 🔭 Ⓢ 🏊 🎾

29 | 28 | 22 | 26 | $700

Pamalican Island | (011-63-2) 759-4040 | fax 759-4044 | 800-477-9180 | www.amanresorts.com | 38 casitas, 2 villas

A "carefully crafted paradise in the middle of the ocean", this "water-centered resort" with "outstanding beach villas" is the "ultrapeaceful getaway" you've been craving; "service is beyond the realm of believable" with some visitors "telling incredible stories" about the staff for months after they return; the white-sand beach is "beautiful", there's a first-rate spa and you can hike or enjoy sailing on the Sulu Sea.

Manila

Makati Shangri-La 🐕 Ⓢ 🏊 🎾

24 | 25 | 23 | 24 | $265

Ayala & Makati Aves. | (011-63-2) 813-8888 | fax 813-5499 | 866-565-5050 | www.shangri-la.com | 605 rooms, 94 suites

Savvy shoppers tout the "location" of this "spectacular spot" "in the middle of Manila's most affluent district" close to a mall and other retail shops; but even inside, this one shines with an impressive atrium, "good dining" and facilities for business travelers; even if the modern rooms come "without character" and a few are frustrated by service that turns "hopeless" at times, they "can't get too angry."

Mandarin Oriental 🔭 Ⓢ 🏊

21 | 26 | 22 | 21 | $280

Makati Ave. | (011-63-2) 750-8888 | fax 817-2472 | www.mandarinoriental.com | 434 rooms, 19 suites

Situated right near the metro in the Financial District, this prestigious chain's Manila outpost garners a mixed bag of comments: "excellent service", the "amazing" East/West-influenced spa and a breakfast buffet with "local specialties" earn praise, but a few say the "not really luxurious" rooms are "tired" and "need updating."

Manila Hotel Ⓗ 🏊 🎾

▽ 21 | 23 | 22 | 20 | $300

1 Rizal Park, Roxas Blvd. | (011-63-2) 527-0011 | fax 527-0022 | www.manila-hotel.com.ph | 498 rooms, 72 suites

Swankly situated next to Rizal Park and overlooking the bay, "one of Asia's most legendary lodgings" has "the feel of Old Manila"; while whiners wait for a renovation of this "fraying-at-the-edges" property, satisfied surveyors say the "classical" decor and selection of restaurants and bars ("make sure you have a drink" there) puts this "grand but dark" dowager at the top of their list.

Peninsula, The [S]🏊 — 24 | 27 | 23 | 25 | $280

Ayala & Makati Aves. | (011-63-2) 887-2888 | fax 815-4825 | 800-223-6800 | www.peninsula.com | 451 rooms, 46 suites

An upscale, international "oasis" in the middle of Makati, the city's business district, this "lovely" chain link scores the most points for its "excellent" service and "see-and-be-seen" lobby; while the extensive spa and "amazing food" also impress, a few say the "spacious" rooms could use some "remodeling."

Poland

Warsaw

Le Royal Méridien Bristol [H]🔭🏊 — 26 | 26 | 24 | 23 | $515

Krakowskie Przedmiescie 42/44 | (011-48-22) 551-1000 | fax 625-2577 | 800-543-4300 | www.lemeridien.com | 169 rooms, 36 suites

Pampered guests revel in the "huge" and "beautiful" rooms at this "true European treasure" on King's Walk, "not too far" from "exciting nightlife" in Old Town Warsaw; expect "one of the best restaurants in town" (Malinowa), an "excellent" staff that reaches "beyond the call of duty" and overall "old-world charm" with "lots of character"; in short, says one believer, "they do everything well."

Marriott 🪣🐕🔭[S]🏊 — 22 | 23 | 20 | 23 | $244

Al. Jerozolimskie 65/79 | (011-48-22) 630-6306 | fax 830-0041 | 800-228-9290 | www.marriott.com | 423 rooms, 95 suites

If you want an "American hotel in the heart" of Warsaw, you've found it in this "modern" chainster; "convenient to the train station and Downtown" (some say "a little too close to the seedy railroad"), it offers "excellent security" and "varied dining."

Rialto, Hotel 🐕🏊 — - | - | - | - | $317

Wilcza 73 | (011-48-22) 584-8700 | fax 584-8701 | 800-323-7500 | www.rialto.pl | 32 rooms, 12 suites

Warsaw's got a hip boutique, thanks to this property lying on the fringes of the central business district and sporting an art deco interior; each room is individually decorated, featuring original furniture and accessories from the early 1900s, while facilities include a fitness center with sauna and steam, a pool, a cigar room and an International restaurant courtesy of chef Kurt Scheller.

Sheraton Hotel & Towers 🪣🐕 — 23 | 22 | 19 | 21 | $262

Ulica B. Prusa 2 | (011-48-22) 450-6100 | fax 450-6200 | 800-325-3535 | www.sheraton.com | 326 rooms, 24 suites

Corporate cronies are "very impressed" with this "modern" business hotel that "does a surprisingly good job of convincing you you're not in Poland anymore" with its "efficient" service, "lovely rooms" ("stay on the business floors") and "great lobby bar"; though the food doesn't get raves and some find it a bit "expensive", most feel it's "worth it."

Portugal

Algarve

Quinta do Lago, Hotel 👪 🔭 ⛳ [S] 🏊 🎾 ∇ 20 | 21 | 15 | 21 | $459

Almancil | (011-351-289) 350-350 | fax 396-393 | www.hotelquintadolago.com | 121 rooms, 20 suites

Modern, well-appointed rooms and suites (one with its own swimming pool and Jacuzzi) and a "beautiful location" recommend this resort situated on 2,000 wooded acres overlooking the Ria Formosa lagoon; "outstanding facilities" for sports lovers include four golf courses, horseback riding, three heated pools, tennis courts, a nearby beach and a spa; add in the "personable" staff and most would "go back in a minute."

Sheraton Algarve at Pine Cliffs Resort 👪 🔭 [S] 🏊 🎾 25 | 24 | 20 | 26 | $442

Praia da Falésia | Albufeira | (011-351-289) 500-100 | fax 501-950 | 800-325-3535 | www.luxurycollection.com | 182 rooms, 33 suites

"Lots of kids" abound at this family-friendly resort perched above "splendid cliffs" and an exclusive Atlantic Ocean beach where elevators "zoom" you down to the sand to "relax for hours" waited on by "friendly, helpful" staffers; the "fantastic environment" includes lots of restaurants (even if they "don't live up to the setting"), golf at the on-site Pine Cliffs course, spa services and exotic Moorish-influenced rooms "with the most comfortable beds you'll ever sleep in", plus the tots will love the Porto Pirata children's club.

Bussaco

Bussaco Palace [H] 🔭 🏊 🎾 16 | 19 | 24 | 20 | $216

Mata do Bussaco | (011-351-23) 193-7970 | fax 193-0509 | www.almeidahotels.com | 58 rooms, 4 suites

This "imposing" Manueline-Gothic former royal hunting lodge in the mountains will "take your breath away", particularly the "unbelievable grounds" - 260 acres of centuries-old natural forest along with "magnificent" formal gardens; enthusiasts "enjoy the peaceful verandas to read and relax" and the "beautiful dining room" serving Bussaco's own wines, but several spoilsports say the stately site "could use freshening up."

Cascais

Albatroz, Hotel [H] 🏊 25 | 26 | 23 | 22 | $429

Rua Frederico Arouca 100 | (011-351-21) 484-7380 | fax 484-4827 | 800-223-6800 | www.albatrozhotels.com | 48 rooms, 11 suites

"Location, location, location" is the lure of this Estoril Coast "gem", a former duke's palace overlooking the "truly picturesque city" of Cascais, "the Cannes of Portugal"; guests who want to "get away from it all" can lounge in the "pristine sanctuary's" "luxurious rooms" (each "fit for a king and his queen"), sit near the oval pool on the wide flagstone terrace, savor the services of a "friendly, attentive" staff and dine on "mouthwatering" fish dishes while taking in "fantastic views" of the bay.

Coimbra

Quinta das Lagrimas 🏊🎾

ROOMS	SERVICE	DINING	FACIL.	COST
-	-	-	-	$188

Coimbra | (011-351-239) 802-380 | fax 441-695 | www.quintadaslagrimas.pt | 49 rooms, 5 suites

A statue of star-crossed lover Ines de Castro greets travelers in the lobby of this 19th-century Relais & Châteaux hotel that's as "pleasant and warm" as Portugal and has hosted kings and dukes; set in the coastal university town of Coimbra, it boasts some of "the finest dining" at Arcadas da Capela, accommodations in palace, garden and spa rooms, and an on-site spa and golf academy.

Lisbon

Bairro Alto Hotel Ⓗ🔭

	ROOMS	SERVICE	DINING	FACIL.	COST
▽	23	21	18	20	$357

Praça Luis de Camoes 8 | (011-351-21) 340-8288 | fax 340-8299 | www.bairroaltohotel.com | 51 rooms, 4 suites

In the city center overlooking both the Tagus River and the main square of Luis de Camoes, this restored 18th-century building features Portuguese-style rooms done in dark woods and rich color palettes; there's a fusion restaurant, a trendy bar, a fitness center and a panoramic terrace.

Four Seasons Hotel Ritz 🍴🐕🔭Ⓢ🏊

ROOMS	SERVICE	DINING	FACIL.	COST
27	27	24	26	$456

Rua Rodrigo da Fonseca 88 | (011-351-21) 381-1400 | fax 383-1783 | 800-332-3442 | www.fourseasons.com | 262 rooms, 20 suites

"Everything" about this "warm and elegant" "highlight of Lisbon" atop one of the city's seven hills is "superlative", from the head-turning local art on the walls to the "beautiful" views; enthusiasts extol the wonderfully "thick beds" in the "large rooms", the "fabulous", "impeccable" service, the "superb food" at Varanda restaurant (voted No. 1 for Food in Lisbon in our *Europe's Top Restaurants* Survey) and the "best-ever fitness facility" with vistas of the Tagus River; the only thing that "could be better" is the location.

[Z] Lapa Palace 🍴Ⓗ🐕🔭Ⓢ🏊

ROOMS	SERVICE	DINING	FACIL.	COST
27	29	25	26	$601

Rua do Pau de Bandeira 4 | (011-351-21) 394-9494 | fax 395-0665 | 800-524-2420 | www.lapapalace.com | 90 rooms, 19 suites

"Life is good" at this 19th-century hilltop château where the "impeccable staff" goes above and beyond to make you feel loved and the "first-rate facilities" feature lots of marble, a "private garden" oasis with a "heavenly pool", an "incredible wellness center, "fantastically appointed rooms" with the "best closets ever" and the "excellent" Ristorante Hotel Cipriani; sure, "it's "a hike" to Downtown Lisbon (a "limo or taxi is essential"), but those who "could live here" don't care.

Palácio Belmonte Ⓗ🔭🏊

ROOMS	SERVICE	DINING	FACIL.	COST
-	-	-	-	$396

Pateo Dom Fradique 14 | (011-351-21) 881-6600 | fax 881-6609 | www.palaciobelmonte.com | 10 suites, 1 apartment

Located on the eastern side of Lisbon's St. George's Castle, this "amazing", but hard-to-find 15th-century structure "in the most beautiful of locations" incorporates part of the city's oldest walls; rebuilt by its French owner, with original tiles and antiques still decorating some rooms, it features a black marble rooftop pool, library and chapel with commanding views of the cityscape and river, and sweet tooths won't want to miss the baked goods at on-site Café Belmonte (it also carries regional wines and cheeses).

Madeira

Reid's Palace 👪 [H] 🐾 🔭 [S] 🏊 🎾

	ROOMS	SERVICE	DINING	FACIL.	COST
▽	26	27	26	28	$681

Estrada Monumental 139 | Funchal | (011-351-291) 717-171 | fax 717-177 | 800-237-1236 | www.reidspalace.com | 128 rooms, 35 suites

It's "heaven on earth" at this Orient-Express hotel above Funchal Bay where the "gorgeous setting" takes you "back in time" to the "gracious living" of the 19th century when it was built; perhaps it may "never be as good as its reputation", which is pretty grand, but it's got that view along with so much "old-world" excellence that it's "still a very special place to stay."

Sintra

Penha Longa Hotel & Golf Resort 👪 [H] 🛏 🔭 ⛳ [S] 🏊 🎾

	ROOMS	SERVICE	DINING	FACIL.	COST
▽	24	25	24	28	$350

Estrada de Lagoa Azul, Linhó | (011-351-21) 924-9011 | fax 924-9007 | www.penhalonga.com | 150 rooms, 44 suites

What's good enough for 15th-century royalty is certainly fine for Ritz regulars and golf enthusiasts who flock to this former monastery in a "beautiful setting" on the Estoril Coast, 20 minutes outside of Lisbon; run by the luxury chain group, it boasts an "impeccable" staff, a "restaurant to die for", a "great Six Senses Spa" and two Robert Trent Jones Jr.-designed courses; most of the luxurious rooms come with views of the south Sintra Mountains.

Tivoli Palácio de Seteais 🍴 [H] 🔭 🏊 🎾

	ROOMS	SERVICE	DINING	FACIL.	COST
	24	26	23	26	$375

Rua Barbosa do Bocage 8 | (011-351-21) 923-3200 | fax 923-4277 | www.tivolihotels.com | 29 rooms, 1 suite

Nicknamed the 'Palace of the Seven Sighs' after 19th-century generals signed a humiliating treaty, this "proud" neoclassical manor, with its mountain backdrop and "magnificent sea view", allows even regular Joes to relish "royal living"; the public areas and rooms showcase "spectacular" frescoes, while the formal gardens have "beautiful topiaries"; the added appeal of a "helpful" staff and "great food and wine" brings its scores up a notch.

Qatar

Doha

Four Seasons 👪 🛏 🔭 [S] 🏊 🎾

	ROOMS	SERVICE	DINING	FACIL.	COST
	-	-	-	-	$583

The Corniche West Bay Complex | (011-974) 494-8888 | fax 494-8282 | www.fourseasons.com | 175 rooms, 57 suites

Looking more like a sculpture than a hotel tower, this "beautiful" outpost of the well-known luxury group lives up to its brand's reputation; the ideal spot if you're looking to park your yacht somewhere (there's a 110-berth marina on the Arabian Gulf), it also impresses with multilevel grotto pools, an extensive spa (with the first hydrotherapy lounge and pools in Qatar) and a fitness center.

	ROOMS	SERVICE	DINING	FACIL.	COST

Ritz-Carlton, The 🏃🚴⚅♨🔍 | – | – | – | – | $302

West Bay Lagoon | (011-974) 484-8000 | fax 484-8484 | 800-241-3333 |
www.ritzcarlton.com | 271 rooms, 103 suites

Providing "classic luxury" and "everything you expect from the
Ritz-Carlton brand", this West Bay Lagoon hotel is somewhat
"isolated" – both an "advantage and a disadvantage" depending on
your perspective, since "you can't go anywhere without getting into a
car or cab"; there's an "excellent, huge" spa and nine restaurants,
along with solid service, which gives you a reason to stay put.

NEW **Sharq Village & Spa** ⚅♨♨ | – | – | – | – | $658

Rass Abu Aboud St. | (011-974) 425-6666 | 800-241-3333 |
www.ritzcarlton.com | 149 rooms, 25 suites

Set on its own island overlooking the Arabian Gulf and minutes from the
Doha Golf Club (home of the Qatar Masters), this new Ritz-Carlton has
plenty of activities and dining options to choose from: nine restaurants
and bars, a spa and modern fitness center, indoor and outdoor swimming
pools and a 235-slip marina; Arabian-inspired rooms feature balconies,
furnishings handmade in Italy and Spain, and plenty of inlaid mahogany,
gold and silverleaf, plus a kids' club brings added appeal for families.

Romania

Bucharest

**JW Marriott Bucharest
Grand Hotel** 🏌♨   ▽ | 22 | 22 | 18 | 23 | $383

Calea 13 Septembrie 90 | (011-40-21) 403-0000 | fax 403-0001 |
www.marriott.com | 379 rooms, 23 suites

Classical music and pastry treats await guests in the "beautiful reception
area" of this chainster tucked behind a somewhat "stark" facade in
Downtown Bucharest; rooms offer "great views of the Danube" and
service is "excellent", and while a few cite lackluster dining, the shopping
and casino lead others to label it "better than you could hope for."

Russia

Moscow

Baltschug Kempinski 🏃⊕🏌⚅♨♨ | 24 | 21 | 21 | 21 | $761

Balchug Ulitsa 1 | (011-7-501) 230-5500 | fax 230-5500 | 800-426-3135 |
www.kempinski.com | 197 rooms, 24 suites, 9 studios

"You don't easily forget" the views at this "safe and swanky" outpost in a
city seeing more hotel development, especially for business travelers;
"just across the bridge from St. Basil's and the Kremlin", its rooms are
"nicely appointed, although on the small side", and feature "thick
down duvets" on "beds so comfortable you don't want to leave them."

Park Hyatt Ararat ⚅♨♨ | 24 | 21 | 19 | 24 | $740

Neglinnaya Ulitsa 4 | (011-7-095) 783-1234 | fax 783-1235 | 800-223-1234 |
www.moscow.park.hyatt.com | 191 rooms, 21 suites

It's "as good as it gets in Moscow" say fans of this "cool" "super-modern"
beauty a pirouette away from the Bolshoi Theater with "great views of

	ROOMS	SERVICE	DINING	FACIL.	COST

the Kremlin" and Red Square; rooms are "fantastic" (if "minimalist") with "great style" and serviced by a "very professional" staff, the gym is "excellent" and the rooftop bar "delights" with its inspiring panoramic view; just "hang on to your wallet" since "everything comes at a price."

Swissôtel Krasnye Holmy ♟☝♨☉🏊

-	-	-	-	$619

Kosmodamianskaya Nab. 52, Bldg. 6 | (011-7-495) 787-9800 | fax 787-9898 | 800-637-9477 | www.moscow.swissotel.com | 207 rooms, 28 suites

Towering 34 floors over the eastern tip of Kremlin Island, this chainster may be the ideal place to get an overview – literally – of Moscow, since you can see the historic Kremlin from your modern, simply designed room before heading to the multitude of palaces, armories and churches just a short walk away; other on-site highlights include the Amrita Spa & Fitness Club with a swimming pool and a solarium, as well as two restaurants offering Italian and Swiss fare; N.B. banquet rooms on the 29th floor have incredible vistas.

St. Petersburg

Astoria, Hotel ⓘ♨☉

21	22	19	19	$560

Bolshaya Morskaya Ulitsa 39 | (011-7-812) 494-5757 | fax 313-5059 | 800-223-6800 | www.lhw.com | 194 rooms, 29 suites

Soak up some "history" at this circa-1912 "grand old hotel" with an "excellent" St. Isaac's Square location near many of St. Petersburg's most popular attractions; inside, there's "lots of character" in the "beautifully restored" art nouveau public spaces and "lovely (albeit small)" rooms, while the staff is deemed "almost invisible and exceedingly prompt" and the "gracious" restaurant "worthwhile"; N.B. there's also a Spa by Clarins and an adjoining casino.

Grand Hotel Europe ⓘ♨♨🏊

23	22	22	23	$510

Nevsky Prospect, Mikhailovskaya Ulitsa 1/7 | (011-7-812) 329-6000 | fax 329-6001 | 800-237-1236 | www.grandhoteleurope.com | 231 rooms, 70 suites

The "best choice in St. Pete for the spoiled traveler", this "beautiful luxury" lodging features a neoclassical facade and a dramatic central atrium with "the feel of Russia all around you"; from "impressive dining" (the "Sunday brunch serves as much caviar as you want") to the late-night bar where "diplomats, movie stars, politicians and business barons" mingle, to the "impeccable" rooms with heated floors in the bathrooms and an "eager and willing staff", it is "a grand hotel indeed."

NEW Kempinski Hotel Moika 22 ♨☉

▽ 20	22	22	21	$648

Moika River Embankment 22 | (011-7-812) 335-9111 | fax 335-9190 | www.kempinski.com | 174 rooms, 23 suites

Live like a czar at this 19th-century glamour palace "superbly located" along the Moika River "just steps" from St. Petersburg's renowned Hermitage Museum; service gets raves as does the "huge red bowl" of caviar offered at the breakfast buffet, but the "small" rooms are especially "disappointing if you don't have a view."

	ROOMS	SERVICE	DINING	FACIL.	COST

Saudi Arabia

Riyadh

Al Faisaliah 🖉🏃🌊 | – | – | – | – | $1250

King Fahad Rd. | (011-966-1) 273-2000 | fax 273-2001 |
www.alfaisaliahhotel.com | 197 rooms, 27 suites

Rosewood has come to Riyadh's city center with this "top-rate" offshoot that's all sleek design and posh amenities, including "excellent",
"personalized" 24-hour butler service, chic rooms decorated in rich
woods (some with separate lounge areas) and see-and-be-seen
scenes at the alfresco Brazilian BBQ, Il Terrazzo, or the slick seafood
eatery, Cristal Grillroom, with views of Al Faisaliah Plaza.

Four Seasons 🏃Ⓢ🌊🔍 | ▽ 27 | 24 | 23 | 26 | $427

Olaya St., Kingdom Centre | (011-966-1) 211-5000 | fax 1211-5001 |
800-819-5053 | www.fourseasons.com | 197 rooms, 52 suites

Laid out on the 10th through 24th floors of Riyadh's Kingdom Centre
("one of the tallest buildings in the Middle East"), this "excellent"
property offers a respite for business travelers; there's a fitness club,
pool, full-service spa, a nearby golf course and tennis, squash and racquetball courts among its amenities, and indoor sports include shopping at the high-end Al Mamlaka mall.

Seychelles

Banyan Tree Ⓢ🌊 | 27 | 28 | 21 | 25 | $1853

Anse Intendance | Mahé Island | (011-248) 383-500 | fax 383-600 |
800-525-4800 | www.banyantree.com | 47 villas

The plantation-style villas are "stellar" at this "honeymoon hideaway"
where you find "heaven in every category" from the "outstanding service" to "one of the world's best spas" featuring steam rooms, indoor and
outdoor showers and treatments utilizing local traditions and ingredients; "man, this place is beautiful" say some struggling to describe the
jungle-covered mountains and wonderful grounds here, but "oh, do you
pay" for it, so pray for sunshine (there's "not much to do if it rains").

Frégate Island Private 🏌🏃Ⓢ🌊🔍 | – | – | – | – | $2775

Frégate Island | (011-49-6102) 501-321 | fax 501-322 | 800-225-4255 |
www.fregate.com | 16 villas

"Feel like you're Brad and Angelina for a week" at this "incredibly expensive" "absolute paradise" on the Indian Ocean, where seven
beaches include "some of the best" you've ever seen and "excellent
service" never disappoints; with just a handful of villas (sporting spectacular views), it seems like "you're the only person on the island", and
"if you love flora and fawna", this should be "your number one choice."

**Lémuria Resort
of Praslin** 🏌🏃⊥Ⓢ🌊🔍 | ▽ 22 | 24 | 23 | 24 | $745

Anse Kerlan | Praslin Island | (011-248) 281-281 | fax 281-001 |
800-735-2478 | www.lemuriaresort.com | 96 suites, 9 villas

"Brush up on your French" and Creole, then head to this Relais &
Châteaux "magical" place that's "perfect for honeymooners" with

"flowers on the bed", "champagne in the evenings" and "tropical paradise" all around; the three-tiered pool is "breathtaking" sigh swimmers, and the "beach is the most beautiful" some have ever seen; it's only a few with higher expectations who find the quarters are "not extraordinary" at this "expensive" spot.

North Island 🐾🏖🏊 | - | - | - | - | $4136

North Island | (011-248) 293-100 | fax 293-150 | www.north-island.com | 11 villas

If you're looking for your own private island vacation, this "amazing" luxe resort that's "absolutely fabulous in every detail" may be the one; a veritable conservation project, it includes an exclusive lodge with just 11 separate, hand-built thatched-roof villas featuring private plunge pools, marble baths, DVD/CD players and walls that open to the crystal blue sea; wildlife abounds (endangered Seychelles species will be reintroduced and given a chance to regenerate here), and service is "dedicated and discreet"; N.B. rates include all meals, most alcohol, scuba, snorkeling, sea kayaking and shore-based fishing.

Taj Denis Island Ⓜ🏖🔍 | - | - | - | - | $1315

Denis Island | (011-248) 321-143 | fax 321-010 | www.tajhotels.com | 23 cottages, 2 villas

A former pirates hideaway, this luxury outpost from Taj Hotels, 30 minutes from Mahé, is set on a 375-acre coral island; accommodations are in cottages and villas designed in natural textures and colors, with vaulted ceilings, attached courtyards and outdoor showers; a bevy of watersports includes windsurfing and fishing, and the hotel can arrange sightseeing excursions.

Singapore

TOPS IN COUNTRY

Conrad Centennial 🏖Ⓢ🏊 | 22 | 22 | 21 | 22 | $312

2 Temasek Blvd. | (011-65) 6334-8888 | fax 6333-9166 | 800-737-1818 | www.conradcentennialsingapore.com | 484 rooms, 25 suites

An "oasis of calm" in the bustling Marina Centre, this "solid" "business hotel" is appreciated for its "doting" staff, "pleasant" modern rooms, prime executive lounge and restaurant providing 24-hour room service; if the overall feel strikes some as "cookie-cutter" ("not much charm"), others consider it an "excellent" alternative to the city's other choices.

Four Seasons 🎾✕🍴🏖Ⓢ🏊🔍 | 26 | 27 | 24 | 24 | $322

190 Orchard Rd. | (011-65) 6734-1110 | fax 6733-0682 | www.fourseasons.com | 214 rooms, 40 suites

"Grace and style" set the tone for this "oasis in the urban sprawl" that's "convenient to busy Orchard Road" but still provides "breathtaking views of the Singapore greenery"; the "pampering" "residential feel" starts with that "polished" service and extends to the "tranquil" rooms with "huge bathrooms" and to the "incredible spa"; but when you see the rates, you may be "thanking God" your "company paid the bill."

Fullerton, The 🫖🏡🔭[S]🏊 24 | 23 | 22 | 24 | $435

1 Fullerton Sq. | (011-65) 6533-8388 | fax 6535-8088 | www.fullertonhotel.com | 379 rooms, 21 suites

It's a "modern classic" argue architectural admirers who've checked into this "magnificently renovated" 1928 building ringed with stately Doric columns in the Civic District; executive types dub it a "stylish" "upscale" choice that's "convenient" for business, and with "charming" service and a "lovely lap pool" (the view while swimming "is hard to beat"), the "venue is ideal for pleasure" travelers too; the main gripe? - rooms that are "too small."

Goodwood Park Hotel [H]🫖🏊 ▽ 18 | 23 | 22 | 21 | $166

22 Scotts Rd. | (011-65) 6737-7411 | fax 6732-8558 | www.goodwoodparkhotel.com | 133 rooms, 98 suites, 3 apartments

"Amid all the new buildings", this "classic hotel" in the shopping district around Orchard and Scotts roads remains one of "the last traces" of Singapore's colonial heritage; set in a "lush park"-like setting and run by an "attentive staff", it's a "relaxing" "oasis" from the city's "heat and bustle", with well-regarded dining options ranging from Continental to Szechuan-style to local seafood (and an "excellent high tea" too); in sum, surveyors say this "historic" spot has "aged well."

Grand Hyatt 🔭[S]🏊🎾 23 | 22 | 21 | 22 | $315

10 Scotts Rd. | (011-65) 6738-1234 | fax 6732-1696 | 800-223-1234 | www.singapore.grand.hyatt.com | 633 rooms, 30 suites

"They really go the extra mile to make you happy" at this business-oriented hotel that's also "a favorite for shopper-tourists" (it's "at the center of things" near the Orchard Road shopping district); the "comfy rooms", especially the "fabulous executive suites", earn praise, while athletes appreciate the "spectacular gym" and "lovely swimming pool"; among the many dining options, the "hip" "Mezza9 is worth a try."

Le Méridien 🏊 18 | 20 | 18 | 18 | $227

100 Orchard Rd. | (011-65) 6733-8855 | fax 6732-7886 | 800-543-4300 | www.lemeridien.com | 387 rooms, 20 suites

"A great place to collapse after a trans-Pacific flight", this "big" hotel that's "convenient to everything on Orchard Road" caters to business travelers; it's built around an open atrium - the lobby is a "work of art" - and facilities include an outdoor pool and the Café Georges, which serves a mix of Western and Asian fare; it's a "decent value", but some surveyors cite "tired" rooms and rate it "average on most counts."

Marina Mandarin 🔭[S]🏊 20 | 22 | 20 | 21 | $284

Marina Sq., 6 Raffles Blvd. | (011-65) 6845-1000 | fax 6845-1001 | 800-223-6800 | www.marina-mandarin.com.sg | 555 rooms, 20 suites

Adjacent to the Suntec Singapore International Convention Centre and surrounded by shopping malls, this contemporary business-friendly tower is "an easy walk to most things"; "the staff is always pleasant", and the Venus Rooms, designed for women travelers, include extra amenities like bath salts and satin hangers, but "try the club floor" for particularly "spacious" accommodations.

	ROOMS	SERVICE	DINING	FACIL.	COST

Meritus Mandarin ⚔🏊🔍

| | ▽ 20 | 16 | 18 | 17 | $331 |

333 Orchard Rd. | (011-65) 6737-4411 | fax 6732-2361 | 800-338-8355 |
www.mandarin-singapore.com | 1166 rooms, 34 suites

Respected as a businessman's refuge, this Singapore mainstay also
entices leisure travelers with its own mall and "one of the best locations" on the shoppers' paradise of Orchard Road; after a day of work
or play, casual diners replenish at the Chatterbox, an eatery "well
known for local cuisine", while those looking to impress snag a table
by the window at Top of the 'M', a revolving restaurant 39 stories high.

Oriental, The ⚔Ⓢ🏊🔍

| | 25 | 25 | 24 | 24 | $238 |

Marina Sq., 5 Raffles Ave. | (011-65) 6338-0066 | fax 6339-9537 |
800-526-6566 | www.mandarinoriental.com | 455 rooms, 72 suites

With "orchids everywhere" and "exceptional" views of the city, you'll
"never want to leave" this Mandarin Oriental "minimalist paradise" in
Singapore's business and entertainment district where a "calm, inspiring", "very Zen vibe" prevails; fans fall for "large and spotless" rooms,
"mind-reading" service, food "without peer" (including Melt's "out-of-
this-world" breakfast buffet and Morton's Steak House, among others), and a "wonderful" pool and spa; muses one reviewer, "is there
such a thing as too nice?"

Pan Pacific ⚔Ⓢ🏊🔍

| | 21 | 23 | 20 | 22 | $211 |

Marina Sq., 7 Raffles Blvd. | (011-65) 6336-8111 | fax 6339-1861 |
800-327-8585 | www.singapore.panpacific.com | 739 rooms, 36 suites

An "outgoing staff" makes guests "feel welcome" from the moment
they step into the "fabulous lobby" beneath a soaring 35-story atrium
at this Singapore "business hotel", which is "well-located" "near the
convention center" and "within a few feet of lots of stores"; other
pluses are its variety of dining options, including a rooftop Cantonese
eatery with "impressive" views, and "chic" rooms outfitted with "plush
beds" to ensure peaceful slumber.

Raffles Hotel ✗ⓗ⒮🏊

| | 25 | 27 | 24 | 24 | $520 |

1 Beach Rd. | (011-65) 6337-1886 | fax 6339-7650 | 800-637-9477 |
www.raffleshotel.com | 103 suites

Oozing "19th-century" "colonial" "charm" and promising "unrivalled"
service, "the trademark Singapore hotel" "still excels at turning op-
pressive equatorial heat into sumptuous luxury"; "elegant" rooms, a
"superb selection of dining" options and a "gem" of a rooftop pool
wow, and although doubters declare it "overpriced" and "overrun with
tourists" slurping Slings, forgiving fans say this "museum" is a "must
on any travel itinerary" and the historic Long Bar is just "as Hemingway
left it – fabulous."

Raffles The Plaza Ⓢ🏊🔍

| | 22 | 23 | 21 | 24 | $310 |

80 Bras Basah Rd. | (011-65) 6339-7777 | fax 6337-1554 | 800-637-9477 |
www.singapore-plaza.raffles.com | 747 rooms, 22 suites

It may "not be the real Raffles", but this Marina Centre modern former
Westin in the Raffles City complex – next door to the historic hotel – still
has a "perfect location" for both shopping and business; with two pools,
tennis courts, yoga and spa services ranging from Thai massage to mud
wraps, the fitness facilities are among "the best", so the athletically
inclined advise staying here and visiting the original "for a drink."

	ROOMS	SERVICE	DINING	FACIL.	COST
Regent, The 🏨⊙♨	22	24	20	21	$179

1 Cuscaden Rd. | (011-65) 6733-8888 | fax 6732-8838 | 800-545-4000 | www.regenthotels.com | 393 rooms, 46 suites

The "staff goes beyond the call of duty to help you with anything" at this "gracious" hotel in the Orchard Road area (perhaps because it's managed by the service-centric Four Seasons chain); the business class find a "quiet" venue "to catch up on work – or rest", and an easy "walk to the main shopping areas"; it's a decent "value for the money" too, though a few feel that "there's better in this town."

	ROOMS	SERVICE	DINING	FACIL.	COST
🔲 **Ritz-Carlton Millenia** ✗♨⊙♨🔍	28	26	25	26	$325

7 Raffles Ave. | (011-65) 6337-8888 | fax 6337-5190 | 800-241-3333 | www.ritzcarlton.com | 530 rooms, 78 suites

"Customer service and exceptional quality reigns" at this "striking" hotel with an impressive modern art collection; "super-spacey" rooms boast the "best bathtubs in the world" set under circular windows "overlooking the city", the "gorgeous" staff is "second to none" and there's a "stellar" gym, "dreamy pool" and "one of the best Sunday brunches in the world"; when real nitpickers complain "nothing tells you you're in Singapore", others quickly respond take a look at the "unbelievable views" – there's no mistaking it.

	ROOMS	SERVICE	DINING	FACIL.	COST
Shangri-La Hotel 🐾♨⊙♨🔍	25	24	23	25	$260

22 Orange Grove Rd. | (011-65) 6737-3644 | fax 6737-3257 | 866-565-5050 | www.shangri-la.com | 719 rooms, 36 suites

"The name says it all" when it comes to this "luxe" Singapore "palace", where "flowers and more flowers" spill from lush gardens into "superb", "spacious" rooms and the staff "goes out of its way to please"; a location that's "tucked away" from the Financial District, an "amazing pool" and "diverse" choice of restaurants make this "business hotel" feel like a "resort"; P.S. big spenders recommend "go for bust and stay in the Valley Wing" where "CEOs and celebs" enjoy privacy and "free-flowing champagne."

	ROOMS	SERVICE	DINING	FACIL.	COST
Sheraton Towers ♨	21	21	20	21	$359

39 Scotts Rd. | (011-65) 6737-6888 | fax 6737-1072 | 800-325-3535 | www.sheraton.com | 396 rooms, 17 suites

"Perhaps the greatest benefit" of this "solid" Singapore hotel is the "easy access" it provides to the food stalls of Hawker Center and shops of Orchard Road; business travelers take in stride its "standard" (some say "dull") rooms given pluses like a "fantastic" pool and "excellent breakfast buffet" that lead many to laud it as an overall "very good value"; N.B. a post-Survey renovation of the rooms, gym and other facilities may outdate the above scores.

	ROOMS	SERVICE	DINING	FACIL.	COST
Swissôtel Merchant Court ♨⊙♨	–	–	–	–	$182

20 Merchant Rd. | (011-65) 6337-2288 | fax 6334-0606 | 800-637-9477 | www.singapore-merchantcourt.swissotel.com | 464 rooms, 6 suites, 6 studios

Located along the Singapore River, this "modern" business-friendly hotel offers complimentary shuttle services to the Financial District, "dedicated service" and rooms with the expected high-tech amenities (the Executive Club ones even have private espresso machines); there's "great walking access to nearby bars and restaurants", or you can enjoy Straits-Chinese and International fare at Ellenborough Market Café.

	ROOMS	SERVICE	DINING	FACIL.	COST

Swissôtel The Stamford 🏃🏻 🐴 Ⓢ 🏖 🔍 | 22 | 23 | 20 | 23 | $299

2 Stamford Rd. | (011-65) 6338-8585 | fax 6338-2862 | 800-637-9477 |
www.singapore-stamford.swissotel.com | 1203 rooms, 59 suites

"The views are heavenly from this tallest hotel" in Singapore (it hosts a
'vertical marathon' race to the top), and the high floors have especially
stellar vistas of the city; the location across from the world-famous
Raffles Hotel in Marina Centre is "convenient for shopping" and for
business travelers (there's an "underground station in the complex"),
while sybarites "like the Amrita Spa", the largest such facility in Asia.

South Africa

TOPS IN COUNTRY

29   Singita | *Kruger Area*
27   Londolozi | *Kruger Area*
26   Cape Grace | *Cape Town*
       Sabi Sabi | *Kruger Area*
       Westcliff | *Johannesburg*

Benmore

Kwandwe Private Game Reserve 🐴 🏖 | - | - | - | - | $714

Benmore | (011-27-11) 809-4300 | fax 809-4400 |
www.kwandwereserve.co.za | 15 suites, 1 house

Expect "exciting viewing" of buffalos, white rhinos and lions at this
"top-of-the-line" Relais & Châteaux Eastern Cape game reserve that's
"ideal for honeymooners" and ardent safari junkies; rooms are divided
among a pair of lodges and a 1905 farmhouse, there are lovely views
of the Great Fish River, the swank restaurant serves "outstanding"
farm-fresh fare and the "superb" staff includes "experienced guides."

Biedouw Valley

Bushmans Kloof
Wilderness Reserve 🐴 Ⓢ | 26 | 25 | 23 | 27 | $279
(aka Bushmans Kloof)

Biedouw Valley | (011-27-27) 482-2627 | fax 482-1011 |
www.bushmanskloof.co.za | 13 rooms, 3 suites, 1 house

After a visit to this "stunningly landscaped" Relais & Châteaux wilderness preserve in a "quiet" location between the Cederberg Mountains
and Karoo Plains, patrons proclaim they'd "surely go back"; among the
"interesting sights" are many "well-preserved" examples of 10,000-
year-old "cave art" and "amazing skies at night", plus the "impeccable
service" and "outstanding" dinners don't disappoint; "as long as you
don't expect to see the Big Five", you'll have a "worthwhile experience."

Cape Town

Bay Hotel, The 🍴 🐴 🏖 | 23 | 24 | 20 | 23 | $351

69 Victoria Rd., Camps Bay | (011-27-21) 430-4444 | fax 438-4433 |
www.thebay.co.za | 68 rooms, 5 suites, 1 villa

"Gorgeous", "commanding views" of "stunning Camps Bay" and "the
spectacular Twelve Apostles" mountains further enhance this "beau-

tiful" Cape Town beach location where "casual elegance" is the hallmark of its "sleek, modern rooms" (though some say they're "overshadowed by the extravagant bathrooms"); "no request is too much for the wonderful staff", plus a "good location" adjacent to shopping spots and "within walking distance of many eateries" means there's a lot more to do than "listen to the sound of the waves from your room."

[Z] Cape Grace 👪 🍴 🔭 [S] 🏊 — 27 | 27 | 25 | 26 | $643

West Quay Rd. | (011-27-21) 410-7100 | fax 419-7622 | 800-223-6800 | www.capegrace.com | 110 rooms, 10 suites, 2 penthouses

The "place to stay in Cape Town", this "first-class", "gracefully aging" "grande dame" in an "absolutely incredible location" "right on the waterfront" is "impeccable without being pretentious" and provides "every amenity" one could want; there's a "super-responsive" staff, a "wonderful spa", an "amazing" restaurant stocking an "incredible" selection of whiskeys and wines and "beautiful", "quiet rooms that help you get over the jet lag."

Cellars-Hohenort Hotel, The 🔭 [S] 🏊 🎾 — 23 | 24 | 23 | 23 | $430

93 Brommersvlei Rd. | Constantia | (011-27-21) 794-2137 | fax 794-2149 | www.cellars-hohenort.com | 32 rooms, 17 suites, 1 villa

Most reviewers laud the "fantastic value", "calm atmosphere" and "beautiful grounds" of this 18th-century "country hotel" in the Constantia wine country, 12 miles west of Cape Town and next to the Kirstenbosch Botanical Gardens; the staff "goes out of its way" and the restaurant is "a destination in itself", but critics contend the "charming" rooms are "kind of small" and they're bothered by too many "pretentious" guests.

Ellerman House 🍴 🛏 🔭 [S] 🏊 — 26 | 27 | 24 | 24 | $744

180 Kloof Rd., Bantry Bay | (011-27-21) 430-3200 | fax 430-3215 | 800-735-2478 | www.ellerman.co.za | 9 rooms, 2 suites, 1 villa

Boasting a "stunning setting overlooking the water", this "small", "exquisite" Relais & Châteaux "jewel" in the residential area of Bantry Bay is especially "wonderful for couples" given its "romantic, secluded" location, "intimate" layout conducive to privacy and "discreet" "personal" service (expect to be "treated like a king and queen"); it also offers "high-caliber" dining, enhanced by a "great wine cellar", and an on-premises spa; N.B. no children under 14 allowed.

Grande Roche 🍴 [H] 🔭 🏊 🎾 — 23 | 27 | 26 | 22 | $355

Plantasie St. | Paarl | (011-27-21) 863-5100 | fax 863-2220 | 800-735-2478 | www.granderoche.co.za | 5 rooms, 29 suites

The "unbelievable food" at Bosman's (the only Relais Gourmand restaurant in Africa) is the true highlight at this "fantastic wine country property", but the "terrific yet understated" staff that "loves to take care of your every need" isn't far behind; a national monument with a manor house surrounded by cottages in "picturesque surroundings", this "true joy" "always exceeds expectations."

Lanzerac Manor & Winery 🍴 [H] 🔭 [S] 🏊 — 23 | 23 | 21 | 22 | $354

Lanzerac Rd. | Stellenbosch | (011-27-21) 887-1132 | fax 887-2310 | www.lanzerac.co.za | 41 rooms, 7 suites

Foodies "definitely recommend" this Stellenbosch venue tucked into South Africa's wine country 40 minutes from Cape Town for its

	ROOMS	SERVICE	DINING	FACIL.	COST

"superb dining" and "wonderful" location for relaxing after a day of tastings; but malcontents maintain the accommodations are "just ok for a luxury resort," which has become "too much of a corporate entertaining venue" anyway.

Mount Nelson Hotel ♀ ✕ Ⓗ Ⓢ ≋ ॐ | 24 | 26 | 25 | 24 | $793 |

76 Orange St. | (011-27-21) 483-1000 | fax 483-1001 | 800-237-1236 | www.mountnelson.co.za | 144 rooms, 57 suites

"Don't miss" the "wonderful tea with cucumber sandwiches" at this "very traditional" stalwart in the shadows of Cape Town's Table Mountain where you'll find a "peaceful oasis" from the "bustle of city life"; "like a good wine", the "Nellie" "continues to age well", providing just the right amount of "grandeur mixed with history" in its "well-appointed" rooms and "world-class amenities"; even the "incredibly responsive" staff that "refreshes your body and soul" makes you "reminicent of life in a bygone era."

Table Bay Hotel, The ♨ Ⓢ ≋ | 26 | 26 | 23 | 25 | $581 |

6 Table Bay Quay | (011-27-21) 406-5000 | fax 406-5787 | 800-223-6800 | www.thetablebay.com | 254 rooms, 75 suites

"Outstanding, attentive service" from a "huge staff" that's "on top of everything" will "make you feel right at home" at this "very modern" "retreat in the middle of beautiful" Cape Town where the "bay views" and backdrop of Table Mountain delight; citing the "large rooms", "fantastic breakfast buffet" and "adjacent shopping" (it's attached to the Victoria & Alfred Waterfront Mall), most describe it as "pricey but worth it."

Franschhoek

Le Quartier Francais ✕ ≋ | 23 | 25 | 28 | 21 | $415 |

16 Huguenot Rd. | (011-27-21) 876-2151 | fax 876-3105 | www.lequartier.co.za | 21 suites

This "oh-so-perfect" Relais & Châteaux "French country boutique" hotel in a charming rural village "has it all", from "pretty rooms" with "clever amenities" to a first-rate staff that provides some of the "best service anywhere"; but what truly makes this *the* place to stay in the wine country" is the "shabby-chic dining room" where "wonderfully fresh ingredients" come together in "delicious" dishes that "rival any great French restaurant" – so even if you don't stay here, "treat yourself to dinner."

Johannesburg

Grace in Rosebank, The ♨ Ⓢ ≋ | 25 | 24 | 22 | 25 | $344 |

54 Bath Ave., Rosebank | (011-27-11) 280-7200 | fax 280-7474 | www.thegrace.co.za | 60 rooms, 13 suites

Expect "uniform politeness" and "superb service" from the "extremely nice", "eager-to-please" staffers ("seems like 10 per guest!") of this "gracious small hotel" located in Rosebank, north of Johannesburg it's a "haven" for weary travelers and offers "wonderful dining" delights – "don't miss" the "amazing breakfast buffet" that's "included" in the cost of your room; N.B. a comp car transports guests anywhere within 10 kilometers (about 6 miles).

Michelangelo, The 🏊 24 | 24 | 21 | 23 | $401

Nelson Mandela Sq. | (011-27-11) 282-7000 | fax 282-7171 | 800-223-6800 | www.legacyhotels.co.za | 218 rooms, 22 suites

Set in a "suburban"-ish area of Johannesburg, this "wonderful establishment" "attached to an amazing shopping center with plenty of options for dining" attracts an "impressive clientele" with a "tasteful villa setting that transports you to Tuscany" ("keep reminding yourself that you are in Africa!"); there are "spacious rooms" with "so much marble" plus "fabulous", "pampering" service, so guests call it "one of the best in Jo-burg."

Park Hyatt 🔭 [S] 🏊 23 | 21 | 19 | 23 | $274

191 Oxford Rd., Rosebank | (011-27-11) 280-1234 | fax 280-1238 | 800-223-1234 | www.johannesburg.park.hyatt.com | 229 rooms, 15 suites

"After dealing with the Jo-burg traffic, it's great to be welcomed home" by the "amazing staff" at this "plush, contemporary hotel" that "mixes glitz and comfort" in the "pleasant neighborhood" of Rosebank (north of Johannesburg); those who prefer "modern accommodations" appreciate its "beautifully designed rooms" and "large suites" graced with "stylish, African-inspired decor" and "warmed by a dozen red roses", plus there's a "very good gym" and "great conference facilities too."

Saxon 🔭 [S] 🏊 ▽ 29 | 29 | 28 | 29 | $666

36 Saxon Rd., Sandhurst | (011-27-11) 292-6000 | fax 292-6001 | www.thesaxon.com | 24 suites

"Only heaven could be better" exalt those who've experienced the "nirvana" of a stay at this ultra-exclusive boutique inn in the "secluded" Johannesburg suburb of Sandhurst, where the top-quality suites, service, fine dining, gardens and pool go way "beyond expectations", and the "new spa is the icing on the cake"; however, with names like Oprah and Beyoncé in the guest register, prospective bookers should have a good idea of what they'll have to shell out for such surpassing luxury.

Westcliff, The 🔭 [S] 🏊 🎾 28 | 25 | 24 | 27 | $301

67 Jan Smuts Ave., Westcliff | (011-27-11) 481-6000 | fax 481-6010 | 800-237-1236 | www.westcliff.co.za | 80 rooms, 35 suites

You'll "think you've died and gone to heaven" after checking into this "spectacular" Orient-Express "hedonistic delight" "built on a hill" outside Jo-burg where the staff works hard to "meet your every need" and the "exquisite" rooms have "bathrooms that you'd want in your home" (try to get one "overlooking" the Zoological Gardens); add in an "excellent" restaurant with "delicious" food, and most "would go back."

Kruger Area

Inyati Private Game Lodge 🍴 🔭 🏊 - | - | - | - | $358

Kruger National Park | (011-27-11) 880-5907 | fax 788-2406 | www.inyati.co.za | 8 rooms, 2 suites

"Beautiful and comfortable" but "not too swanky", this "authentic" safari spot is located in the famed Sabi Sand reserve next to Kruger National Park; guests enjoy top-notch cuisine, "affable hosts" and sightings of the Big Five as well as other wildlife, thanks to the expert guides; rates for the luxury chalets include meals, game drives, sundowners, foot treks and more, making this one of the "best bargains" in the region.

	ROOMS	SERVICE	DINING	FACIL.	COST

☑ Londolozi Private
Game Reserve ✕ ⚭ ≋

| | 28 | 28 | 25 | 26 | $974 |

Sabi Sand Reserve | (011-27-11) 809-4300 | fax 809-4400 |
800-735-2478 | www.ccafrica.com | 14 suites, 22 chalets

It's "worth every penny" to stay at this "exciting" Relais & Châteaux "dream safari camp" on the edge of Kruger National Park, known for its "outstanding rangers", "spectacular game drives" (you'll see "herds of rhinos, lions and elephants"), "fabulous food" and "lavish" suites that are "as luxurious as any in New York or Paris"; all in all, "if you're willing to pay for the best", "you'll never look at camping in the wilderness in the same way again."

MalaMala Game Reserve ✕ ⚭ ≋

| | 25 | 29 | 23 | 26 | $500 |

KwaZulu-Natal | (011-27-11) 442-2267 | fax 442-2318 |
www.malamala.com | 10 rooms, 15 suites

Experience "South Africa at its best" – "unbeatable" wildlife, "luxury" and "beauty in the bush" – at this "exquisite game reserve" with "superb facilities" in three distinct camps where the "courteous" staffers and "excellent animal trackers" "treat you like a prince" and make this a truly "unforgettable experience"; with such "exemplary" service and amenities, the food seems "lackluster" by comparison – but that's just nitpicking because overall this is "what you've fantasized about."

Ngala Private Game Reserve ⚭ ≋

| | 23 | 26 | 23 | 23 | $974 |

Kruger National Park | (011-27-11) 809-4300 | fax 809-4400 |
800-525-4800 | www.ccafrica.com | 20 cottages, 6 tents

The "trackers make an experience here worth every penny" say pleased patrons of this "magical" safari setting in Kruger National Park where "every detail is accounted for" and some report they "had four out of the Big Five" game sightings in their first two days; accommodations are in thatched cottages or in the nearby tented camp.

Phinda Private Game Reserve ⚭ ≋

| | 27 | 28 | 23 | 25 | $582 |

KwaZulu-Natal | (011-27-11) 809-4300 | fax 809-4400 | 800-525-4800 |
www.phinda.com | 52 suites, 4 cottages, 4 tents

You'll feel "like the top lion" at this "luxury bush resort" set in six different lodges "in the wilds" of KwaZulu-Natal; you "won't want to leave" the "chic" rooms (some with "private plunge pools"), but you will to view "elephants, rhinos" and other "stunning sights" on "terrific safari rides" led by "enthusiastic trackers"; the food doesn't get as many raves, but overall most say it's "worth every cent."

Sabi Sabi Private
Game Reserve ⚭ Ⓢ ≋

| | 28 | 25 | 26 | 25 | $512 |

Sabi Sand Reserve | (011-27-13) 735-5261 | fax 735-5081 |
www.sabisabi.com | 52 suites

"You can see the Big Five" (lions, elephants, rhinos, leopards and buffalos) at this "heavenly", "almost-too-perfect" "refuge" that's four venues in one – the "spectacular" Earth Lodge with luxury suites, the colonial-themed Selati Camp, the contemporary African-themed Bush Lodge and the more exclusive Little Bush Lodge; with "rooms the size of your house", an "unobtrusive and delightful staff" and "plentiful game" ("breakfast with giraffes just off your veranda"), most guests "can't say enough" about their stay.

	ROOMS	SERVICE	DINING	FACIL.	COST

☒ Singita ✕ ♨ ≋

| | 29 | 29 | 29 | 29 | $1022 |

Kruger National Park & Sabi Sand Reserve | (011-27-21) 683-3424 |
fax 683-3502 | www.singita.com | 24 suites

Expect "A-list treatment" "from the moment you arrive" at this "absolutely flawless" Relais & Châteaux safari compound with lodges in both Kruger National Park and Sabi Sand Reserve that's "almost untouchable" by the competition (and voted the world's No. 1 Small Hotel as well as No. 1 for Rooms in this Survey); given its "stunning" quarters designed with "native materials", "superb" dining, "plush" facilities and a "staff so friendly, you swear you're visiting someone's home" ("never had better service in my life"), awestruck admirers proclaim this "high-end" "piece of heaven" "the best hotel anywhere on the planet."

Thornybush Game Lodge ♛ ♨ ⓢ ≋

| ▽ | 26 | 28 | 24 | 24 | $945 |

Guernsey Rd., Limpopo | Thornybush Game Reserve |
(011-27-11) 883-7918 | fax 883-8201 | www.thornybush.co.za |
18 rooms, 2 suites

With a maximum occupancy of 40 people, this "amazing" lodge with "super-friendly" staffers located adjacent to Kruger National Park has a Guerlain spa, swimming pool, library and views over a rather active watering hole for Big Five game, in addition to offering both dawn and dusk safari drives that are "beyond belief" and a "life-changing experience" for some; the "beautiful" accommodations (including two family suites) feature outdoor showers and private decks overlooking the seasonal Monwana River – you may just "hear the roar of lions" at night.

Ulusaba
Private Game Reserve ♛ ♨ ⓢ ≋ 🔍

| ▽ | 25 | 28 | 25 | 27 | $1145 |

Sabi Sand Reserve | (011-27-13) 735-5460 | 800-225-4255 |
www.ulusaba.com | 18 rooms

Richard Branson applies the "over-the-top" luxury of his Virgin Limited Edition brand to Big Five game watching at this "exciting" pair of lodges spread over 10,000 acres in South Africa's Sabi Sands Reserve, bordering Kruger National Park; in addition to "spectacular" safaris led by "informative guides", privileged patrons enjoy fitness and spa services, star-gazing from an observatory and "bush nights" featuring "wonderful food" and tribal dancers in the open air, all of which add up to "memories" one could "never forget."

Plettenberg Bay

Plettenberg, The ♨ ⊥ ⓢ ≋

| | 26 | 25 | 25 | 22 | $401 |

40 Church St. | (011-27-44) 533-2030 | fax 533-2074 |
www.collectionmcgrath.com | 24 rooms, 12 suites, 2 houses

"It doesn't get any better" than this small Relais & Châteaux South African sanctuary "perched on a cliff" overlooking the Indian Ocean, so "book a suite", head to the "outstanding" seaside restaurant, ask a "charming" server to recommend something from the "creative chef" and let the "sounds of the crashing waves" roll over you; besides a pool and spa, there are "no real facilities" to speak of, but scuba diving, nature preserves and animal refuges are nearby; N.B. no children under 12.

Tsala Treetop Lodge 🔭🏊

ROOMS	SERVICE	DINING	FACIL.	COST
▽ 29	24	24	22	$767

off Hwy. N2 | (011-26-44) 532-8228 | fax 532-7587 | 800-735-2478 | www.tsala.co.za | 10 suites

This Relais & Châteaux "luxury treehouse" "for grown-ups" is "a bit out of the way but worth the trip", owing to its "idyllic setting" "at the top of a hill" overlooking the Tsitsikamma forest and its "unbelievably beautiful" rooms "built into the trees" with private decks and hot tubs"; "amazing" food and "gracious" service" make the "romantic" experience even more "sublime."

Sun City

Palace of the Lost City, The 👪🔭⛳Ⓢ🏊🎾

ROOMS	SERVICE	DINING	FACIL.	COST
26	21	21	26	$623

Sun City | (011-27-14) 557-4307 | fax 557-3111 | 800-223-6800 | www.lhw.com | 322 rooms, 16 suites

"'Over the top' is too mild to describe this amazing resort" in South Africa's North West Province, a "fantasy hotel complex" that's a "cross between Las Vegas, Disneyland and Atlantic City"; the "opulence" of its "fairyland" facilities "can't be beat", "the service is something else" and the "fabulous rooms" "must be seen to be believed", though with "everything from tennis and golf" to "tremendous pools", you may spend little time indoors.

South Korea

Seoul

Grand Hyatt 🔭Ⓢ🏊🎾

ROOMS	SERVICE	DINING	FACIL.	COST
20	23	21	22	$370

747-7 Hannam-dong | Yongsan-gu | (011-82-2) 797-1234 | fax 798-6953 | 800-223-1234 | www.seoul.grand.hyatt.com | 554 rooms, 47 suites

The "most popular club in town" (JJ Mahoney's) makes this "excellent business property" a "happening" place where the "jet set and movie stars hang out"; an "out-of-the-way location makes it tough to get to" but you're rewarded with an "unparalleled view over Han River" and Downtown Seoul and a "friendly staff"; too bad a few find rooms "teeny and showing their age"; N.B. the outdoor pool is an ice rink in winter.

Grand InterContinental 🏊

ROOMS	SERVICE	DINING	FACIL.	COST
23	23	22	23	$435

159-8 Samseong-dong | Gangnam-gu | (011-82-2) 555-5656 | fax 559-7990 | 888-424-6835 | www.intercontinental.com | 272 rooms, 263 suites

The "great location" at the Korea World Trade Centre complex is the feature some "like best" about this property, since "everything is in walking distance"; business types love the "roomy" quarters with "the latest technology" and "every imaginable amenity", while the "friendly personnel" "meet all their needs", and leisure lodgers like the proximity "right by the biggest mall."

Lotte Hotel 🏊

ROOMS	SERVICE	DINING	FACIL.	COST
19	22	18	19	$325

1 Sogong-dong | Jung-gu | (011-82-2) 771-1000 | fax 752-8602 | www.lottehotel.co.kr | 1184 rooms, 295 suites

The "convenient" Downtown location and plethora of dining choices of this "mega hotel" in the business district, as well as its proximity to shopping, mean it's decent for business and leisure folks alike who find a "memorable room in a busy" lodging, especially since a renovation last year; solid service brings it all together, so "if huge works" for you, try it.

Ritz-Carlton, The 👨Ⓢ⛲

| 22 | 24 | 22 | 22 | $215 |

602-4 Yeoksam-dong | Gangnam-gu | (011-82-2) 3451-8000 | fax 3451-8282 | 800-241-3333 | www.ritzcarlton.com | 363 rooms, 47 suites

"Everything is enjoyable" at this property in an "incredible location" in the Gangnam business district where you can "enjoy the nearby active nightlife" then return for "full-time pampering" and "outstanding" restaurants; although a few sour sorts say the rooms are not up to snuff (they "need a face-lift"), they're "bigger than normal for Asia", at least.

Shilla, The 👨Ⓢ⛲⚲

| 23 | 25 | 23 | 24 | $246 |

202 Jangchung-dong | Jung-gu | (011-82-2) 2233-3131 | fax 2233-5073 | 800-223-6800 | www.shilla.net | 472 rooms, 35 suites

An "outstanding" staff that's "always willing to help" makes this "upscale" stalwart a "heavenly" way to do Seoul; cutting a wide swathe into a hillside in the Jung-gu neighborhood, its abundant attractions include two pools, a "phenomenal spa", a garden that's perfect for a "meditative" stroll, an "extensive duty-free" mall and a "complex of excellent restaurants"; most agree that the rooms are "comfortable", but some suggest "it may be time to update" them now that the lobby's been renovated.

Westin Chosun 👨⛲

| 23 | 23 | 19 | 22 | $460 |

87 Sogong-dong | Jung-gu | (011-82-2) 771-0500 | fax 752-1443 | 800-937-8461 | www.westin.com | 434 rooms, 19 suites

"Like ants to a sugar cube", road warriors "always look forward to" this "old-time favorite" "right in the thick of things" where the rooms are "modern" and "one of the best-trained staffs" is "especially helpful to Americans"; it's "steps away from shopping and City Hall", and the "refreshing French restaurant makes you forget you're in Korea", so even if some say "it's a bit noisy", most conclude it's "reliable."

W Seoul-Walkerhill 🍴👨Ⓢ⛲⚲

▽ | 21 | 24 | 22 | 23 | $487 |

21 Gwangjang-dong | Gwangjin-gu | (011-82-2) 2022-0000 | fax 2022-0103 | 877-946-8357 | www.whotels.com | 223 rooms, 29 suites

"Easy smiles" from staffers who "go out of their way to make sure you love South Korea" "follow you everywhere" at this sleek, "sexy" trendsetter situated "a bit far" from Downtown Seoul on the slopes of Mount Acha; if you take a "big loss" in the adjacent casino, you can let it all go in the "amazing" spa's outdoor tubs before filling up at its "above-average" restaurants (which "tend to cater to Western palates") and retiring to your "stylish", "perfectly serviceable" room.

Spain

TOPS IN COUNTRY

26	Hostal/Gavina	*Costa Brava*
25	Arts	*Barcelona*
	Ritz	*Madrid*
24	Marbella Club	*Costa del Sol*
	Alfonso XIII	*Seville*

ROOMS | SERVICE | DINING | FACIL. | COST

Barcelona

Arts, Hotel ☕🐕🔭Ⓢ🏊

Rooms	Service	Dining	Facil.	Cost
28	24	24	26	$616

Carrer de la Marina 19-21 | (011-34-93) 221-1000 | fax 221-1070 | 800-241-3333 | www.ritzcarlton.com | 397 rooms, 58 suites, 27 apartments

"Sleek, sexy and gorgeous" gush guests of this "high-style", modern aerie with "incredible architecture" and "magnificent" vistas over the Barcelona port; "luxurious rooms" feature "cool toys" like Bang & Olufson stereos and bathrooms so large "you could spend a long weekend" there, but most head out to enjoy the spa, casino, "hippest" beachside pool and "fab" fair at Sergi Arola's Catalan restaurant; P.S. "if you're looking for surrounding nightlife", this "quiet" location "isn't the place."

Casa Camper 🔭

Rooms	Service	Dining	Facil.	Cost
-	-	-	-	$284

Carrer Elisabets 11 | (011-34-93) 342-6280 | fax 342-7563 | www.camper.com | 20 rooms, 5 suites

Located in the up-and-coming Raval district, this "unique" boutique courtesy of the Camper shoe biz family is set in a 19th-century building with views over Tibidabo and the Macba; the facilities are pretty simple, but they're "filled with playful and thoughtful touches" like a pillow menu in rooms, on-site bikes to borrow and a 24-hour buffet with free snacks for night owls.

Claris Hotel Ⓗ🐕🔭Ⓢ🏊

Rooms	Service	Dining	Facil.	Cost
21	22	18	21	$539

Pau Claris 150 | (011-34-93) 487-6262 | fax 215-7970 | www.derbyhotels.com | 84 rooms, 24 suites, 16 duplexes

A "stylish" mix of the old and the new, this Eixample boutique hotel looks from the outside like the 19th-century palace it once was, but walk into the "stunning" lobby and you're surrounded by "modern" furnishings and decor; similarly, "ultracool" rooms expressing a "hip" aesthetic coexist with an "in-house museum with Egyptian artifacts"; loungers laud the "lovely" rooftop pool and cafe, a "heavenly oasis in the middle of the city", and enjoy the "excellent" central location.

Le Méridien 🐕🔭

Rooms	Service	Dining	Facil.	Cost
22	21	18	18	$515

Ramblas 111 | (011-34-93) 318-6200 | fax 301-7776 | 800-543-4300 | www.lemeridien.com | 193 rooms, 40 suites

"Beautiful", "ultramodern" chambers with "heated bathroom floors" and "plenty of storage" "feel cozier than home" at this "fabulous" spot; service is mostly "fine", and "delicious tapas" in the "fantastic" lobby bar are perfect for a "post-Gaudí fix" (although it may be "better to dine locally"), but an "unbeatable" location "near the top of Las Ramblas" trumps all; P.S. renovations continue through mid 2007, so try to stay in the completed portion – and "ask for an extra-large balcony."

Majestic, Hotel Ⓗ🔭🏊

Rooms	Service	Dining	Facil.	Cost
22	25	20	21	$390

Paseo de Gracia 68 | (011-34-93) 488-1717 | fax 487-9790 | www.hotelmajestic.es | 272 rooms, 30 suites, 1 apartment

Situated on the swank Passeig de Gràcia in Barcelona's elegant shopping district in Eixample, this "good business-class hotel" with "excellent service" is "perfect for city-based travelers"; surveyors suggest you pause a few minutes to take in the "beautiful lobby" with its collection of contemporary and avant-garde art before heading to your "gorgeously decorated" suite or to the rooftop pool and patio for panoramic metropolitan vistas; the highly regarded restaurant, Drolma, which offers a cutting-edge, modern Catalan menu from chef Fermi Puig, is "rather expensive."

Neri Hotel & Restaurante ⑪Ⓜ️♨️ | – | – | – | – | $390 |

Sant Sever 5 | (011-34-93) 304-0655 | fax 304-0337 | www.hotelneri.com | 14 rooms, 8 suites

Set in a "stunning" former 18th-century palace, this hotel in a "great" Barri Gòtic location has a certain "*Jetsons*-meets-Count-Dracula feel" to its modern/old-world decor; rooms are a "sea of tranquility" with "lovely" bathrooms, original artwork and flat-screen TVs, while chef Jordi Ruiz (previously of El Bulli) heads up the Mediterranean restaurant that overlooks Plaza Sant Felip, serving dishes melding the flavors of medieval regional cooking.

Omm, Hotel ♨️≋ | 22 | 20 | 26 | 24 | $273 |

Rossello 265 | (011-34-93) 445-4000 | fax 445-4004 | www.hotelomm.es | 79 rooms, 12 suites

It's all sleek Barcelona design for the "fashionista crowd" at this "luxuriously minimalist" cosmopolitan hotel in the Eixample area where a rooftop pool and sundeck features choice views of Gaudí's Casa Milà and the shops at Passeig de Gràcia; "every detail is interesting and thoughtful", from rooms with white acrylic walls and black mod chairs to the "excellent" on-site eatery, Moo (from the respected restaurateurs, the Roca brothers), to the high-tech nightclub, Ommsesion; better yet, the "height of cool" comes with "friendly and attentive" service.

Palace, Hotel ✕✿♨️ | 22 | 24 | 21 | 21 | $502 |

Gran Via de les Corts Catalanes 668 | (011-34-93) 510-1130 | fax 318-0148 | www.hotelpalacebarcelona.com | 79 rooms, 41 suites

Aficionados of "old-school Europe at its finest" consider a stay at this "splendid" stalwart in Eixample a "first-rate experience", citing "gorgeous" accommodations outfitted with "world-class elegance" (e.g. intricately tiled 'Roman baths', bouquets of "calming calla lilies", "great gizmos" like CD players); they also adore "gracious" attendants, chef Romain Fornelli's "wonderful" Catalan-French cuisine at Caelis and a central location that's ideal "for a walking tour of the Gaudí buildings"; cutting-edgers, however, find the chambers "out of place in trendy Barcelona."

Rey Juan Carlos I, Hotel Ⓢ≋ | 23 | 20 | 19 | 23 | $418 |

Ave. Diagonal 661-671 | (011-34-93) 364-4040 | fax 364-4264 | 800-223-6800 | www.hrjuancarlos.com | 375 rooms, 37 suites

"Outstanding gardens" and a "soaring" glass lobby with internal balconies are the "highlights" of this "left-of-center" hotel in the Zona Universitaria that loyal royalists dub a "great place for meetings" owing to its "nicely appointed" rooms and "amazing facilities, in particular the spa/gym" and three swimming pools; meanwhile, fault-finders fret that food is "fairly average" and would-be walkers whine that the location is "too far away from the city center", with "little to see in the immediate area" – still, "if you expect to taxi or metro to other spots", the Rey's A-ok.

Bilbao

MiróHotel 👓 [S]

ROOMS	SERVICE	DINING	FACIL.	COST
-	-	-	-	$234

Alameda Mazarredo 77 | (011-34-94) 661-1880 | fax 425-5182 | 800-337-4685 | www.mirohotelbilbao.com | 50 rooms

The concept of Spanish fashion designer Antonio Miró, this "chic" minimalist hotel with a "great location" near the Guggenheim offers expansive "high-tech" rooms fitted out with beige walls and black marble bathrooms plus flat-screen TVs, DVD players and "amazing views"; the gym is sleek and chic, while the bar, the lobby, the dining room and the library - all mostly black and white, with a few colorful accents - are airy, ultramodern spaces where guests can socialize, read the paper or have coffee, attended by a young and friendly staff.

Costa Brava

Hostal de la Gavina 👓 [S] 🏊 🎾

ROOMS	SERVICE	DINING	FACIL.	COST
26	26	25	27	$363

S'Agaró | (011-34-972) 321-100 | fax 321-573 | 800-223-6800 | www.lagavina.com | 56 rooms, 16 suites

The service at this "beautiful property" with a "breathtaking setting" on the Iberian peninsula sets the stage for a "romantic" and "peaceful" vacation; there's a "wonderful swimming pool", restaurants that serve fresh, locally caught seafood and rooms with marble floors and hand-carved ebony furniture; only energetic types have trouble with the "too quiet" atmosphere, but most patrons are quite satisfied sitting atop this "lap of luxury."

Costa del Sol

Kempinski Resort Estepona 🏠 👓 🏊 🎾

	ROOMS	SERVICE	DINING	FACIL.	COST
▽	26	22	20	24	$449

Carretera de Cádiz, Km. 159, Playa el Patron | Estepona | (011-34-95) 280-9500 | fax 280-9550 | 800-426-3135 | www.kempinski.com | 133 rooms, 15 suites

A vast pool system with cascading waterfalls and acres of "breathtaking" landscaped gardens surround this Costa del Sol enclave where accommodations include rooms with marble baths and deluxe apartment-style suites, leafy balconies and satellite TVs; there is "professional, personal" service, plus views from the Mediterranean restaurants' outdoor seating areas that range from Gibraltar to the African coastline.

Marbella Club Hotel, Golf Resort & Spa 👓 [S] 🏊

ROOMS	SERVICE	DINING	FACIL.	COST
25	24	24	25	$595

Blvd. Príncipe Alfonso von Hohenlohe | Marbella | (011-34-952) 822-211 | fax 829-884 | 800-223-6800 | www.marbellaclub.com | 84 rooms, 37 suites, 16 villas

A "playground" for the "Euro jet set", this Marbella resort on the Costa del Sol is "right out of a Grace Kelly/Cary Grant movie" with "magnificent" facilities and grounds, "spacious", "elegant" rooms, a "great golf course" and some of the "best food" in Spain, including a "fabulous" brunch "worth every penny"; better yet, "no request is too large" for the "attentive" staff - no wonder those who "love it" exclaim "I want to live here!"

	ROOMS	SERVICE	DINING	FACIL.	COST

Puente Romano, Hotel ♨≋✎ | 23 | 23 | 22 | 25 | $521

Carretera de Cádiz, Km. 177 | Marbella | (011-34-952) 820-900 |
fax 775-766 | 800-223-6800 | www.puenteromano.com | 212 rooms,
81 suites

Families find this Andalusian-style resort named after a nearby ancient bridge "absolutely top shelf"; 10 tennis courts make this "Spanish Wimbledon" a "tennis player's paradise", but non-racketeers are also able to "manage very nicely" by strolling through "lovely" subtropical gardens, basking by the "beautiful ocean" or enjoying three pools, fishing, sailing or riding horseback; ask the "nice" staffers for a room on the top floor to get a view from your private balcony; N.B. there's a children's program during the summer months.

Granada

Barceló La Bobadilla, | ▽ 28 | 26 | 25 | 27 | $329
Hotel ✕✦ⓢ≋✎

Loja | (011-34-958) 321-861 | fax 321-810 | 800-223-6800 |
www.la-bobadilla.com | 26 rooms, 44 suites

"Secluded from the overbuilt coast", seemingly "in the middle of nowhere", this 1,000-acre estate modeled after a Moorish village (with arabesque arches, flower-filled courtyards and marble colonnades) is an "unbelievably romantic" place; its rugged expanses allow for such "family-oriented" activities as archery, horseback riding, skeet shooting, hot-air ballooning and bird-watching, while indoors there are saunas, steam rooms, lounges and "fantastic" rooms; "impeccable service" and "outstanding food and wine" round out the picture.

Parador de Granada ⓗ♨ | 21 | 22 | 22 | 21 | $330

Real de la Alhambra | (011-34-958) 221-440 | fax 222-264 |
www.parador.es | 34 rooms, 2 suites

Regulars relish the "fabulous" history of this "ethereal" palace hotel in the midst of Grenada's 12th-century Alhambra, where guests are waited on by "helpful" staffers and savor dinner on the terrace with "hot chocolate and churros . . . mmm"; but you "don't come for" the "tiny" "Moorish-style" rooms (it's "like going to summer camp") say those who choose to focus on the "spectacular" location instead.

Madrid

AC Santo Mauro, Hotel ⓗ♨≋ | 25 | 24 | 23 | 23 | $583

Zurbano 36 | (011-34-91) 319-6900 | fax 308-5477 |
www.achotelsantomauro.com | 34 rooms, 17 suites

A "wonderful staff" delivering "personal service" helps make this "intimate", "stylish and reserved" Chamberí district hotel *the* place to stay" in Madrid; a 19th-century duke's palace with "classic decor", it encompasses "funky" rooms, an indoor pool, a reading room and "fabulous food" served in the book-lined dining room or "lovely little garden."

Adler Hotel ♨ | - | - | - | - | $522

Calle Velazquez 33 | (011-34-91) 426-3220 | fax 426-3221 |
www.adlermadrid.com | 45 rooms

A dynamic mix of old and the new, this refurbished neoclassical boutique hotel holding court in the chichi Barrio Salamanca boasts an "ex-

ROOMS	SERVICE	DINING	FACIL.	COST

cellent" location, "beautiful" rooms and an "outstanding" staff; travelers can treat themselves to a Mediterranean feast at the intimate Adler restaurant and a decadent in-room massage, or venture outdoors to splurge at nearby designer shops and peruse the eye-popping treasures of the Prado and Thyssen-Bornemisza Collection.

De Las Letras, Hotel 🔭

	ROOMS	SERVICE	DINING	FACIL.	COST
▽	25	22	23	18	$317

Gran via 11 | (011-34-91) 523-7980 | fax 523-7981 | www.epoquehotels.com | 101 rooms

Fans of this "sleek" choice in the middle of Madrid are afraid to talk about it for "fear it will become wildly popular" due to its "very modern", "high-tech" rooms, "fabulous hangout bar" and "terrific breakfast buffet"; an "amazing" rooftop hot tub and a "helpful" staff are added pluses, but just be prepared for "street noise."

Hesperia 🍴

	ROOMS	SERVICE	DINING	FACIL.	COST
▽	20	24	22	19	$496

Paseo de la Castellana 57 | (011-34-91) 210-8800 | fax 210-8899 | 800-223-6800 | www.hesperia-madrid.com | 137 rooms, 34 suites

"From the minute you exit the taxi to the second you check out", the service at this "elegant" retreat in central Madrid pampers patrons; you'll have "one of the best meals" at chef Santi Santamaría's skylit Santceloni (voted No. 1 for Food in Madrid in our *Europe's Top Restaurants* Survey) and delicious after-dinner drinks at the"hip" Scotch Piano Bar, but the rooms are not up to the same standard.

InterContinental 🐕🔭Ⓢ

ROOMS	SERVICE	DINING	FACIL.	COST
20	22	18	20	$279

Paseo de la Castellana 49 | (011-34-91) 700-7300 | fax 319-5853 | 800-327-0200 | www.madrid.intercontinental.com | 279 rooms, 28 suites

The rooms are "excellent" at this "great business hotel" in Paseo de la Castellana with "easy access to everything and everywhere", and "reliable" multilingual staffers who "go all out to make sure everything is just right"; road warriors get high-speed Internet access, a 24-hour gym and views in the eighth-floor solarium.

Puerta America, Hotel 🏊

ROOMS	SERVICE	DINING	FACIL.	COST
-	-	-	-	$263

Ave. America 41 | (011-34-91) 744-5400 | fax 744-5401 | www.hotelpuertamerica.com | 308 rooms, 34 suites

In a bold aesthetic move, the Silken Group commissioned 12 designers to fashion this modernist boutique hotel, "the coolest" some have "ever seen"; each "otherworldly" floor reflects the style of a different artist, be it ultramod or avant-garde, from backlit mirrors to lounges that appear to float in the clouds ("it's hard to imagine a place like this other than on a movie set"), but the staff in this "highly original" lodging is "not ready for prime time"; N.B. there's an on-site spa and indoor pool.

Ritz, Hotel Ⓗ🐕🔭Ⓢ

ROOMS	SERVICE	DINING	FACIL.	COST
24	26	24	23	$634

Plaza de la Lealtad 5 | (011-34-91) 701-6767 | fax 701-6776 | 800-237-1236 | www.ritzmadrid.com | 137 rooms, 30 suites

A "monument to gracious living", this "fancy with a capital F" Orient-Express baroque palace near the Prado Museum in El Centro gets the nod for "extremely formal, old-school service" (white-gloved elevator operators) and decor that's a "throwback in time" (silk on the walls); though critics complain it's a little "low on facilities" and some of the rooms seem "faded", most just "want to be seen" at this "dowager" enjoying the "excellent" Spanish-International restaurant, Goya.

	ROOMS	SERVICE	DINING	FACIL.	COST
Villa Magna, A Park Hyatt Hotel ✕ 💆 👁	22	22	20	20	$525

Paseo de la Castellana 22 | (011-34-91) 587-1234 | fax 431-2286 | 800-223-1234 | www.villamagna.park.hyatt.com | 164 rooms, 18 suites

This "very plush", "first-rate business" hotel "in the middle of Salamanca, a posh residential and upscale shopping district" (where everything from El Prado to the city's business district is "easily accessible"), qualifies as "a sure bet"; the "attractive" rooms are "well appointed", the "excellent concierge" and "polite staff" are consistently "helpful" ("scored me great tickets to the bullfights") and its two "excellent restaurants" - Tse-Yang and the "unparalleled" Le Divellec - "add to the joys of staying here."

	ROOMS	SERVICE	DINING	FACIL.	COST
Villa Real 💆	24	26	20	21	$515

Plaza de las Cortes 10 | (011-34-91) 420-3767 | fax 420-2547 | www.derbyhotels.es | 98 rooms, 17 suites

"Exceptionally friendly service" has guests smiling in this boutique hotel "marvelously located" "in the heart" of Madrid within "walking distance of the Prado", the Thyssen-Bornemisza Collection and the Stock Exchange; a respected art collection fills the "sumptuous" public spaces (including Warhols in the restaurant/bar East 47), and even though some rooms are "lovely duplexes with terraces" and others are "smallish" singles, they're all "well appointed" with "modern furniture" and high-speed Internet access.

	ROOMS	SERVICE	DINING	FACIL.	COST
Wellington, Hotel 🏊	▽ 20	20	22	20	$363

Velázquez 8 | (011-34-91) 575-4400 | fax 576-4164 | www.hotel-wellington.com | 264 rooms, 28 suites

Value-minded visitors venerate this "very nice hotel for the money" because it's in the Salamanca district near shopping and not too far from museums yet "quiet" and "comfortable"; a "helpful" staff, "smallish but luxe" quarters and a "great" courtyard pool "for cooling off" are other facets of this old-school "jewel" - but a rear guard of reviewers regard it as "unremarkable" and beef the Wellington "needs a face-lift"; N.B. a new spa opens in 2007.

	ROOMS	SERVICE	DINING	FACIL.	COST
Westin Palace [H] 💆 👁	25	24	21	23	$565

Plaza de las Cortes 7 | (011-34-91) 360-8000 | fax 360-8100 | 800-937-8461 | www.westin.com | 438 rooms, 27 suites

"Grand" architecture that includes a glass dome, an "incomparable" location in central Madrid overlooking the Neptune Fountain and an "eagerly helpful" staff make guests at this palace hotel "feel like kings and queens" - even if they have to drain the royal treasury to pay the bill; quarters are "huge" with those signature "Heavenly" beds, a "beautiful lounge with live pianist" offers "delicious drinks" and exercise buffs relish the city vistas at the gym.

Mallorca

	ROOMS	SERVICE	DINING	FACIL.	COST
La Residencia 👪 [H] 👁 [S] 🏊 🎾	▽ 23	25	25	22	$641

Son Canals | Deià | (011-34-971) 639-011 | fax 639-370 | 800-237-1236 | www.hotel-laresidencia.com | 44 rooms, 23 suites

For calm "on an otherwise crazy island", trek to this "superb retreat" in a "pretty" Mallorcan village (about 20 miles outside Palma) and let an "outstanding" staffer show you to your "charming" room filled with local antiques; its mountain locale means there's a "lack of beach" and "not much in the way of grounds", but "a series of pools on various levels", "lovely" meals served outside, a spa and sheer "peace" have most guests declaring it "heaven."

Mardavall Hotel & Spa 👫 Ⓢ 🏊

ROOMS	SERVICE	DINING	FACIL.	COST
-	-	-	-	$485

Passeig Calvià | Palma de Mallorca | (011-34-971) 629-629 | fax 629-630 | 800-325-3589 | www.mardavall-hotel.com | 44 rooms, 89 suites

You may "fall in love" with the "dreamy" rooms at this "bastion of luxury" - "each different and charming" - that boast "flat-screen TVs to watch from the bathtub" and "remote-controlled drapes"; some find "high-end relief" in the "amazing" spa that takes you "far away from the maddening Mallorca crowd", others by the staff that "totally knocks itself out" in order to assist you; so "the only negative is the lack of an on-site beach" (it's about 10 minutes away).

Son Brull Hotel & Spa 🔭 🏊 🎾

ROOMS	SERVICE	DINING	FACIL.	COST
-	-	-	-	$278

Carretera Palma-Pollença | Pollença | (011-34-97) 153-5353 | fax 153-1068 | www.sonbrull.com | 16 rooms, 7 suites

Set in an 18th-century monastery, this member of Relais & Châteaux blends a country chalet design with a sleek, boutique feel; cleanly designed rooms, two with their own private terraces, have hydrobaths, and the facilities include indoor and outdoor pools, tennis courts, a nearby Robert Trent Jones Jr.-designed golf course and a spa with a *hammam*; among the other activities guests can arrange are kayaking, canoeing, fishing, group cooking lessons and wine seminars.

San Sebastián

Maria Cristina, Hotel [H] 🐕 🔭 Ⓢ 🏊

ROOMS	SERVICE	DINING	FACIL.	COST
25	23	20	21	$555

Calle Oquendo 1 | (011-34-943) 437-600 | fax 437-676 | 800-325-3589 | www.luxurycollection.com | 109 rooms, 27 suites

Maybe it's because San Sebastián is such a "sleeper", but folks don't seem to want to get out of the "amazingly comfortable beds" in the almost "perfect rooms" of this "charming", "centrally located" "palace"; but they rise and shine for the "incredible buffet" ("bring an appetite" for the hearty Basque cuisine), the spa and the indoor heated pool, all with service that's "knowledgeable and helpful" (although there are a few reports of "unaccommodating" staffers).

Seville

Alfonso XIII, Hotel 🍴 [H] 🏊

ROOMS	SERVICE	DINING	FACIL.	COST
26	24	22	24	$839

San Fernando 2 | (011-34-95) 491-7000 | fax 491-7099 | 800-937-8461 | www.alfonsoxiii.com | 128 rooms, 19 suites

This "enchanting" Moorish palace commissioned by the king in 1929 is an "exceptional" "landmark" where "even the elevators are classy" and entering the "gorgeous lobby" is "like walking into a fantasy where everything is either gilded, marbled or velveted"; private quarters boast touches like "swoon-inducing arches over your bed", silk-and-linen-covered walls and ornately tiled baths, and the "wondrous" staff is "quietly attentive"; the restaurant in the Mudejar courtyard during the summer is "lovely" as well.

	ROOMS	SERVICE	DINING	FACIL.	COST

Hacienda Benazuza elBullihotel ✕ⓘ♨≋🔍   ▽ 24 | 25 | 25 | 22 | $502

Virgen de las Nieves, Sanlúcar la Mayor | (011-34-95) 570-3344 | fax 570-3410 | www.elbullihotel.com | 26 rooms, 18 suites

An ancient Moorish farmhouse dating back to the 10th century houses this "super-luxury" hotel in the Spanish countryside not far from Seville where the "romantic" setting is "perfect for weddings and celebrations"; others just come for "a weekend away from it all", relaxing to "the cool sound of fountains in the hidden garden" and enjoying the "dreamlike facilities"; chef Raphael Morales has taken over from Ferràn Adrià, but the latter's "influence is very noticeable" in the "nouvelle cuisine" – just beware this one's "not for the faint of wallet."

Sri Lanka

Amangalla 👫♀♨Ⓢ≋   - | - | - | - | $500

10 Church St. | Galle | (011-94-91) 223-3388 | fax 223-3355 | 800-477-9180 | www.amanresorts.com | 20 rooms, 8 suites, 1 house

This Amanresorts deluxe property (two hours west of sister beach resort Amanwella) is perfectly situated for exploring the adjacent historic Galle Fort, a UNESCO World Heritage site; its highlights include a full-service spa focusing on Sri Lankan Ayurvedic healing treatments, rooms with four-poster king-size beds, a two-story house decked out with original antiques, a formal dining room serving local and European cuisine amid colonial period furnishings and an outdoor pool with shaded cabanas.

Amanwella 👫♨≋   - | - | - | - | $650

Bodhi Mawatha, Wella Wathuara, Godellawela | Tangalle | (011-94-47) 224-1333 | fax 224-1334 | 800-477-9180 | www.amanresorts.com | 30 suites

Amanresorts opened this small beachfront lodging on a crescent-shaped cove surrounded by palm trees 62 miles south of Colombo; many suites boast a private terrace, plunge pool, floor-to-ceiling glass windows and sliding doors that open to stunning sea views, and there's an on-site Asian-Mediterranean restaurant as well as outdoor spa treatments; nearby activities include nature walks in Wella Wathuara, historic sightseeing at Mulgirigalla Rock Temple 35 minutes north and rare bird-watching opportunities in Bundala National Park, 75 minutes east.

St. Barts

Carl Gustaf ☕♀♨≋   24 | 24 | 27 | 22 | $1004

Rue des Normands | Gustavia | (011-590-590) 297-900 | fax 278-237 | 800-457-4000 | www.carlgustaf.com | 14 suites

With kitchenettes, minibars, DVD players, private terraces and individual plunge pools, devotees assert "there's no need to leave" the "fabulous" villas at this "romantic", "hoity-toity" refuge on the slopes of St. Barts; for those who do venture out, however, there's a world-class French-Caribbean restaurant with picturesque landscapes of the harbor and a hilltop bar with live music that's "great for drinks at sunset"; but the bird's-eye view has its price – "a lot of steps to climb" and a long trek to the beach.

Christopher Hotel 🏨♨♒

| | 20 | 22 | 19 | 20 | $1103 |

Pointe Milou | (011-590-590) 276-363 | fax 279-292 | 800-763-4835 | www.hotelchristopherstbarth.com | 39 rooms, 2 suites

It's "perfect for a romantic vacation" exclaim escapists about this "reasonably priced" seaside hotel nestled in a "beautiful", "remote location on an island that can elsewhere be congested"; the staff is "friendly", and a "wonderful" infinity pool makes up for the lack of a beach, but given "standard fare" and "small rooms", dissers deem it "middle of the road."

Eden Rock 🏨♨♒

| | 24 | 23 | 25 | 23 | $1024 |

Saint-Jean Baie | (011-590-590) 297-999 | fax 278-837 | 877-563-7105 | www.edenrockhotel.com | 22 suites, 4 cottages, 4 houses, 3 cabins

A "*très chic*", "old-time Hollywood" haven, this Relais & Châteaux promontory features unique offerings like a 'Howard Hughes suite', an art gallery and a clothing store; the location on one of the island's "longest stretches of beach" means you can "watch the surf for celebrities" and enjoy beautiful views of Baie de St. Jean, plus the "dynamite fare" leads some to proclaim it's "better to dine here" than it is to stay.

François Plantation ✕🏨♒

| | ▽ 24 | 25 | 29 | 22 | $595 |

Colombier | (011-590-590) 298-022 | fax 276-126 | 800-207-8071 | www.francois-plantation.com | 12 cottages

The prospect of "superb dining" entices eager eaters to this "elegant" aerie, where a dozen fruit-hued houses "perched high atop a bluff" and a hilltop pool all provide "beautiful views of the island" and create a mood of "total serenity"; meanwhile, correspondents who crave excitement wistfully observe it's a "little out of the way" (and a few "miles from the beach").

Guanahani & Spa, Hotel 🏨Ⓢ♒🔍

| | 23 | 22 | 22 | 22 | $747 |

Grand Cul de Sac | (011-590-590) 276-660 | fax 277-070 | 800-223-6800 | www.leguanahani.com | 35 rooms, 35 suites

"Relaxation and pampering" await visitors at this "excellent" self-contained resort, a "class-act" colony of colorful cottages where the rooms are filled with "luxury toiletries", the "calm" beach is "clean and welcoming" and the "beautiful bartenders" serve up "amazing drinks in a peaceful setting"; a "friendly", "capable" staff is "anxious to satisfy your every whim", and although "wonderful breakfasts" elicit 'ooh-la-la's', grumbling gastronomes grouse that most of the "standard" food "leaves something to be desired."

Isle de France ✕🏖🏨Ⓢ♒🔍

| | 26 | 24 | 24 | 24 | $674 |

Anse de Flamands | (011-590-590) 276-181 | fax 278-683 | 800-810-4691 | www.isle-de-france.com | 12 rooms, 8 suites, 12 bungalows, 1 cottage

This small, "chichi" bayfront hot spot is a "wonderful place to unwind" in a "very European" atmosphere that includes a "delicious French restaurant", "pristine beach", full-service Molton Brown spa, two freshwater pools, yoga classes and even weekly fashion shows; a "friendly staff" and "tasteful" cottages with oversized marble baths are further reasons to go to this "heaven"; N.B. closed from the beginning of September to mid-October.

	ROOMS	SERVICE	DINING	FACIL.	COST
La Banane 👪🐕🏊	▽ 23	23	22	18	$1057

Baie de Lorient | (011-590-590) 520-300 | fax 276-844 | www.labanane.com | 9 bungalows

Surrounded by hibiscus, jasmine and bougainvillea, "the nicest small hotel on St. Barts" encompasses just nine "gorgeous", colorful bungalows with private terraces - and names to match (watermelon, grape, kiwi, etc.); with a "super-attentive" staff that "accommodates your every whim", two pools and a library to grab the latest read, this "simple offering" is "absolute paradise" to many.

	ROOMS	SERVICE	DINING	FACIL.	COST
Le Toiny 🍴💻🐕🔭🏊	28	27	27	24	$1057

Anse de Toiny | (011-590-590) 278-888 | fax 278-930 | 800-735-2478 | www.hotelletoiny.com | 15 cottages

"Splurge and enjoy" this "romantic" and "secluded" Relais & Châteaux hideaway where the "exquisite" villas are "the ultimate in civilized hedonism" with "all the amenities" you could ask for, including open-air showers, private plunge pools and high-tech electronics; a "fabulous staff" is as good as the view, which includes movies stars and moguls who don't mind its "out-of-the-way" location, but if you don't have a "lottery ticket" to "cash in", just come for dinner - it'll be your "best meal on the island."

	ROOMS	SERVICE	DINING	FACIL.	COST
Manapany, Hôtel 🔭🏊🎾	▽ 21	20	22	22	$920

Anse de Cayes | (011-590-590) 276-655 | fax 277-528 | www.lemanapany.com | 46 cottages

On a "nice quiet beach away from the bustle" sits this "secluded" cottage cluster with "flowers everywhere"; partisans praise the "charming", "friendly" staff, the "great" pool and the restaurant's hearty brunch (during high season), but foes fret it's "too windy on this part of the island", the adjacent seashore is "only fair" and the property as a whole can seem "a little run-down."

St. Kitts & Nevis

Nevis

	ROOMS	SERVICE	DINING	FACIL.	COST
[Z] **Four Seasons** 👪🍴🔭⛳Ⓢ🏊🎾	27	27	25	27	$655

Pinney's Beach, Charlestown | (1-869) 469-1111 | fax 469-1112 | 800-332-3442 | www.fourseasons.com | 196 rooms, 40 villas

Framed by "aqua waters" and "cloud-shrouded" mountain peaks, this "glorious" and "serene" resort, which underwent a $10 million overhaul in 2006, makes guests feels as if they're on their "own *Fantasy Island*"; fans laud the "large" and "inviting plantation-style rooms", a staff that's "right out of a movie" and "the best golf experience" they've ever had (the "ball-stealing monkeys" notwithstanding); dining is "classy", though some wish there were more options.

	ROOMS	SERVICE	DINING	FACIL.	COST
Montpelier 🔭🏊🎾	22	28	28	25	$480

Nevis | (1-869) 469-3462 | fax 469-2932 | www.montpeliernevis.com | 16 rooms, 1 suite

"If it was good enough for Princess Di, it should be over the edge for us commoners" reason royalty-watchers who relish this "gorgeous location with service and dining to match"; set in an 18th-century hilltop

| | ROOMS | SERVICE | DINING | FACIL. | COST |

sugar mill with "spectacular views of the ocean and lush green hills", it achieves true noteworthiness through its "fantastic restaurant" with "definitely the best food on the island" and a staff that "treats you like family"; the rooms are a "bit disappointing" compared to the rest, but the rest really makes you sigh "this is the life."

**Nisbet Plantation
Beach Club** ✕ⓗⓢ☄⚲

| 20 | 27 | 25 | 20 | $550 |

St. James Parish | (1-869) 469-9325 | fax 469-9864 | 800-742-6008 | www.nisbetplantation.com | 14 rooms, 22 suites

A "warm and attentive" staff that "remember guests" is the high point of this "intimate" and "very British" boutique hotel named for former plantation resident Fanny Nisbet (aka *Mrs.* Admiral Horatio Nelson); taking full advantage of its 30 oceanfront acres "away from the crowds", it boasts a pool and two restaurants on the beach where diners can enjoy the "freshest seafood around" with their "toes in the sand."

St. Lucia

Anse Chastanet Resort ⓜⓢ⚲

| 26 | 25 | 21 | 24 | $545 |

Soufrière | (1-758) 459-7000 | fax 459-7700 | 800-223-1108 | www.ansechastanet.com | 49 rooms

You may "burn your return plane ticket" after a stay at this "secluded" "hilltop hideaway" with "huge", "fabulous", "rustic" rooms that evoke the *"Swiss Family Robinson"* ("no TVs or radios") and feature "stunning" Piton views; the "special", "experienced" staff "makes you feel as though you're the only guests", "adventurous nature lovers" laud the "great snorkeling" and sentimental sorts say it's "one of the most romantic."

**Jalousie
Plantation, The** ⚑⚑ⓜⓢ☄⚲

| 25 | 23 | 18 | 24 | $450 |

Bay St. | Soufrière | (1-758) 456-8000 | fax 459-7667 | 800-544-2883 | www.thejalousieplantation.com | 25 rooms, 58 suites, 34 villas

"For natural beauty", this "secluded" rainforest resort with a "picture-perfect backdrop" of the majestic Pitons "can't be beat"; enjoy the view from "your own personal plunge pool" at one of the "lovely" villas "spread out over the hillside", or partake in "superb" water-sports including the "best snorkeling" off their "quiet beach"; though the staff is "so attentive you want to take them home", leave behind the "expensive", "just ok" food; N.B. a nonintrusive room renovation (to be completed in 2008) may outdate the above Rooms score.

Ladera ✕ⓢ☄

| 27 | 26 | 25 | 23 | $550 |

Soufrière | (1-758) 459-7323 | fax 459-5156 | 800-738-4752 | www.ladera.com | 19 suites, 6 villas

"Waking up to a bird singing on your nightstand" is a distinct possibility given this "unforgettable" tropical resort's "unusual" yet "magical open-air rooms" that, literally, have no fourth wall; "reborn" guests rave about the "breathtaking" views of the Pitons and Caribbean Sea, "exceptional" service and "the best chef on the island", but some find the "remote" location makes them feel more "captive" than captivated; N.B. there are no children under 15 permitted except during Christmas/New Year seasons.

Sandals Grande St. Lucian Spa & Beach Resort 🏋 Ⓢ 🏊 🎾 — 22 | 23 | 21 | 24 | $400

Gros Islet | (1-758) 455-2000 | fax 455-2001 | 800-726-3257 | www.sandals.com | 272 rooms, 11 suites

"Sun and sand", "gorgeous" grounds and "amazing amenities" (as well as the capacity to "share those of the other Sandals resorts on the island") captivate couples only at this "all-inclusive that really does have it all"; the "delightful" staff provides "wonderful" service, the rooms afford "fabulous views" and while a few fume it's "not worth the price tag", others wouldn't hesitate to "recommend it to honeymooners"; N.B. butler service is available.

Sandals Regency St. Lucia Golf Resort & Spa Ⓢ 🏊 🎾 — 22 | 23 | 21 | 24 | $390

Castries | (1-758) 452-3081 | fax 452-1012 | 800-726-3257 | www.sandals.com | 205 rooms, 116 suites, 6 villas

"Package honeymooners" and "party-loving couples" exude "airs of happiness" at this all-inclusive "Americanized tropical vacation spot" that's like "*The Love Boat* but on land"; "excellent" facilities (nine-hole golf course, health club, St. Lucia's largest pool) and activity directors that "go the extra mile" provide for "everything you'd want to do" including "worthwhile" snorkeling trips and "fabulous in-room couples massages"; Sandalistas savor numerous dining options as well, though dissenters dub the food "average."

Windjammer Landing Villa Beach Resort 👪 🐕 🏋 Ⓢ 🏊 🎾 — ▽ 22 | 21 | 17 | 18 | $350

Labrelotte Bay | Castries | (1-758) 456-9000 | fax 452-9454 | 800-743-9609 | www.windjammer-landing.com | 42 rooms, 213 villas

There's "plenty of room to roam" in this resort village "built into the side of a mountain", both on the brick pathways and in the "huge", "private" rooms and villas (many with plunge pools); children's programs, "multiple beach activities" and a "good value for the price" attract families with kids, but not "those wanting calm and sophistication or a gourmet meal" since there's "noise all around the pool" and "average" dining.

St. Maarten

Oyster Bay Beach Resort 👪 🐕 🏋 🏊 — 21 | 20 | 18 | 22 | $250

10 Emerald Merit Rd., Oyster Bay | (011-599) 543-6040 | fax 543-6695 | 866-978-0212 | www.oysterbaybeachresort.com | 158 rooms, 20 suites

"Straight out of a miniseries", this dramatic resort, with an "excellent location and layout", affords "spectacular" views of Dawn Beach as well as "beautiful" grounds and an infinity pool; they've put "an inordinate amount of money into upgrading", but some still say it's too "far from everything" and "not up to the hype."

Wyndham Sapphire Beach Club & Resort 🐕 🏋 🏊 — 21 | 20 | 18 | 21 | $350

Lowlands 147, Cupecoy Beach | (011-599) 545-2179 | fax 545-2178 | 800-822-4200 | www.wyndham.com | 165 rooms, 14 villas

This "wonderful facility" provides "all the amenities": a "pleasant" staff that's "too good", "spacious", "first-class rooms", "convenient" location,

	ROOMS	SERVICE	DINING	FACIL.	COST

"lively entertainment" and a "beautiful", "pristine beach"; though it's lost its luster for some due to "views of tourists' cruise ships" and "so-so food", more report an "enjoyable stay."

St. Martin

La Samanna ✕⊟♨③🏊🔍 | 25 | 25 | 25 | 25 | $950 |

Baie Longue | (011-590-590) 876-400 | fax 878-786 | 800-237-1236 | www.lasamanna.com | 18 rooms, 57 suites, 6 villas

"Stay with the stars and get the same treatment" at this "secluded" "total luxury" resort popular with publicity-shy celebs, as well as googly-eyed honeymooners; just a short drive from tony Marigot and Grand Case, the "sublime" Orient-Express spot is surrounded by "exquisite gardens" and "the most spectacular views of the Caribbean"; fans give props to the "large but simple" rooms, "world-class French cuisine" and "outstanding" service, but anti-Samites find it just plain "overrated."

L'Habitation de Lonvilliers 👪🍴♨🏊🔍 | 21 | 19 | 20 | 22 | $475 |

Anse Marcel | (011-590-590) 876-700 | fax 873-038 | 888-790-5264 | www.habitationstmartin.com | 187 rooms, 12 suites, 34 family rooms

"On a beautiful bluff" with a "panoramic view" of the "cozy cove", this "colonial-style" resort offers patrons tennis courts and a French Creole eatery set on "enough grounds to film *Survivor*"; although there are "beautiful beaches" nearby, it's a car "ride away from everything" – "great if you want to get away from it all", but not if the mediocre fare and "too laid-back" service forces you to "go over the hill to eat in town."

Sweden

Jukkasjärvi

ICEHOTEL 🍴 | ▽ 24 | 25 | 21 | 26 | $409 |

Marknadsvägen 63 | (011-46-980) 66800 | fax 66890 | www.icehotel.com | 35 rooms, 25 suites, 56 cabins

For a "magical", "once-in-a-lifetime experience", "nothing compares" to this "amazing" "gimmick", "built every year" from ice in a Swedish village north of the Arctic Circle; dog sledding and snowmobiling fill the days, and nights are spent staving off the chill with "reindeer stew" and "lashes of vodka with lingonberry juice" before slipping into a thermal sleeping bag atop animal pelts and a frozen bed; there are year-round cabins, but just "one night is enough to provide memories forever."

Stockholm

Berns Hotel ⊕♨ | 18 | 19 | 18 | 17 | $350 |

Näckströmsgatan 8 | (011-46-8) 5663-2200 | fax 5663-2201 | www.berns.se | 61 rooms, 4 suites

"Central to all that's hip" in Stockholm, this "too cool" boutique hotel whose "grand" shell is overlaid with a "trendy" gloss attracts a "youthful clientele" who gather for the "hopping" bar scene ("great if you're in advertising or wear Armani") as well as the "fantastic" Asian fare; rooms are "small", but "modernity and amenities" compensate.

	ROOMS	SERVICE	DINING	FACIL.	COST

Grand Hôtel 🔱Ⓢ

| 21 | 23 | 20 | 21 | $540 |

Södra Blasieholmshamnen 8 | (011-46-8) 679-3500 | fax 611-8686 | 800-223-6800 | www.grandhotel.se | 343 rooms, 33 suites

Subjects who bow to this Stockholm "grande dame" with a "perfect location" "on the harbor facing the royal palace" feel like crowned heads themselves given the staff's "polish and good cheer" as well as the "large" suites with "antiques everywhere" (though many report that the "smallish" regular rooms "need updating"); what's more, its restaurant offers a "sensational smorgasbord" and the "elegant" bar is "not to be missed"; N.B. a new eatery is scheduled to open in spring 2007.

Hotel J 🔱

| - | - | - | - | $262 |

Ellensviksvagen 1 | (011-46-8) 601-3000 | fax 601-3009 | www.hotelj.com | 40 rooms, 5 suites

Newport meets Stockholm in this small hotel 15 minutes from the city center named for the America's Cup's fabled J-class yachts; guests arrive by ferry to this sleek spot, whose interior incorporates New England nautical design and most rooms feature balconies or patios; a tranquil garden and fireplace in the 'living room' lounge are further draws.

Rival 🔱

| - | - | - | - | $334 |

Mariatorget 3 | (011-46-8) 5457-8900 | fax 5457-8924 | www.rival.se | 97 rooms, 2 suites

Abba legend Benny Andersson remade this 1937 art deco hotel facing leafy Mariatorget Square with "pop-oriented design" and created a "hip and happening" focal point for the trendy Sodermalm neighborhood; there's a "raucous bar scene on the weekends", a cafe/bakery, a red velvet-draped movie theater and "chic", "well-thought-through" rooms serviced by a "helpful", "youthful" staff .

Stallmastaregarden Hotel ⊕🔱

| - | - | - | - | $350 |

Annerovägen 2, Nortull | (011-46-8) 610-1300 | fax 610-1340 | www.stallmastaregarden.se | 46 rooms, 3 suites

An offshoot of a traditional Swedish restaurant (circa 1638) that sits adjacent to it on a lakefront park just outside the main part of Downtown, this seven-year-old hotel is set in a "charming" building with spare simple rooms; nab a suite with water views and enjoy the "bucolic" setting.

Switzerland

TOPS IN COUNTRY

26	Beau-Rivage Palace	*Lausanne*
	Victoria-Jungfrau	*Interlaken*
25	Baur au Lac	*Zurich*
24	Badrutt's Palace	*St. Moritz*
	Widder	*Zurich*

Berne

Bellevue Palace ⊕🔱

| ∇ 26 | 26 | 25 | 24 | $448 |

Kochergasse 3-5 | (011-41-31) 320-4545 | fax 311-4743 | 800-223-6800 | www.bellevue-palace.ch | 100 rooms, 30 suites

It's "very satisfying" to stay at this hotel that exudes "class, class, class" adjacent to the Swiss parliament near the main shopping area and the official residence for visiting dignitaries; golf, riding and tennis are nearby, and some of the "outstanding rooms" have views of the Bernese Alps along with granite "baths bigger than your kitchen back home"; the Bellevue Grill and Terrasse, an open-air restaurant with panoramic vistas of the Alps, offer French fare.

Geneva

Beau-Rivage, Hôtel 🍴🐕🔭 24 | 25 | 24 | 22 | $597

13 Quai du Mont-Blanc | (011-41-22) 716-6666 | fax 716-6060 | 800-323-7500 | www.beau-rivage.ch | 82 rooms, 11 suites

The restaurants may be "what set this understated hotel apart", since Patara serves "some of the best Thai food outside Bangkok" and Le Chat-Botté offers "very good" French cuisine "overlooking Lake Geneva"; loyalists also like this 1865 veteran's "old-fashioned service", it's just too bad a few find some rooms in need of "a face-lift."

d'Angleterre, Hotel 👪[H]🐕🔭🎾 25 | 25 | 22 | 21 | $522

17 Quai du Mont-Blanc | (011-41-22) 906-5555 | fax 906-5556 | 800-223-6800 | www.dangleterrehotel.com | 39 rooms, 6 suites

Worker-bees believe this is the "perfect place to stay on business", with "well-appointed", "rather large" rooms, "quick Internet connections", "great service" and "decent" enough fare at Windows; but the more demanding are dissatisfied, deeming it "well over its prime", offering "hit-or-miss" accommodations and just "ok" facilities; at least a few find "no better view of the lake" from the deluxe suites.

Four Seasons Hotel des Bergues 🍴🐕🔭 25 | 26 | 23 | 22 | $593

33 Quai des Bergues | (011-41-22) 908-7000 | fax 908-7400 | 800-332-3442 | www.fourseasons.com | 61 rooms, 42 suites

The renovation that turned it into a Four Seasons "did wonders" for this 1834 landmark situated where the Rhône meets Lake Geneva, according to surveyors smitten with its "outstanding" service, "luxurious" rooms furnished in the Louis Philippe style, "sophisticated" public spaces and "world-class" Italian restaurant; the crowd's "strictly business" (though children are made to feel welcome with a cache of gifts and amenities), and tabs can be "very expensive" - but at least all agree "you get what you pay for."

La Réserve 🔭Ⓢ🏊 ▽ 25 | 25 | 25 | 25 | $821

301 Rte. de Lausanne | Bellevue | (011-41-22) 959-5959 | fax 959-5960 | 800-223-6800 | www.lareserve.ch | 85 rooms, 17 suites

A complete makeover by Parisian decorator Jacques Garcia makes this "heaven on the shores of Lake Geneva" a "relaxing" choice; it features a spa and wellness center with an indoor and outdoor pool, sauna, salon, tennis courts, massage and a child-care center, plus offers dining at Tsé-Fung, a well-known Chinese restaurant that's a "favorite" of some reviewers.

Mandarin Oriental Hotel du Rhône 🔭 24 | 25 | 23 | 23 | $635

1 Quai Turrettini | (011-41-22) 909-0000 | fax 909-0010 | 866-526-6567 | www.mandarinoriental.com | 166 rooms, 24 suites

This "high-end hotel" on the Right Bank of the Rhône may "seem a little stiff at first, but boy, does it have style" say sybarites, who insist "it

	ROOMS	SERVICE	DINING	FACIL.	COST

sets the standard for chain hotels" with its "very good service", "spacious rooms", "first-class" French-Mediterranean at Le Neptune and "enjoyable bar"; sure, it's "very expensive", but it's also "discreet" enough for business travelers.

President Wilson, Hotel 🔭 Ⓢ 🏊

ROOMS	SERVICE	DINING	FACIL.	COST
21	22	20	21	$655

47 Quai Wilson | (011-41-22) 906-6666 | fax 906-6667 | 800-325-3589 | www.hotelpwilson.com | 190 rooms, 45 suites

You'll feel "genuinely welcomed" by the "superb staff" at this "modern" hotel on the waterfront promenade where some of the rooms boast "grand views of the lake"; there's "marvelous dining" at the Lebanese L'Arabesque and the Asian fusion Spice's restaurants, and "renovated rooms are nice", but it may not be presidential enough for some penny-pinchers who pout it's "not worth the price."

Gstaad

Gstaad Palace 👫 Ⓗ 🐕 🔭 Ⓢ ⛷ 🏊 🎾

	ROOMS	SERVICE	DINING	FACIL.	COST
▽	25	26	25	28	$796

Palacestrasse | (011-41-33) 748-5000 | fax 748-5001 | 800-223-6800 | www.palace.ch | 64 rooms, 36 suites

One reviewer sighs, "we should sell our house and move in" to this "magical" place "on top of a mountain" in the Swiss Alps; whether it's "pretentious" or "just drips with money", the hotel earns praise for the "Swiss care with Italian flair" taken by the family who have owned it since 1913, grooming "the best-ever" staff, "amazing" suites, a full-service spa and copious recreation options (for kids too); N.B. closed mid-September to mid-December.

Interlaken

[Z] Victoria-Jungfrau Grand Hotel & Spa Ⓗ 🐕 🔭 Ⓢ 🏊 🎾

ROOMS	SERVICE	DINING	FACIL.	COST
25	26	25	26	$373

Höheweg 41 | (011-41-33) 828-2828 | fax 828-2880 | 800-223-6800 | www.victoria-jungfrau.ch | 107 rooms, 105 suites

Many of the "large, old-world" rooms at this 1895 grande dame - "a marvelous blending of Victorian and modern architecture" - offer "breathtaking" Alps views to accompany "the whole upper-crust thing" ("not much humor" here); you'll also get "superlative European dining", the "world's very best hot chocolate" and a "huge", "world-class" spa, so some say "there might not be a reason to leave" except for the ski slopes "an hour away."

Lausanne

Beau-Rivage Palace 👫 ✕ Ⓗ 🐕 🔭 Ⓢ 🏊 🎾

ROOMS	SERVICE	DINING	FACIL.	COST
26	27	25	26	$390

Place du Port 17-19 | (011-41-21) 613-3333 | fax 613-3334 | 800-223-6800 | www.brp.ch | 140 rooms, 29 suites

"It doesn't really get better than this dreamy palace on the lake" laud loyalists of this "airy and splendid" spot built in 1865 that has "all the bells and whistles": a "superb location", the "most beautiful spa in Switzerland", "spectacular service" and "wonderful food", including "delicious buffet lunches"; just "be sure to get one of the renovated rooms", which are "light years ahead of the older" ones.

	ROOMS	SERVICE	DINING	FACIL.	COST
Lausanne Palace & Spa Ⓗ🐕🔭Ⓢ🏊	24	24	21	25	$414

Grand-Chêne 7-9 | (011-41-21) 331-3131 | fax 323-2571 | 800-223-6800 | www.lausanne-palace.com | 123 rooms, 31 suites

"It's sublime to slip on a hotel bathrobe and take the elevator" straight to the country's "best urban spa" at this "sumptuous" "grande dame"; it's "one of the most beautiful in the world", with a "fantastic location", "amazing" service and "classic" rooms, some with a "gorgeous view of the lake"; return revelers suggest visiting around the holidays, "when the hotel is covered in lights."

Lugano

	ROOMS	SERVICE	DINING	FACIL.	COST
Villa Principe Leopoldo & Residence Ⓗ🔭🏊🎾	▽ 27	26	27	23	$489

Via Montalbano 5 | (011-41-91) 985-8855 | fax 985-8825 | 800-735-2478 | www.leopoldohotel.com | 107 rooms, 10 suites

In an "outstanding location" "not far from Milan", this "unbelievably" "romantic" Relais & Châteaux hotel (the former residence of Prince Frederic Leopold) "built into the side of a valley" overlooks "spectacular" views of Lake Lugano; service is "very energetic", the restaurant "fabulous" and the rooms "elegant" and "beautifully decorated", even if some "need a little added zip"; the only thing it "needs" is a spa.

Montreux

	ROOMS	SERVICE	DINING	FACIL.	COST
Raffles Le Montreux Palace 👪🍴Ⓗ🍳🐕🔭Ⓢ🏊	25	23	22	25	$324

Grand Rue 100 | (011-41-21) 962-1212 | fax 962-1717 | 800-637-9477 | www.montreux-palace.com | 187 rooms, 48 suites

"Lovely, lovely, lovely" describes the "magnificent rooms" with "spectacular views" of either Lake Geneva or the Alps, "European decadence" and "old-fashioned graciousness" of this "glamorous yet completely modern" hotel "right in the heart of fabulous and fun Montreux"; in addition, dining on Asian-enhanced French fare at Jaan is "out of this world" ("don't skip dessert") and "spa facilities are great."

St. Moritz

	ROOMS	SERVICE	DINING	FACIL.	COST
Badrutt's Palace 👪Ⓗ🔭Ⓢ⛷🏊🎾	22	25	25	25	$1260

Via Serlas 27 | (011-41-81) 837-1000 | fax 837-2999 | 800-223-6800 | www.badruttspalace.com | 135 rooms, 30 suites

Arriving here is "like walking into a James Bond movie" say fans of this 1896 chalet that's "the place to be" in this swanky ski resort "as long as you can stand all the glitz"; expect "spectacular service" (the "Rolls-Royce to the train station is an added treat"), a "magical lobby" "with panoramic views" and "three-hour" "luxe and lovely" dinners, but rooms "vary enormously", "from cramped to cavernous."

	ROOMS	SERVICE	DINING	FACIL.	COST
Kempinski Grand Hôtel des Bains 👪Ⓗ🍳🐕🔭Ⓢ⛷🏊🎾	-	-	-	-	$750

Via Mezdi 27 | (011-41-81) 838-3838 | fax 838-3000 | 800-426-3135 | www.kempinski.com | 136 rooms, 48 suites

Built in 1864 as a Grand Hotel, this "totally renovated" seasonal icon sits directly above the Mauritius spring, the source of St. Moritz's healthy reputation; accordingly, its "fantastic" spa offers an extensive roster of beauty and wellness services, while a new center (opening mid-2007) will focus on modern treatments and preventative medicine; a two-floor kids' club keeps tots occupied, while non-spa-goers enjoy the on-site casino, sailing, relaxing by the in-room fireplaces and the Mediterranean cuisine.

Kulm Hotel 👪 [H] 🏋 [S] 🏊 🎾 ▽ 23 | 24 | 21 | 26 | $431

Via Veglia 18 | (011-41-81) 836-8000 | fax 836-8001 | 800-223-6800 | www.kulmhotel-stmoritz.ch | 138 rooms, 35 suites

The first to open in St. Moritz, in 1856, this "fine old-world hotel" in a "beautiful setting" overlooking the lake and mountains of Engadine and close to the railway station boasts "excellent food and service", "front-facing rooms with great views" and small balconies where "you can relax"; there are also plenty of sports, ranging from downhill skiing to ice skating in the winter and golf, tennis, hiking, horseback riding and biking; N.B. too bad it's closed from early April to the end of June and early/mid-September to early December.

Vitznau

Park Hotel [H] 🐕 🏋 [S] 🏊 🎾 ▽ 24 | 22 | 25 | 25 | $530

Seestrasse | (011-41-41) 399-6060 | fax 399-6070 | 800-323-7500 | www.parkhotel-vitznau.ch | 71 rooms, 32 suites

"This is paradise" in a "perfect location on Lake Lucerne" posit patrons pleased by the "remote" mountainous setting and the "first-class", "understated service"; it all "breathes classic style", from the "luxurious" rooms with "magnificent" bathrooms, to the "indoor/outdoor pool" to the lakeside dining complete with "panoramic views"; N.B. open seasonally from mid-April to the end of October.

Zermatt

Grand Hotel Zermatterhof [H] 🐕 🏋 [S] 🏊 23 | 26 | 24 | 22 | $630

Bahnhofstrasse 55 | (011-41-27) 966-6600 | fax 966-6699 | 800-323-7500 | www.zermatterhof.ch | 58 rooms, 26 suites

"Prepare to be pampered" by a "friendly" staff ("getting picked up at the train station in a horse-drawn carriage adds to the appeal") at "simply the best" hotel in Zermatt, an 1879 gem with "atmospheric", "old-fashioned" accommodations and "superb food"; "get a room facing the Matterhorn for the most incredible view of the mountain", and then head out for glacier skiing; N.B. no cars are allowed in the village, and the hotel is closed in October, November and May.

Mont Cervin Palace 👪 [H] 🛏 🐕 🏋 [S] 🏊 ▽ 23 | 28 | 25 | 26 | $646

Bahnhofstrasse 31 | (011-41-27) 966-8888 | fax 966-8899 | 800-223-6800 | www.seilerhotels.com | 87 rooms, 32 suites, 14 apartments

Get set for "incredible hospitality" at this "romantic, luxury hotel" with "spectacular views of the Matterhorn"; rooms are located in three interconnected buildings, the decor is "simply beautiful", the food is "wonderful", the spa offers a variety of treatments and the "central location for walking tours of Zermatt", as well as mountain railways leading to skiing and hiking, means it's "convenient"; N.B. closed May to mid-June and early October to the end of November.

Zurich

Baur au Lac 🍴 [H] ♨ 🔭

ROOMS	SERVICE	DINING	FACIL.	COST
26	26	24	24	$646

Talstrasse 1 | (011-41-1) 220-5020 | fax 220-5044 | 800-223-6800 | www.bauraulac.ch | 83 rooms, 42 suites

"A Zurich tradition" since 1844, this "polished" "old-world" "business hotel" has almost perfected "crisp, pleasant" and "efficient Swiss-German service" in an "ideal" location on the Zurichsee; "everything is spotless" in "the world's quietest city hotel", including the "tastefully decorated" rooms and the "enchanting" outdoor cafe (open in summer); the only criticism ranges from "a little dull" to "only slightly snooty."

Eden au Lac, Hotel 🔭 🏊

ROOMS	SERVICE	DINING	FACIL.	COST
24	26	23	22	$348

Utoquai 45 | (011-41-44) 266-2525 | fax 266-2500 | www.edenaulac.ch | 45 rooms, 5 suites

This art nouveau "jewel" "overlooking Lake Zurich" is a "charming" choice "when in Zurich for business", but it suits leisurites as well since it's within walking distance of the Opera House, Bahnhofstrasse and other Zurich hot spots; the "service is beyond thoughtful (they're almost clairvoyant)", you "won't want to miss a meal" and the "amazing views" astound (most rooms have balconies or terraces with city, lake or mountain vistas).

Park Hyatt ♨ [S]

ROOMS	SERVICE	DINING	FACIL.	COST
26	24	22	24	$679

Beethoven-Strasse 21 | (011-41-43) 883-1234 | fax 883-1235 | www.park.hyatt.com | 130 rooms, 12 suites

The first Hyatt in Switzerland, this "quiet and refined" city center hotel touts "ultramodern" technology and conference capability first, and comfort and design a close second; there's a "cool bar where you can trade stories with movers and shakers" and "unusually spacious" rooms with rich wood tones, soft lighting and "amazing bathrooms" with oversized soaking tubs and "sliding windows" to "watch TV while enjoying a bubblebath"; it's all "smooth, hip and discreet."

Widder Hotel [H] ♨ 🔭

ROOMS	SERVICE	DINING	FACIL.	COST
26	24	24	23	$406

Rennweg 7 | (011-41-44) 224-2526 | fax 224-2424 | 800-223-6800 | www.widderhotel.com | 42 rooms, 7 suites

The rooms at this "sleek property" comprised of eight restored historic townhouses are quite likely the "most charming and fascinating" in all of Switzerland, if not "the world", say style mavens marveling at the "refreshing architecture" that combines "old with new" ("*Heidi* meets *The Jetsons*"); it all "works smoothly" here thanks to the "professional staff" and "state-of-the-art" facilities, and most find the International cuisine at Widder "lovely."

Syria

Damascus

Four Seasons 🍴 ♨ 🔭 [S] 🏊

	ROOMS	SERVICE	DINING	FACIL.	COST
▽	26	25	25	25	$265

Shukri Al Quatli St. | (011-963-11) 339-1000 | fax 339-0900 | www.fourseasons.com | 231 rooms, 66 suites

"Combining local charm and excellent service", this new "scene" in Downtown Damascus located beside a lovely public garden and historic mosque is "the only real five-star hotel" here, say early fans who "hang out" with the city's "pretty people"; you'll "stuff your face" at the wonderful Al Halabi restaurant, enjoy pampering at the Balloran Spa and cool off in an outdoor pool.

Taiwan

Taipei

Grand Formosa Regent [S] 🏊 | 23 | 23 | 22 | 22 | $226

41 Chung Shan N. Rd., Sec. 2 | (011-886-2) 2523-8000 | fax 2523-2828 | 800-545-4000 | www.regenthotels.com | 479 rooms, 60 suites

"You feel like you're in the center of what's happening" at this "convenient", "pleasant" resort with an "attentive" staff that provides "everything you desire"; rooms are "lovely" in a "big-hotel kind of way", the amenities are "great" (including a spa and rooftop pool) and restaurant Lan Ting is especially "good", but a few "disappointed" guests grouse it's "nothing special for the price."

Grand Hyatt 🛏 🔭 [S] 🏊 | 24 | 23 | 23 | 23 | $400

2 Song Shou Rd. | (011-886-2) 2720-1234 | fax 2720-1111 | 800-223-1234 | www.taipei.grand.hyatt.com | 604 rooms, 252 suites

The "all-white marble lobby with a humongous floral display" makes a "grand" first impression at this "large", "modern" hotel whose "central location" by the convention center makes it a boon to "business travelers"; "spacious, well-appointed" rooms, a "very good" gym and swimming pool, "first-class" service and "excellent restaurants" are other reasons it's considered among the "top in Taipei."

Shangri-La's Far Eastern Plaza Hotel 🔭 [S] 🏊 | 25 | 25 | 23 | 24 | $230

201 Tun Hwa S. Rd., Sec. 2 | (011-886-2) 2378-8888 | fax 2377-7777 | 866-565-5050 | www.shangri-la.com | 367 rooms, 53 suites

The "plush" rooms featuring the "softest cotton sheets" are "excellent for business or pleasure" at this hotel some believe is the "best in town"; the staff "makes you feel special" ("it welcomed me as a regular on my second visit"), the facilities include a spa and "fantastic" rooftop pool and the many "good" restaurants provide a range of cuisines from Cantonese to Japanese to Italian.

Sherwood, The 🔭 [S] 🏊 | 24 | 25 | 20 | 22 | $231

111 Ming Sheng E. Rd., Sec. 3 | (011-886-2) 2718-1188 | fax 2713-0707 | 800-223-6800 | www.sherwood.com.tw | 301 rooms, 44 suites

"Luxurious comfort" defines this "relaxing" hotel with a "terrific location" on a "busy street" in the Financial District; featuring "wonderful rooms" that are "great for business entertaining", "spectacular" artwork and a spa, gym and restaurants when you're ready to "relax", it's considered by connoisseurs to be "one of the nicest" lodgings in the country.

Westin 👪 🏊 | 23 | 21 | 19 | 21 | $250

133 Nanking E. Rd., Sec. 3 | (011-886-2) 8770-6565 | fax 8770-6555 | 800-937-8461 | www.westin.com | 246 rooms, 42 suites

Fans appreciate this solid "business hotel" with "spacious" accommodations, "luxurious beds", "hospitable" service and a "fantastic morning breakfast buffet"; but others only see the "plain lobby" and "drab" decor, finding "nothing special" overall.

Tanzania

Dar es Salaam

Kilimanjaro Hotel Kempinski
Dar es Salaam ⑨▨

`- | - | - | - | $175`

Kivukoni St. | (011-255-22) 213-1111 | fax 212-0777 | www.kempinski.com | 165 rooms, 15 suites

Notable names from Nelson Mandela to Michael Jackson have rested at "The Kili", a local landmark since 1965; the stylish, well-appointed rooms feature high-speed and WiFi access, 29-inch flat-screen TVs and spacious bathrooms with both soaking tubs and rainforest showers; Southeast Asian and Continental restaurants, a 20-meter pool with private sundeck, a spa and the panoramic Summit Bar help business travelers enjoy their downtime.

Lake Manyara National Park

Lake Manyara Serena
Safari Lodge ▨▨

`20 | 22 | 20 | 20 | $410`

Mto Wa Mbu Escarpment | (011-255-27) 253-9160 | fax 253-9163 | www.serenahotels.com | 53 rooms, 1 suite

High on a bluff on the edge of the Mto Wa Mbu Escarpment, this "charming", lodge of "attractive" thatched-roof huts is a "surprising oasis"; some call the service "average" and the food "nothing to write home about", but all agree the "gorgeous infinity pool" "overlooking the [Great Rift] Valley", which appears "as though it drops off the earth", is a slice of "heaven" and provides "the perfect photo op."

Ngorongoro

Ngorongoro Crater Lodge ✕▨

`26 | 26 | 24 | 25 | $730`

Ngorongoro Crater | (011-255-27) 253-7038 | fax 253-7039 | 888-882-3742 | www.ngorongorocrater.com | 30 suites

Perched on the rim of a collapsed volcano, this "fantastic place" comprising three "relaxing, serene" camps epitomizes "elegance in the bush", with "over-the-top luxury" that includes "superb service" from a "private butler" in each of its "large, comfortable" colonial-meets-Maasai suites, some of which feature "perfectly positioned bathtubs overlooking the crater"; the "incredible location" right "in the middle of spectacular wildlife" makes it "convenient for safaris", but you might even see "game literally at the doorstep" (fret not: security guards escort you to and from your room at night).

Ngorongoro Serena Safari Lodge ▨

`23 | 24 | 20 | 23 | $490`

Ngorongoro Crater | (011-255-27) 253-7050 | fax 253-7056 | www.serenahotels.com | 74 rooms, 1 suite

"Feel like you've stepped into a scene from *Out of Africa*" at this "unique lodge" in a "fabulous location" with "sweeping views" of the "fantastic Ngorongoro crater", a two-and-a-half-million-year-old remnant of a now-extinct volcano; visitors "love the balconies" with walls

	ROOMS	SERVICE	DINING	FACIL.	COST

of stone that grace each of the "clean rooms", not to mention the "friendly staff"; all told, it's a "great place to relax after a safari"; P.S. when packing, "remember the altitude" (7,500 feet) – you might not expect it, but "it can get cold here!"

Serengeti National Park

Serengeti Serena Safari Lodge 🏨 ⛵

| 22 | 24 | 22 | 22 | $410 |

Serengeti | (011-255-28) 262-2612 | fax 262-1520 | www.serenahotels.com | 65 rooms, 1 suite

"Lovely rooms made to look like traditional Maasai huts" serve as your base when you visit this "oasis in the middle of a sea of grass", "one of the best in the Serengeti" National Park; a "friendly" staff and "good food" are additional draws, though many insist that "the animal experience is the main attraction here" ("I woke up one morning to find a zebra staring into my room – very cool!").

Zanzibar

Mnemba Island Lodge 🏨

| - | - | - | - | $975 |

Mnemba Island | (011-27-11) 809-4300 | fax 809-4400 | 888-882-3742 | www.ccafrica.com | 10 cottages

Few have experienced this "snorkelers' and divers' paradise" in the Indian Ocean northeast of Zanzibar ("getting there is quite an adventure") but those who have say it's a "trip of a lifetime" filled with soft white-sand beaches, top-shelf service and luxurious accommodations in palm-fronded cottages; it's so "fabulous all around" that even the out-of-this-world rates are "worth it"; N.B. closed April and May.

Zamani Kempinski 🏨 ⓢ ⛵

| - | - | - | - | $350 |

Kiwengawa | (011-255-77) 444-4477 | fax 744-4488 | www.kempinski.com | 100 rooms, 10 suites, 7 villas

This deluxe beachfront resort in Zanzibar, 25 miles from the coast of Tanzania, uses the spectacular views of the Indian Ocean to the utmost with luxe rooms that each have a private terrace; on-site facilities include a pool, several restaurants, a spa and upscale boutiques.

Thailand

TOPS IN COUNTRY

28 | Four Seasons Tented | *Golden Triangle*
Four Seasons | *Chiang Mai*
Peninsula | *Bangkok*
27 | Oriental | *Bangkok*
Amanpuri | *Phuket*

Bangkok

TOPS IN CITY

28 | Peninsula
27 | Oriental
26 | Sukhothai
Four Seasons
24 | Conrad

	ROOMS	SERVICE	DINING	FACIL.	COST

Banyan Tree 🏨⑤≋
| | 23 | 24 | 22 | 24 | $360 |

21/100 S. Sathorn Rd., Tungmahamek, Sathorn | (011-66-2) 679-1200 |
fax 679-1199 | 866-822-6926 | www.banyantree.com | 216 suites

This "modern", "all-suites" "business hotel" is "beautifully laid out"
and "filled with orchids" (request your rooms on a high floor and "feel like
you're sleeping in the clouds"); sybarites indulge themselves with the
"seaweed wrap, loofah scrub and lomi-lomi massage" 39 stories up at
the Banyan Tree Spa, enjoying a respite from the heat, then head for the
61st-floor Vertigo Grill "for the views" and the opportunity "to be seen."

Conrad 🐾🏨⑤≋🔍
| | 26 | 25 | 23 | 23 | $149 |

87 Wireless Rd. | (011-66-2) 690-9999 | fax 690-9000 | 800-445-8667 |
www.conradhotels.com | 371 rooms, 21 suites

In "a city spoiled for choice", tony travelers tend toward this high-
"caliber" spot that "oozes style", especially in its modern rooms featuring "divine", "erotic bathrooms" "with a view" (separated from the
beds by a glass wall); "superb" service, an "oasis" of a rooftop pool
(it's "surprisingly chilly") and "excellent dining" leave loyalists of this
chain sighing "if only all Conrads could be" so good.

Dusit Thani 🏨⑤≋
| | 23 | 26 | 23 | 23 | $170 |

946 Rama IV Rd. | (011-66-2) 236-9999 | fax 236-6400 | 800-223-6800 |
www.dusit.com | 491 rooms, 26 suites

You'll encounter the "friendliest staff you'll ever meet" at this "fine
Thai-run hotel" that also boasts a "convenient location", "excellent
spa" and a "wide variety" of dining options; but naysayers note that
the onetime "grande dame of Bangkok" is "not the property it once
was", now "looking slightly shabby with age."

Four Seasons ✕🍴🏨⑤≋
| | 26 | 27 | 25 | 26 | $280 |

155 Rajadamri Rd. | (011-66-2) 250-1000 | fax 253-9195 | 800-332-3442 |
www.fourseasons.com | 327 rooms, 18 suites, 8 cabanas

"Classic style and sophistication" plus "impeccable", "gracious" service win over converts to this "awesome" lodging centrally located and
well-connected to major spots by SkyTrain; an "older" outpost of the
luxury hotel group, it renovated all of its "beautiful" rooms (with "pos-
itive results") so "everything" is "fabulous" now, including the "amazing terrace for dining" and the tranquil "pool with waterfall."

Grand Hyatt Erawan ⑤≋🔍
| | 23 | 24 | 22 | 23 | $250 |

494 Rajdamri Rd. | (011-66-2) 254-1234 | fax 254-6308 | 800-223-1234 |
www.bangkok.grand.hyatt.com | 336 rooms, 38 suites, 6 cottages

A "gracious staff" offering "friendly service" makes this "serene" hotel
a "good retreat from the heat, humidity and noise of Bangkok", with its
"understated rooms" and "perfect location" near shopping and the
SkyTrain; in short, it's "great for the American who likes the Hyatt
touch, and par for the international traveler who expects more from
grand hotels in Thailand."

Metropolitan ⑤≋
| | ▽ 25 | 24 | 23 | 21 | $240 |

27 S. Sathorn Rd., Tungmahamek, Sathorn | (011-66-2) 625-3333 |
fax 625-3300 | 800-337-4685 | www.metropolitan.como.bz |
169 rooms, 12 suites

The "sleek, clean" look of this "hip" "modern oasis" reminds some o
a "fashion runway", with original artwork, native woods and "spacious

quarters" boasting "excellent amenities" (goosedown comforters, Egyptian linens); other draws include a staff that "caters to your needs", a "really outstanding" restaurant and the "best spa"; could it possibly be "the perfect hotel"? ask trendsetters – well, maybe not quite, but it's definitely the "sharp and sexy" choice in this town.

Z Oriental, The 🏨✕⑪♨Ⓢ≋☜ | 27 | 29 | 27 | 27 | $370

48 Oriental Ave. | (011-66-2) 659-9000 | fax 659-0000 | 866-526-6567 | www.mandarinoriental.com | 393 rooms, 39 suites

"They knew our names on arrival, not after check-in" writes one incredulous guest of "the only addictive hotel in the world" where "everything is perfect" and "expectations" are routinely "exceeded"; this riverside flagship with "floral aromas" in the lobby, "luxurious" rooms with butler service that's "beyond intuitive", a "super spa" and a "gorgeous buffet overlooking the water" is "still one of the finest in the world" and causes "serious withdrawal symptoms" at check-out.

Z Peninsula, The 🏨✕♨Ⓢ≋☜ | 29 | 28 | 26 | 28 | $260

333 Charoennakorn Rd. | (011-66-2) 861-2888 | fax 861-1112 | 800-223-6800 | www.bangkok.peninsula.com | 304 rooms, 66 suites

"High tech" meets "Thai culture" at this "wonderful property" on "the far side of the river" where you can "live like a king and queen"; guests get "beautiful" rooms with button-touch controls, "first-rate dining", a "stunning pool area" and "outstanding service"; those who complain about being far "from most of the action" can ferry to the busy tourist sites and come right back to enjoy true "tranquility" and "amazing" city and Chao Phraya River views.

Plaza Athénée 🏨Ⓢ≋ | ▽ 27 | 27 | 25 | 27 | $165

Wireless Rd. | (011-66-2) 650-8800 | fax 650-8500 | 800-543-4300 | www.starwoodhotels.com | 354 rooms, 24 suites

This "superior" glass tower serves as an oasis of "calm" amid the Downtown Bangkok bustle, starting with its "genteel" look and feel and continuing with its "exceptional" service and top-drawer dining options; upstairs, "spacious" rooms with "all the expected amenities in place" marry "convenience" and classic Thai design, adding up to stays that are considered "as good as you can get" – especially "for the price."

Royal Orchid Sheraton Hotel & Towers ♨Ⓢ≋☜ | 23 | 24 | 22 | 22 | $200

2 Charoen Krung Rd. Soi 30, Siphya, Bangrak | (011-66-2) 266-0123 | fax 236-8320 | 800-325-3535 | www.sheraton.com | 667 rooms, 73 suites

A "very central location" and the convenience of an "adjacent exotic shopping center" are the selling points of this "otherwise unassuming" "big convention hotel", where the rooms may be on the "sterile" side, but they "all have views of the fascinating Chao Phraya River"; given the "reasonable" prices, penny-pinchers call it a "good value."

Shangri-La Hotel ♨Ⓢ≋☜ | 24 | 25 | 23 | 24 | $270

89 Soi Wat Suan Plu, New Rd. | (011-66-2) 236-7777 | fax 236-8579 | 866-565-5050 | www.shangri-la.com | 743 rooms, 56 suites

"Like a spa that pampers your whole being instead of just your body", this "little patch of paradise" boasts a "gracious, accommodating staff" that takes care of "everyday tasks" as well as being "generous with room upgrades"; request a riverfront view and praise the "sumptuously landscaped" pool and "lovely grounds" (think "the palace in *The King and I*"), though some aesthetes say the interior is in need of a "face-lift."

Sheraton Grande Sukhumvit 👬 🏊 Ⓢ 🌊

| 25 | 24 | 22 | 22 | $210 |

250 Sukhumvit Rd. | (011-66-2) 649-8888 | fax 649-8000 | www.luxurycollection.com | 383 rooms, 37 suites

"It's not the Sheraton you're used to" say those who believe this "refined" outpost is "considerably better than the ones you find in the U.S." due to its "very luxurious rooms" (some with butlers), "well-trained, welcoming staff" with the "friendliest of smiles" and "rooftop pool" that's "the perfect spot to unwind" (as is the on-site spa); its location just minutes from the Asok Sky Train is "ideal for business travelers", and the five restaurants offer some pretty "fabulous" dining.

🔢 Sukhothai, The ✕ 🏊 Ⓢ 🌊 🔍

| 27 | 27 | 27 | 25 | $290 |

13/3 S. Sathorn Rd., Tungmahamek, Sathorn | (011-66-2) 344-8888 | fax 344-8899 | 800-223-6800 | www.sukhothai.com | 132 rooms, 82 suites

"Everything is so hushed" at this "genteel" hotel that "heads will turn if a pin drops" posit patrons enthralled by the "Zen atmosphere"; the "refined style" is coupled with "warmth of service", while rooms with "traditional materials" and baths sporting "amazing shower jets" are further "wonderful features"; when it's time to dine, the "heavenly" Celadon comes through with "incredible" fare.

Chiang Mai

🔢 Four Seasons 👬 ✕ 🌿 🏊 Ⓢ 🌊 🔍

| 29 | 29 | 26 | 29 | $450 |

502 Moo 1, Mae Rim-Samoeng Old Rd., Mae Rim | (011-66-53) 298-181 | fax 298-189 | www.fourseasons.com | 16 suites, 64 pavilions

Deep in the terraced mountains, "out of the way" from the "city's nightlife", this "truly superior resort" with "gracious service" and "absolutely gorgeous" surroundings gives even cynics trouble "imagining a more romantic" spot; "fantastic rooms in the jungle", a "world-class" spa and "amazing" restaurants is "a fairy tale come true" for most; P.S. "don't miss the sun setting over the infinity pool."

Golden Triangle

Anantara Resort & Spa Golden Triangle 🏊 Ⓢ 🌊 🔍

| 24 | 25 | 22 | 25 | $350 |

229 Moo 1, T Wiang | Chiang Saen | (011-66-53) 784-084 | fax 784-090 | www.anantara.com | 58 rooms, 1 suite

Given the setting on the Golden Triangle (where Myanmar, Laos and Thailand meet), this "unique resort" offers a tour that visits three countries in a day – if guests can tear themselves away from the "gorgeous rooms and pool" with "splendid views" and "first-class" service; other on-site draws are the Mandara spa and several restaurants.

🔢 Four Seasons Tented Camp Golden Triangle 🏊 Ⓢ 🌊

| 29 | 29 | 27 | 28 | $1557 |

Chiang Rai | (011-66-53) 652-191 | fax 652-189 | 800-819-5053 | www.fourseasons.com | 15 tents

"Coming here for your honeymoon may be reason enough to get married" say smitten sojourners starstruck by this "amazing" resort reachable by riverboat through a bamboo forest in northern Thailand; "where else can you see three different countries while having a sip of your gin and tonic" then retire to a "luxurious" tented room with "lovely" hand-hammered copper tubs?; the "food and service are excellent too", and "don't miss the elephant ride" or a swim in the pool with views of the Ruak River; it's all a "double wow" "once-in-a-lifetime experience"; N.B. offers all-inclusive three- and four-night vacations.

Hua Hin

Chiva-Som International Health Resort 🔭Ⓢ🏊

Rooms	Service	Dining	Facil.	Cost
23	27	22	28	$760

73/4 Petchkasem Rd. | (011-66-32) 536-536 | fax 511-154 | 800-525-4800 | www.chivasom.com | 33 rooms, 7 suites, 17 pavilions

"Come prepared to relax" at this luxury spa in "unspoiled Hua Hin" offering an "array of services" geared toward "healthy", "cleansing" living administered by lots of "warm" folks (credit the "huge staff-to-guests ratio"); there's "not much to do" other than indulge in the extensive programs, so enjoy your "daily massage" (or "pummeling" depending on who's talking), nibble on the Thai-inflected fare and "be discreet when you bump into celebs and rock stars"; N.B. no kids under 16 are allowed.

Evason Hua Hin Resort & Six Senses Spa 👫🫖🔭Ⓢ🏊🎾

Rooms	Service	Dining	Facil.	Cost
-	-	-	-	$150

9 Moo 3, Paknampran Beach | Prachuap Khiri Khan | (011-66-32) 632-111 | fax 632-112 | 800-525-4800 | www.sixsenses.com | 145 rooms, 40 villas

Set on 20 acres of tropical grounds, this Six Senses resort offers "absolute luxury without pretense" and "all of what you need to get away from your busy life" including villas with private plunge pools and outdoor bathtubs, an on-site holistic spa offering open-air treatment facilities, an outdoor beachside eatery focusing on wood-fired pizza by day and seafood by night and a dinner-only formal Asian fusion spot; most fans "really enjoy" themselves, but all that joy "comes with a price."

Koh Samui

[NEW] Four Seasons Resort 🏊🎾

Rooms	Service	Dining	Facil.	Cost
-	-	-	-	$600

219 Moo 5, Angthong | (011-66-77) 243-000 | fax 243-002 | www.fourseasons.com | 61 villas, 2 houses

The fourth Four Seasons resort in Thailand, this hillside newcomer at Laem Yai peninsula features secluded villas built on stilts above sea level among coconut and mango trees, each with its own infinity pool, outdoor space and Gulf of Siam views; five spa pavilions offer indoor and outdoor treatment areas and therapies focused on holistic Thai-based remedies, a separate yoga area is open all day for private and group sessions and a private white-sand beach beckons; local specialties along with Italian dishes are served indoors and out at Lan Tania restaurant.

Le Royal Méridien Baan Taling Ngam 🫖🔭Ⓢ🏊🎾

Rooms	Service	Dining	Facil.	Cost
25	24	24	22	$595

295 Moo 3, Taling Ngam Beach | (011-66-77) 429-100 | fax 423-220 | 800-543-4300 | www.lemeridien.com | 38 rooms, 2 suites, 30 villas

With a "breathtaking" cliffside setting on the west side of Koh Samui Island, this "calming", "idyllic" chain hideaway is a "fantastic" choice; the views from the rooms are "gorgeous", the "amazing" spa offers indoor and outdoor treatment suites and the dining, albeit "limited", includes a "great breakfast buffet"; although it's "a long taxi ride to town and a hike downhill to the beach", some are so enamored with the tropical grounds and "awesome" infinity pool, they'd "hate to leave" anyway.

Napasai ♨ⓢ≈⚲

				$640
-	-	-	-	

65/10 Ban Tai, Maenam, Suratthani | (011-66-77) 429-200 | fax 429-201 | www.pansea.com | 55 cottages, 14 villas

Nestled among cashew, palm and coconut trees on the northern coast of Koh Samui, this tropical resort from the luxe brand Orient-Express features a design with plenty of silk, wood and bamboo; quarters include a two-bedroom private villa with pool, a beachfront family cottage and a seaview cottage, and the on-site spa offers treatments based on traditional Thai and Oriental philosophies.

Phuket

☒ Amanpuri ✕🐾ⓢ≈⚲

28	28	25	27	$680

Pansea Beach | (011-66-76) 324-333 | fax 324-100 | 800-477-9180 | www.amanresorts.com | 40 pavilions, 31 villas

"Stunning doesn't begin to describe" this flagship Aman resort that's nestled in a coconut plantation on the west coast of Phuket; every villa "is like a private home", the "restaurants are unbelievably wonderful" and the enormous pool is tiled in midnight blue; further fueling fans who "never want to leave" this "peaceful" "paradise discovered" is the staff's "absurd attention to detail" – "if even your toe gets touched by the sun, your umbrella will be readjusted."

☒ Banyan Tree ♥🐾♨▙ⓢ≈⚲

27	26	24	26	$950

33 Moo 4, Srisoonthorn Rd. | (011-66-76) 324-374 | fax 324-375 | 866-822-6926 | www.banyantree.com | 123 villas

"Tiny touches of luxury abound" at this "gorgeous property" in the Laguna Phuket complex of five resorts where "beautifully furnished" villas are decorated with Thai artwork and the "charming staff" that "doesn't speak above a whisper" "fills your private pool with orchids"; you'll find "the best massages in the world" at the "amazing" spa, access to all the facilities (golf, watersports, etc.) of the other five hotels and "good", if "not gourmet" food.

Chedi, The ♥♨ⓢ≈⚲

21	22	21	20	$599

118 Moo 3, Choeng Talay | (011-66-76) 324-017 | fax 324-252 | www.ghmhotels.com | 92 rooms, 16 suites

Stay "right next door" to the Amanpuri and share the "same beautiful beach" for less money at this "intimate" hotel consisting of "understated" thatched cottages perched on a hillside that might be "not quite as luxe" as its famed neighbor but is still "more than sufficient."

Evason Phuket Resort & Spa ♥♨ⓢ≈⚲

				$370
-	-	-	-	

100 Vised Rd., Moo 2, Tamboi Rawai, Muang District | (011-66-76) 381-0100 | fax 381-018 | www.sixsenses.com | 213 rooms, 40 suites, 7 villas

Facing the Andaman Sea on 64 acres of tropical gardens, this resort or Rawai Beach "never fails to disappoint"; there's a Six Senses Spa (outdoor massages in grass-roofed huts), "very romantic" rooms including "secluded pool villas" and a Honeymoon Villa on the nearby private Bon Island; dining options encompass an International eatery, a seaview Thai with live music, a fusion spot and a beachside casual restaurant.

JW Marriott Resort & Spa 👪 🔭 Ⓢ 🏊 🎾

Rooms	Service	Dining	Facil.	Cost
26	24	23	25	$530

231 Moo 3, Mai Khao Beach, Talang | (011-66-76) 338-000 | fax 348-348 | 800-228-9290 | www.marriott.com | 252 rooms, 13 suites

"On a magic beach" at the end of Phuket sits this "better-than-expected" "gem" with a "gorgeous" spa, "hop-to" service, "grand" rooms with polished wooden floors, balconies and "fantastic silk bedding", and an "outstanding" array of dining and leisure options; it's "far" from the action in Phuket, which is fine for those who have no trouble "staying put" in this "excruciatingly comfortable" spot.

Rayavadee 🔭 Ⓢ 🏊 🎾

Rooms	Service	Dining	Facil.	Cost
▽ 27	26	21	27	$567

214 Moo 2, Tambol Aonang, Amphur Muang | Krabi | (011-66-75) 620-740 | fax 620-630 | www.rayavadee.com | 94 pavilions, 9 villas

"Take a private boat to your private resort? count me in!"; this "absolutely magical" Krabi resort (an hour from Phuket) consistently charms with "amazing" guest quarters in separate two-story bungalows sporting coconut-shaped tops and amenities like brandy at turndown, "service so good you gasp" and "some of the most beautiful beaches in Thailand"; while a few faultfinders feel "food could be better", the private dinners by a cave are still "very romantic."

Sheraton Grande Laguna 👪 🐾 🔭 ⛳ Ⓢ 🏊 🎾

Rooms	Service	Dining	Facil.	Cost
24	23	21	26	$269

10 Moo 4, Srisoonthorn Rd., Tambol Cherng Talay, Talang | (011-66-76) 324-101 | fax 324-108 | 800-325-3589 | www.luxurycollection.com | 222 rooms, 183 villas

Set around lagoons and a "wonderful" serpentine pool, this "family-friendly" resort is "huge", "so be prepared to walk" or hop a golf cart to get around; vacationers can choose among an "amazing" array of accommodation, recreation and dining options, including an "excellent" pool and "busy" beach, but some are brought down by the location that's a bus or boat ride from "anything authentically" Thai and warn that the newer rooms are "much nicer than the slight dated" older ones.

Turkey

Antalya

Hillside Su Ⓢ 🏊 🎾

Rooms	Service	Dining	Facil.	Cost
-	-	-	-	$496

Konyaalti | (011-90-242) 249-0700 | fax 249-0707 | 800-337-4685 | www.hillside.com.tr | 200 rooms, 41 suites

Step into an updated version of the 1970s at this "fabulous", "sexy" seaside hotel where glittering disco balls dominate the lobby and a clean, all-white design (with flashes of red and black) sets the tone; there's "fantastic use of lights" both in the "beautiful rooms" with state-of-the-art amenities and on the "outside of the building", the staff knows how to "pamper in style" and the "cool" beach bar is "a people-watcher's paradise."

	ROOMS	SERVICE	DINING	FACIL.	COST

Bodrum

Kempinski Hotel
Barbaros Bay Bodrum 🏌🏊♨🅢⛵⛴

▽ 27 | 24 | 20 | 26 | $542

Kizilagac Koyu, Gerenkuyu Mevkii Yaliciftlik | (011-90-252) 311-0303 | fax 311-0300 | www.kempinski.com | 148 rooms, 25 suites

The balcony of every room in this "reliable" outpost boasts "extraordinary" views of the Aegean Sea, while the decor features furnishings from around the globe; although the central draw for many may be the "extraordinary" Six Senses Spa with Turkey's only Watsu chamber (for water-based treatments), the private suites to rent by the day, the indoor pool and Bodrum's largest outdoor pool are further enticements.

Marmara, The ♨♨🅢⛴♦

25 | 22 | 21 | 23 | $360

Yokusbasi, Mah Suluhasan Cad 18 | (011-90-252) 313-8130 | fax 313-8131 | 800-525-4800 | www.themarmarahotels.com | 83 rooms, 17 suites

A "stunning" "medieval-style castle" with a "magnificent hilltop" setting "looking down onto the water and fortress" houses this hotel that boasts an "airy and eclectic interior", tile-floored rooms and service that's "friendly but slow"; the "views of Bodrum at sunset" mean you must "go to the poolside bar for at least one round of cocktails" and listen to the DJ play "cool tunes"; this one may very well be a "must-stop respite on the coast."

Istanbul

Çiragan Palace
Kempinski ✕⊕🐾♨🅢⛴

26 | 25 | 25 | 27 | $480

Çiragan Caddesi 32 | (011-90-212) 326-4646 | fax 259-6687 | 800-426-3135 | www.ciraganpalace.com | 284 rooms, 31 suites

You'll be "treated like a sultan" at this "opulent", baroque hotel that's set in an "incredibly restored" "actual palace" in Besiktas; the rooms are, not surprisingly, "fit for royalty", and the "fabulous location" means some quarters have "stunning views of the Bosphorus"; other highlights are the "breathaking infinity pool" that appears to flow into the sea and "delicious food" that includes Turkish-Ottoman cuisine at Tugra and a Sunday brunch that's an "incredible" "feast for the eyes" and stomach.

Conrad 🐾♨⛴♦

19 | 19 | 19 | 19 | $490

Barborros Blvd., Yildiz Caddesi | (011-90-212) 227-3000 | fax 259-6667 | 800-445-8667 | www.conradistanbul.com | 560 rooms, 35 suites

This "treasure" in Besiktas next to the Yildiz Palace and overlooking the Bosphorus and Sea of Marmara boasts a "marvelous marble lobby", an "enthusiastic staff" that offers "friendly and cordial service" and a "fantastic fitness center"; while there's a "fabulous view from the terrace on the club level", rooms themselves strike a few as "antiseptic" and the property is frequently a "convention site for conferences."

Four Seasons ✕⊕♨♨

28 | 29 | 25 | 26 | $420

Tevkifhane Sokak 1 | (011-90-212) 638-8200 | fax 638-8210 | 800-332-3442 | www.fourseasons.com | 51 rooms, 14 suites

"Probably the best prison stay in Turkey" say guests who don't mind an extended term at this "well-done conversion" of the neoclassical Sultanahmet lock-up; "full of color and style" and "within walking distance to almost anything", including the Blue Mosque and Topkapi Palace, it boasts that "legendary Four Seasons service" "as good as anywhere in Asia", "delicious" "cuisine to match" and a truly "peaceful" atmosphere, so most wouldn't mind being inmates at this one; P.S. the only thing it "lacks" is a swimming pool.

Hyatt Regency 👥🏊🔍

| 25 | 25 | 22 | 26 | $335 |

Taskisla Caddesi 1 | (011-90-212) 368-1234 | fax 368-1000 | 800-223-1234 | www.istanbul.regency.hyatt.com | 325 rooms, 28 suites, 7 apartments
In a "convenient" financial district location "slightly removed from the center of town", this "sleek, but warm" business hotel is "outstanding in every way", with "Asian-style" decor and a "resourceful" staff, including "fantastic" concierge service; "one could get used to life" in this "very relaxed" lodging where the Turkish bath "should not be missed."

Ritz-Carlton, The 👥Ⓢ🏊

| 27 | 24 | 22 | 23 | $330 |

Suzer Plaza, Elmadag, Askerocagi Caddesi 15 | (011-90-212) 334-4444 | fax 334-4464 | 800-241-3333 | www.ritzcarlton.com | 220 rooms, 24 suites
This luxury outpost in the Dolmabahce neighborhood overlooks the Bosphorus and offers lots of glass mosaic tiles and teak-wood columns, rooms "you won't want to leave" with "beautiful views", a spa with a Turkish *hammam*, a Mediterranean-Ottoman restaurant and the usual "excellent" staff that will "do anything for you"; though some take issue with a building that "sticks out like a sore thumb" above the mosques, it's the "signature service" that soars even higher.

Swissôtel The Bosphorus 👁👥Ⓢ🏊🔍

| 25 | 25 | 23 | 25 | $444 |

Bayildim Caddesi 2 | (011-90-212) 326-1100 | fax 326-1122 | 800-637-9477 | www.istanbul.swissotel.com | 474 rooms, 23 suites
On a hilltop overlooking the Bosphorus, this "modern" conference hotel offers "large, comfortable" rooms, many with "killer views" (which "cost extra"), a "peaceful" pool area and a "magnificent" rooftop bar; the breakfast "spread" on the terrace earns points for "beautiful pastries" and, again, "incredible" vistas, but the hotel's location "north of the old city among a cluster of skyscrapers" is "not great."

Turks & Caicos

NEW Amanyara 👥🏊🔍

| ▽ 29 | 28 | 25 | 29 | $1350 |

Northwest Point | Providenciales | (1-649) 941-8133 | fax 941-8132 | 866-941-8133 | www.amanresorts.com | 40 pavilions
Some say this "brand-new", "off-the-beaten-track" "paradise" is the "best Aman resort" they've ever been to; accommodations are in airy and spacious timber-shingled pavilions with terraces, pond or ocean views, flat-screen TVs and personal bars, and the service and dining get high scores as well (they "should be great" with a "price tag" like this); but "you'd better like who you're with" at this "heaven on earth" since it's practically like being on a "deserted isle."

Grace Bay Club 👫👥Ⓢ🔍

| 25 | 24 | 23 | 25 | $785 |

Providenciales | (1-649) 946-5050 | fax 946-5758 | 800-946-5757 | www.gracebayclub.com | 21 suites, 38 villas
It feels "like you're among a handful of people" at this "small" Provo resort with a "romantic-beyond-words" restaurant on "one of the loveli-

est beaches in the Caribbean"; the "elegant villas" with "stellar balconies and baths", an on-site spa with Asian- and European-influenced treatments and a staff that "tries very hard" (though "doesn't always get it right") lead to almost "complete relaxation" – no wonder "Hollywood stays" here (albeit "at Rodeo Drive prices"); N.B. a renovation of the main building's rooms should be complete by April 2007.

Ocean Club/Ocean Club West 🏌🏖🏋⛱�️🌊🔍

| 17 | 17 | 16 | 19 | $360 |

Providenciales | (1-649) 946-5880 | fax 946-5845 | 800-457-8787 | www.oceanclubresorts.com | 86 suites

Families looking for a reasonably priced getaway – "relatively" speaking, anyway – find one at these "lovely and charming" sister resorts on Grace Bay; "comfortable apartment-style" accommodations feature fully equipped kitchens and some have washers and dryers, while the "beautiful" white-sand beaches are "the perfect place to chill out with the kids"; but detractors find the savings don't make up for the "far-from-luxurious" atmosphere and "lack of" good "dining choices."

Parrot Cay ✗🏖🎣�️🌊🔍

| 25 | 24 | 23 | 25 | $680 |

Parrot Cay | (1-649) 946-7788 | fax 946-7789 | 877-754-0726 | www.parrotcay.como.bz | 42 rooms, 4 suites, 6 houses, 8 villas

There's "nothing else like it in the western hemisphere" hail "hip" habitués of this "nearly flawless" resort where the "flourlike" sand on the "mostly deserted beach" and the "gorgeous grounds" with "beautiful infinity pool" create a "peaceful" "paradise"; other "heavenly" features include "incredible cuisine", "chic", "pristine" white rooms, "unobtrusive" service, "excellent" spa treatments and "celebrity eye candy", though the prices are not so sweet.

United Arab Emirates

Dubai

🅉 Burj Al Arab 🏌✗🏖🏋�️🌊

| 29 | 28 | 25 | 28 | $1497 |

Jumeirah Beach | (011-971-4) 301-7777 | fax 301-7000 | 877-854-8051 | www.burj-al-arab.com | 202 suites

"Over-the-top" and "extravagant" don't begin to describe this "ostentatious" "pleasure palace" shaped like a sail and floating on its own man-made island; the decor – "gold galore" – is "tacky but in a splendid way" as are the "palatial" two-story suites complete with laptops and printers, personal butlers, pillow menus and "mind-boggling" views that only the world's tallest hotel could offer; dining is also 24-karat, but it's the staff that "constantly look for ways to please you" that truly makes it the "eighth wonder of the world."

Grosvenor House ✗🏋�️🌊

| ▽ 26 | 22 | 24 | 24 | $665 |

Sheikh Zayed Rd. | (011-971-4) 399-8888 | fax 399-8444 | www.lemeridien.com | 174 rooms, 43 suites

The sky's the limit for this "absolutely wonderful" "sleek and modern" tower with breathtaking views of the Dubai skyline and Arabian Sea; it features "beautiful rooms" with "fantastic flat-screen" satellite TVs and lavish furnishings, 24-hour butler service and an "excellent" restaurant run by Gary Robinson, former personal chef to Prince Charles; there's also a stellar spa and health club on-site.

Jumeirah Beach Hotel ♀♂☕🐎Ⓢ🏖🔍 | 23 | 24 | 22 | 26 | $920

Jumeirah Beach | (011-971-4) 348-0000 | fax 348-2273 | 877-854-8051 | www.jumeirahbeachhotel.com | 551 rooms, 48 suites, 19 villas

A magic kingdom of a different sort, this "very busy" "Florida-type family resort" on the Arabian Sea has plenty to keep guests entertained including tennis courts, five pools, a diving center, an "unparalleled" shopping mall and unlimited access to Wild Wadi Water Park next door; after refueling at one of 16 "fantastic" themed restaurants and being catered to by an "extremely friendly and well-trained staff", exhausted guests can retire to their rooms, which some feel, are "getting a little tired" too.

Jumeirah Emirates Towers 🐎Ⓢ🏖 | ▽ 28 | 27 | 23 | 25 | $680

Sheikh Zayed Rd. | (011-971-4) 330-0000 | fax 330-3030 | 877-854-8051 | www.jumeirahemiratestowers.com | 360 rooms, 40 suites

Situated in the heart of Dubai's commercial district, this "opulent, luxury" hotel caters to on-the-go corporate types with a 24-hour business center, meeting rooms and helicopter transfers to and from the airport, but it also appeals to leisurites who love the "eclectic" European-style decor, "welcoming and accommodating" staff, proximity to "high-end" shopping, 15 "fabulous" restaurants and Vu's Bar, a "happening spot" with "excellent views" and lots of "sheikhs and supermodels"; N.B. there's free transport to the beach.

Le Royal Méridien Beach Resort & Spa ♀♂🐎Ⓢ🏖🔍 | ▽ 24 | 24 | 24 | 26 | $715

Al Sufouh Rd., Jumeirah Beach | (011-971-4) 399-5555 | fax 399-5999 | 800-543-4300 | www.lemeridien.com | 444 rooms, 54 suites, 1 apartment, 1 penthouse

"A great place to recharge your batteries", this "incredibly luxurious hotel" with "beautiful grounds", impressive accommodations (some with views of Jumeirah Beach) and "all the facilities imaginable" offers "one of Dubai's best spas", not to mention a "fantastic" fitness center, a "friendly staff" and a "huge number of restaurants covering food from many parts of the world"; "especially good" is Fusion, featuring a mixture of different Asian cuisines, and if you stop by Al Khaima you can "order an apple-flavored shishah water pipe, sit back" and enjoy "a truly relaxing experience."

☑ One & Only Royal Mirage ♀♂🐎Ⓢ🏖🔍 | 26 | 27 | 26 | 27 | $381

Jumeirah Beach | (011-971-4) 399-9999 | fax 399-9998 | 866-552-0001 | www.oneandonlyresorts.com | 367 rooms, 101 suites, 3 villas

Three distinct properties – The Palace, Arabian Court and "the ultimate", Residence & Spa – comprise this "superb" "luxury" resort reminiscent of old Arabia, where "better than first-class" service makes anyone "feel royal"; lushly landscaped gardens, soothing water features and "one of the best beaches in Dubai" create a "dream oasis", while Givenchy Spa is "*the* place to be pampered"; nicely appointed rooms with satellite TVs, seven restaurants and a happening nightclub mean there's "no need to go outside the hotel complex."

	ROOMS	SERVICE	DINING	FACIL.	COST

Park Hyatt ✕ ⟟ ⓢ ≋

▽ 23	21	23	25	$306

Al Garhoud Rd. | (011-971-4) 602-1234 | fax 602-1235 |
www.dubai.park.hyatt.com | 225 rooms, 43 suites

Adjacent to the Dubai Creek Golf & Yacht Club, this luxurious water-front hotel is close to the city center, shopping and business areas; the on-site Amara spa offers a variety of massage and beauty treatments, three restaurants feature wood-fired ovens and open kitchens, rooms have LCD TVs and high-speed Internet access and there's an 18-hole golf course, plus a secluded swimming pool set among palm trees.

Ritz-Carlton, The ♙♙ⓢ≋↘

25	26	24	22	$558

Jumeirah Beach | (011-971-4) 399-4000 | fax 399-4001 | 800-241-3333 |
www.ritzcarlton.com | 125 rooms, 13 suites

Perched on prime beachfront, this Mediterranean-style hideaway offers "all the protection you need from the heat" and "surrounding building work", namely, a "stunning" Balinese spa, a "mega-pool" with swim-up bar and "huge" rooms with Jacuzzis and DVD players; devotees also applaud its "top-notch" eateries and "superb" staff, but critics say there's nothing relaxing about being "in a construction zone."

Shangri-La Hotel ♙ⓢ≋↘

▽ 27	25	21	21	$212

Sheikh Zayed Rd. | (011-971-4) 343-8888 | fax 343-8886 |
www.shangri-la.com | 271 rooms, 30 suites, 126 apartments

In the multipurpose Al-Jaber skyscraper lies this "top-notch" business hotel with "attentive and caring" service, "some of the best dining in the UAE", rooms with city or sea views, a club floor, a fitness center and a spa facility with a holistic approach to health and beauty; given Dubai's reputation as the shopping capital of the Middle East, there are also plenty of malls and souks nearby.

United Kingdom – England

Berkshire

Cliveden House ⊕≋♙ⓢ≋

28	25	24	27	$590

Cliveden | Taplow | (011-44-1628) 668-561 | fax 661-837 | 800-747-6917 |
www.clivedenhouse.co.uk | 23 rooms, 15 suites, 1 cottage

"Feel like an 18th-century lord" in the "elegant" rooms with "unforgettable" river views at this "sublime" "grand manor" that's "steeped in history" (and a little "scandal") in Taplow on the River Thames; from the "majestic" lobby to the "perfectly manicured" gardens to the "butler-style" staff (they'll "unpack your bags") to the "superb" cuisine at Waldo's restaurant, "you'll get your money's worth", even if the prices "eat right through your wallet."

Vineyard at Stockcross, The [S] 🏊 — 22 | 23 | 25 | 21 | $531

Newbury | (011-44-1635) 528-770 | fax 528-398 | 800-735-2478 | www.the-vineyard.co.uk | 32 rooms, 17 suites

Cuisine's the thing at this Newbury "hideaway" that's "worth" visiting for a "wine-and-dine vacation" thanks to chef John Campbell's "first-rate" European restaurant offering an "excellent" tasting menu and a "great wine list" "from a "massive" collection of more than 2,000 international labels; even though the "amazing" food is why you're here, the digs are "charming", the spa with an indoor pool is "lovely" and service is "spot on" as well.

Chester

Chester Grosvenor & Spa, The [H] 🔭 [S] — 22 | 24 | 21 | 20 | $374

Eastgate | (011-44-1244) 324-024 | fax 313-246 | 800-525-4800 | www.chestergrosvenor.co.uk | 66 rooms, 14 suites

A "fine place for a British-cum-Roman" holiday, this "gracious" "in-town hotel" in a historic building is hailed for its "friendly staff", the "best food" around served in the Arkle restaurant (along with two less formal options), "awesome", "top-of-the-line" rooms, "pleasant" public areas and an "au courant" spa.

Cornwall

Lugger Hotel, The [H] 🔭 [S] — - | - | - | - | $492

Portloe | (011-44-1872) 501-322 | fax 501-691 | www.luggerhotel.com | 20 rooms, 1 cottage

Loyalists "hope not too many people discover" this small 17th-century inn "in a tiny coastal village" surrounded by cliffs with views of Portloe Harbor; with a shady past as a smuggler's hangout, it's now one of the "very best" bases for "touring Cornwall", featuring modern, crisply decorated rooms, a spa, a "great" restaurant that spotlights local seafood and "inobtrusive service"; N.B. no kids under 12 permitted.

Cotswolds

Bath Priory Hotel 🫖 🔭 [S] 🏊 — 24 | 24 | 23 | 21 | $482

Weston Rd. | Bath | (011-44-1225) 331-922 | fax 448-276 | 800-525-4800 | www.thebathpriory.co.uk | 27 rooms, 4 suites

"Like a page out of *Country Living*", this "charming" hotel just outside city center offers an "unforgettable experience" including "superb" dining spotlighting produce from the property's "lovely garden"; rooms are "spacious" and "beautiful" (if heavy on the "chintz"), the staff "treats you like family" and the grounds (with indoor and "attractive" outdoor pools) are "wonderful."

Buckland Manor [H] 🔭 🎾 — 25 | 25 | 26 | 22 | $492

near Broadway | Buckland | (011-44-1386) 852-626 | fax 853-557 | 800-735-2478 | www.bucklandmanor.co.uk | 13 rooms

Partisans "sing the praises of the wondrous staff" and advise "bring your camera to catch every angle" of this centuries-old "great manor home" set on 10 acres of gardens, streams and waterfalls; as befits a Relais & Châteaux property, the "charming" individually decorated rooms are "unbelievable", the food's "fabulous" and the location's ideal for touring nearby historic homes; N.B. no children under 12 allowed.

Calcot Manor ♿ⓌⓈ🏊🔍 | ▽ 21 | 23 | 20 | 21 | $521

near Tetbury | (011-44-1666) 890-391 | fax 890-394 | www.calcotmanor.co.uk | 28 rooms, 5 suites

It's been around awhile, but this chintz-free country house hotel set "in one of the nicest parts of England" (100 miles west of London) in the Cotswolds has "loads of things to do" including enjoying a "fabulous" 7,000-sq.-ft. spa and "fantastic" kids' club and full-time nursery "for families wanting a break" from the little ones, a "very helpful" staff and some "wonderful" food at the glass-enclosed restaurant; rooms are in a collection of converted barns and farmhouses (some dating to the 13th century), plus larger cottages are also available.

Cowley Manor ⓌⓌ🏊Ⓢ🏊 | 26 | 21 | 20 | 25 | $452

near Cheltenham | Cowley | (011-44-1242) 870-900 | fax 870-901 | www.cowleymanor.com | 30 rooms

"The perfect country retreat" may well be the "stunning blend of old world and new" at this "splendid manor house" set above lakes and ponds with 55 acres of formal gardens (reputedly where Lewis Carroll met Alice Liddell); the "sophisticated", "superb" rooms feature "contemporary" decor, the "communal areas are great", the service is "warm", the spa provides "high-standard treatments" and the food is "excellent"; be forewarned, though: "leaving is heart-wrenching."

Le Manoir aux Quat'Saisons ✕Ⓦ🏊🏊 | 25 | 27 | 28 | 21 | $816

Church Rd. | Great Milton | (011-44-1844) 278-881 | fax 278-847 | 800-237-1236 | www.manoir.com | 19 rooms, 13 suites

Famed chef Raymond Blanc has created an "air of opulence" amid "metropolitan luxury in the English countryside" at this Relais & Châteaux resort; it's "beautiful, genteel and lovely . . . and that's just the food" – modern French "in superlative style" that's "ludicrously good"; rooms are "quite excellent" and the "relaxing atmosphere" is "something to look at" – "perfection but at a price that hurts!"

Lower Slaughter Manor Ⓦ🏊🏊🔍 | ▽ 24 | 24 | 26 | 20 | $452

Lower Slaughter | (011-44-1451) 820-456 | fax 822-150 | www.lowerslaughter.co.uk | 13 rooms, 3 suites

"If you want to get away, this is the place" say connoisseurs of "Cotswolds' charm" who've stayed at this "delightful country house" with "beautiful grounds", "elegant" rooms, "excellent" service from a "wonderful" staff and a "fantastic restaurant" with a "good wine list"; overall, most say it's "simply a delight to spend time" here; N.B. a nearby golf course offers discounted greens fees to guests.

Lucknam Park Hotel ✕Ⓦ🏊Ⓢ🏊🔍 | ▽ 24 | 29 | 27 | 27 | $482

Colerne | Chippenham | (011-44-1225) 742-777 | fax 743-536 | 800-735-2478 | www.lucknampark.co.uk | 28 rooms, 13 suites

The "friendly", "impeccable" staff makes you "feel like you're the lord of the manor" at this "truly great" Relais & Châteaux resort that reflects "the best of the British countryside"; its 500 acres of grounds are "gorgeous" with a spa, pool and equestrian center, the food is "superb" (under chef Hywel Jones) and the "old-fashioned" rooms are "beautiful", some made more so by a "fireplace ablaze on a snowy evening."

Lygon Arms, The ⊕❄♨⊚☕🔍 | 20 | 21 | 21 | 20 | $450

High St. | Broadway | (011-44-1386) 852-255 | fax 854-470 | www.thelygonarms.co.uk | 60 rooms, 9 suites

Look forward to being "totally pampered" by a "mind-reading staff" during your "utterly enchanting" stay at this "archetypical English" circa-1532 country inn whose past guests include Charles I and Oliver Cromwell; some of the rooms in both the old and newer sections feature "wonderful four-poster beds with the softest linens", the grounds are "gorgeous" and the spa's "fantastic."

Royal Crescent Hotel, The ⊕❄♨Ⓢ☕ | 24 | 24 | 22 | 23 | $570

16 Royal Crescent | Bath | (011-44-1225) 823-333 | fax 339-401 | 888-295-4710 | www.royalcrescent.co.uk | 29 rooms, 16 suites

"The last word in 18th-century elegance" may be this "fabulous hotel" situated in a crescent of Georgian mansions in a "lovely city"; the "elegant" rooms are named after notable town residents (the "Jane Austen suite is wonderful"), the staff's "courteous", the restaurant serves "superb" food and the spa is "first rate"; "even though your wallet takes a bath", most maintain it's "worth it."

Thornbury Castle ⊕❄♨ | 27 | 26 | 25 | 25 | $391

Castle St. | Thornbury | (011-44-1454) 281-182 | fax 416-188 | www.thornburycastle.co.uk | 21 rooms, 4 suites

"Modern amenities in medieval splendor" characterize this nearly 500-year-old "beautiful castle in a charming town"; for an "incredible experience", guests can "sleep in the same room once inhabited by Henry VIII and Anne Boleyn" (the first owner was beheaded by the King), sip cocktails in the "manicured" Tudor gardens and enjoy "world-class service"; among the activities to enjoy are nearby clay pigeon shooting, on-site falconry and the "perfect high tea."

Whatley Manor ❄♨Ⓢ | ▽ 23 | 22 | 21 | 24 | $551

Easton Grey | Malmesbury | (011-44-16) 6682-2888 | fax 6682-6120 | www.whatleymanor.com | 15 rooms, 8 suites

An "unbeatable attention to detail" defines this "quaint" and "luxurious" Relais & Châteaux "regional" favorite, located near Bath in a "beautiful setting" with "extensive gardens"; "unlike any other in the U.K.", the "huge", award-winning Aquarias Spa – offering La Prairie treatments, water circuits, thermal cabins and more – is "worthy of a particular mention"; "superb rooms" feature Bang & Olufsen stereos, heated floors and antique furnishings, while "sublime service" keeps the vibe "relaxed"; summer "breakfast in the garden" is "a must."

Cumbria

Holbeck Ghyll 🖉❄♨Ⓢ | 23 | 25 | 22 | 21 | $374

Holbeck Ln. | Windermere | (011-44-15) 3943-2375 | fax 3943-4743 | www.holbeckghyll.com | 22 rooms, 1 suite

A warm welcome awaits guests in the oak-paneled entrance hall of this "amazing" 19th-century Lake District charmer with a "magnificent location" boasting "stunning views" of Lake Windermere and the Langdale Fells; fans love the "top-class" dining (with extensive wine lists and outdoor seating in warm weather), the "tranquil" atmosphere that includes an inglenook fireplace and the "quality service to match" it all.

Sharrow Bay Country House ⊕🕌 | 27 | 25 | 28 | 19 | $413

Lake Ullswater | Penrith | (011-44-1768) 486-301 | fax 486-349 | 800-735-2478 | www.sharrowbay.co.uk | 17 rooms, 7 suites

You'll "feel like a guest at a country house" when you're walking around this "delightful" Lake District Relais & Châteaux hotel (a private home in the 1800s) with "gorgeous views" and a "friendly, faultless staff"; "breakfast is spectacular" and it's "oh-so-British" all around, but some deem this "precious" place "chintzy", so they take "lots of great hikes" to "make up for it"; N.B. no kids under 13 allowed.

Devon

Bovey Castle 👫⊕🕌🛏️⛵🔍 | ▽ 23 | 21 | 22 | 26 | $590

Dartmoor National Park | North Bovey | (011-44-1647) 445-016 | fax 445-020 | www.boveycastle.com | 55 rooms, 10 suites

Located on "glorious" grounds within Dartmoor National Park in Devon, this "fabulous" resort housed in an early-20th-century building with 1920s decor successfully incorporates "modern amenities without losing any of its character"; the "rooms are cozy", the food is "high quailty" and there's "so much to do on the estate – fishing, riding, falconry" and playing golf; though a few find it "expensive for what it is", others insist it's an "ideal way to spend a weekend in the countryside."

☑ Gidleigh Park ✕🕌🔍 | 28 | 29 | 28 | 26 | $757

Chagford | (011-44-1647) 432-367 | fax 432-574 | 800-735-2478 | www.gidleigh.com | 21 rooms, 1 cottage

"Food, glorious food" sing enchanted epicures who find their "favorite restaurant" "on the planet" at this recently renovated Relais & Châteaux 45-acre Tudor "retreat", a piece of "heaven in Devon" blessed by chef Michael Caine's "exceptional French" restaurant and "incredible wine selection"; "luxurious rooms", "gorgeous gardens" and "outstanding service" further justify "astronomical prices."

Hampshire

Chewton Glen ⊕🕌Ⓢ⛵🔍 | 26 | 25 | 26 | 27 | $993

Chewton Farm Rd. | New Milton | (011-44-1425) 275-341 | fax 272-310 | 800-344-5087 | www.chewtonglen.com | 35 rooms, 23 suites

"As good as it gets in country-house living", this "quintessentially English" Relais & Châteaux resort in New Milton, "where the rich and famous arrive by helicopter", is a "serene respite" with "unique" rooms, "glorious" gardens, "superb" tennis, an "amazing" Molton Brown spa, a nine-hole golf course and a "hand-trimmed croquet pitch"; guests further gush over the "immaculate" service "without pretension", "exquisite" dining and a high tea that will "make an American a true Brit."

**Four Seasons
Dogmersfield Park** 👫🐾🕌Ⓢ⛵🔍 | ▽ 27 | 25 | 22 | 26 | $541

Dogmersfield Park, Chalky Ln. | Dogmersfield | (011-44-1252) 853-000 | fax 853-010 | 800-332-8442 | www.fourseasons.com | 111 rooms, 22 suites

"Highly recommended" for "harried travelers", this "beautiful restoration of a country home" in Hampshire is a "delightful oasis" with a "spectacular pool and grounds", an "excellent" spa and rooms with "chandeliers and tapestry wall hangings"; even if the dining isn't on par with the rest and it's a bit too "sprawling" for some, it "oozes quality" for those wanting "a weekend escape from London."

Hertfordshire

Grove, The 👪 [H] 🏋 ⛳ [S] 🏊 🎾 — 23 | 22 | 21 | 25 | $492

Chandler's Cross | (011-44-1923) 807-807 | fax 221-008 | 800-223-6800 | www.thegrove.co.uk | 215 rooms, 12 suites

Situated on 300 acres, this "awesome" hotel set in an early-18th-century building just 30 minutes from central London has been reborn as a "hip" country-house lodging with an eccentric interior design and "palatial" rooms, outfitted with plasma TVs and other ultramod amenities; some say it's "well worth the journey" for the "outstanding level of service", the on-site Sequoia spa and "one of the best" golf courses, but others find the "modern design" a "bit odd" and "impractical", like "a corporate vision of what it is to be quirky."

London

TOPS IN CITY

26 Lanesborough
25 Claridge's
24 Four Seasons Canary Wharf
Dorchester
Connaught

Athenaeum Hotel & Apartments 🛏 🐕 🏋 [S] — 21 | 23 | 17 | 18 | $580

116 Piccadilly | (011-44-20) 7499-3464 | fax 7493-1860 | 800-335-3300 | www.athenaeumhotel.com | 112 rooms, 12 suites, 33 apartments

Fans of this staple rave about its "perfect location on Piccadilly" - "across from Green Park" and near "the shopping district of Knightsbridge" - as well as the "top-of-the-line service", "24-hour" health club with Jacuzzi and a whiskey bar that's among the "best in London"; less popular are the rooms, which, while "quiet", "modern" and outfitted with "chic bathrooms", can be "tiny"; for more space, stay in one of the apartments located in several Edwardian townhouses.

Berkeley, The 🍴 🛏 🏋 [S] 🏊 — 23 | 24 | 24 | 23 | $902

Wilton Pl. | (011-44-20) 7235-6000 | fax 7235-4330 | 800-637-2869 | www.the-berkeley.co.uk | 149 rooms, 65 suites

A "very traditional" and "proper" Knightsbridge "haven", this veteran overlooking Hyde Park wins the "best of breed" nod from fervent fans for its "attentive" service, rooms with "plush beds" and "luxury marble bathrooms", and "gorgeous" top-floor pool; with "exquisite" French dining at chef Marcus Wareing's Pétrus, a "rich and famous" scene at Blue Bar and proximity to Harrods, it "doesn't come cheap."

Blakes Hotel 🍴 🛏 🐕 🏋 — 22 | 24 | 21 | 17 | $403

33 Roland Gardens | (011-44-20) 7370-6701 | fax 7373-0442 | 800-926-3173 | www.blakeshotels.com | 36 rooms, 9 suites

Blokes love this "discreet", "super-cool, super-chic, super-expensive" boutique hotel in residential South Kensington that some consider the "sexiest, most romantic" in London; "exotic" (though "small") rooms designed by owner Anouska Hempel are individually decorated, there's a "creative" Pacific Rim fusion restaurant via chef Neville Campbell and the "helpful" staff brings it all together; a few, however, find "too much attitude."

Brown's Hotel ⊕♨Ⓢ

22	24	22	19	$560

30 Albemarle St. | (011-44-20) 7493-6020 | fax 7493-9381 | www.brownshotel.com | 102 rooms, 15 suites

"After being closed for over a year", this "remodeled and rejuvenated London classic" – now part of the Rocco Forte group – is back and "better than ever", offering spacious rooms and bathrooms with "modern amenities" like "plasma TVs", "impeccable" service from a staff that, "when it knows you, treats you like family" and a "posh"-but-not-pretentious vibe; along with its "great shopping and walking location", pluses include the notable restaurant, "fabulous", trendy bar and a rave-worthy "high tea" that "is like something out of a Merchant Ivory film."

Cadogan, The ⊕⌇♨

19	21	16	16	$659

75 Sloane St. | (011-44-20) 7235-7141 | fax 7245-0994 | 877-783-4600 | www.cadogan.com | 55 rooms, 10 suites

Transformed by hotel designer Grace Leo-Andrieu (Montalembert in Paris), this 1887 landmark offers an "understated" and "sexy" option in an "amazing" Knightsbridge location for "seeing all of London"; the spot where Oscar Wilde was arrested for indecent acts now offers "distinctive" rooms with either contemporary or classic English decor, "gracious service" and a "wonderful low-key afternoon tea", plus a British restaurant and a fun red-glass bar sporting ostrich-leather chairs.

Capital Hotel

-	-	-	-	$383

22 Basil St. | (011-44-20) 7589-5171 | fax (011-44-20) 7255-0011 | www.capitalhotel.co.uk | 41 rooms, 8 suites

Located in the Knightsbridge area, steps from Harrods, Harvey Nichols and the designer boutiques of Sloane Street, this family-run hotel draws particular notice for its legendary New French restaurant, under the auspices of chef Eric Chavot; but the classical rooms, with Egyptian cotton bedding and marble baths, plus the attached serviced apartments, are solid options for short- and long-term stays as well.

Charlotte Street Hotel ♨

23	23	22	22	$403

15 Charlotte St. | (011-44-20) 7806-2000 | fax 7806-2002 | 800-553-6674 | www.charlottestreethotel.com | 39 rooms, 13 suites

"Perfectly" located for "the British Museum, Chinatown and a night out", this Bloomsbury spot manages to be both "very hip" and "cozy and comfortable", offering a "home-on-the-road" atmosphere that makes guests feel like they "really live in London"; "first-class" rooms designed by Kit Kemp, "great amenities" and "professional service" earn traveler raves, while local "media and film types" come for the "screening room" and "cool bar."

Claridge's ✕⊕Ⓢ

25	26	24	24	$1001

Brook St. | (011-44-20) 7629-8860 | fax 7499-2210 | 800-637-2869 | www.theclaridgeshotellondon.com | 143 rooms, 60 suites

"Gorgeous, darling, gorgeous" gush guests of this "old-line" Mayfair "legend" near top shops and theaters that "remains the hotel to which others should aspire"; service that's "second to none" includes an "old-fashioned" elevator operator, and each room is "quirkily but luxuriously decorated" – beds are "made in heaven" and "the showerheads alone are worth the stay"; foodies recommend booking "well in advance" to experience chef Gordon Ramsay's "world-class" Modern European fare.

Connaught, The ✕ ⓗ 🗠 ⓢ

| 24 | 27 | 25 | 22 | $902 |

Carlos Pl. | (011-44-20) 7499-7070 | fax 7495-3262 | 800-637-2869 | www.theconnaughthotellondon.com | 69 rooms, 23 suites

You half expect James Bond to appear at this "clubby", "top-flight" Mayfair "treasure" that's the kind of place "you imagine spies meet to trade secrets"; it's got close to "perfect" service, "beautifully appointed", antiques-filled rooms and "outstanding" dining thanks to chef Angela Hartnett; even those who say it's "stodgy" and "tired" agree "you must" go for an "inventive" cocktail at the "hidden-away" bar.

Conrad 🖎 🗠 🛢 🏊

| 25 | 23 | 19 | 22 | $409 |

Chelsea Harbour | (011-44-20) 7823-3000 | fax 7351-6525 | 800-445-8667 | www.conradhotels.com | 160 suites

If you "ask for a room overlooking the harbor", you won't mind the "out-of-the-way location" in Chelsea of this "great property" with "large, American-sized" "comfortable suites" and "crisp, modern and posh British style"; just a few report "distant" service from a "staff shipped from Madame Tussaud's."

Covent Garden Hotel ⓢ

| 25 | 25 | 20 | 23 | $383 |

10 Monmouth St. | (011-44-20) 7806-1000 | fax 7806-1100 | 800-553-6674 | www.coventgardenhotel.co.uk | 51 rooms, 7 suites

A "small", "tranquil hotel in a raucous location" near the shops and theaters of Covent Garden, this "trendy" but "charming" boutique features "beautifully appointed" quarters and "outstanding" service (the "best concierge experience I've ever had"); it also boasts a beauty room and gym, and though a few dis the dining as "subpar", there's a "world of food and entertainment" nearby.

Dorchester, The ⓗ 🛢 ⓢ

| 25 | 26 | 24 | 23 | $1032 |

Park Ln. | (011-44-20) 7629-8888 | fax 7409-0114 | 800-727-9820 | www.dorchesterhotel.com | 197 rooms, 53 suites

It's "tops, tops, tops", old bean, at this "star-studded" landmark in Mayfair where the "luxurious" rooms have "fat, plushy beds" that you "can't wait to get back to", and the "kind" staff "knows what you want before you do"; try a Thai massage in the spa, then dine at China Tang and "all will be well with the world"; N.B. Alain Ducasse plans a new restaurant here this year.

Dorset Square Hotel

| 22 | 22 | 18 | 18 | $295 |

39 Dorset Sq. | (011-44-20) 7723-7874 | fax 7724-3328 | www.dorsetsquare.co.uk | 34 rooms, 3 suites

For travelers who want to escape the "large business hotels" in London, this boutique option with unique rooms that "vary in size" but are "charming", "cozy and comfortable" offers a "great value"; "very private and personal" service, a restaurant that features produce from Dorset County farmers and an "excellent location" close to intriguing shops on Marylebone High Street (as well as the Sherlock Holmes Museum) are further draws.

	ROOMS	SERVICE	DINING	FACIL.	COST

Dukes Hotel 🏨Ⓢ
| 21 | 26 | 19 | 21 | $659 |

35 St. James's Pl. | (011-44-20) 7491-4840 | fax 7493-1264 |
800-381-4702 | www.dukeshotel.com | 78 rooms, 12 suites

"Tucked away in a charming cul-de-sac", this "fabulous", "homey",
"clublike" hotel is "worth the trip" to the St. James's area; the "first-
rate staff" supplies a "warm welcome to weary travelers" who enjoy
the "small" but "comfortable", "lovely" rooms, and no one should
leave without repairing to the wood-paneled bar for what may be the
"best martini in town."

51 Buckingham Gate 🏨Ⓢ
| 24 | 26 | 18 | 21 | $708 |

51 Buckingham Gate | (011-44-20) 7769-7766 | fax 7233-5014 |
www.51-buckinghamgate.com | 12 suites, 74 apartments

"Homey and inviting" apartments within "walking distance to the
palace" lure travelers to this "stylish" "jewel" in Westminster where
guests knock around "spacious kitchens" and enjoy "extremely
helpful" service (which can include a personal butler); there's a
"must-try" spa and French, British and Indian restaurants, and connoisseurs appreciate the discreet off-street entrance apparently
favored by "stars and VIPs."

47 Park Street 🏨
| 27 | 27 | 19 | 21 | $713 |

47 Park St. | (011-44-20) 7491-7282 | fax 7491-7281 | 800-228-9290 |
www.47parkstreet.com | 49 suites

Kick back and spread out in this "oasis in Mayfair", an elegant
Edwardian residence-hotel that's a real "home away from home" featuring rooms with "plenty of space" – basically a full "London apartment to accommodate the family" – superior service and "excellent"
dining at Le Gavroche restaurant; be prepared for a time-share sales
pitch at this Marriott club (a setup that can seem "peculiar"), but at
least it's "not pushy."

Four Seasons 🏨✕🏨
| 24 | 26 | 23 | 22 | $739 |

Hamilton Pl., Park Ln. | (011-44-20) 7499-0888 | fax 7493-1895 |
800-332-3442 | www.fourseasons.com | 193 rooms, 26 suites

For a "slice of heaven" in Mayfair head to this "spectacular" spot
boasting "unbelievable service" "with a smile but without the
arrogance" and a concierge who "can arrange anything"; kudos go to
the "great tearoom", Lanes Restaurant and "well-appointed" rooms
with baths like "mini-spas", but a few find this outpost "somewhat
ordinary" for the luxury hotel group, citing "dated decor" that "needs
to be redone."

Four Seasons Canary Wharf 🏨✕🏨Ⓢ
| 26 | 26 | 22 | 24 | $625 |

46 Westferry Circus | (011-44-20) 7510-1999 | fax 7510-1998 |
www.fourseasons.com | 128 rooms, 14 suites

"Sleek" and sassy, this "modern" Canary Wharf outpost offers "perfect comfort on a business trip": "top-notch gym facilities", a "spectacular" infinity pool "overlooking the Thames", "huge" rooms with
views, a "warm, wonderful staff" and a "very convenient" location
near London's financial center (it can get "boring at night" though);
the only negative, say a few, is a restaurant that leaves "something
to be desired."

	ROOMS	SERVICE	DINING	FACIL.	COST

Goring, The ⑪ | 23 | 26 | 25 | 22 | $639

Beeston Pl., Grosvenor Gardens | (011-44-20) 7396-9000 | fax 7834-4393 |
www.goringhotel.co.uk | 61 rooms, 6 suites

Since 1910, this family-owned "wonderful sleeper" with a "brilliant location" in Victoria has served as a "home away from home" for staunch supporters of its "cheerful" but "polished" staff's "staggering attention to detail" as well as its "warm atmosphere" embodied in "elegant" rooms; the eponymous restaurant serves "fantastic" Traditional British fare, adding to the "old English charm" of the experience.

Halkin, The ♨ | 24 | 26 | 21 | 21 | $688

5 Halkin St. | (011-44-20) 7333-1000 | fax 7333-1100 | 800-223-6800 |
www.halkin.co.uk | 30 rooms, 11 suites

"Chic" and "high-tech", this Belgravia boutique hotel near Hyde Park offers "immaculate" accommodations that have what may be the "largest bathrooms in London", a "brilliant, cheerful" staff that "goes out of its way to help" and Thai cuisine served up by chef David Thompson at Nahm restaurant; though it's tucked away in a residential nabe where there's "not much activity", it's right near a tube stop.

Hempel, The ✗ ⊗ ♨ | 23 | 20 | 19 | 21 | $521

31-35 Craven Hill Gardens | (011-44-20) 7298-9000 | fax 7402-4666 |
www.the-hempel.co.uk | 37 rooms, 5 suites, 5 apartments

"Zen" before Zen was hip, this "serene" "sleeper" in residential Bayswater was crafted by Brit designer Anouska Hempel and features "lovely, bright", "extremely white" "minimalist rooms", complemented by a "beautiful" geometric garden setting; despite the "inconvenient location", it's an "escape" for "young", savvy types, who appreciate the "chichi" design, the "killer", coolly sophisticated I-Thai restaurant (fusing Thai, Italian and Japanese) and the overall "good value."

Jumeirah Carlton Tower ♨ ⓢ ≋   ▽ | 22 | 21 | 20 | 24 | $942

1 Cadogan Pl. | (011-44-20) 7235-1234 | fax 7235-9129 | 877-854-8051 |
www.jumeirah.com | 161 rooms, 59 suites

"Well-located" in Knightsbridge, with "Harrods and Harvey Nichols nearby", this "elegant" spot has enjoyed ongoing upgrades since joining the Jumeirah family; new Garden Rooms and meeting spaces, a Gilt Champagne Lounge, redone public spaces and a "world-class gym" with spa and "huge stainless-steel swimming pool" are overseen by an "attentive and competent" staff, while business travelers appreciate the "great" Rib Room & Oyster Bar.

Jumeirah Lowndes, The ⓢ | - | - | - | - | $639

21 Lowndes St. | (011-44-20) 7823-1234 | fax 7235-1154 | 877-854-8051 |
www.jumeirahlowndeshotel.com | 87 rooms, 14 suites

Some visitors find a "great boutique-style" hotel with "top-notch" service when they stay at this small spot near Harvey Nichols and Harrods in Knightsbridge; it closed briefly for renovations last year, so you'll find a fresher look to the "well-appointed" rooms and public areas.

K West Hotel & Spa ♨ ⓢ   ▽ | 20 | 19 | 17 | 22 | $492

Richmond Way | (011-44-87) 0027-4343 | fax 0811-2612 |
www.k-west.co.uk | 208 rooms, 12 suites

Admirers of this "low-key hotel in residential" West Kensington cite its "quiet", "ultramodern" accommodations with "fabulous beds", "great amenities" including "all the Internet you can eat" and "impressive spa" as well as "yummy breakfasts" in an "elegant" dining room; the "disappointed", however, deem the chambers "dark", the location "inconvenient" and the "dot-com boutique concept a bit passé."

Landmark London, The ⑪🌊♨️Ⓢ🏊 | 23 | 22 | 20 | 22 | $875

222 Marylebone Rd. | (011-44-20) 7631-8000 | fax 7631-8080 | 800-323-7500 | www.landmarklondon.co.uk | 252 rooms, 47 suites

Set in a "beautifully restored building", this "revived" Marylebone classic boasts an "old-world feel" and "fantastically large rooms" – particularly for "central London" – as well as a "convenient" location for business with "close proximity to Paddington Station" and Regent's Park; though the food "is nothing to write home about", the "perfect execution" of the atrium "Winter Garden" and service that's "the epitome of British" help create "a welcome refuge from the outside world."

Lanesborough, A St. Regis Hotel ⑪🌊♨️Ⓢ | 27 | 28 | 25 | 24 | $780

1 Lanesborough Pl. | (011-44-20) 7259-5599 | fax 7259-5606 | 800-999-1828 | www.lanesborough.com | 50 rooms, 46 suites

"You've really arrived when you arrive" at this "utter delight" in Belgravia across from Hyde Park, where "outrageously helpful" staffers who "know their business" "set the standard" for service "beyond belief" amid "traditional grandeur"; the "antiques-filled" rooms with "cutting-edge technology" are worth leaving for "lovely" breakfasts and high tea (a "required stop") in the "beautiful" conservatory, and for the Library Bar's "fantastic atmosphere"; if only it weren't "so expensive."

Mandarin Oriental Hyde Park ✕♨️Ⓢ | 24 | 25 | 23 | 23 | $749

66 Knightsbridge | (011-44-20) 7235-2000 | fax 7235-2001 | 800-526-6566 | www.mandarinoriental.com | 177 rooms, 23 suites

Be "treated like an emperor" at this "opulent jewel", a remade 1889 gentlemen's club a "two-minute walk" from Harrods, where "attention to detail is incredible" and a "truly memorable stay" can be had; regulars recommend the "excellent park view rooms" (avoid facing "noisy" Knightsbridge), the "outrageously priced" spa ("worth it"), the "very cool" Adam Tihany–designed bar ("be seen in the scene") and chef Chris Staines' "fantastic" French–Modern European Foliage restaurant.

Metropolitan ✕🌊♨️Ⓢ | 21 | 19 | 23 | 19 | $629

Old Park Ln. | (011-44-20) 7447-1000 | fax 7447-1100 | 800-337-4685 | www.metropolitan.co.uk | 132 rooms, 18 suites, 19 apartments

"Über-modern" design is "applied in a thick paste" at this "slightly too hip" Mayfair boutique whose "big plus" is the "awesome" Nobu restaurant and a "super" location "next to the tube"; but some say the "stylishly dressed" staff has "too much attitude" and "spartan" rooms "can be loud on lower floors" near the "noisy" lobby, so although it may "work for some" it "doesn't work" for others.

Milestone Hotel & Apartments 🌊🌊♨️🏊 | 23 | 26 | 21 | 22 | $492

1 Kensington Ct. | (011-44-20) 7917-1000 | fax 7917-1010 | 800-223-6800 | www.milestonehotel.com | 45 rooms, 12 suites, 6 apartments

A Victorian building in a "fabulous location" opposite Kensington Palace, one of London's "best" small hotels "treats you like returning royalty" with "flawless", "personalized" service that "never wavers"; "tasteful" and "different" rooms with "all the little extras" are "overstuffed with stuff" and equipped with "Rube Goldberg" bathrooms, though some are "a bit snug" ("bigger rooms are in back"); families find "a welcome haven" in the apartments, and there's "a nice English bar."

One Aldwych [H] 🔭 [S] 🏊 22 | 24 | 23 | 24 | $708

1 Aldwych | (011-44-20) 7300-1000 | fax 7300-1001 | 800-223-6800 | www.onealdwych.com | 93 rooms, 12 suites

"Even if you're not staying" at this "swank" property with an "excellent Covent Garden" location, the "see-and-be-seen" lobby bar is "not to be missed" and the restaurants are "outstanding"; the "stylish" rooms are "small but fantastically comfortable", service is "fabulous" and "unpretentious" and the "beautiful" pool with its underwater soundtrack is "recommended for stressed travelers"; naturally, it's a "bit pricey", but this "grand duke of 'cool Britannia' sets the standard."

Ritz, The 👪 🍴 [H] 🔭 24 | 26 | 22 | 24 | $668

150 Piccadilly | (011-44-20) 7493-8181 | fax 7493-2687 | 877-748-9536 | www.theritzlondon.com | 113 rooms, 20 suites

"Don't forget your jacket and tie" when you stay at this "classic" "ideal" in Piccadilly - definitely a "tradition" you should try "before you die"; if you can't afford an overnight at this "set of *Lifestyles of the Rich and Famous*", "at least have the decency to take your mother to tea" to "be seen", or to dinner in the "magnificent" "formal" Ritz restaurant; while a few are "put off" by the "stiff upper lips" among the "pompous staff" and the overall "stuffy" air, the majority finds it "lives up to its reputation" so "what else need be said?"

Sanderson 🍴 🛁 [S] 23 | 18 | 22 | 21 | $472

50 Berners St. | (011-44-20) 7300-1400 | fax 7300-1401 | 800-634-1444 | www.morganshotelgroup.com | 136 rooms, 12 suites, 1 penthouse, 1 apartment

"Life's a party" at this "spectacular" West End/Soho Morgans Hotel, due in part to the "tragically hip" Long and Purple bars "frequented by the fashion and media crowds", "surreal" Philippe Starck-designed rooms and the "transporting" Agua spa; too bad the "disorganized", "slow" service mars the overall effect; N.B. post-Survey, Alain Ducasse's Spoon restaurant was replaced by Zak Palaccio's Malaysian eatery, Suka.

Savoy, A Fairmont Hotel 🍴 [H] 🔭 [S] 🏊 22 | 24 | 24 | 23 | $391

Strand | (011-44-20) 7836-4343 | fax 7240-6040 | 888-590-9900 | www.fairmont.com | 218 rooms, 45 suites

For an enjoyable stay at this "slightly funky" "grande dame" (circa 1899) "ask for one of the renovated rooms" "overlooking the Thames" since the "faded" hotel's "resurrection" by the Fairmont Group has "a long way to go" (quarters are "a bit hit-or-miss"); nevertheless, service is "exemplary" and the Strand location "brilliant" for "a night at the theater", plus, you'll "never forget" dinner at Marcus Wareing's Savoy Grill.

Sheraton Park Tower 🔭 22 | 20 | 18 | 20 | $786

101 Knightsbridge | (011-44-20) 7235-8050 | fax 7235-8231 | 800-325-3589 | www.luxurycollection.com | 242 rooms, 38 suites

The Knightsbridge location near "excellent shopping and transportation" and an "incredible staff" "saves" this otherwise "forgettable"

Sheraton; though the "dependable" rooms "seem bigger than they are" (some have "almost a 180-degree view of London"), a few say the food's "pitiful" and the decor "very plain."

Sofitel St. James ⓗ❄️🏨   24 | 22 | 18 | 20 | $600

6 Waterloo Pl. | (011-44-20) 7747-2200 | fax 7747-2210 | 800-763-4835 | www.sofitelstjames.com | 166 rooms, 20 suites

With its "gorgeous, well-appointed rooms" featuring "fancy" bath fixtures, "excellent" Piccadilly location near the cultural and tourist attractions and "accommodating" service, this hotel in a "grand building" (formerly a bank) is a solid choice; there's also "delicious" French fare in the Brasserie Roux and a "trendy" bar.

Soho Hotel, The 🍽️🏨Ⓢ   26 | 22 | 19 | 21 | $521

4 Richmond Mews | (011-44-20) 7559-3000 | fax 7559-3003 | 800-553-6674 | www.sohohotel.com | 85 rooms, 6 apartments

Best known for their Charlotte Street and Covent Garden hotels, the Firmdale group (aka Tim and Kit Kemp) has miraculously transformed a former car park in a quiet corner of central Soho into "the most stylish hotel in London" with "funky, large bedrooms", a "bar heaving with Soho media types" and "witty" decor "from the giant bronze cat in the lobby to the clever details throughout"; sure, the staff can be "too cool to acknowledge your presence" and the food just "so-so", but in such a "gorgeous" venue you can't help but have a "great time."

Stafford, The ⓗ🏨   23 | 26 | 22 | 21 | $600

St. James's Pl. | (011-44-20) 7493-0111 | fax 7493-7121 | 800-525-4800 | www.thestaffordhotel.co.uk | 69 rooms, 12 suites

"Incredible", "highly personalized service" from the "excellent porters" to the "best concierge in the world" is the hallmark of this "clubby" "home away from home" just off Green Park; the "posh" yet "cozy" accommodations are "individually decorated", and the "American Bar is a wonderful gathering place" (the 350-year-old wine cellar merits a tour).

St. Martins Lane 🍽️Ⓢ   20 | 18 | 20 | 18 | $433

45 St. Martin's Ln. | (011-44-20) 7300-5500 | fax 7300-5501 | 800-634-5500 | www.morganshotelgroup.com | 200 rooms, 2 suites, 1 penthouse, 1 apartment

"Light, airy and modern", this "Ian Schrager classic" (part of the Morgans Hotel Group and sister to the Sanderson) "continues to please the cool crowd" with its "great" Asia de Cuba restaurant, "popular bar" and Covent Garden location in the "smack-center of the theater district"; "designed by Philippe Starck", the lobby is "a playground for adults", while the "stylish but tiny" rooms feature the "best showers in London" and "multicolor" lighting that's changeable "to reflect your mood"; still, that "groovier-than-thou service" and an in-room setup that's "not functional for working" leaves some surveyors snapping "style over substance."

Stoke Park Club ⓗ🏨♨️Ⓢ⛳🏊🔍   ▽ 23 | 21 | 18 | 27 | $560

Park Rd., Stoke Poges | (011-44-1753) 717-171 | fax 717-181 | 800-525-4800 | www.stokeparkclub.com | 17 rooms, 4 suites

Located outside Windsor, just seven miles from Heathrow Airport, this 350-acre estate with a storied history is a "great place to spend a weekend" with "jaw-droppingly beautiful grounds and vistas" and the

27-hole Stoke Poges golf course on-site; the "sumptuous interior doesn't disappoint" either with an "amazing gym and spa" and individually decorated rooms flush with antiques, original artwork and satellite TVs; N.B. of note to movie buffs: several scenes in the James Bond movies *Goldfinger* and *Tomorrow Never Dies* were shot here.

Threadneedles ⓗ

| 21 | 23 | 15 | 18 | $560 |

5 Threadneedle St. | (011-44-20) 7657-8080 | fax 7657-8100 | www.theetoncollection.com | 58 rooms, 8 suites, 3 studios

Set in a converted 1865 bank right near the Tower of London and St. Paul's Cathedral, this "great little niche hotel" scores points for "excellent" service, a "central location" and rooms with "immensely comfortable beds" and "positively luxurious" limestone bathrooms; but guests give middling ratings to the European-Med restaurant, and warn "if you're looking for nightlife, stay elsewhere."

Trafalgar, The ♨

| 19 | 20 | 16 | 17 | $407 |

2 Spring Gardens | (011-44-20) 7870-2900 | fax 7870-2911 | 800-445-8667 | www.hilton.co.uk | 127 rooms, 2 suites

"Decent but lacks the final touch" is the word on this Trafalgar Square property with "nice-sized", "minimalist" rooms, "at least by London's standards", and "very modern decor" with the "attendant attitude from the chic staff"; a "popular" rooftop bar with "fantastic" views lends to the scene of the "young and hip who mingle to music in the lobby", but faultfinders fret that it has "not lived up to its promise."

22 Jermyn Street ⌇♨

| 22 | 22 | – | 16 | $433 |

22 Jermyn St. | (011-44-20) 7734-2353 | fax 7734-0750 | 800-682-7808 | www.22jermyn.com | 5 rooms, 13 suites

"Location, location, location" along with "lovely", "small" rooms" are part of the "charm" of this "small" but "cozy" "gem" of a townhouse in the St. James's area near Piccadilly, right in the "middle of the action" (which means it can get a little "noisy"); the "superb" staff that "will do anything to help" makes it "tough to say cheerio", unless it's to go out for dinner, since there's no bar or restaurant on-site.

West Sussex

Amberley Castle ⓗ♨⌐☍

| 24 | 26 | 24 | 23 | $324 |

Amberley | (011-44-1798) 831-992 | fax 831-998 | 800-735-2478 | www.amberleycastle.co.uk | 13 rooms, 6 suites

It's all "absolutely fabulous" at this "true castle" built in 1103, a "stunning" medievel "getaway" in "quaint" Amberley that lets you "play Henry VIII for a day – but just take one wife"; the verdant Relais & Châteaux lodging "is nothing short of amazing", charmed by white "roaming peacocks", croquet lawns and a thatched-roof treehouse; as befits royalty, rooms are "large and comfortable" with Jacuzzi baths, the service is "discreet" and you can relish dinner in the armor-adorned hall; N.B. no children under 12.

Gravetye Manor ⓗ♨

| 24 | 25 | 26 | 22 | $433 |

Vowels Ln. | East Grinstead | (011-44-1342) 810-567 | fax 810-080 | 800-735-2478 | www.gravetyemanor.co.uk | 18 rooms

"You feel as though Christopher Robin will pop out of the woods" at any moment at this "totally charming" Relais & Châteaux Elizabethan stone mansion, a "romantic country house" with "beautiful English gardens", a "splendid staff" that always supplies "excellent service" and "lovely rooms"; the food may be "pricey" for some wallet-watchers, but the majority finds it all simply "outstanding."

York

Middlethorpe Hall ⑪🔒Ⓢ♨ ▽ | 22 | 22 | 25 | 21 | $354

Bishopthorpe Rd. | (011-44-1904) 641-241 | fax 620-176 | www.middlethorpe.com | 25 rooms, 4 suites

Surrounded by 20 acres of "lovely grounds" in York and "convenient" to the local racecourse, this country getaway offers "well-furnished", individually decorated rooms in a "formal" 17th-century manor house once owned by diarist Lady Mary Wortley Montagu; "old-world charm" prevails, from the paneled walls of the 3 AA Rosette restaurant to the extensive spa and 40-ft. indoor pool.

United Kingdom - Scotland

Ayrshire

☑ **Westin Turnberry** 24 | 26 | 23 | 28 | $737
Resort, The 🍴⑪🎾🔒⊥Ⓢ♨🔍

Turnberry | (011-44-1655) 331-000 | fax 331-706 | 800-937-8461 | www.turnberry.co.uk | 207 rooms, 3 suites, 9 cottages

Duffers declare this Scottish "gem" "out in the middle of nowhere" is "the place to be for great golf" on "one of the world's finest" courses – site of multiple British Opens; but even nonswingers "love" to "soak up the atmosphere", visit the "nicest spa", enjoy archery and falconry and dine on "excellent breakfasts", plus there's also a "respectful staff."

Edinburgh

Balmoral, The 🍴⑪🎾🔒Ⓢ♨ 23 | 23 | 22 | 22 | $593

1 Princes St. | (011-44-131) 556-2414 | fax 557-8740 | 800-223-6800 | www.thebalmoralhotel.com | 168 rooms, 20 suites

A member of the Rocco Forte group, this "spectacular", "grand old European" hotel in a "superb" location delivers "the royal treatment" "without being stuffy"; go to the bar that stocks 50 brands of scotch and down a few before heading to the "splendid" "completely redone" rooms where there's "fruit, bottled water and a robe and slippers" ("get a corner unit if you can"); some say they could "spend weeks" at this "crown jewel of Edinburgh", especially given the spa and chef Jeff Bland's Number One restaurant.

Fort William

Inverlochy Castle ⑪🔒🔍 27 | 28 | 27 | 25 | $806

Torlundy | (011-44-1397) 702-177 | fax 702-953 | 888-424-0106 | www.inverlochycastlehotel.com | 13 rooms, 4 suites

It "would be hard to find a more perfect spot" in which to enjoy a "fantasy world of old-school elegance" than this 19th-century Relais & Châteaux "true Scottish castle at the foot of the Highlands"; it's "excellent in every respect" – an "idyllic setting", "sublime service", "spectacular food" at chef Matthew Gray's restaurant, "amazing fishing on the lake" and service that "couldn't be better" - so even if a few would like to see the decor "updated", it "knocks the socks off" most.

Glasgow

Malmaison Ⓗ 🐕

	ROOMS	SERVICE	DINING	FACIL.	COST
▽	21	21	16	16	$305

278 W. George St. | (011-44-141) 572-1000 | fax 572-1002 | www.malmaison-glasgow.com | 64 rooms, 8 suites

A converted Greek Orthodox church is the setting for this "trendy boutique" hotel centrally located within easy walking of "all of the city's hot spots"; the staff couldn't be more "charming", and even if some of the "stylish" rooms are "impossibly small", they have "all the amenities you could ask for", as well as "out-of-this-world" showers; it's "original" say impressed worshipers, making it "worth a repeat visit", especially after the refurbishment of all rooms was completed in March 2005; N.B. don't miss the Champagne Bar and Brasserie in the vaulted basement.

One Devonshire Gardens Ⓗ

ROOMS	SERVICE	DINING	FACIL.	COST
26	25	23	20	$275

1 Devonshire Gardens | (011-44-141) 339-2001 | fax 337-1663 | www.onedevonshiregardens.com | 32 rooms, 3 suites

Set in five townhouses on the West End, this "wonderful surprise" of an "intimate hotel" with "impeccable", "incredibly friendly service" and some of the "nicest rooms you've ever seen" with "great bathroom fixtures" has enthusiasts exclaiming it's "absolutely the best Glasgow has to offer"; try the "traditional Scottish breakfast" and "get rid of any chill by warming yourself in the tearoom next to a crackling fire"; N.B. fans also like dining at chef David Clark's Restaurant No. 5.

Inverness

Culloden House Hotel

ROOMS	SERVICE	DINING	FACIL.	COST
24	26	24	20	$472

Culloden | (011-44-1463) 790-461 | fax 792-181 | www.cullodenhouse.co.uk | 23 rooms, 5 suites

"Pure Scotland" down to the plasterwork details, this "idyllic", "historic" North Highlands mansion in Inverness where "Longhorn cows greet you hello" takes you "away from present-day life"; wayfarers feel like "royalty" in the "wonderfully spacious" rooms and antiques-adorned premises "filled with treasures", and the "unique" experience continues when "a piper plays during cocktail hour" (from May to October).

Perthshire

[Z] Gleneagles Ⓗ 🐕 🔭 ⛳ Ⓢ 🏊

ROOMS	SERVICE	DINING	FACIL.	COST
24	26	24	28	$698

Auchterarder | (011-44-1764) 662-231 | fax 662-134 | 866-881-9525 | www.gleneagles.com | 250 rooms, 16 suites

"Amazing", even if you don't like golf, this Perthshire resort with three "wonderful" courses appeals to everyone since there are "more activities" on the "stunning grounds" "than you can shake a club at": a "kid-friendly" mini-course, falconry, clay shooting, archery, off-road driving, an "ultra modern" fitness center and a "lovely spa", to name a few; "fantastic" rooms are filled with "old-world charm", the food is "fabulous" and the "superb staff" pulls it all together.

	ROOMS	SERVICE	DINING	FACIL.	COST

St. Andrews

Old Course Hotel, Golf Resort & Spa 🏌🍴♨🛁⛴☉🏊 | 23 | 23 | 21 | 27 | $678 |

St. Andrews, Kingdom of Fife | (011-44-1334) 474-371 | fax 477-668 | 800-223-6800 | www.oldcoursehotel.co.uk | 109 rooms, 35 suites

If you want "Old Course tee times" and "the best view a golfer could ask for", head to this historic "birthplace" of the game and get in on the action; even nonduffers are delighted by the "history" of it all, along with "sublime" sea views, a "don't-miss bar" and renovated rooms; the drawback for some is that the "eager-to-please" staff of "young" employees "can't seem to get its arms around good service."

United Kingdom – Wales

Cardiff

St. David's Hotel & Spa, The ♨☉🏊   ▽ | 22 | 19 | 18 | 24 | $485 |

Havannah St. | (011-44-2920) 454-045 | fax 487-056 | 800-223-6800 | www.thestdavidshotel.com | 116 rooms, 16 suites

Hotelier "Rocco Forte did it again" with this "bayside modern monument" that features a truly "excellent spa" with all the right hydrotherapy treatments and a "pool-sized hot tub"; it has a glass-backed atrium, all of the rooms have views over Cardiff Bay or the ocean from their wood-deck balconies and Tides Grill serves Welsh and English cuisine.

Llandudno

☑ Bodysgallen Hall ♨☉🏊⚲ | 26 | 28 | 26 | 27 | $324 |

Pentywyn Rd. | (011-44-1492) 584-466 | fax 582-519 | www.bodysgallen.com | 17 rooms, 16 suites

Two hundred acres of "beautiful gardens and woods" surround this "lovely place", where guests can feel like the "lady of the manor for a few days"; individually designed rooms are set in a "wonderful old house", which dates to the 13th century and boasts views "all the way to Conway Castle", while luxe cottages and suites dot the grounds; the gourmet restaurant and extensive spa, "afternoon tea in a stately sitting room" and the staff's "Welsh smiles" help "restore the soul."

United States

TOPS IN COUNTRY

29	Four Seasons/Hualalai	*Hawaii*
28	Peninsula	*Chicago*
	Four Seasons Wailea	*Hawaii*
27	Four Seasons	*Chicago*
	Mandarin Oriental	*Miami*
	Peninsula	*Los Angeles*
	Four Seasons	*Las Vegas*
	Halekulani	*Hawaii*
	Four Seasons	*New York City*
	Ritz-Carlton	*Orlando*

Atlanta

Four Seasons 🍴🐾🏋[S]🏊 26 | 27 | 26 | 25 | $315

75 14th St. | 404-881-9898 | fax 404-873-4692 | 800-819-5053 | www.fourseasons.com | 226 rooms, 18 suites

"Even for a Four Seasons, it's good" gush fans of this metropolitan "oasis" touted for "elegance" all around; commodious, "comfortable rooms" ("take one with a terrace"), a "gargantuan marble lobby", "impressive health club with indoor saltwater pool" and a "staff that treats you as though you live there" are all part of the "true luxury experience", augmented by "great food" from Park 75, one of Atlanta's finest eateries; best of all, its Midtown location - near offices, the High Museum and the symphony - "caters to the business traveler" and arts lovers alike.

InterContinental Buckhead 🍴🐾🏋[S]🏊 25 | 23 | 19 | 24 | $329

3315 Peachtree Rd. NE | 404-946-9000 | fax 404-946-9001 | www.intercontinental.com | 401 rooms, 21 suites

"Your stay will be comfy and your needs will be met" at this hotel "in the middle of Buckhead" touted for rooms with "hip furniture", sheets that "cost more than a plane ticket" and "deep-soaking tubs" - "the bath products ain't bad either"; public spaces include a "beautiful lobby", 25,000-sq.-ft. garden and the "best 24-hour restaurant in the city" ("where else can you get pig's trotters at 3 AM?"); skeptics snap at the "snobby" service and "way too high" prices, but most deem this "plush tower" "an amazing place to stay."

Ritz-Carlton, The 🍴🏋 24 | 24 | 23 | 22 | $395

181 Peachtree St. NE | 404-659-0400 | fax 404-688-0400 | 800-241-3333 | www.ritzcarlton.com | 422 rooms, 22 suites

"If you have to be in Downtown Atlanta", old hands say head to this "centrally located", large "luxury" hotel, as it "blows away its neighbors" with "wonderful" rooms and service that "has that typical Ritz efficiency" ("they take especially good care of solo females"); however, several say this twentysomething's somewhat "worn", hence "lacking the 'wow' that would make it appeal to anyone but a business traveler."

Ritz-Carlton Buckhead 🍴🐾🏋🏊 24 | 25 | 25 | 23 | $479

3434 Peachtree Rd. NE | 404-237-2700 | fax 404-239-0078 | 800-241-3333 | www.ritzcarlton.com | 524 rooms, 29 suites

"Right in the heart of everything" in Buckhead, this "gracious, reliable" hotel "exudes a distinct Southern charm" with its "beautifully appointed" rooms ("some small", but still "extremely comfortable") and "wonderful" staff that "greets you by name"; the "superb" fare, from "fantastic breakfasts to hedonistic teas to elaborate gourmet dinners", "makes going out unnecessary", and live "music and dancing" in the "best lobby bar anywhere" adds to the "indulgent experience."

Westin Buckhead 🐾🏋🏊 25 | 24 | 22 | 25 | $359

3391 Peachtree Rd. NE | 404-365-0065 | fax 404-365-8787 | www.westin.com | 354 rooms, 11 suites

"If you have to do business in Buckhead, this is the place to stay" insist fans of this "stylish" glass-fronted hotel with a "good layout" ("everything works"), which is "so convenient to the shopping" in Lenox Mall across the way; proponents feel pampered by large-windowed "rooms that are the standard Westin quality with their Heavenly everything" brand of bath, bed and even cribs, plus "top-notch fitness facilities"; "dining is limited to the lobby restaurant", but since it's a Palm steakhouse, maybe that's not so bad.

Boston

Boston Harbor Hotel 👪🍴🏠🔭Ⓢ🏊

Rooms	Service	Dining	Facil.	Cost
25	24	23	24	$485

70 Rowes Wharf | 617-439-7000 | fax 617-951-9307 |
800-752-7077 | www.bhh.com | 204 rooms, 26 suites

Enjoy "gorgeous views of the harbor" and a no-tipping policy at this waterfront hotel where the "rooms are expansive", "service is impeccable" and "chef Daniel Bruce of the amazing Meritage Restaurant" is "world-class at matching food and wine"; though the nearby Big Dig construction can be annoying, a stay is "worth every penny per night" - even getting here from Logan International on the water ferry is "a joy" that avoids Boston's notorious airport traffic.

Fifteen Beacon 🍴🏠🔭 (aka XV Beacon)

Rooms	Service	Dining	Facil.	Cost
27	26	26	22	$350

15 Beacon St. | 617-670-1500 | fax 617-670-2525 | 877-982-3226 |
www.xvbeacon.com | 57 rooms, 3 suites

"As cool a hotel as you can find", this "interior-design marvel" on Beacon Hill is "very hip in a Back Bay way" (e.g. "dark" "high-style" decor in a 1903 beaux arts building); each of the "wonderfully big" guestrooms is unique, and stocked with "all the essentials: fireplace, great stereo, remote-controlled everything"; The Federalist restaurant "is hard to beat", and the service is "white-glove all the way", including the free Lexus limos that whisk guests "anywhere in Downtown and to the airport."

[Z] Four Seasons 👪🍴🏠🔭🏊

Rooms	Service	Dining	Facil.	Cost
27	27	27	25	$475

200 Boylston St. | 617-338-4400 | fax 617-423-0154 | 800-332-3442 |
www.fourseasons.com | 197 rooms, 76 suites

"A foolproof choice" "for every season" rave reviewers about this "recently remodeled" Back Bay beauty; granted, "prices are insane", but the "location is second to none" (the Commons' famed "swan boats are a short walk away") and the rooms, though a tad "small", are "well organized and outfitted"; partake of the "superb" cuisine - you can work the calories off at "the best gym facility in the state" - and enjoy a staff system that's "always a step - no, a leap - ahead": even "at 2 AM, room service [delivers] a gourmet meal."

Ritz-Carlton Boston Common 🍴🏠🔭Ⓢ🏊

Rooms	Service	Dining	Facil.	Cost
26	26	23	24	$579

10 Avery St. | 617-574-7100 | fax 617-574-7200 | 800-241-3333 |
www.ritzcarlton.com | 150 rooms, 43 suites

"Posh and cool", this hotel (now the only Ritz-Carlton in Boston since the takeover by Taj Hotels of the original one) is "as cutting-edge as its Ladder District neighborhood"; professional "sports teams stay here" (it can get "noisy" when the buses pull up), but you don't have to be Derek Jeter for the "staff to cater to your every whim" or to enjoy the lavish Sports Club/LA gym, "just an elevator ride away."

	ROOMS	SERVICE	DINING	FACIL.	COST

Taj Boston ♯♯✕☇ᴙ
(fka The Ritz-Carlton)

| | 24 | 26 | 24 | 23 | $499 |

15 Arlington St. | 617-536-5700 | fax 617-536-1335 | 877-482-5267 |
www.ritzcarlton.com | 228 rooms, 45 suites

"Still the grande dame of Boston hotels", "dripping" with crystal and gold, this former Ritz-Carlton is now a Taj hotel (possibly outdating the above scores); you can still expect those "beautiful, roomy and spotless" chambers, a "perfect setting overlooking the Boston Public Gardens" and "steps away from shopping" and "fantastic" dining from tea to bar fare; in short, it's a "comfy, inviting respite from the city."

Chicago

TOPS IN CITY

28 Peninsula
27 Four Seasons
26 Ritz-Carlton

Burnham, Hotel ⊕☇ᴙ

| | 25 | 24 | 22 | 19 | $229 |

1 W. Washington St. | 877-294-9712 | fax 312-782-0899 | 866-690-1986 |
www.burnhamhotel.com | 103 rooms, 19 suites

A "historic landmark" in an "amazingly gorgeous" restored building (one of the world's first skyscrapers, built by Daniel Burnham in 1894), this "atmospheric" Kimpton "boutique hotel" offers "a good Loop location" for business or visiting Millennium Park, theaters and shopping; "pet-friendly" rooms are "small, but beautifully furnished" (suites overlook Grant Park and Lake Michigan), the staff "knows and takes care of its repeat" visitors and the "charming [American] bistro" has a "great bar."

🆕 Conrad ☇ᴙ
(fka Le Méridien)

| | 27 | 22 | 21 | 23 | $525 |

521 N. Rush St. | 312-645-1500 | fax 312-645-1550 | 800-543-4300 |
www.conradhotels.com | 278 rooms, 33 suites

With a "dynamite location" "in the middle of everything" above Westfield North Bridge on Michigan Avenue ("you can get to Nordstrom without stepping outside"), this former Le Méridien is great for shoppers and has "all the modern amenities a business traveler needs"; there are "spacious, well-kept" rooms with "amazing" bathrooms that "you could live in" if it wasn't that you'd "miss the superb bed", but opinion is mixed on service: some say it's "warm" and "attentive", others "stuffy"; N.B. the new Eclectic restaurant is still a work-in-progress.

Fairmont ☇ᴙ☺☲

| | 23 | 24 | 21 | 22 | $339 |

200 N. Columbus Dr. | 312-565-8000 | fax 312-565-1032 |
800-441-1414 | www.fairmont.com | 626 rooms, 66 suites

This "comfortable" convention/conference facility "a block from the stunning new Millennium Park" "doesn't seem as hectic as some of the other Downtown properties" – perhaps since it's "not on the Mag Mile, but close"; "well-appointed rooms" "with nice views of the lake by Navy Pier" are "slightly dated", but there are "beautiful facilities" available "for weddings and meetings", the Eclectic "swanky" Aria restaurant and a "helpful staff"; in short, it's an "entirely adequate"

	ROOMS	SERVICE	DINING	FACIL.	COST

"mass-market business hotel" offering "nothing over the top"; P.S. it's "attached to a wonderful fitness club" – but you "must pay."

☑ Four Seasons ♨✗♒♨Ⓢ≋

| 27 | 28 | 27 | 27 | $430 |

120 E. Delaware Pl. | 312-280-8800 | fax 312-280-1748 | 800-332-3442 | www.fourseasons.com | 175 rooms, 168 suites

"Top-notch pampering" makes travelers "never want to leave" this "posh", "pitch-perfect" "city hotel" "right on the Magnificent Mile", where "traditional" rooms with "amazing" views of the Michigans (Avenue and Lake) are serviced by "visits from the martini man"; the "terrific" "bells and whistles" include "wonderful" New American dining at Seasons, a "fabulous spa" and gym, "great pool", "relaxing bar" and "beautiful public rooms."

Monaco, Hotel ♒♨

| 24 | 23 | 18 | 21 | $209 |

225 N. Wabash Ave. | 312-960-8500 | fax 312-960-1883 | 800-397-7661 | www.monaco-chicago.com | 170 rooms, 22 suites

With a "convenient" Loop "location that's not too touristy but right in the middle of it all", the Kimpton Group's "offbeat" boutique hotel represents a "hip" but "comfortable" "alternative to the large chains"; most "rooms are on the petite side", but they have "wonderful beds" and "fun, vibrant decor" (including "goldfish to keep you company"); sojourners traveling solo say the "South Water Kitchen is a pleasant place to sit at the bar and enjoy a good meal" – if you're not too full from the "complimentary breakfast and evening hors d'oeuvres."

☑ Park Hyatt ♨✗♒♨Ⓢ≋

| 27 | 26 | 25 | 26 | $525 |

800 N. Michigan Ave. | 312-335-1234 | fax 312-239-4029 | 800-778-7477 | www.parkhyatt.com | 173 rooms, 15 suites

"Zen garden meets corporate boardroom" at this "sleek" yet "serene oasis" with an "unbeatable location" facing "the old Water Tower" from which you can "walk to everything"; you'll return to a "dreamy room" with "appointments to die for" (the "poufy beds" are "instantly engulfing") and a "friendly staff that shows you are welcome here – always"; the "outstanding pool, fitness center" and Tiffani Kim spa, plus New French cuisine at NoMI ("one of Chicago's best restaurants"), help make this "winner" "well worth the tariff."

☑ Peninsula, The ✗♒♨Ⓢ≋

| 29 | 28 | 27 | 28 | $490 |

108 E. Superior St. | 312-337-2888 | fax 312-751-2888 | 866-288-8889 | www.peninsula.com | 256 rooms, 83 suites

The "wow factor" would "make a sultan swoon" at this high-priced but "near-perfect", "star-studded" River North property, voted the No. 1 Hotel in the U.S.; the "pampering par excellence" extends to "glorious rooms" that include "tubs for two" with "built-in TV", "clairvoyant, unobtrusive service" and "outstanding food in the restaurants"; there's a "knockout" gym (lift weights "next to a wall of windows overlooking Lake Michigan") and a "spa to make your worries melt away" – though fans find "you look better [just] standing in their lobby."

Renaissance ♒♨Ⓢ≋

| 24 | 21 | 19 | 22 | $529 |

1 W. Wacker Dr. | 312-372-7200 | fax 312-372-0093 | 800-468-3571 | www.renaissancehotels.com | 513 rooms, 40 suites

"At the head of State Street", this "absolutely solid" "Downtown business hotel" boasts a "location convenient to everything" "inside the

Loop"; the "nicely appointed rooms" - "many with views" - are "comfortable", even "chic" (thanks to recent renovations), and the staff's "very good"; though the food is merely "ok" in the restaurants ("one upscale, one the kids will love"), "the lounge is a great place to relax" - or "if you get tired walking along the river, there is a lovely pool."

[Z] Ritz-Carlton (A Four Seasons Hotel) 🍴🏠👪🔭Ⓢ🏊 26 | 27 | 26 | 25 | $390

160 E. Pearson St. | 312-266-1000 | fax 312-266-1194 | 800-621-6906 | www.fourseasons.com | 344 rooms, 91 suites

Among "the top-flight hotels on Michigan Avenue", this "old-world-elegant" "class act" constitutes "a perfect business"-traveler venue that's also "lovely for shopping" mavens, as it's perched "above the Water Tower Place indoor mall"; "beautifully appointed rooms" with "sleek contemporary bathrooms" and "world-class views" lure loyalists, along with an "impressive, responsive staff", New French fare that's "still among the best in town" and a "grand-hotel" "lounge and lobby area"; and if a few feel this "tasteful establishment" is "not exciting", to most she's "still great."

Sofitel 👪🔭 27 | 24 | 23 | 23 | $425

20 E. Chestnut St. | 312-324-4000 | fax 312-324-4026 | 877-813-7700 | www.sofitel.com | 382 rooms, 33 suites

"Contemporary luxury with a European feel" lurks "in the heart of the Gold Coast" at this "smart, sophisticated" scene of "beautiful", "futuristic" furnishings, "fresh flowers throughout", "gorgeous suites" and "airy rooms" "with real character" (and "magnificent beds"); factor in French cooking at the Café des Architectes - so fine that some surveyors "go here to eat even when staying elsewhere" - and "cordial" service, and vets vote it a "very good value for the business traveler if you don't need a pool and spa."

Dallas/Ft. Worth

Adolphus, The 🍴Ⓗ🔭 24 | 25 | 26 | 23 | $188

1321 Commerce St. | Dallas | 214-742-8200 | fax 214-651-3561 | 800-221-9083 | www.hoteladolphus.com | 400 rooms, 22 suites

Built by (and named for) a local beer baron in 1912, this "first-class" Downtown hotel is anything but Busch league thanks to the "outstanding" French Room (voted Dallas' No. 1 Restaurant in our *Texas Restaurants* Survey), serving "magnificent food", and a staff that greets guests "like returning family"; "luxurious" rooms have the "feel of a bygone era" plus 21st-century perks like WiFi and flat-panel TVs; overall, it may be "a bit stuffy", but it's the "ultimate in elegance"; N.B. ongoing renovations were slated to be completed post-Survey.

Crescent Court, A Rosewood Hotel 🍴🏠👪🔭Ⓢ🏊 25 | 25 | 23 | 24 | $380

400 Crescent Ct. | Dallas | 214-871-3200 | fax 214-871-3272 | 800-654-6541 | www.crescentcourt.com | 191 rooms, 29 suites

"Grand in scale and aspirations", this stalwart "in a chichi shopping district" near Downtown is a "trendy yet classic" stay; a "gracious staff" and "gorgeous lobby" welcome visitors who rhapsodize about the hotel's "great gym", 22,000-sq.-ft. spa and "fabulous people-watching" ("look for celebs in the elevators") and point out that the recent arrival of Japanese-Peruvian hot spot Nobu "dramatically improves dining options"; you can expect "stylish", "splendid" rooms with great amenities as well.

[Z] Four Seasons Las Colinas 👫🍴🐕🔭⛳Ⓢ🏊🎾

ROOMS	SERVICE	DINING	FACIL.	COST
26	27	23	28	$340

4150 N. MacArthur Blvd. | Irving | 972-717-0700 | fax 972-717-2550 | 800-332-3442 | www.fourseasons.com | 377 rooms, 20 suites

"Laid-back but stylish", this outpost of the luxe hotel group in suburban Irving (between DFW Airport and Downtown Dallas) delights duffers with its "tournament-quality" links, but there's much more: a "huge, first-class gym", an "expansive" free-form outdoor pool, courts for tennis, racquetball and squash, a "spa that truly takes you away" and "exceptional" service; though the "food doesn't match" the other elements here, overall it's a "truly grand" experience.

Mansion on Turtle Creek, The 🍴🐕🔭🏊

ROOMS	SERVICE	DINING	FACIL.	COST
26	27	27	24	$405

2821 Turtle Creek Blvd. | Dallas | 214-559-2100 | fax 214-528-4187 | 888-767-3966 | www.mansiononturtlecreek.com | 127 rooms, 16 suites

The "pampering service" is "so phenomenal you think you're in Asia", but this Uptown "heaven on earth" is "as Classic Dallas as big hair and rhinestones"; regulars rhapsodize about this "lovely" 1925 mansion's "impeccably decorated" rooms, all with balconies, the "small" "shaded" rooftop pool with adjacent bar and the "truly gourmet" Southwestern cuisine (even now that "star chef" Dean Fearing is gone); "reliable excellence" has guests "above the clouds every time", especially if they "bring someone else's wallet."

Zaza, Hotel 🔭Ⓢ🏊

ROOMS	SERVICE	DINING	FACIL.	COST
26	22	23	22	$259

2332 Leonard St. | Dallas | 214-468-8399 | fax 214-468-8397 | 800-597-8399 | www.hotelzaza.com | 152 suites

A "destination in itself" - and "the current place to be seen" - this "hip", "artistic" Uptown venue is "perfect for the under-35" demo; "colorful" suites done in "modern, retro and exotic" styles "excite", while Urban Oasis' "great bar scene" and the Asian-Med eatery Dragonfly abound with "pretty people"; traditionalists tsk that it "tries too hard to be trendy", saying amenities and service lag behind the "comfort and communal ease" of the rooms.

Hawaii

[Z] Fairmont Kea Lani 👫🫖🔭Ⓢ🏊🎾

ROOMS	SERVICE	DINING	FACIL.	COST
27	26	25	27	$425

4100 Wailea Alanui Dr. | Wailea | 808-875-4100 | fax 808-875-1200 | 800-441-1414 | www.fairmont.com | 413 suites, 37 villas

Like "a beautiful Moorish village" set "right on the luxe" Wailea strip, this suites-only "white wonderland" scores big for its "sweet" "spacious" quarters with "balconies, ocean views" and "wonderful bathrooms" that "provide the best bang for your buck" this side of the island; the "spectacular" staff is "always kind, friendly and accommodating", "the beach and pools are beautiful" (the adult-only one means "you can relax in peace") and some claim "Nick's Fish House is the best restaurant" in the area; P.S. the "expensive" "private villas are worth it."

	ROOMS	SERVICE	DINING	FACIL.	COST

☑ Four Seasons Resort Hualalai ♥️✕🍴♨️👥🛎️☉🏊🔍

| 29 | 29 | 27 | 29 | $695 |

100 Kaupulehu Dr. | Kaupulehu-Kona | 808-325-8000 | fax 808-325-8200 | 888-336-5662 | www.fourseasons.com | 212 rooms, 30 suites, 1 villa

"Every need is anticipated" at this "flawless" "low-key" "worth-the-splurge" "slice of heaven", rated the world's top Resort; "gorgeous rooms" (some have outdoor lava rock showers), "the best spa east of Mekong" (it was also rated No. 1 Destination Spa), a "snorkeling pool stocked with fish and manta rays", a "very private golf course" that you'll "feel like you own" and "fantastic meals on the beach" will bring you "closer to paradise than you've ever been on earth"; so what if "the beach is not great for swimming"? – you can spot whales frolicking in the winter months as well as celebrities like Dustin Hoffman and Heather Locklear sunning themselves at one of several pools.

☑ NEW Four Seasons Resort Lanai at Manele Bay ♥️✕👥🛎️☉🏊🔍

| 27 | 26 | 25 | 27 | $395 |

1 Manele Bay Rd. | Lanai City | 808-565-7700 | fax 808-565-2483 | www.fourseasons.com | 215 rooms, 21 suites

"You feel like you're on your own private island" at this "secluded corner of paradise" (now managed by Four Seasons), a "low-key, romantic" "getaway" on this less-visited neighbor island with "impeccable service" and "larger-than-average rooms" from which you can "often spot dolphins jumping"; there's an "excellent" golf course on-site with "ocean views from every hole" (and access to the course at sister property Lodge at Koele), a "gem of a bay" with "great snorkeling", "outstanding" dining and even "a sunglass valet who cleans your shades while you bask in the sun"; in sum, it's a "perfect honeymoon spot" where you can't "ask for anything more."

☑ Four Seasons Wailea ♥️✕🍴👥🛎️☉🏊🔍

| 27 | 29 | 27 | 28 | $440 |

3900 Wailea Alanui Dr. | Wailea | 808-874-8000 | fax 808-874-2244 | 800-334-6284 | www.fourseasons.com | 305 rooms, 75 suites

"Being asked 'would you care for a frozen strawberry?' while lounging by the pool" pretty much sums up the out-of-this-world service at this "perfect honeymoon spot" where "every room comes with a huge bathroom" (and should benefit from the "subtle update" now underway) and the "beach and free poolside cabanas" are "amazing"; add in the "gorgeous spa", "orgasmic breakfast buffets" and "stellar alfresco dining at Spago", and this Wailea outpost is a "place to be seen."

☑ Grand Hyatt ♥️👥🛎️☉🏊🔍

| 25 | 25 | 23 | 28 | $455 |

1571 Poipu Rd. | Koloa | 808-742-1234 | fax 808-742-1557 | 800-233-1234 | www.kauai.hyatt.com | 565 rooms, 37 suites

"Tasteful architecture, beautiful, tropical gardens, meandering pools" (with "fantastic slides") and "friendly service" make this Poipu resort a "great" choice "for a family vacation, honeymooners or anyone" – except, admittedly, "in the high season, when you'll have to fight through the kids for a chair at the pool"; though faultfinders feel the "food should be better for the price" and the atmosphere can seem "corporate" at times, that's more than made up for by the "terrific spa", "unbelievable golf course", rooms equipped with "lava rock showers" and "gentle, perfumed breezes" everywhere.

U.S. - HAWAII

Grand Wailea Resort ♀♥ 👫 Ⓢ ≋

	ROOMS	SERVICE	DINING	FACIL.	COST
	25	23	23	28	$495

3850 Wailea Alanui Dr. | Wailea | 808-875-1234 | fax 808-879-4077 |
800-888-6100 | www.grandwailea.com | 728 rooms, 52 suites

Step into this "huge mega-resort" with "winding paths through lush gardens" "on a beautiful" strip of Wailea Beach and be blown away by the "wonderful open-air lobby" and the "eye-catching art and sculptures"; the "spa is one of the best" and "most opulent in the world" say its fans, and "everyone needs to swim" in the "incredible" pool "once in their lives" (good luck getting the kids out); but some advise "if you're looking for a quiet romantic getaway", this "pleasure dome" "overcrowded with families" "may not be the place for you."

☑ Halekulani ♀♥ ✕ 👫 Ⓢ ≋

	ROOMS	SERVICE	DINING	FACIL.	COST
	27	28	28	26	$435

2199 Kalia Rd. | Honolulu | 808-923-2311 | fax 808-926-8004 |
800-367-2343 | www.halekulani.com | 412 rooms, 43 suites

"All staff members mysteriously know your name" at this "diamond on the beach" that's "an island of peace in Waikiki's cauldron of confusion"; regulars report it's "always perfect after all these years" with "elegant" "service and facilities that can't be beat" including the "delectable" oceanside New French restaurant, La Mer, and a "to-die-for" Sunday brunch at Orchids; add in "meticulous housekeeping", a pool that's a "treasured work of art" and rooms with "high-tech" touches, and most can ignore the numerous brides with their "entourage of photographers" traipsing the grounds.

☑ Kahala Hotel & Resort, The ♀♥ ✕ 👫 Ⓢ ≋ ⚲

	ROOMS	SERVICE	DINING	FACIL.	COST
	26	26	26	26	$675

5000 Kahala Ave. | Honolulu | 808-739-8888 | fax 808-739-8800 |
800-367-2525 | www.kahalaresort.com | 316 rooms, 29 suites

"Apartment-sized rooms with mahogany poster beds and 450-thread-count sheets", a "mesmerizing dolphin lagoon", "excellent restaurants", a "glorious spa" and "a gorgeous beach" make this "former Mandarin Oriental" "just a 15-minute drive from Waikiki" in a "luxe residential area" "the gold standard" on Oahu; add in the "very friendly service" and most say they "want to retire to" this "romantic getaway."

Princeville Resort ♀♥ 👫 Ⓛ Ⓢ ≋ ⚲

	ROOMS	SERVICE	DINING	FACIL.	COST
	25	25	24	25	$500

5520 Ka Haku Rd. | Princeville | 808-826-9644 | fax 808-826-1166 |
800-826-4400 | www.princeville.com | 201 rooms, 51 suites

"Leave your window open to listen to the waves crashing" at this "honeymooner's paradise", a "gem of all gems" "perched on a cliff overlooking Hanalei Bay" with "drop-dead views of Bali Hai"; from the "amazing service" to the "fantastic beach" to the "world-class golf" to the "swim-up bar" at the infinity pool, this is a "very impressive" spot; but a few cutting-edgers concur that the rooms may need a modern "update" since the bathrooms' once "cool" liquid crystal opaque shower wall that clears for ocean viewing is "kind of 'disco' now."

☑ Ritz-Carlton Kapalua ♀♥ ✕ 👫 Ⓛ Ⓢ ≋ ⚲

	ROOMS	SERVICE	DINING	FACIL.	COST
	25	26	24	26	$475

1 Ritz-Carlton Dr. | Kapalua | 808-669-6200 | fax 808-665-0026 |
800-262-8440 | www.ritzcarlton.com | 490 rooms, 58 suites

"A golfer's paradise", this "fabulous resort" in a "secluded location" with "unmatched views" has Ritz regulars raving; from the "first-class" service to the "gorgeous facilities" that include "spacious grounds", a "unique multi-tiered pool", an "amazing" spa and the "excellent" Asian-inspired Banyan Tree restaurant, it's "outstanding in every way"; still, a few who find it "below expectations" are put off by the "howling wind", the "hike" to the beach and the somewhat "stiff" staff.

Houston

Four Seasons ✕ ✻ 👪 ⓢ ≋ | 24 | 25 | 24 | 24 | $330 |

1300 Lamar St. | 713-650-1300 | fax 713-652-6220 | 800-332-3442 | www.fourseasons.com | 289 rooms, 115 suites

Located two blocks from Downtown's convention center, this luxe lodging evinces "Texas hospitality with class" report respondents who rave about "splendid" management, a "truly service-oriented" staff (the "fabulous" concierge "planned my entire visit") and the "exceptional" Quattro restaurant boasting an "impressive wine cellar"; other highlights include "huge" rooms with flat-panel TVs and WiFi, a 24-hour gym and a "wonderful" spa, but just a few find, though it's one of the best in town, it "doesn't live up to the usual Four Seasons standards."

Houstonian, The ✻ 👪 ⓢ ≋ ✎ | 22 | 25 | 22 | 26 | $315 |

111 N. Post Oak Ln. | 713-680-2626 | fax 713-680-2992 | 800-231-2759 | www.houstonian.com | 280 rooms, 7 suites

"Tucked away" on 18 verdant acres, this "elegant" venue near the Galleria and Memorial Park feels like a "country retreat in the middle of the city"; visitors "relax even while on business" thanks to a "spectacular" spa and "excellent" health club (with play areas "perfect" for kids); staffers "aim to please and hit their mark", but some say the rooms "need sprucing up."

Lancaster, The 👪 | 20 | 24 | 25 | 18 | $270 |

701 Texas Ave. | 713-228-9500 | fax 713-223-4528 | 800-231-0336 | www.thelancasterhouston.com | 83 rooms, 10 suites

"Conveniently" located in Downtown's Theater District, this "intimate" 1926 "jewel" is a "refreshing" "alternative to the big hotels"; aficionados adore "first-class service all the way", applaud the "fine kitchen" at New American eatery Bistro Lancaster and quip that the "pretty", "Brit-style" rooms feature "enough chintz to gag a Sloane Ranger"; free local transport by town car for guests is a bonus.

Omni ✻ ✕ ✻ 👪 ≋ ✎ | 20 | 21 | 22 | 22 | $349 |

4 Riverway | 713-871-8181 | fax 713-871-0719 | 800-843-6664 | www.omnihotels.com | 345 rooms, 33 suites

"Location, location, location" sells surveyors on this parkside veteran near the Galleria mall – one can "relax" "after a hard day in the shops" with a "great meal" of New American cuisine at Noe, a dip in the "impressive" pools (the heated one features underwater music), an evening of darts and dancing at the Black Swan Pub or a trip to the spa; just a few say "comfortable" rooms "need a makeover."

St. Regis ✻ 👪 ⓢ ≋ | 25 | 27 | 24 | 22 | $480 |

1919 Briar Oaks Ln. | 713-840-7600 | fax 713-840-8036 | 877-787-3447 | www.stregis.com | 179 rooms, 53 suites

"Classy and elegant", "exactly as expected" laud loyalists of this "outstanding" "grande dame" near the Galleria and the River Oaks neigh-

ROOMS | SERVICE | DINING | FACIL. | COST

borhood; "superb" staffers are the embodiment of "Southern hospitality" at its best, while The Remington restaurant is renowned for "divine" New American cuisine and its "wonderful bar"; "traditionally styled", "well-appointed" rooms have "amazing" beds, but light sleepers wish for "better insulation" since the trains passing nearby "can drive you nuts."

Las Vegas

TOPS IN CITY

27 Four Seasons
Bellagio
26 Wynn

[Z] Bellagio Hotel 🍴🔭[S]🏊 27 | 24 | 28 | 28 | $359

3600 Las Vegas Blvd. S. | 702-693-7111 | fax 702-693-8546 | 888-987-6667 | www.bellagio.com | 3421 rooms, 512 suites, 9 villas

"Top-of-the-line in every respect", this landmark is "as close to tasteful as one gets in Las Vegas", offering guests a "classic rather than plastic" experience at a true resort, "not a casino with rooms"; "plush" accommodations - the fountain views are "well worth the extra cost" - add to the "va-va-voom" factor, as do the "outstanding" public areas with "spectacular" flowers, an "astounding collection" of "first-class" restaurants and "fantastic shopping"; the newly renovated, 55,000-sq.-ft. spa is "phenomenal", and though critics complain "check-in is always a nightmare", the majority sums it up in "two words: the best."

Caesars Palace 🔭[S]🏊 21 | 19 | 23 | 24 | $200

3570 Las Vegas Blvd. S. | 702-731-7110 | fax 702-866-1700 | 800-634-6661 | www.caesarspalace.com | 3348 rooms

"The grand old" ruler "continues to satisfy" with a "convenient" Strip location, "the prettiest swimming pool in Vegas", "to-die-for shopping" at the adjacent Forum Shops and a "top-of-the-line restaurant selection" that runs from "fast food to superb" (an outpost of NYC's Rao's was to open in December 2006); voters say the newer Augustus Tower rooms are "fit for a king" with "spectacular" marble bathrooms and "better amenities" than the "run-down" older rooms, and while loyalists rave it "still manages to get it right", brutish types bemoan that this "too crowded" emperor of Sin City is "riding on the coattails of his past success."

[Z] Four Seasons 🍴🐕🔭[S]🏊 28 | 28 | 26 | 27 | $305

3960 Las Vegas Blvd. S. | 702-632-5000 | fax 702-632-5195 | www.fourseasons.com | 338 rooms, 86 suites

"A casino-free oasis of calm and elegance" amid the "insanity of the Strip", this "stunning", "concierge-class" "gem" on the top floors of Mandalay Bay Resort is "supremely elegant" with renowned eateries and "fabulous", recently renovated rooms featuring "stellar views" and "lovely amenities"; fans say a "private lobby entrance" and "secret casino" passage make you "feel like a celebrity", and that the "top-shelf" staff has "pampering down to a science"; if a few fusspots lament it's "a little ways down from the action", insiders say its "above-it-all" location makes them feel "wonderfully excluded" from the "unwashed masses."

	ROOMS	SERVICE	DINING	FACIL.	COST

Green Valley Ranch Resort & Spa 🏨 🍴 👥 ⑤ 🏊

| 25 | 23 | 20 | 25 | $500 |

2300 Paseo Verde Pkwy. | Henderson | 702-617-7777 | fax 702-617-7778 |
866-782-9487 | www.greenvalleyranchresort.com | 325 rooms, 73 suites
"A short drive" from the "cha-ching of the slots" on the Strip, this
"luxurious-without-being-pretentious" resort in Henderson is an "oasis in the land of neon"; with "big fluffy beds", a "pool out of a Chanel
No. 5 commercial" and "awesome Mediterranean flair", it has "all
you'll ever need", including "beautiful public spaces", plus a "very cool
spa" and "restaurants, grounds and shopping much nicer than expected"; although critics cite "mediocre service", the majority has a
"relaxing, enjoyable" time.

JW Marriott Resort & Spa 🍴 👥 ⑤ 🏊

| 25 | 21 | 18 | 24 | $269 |

221 N. Rampart Blvd. | 702-869-7777 | fax 702-869-7339 | 877-869-8777 |
www.jwlasvegasresort.com | 471 rooms, 77 suites
Surrounded by championship golf courses and "impeccable grounds"
in upscale Summerlin, this "gorgeous" resort is a "great" off-Strip "alternative" with an "outstanding spa", "amazing pool" and "friendly
staff"; the "well-appointed" "capacious" accommodations have
"bathrooms bigger than some hotel rooms", with "nice additions"
such as rainfall showerheads and Jacuzzi tubs; if some cite food quality as the chain property's "weakest link" and gripe "it's too far from
town", fans who appreciate a "quiet, smaller casino" and "the ultimate
in relaxation" say "just leave me here for the rest of my days."

Loews
Lake Las Vegas Resort 🏨 👥 � ⑤ 🏊 🔍

| 22 | 22 | 20 | 25 | $329 |

101 Montelago Blvd. | Henderson | 702-567-1234 | fax 702-567-6103 |
800-233-1234 | www.lakelasvegas.hyatt.com | 454 rooms, 39 suites
An "oasis" located a half-hour from Sin City, this "tasteful" Moroccan-
inspired former Hyatt Regency resort "leaves the tackiness of the Strip
behind" and offers "activities for every age", including access to two
"great" Jack Nicklaus–designed golf courses, "family-friendly" pools
and a small beach with paddle boating; "gorgeous" views of the lake,
a "small" but "excellent" spa and "good" dining options are draws,
and though the waterside cottages are "fabulous", critics say the
"fairly average" regular rooms are "a disappointment for the price";
N.B. the post-Survey management change may outdate some of
the above scores.

Mandalay Bay Resort ✗ 👥 ⑤ 🏊

| 24 | 20 | 24 | 26 | $259 |

3950 Las Vegas Blvd. S. | 702-632-7777 | fax 702-632-7328 | 877-632-7000 |
www.mandalaybay.com | 3200 rooms, 1120 suites
Popular with the "twenty- to thirtysomething crowd", this "classy"
spot with a "non-Vegas" feel is, paradoxically, "everything you want"
in a Sin City resort – "outstanding" bars, the "best pools in town" and
an "awesome spa"; though it's "a little too far from mid-Strip" for
some, fans say the monorail "makes transportation easy" and the "array of restaurants" and activities means you might "never venture outside the property" (the newest hot spot eatery is Michael Mina's
StripSteak); rooms are "ultra-contemporary", and those in the more
upscale THEhotel tower offer "spacious suites with big-screen TVs", so
it's "only the service that keeps it from becoming a world-class resort."

	ROOMS	SERVICE	DINING	FACIL.	COST

Z Ritz-Carlton

| 27 | 26 | 23 | 25 | $339 |

Lake Las Vegas ✳ 🐾 🛁 ⬆ ⑤ 🏊

1610 Lake Las Vegas Pkwy. | Henderson | 702-567-4700 | fax 702-567-4777 | 800-241-3333 | www.ritzcarlton.com | 314 rooms

Offering "gorgeous rooms" with "lovely views" and service that "lives up to all Ritz-Carltons", this "palace in the desert" on Lake Las Vegas in Henderson is a "true gem" away from the "bustle of the Strip"; guests say concierge-level suites "on a bridge over the lake" are a "decadent" "splurge" and that "golf enthusiasts" should "come one, come all" for the Jack Nicklaus–designed links, but others want "more restaurant choices" and feel "stranded" if they don't have a car.

Venetian Hotel ✗ 🛁 ⑤ 🏊

| 27 | 22 | 25 | 26 | $899 |

3355 Las Vegas Blvd. S. | 702-414-1000 | fax 702-414-1100 | 877-283-6423 | www.venetian.com | 4027 suites

Offering "magnificent" standard rooms ("the nicest in town"), this "explosion of old-world Venice" in the "heart of the Strip" dazzles with "all the amenities you could ask for", including the "unbeatable" Canyon Ranch Spa, a "don't-miss" Guggenheim museum, "wondrous" dining (the newest is Thomas Keller's Bouchon) and "unbelievable" shopping" options along the Grand Canal ("with singing gondoliers"); still, if critics cite "hot and cold" service or snipe that you'll need "roller blades" to get to the exclusive Venezia Tower, supporters say their "top-notch" "favorite" is "almost as nice as the real thing, though much glitzier"; N.B. a third tower, Palazzo, is expected to open in late 2007.

Z NEW Wynn Las Vegas

| 28 | 23 | 26 | 27 | $319 |

Casino Resort ✗ 🛁 ⬆ ⑤ 🏊

3131 Las Vegas Blvd. S. | 702-770-7100 | fax 702-770-1510 | 888-320-9966 | www.wynnlasvegas.com | 2108 rooms, 608 suites

This one-year-old, "worth-the-billions" "gem" sets a "new standard" on the Strip for "undeniable luxury" with "huge", "museum-quality rooms", "out-of-this-world" parlor suites and 19 "top-notch" restaurants that create a "feast for the eyes and the stomach"; "perfect for couples" and "well-heeled business travelers" ("not for kids"), it's "more elegant and quieter" than other "mega-casinos" with "bold, fanciful" touches and a "breathtaking" golf course ("the only in-town links left"); still, if critics grump it's "overblown" and complain of "sky-high prices", regulars retort this "work of art" "is a Wynner for sure."

Los Angeles

TOPS IN CITY

27 Peninsula
    Bel-Air
26 Four Seasons Beverly Hills
25 Beverly Hills Hotel
    Raffles L'Ermitage

Z Bel-Air, Hotel ✗ ⊕ 🐾 🏊

| 27 | 28 | 27 | 26 | $395 |

701 Stone Canyon Rd. | Bel-Air | 310-472-1211 | fax 310-476-5890 | www.hotelbelair.com | 52 rooms, 39 suites

"With trumpet swans heralding your arrival", "it can't get any better than this" "dowager of LA hotels" in the "quiet residential area" of

Bel-Air; though its "intuitive staff" caters to "stars galore", "it's the utmost in luxury for those who don't want to be seen", as the "refined", "romantic" rooms are all in "secluded" bungalows; if you venture forth (even the spa treatments come to you), you'll find "possibly the best French restaurant in town", "an intimate bar with piano music", "enchanting gardens" and a sceney pool; "if you have to ask, you can't afford it" – but this is "old-world hospitality at its best."

Beverly Hills Hotel & Bungalows

26	26	24	25	$440

9641 Sunset Blvd. | Beverly Hills | 310-276-2251 | fax 310-887-2887 | www.beverlyhillshotel.com | 166 rooms, 38 suites, 21 bungalows
"A true classic that has gotten better over the years", Beverly Hills' "pink and green icon" with "an exclusive 1950s country club feel" is "what a luxury hotel should be"; though there are "celebs everywhere" (especially at the Polo Lounge, still "the place to see and be seen"), the staff "treats everyone special" "even if you're out of your usual element"; those "in need of a luxury fix won't be disappointed with the pool or spa", and "the rooms are fabulous, with fresh flowers"; so if modernists moan it all "feels old", others respond where else can you "sip champagne with the oldies, the trendy and anyone else in-between"?

Beverly Wilshire

25	26	24	24	$455

9500 Wilshire Blvd. | Beverly Hills | 310-275-5200 | fax 310-274-2851 | 800-545-4000 | www.fourseasons.com | 280 rooms, 115 suites
"A class act all the way", this "timeless landmark", where you can "live out" your *Pretty Woman* fantasies, is "everything a hotel should be" with a location "in the heart of Beverly Hills" and "Rodeo Drive at the front door"; "spacious suites" have "amazingly comfortable beds" and L'Occitane toiletries, the "staff can't do enough for you" and the "food is always top-notch" (Wolfgang Puck recently opened Cut steakhouse); P.S. it's still one of the best spots in town for "spotting celebrities."

Casa Del Mar, Hotel

25	24	22	24	$450

1910 Ocean Way | Santa Monica | 310-581-5533 | fax 310-581-5503 | 800-898-6999 | www.hotelcasadelmar.com | 125 rooms, 4 suites
"How could you not love a hotel that supplies your very own teddy bear and rubber ducky?" demand devotees of this "beautifully restored grande dame" "right on the beach in Santa Monica"; now "blending an old-time glamorous feel with modern amenities", its features range from "sinfully comfortable" rooms with hydrotherapy tubs to a spa that does outdoor massages by the "secluded rooftop pool"; some opine it's "overpriced for what you get", but "if you can't afford the daily rate, just visit the bar" – a perfect spot for "sipping cocktails while watching the sunset."

Chateau Marmont

21	21	21	21	$435

8221 Sunset Blvd. | Hollywood | 323-656-1010 | fax 323-655-5311 | 800-242-8328 | www.chateaumarmont.com | 11 rooms, 23 suites, 9 cottages, 4 bungalows
"Oozing with history, legends and '30s charm", this perpetually "hot hipster spot" in the Hollywood Hills allows you to "rub elbows with the rich and famous" amid "funky" Gothic decor; "some rooms are amazing" while others are "sparse", and service can act "too cool for

school", but "lunch in the garden is quite beautiful" and there's an "outdoor bar that's the best in town"; so let cynics snap "it's over-hyped and overpriced" – to most, this offers "a unique Hollywood experience" ("if you can get a reservation").

Disney's Grand Californian Hotel & Spa 👫 🍴🛎Ⓢ 🌊

| 22 | 24 | 23 | 26 | $500 |

1600 S. Disneyland Dr. | Anaheim | 714-635-2300 | fax 714-300-7300 | www.disneyland.com | 705 rooms, 40 suites

"California Adventure theme park is your backyard" at this "huge" Anaheim resort, architecturally a "redwood paradise" with a "drop-dead stunning lobby" and "rustic" "Craftsman theme"; this being the work of the "Disney imagineers", it's no wonder there are "wonderful activities" for kids and it's staffed by a highly "friendly crew" – though there's "surprisingly amazing dining at the Napa Rose" too; skeptics snap "it's overpriced, considering its small, unimpressive rooms" (though "kids love the bunk beds"), but they admit the location "makes the Disneyland thing very easy."

Fairmont Miramar ⑪🍴🛎🌊

| 23 | 22 | 19 | 23 | $359 |

101 Wilshire Blvd. | Santa Monica | 310-576-7777 | fax 310-458-7912 | 866-540-4470 | www.fairmont.com | 209 rooms, 61 suites, 32 bungalows

"Just a short walk from all the action in Santa Monica", this Jazz Age hotel "with historical charm and character" is "a tropical oasis surrounded by lush gardens" and an "awe-inspiring" century-old fig tree; "a wonderful place to begin your honeymoon", it offers "super ocean views from the tower rooms", though many "prefer the little cottages around the koi pond and waterfall"; and if some say it's "still a convention hotel at heart", citing "ok food" and "prompt but impersonal service", "the beach location makes up for a lot."

🇿 Four Seasons Beverly Hills ✗🍴🛎Ⓢ🌊

| 26 | 27 | 26 | 26 | $395 |

300 S. Doheny Dr. | Beverly Hills | 310-273-2222 | fax 310-859-3824 | 800-332-3442 | www.fourseasons.com | 185 rooms, 100 suites

You'll "feel like a star (plus, you're guaranteed to see several of them)" at this "wonderful cocoon in Beverly Hills"; "elegant without being stuffy", it features "beds you'll never want to get out of" – though when you do, there's "excellent food" ("lunch on the patio is among life's sacred pleasures"), "a spectacular rooftop pool", "outdoor gym facilities" and "friendly concierges who can get you into the top places"; it's "a bit out of the way", but otherwise this "posh"-priced place is "perfect, as it should be."

Hilton Checkers ✗🛎Ⓢ🌊

| 21 | 23 | 22 | 20 | $350 |

535 S. Grand Ave. | 213-624-0000 | fax 213-626-9906 | www.hilton.com | 183 rooms, 5 suites

The "best-kept secret in Downtown LA" believe business types of this "beautifully restored" 1920s Spanish Moor–style hotel; radiating a "quaint", "quiet quality", it's "convenient to the courts" and offices, and offers "small" but "plush rooms", a "penthouselike lap pool and hot tub", "luxe" restaurant and "helpful staff"; however, some carp the facilities "close way too early", and since it's "Downtown, there's nothing to do at night."

	ROOMS	SERVICE	DINING	FACIL.	COST

Le Merigot Beach Hotel & Spa 林 ⚮ ♨ ⓢ ≈

| 24 | 24 | 21 | 23 | $369 |

1740 Ocean Ave. | Santa Monica | 310-395-9700 | fax 310-395-9200 | 800-228-9290 | www.lemerigothotel.com | 160 rooms, 15 suites

"The bargain of the four beachfront Santa Monica hotels", this "first-class" resort has an "unbeatable" location within "walking distance" of the Third Street Promenade and the pier; offering "luxurious" rooms ("though not many oceanfront") with "incredible service and warmth", a "great" spa and "terrific views from the patio restaurant", it "makes you feel like you've been to the South of France"; though some say its "strangely formal" vibe makes it "more a business hotel", others comment there's "absolutely nothing not to like."

Loews Santa Monica Beach 林 ⚮ ♨ ⓢ ≈

| 21 | 20 | 18 | 23 | $399 |

1700 Ocean Ave. | Santa Monica | 310-458-6700 | fax 310-458-6761 | 800-235-6397 | www.loewshotels.com | 323 rooms, 19 suites

Guests say this "wonderful" oceanfront resort close to the pier and restaurants is "good for families" and provides "solid service" that "makes you feel welcome"; there are "beautiful retro-styled rooms" with "comfortable bedding" and "unimpeded views of the beach" from higher floors ("just don't get stuck on the alley wing"), but critics question its "convention-hotel feel."

Mondrian ✕ ⚭ ♨ ⓢ ≈

| 20 | 19 | 24 | 21 | $335 |

8440 Sunset Blvd. | West Hollywood | 323-650-8999 | fax 323-650-5215 | 800-525-8029 | www.morganshotelgroup.com | 40 rooms, 197 suites

It's all "still going on" at Ian Schrager's Sunset Strip spot where "siz-able suites" in "subtle whites" with "spectacular" skyline vistas draw a "young, moneyed crowd"; Skybar is among the "hottest nightspots in town", and the "amazing" (and "pricey") Asia de Cuba restaurant is "still tops" and a "great place to stargaze"; and even if detractors dis a staff with "attitude" ("45 minutes to get your car from the valet!"), most surveyors agree that "the people and the views are beautiful - but the latter aren't surgically enhanced."

Park Hyatt 林 ♨ ⓢ ≈

| 23 | 23 | 19 | 22 | $400 |

2151 Ave. of the Stars | Century City | 310-277-1234 | fax 310-785-9240 | 800-233-1234 | www.parkhyattlosangeles.com | 212 rooms, 151 suites

"A haven of civility" with "great views of the Hollywood Hills", this "subdued gem" is "close to everything in chic" Century City, a "great location for business or a weekend shopping spree"; the "spacious rooms" have "modern furniture" and "luxurious balconies", there's a "lovely rooftop pool deck" and an "excellent spa"; but a few guests grumble that this "plain-Jane" "needs a face-lift" since she's got "nothing very special" going on.

☑ Peninsula Beverly Hills 林 ✕ ⚭ ⚮ ♨ ⓢ ≈

| 28 | 28 | 26 | 27 | $595 |

9882 S. Santa Monica Blvd. | Beverly Hills | 310-551-2888 | fax 310-788-2319 | 800-462-7899 | www.peninsula.com | 144 rooms, 36 suites, 16 villas

"An oasis at the eastern end of Beverly Hills", this "glitzy classic" is "five-star by every measure" from the rooms with "the most comfortable beds you'll ever sleep in" ("guest initials are embroidered on the pillows") and "spectacular bathrooms" to the rooftop "pool scene" with "beautiful people-watching", "fantastic massages", "top-notch dining" and "the best afternoon tea"; but enthusiasts note it's the "dedication to serving all with equal attentiveness" that makes it "the crème de la crème" in LA.

Raffles L'Ermitage ✕🕭🐎🛁☉🏊

| 28 | 27 | 22 | 25 | $498 |

9291 Burton Way | Beverly Hills | 310-278-3344 | fax 310-278-8247 | 800-800-2113 | www.raffles.com | 104 rooms, 15 suites
"Serene, understated elegance" and a convenient location "in a residential area on the border of Beverly Hills" have made this "small, intimate" hotel "a favorite" with guests who like the close proximity to Rodeo Drive and nearby chic restaurants; "exceptionally luxurious rooms", "fabulous products in the bath" and touches like "curbside check-in" and "business cards for guests" are a few ways "they make you feel like a celebrity", plus "a lovely rooftop pool" and "a stunning outdoor patio" bring it close to "perfection."

Ritz-Carlton Huntington Hotel & Spa ♨✕🐎🛁☉🏊🔍

| 25 | 25 | 24 | 25 | $399 |

1401 S. Oak Knoll Ave. | Pasadena | 626-568-3900 | fax 626-568-3700 | 800-241-3333 | www.ritzcarlton.com | 358 rooms, 26 suites, 8 cottages
Situated on "spectacular grounds" in the "heart of Pasadena" at the foothills of the San Gabriel Mountains, this "grand, historic" Mediterranean-style "gem" offers "old-world (but not stale)" elegance in a "peaceful", *très riche* "estatelike" setting; "luxurious" rooms, a "first-rate" spa, "lavish" Sunday brunch and "unbeatable service" win devotion, but a few warn that this "getaway from La La Land" "isn't within walking distance of anything"; P.S. a recent $19-million refurbishment meets with "Ritz-Carlton standards."

Ritz-Carlton Marina del Rey 🛁☉🏊🔍

| 24 | 26 | 24 | 23 | $439 |

4375 Admiralty Way | Marina del Rey | 310-823-1700 | fax 310-823-2403 | 800-241-3333 | www.ritzcarlton.com | 281 rooms, 23 suites
If you've "got to be near LAX" but want "everything you'd expect" from a luxury lodging, head to this "pretty setting" in Marina del Rey, where "nice harbor views", an "exquisite pool", "outstanding dining" and "attentive" service win praise; but Ritz regulars report that "small rooms" (spring for the "nice club level" for extra amenities) and a somewhat "dated" feel make this one "not as fancy as others in the chain."

Shutters on the Beach ✕🕭🛁☉🏊

| 26 | 24 | 24 | 25 | $480 |

1 Pico Blvd. | Santa Monica | 310-458-0030 | fax 310-458-4589 | 800-334-9000 | www.shuttersonthebeach.com | 186 rooms, 12 suites
A "getaway for the well-heeled" in Santa Monica, this veteran may be "the most charming hotel on the whole West Coast"; its "idyllic" beachfront location makes it "the epitome of laid-back elegance", and "dreamy", "luxurious" rooms that "feel like Nantucket" offer "many personal touches"; a "not-to-be-missed" Sunday brunch and "life-changing" spa massages please too, and though the star-struck say that with "celebrities around all the time", "it's one of the best in LA", insiders insist "if you get a room with parking lot views you might as well be in Tulsa."

	ROOMS	SERVICE	DINING	FACIL.	COST

Viceroy ✦🏊🏖

| 22 | 20 | 21 | 22 | $359 |

1819 Ocean Ave. | Santa Monica | 310-260-7500 | fax 310-260-7515 |
800-670-6185 | www.viceroysantamonica.com | 144 rooms, 18 suites

An "art deco fun house" is how some voters describe this "see-and-be-seen" boutique hotel near "all good things in Santa Monica"; featuring "cool, all-white-themed" accommodations and "wonderful" bathrooms with "oodles of mirrors", it also offers a "hip, poolside bar scene" ("the Westside version of Skybar"); while detractors question the "fatally trendy" vibe, iffy service and a structure whose "common bones" ("low ceilings, small rooms") mean "all style, no comfort", fans insist this spot is a "class act."

W Westwood ✕✦🏊🅂🏖

| 23 | 21 | 20 | 23 | $550 |

930 Hilgard Ave. | Westwood | 310-208-8765 | fax 310-824-0355 |
877-946-8357 | www.whotels.com | 258 suites

Former UCLA dorms are now "sleek", "comfortable" rooms at this "chic-from-every-angle" "hangout" in the "heart of Westwood", where "stylish attendants" and "lots of bling and pretty people" make for a "pure-LA" atmosphere; a "happening" lobby bar, standout restaurant, "delightful", newly remodeled Bliss Spa and WiFi-enabled poolside cabanas add to the draw; still, critics warn of a "cooler-than-thou" crowd "overrun with poseurs" that can make the public spaces feel "like a bad B-movie" in the evenings.

Miami

TOPS IN CITY

27 Mandarin Oriental
        Four Seasons
25 Setai

Biltmore Hotel, The ✕🅗🏋🅛🅢🏖🅠

| 23 | 24 | 25 | 26 | $399 |

1200 Anastasia Ave. | Coral Gables | 305-445-1926 | fax 305-913-3152 |
800-727-1926 | www.biltmorehotel.com | 280 rooms, 6 suites

"Expect Humphrey Bogart to step out from behind the giant birdcages in the lobby" at this "phenomenal" National Historic Landmark in "suburban Coral Gables", where a visit will make "you feel like you've gone back in time" to the hotel's birth in 1926; from the "gorgeous hand-painted ceilings and antique furniture" to the "magnificent", "endless pool" (the largest in the continental U.S.) to the "superb" Palme d'Or restaurant, which serves "the best Sunday brunch in Miami", most love this "old classic", even if a few say she "shows her wrinkles" despite recent renovations.

Fisher Island
Hotel & Resort ✦🅗🏌✦🏋🅛🅢🏖🅠

| 25 | 26 | 22 | 27 | $575 |

1 Fisher Island Dr. | Miami Beach | 305-535-6080 | fax 305-535-6003 |
800-537-3708 | www.fisherisland.com | 2 rooms, 49 suites, 7 villas,
3 cottages

"Live like a Vanderbilt" at one of the clan's former homes, a "posh" 1928 mansion on Fisher Island, "the most charming and unique island in America" (about a seven-minute ferry ride from the mainland); "drive your golf cart everywhere" around the suites and villas, The Links championship course, 18 tennis courts, five pools, 22,000-sq.-ft. spa and seven restaurants, including a "fantastic oceanside bar serving fresh sushi and shellfish"; the "service is unbelievable" ("ask and ye shall receive"), making this a "blissful oasis", even if there's "too many people at peak times."

☑ Four Seasons 👫🐾🚭🏋🍸Ⓢ🌊 | 28 | 27 | 25 | 27 | $425

1435 Brickell Ave. | 305-358-3535 | fax 305-358-7758 | 800-819-5053 | www.fourseasons.com | 182 rooms, 39 suites

Sure, this tower of glass and granite sits "in the middle of the Financial District" – perfect for business, "out of the way" for pleasure – but you'll probably "never leave" when you get a load of the "breathtaking views", "unbelievable pools" (reserve a cabana "early in the morning"), "best fitness center", "wonderful amenities" and, of course, the "first-rate", "discreet" service; add in the "incredible rooms" with an "excellent" restaurant and "you'll need a fat wallet" for this one.

Grove Isle Hotel & Spa ✕🚭🏋Ⓢ🌊🎾 | 26 | 22 | 25 | 23 | $689

4 Grove Isle Dr. | Coconut Grove | 305-858-8300 | fax 305-858-5908 | 800-884-7683 | www.groveisle.com | 49 rooms

"You'll feel like you're in your own little paradise" at this "enchanting", "romantic" Relais & Châteaux hotel on a "nearly private island" "in the middle of Biscayne Bay", where "no neon and no salsa" contribute to the "quiet" atmosphere; "casual but lush" rooms, a "heavenly spa" and "moon-kissed" "dining on the water" at the "delightful" oceanfront Baleen (the "highlight of a visit") have some guests smitten.

☑ Mandarin Oriental ✕🚭🏋Ⓢ🌊 | 29 | 27 | 27 | 27 | $675

500 Brickell Key Dr. | 305-913-8288 | fax 305-913-8300 | 866-888-6780 | www.mandarinoriental.com | 296 rooms, 31 suites

It may be located "on its own little Key" in the Brickell Area, but this "Zen-sational" hotel is "truly a glimpse into the Orient", with "gorgeous, Asian-influenced rooms" that have "breathtaking views" – "even from the showers" in some cases; while service is "abundant and soothing" everywhere, it especially shines in the "quite lovely spa", offering unique treatments" and in Azul restaurant, whose "creative" Asian-Med cuisine "dances on your taste buds"; the "only negative is that it's not on the beach", and the "small" "pool's an afterthought" – but for "spectacular without the glitz", this is the place.

Ritz-Carlton Coconut Grove ✕🏋Ⓢ🌊 | 25 | 25 | 23 | 24 | $399

3300 SW 27th Ave. | Coconut Grove | 305-644-4680 | fax 305-644-4681 | 800-241-3333 | www.ritzcarlton.com | 98 rooms, 17 suites

The "superb rooms" and "excellent service without attitude" at this Italian Renaissance–style boutiquey outpost of the venerable chain are two of the many highlights that draw regulars, especially those who want to be in the "hippest area of town" with "great shopping right out the door" and "far from the maddening South Beach crowd"; with "lots of treats in the lobby" and "exceptional" food at Bizcaya, it's a good thing there's a full-service spa and gym to work the calories off.

☑ Ritz-Carlton Key Biscayne 👫✕🚭🏋Ⓢ🌊🎾 | 25 | 26 | 23 | 26 | $389

455 Grand Bay Dr. | Key Biscayne | 305-365-4500 | fax 305-365-4505 | 800-241-3333 | www.ritzcarlton.com | 342 rooms, 60 suites

"Secluded from the rest of Miami" on Key Biscayne, this "stunning" oceanfront "hideaway" makes you "feel like you're in another world" where the "exotic" location emits "a tropical breeze of elegance", "service is king" and "you're likely to see a celebrity"; "plenty of things to do", like tennis, volleyball, bocce and croquet, mean it's "very family-oriented", but that also translates to "tons of kids in the pool"; good thing there's an "extraordinary spa and gym", "bright and airy rooms" and satisfying dining at Cioppino.

Ritz-Carlton South Beach ♥♥✕♥♨♥♨

25	24	23	25	$409

1 Lincoln Rd. | Miami Beach | 786-276-4000 | fax 786-276-4001 | 800-241-3333 | www.ritzcarlton.com | 334 rooms, 41 suites

Looking quite "unlike a traditional Ritz", this site "in the middle of the South Beach action" (and actually "on the beach", unlike some) "preserves many features of the original 1953 Morris Lapidus-designed Dilido hotel", while adding such "modern amenities as a 16,000-sq.-ft. spa, high-speed Internet access in all rooms, a multimillion-dollar art collection and VIP cabanas along an infinity-edge pool where tanning butlers shoot SPF lotion out of holsters"; "the food's very good", the staff offers the chain's "typical, high-end service" and "even the small rooms are big here", but many recommend "upgrading to the club level for access to the lounge and private concierge."

Setai, The ♨♥♨♥♨

26	24	25	26	$900

2001 Collins Ave. | Miami Beach | 305-520-6000 | fax 305-520-6600 | www.setai.com | 125 suites

"An oasis from the fast-paced Miami Beach scene", this "Asian-inspired", earth-toned hotel and adjoining residential tower is "insanely great", boasting "rooms decorated to perfection", a "beautiful bar under the stars" and "three overflowing waterholes you can pool-hop between"; "courteous, efficient" staffers "cater to your every whim"; just "bring buckets of money – you'll need it."

Victor, Hotel ♥♨♥♨

23	24	24	24	$345

1144 Ocean Drive | Miami Beach | 305-428-1234 | fax 305-421-6281 | www.hotelvictorsouthbeach.com | 39 rooms, 33 rooms, 7 bungalows, 5 suites

With its "spectacular jellyfish tank", "the lobby is an experience" at this "still new" *très cool* hotel situated on what some call "the best spot on South Beach", "fronting the beach, yet far from the 'touristy' section of Ocean Drive"; the fin-themed "fanciful decor" continues throughout the property, from the "sexy swimming pool" to the "small but elegant rooms"; "the employees are hip, yet accommodating", and foodies flip for restaurant Vix where the "chef outdoes himself" with his "innovative" yet heartwarming touches, like serving "homemade chocolate lollipops" at the end of each meal.

New Orleans

Omni Royal Orleans ♥♥✕♨♨

22	23	22	22	$295

621 St. Louis St. | 504-529-5333 | fax 504-529-7089 | 800-843-6664 | www.omniroyalorleans.com | 321 rooms, 25 suites

"From the chicory in the coffee to the French Quarter location, this is New Orleans" say visitors "staggering back from Bourbon Street" to their accommodations in this "beautiful hotel"; the Rib Room is an "excellent" place to dine, particularly on Friday afternoons amid the long-lunching locals, but for those who find "too small" rooms, the only real advantage here is the "rooftop pool and bar" with "great views."

Ritz-Carlton, The ⚭✕🍸🛁Ⓢ♨⛵

					$419
	-	-	-	-	

921 Canal St. | 504-524-1331 | fax 504-524-7233 | 800-241-3333 | www.ritzcarlton.com | 490 rooms, 37 suites

Located on the famous French Quarter's Canal Street, this luxury outpost has reopened post-Katrina, with a freshened look that includes a newly renovated 25,000-sq.-ft. spa, four dining/lounge facilities and eight new meeting rooms (for a total of 35,000 sq. ft. of conference space); rooms feature terry cloth robes and Italian marble baths and there's a comprehensive on-site fitness facility.

Royal Sonesta ⚭⛵

20	20	20	21	$349

300 Bourbon St. | 504-586-0300 | fax 504-586-0335 | 800-766-3782 | www.royalsonestano.com | 478 rooms, 22 suites

Its "balcony quarters put you in the heart of the action" "overlooking Bourbon Street", but "if the partying is too much", this "lovely property's" "serene courtyard with pool and bar" can help you feel like the bead throwing is "a thousand miles away"; while "some rooms are top-notch and others need work", a "staff that labors tirelessly to fill the gaps left by the hurricane" is uniformly "impressive."

Soniat House Ⓗ⚭

27	25	16	20	$265

1133 Chartres St. | 504-522-0570 | fax 504-522-7208 | 800-544-8808 | www.soniathouse.com | 23 rooms, 10 suites, 1 cottage

"The most beautifully appointed rooms in Louisiana" come courtesy of hoteliers who also own the antiques store adjacent to this "enchanting" Vieux Carré boutique; "get a suite with a Jacuzzi" and "a balcony overlooking Chartres Street", "enjoy the lovely living-room honor bar", "do not pass on the breakfast biscuits and preserves" in the "courtyard garden", revel in the "wonderful, old-style service" and let yourself "live like a (wealthy) local."

🆉 Windsor Court Hotel ⚭✕🎬🍸⚭⛵

27	28	27	26	$450

300 Gravier St. | 504-523-6000 | fax 504-596-4513 | 800-262-2662 | www.windsorcourthotel.com | 266 suites, 58 rooms

With their signature "sense of grace and style" "in spite of the devastation", the "impeccable" staff at "New Orleans' premier hotel" "makes you feel like a king", "providing exactly what you want" before you even know it; though some rooms might be a bit "worn", "luxurious" suites and other "elegant" facets lead guests to conclude that "this gem is still full of luster"; N.B. chef Michael Collins is top toque at the highly rated New Orleans Grill.

🆕 W New Orleans 🍸⚭⛵

23	21	18	20	$459

333 Poydras St. | 504-525-9444 | fax 504-581-7179 | 877-946-8357 | www.whotels.com | 400 rooms, 23 suites

"Strangely chic" for its CBD location "next to the historic but down-at-the-heels" Mothers Restaurant, this boutique-y "escape from the typical business mega-hotels" is a "modern", "interesting and fun" place to bed, or perch on a couch indoors or out and sip among the "hip"; some of the rooms are "nicer and larger than the typical W's", and the service is more "welcoming", but there are still those "edgy, dark" quarters.

New York City

TOPS IN CITY

27 Four Seasons
Mandarin Oriental
Ritz-Carlton Central Park

26 St. Regis
Ritz-Carlton Battery Park

	ROOMS	SERVICE	DINING	FACIL.	COST
Carlyle, The 🫖🐕🔭	24	27	24	23	$650

35 E. 76th St. | Manhattan | 212-744-1600 | fax 212-717-4682 | 888-767-3966 | www.thecarlyle.com | 122 rooms, 57 suites

"Kings, queens, presidents, celebrities" - and you - can be "spoiled" by the "wonderful" staff at this Upper East Side "grande dame" that epitomizes "old New York at its finest"; the decor's "glamorous", the rooms are "elegant" and there's "nothing more sumptuous than a night at the Café Carlyle", which showcases "fantastic" performers like Elaine Stritch; admittedly, you'll "spend a fortune", but its many "repeat" guests prove it's "worth the bucks."

	ROOMS	SERVICE	DINING	FACIL.	COST
Chambers 🍴🐕🔭	21	21	24	21	$450

15 W. 56th St. | Manhattan | 212-974-5656 | fax 212-974-5657 | 866-204-5656 | www.chambersnyc.com | 60 rooms, 5 suites, 12 studios

"Lovely" public spaces featuring "beautiful artwork", "chic", "minimalist" rooms, one of the "best restaurants in the city" (Geoffrey Zakarian's Town) and "excellent" service distinguish this "hip" David Rockwell-designed Midtowner located just off Fifth Avenue; amenities like "amazing" rain shower fixtures and flat-screen TVs help offset complaints about the "oh-so-tiny" "trendy" accommodations.

	ROOMS	SERVICE	DINING	FACIL.	COST
[Z] **Four Seasons** 🍴🐕🔭Ⓢ	28	28	26	27	$675

57 E. 57th St. | Manhattan | 212-758-5700 | fax 212-758-5711 | 800-332-3442 | www.fourseasons.com | 305 rooms, 63 suites

"The best of the best" in NYC, this Midtown "modern work of art" courtesy of architect I.M. Pei "sets the standard" from the "dramatic lobby" to the "extraordinary", "luxurious" accommodations featuring "great soaking bathtubs" to the "unmatched level of service" from a staff that seems to fulfill your "every wish"; an "excellent" spa facility, "wonderful" bar and "lovely" views of Central Park are other reasons you'll see celebrities and "swanky" folks "wandering through" - it's a "must-stay" for some, "cost be damned"; N.B. the post-Survey opening of restaurant L'Atelier de Joël Robuchon is not reflected in the above Dining score.

	ROOMS	SERVICE	DINING	FACIL.	COST
Library Hotel	23	23	18	24	$335

299 Madison Ave. | Manhattan | 212-983-4500 | fax 212-499-9099 | 877-793-7323 | www.libraryhotel.com | 57 rooms, 3 suites

Literary lions "love" the "charming theme" of this "lovely" Midtown "sanctuary" where each floor represents a different "library classification" including "reference books, fiction", even "erotica"; the rooms are "comfy" and "calming" (although "small"), and the "helpful" staff seems "happy" to be there; what's more, the "rooftop terrace is a little garden of Eden in the city", and "complimentary breakfast and afternoon wine and cheese" make it an "affordable getaway."

	ROOMS	SERVICE	DINING	FACIL.	COST
Lowell, The 🐕🔭	27	26	23	22	$495

28 E. 63rd St. | Manhattan | 212-838-1400 | fax 212-319-4230 | 800-221-4444 | www.lowellhotel.com | 23 rooms, 47 suites

An "unbeatable location" ("two blocks from Barneys!"), "beautiful" accommodations with an "English country house" feel, "glorious" bathrooms and "fantastic" service from the "kind" staff make this "intimate" Upper Eastsider a "diamond among the rhinestones"; "power" dining at the Post House adds to the "crème de la crème" experience.

	ROOMS	SERVICE	DINING	FACIL.	COST
[Z] Mandarin Oriental 🍴🐕🔭Ⓢ🏊	28	27	26	28	$725

80 Columbus Circle | Manhattan | 212-805-8800 | fax 212-805-8882 | 866-801-8880 | www.mandarinoriental.com | 200 rooms, 48 suites

You may "say 'sayonara'" to the competition after being "spoiled" at this "world-class", "luxury" property in the Time Warner Center on Columbus Circle; the "gorgeous" rooms offer the "best technology and home entertainment", "exceptional amenities" and "panoramic" vistas, the service is "incomparable" and the "top-notch spa and fitness facilities" include a "beautiful" pool; even though you'll pay "astronomical prices", especially at the "amazing" restaurant, Asiate, it's "the place to splurge in NYC."

	ROOMS	SERVICE	DINING	FACIL.	COST
Mercer, The 🍴🐕🔭	23	20	23	20	$440

147 Mercer St. | Manhattan | 212-966-6060 | fax 212-965-3838 | 888-918-6060 | www.mercerhotel.com | 60 rooms, 15 suites

"Everything a chic SoHo hotel should be", this "celebrity" stronghold offers "elegant" rooms "tastefully decorated" by Christian Liaigre as well as "lovely" dining at Jean-Georges Vongerichten's Mercer Kitchen and a guests-only lounge accessorized with "great-looking people" ("you may spot" a celebrity or two); though a few detect a "bit of attitude" from the staff, more maintain "if you can afford to stay here, all your needs will be met."

	ROOMS	SERVICE	DINING	FACIL.	COST
New York Palace Ⓗ🐕🔭Ⓢ	25	25	21	24	$720

455 Madison Ave. | Manhattan | 212-888-7000 | fax 212-303-6000 | 800-697-2522 | www.newyorkpalace.com | 825 rooms, 73 suites

"Luxurious without being fussy", this Midtown art deco palace earns kudos for its "beyond fantastic" concierge desk and a staff that makes "you feel like you're the most important guest they've had all day"; further notice goes to the "lovely" common areas and the "golden" Gilt restaurant (in the Villard Mansion space that formerly housed Le Cirque); though some quibble over "nothing special" standard rooms, the "superb" "tower rooms are borderline luxurious" and "well worth" the price.

	ROOMS	SERVICE	DINING	FACIL.	COST
Peninsula, The 🐕🔭Ⓢ🏊	26	26	23	25	$725

700 Fifth Ave. | Manhattan | 212-956-2888 | fax 212-903-3949 | 800-262-9467 | www.peninsula.com | 185 rooms, 54 suites

Offering "everything you'd expect from a five-star establishment in a five-star city", this "quiet" Midtown choice is "practical for business travelers and shoppers" who love its central Fifth Avenue location (high-end shops, St. Patrick's Cathedral, Central Park within walking distance), "fabulous" rooftop bar and "very attentive", "everyone-knows-your-name" service; though some tout the "extremely well-appointed rooms" boasting "large baths" and bedside consoles that operate TVs and lights, others say the "luxurious" spa and rooftop in-door pool ("a dreamy escape") definitely outshine the quarters.

Pierre New York, The ♨ ✦♨ | 23 | 26 | 23 | 23 | $610 |

2 E. 61st St. | Manhattan | 212-838-8000 | fax 212-940-8109 | 800-223-6800 | www.tajhotels.com | 150 rooms, 51 suites

Loyalists love this "landmark" hotel in a "fantastic location" "right across from Central Park" that's "as classy as they come", with "sensational service" ("nothing is too much for the staff") and "elegant" styling; while a few say this "grand old dame" is looking a "bit saggy", she's about to get a shot of "needed Botox" via renovations by new managers, the Taj Group – "after that, look out", she may become "the hottest" chick in town.

Plaza Athénée, Hôtel ♨ ✕ ✦♨ | 25 | 26 | 24 | 22 | $535 |

37 E. 64th St. | Manhattan | 212-734-9100 | fax 212-772-0958 | 800-447-8800 | www.plaza-athenee.com | 114 rooms, 35 suites

A "cozy yet luxurious oasis off Madison Avenue", this European-style boutique Eastsider "in a real neighborhood" finds favor for a "discreet" staff that "really makes you feel at home", a "fine restaurant", Arabelle, with "one of the best Sunday brunches" around, and "lovely" rooms that include some suites with outdoor balconies; business types tout it as "a great place for hosting conferences for the upper elite", while leisure-ites love the "charming" location near high-end shopping and Central Park; N.B. don't miss a drink in the romantic Bar Seine.

Regency, The ♨ ⊟ ✦♨ | 22 | 23 | 21 | 20 | $329 |

540 Park Ave. | Manhattan | 212-759-4100 | fax 212-826-5674 | 800-233-2356 | www.loewshotels.com | 266 rooms, 85 suites

"Everyone gets the superstar treatment" at this Upper East Side "clubby" "classic" on Park Avenue; with its "famous power breakfasts", afternoon wine in the Library, "accommodating staff" and "perfect", "wish-fulfillment address", it's particularly "impressive for out-of-town business" clients; just a few nitpickers natter about some rooms needing "refurbishing"; N.B. don't miss pop-vocalist Michael Feinstein at his namesake cabaret five nights a week.

Ritz-Carlton Battery Park ♨ ✦♨Ⓢ | 28 | 26 | 24 | 25 | $550 |

2 West St. | Manhattan | 212-344-0800 | fax 212-344-3801 | 800-241-3333 | www.ritzcarlton.com | 259 rooms, 39 suites

You have to travel pretty far south for "the best view in the world", but this "exceptional" Battery Park bastion at the tip of Manhattan is so "fabulous in every way" it's "worth it"; from the "impeccable" service to the "fantastic" 14th-floor Rise bar to the "large and luxurious rooms" (Liberty View ones come "with a telescope to scan NY Harbor"), this is "*the* place to stay" "if you have business Downtown"; just be warned, although it's convenient to a few major attractions (Ellis Island, the former World Trade Center site), it's a "$20 taxi ride to Midtown" – and "good luck getting a cab after hours"; N.B. look for weekend bargains.

⬛ Ritz-Carlton Central Park ✕ ✦♨Ⓢ | 28 | 28 | 25 | 26 | $895 |

50 Central Park S. | Manhattan | 212-308-9100 | fax 212-207-8831 | 800-241-3333 | www.ritzcarlton.com | 213 rooms, 48 suites

Expect both "stunning" park views and "stunning" service at this "absolutely wonderful" outpost of the luxury group, where the staff pays "attention to minute details" and the "top-notch" Midtown location means easy strolls to Central Park across the street; "spacious rooms" with "gigantic bathrooms", "Frédéric Fekkai hair products" and sound-proof windows, as well as a "to-die-for" spa and "fabulous" food at Atelier win praise, but most are more impressed that "the hotel car is a Maybach" – no wonder there are so many "celebrity sightings" here.

Sherry-Netherland, The 🏨

| 26 | 27 | 22 | 21 | $499 |

781 Fifth Ave. | Manhattan | 212-355-2800 | fax 212-319-4306 | 877-743-7710 | www.sherrynetherland.com | 30 rooms, 20 suites
Look for the signature clock that marks the Fifth Avenue entrance of this circa-1927 hotel just "steps away from Central Park" that boasts an "Old New York" "residential feel" with hand-loomed carpets, custom-made crystal chandeliers and white-gloved elevator attendants (there are private residences here as well); better yet, say those who "highly recommend it", "they don't nickel-and-dime you", providing "a lot of free amenities" like breakfasts and newspapers.

Sofitel 🏨

| 25 | 24 | 21 | 22 | $609 |

45 W. 44th St. | Manhattan | 212-354-8844 | 212-354-2480 | www.sofitel.com | 346 rooms, 52 suites
"Tucked away on a side street" in a "superb location" just a few minutes' walk from Times Square, this "tasteful", "understated" European Midtowner is a pleasant "surprise" for those who've discovered it; "large", "reasonably priced rooms (for NYC at least)" with "swanky bathrooms" and "great toiletries", a "friendly staff that can't do enough" and an art deco French-Asian restaurant with an outdoor terrace prompt many patrons to "stay there again."

Ⓩ St. Regis ✕⊛🕭🏨Ⓢ

| 27 | 27 | 25 | 25 | $760 |

2 E. 55th St. | Manhattan | 212-753-4500 | fax 212-787-3447 | 877-787-3447 | www.stregis.com | 229 rooms
"Live it up with dignitaries and diplomats" at this "swell-egant" Midtown "favorite" "in the center of everything", where the "best service in town" includes a "truly outstanding staff", "wonderful butlers" and "complimentary overnight ironing and shoe shines"; "opulence abounds", from the "crystal chandeliers in the rooms" (many with "great views of Central Park") to the "hundreds of extras", to the "must"-stop King Cole bar, but going "first class all the way" means you might have to "take out a second mortgage"; N.B. star chef Alain Ducasse is slated to move his restaurant here in spring 2007.

Trump International Hotel & Tower ✕🕭🏨Ⓢ⚓

| 26 | 25 | 25 | 24 | $695 |

1 Central Park W. | Manhattan | 212-299-1000 | fax 212-299-1150 | 888-448-7867 | www.trumpintl.com | 39 rooms, 128 suites
"From the curb to the room, you're made to feel welcome" by an "impeccable staff" at this Columbus Circle "gem" "that's as slick as the Donald's hair"; with "one of the greatest locations on earth" right on Central Park West, it's a "favorite place for celebrities", with "massive rooms" boasting "views of the Park" and "fully stocked kitchenettes", plus the "to-die-for" Jean Georges (one of the top-rated restaurants in our *NYC Restaurants* Survey); add in "no shortage of gold or marble" and regulars rhetorically ask "what's not to like?"

	ROOMS	SERVICE	DINING	FACIL.	COST

Waldorf-Astoria & Towers Ⓗ🐾Ⓢ

| 21 | 23 | 21 | 22 | $599 |

301 Park Ave. | Manhattan | 212-355-3000 | fax 212-872-7272 |
800-925-3673 | www.waldorfastoria.com | 1175 rooms, 250 suites

This "classic" Midtown art deco "treasure" is "still the one" say its
many fans who take a "graceful, elegant" "walk back in time" when-
ever they stay here; with "exceptional service", "truly outstanding
public areas" and "historic ambiance", there's "no other hotel like it",
but even admirers admit the rooms "have seen better days" (the separate Towers gets higher praise) and complain that the "lobby loaded
with tourists" is "busier than nearby Grand Central Station" – so "don't
expect too much" from this "dowager", just "love it for what it is."

W Union Square ✕🐾

| 22 | 22 | 22 | 21 | $689 |

201 Park Ave. S. | Manhattan | 212-253-9119 | fax 212-253-9229 |
877-946-8357 | www.whotels.com | 254 rooms, 16 suites

"The best W in NYC", this outpost set in a "historic building" in the
"heart of Union Square", within "walking distance to SoHo, Chelsea,
the subway" and "some of the city's treasured restaurants", has a "location that can't be beat"; regulars appreciate the chain's typical
"style and attitude" with "music, food and drinks under one roof": "access to Rande Gerber's Underbar", chef Todd English's "superb"
Olives and lots of "great people-watching" in a lounge with floor-to-
ceiling windows; the "minimalist" rooms are "inviting", as well, but
older folks say "if you're over 30 you may as well be 80 when you're in
the lobby bar filled with imbibing twentysomethings searching for
their next significant others."

Orlando

Disney's Animal Kingdom Lodge 🚹🐾🏊

| 23 | 24 | 23 | 27 | $335 |

2901 Osceola Pkwy. | Lake Buena Vista | 407-938-3000 |
www.disneyworld.com | 1274 rooms, 19 suites

Guests say "waking up to giraffes looking in your window" at this
"African palace" with an "awe-inspiring" lobby is like going "on safari
in Florida", especially if you "splurge" for a "pricey" Savannah view to
ensure "exotic animals right off your balcony" ("with no zoo smells");
other highlights are the "friendly staff" that includes "storytellers
around an outdoor fire pit", two "incredible" restaurants featuring a
"not-to-be-missed" buffet at one and a "large South African wine list"
at the other, and a "great" expansive pool area; even if it's "a bit away"
from "the rest of 'the World'", to many it's "the king of the jungle
of Disney hotels."

Disney's Grand Floridian Resort & Spa 🚹🐾🛏⬆Ⓢ🏊🔍

| 24 | 25 | 24 | 26 | $555 |

4401 Floridian Way | Lake Buena Vista | 407-824-2421 | fax 407-824-3186 |
www.disneyworld.com | 837 rooms, 25 suites

An "amazing" Victorian-style resort with "breathtaking" views of
Cinderella's Castle across the lagoon, this "grande dame of Disney hotels" located "two minutes from the Magic Kingdom" by monorail is
"stunning inside and out"; offering a "variety of room types" that take
advantage of architectural details like sloping ceilings, garrets, etc.,
it's "well-suited for adults with or without kids"; the on-site Victoria &

Albert's restaurant is "one of the best", and if enthusiasts rave of a "fabulous spa", "exceptional" service and a "luxurious", "magical" setting, they also warn you should "expect to pay for it."

Disney's Yacht Club Resort 添盖鱼 | 24 | 24 | 22 | 26 | $415 |

1700 Epcot Resort Blvd. | Lake Buena Vista | 407-934-7000 |
fax 407-934-3450 | www.disneyworld.com | 610 rooms, 11 suites
"Outstanding service" and an "awesome" waterfront location "within walking distance to Epcot" make this New England–themed resort "great for families"; "well-appointed" rooms with nautical motifs and "beautiful views" are "a bit classier" than those at its sister Beach Club next door, but the highlight here is the same: the "fantastic" sand-bottomed pool and three-acre "mini-water park"; though meat eaters tout the "filet mignon you can cut with a fork" at The Yachtsman Steakhouse, penny-pinchers pout that "for the price" they "expected larger" quarters and more dining options.

JW Marriott
Grande Lakes 添船上③盖鱼 | 25 | 24 | 22 | 27 | $469 |

4040 Central Florida Pkwy. | 407-206-2300 | fax 407-206-2301 |
800-228-9290 | www.marriott.com | 934 rooms, 64 suites
"An oasis of calm and luxury" amid the South "Orlando kitsch", this property is "an outstanding convention venue", but also "a great place for golfers" and any "adult who wants to get away from all the noise" (you'll "need to rent a car" to visit Disney World, SeaWorld and Universal Studios); notable features include a "relaxing lazy-river pool area", "beautiful sweeping grounds, a spacious lobby" and a "phenomenal" spa/exercise facility "shared with the adjacent Ritz-Carlton Grande Lakes"; the rooms are "comfortable" and the "staff friendly", but some suggest hitting the Ritz for dining as well.

Z Ritz-Carlton
Grande Lakes 添×船上③盖鱼 | 28 | 27 | 25 | 28 | $390 |

4012 Central Florida Pkwy. | 407-206-2400 | fax 407-206-2401 |
800-241-3333 | www.ritzcarlton.com | 520 rooms, 64 suites
Its South Orlando location is "in the middle of nowhere, but who cares?" when you've got "the best of the Ritz-Carltons in Florida" say surveyors who swoon over this "super-sized, yet surprisingly intimate" "Italian palace–like" resort filled with "everything you never knew you needed, [like] a chilled towel and lemonade upon check-in", "divine bathtubs" in the "amazing rooms", "outstanding" New World cuisine at Norman's, "top-notch activities" and an "Epcot of spas combining services from around the world"; "and if a movie and popcorn at the pool is not enough, the JW Marriott next door has an awesome lazy river"; P.S. the "wonderful" staff "takes care of kids as if they're the ones paying the bill."

Philadelphia

Z Four Seasons 添×岸船③盖 | 27 | 28 | 27 | 26 | $355 |

1 Logan Sq. | 215-963-1500 | fax 215-963-9562 | 866-516-1100 |
www.fourseasons.com | 356 rooms, 8 suites
"You can't find better service in the City of Brotherly Love" than at this "supremely tasteful" hotel on Ben Franklin Parkway, where the "flaw-

less" staff "pampers" every guest, from "power-broking attorneys with cigars" to "babies" with binkies; newly renovated "spacious rooms", a "divine pool", a "great location for museums" and the Fountain Restaurant's "outstanding" fare (it was voted No. 1 in our *Philadelphia Restaurants* Survey) are other reasons to stay here.

Park Hyatt at the Bellevue 👪 ✗ [H] 🔭 [S] — 23 | 23 | 23 | 22 | $350

200 S. Broad St. | 215-893-1234 | fax 215-732-8518 | 800-233-1234 | www.parkphiladelphia.hyatt.com | 159 rooms, 13 suites

"Champagne at check-in starts your trip off right" at this 1904 "historic" "queen" that delivers a "mix of grandeur and homelike comfort", particularly in the renovated 19th-floor lounge and cafe beneath the "stained-glass dome"; though they "vary in size, shape and arrangement", the "high-ceilinged rooms" are all "clean and comfortable", and the Avenue of Arts location is convenient to "museums, performing arts and galleries, as well as shopping."

Rittenhouse, The ✗ 🐕 🔭 [S] 🏊 — 27 | 26 | 26 | 24 | $420

210 W. Rittenhouse Sq. | 215-546-9000 | fax 215-732-3364 | 800-635-1042 | www.rittenhousehotel.com | 87 rooms, 11 suites

It's "first class all the way" at this wonderfully located, "classy, small" Center City hotel where you'll peer out onto "one of the prettiest squares on the Eastern seaboard" from the "many windows" of your "luxurious", "oversized" room - just "an elevator ride" up from "Jean-Marie Lacroix's magnificent restaurant"; named after the adjacent park, it also "impresses" with its "gracious" staff and "resort-level spa", leading some to admit they "wouldn't stay anywhere else in Philly."

Ritz-Carlton, The ✗ [H] 🐕 🔭 [S] — 24 | 24 | 22 | 23 | $300

10 Ave. of the Arts | 215-523-8000 | fax 215-568-0942 | 800-241-3333 | www.ritzcarlton.com | 298 rooms, 32 suites, 1 penthouse

"Tea in the rotunda is a must", as the "magnificent lobby" of this "converted beaux arts bank building" "has all the wow factor that you'd expect" from the luxury chain; the "plush eye-candy" public facilities are nearly matched by the rooms, which, while a "bit small", have "marble baths" ("bathrobes are the tops"); but a few advise "make sure you stay on the club level" for the best service.

Sofitel 👪 🐕 🔭 — 25 | 23 | 20 | 21 | $300

120 S. 17th St. | 215-569-8300 | fax 215-564-7452 | www.sofitel.com | 238 rooms, 68 suites

"A terrific, centrally located choice for touring Philly" is this Center City property owned and operated by a "fabulous" French company; there's "no pool to cool off in" and it's "not fancy", but the "sharp staff" helps make the bar a popular pit stop for visiting "singles", who look past the "perfunctory" lobby to "comfortable" rooms featuring "European decor" and "to-die-for" baths with "top-class toiletries, towels and robes."

Phoenix/Scottsdale

[Z] **Boulders, The** 🐕 🔭 ⛳ [S] 🏊 🎾 — 26 | 25 | 23 | 27 | $129

34631 N. Tom Darlington Dr. | Carefree | 480-488-9009 | fax 480-488-4118 | 800-553-1717 | www.theboulders.com | 160 casitas, 55 villas

"A Zen-like retreat" that's "perfectly meshed into its Sonoran Desert setting" outside Scottsdale, this "enchanting oasis" is "a treat for the senses"; "fantastic" for golfers and "a highly desirable" spot even for non-duffers (try a "massage of a lifetime" at the "incredible" Golden Door Spa), it boasts "beautiful grounds", "dramatic views", "luxurious" casitas in which you "could live forever", a staff that "goes out of its way" and "excellent" dining.

[Z] Four Seasons Resort Troon North 👪🐕🔭⛳Ⓢ🏊🎾

Rooms	Service	Dining	Facil.	Cost
27	27	25	27	$495

10600 E. Crescent Moon Dr. | Scottsdale | 480-515-5700 | fax 480-515-5599 | 888-207-9696 | www.fourseasons.com | 188 rooms, 22 suites

"Understated" "luxury is seamlessly integrated with the desert" at this Scottsdale resort whose "Pinnacle Peak views" make it the "perfect remote location for a relaxing getaway"; the often-"cavernous" "casitas provide a Southwest feel with all the modern comforts, plus extras like a stargazing chart and fireplaces" ("splurge for a room with a plunge pool"); regulars report it might "not be up to the usual" high standards of this chain, but most praise the staff's "pampering beyond your dreams", down to "remembering your seven-year-old's favorite juice."

[Z] Phoenician, The 👪🍴🔭⛳Ⓢ🏊🎾

Rooms	Service	Dining	Facil.	Cost
26	26	25	28	$625

6000 E. Camelback Rd. | Scottsdale | 480-941-8200 | fax 480-947-4311 | 800-888-8234 | www.thephoenician.com | 474 rooms, 66 suites, 107 casitas, 7 villas

It's "a bit on the ostentatious side" ("marble, in Arizona?"), but "everything is amazing" at this "huge" hotel at the base of Camelback Mountain; the "service is so good, it's scary", whether in your "opulent", "exceptionally large" chamber ("you could get lost in the bathroom"), at the spa ("an experience not to be missed"), at "Mary Elaine's, the ultimate in fine dining", or on the golf courses that are "challenging enough for experienced players without being beyond hope for weekend hackers"; "you'll certainly pay the price for all this" - "a pack of canned soda is equal to a car payment" - but go ahead, "indulge yourself" with some "heaven in the desert."

[Z] Royal Palms Hotel & Casitas 🍴🐕🔭Ⓢ🏊

Rooms	Service	Dining	Facil.	Cost
26	26	28	25	$429

5200 E. Camelback Rd. | Phoenix | 602-840-3610 | fax 602-840-6927 | 800-672-6011 | www.royalpalmshotel.com | 63 rooms, 44 casitas, 5 villas, 7 suites

"Unbelievably serene", this "quintessential Old Phoenix resort" from the '40s just may be the "best-kept secret in Arizona"; though "set in the lap of Camelback Mountain", the "relatively small" retreat has a "romantic", "European-hotel" air: "gorgeous" grounds dotted with outdoor fireplaces, the "phenomenal T. Cook's" Med restaurant, a "gracious staff that goes out of its way" and such "special touches" as "rose petals on the bed" and "the scent of orange blossoms" in the air; just "make sure you get a casita and not a standard room", or else the "picturesque" can be "cramped."

[Z] Sanctuary on Camelback Mountain 🏨🐕Ⓢ🏊🎾

Rooms	Service	Dining	Facil.	Cost
25	24	25	26	$425

5700 E. McDonald Dr. | Paradise Valley | 480-948-2100 | fax 480-483-7314 | www.sanctuaryoncamelback.com | 98 casitas, 6 houses

"Chic, hip and at the same time relaxing", this "classy" resort "nestled at the foot of Camelback Mountain" is "perfect" for "hiding from the rest of the world" (indeed, one guest "saw Bono, Britney and Jennifer Aniston - all in just two visits"); pampering prevails, whether in the "swanky rooms", at "the most amazing spa" - where the "watsu water massage is to die for" - on the "great tennis" courts or in the restaurant, which serves "delicious food highlighted by gorgeous views"; "come dressed to impress", but "don't bring the kids" (they're welcome, but the "serene" scene may bore them).

San Francisco

TOPS IN CITY

27 Ritz-Carlton
26 Four Seasons
St. Regis

Campton Place Hotel 🍴🐕🔭Ⓢ

ROOMS	SERVICE	DINING	FACIL.	COST
23	25	26	20	$425

340 Stockton St. | 415-781-5555 | fax 415-955-5536 | 866-332-1673 | www.camptonplace.com | 100 rooms, 10 suites

Gourmands gush that dinner is a "three-hour work of art" at the "exquisite" restaurant in this "intimate" boutique hotel in a "close-to-everything" location at the tip of Union Square; an "attentive staff" that "couldn't be nicer or more gracious" and "plush" rooms (though "a bit small" some complain) further make this one of the "most charming hotels in the city"; P.S. the dining room also serves the "best breakfast in town."

Fairmont 🐕🔭Ⓢ

ROOMS	SERVICE	DINING	FACIL.	COST
22	24	20	22	$319

950 Mason St. | 415-772-5000 | fax 415-772-5013 | 800-441-1414 | www.fairmont.com | 529 rooms, 62 suites

"Guests are treated like royalty" at this "belle of the ball" perched atop Nob Hill, where rooms in the original 1907 building sport an "old-world" elegance and those in the newer tower have "awesome" views of the city and the "nightly fog that envelops the upper floors"; though detractors say this "old lady" is a "bit down at the heels", loyalists laud her as "first-class" in most respects; P.S. the tiki-"kitschy" Tonga Room bar is an "SF don't-miss."

[Z] Four Seasons 👫🐕🔭Ⓢ🏊

ROOMS	SERVICE	DINING	FACIL.	COST
26	28	25	27	$430

757 Market St. | 415-633-3000 | fax 415-633-3009 | 800-332-3442 | www.fourseasons.com | 231 rooms, 46 suites

"I left my heart" here declare devotees of this "fabulous" SoMa/Union Square property with "all of the expected bells and whistles" the chain is famous for: an "impeccable" staff that's "always one step ahead" with "special touches" ("personal notes, fresh fruit, truffles"), "beautiful" rooms and a fitness facility that "can't be beat" "even if you're not a health nut"; in fact, guests "can't find a thing wrong with it", other than the "crazy-high" price, which some call "worth it" for the "epitome of modern luxury."

Huntington Hotel & Nob Hill Spa Ⓗ🫖🔭Ⓢ🏊

ROOMS	SERVICE	DINING	FACIL.	COST
23	24	23	23	$350

1075 California St. | 415-474-5400 | fax 415-474-6227 | www.huntingtonhotel.com | 96 rooms, 40 suites

"Take me back to a time of quiet elegance" sigh devotees of this "completely refined" hotel that boasts white-gloved doormen and a "top-of-the-world" Nob Hill perch overlooking "beautiful" Huntington Park; the "attentive" staff is "exemplary in kindness", and though fans say the "old-fashioned" rooms are "beautifully appointed", some feel they're "uneven" and "need a makeover"; still, a "first-rate" spa with a "stunning" indoor pool and a "grand" outdoor deck provides a "rejuvenating oasis."

Lafayette Park Hotel & Spa 🔭Ⓢ🏊 24 | 22 | 22 | 22 | $249

3287 Mt. Diablo Blvd. | Lafayette | 925-283-3700 | fax 925-284-1621 | 800-368-2468 | www.lafayetteparkhotel.com | 128 rooms, 12 suites

You'll enjoy "city-level quality in the suburbs" when you stay at this East Bay "European"-style hotel, with its French-château architecture, three-story domed lobby, "gorgeous, seductive pool", "well-appointed, but small spa" ("request a treatment room that's not over the pool pump"), "great restaurant" and "inviting rooms"; but cautious critics counter the "pleasant" service is "not outstanding", summing it up as simply "nice for its location" 30 minutes from San Francisco.

Mandarin Oriental 🍴🐾🔭 27 | 27 | 24 | 24 | $545

222 Sansome St. | 415-276-9888 | fax 415-276-9600 | 800-622-0404 | www.mandarinoriental.com | 151 rooms, 7 suites

Fans say a stay at this "elegant" "modern classic" in the Financial District is like "floating above the city in a palace" as the "fog rolls in below you"; "exquisite" rooms "with a touch of the Orient" yield "world-class" vistas from "bridge to bridge" ("some from the bathtubs"), and a "superb" staff "makes you feel like an emperor" "from the moment you arrive"; the "terrific" Silks restaurant pleases as well, confirming that this "true delight" is "top-notch in every respect" - "now if it could only have a spa."

Palomar, Hotel 🍴🐾🔭 23 | 23 | 25 | 19 | $309

12 Fourth St. | 415-348-1111 | fax 415-348-0302 | 877-294-9711 | www.hotelpalomar.com | 182 rooms, 16 suites

This boutique hotel "puts the *chi* in chichi" exclaim fans of their "absolute favorite" with a "great location" near Union Square, SoMa and the Financial District; the exterior is the "epitome of old San Francisco architecture", and the accommodations are "gorgeous", from the "groovy animal-print rugs" to the "huge, two-person whirlpool baths"; guests also rave about the staff that "will call you by name", the "fantastic" Fifth Floor Restaurant and the "hip" vibe, making it the ultimate "21st-century hotel."

[Z] **Ritz-Carlton, The** 🍴🔭Ⓢ🏊 26 | 28 | 27 | 26 | $495

600 Stockton St. | 415-296-7465 | fax 415-291-0288 | 800-241-3333 | www.ritzcarlton.com | 294 rooms, 42 suites

It's "the finest hotel in the city", "as close to perfection as you can get" say its loyal fans who cite "beautiful decor", "absolutely superb service" and an all-around aura of "luxe" that "makes you feel like a king" - "beg, borrow or steal to be on the club level" because "they know how to pamper" you with "attention only meant for the upper crust"; a recent $12.5-million renovation brought the "elegant" rooms with "cushy feather beds" "back to their majesty" and there's an "amazing" restaurant, so "other than the hike up and down Nob Hill", there's no reason not to "highly recommend" it.

[Z] [NEW] St. Regis 🐕 👓 Ⓢ 🏊 | 28 | 25 | 26 | 27 | $529

125 Third St. | 415-284-4000 | www.stregis.com | 214 rooms, 105 condos, 46 suites

A "spectacular addition to the hotel scene", this "grown-up" hotel next door to the SF MoMA incorporates the historic Williams Building and hits just the right notes with its "cool, Zen-like" feel; "modern" rooms with 42-inch plasma TVs, "exceptional baths" and "remote controls that do everything" from operating window blinds to ordering "butler service" beckon guests to "relax", plus there's a Remède spa that's "pure luxury" and a "fine" New American eatery, ame, from the team behind St. Helena's famed Terra Restaurant.

Vitale, Hotel 🐕 👓 | 26 | 23 | 22 | 26 | $279

8 Mission St. | 415-278-3700 | fax 415-278-3750 | 888-890-8688 | www.hotelvitale.com | 8 suites, 191 rooms

This two-year-old Embarcadero hotel is "front and center of a lot of great things" - it's "across the street from the Ferry Building" (a gourmet's mecca), near the Financial District and in perfect position to view "the sun rising over San Francisco Bay and the bridge"; "contemporary" rooms (some with "killer views") come with "exquisite amenities" (Fresh brand bath products, 440-thread-count European linens), and chef Paul Arenstam's "excellent" Americano restaurant incorporates ingredients from the Farmers Market across the street; P.S. don't miss the "rooftop spa" with outdoor soaking tubs.

Seattle

Bellevue Club Hotel 🐕 👓 Ⓢ 🏊 🎾 | 27 | 26 | 22 | 28 | $235

11200 SE Sixth St. | Bellevue | 425-454-4424 | fax 425-688-3197 | 800-579-1110 | www.bellevueclub.com | 64 rooms, 3 suites

"As good as it gets on the Eastside", this "high-end" Bellevue boutique "just five miles across the lake from Seattle" is attached to a tony private athletic club with a "truly great" gym and "wonderful" spa treatments; "immaculate rooms" feature "high ceilings", "courteous" service includes a handy limo "for dining and shopping", there's "great art throughout" the property and even the food is "top-notch"; some insist this one is "better than most anywhere."

Fairmont Olympic 👪 ✕ Ⓗ 🐕 👓 Ⓢ 🏊 | 24 | 25 | 24 | 25 | $419

411 University St. | 206-621-1700 | fax 206-623-2271 | 800-821-8106 | www.fairmont.com | 234 rooms, 216 suites

Seattle's most elegant "matriarch" for generations, this "magnificent" historic Italian Renaissance hotel has a "gorgeous" lobby full of "comfy" spots to "people-watch", a stellar piano bar, "beautiful" luxuriously appointed rooms with beds that "have you dreaming in no time" and a staff that "treats you like royalty"; the indoor pool and health club are the "best" and The Georgian Court restaurant is a "classy" spot for breakfast or dinner.

Inn at Langley, The ✕ Ⓗ 👓 Ⓢ | 25 | 24 | 28 | 20 | $265

400 First St. | Langley | 360-221-3033 | fax 360-221-3033 | www.innatlangley.com | 22 rooms, 2 suites, 2 cottages

The "exquisite" meals by chef/general manager Matt Costello "can't be beat", and in fact are the standout feature of this "wonderful" "tiny hideaway" built on a bluff in the art community of Whidbey Island; its "totally Zen" rooms feature "glorious water views", outdoor balconies, whirlpool tubs and wood-burning fireplaces, and there's a "wonderful spa" under separate ownership; nevertheless, some say it's mostly "worth going" for the "dining experience."

Salish Lodge & Spa ✕ ♨ Ⓢ
25 | 24 | 25 | 25 | $529

6501 Railroad Ave. SE | Snoqualmie | 425-888-2556 | fax 425-888-2533 | 800-272-5474 | www.salishlodge.com | 85 rooms, 4 suites

Curl up in front of the "roaring" wood-burning fireplace in your "rustic" room with "incomparable" views of Snoqualmie Falls at this "pricey" outpost 45 minutes from Downtown Seattle; the "amazing location" (once a star in the TV show *Twin Peaks*) is complemented by "manicured gardens" and "warm service", plus the accommodations come with whirlpools for two and "pillow menus" offering 16 fluffy choices – all in all, it's a "cozy way to spend a chilly weekend."

Willows Lodge ✕ ♨ Ⓢ
27 | 23 | 27 | 22 | $195

14580 NE 145th St. | Woodinville | 425-424-3900 | 877-424-3930 | www.willowslodge.com | 80 rooms, 6 suites

With a "winning spa, a prime location in Washington wine country (30 minutes from Seattle) and two excellent restaurants" (Barking Frog and the "ultra-superior" Herbfarm), this modernist "Pacific Northwest lodge" in Woodinville, 30 minutes from Seattle, is an "amazing" "getaway"; "bucolic" grounds, "modern", "romantic" rooms with fireplaces and luxe bathrooms and a "wonderful staff" give you "everything you need for a perfect weekend."

Washington, DC

Fairmont ♯ ♨ ♨ Ⓢ ≈
23 | 24 | 21 | 22 | $619

2401 M St. NW | Washington | 202-429-2400 | fax 202-457-5089 | 800-257-7544 | www.fairmont.com | 392 rooms, 23 suites

With a "stylish" West End location, "straddling Georgetown, the CBD" and "tourist sites", this large property is a "great value if you don't feel like paying for the Ritz or Four Seasons" but still want "every amenity" – "large, airy rooms", "excellent service" and "charming public spaces"; the flower-filled courtyard and a "legendary" Sunday brunch help set it "apart from the ordinary business hotel", although one live-wire laments it "lacks verve."

Four Seasons ✕ ♨ ♨ Ⓢ ≈
25 | 26 | 25 | 25 | $565

2800 Pennsylvania Ave. NW | Washington | 202-342-0444 | fax 202-944-2076 | 800-332-3442 | www.fourseasons.com | 160 rooms, 51 suites

"Terrific" even before a recent makeover, this "nearly flawless" "favorite" "right on the edge of Georgetown" offers "elegant", "understated luxury" that's "appropriately staid for DC"; though great for "celebrity spotting", the "institution's" "incredible" staff "caters to everyone" (including the children) with "a warm welcome", and "outrageously wonderful" dining, rooms with "42-inch flat-screen TVs" (the east wing's were refurbished under a design by Pierre-Yves Rochon of Paris' Hôtel George V) plus a "fabulous" spa and fitness center round out this "oasis."

	ROOMS	SERVICE	DINING	FACIL.	COST

Hay-Adams, The ✗⊕🛏♨ | 25 | 26 | 24 | 22 | $400

800 16th St. NW | Washington | 202-638-6600 | fax 202-638-2716 |
800-424-5054 | www.hayadams.com | 125 rooms, 20 suites

"Try not to bump into too many celebrities and newsmakers" at this
"old-fashioned charmer" that "exudes elegance from every crystal of
its many chandeliers" situated "across the park from the ultimate
Washington address"; indeed, "if you were any closer to the White
House, you'd be sleeping in the Lincoln bedroom", rather than in this
"oasis of calm" where the "gracious" staff knows you by name" and
there are "beautifully appointed" rooms; "DC's power-azzi" line the
Lafayette Room where "formal" meals are "wonderfully prepared."

☑ Inn at Little Washington, The ✗♨ | 27 | 29 | 29 | 23 | $615

309 Middle St. | Washington | 540-675-3800 | fax 540-675-3100 |
800-735-2478 | www.theinnatlittlewashington.com | 10 rooms,
5 suites, 2 houses

"All it's cracked up to be and more" swear sybarites about the "ultimate dine-and-stay experience" "choreographed" at this über-
"romantic" Virginia "getaway", a little over an hour from the Capitol;
its proprietors provide legendary "attention to detail" with "uniquely
furnished" rooms, "luxurious" amenities and "theatrical" service in its
"incomparable" Relais Gourmand New American restaurant.

Jefferson, The ✗🛏♨≋ | 22 | 25 | 21 | 20 | $509

1200 16th St., NW | Washington | 202-347-2200 | fax 202-331-7982 |
866-270-8102 | www.thejeffersonwashingtondc.com | 70 rooms, 30 suites

"Quiet elegance" is the hallmark of this "romantic", "unflashy" beaux
arts–inspired boutique "from a different era", where a "discreet,
prompt and efficient" staff "always bends over backwards" for guests
and the "charming if small rooms" are moments from the White
House, museums and the Mall; guests can peruse documents from
the third president while enjoying a "sublime afternoon tea" in a "gorgeous setting", or dine in the namesake New American restaurant.

Mandarin Oriental 🛏♨Ⓢ≋ | 27 | 25 | 25 | 25 | $445

1330 Maryland Ave. SW | Washington | 202-554 8588 | fax 202-554 8999 |
888-888-1788 | www.mandarinoriental.com | 348 rooms, 52 suites

"Divine is the only word to describe" the "exquisite suites" with "views
to die for" and "attentive-without-being-obsequious" service at this
"oasis of tranquility" with its "absolutely stunning facilities" including
a "glitzy" lobby, "trendy" dining rooms (most notably, the New
American "gastric delight", CityZen) and "huge well-appointed spa";
even a "middle-of-nowhere location" in South West doesn't bother
most – where else can you "dine and look at the Jefferson Memorial"?

Monaco, Hotel 🛏♨ | 23 | 21 | 20 | 21 | $409

700 F St. NW | Washington | 202-628-7177 | fax 202-628-7277 |
800-649-1202 | www.monaco-dc.com | 168 rooms, 16 suites

"Stately and grand on the outside, funky on the inside", this "fascinating"
Kimpton conversion of an early-19th-century post office "in the heart of
the action" (Penn Quarter) boasts "20-ft. ceilings", "stunning hallways"
and "stylish" rooms that maintain the "original architectural details"; it's
a "short walk to some of the better DC dining spots" or you can feast
in-house on New American fare in "chic" Poste-Modern Brasserie.

	ROOMS	SERVICE	DINING	FACIL.	COST

Ritz-Carlton, The 🏃 🛏 🛁 ⓈⒶ
27 | 27 | 24 | 26 | $399

1150 22nd St. NW | Washington | 202-835-0500 | fax 202-835-1588 | 800-241-3333 | www.ritzcarlton.com | 267 rooms, 33 suites

"Exemplary", "detail-oriented" "service is the difference" at this "classy-without-being-stuffy" West Ender where "guests are made to feel like visiting diplomats" – especially on the "incredible" private club level; after taking advantage of the "huge and well-equipped" on-site Sports Club/LA, residents relax in "elegant", "well-appointed" rooms with "lavish and luxurious" bathrooms before heading down-stairs for "strong drinks" in the celebrity-filled bar.

Ritz-Carlton Georgetown 🛏 🛁 Ⓢ
27 | 27 | 24 | 24 | $650

3100 South St. NW | Washington | 202-912-4100 | fax 202-912-4199 | 800-241-3333 | www.ritzcarlton.com | 53 rooms, 33 suites

An "easy walk to the shops and to the waterfront", Georgetown's "sexy" "boutique" "classic" "uniquely" fashioned from "an old incinerator" strikes surveyors as "quite hip and modern for a Ritz" – from its "younger staff" to the "innovative design" of its "spacious" rooms to the "swank bar that makes you feel like you're in NYC"; "escape" the crowds at the "absolutely divine" spa or the "wonderful" Fahrenheit restaurant – "one of DC's most interesting venues."

Sofitel Lafayette Square ✕ 🛏
25 | 24 | 21 | 21 | $280

806 15th St. NW | Washington | 202-730-8800 | fax 202-730-8500 | 800-763-4835 | www.sofitel.com | 220 rooms, 17 suites

"Updated, modern" rooms "with a French accent", ultra"comfortable" beds and "great" baths with "wonderful Roger & Gallet toiletries" score points among patrons of this boutique "just steps from the White House"; "efficient" (if sometimes "snooty") service and a "quiet" location (too "isolated on weekends" for tourists) make it a good business hotel, plus a few find the New French restaurant, Café 15, "superb."

Willard InterContinental ⒽⓍ Ⓢ
24 | 25 | 23 | 24 | $575

1401 Pennsylvania Ave. NW | Washington | 202-628-9100 | fax 202-637-7326 | 800-327-0200 | www.interconti.com | 283 rooms, 41 suites

"No other hotel in DC has the history" of this "granddaddy of old-world charm" (it's where "Lincoln slept" and "M.L. King wrote the 'I Have a Dream' speech"); "gracious" service, "generous" rooms, an "excellent new spa", "one of America's great bars" (the Round Robin), "amazing ballrooms" and "a location convenient to all the National Mall Museums" appeal to an "older" crowd.

Uruguay

Carmelo

☑ Four Seasons 🏃 🛁 Ⓐ 🔍
28 | 27 | 24 | 28 | $290
(aka HCU)

Ruta 21, Km. 262 | (011-598-5) 429-000 | fax 429-001 | www.fourseasons.com | 24 suites, 20 bungalows

"Who knew that nirvana is in Uruguay" on the banks of the Rio de la Plata?; "a wonderful surprise", this "secluded" outpost in a eucalyptus and pine forest is "worth going to Uruguay for", drawing guests who want to "stay forever" for the "excellent golf", "amazing horseback riding school", "gorgeous" spa and "huge", two-level suites and bungalows, each with their own terrace; oh, and of course, the staff is "exceptional."

Punta del Este

Conrad Resort & Casino 🏌🔭🏊🔍 22 | 20 | 19 | 23 | $340

Avenida Biarritz y Artigas, Parada 4, Playa Mansa |
(011-598-42) 491-111 | fax 489-999 | 800-445-8667 |
www.conradhotels.com | 302 rooms, 24 suites

"A bit (ok, a lot) like Las Vegas", this "fantastic resort" features a "casino that's lots of fun", as well as "evening shows that are on par" with any Sin City production; of course, entertainment isn't the only thing that makes it one of the "most exciting places in South America" – the "modern facility" also offers "impeccable rooms", some with "breathtaking views" of the ocean, a "superb" staff and a trio of dining options.

Venezuela

Caracas

Tamanaco InterContinental 🔭🏊🔍 18 | 19 | 21 | 21 | $219

Final Av. Principal de las Mercedes | (011-58-212) 909-7111 |
fax 909-7116 | 888-424-6835 | www.intercontinental.com |
503 rooms, 32 suites

"Easily the tops in Caracas", this hotel is a "jewel" say fans who like to keep it a "hidden secret"; "high-class service", a location in fashionable Las Mercedes, "decent" dining and "above-average rooms" make it "worth a stay", though some add it could use "a face-lift."

Vietnam

Hanoi

Hilton Opera 🔭🏊 22 | 24 | 19 | 20 | $175

1 Le Thanh Tong St. | (011-84-4) 933-0500 | fax 933-0530 | 800-445-8667 |
www.hanoi.hilton.com | 256 rooms, 13 suites

Fans of this "modern hotel in a great location" adjacent to the Opera House consider it a "comfortable" place to stay in a "fascinating city" full of French influences; it has a "beautiful" fitness facility and "excellent service", but a few feel this "massive" Hilton can be a "bit impersonal."

Sofitel Metropole ⓗ🏊 24 | 25 | 25 | 23 | $391

15 Ngo Quyen St. | (011-84-4) 826-6919 | fax 826-6920 |
800-763-4835 | www.sofitel.com | 201 rooms, 31 suites

It feels "like you've stepped back in history" at this "grand old" French-colonial "throwback" that "oozes class and tradition"; the "friendly" staff is "top-notch", rooms offer a "wonderful bit of history", especially if you arrange to "stay in the property's old wing", and the "amazing food" includes an "unbelievable breakfast buffet"; just "remember to leave the grounds and explore Hanoi a bit."

	ROOMS	SERVICE	DINING	FACIL.	COST

Ho Chi Minh City

NEW Park Hyatt Saigon

| – | – | – | – | $240 |

2 Lam Son Sq., District 1 | (011-84-8) 824-1234 | fax 823-7569 |
www.park.hyatt.com | 231 rooms, 21 suites

This dramatic, contemporary luxury outpost in Lam Son Square near the Opera House features colonial-style rooms with hardwood floors, white marble baths with rain showers and flat-screen TVs; other highlights include a business center with a technology concierge, a spa with an outdoor pool in a landscaped garden, a casual Italian eatery with alfresco dining and a second restaurant offering Vietnamese and Western fare.

Sofitel Plaza Saigon ⊕♨♒

| 23 | 24 | 20 | 20 | $234 |

17 Le Duan Blvd. | (011-84-8) 824-1555 | fax 824-1666 |
800-763-4835 | www.sofitel.com | 279 rooms, 11 suites

"If you need a little more luxury, this is the hotel to use" say business types who tout the central location, the fare at "one of the better hotel restaurants" and the "excellent" service; rooms, however, are "a bit on the small side", so some head to the rooftop pool and enjoy "great views of the whole city" before walking to the nearby Notre Dame Cathedral and Reunification Palace.

Nha Trang

Evason Hideaway at Ana Mandara 🚻♨Ⓢ♒🔍

| 24 | 26 | 22 | 23 | $282 |

Beachside Tran Phu Blvd. | (011-84-58) 522-222 | fax 524-704 |
www.six-senses.com | 70 rooms, 4 suites

There's a mind-reading staff and "lemongrass wafting through the air to inspire relaxation" at this "ultrachic boutique hotel" that makes you feel like you're "living in a dream" – one accessible only by boat, that is; "luxury cottages" with terraces and "private outdoor showers" are tucked into the "beautiful gardens" or perched on the "spectacular" beach, while other high-end temptations such as "top-rate" food, outdoor salas at the Six Senses Spa and an array of water sports prompt rich ramblers to recommend a visit "before Nha Trang gets overdeveloped."

Zambia

Livingstone

Royal Livingstone 🚻♨♒

| ▽ 25 | 27 | 22 | 25 | $480 |

Mosi-Oa-Tunya Rd. | (011-260-3) 321-122 | fax 321-128 |
www.suninternational.co.za | 169 rooms, 4 suites

"Monkeys and zebras roaming" outside your "charming" Edwardian-style room and a location "within walking distance of Victoria Falls" bring visitors back to this David Livingstone–inspired resort complex of many buildings nestled along the great Zambezi River; further draws are the "lush" grounds with "stunning" water views and "very friendly staff", but some surveyors are less impressed with the "overpriced" dining.

Zimbabwe

Victoria Falls

Victoria Falls Hotel ⊕ ♨ ≈ ◈ | 20 | 23 | 19 | 21 | $322 |

10 Mallet Dr. | (011-263-13) 44751 | fax 42354 | 800-223-6800 |
www.victoriafallshotel.com | 143 rooms, 18 suites

Over a century old, this "stately" "grande dame" in a "fabulous location" overlooking the mists of Victoria Falls has its "old-world"
"colonial charm still intact"; the "heavenly" staff "treats guests like
royalty", the "grounds are wonderful", the "views are magnificent"
and the food is "delicious"; still, some find it a bit "stuffy" and "faded."

Victoria Falls Safari Lodge ♨ ⓢ ≈ | 21 | 22 | 19 | 22 | $394 |
(aka VFSL)

Stand 471, Squire Cummings Rd. | (011-263-13) 43211 | fax 43205 |
www.vfsl.com | 66 rooms, 6 suites

Set high on a plateau adjacent to the Zambezi National Park and two-
and-a-half miles from Victoria Falls, this "very good hotel" is an "exotic" break from the everyday; sampling local delicacies while "eating
outside under the wooden roof" of the Boma restaurant and "watching
elephants and buffalos drink in the pond is amazing" and contributes
to the "hypnotizing atmosphere"; just remember that "the warnings
about locking your doors to prevent monkeys and baboons from
getting in are for real!"

INDEXES

Hotel Types

Indexes list the best in each category. Listings are arranged by country and are followed by nearest major city where needed. ☒ indicates places with the highest ratings, popularity and importance.

ALL-INCLUSIVE

ANTIGUA
Curtain Bluff
Jumby Bay
Sandals Resort
St. James's Club

ARUBA
Divi Aruba Beach

AUSTRALIA
Bedarra Island | *Great Barrier Reef*
Voyages Lizard Island | *Great Barrier Reef*
Wilson Island | *Great Barrier Reef*

BAHAMAS
Club Med
Musha Cay
Sandals Royal

BELIZE
Cayo Espanto | *San Pedro*

BERMUDA
Pink Beach Club

BHUTAN
Amankora | *Paro*

BOTSWANA
Abu Camp | *Okavango Delta*
Camp Okavango | *Okavango Delta*
Chief's Camp | *Okavango Delta*
Chobe Chilwero | *Chobe National Park*
Khwai River Lodge | *Okavango Delta*
☒ Mombo Camp | *Okavango Delta*
Savute Elephant Camp | *Chobe National Park*

BRITISH VIRGIN ISLANDS
Biras Creek Resort | *Virgin Gorda*
Guana Island | *Virgin Gorda*
Necker Island | *Virgin Gorda*
Peter Island | *Peter Island*

CANADA
Alive Health | *Canadian Rockies*
Kingsbrae Arms | *St. Andrews*

CHILE
Explora En Atacama | *Atacama*
Explora En Patagonia | *Patagonia*

COSTA RICA
La Paloma Lodge | *Osa Peninsula*

DOMINICAN REPUBLIC
Excellence Punta Cana

FIJI
Turtle Island
Vatulele Island

FRANCE
Château Eza | *Côte d'Azur*
Évian Royal Palace | *Haute-Savoie*
Grand Cap-Ferrat | *Côte d'Azur*

GREECE
Elounda Mare | *Crete*

GRENADINES
Petit St. Vincent | *Petit St. Vincent*

IRELAND
Dromoland Castle | *County Clare*

ISRAEL
☒ Carmel Forest Spa | *Haifa*

JAMAICA
Beaches Boscobel | *Ocho Rios*
Couples Sans Souci | *Ocho Rios*
Couples Swept Away | *Negril*
Grand Lido | *Negril*
Grand Lido Braco | *Montego Bay*
Sandals | *Montego Bay*
Sandals Dunn's River | *Ocho Rios*
Sandals Grande | *Ocho Rios*
Sandals Negril Beach | *Negril*

KENYA
Giraffe Manor | *Nairobi*
Governor's Camp | *Masai Mara Game Reserve*

Kichwa Tembo | *Masai Mara Game Reserve*
Little Governor's | *Masai Mara Game Reserve*
Mara Serena | *Masai Mara Game Reserve*

MEXICO
NEW Excellence Riviera | *Cancún*
Iberostar | *Cancún*
La Jolla/Mismaloya | *Puerto Vallarta*
Rancho La Puerta | *Baja Peninsula*
Z Royal Hideaway | *Playa del Carmen*
Secrets Capri | *Cancún*

MOROCCO
La Gazelle d'Or | *Taroudant*

NEW ZEALAND
Z Blanket Bay | *Queenstown*
Huka Lodge | *Taupo*
Z Kauri Cliffs | *Kerikeri*
Z Wharekauhau | *Featherston*

SEYCHELLES
Frégate Island
North Island

SOUTH AFRICA
Bushmans Kloof | *Biedouw Valley*
Inyati/Game Lodge | *Kruger Area*
Kwandwe/Game Reserve | *Benmore*
Z Londolozi | *Kruger Area*
MalaMala | *Kruger Area*
Z Singita | *Kruger Area*
Ulusaba/Game Reserve | *Kruger Area*

ST. LUCIA
Sandals Grande
Sandals Regency

TANZANIA
Mnemba Island | *Zanzibar*
Ngorongoro Crater | *Ngorongoro*
Ngorongoro Serena | *Ngorongoro*

THAILAND
Z Four Seasons Tented | *Golden Triangle*

UNITED STATES
Le Merigot Beach | *Los Angeles*

BEACH RESORT

ANGUILLA
CuisinArt Resort
Malliouhana

ANTIGUA
Carlisle Bay
Curtain Bluff
Jumby Bay
Sandals Resort
St. James's Club

ARUBA
Aruba Resort
Divi Aruba Beach
Marriott Resort
Marriott's/Ocean Club
Radisson Resort
Renaissance

AUSTRALIA
Bedarra Island | *Great Barrier Reef*
Dunk Island | *Great Barrier Reef*
Z Hayman Island | *Great Barrier Reef*
Hyatt Regency | *Sunshine Coast*
Sebel Reef House | *Great Barrier Reef*
Sheraton Mirage | *Gold Coast*
Sheraton Mirage | *Great Barrier Reef*
Voyages Lizard Island | *Great Barrier Reef*

BAHAMAS
Atlantis
Club Med
Four Seasons
Musha Cay
Z One & Only
Pink Sands
Sandals Royal
Westin Our Lucaya

BARBADOS
Cobblers Cove
Coral Reef Club
Crane
Z Sandy Lane

BELIZE
Kanantik Reef | *Dangriga*
Turtle Inn | *Placencia*

BERMUDA
Cambridge Beaches
Elbow Beach
Fairmont Southampton
Pink Beach Club
Reefs

BRAZIL
Sheraton | *Rio de Janeiro*

BRITISH VIRGIN ISLANDS
Biras Creek Resórt | *Virgin Gorda*
Bitter End | *Virgin Gorda*
Guana Island | *Virgin Gorda*
Little Dix Bay | *Virgin Gorda*
Long Bay Resort | *Tortola*
Peter Island | *Peter Island*

CANADA
Aerie | *Victoria*
Fairmont Algonquin | *St. Andrews*
Rimrock | *Canadian Rockies*

CAYMAN ISLANDS
Hyatt Regency
🅩 Ritz-Carlton

COSTA RICA
La Paloma Lodge | *Osa Peninsula*
Los Sueños Marriott | *Puntarenas*
Paradisus | *Guanacaste*
Punta Islita | *Guanacaste*

CURAÇAO
🅩 Kura Hulanda
Marriott Beach

CYPRUS
Anassa | *Polis*

DOMINICAN REPUBLIC
Casa de Campo
Punta Cana

EGYPT
🅩 Four Seasons | *Red Sea*
Oberoi Sahl Hasheesh | *Red Sea*
Ritz-Carlton | *Red Sea*

FIJI
Shangri-La's Fijian
Sheraton
Vatulele Island
Wakaya Club
NEW Westin Denarau

FRANCE
🅩 Four Seasons Resort | *Provence*
Grand Cap-Ferrat | *Côte d'Azur*
La Réserve/Beaulieu | *Côte d'Azur*
Martinez | *Côte d'Azur*

FRENCH POLYNESIA
Bora Bora Lagoon | *Bora Bora*
Bora Bora Pearl | *Bora Bora*
InterContinental | *Moorea*
Le Méridien | *Bora Bora*
Le Méridien | *Tahiti*
Le Taha'a | *Taha'a*

GREECE
Astir Palace | *Athens*
🅩 Blue Palace Resort | *Crete*
Elounda Beach | *Crete*
Santa Marina | *Mykonos*
Vedema Resort | *Santorini*

GRENADINES
Cotton House | *Mustique*
Petit St. Vincent | *Petit St. Vincent*
Raffles Resort | *Canouan Island*

INDONESIA
🅩 Amankila | *Bali*
🅩 Amanusa | *Bali*
Banyan Tree | *Bintan*
🅩 Four Seasons Jimbaran Bay | *Bali*
Grand Hyatt | *Bali*
InterContinental | *Bali*
Laguna Resort | *Bali*
Le Méridien Nirwana | *Bali*
🅩 Ritz-Carlton | *Bali*

ITALY
Buca di Bacco | *Amalfi Coast*
🅩 Cala di Volpe | *Sardinia*
Capri Palace | *Amalfi Coast*
Des Bains | *Venice*
🅩 Il San Pietro | *Amalfi Coast*
Le Sirenuse | *Amalfi Coast*
Palazzo Sasso | *Amalfi Coast*
Pitrizza | *Sardinia*
Romazzino | *Sardinia*
Santa Caterina | *Amalfi Coast*
🅩 Villa d'Este | *Lake Como Area*

JAMAICA
Beaches Boscobel | *Ocho Rios*
Couples Sans Souci | *Ocho Rios*

subscribe to zagat.com

Couples Swept Away | *Negril*
Grand Lido | *Negril*
Grand Lido Braco | *Montego Bay*
Half Moon | *Montego Bay*
Ritz-Carlton Golf | *Montego Bay*
Rose Hall Resort | *Montego Bay*
Round Hill | *Montego Bay*
Sandals | *Montego Bay*
Sandals Dunn's River | *Ocho Rios*
Sandals Grande | *Ocho Rios*
Sandals Negril Beach | *Negril*
Tryall Club | *Montego Bay*

MALAYSIA
Ⓩ Datai | *Langkawi*
Four Seasons | *Langkawi*
Pangkor Laut | *Langkawi*
Tanjong Jara | *Penang*

MALDIVES
Banyan Tree
Four Seasons/Kuda Huraa
NEW Four Seasons/Landaa Giraavaru
Soneva Fushi
Taj Exotica
NEW W Retreat & Spa

MAURITIUS
Le Prince Maurice
Le Saint Géran
Le Touessrok
Oberoi
Taj Exotica

MEXICO
Aventura Spa | *Cancún*
Casa Del Mar | *Baja Peninsula*
CasaMagna Marriott | *Cancún*
CasaMagna Marriott | *Puerto Vallarta*
Dreams Los Cabos | *Baja Peninsula*
Dreams | *Cancún*
Dreams | *Puerto Vallarta*
Ⓩ Esperanza | *Baja Peninsula*
Fairmont Pierre | *Acapulco*
Fairmont/Princess | *Acapulco*
Fiesta Americana | *Baja Peninsula*
Fiesta Americana | *Cancún*
Ⓩ Four Seasons | *Punta Mita*
Gran Meliá | *Cancún*

Hilton Beach | *Cancún*
Iberostar | *Cancún*
JW Marriott | *Cancún*
La Jolla/Mismaloya | *Puerto Vallarta*
Las Alamandas | *Manzanillo*
Las Brisas | *Acapulco*
Las Brisas | *Ixtapa*
Las Hadas | *Manzanillo*
Ⓩ Las Ventanas | *Baja Peninsula*
Le Méridien | *Cancún*
Maroma | *Cancún*
Omni | *Cancún*
Ⓩ One & Only | *Baja Peninsula*
Ⓩ Ritz-Carlton | *Cancún*
Ⓩ Royal Hideaway | *Playa del Carmen*
Twin Dolphin | *Baja Peninsula*
Villa del Sol | *Zihuatanejo*
Westin | *Cancún*

NEPAL
Le Méridien | *Kathmandu*

NEW ZEALAND
Ⓩ Kauri Cliffs | *Kerikeri*

OMAN
Shangri-La | *Muscat*

PALAU
Palau Royal Resort | *Koror*

PHILIPPINES
Amanpulo | *Cuyo Islands*
Shangri-La | *Cebu*

PORTUGAL
Quinta do Lago | *Algarve*
Sheraton Algarve | *Algarve*

QATAR
NEW Sharq Village & Spa | *Doha*

SEYCHELLES
Banyan Tree
Frégate Island
Lémuria Resort
Taj Denis Island

SOUTH AFRICA
Palace of the Lost City | *Sun City*

SPAIN
Marbella Club | *Costa del Sol*
Mardavall | *Mallorca*

SRI LANKA
Amanwella

ST. BARTS
Eden Rock
Guanahani & Spa

ST. KITTS & NEVIS
Z Four Seasons | *Nevis*

ST. LUCIA
Anse Chastanet
Jalousie Plantation
Ladera
Sandals Grande
Sandals Regency
Windjammer Landing

ST. MAARTEN
Oyster Bay Beach
Wyndham Sapphire

ST. MARTIN
La Samanna
L'Habitation/Lonvilliers

SWITZERLAND
Kempinski Grand | *St. Moritz*

TANZANIA
Mnemba Island | *Zanzibar*

THAILAND
Z Amanpuri | *Phuket*
Z Banyan Tree | *Phuket*
Chedi | *Phuket*
Chiva-Som | *Hua Hin*
Evason | *Hua Hin*
Evason | *Phuket*
NEW Four Seasons Resort | *Koh Samui*
JW Marriott | *Phuket*
Le Royal Méridien | *Koh Samui*
Rayavadee | *Phuket*
Sheraton Grande | *Phuket*

TURKS & CAICOS
NEW Amanyara
Grace Bay Club
Ocean Club/West
Parrot Cay

UNITED ARAB EMIRATES
Z Burj Al Arab | *Dubai*
Jumeirah Beach | *Dubai*

Le Royal Méridien | *Dubai*
Z One & Only | *Dubai*

UNITED STATES
Casa Del Mar | *Los Angeles*
Z Fairmont Kea Lani | *Hawaii*
Fisher Island | *Miami*
Z Four Seasons/Hualalai | *Hawaii*
Z NEW Four Seasons/Lanai | *Hawaii*
Z Four Seasons Wailea | *Hawaii*
Z Grand Hyatt | *Hawaii*
Grand Wailea Resort | *Hawaii*
Z Halekulani | *Hawaii*
Z Kahala | *Hawaii*
Loews Santa Monica | *Los Angeles*
Princeville Resort | *Hawaii*
Z Ritz-Carlton Kapalua | *Hawaii*
Z Ritz-Carlton Key Biscayne | *Miami*
Ritz-Carlton South Beach | *Miami*

URUGUAY
Conrad Resort | *Punta del Este*
Z Four Seasons | *Carmelo*

VIETNAM
Evason Hideaway | *Nha Trang*

BED & BREAKFAST/INN

CANADA
Z Hastings House | *Vancouver*
Pillar and Post Inn | *Niagara Falls*
Sooke Harbour | *Victoria*
Wickaninnish Inn | *Victoria*

COSTA RICA
Finca Rosa Blanca | *San José*

DENMARK
Sonderho Kro | *Copenhagen*

FRANCE
Château de Noirieux | *Loire*
La Bastide/Moustiers | *Provence*
Le Moulin/L'Abbaye | *Dordogne*
Les Deux Abbesses | *Haute-Loire*
Le Vieux Logis | *Dordogne*
Oustau Baumanière | *Provence*

ITALY
Inn at Spanish Steps | *Rome*

JAMAICA
Jamaica Inn | *Ocho Rios*

JAPAN
Tawaraya Ryokan | *Kyoto*

MEXICO
Casa/Sierra Nevada | *San Miguel de Allende*

SOUTH AFRICA
Lanzerac Manor | *Cape Town*

UNITED KINGDOM - ENGLAND
Ⓩ Gidleigh Park | *Devon*
Lower Slaughter | *Cotswolds*
Lygon Arms | *Cotswolds*
Sharrow Bay | *Cumbria*
Whatley Manor | *Cotswolds*

UNITED KINGDOM - SCOTLAND
Culloden House | *Inverness*

UNITED STATES
Inn at Langley | *Seattle*
Ⓩ Inn/Little Washington | *Washington, DC*
Willows Lodge | *Seattle*

BOUTIQUE

ARGENTINA
NEW Cavas Wine Lodge | *Agrelo*

AUSTRALIA
Lilianfels Blue Mtns. | *Blue Mountains*
Sir Stamford | *Sydney*

AUSTRIA
Goldener Hirsch | *Salzburg*
Imperial | *Vienna*

BAHAMAS
Rock House

BARBADOS
Lone Star

BELGIUM
Heritage, Hotel | *Brugges*

CAMBODIA
Shinta Mani | *Siem Reap*

CANADA
NEW Adara | *Canadian Rockies*
Auberge du Vieux-Port | *Montréal*
Auberge Saint Antoine | *Québec City*

Dominion 1912 | *Québec City*
Kingsbrae Arms | *St. Andrews*
La Pinsonnière | *Québec City*
Le Germain | *Montréal*
Loews Hotel Vogue | *Montréal*
Opus | *Vancouver*
Wedgewood | *Vancouver*

CHINA
Jia | *Hong Kong*
Mandarin Oriental/Landmark | *Hong Kong*

CYPRUS
Almyra | *Paphos*

CZECH REPUBLIC
Savoy | *Prague*

ESTONIA
Three Sisters | *Tallinn*

FRANCE
Astor Saint-Honore | *Paris*
Château de Bagnols | *Rhône*
Château de Marçay | *Loire*
Château Eza | *Côte d'Azur*
Costes | *Paris*
de Crillon | *Paris*
d'Europe | *Provence*
de Vendôme | *Paris*
Domaine/Hauts de Loire | *Loire*
du Petit Moulin | *Paris*
Ⓩ La Maison Troisgros | *Loire*
Lancaster | *Paris*
Ⓩ Michel Bras | *Aveyron*
Montalembert | *Paris*
Murano Urban | *Paris*
Negresco | *Côte d'Azur*
Pavillon de la Reine | *Paris*
Ⓩ Plaza Athénée | *Paris*
Raphael | *Paris*
Relais Christine | *Paris*
Saint James | *Paris*

GERMANY
Eisenhut | *Rothenburg*
Schloss. Bühlerhöhe | *Baden-Baden*
25hours | *Hamburg*

INDONESIA
Dharmawangsa | *Jakarta*
Viceroy Bali | *Bali*

IRELAND
Clarence | *Dublin*
Morgan | *Dublin*
Morrison | *Dublin*
Park Hotel Kenmare | *County Kerry*

ITALY
Beacci Tornabuoni | *Florence*
Bulgari Milan | *Milan*
Caesar Augustus | *Amalfi Coast*
Ca'Pisani | *Venice*
Eden Roc | *Amalfi Coast*
Gallery Hotel Art | *Florence*
Helvetia & Bristol | *Florence*
Il Sole Di Ranco | *Milan*
Lord Byron | *Rome*
Luna | *Venice*
Lungarno | *Florence*
Monaco | *Venice*
Park Hyatt | *Milan*
Regency | *Florence*
Relais La Suvera | *Siena*
Straf | *Milan*

JAMAICA
Jamaica Inn | *Ocho Rios*

JAPAN
Four Seasons/Marunouchi | *Tokyo*
Hiiragiya Ryokan | *Kyoto*

MEXICO
Antigua Villa | *San Miguel de Allende*
Casa Natalia | *Baja Peninsula*
Habitá | *Mexico City*
Secreto | *Cancún*

MOROCCO
Ksar Char-Bagh | *Marrakech*

NETHERLANDS
Dylan | *Amsterdam*
Le Méridien | *The Hague*
Seven One Seven | *Amsterdam*

POLAND
Rialto | *Warsaw*

PORTUGAL
Bairro Alto | *Lisbon*
Palácio Belmonte | *Lisbon*

SOUTH AFRICA
☑ Cape Grace | *Cape Town*
Ellerman House | *Cape Town*
Le Quartier Francais | *Franschhoek*
Plettenberg | *Plettenberg Bay*
Saxon | *Johannesburg*

SOUTH KOREA
W Seoul-Walkerhill | *Seoul*

SPAIN
Adler | *Madrid*
Casa Camper | *Barcelona*
Claris | *Barcelona*
Neri | *Barcelona*
Omm | *Barcelona*
Palace | *Barcelona*
Puerta America | *Madrid*
Son Brull | *Mallorca*
Villa Magna | *Madrid*

ST. KITTS & NEVIS
Montpelier | *Nevis*

SWEDEN
Berns Hotel | *Stockholm*
Hotel J | *Stockholm*
Rival | *Stockholm*
Stallmastaregarden | *Stockholm*

SWITZERLAND
Eden au Lac | *Zurich*

UNITED KINGDOM - ENGLAND
Bath Priory | *Cotswolds*
Blakes | *London*
Capital Hotel | *London*
Charlotte St. | *London*
Covent Garden | *London*
Dorset Square | *London*
51 Buckingham Gate | *London*
Hempel | *London*
Milestone | *London*
One Aldwych | *London*
Royal Crescent | *Cotswolds*
Sanderson | *London*
Soho Hotel | *London*
St. Martins Lane | *London*
Threadneedles | *London*
22 Jermyn St. | *London*

subscribe to zagat.com

UNITED KINGDOM – SCOTLAND
One Devonshire | *Glasgow*

UNITED STATES
☑ Bel-Air | *Los Angeles*
Bellevue Club | *Seattle*
Burnham | *Chicago*
Campton Place | *San Francisco*
Chambers | *New York City*
Chateau Marmont | *Los Angeles*
Fifteen Beacon | *Boston*
Grove Isle | *Miami*
Huntington | *San Francisco*
Jefferson | *Washington, DC*
Lancaster | *Houston*
Le Merigot Beach | *Los Angeles*
Library | *New York City*
Lowell | *New York City*
Mansion/Turtle Creek | *Dallas/Ft. Worth*
Mercer | *New York City*
Monaco | *Chicago*
Monaco | *Washington, DC*
Mondrian | *Los Angeles*
Palomar | *San Francisco*
☑ Park Hyatt | *Chicago*
Plaza Athénée | *New York City*
Rittenhouse | *Philadelphia*
Ritz-Carlton | *New Orleans*
Setai | *Miami*
Sherry-Netherland | *New York City*
Sofitel | *Philadelphia*
Sofitel | *Washington, DC*
Viceroy | *Los Angeles*
Victor | *Miami*
W Westwood | *Los Angeles*
Zaza | *Dallas/Ft. Worth*

BUSINESS-ORIENTED

ARGENTINA
Park Tower | *Buenos Aires*

AUSTRALIA
Four Seasons | *Sydney*
Grand Hyatt | *Melbourne*
Observatory | *Sydney*
Park Hyatt | *Sydney*
Westin | *Sydney*

BELGIUM
Royal Windsor | *Brussels*

BERMUDA
Fairmont Hamilton
Waterloo House

BRAZIL
InterContinental | *São Paulo*

CANADA
Four Seasons | *Vancouver*
Laurel Point | *Victoria*
Le Royal Méridien | *Toronto*
Metropolitan | *Vancouver*
Omni | *Montréal*
Park Hyatt | *Toronto*

CHILE
San Cristobal Tower | *Santiago*

CHINA
Conrad Int'l | *Hong Kong*
Kerry Centre | *Beijing*
Kowloon Shangri-La | *Hong Kong*
Mandarin Oriental | *Hong Kong*
Ritz-Carlton | *Hong Kong*
St. Regis | *Beijing*
☑ St. Regis | *Shanghai*

EGYPT
Conrad | *Cairo*
Four Seasons/First Residence | *Cairo*

FRANCE
Hyatt Reg./de Gaulle | *Paris*
InterContinental | *Paris*

GERMANY
Hyatt Regency | *Cologne*
Kempinski/Bristol | *Berlin*

INDIA
Oberoi Grand | *Calcutta*
Taj Palace | *New Delhi*

INDONESIA
Mandarin Oriental | *Jakarta*

IRELAND
Fitzwilliam | *Dublin*

ISRAEL
King David | *Jerusalem*
Regency | *Jerusalem*

ITALY
Bauer | *Venice*
☑ Four Seasons | *Milan*
Savoy | *Florence*
Westin Palace | *Milan*

JAPAN
Grand Hyatt | *Tokyo*

JORDAN
☑ Four Seasons | *Amman*

KENYA
Norfolk | *Nairobi*

MALAYSIA
Mandarin Oriental | *Kuala Lumpur*

MEXICO
☑ Four Seasons | *Mexico City*
JW Marriott | *Mexico City*
Marquis Reforma | *Mexico City*
Nikko | *Mexico City*

NETHERLANDS
Okura | *Amsterdam*

NORWAY
Grand | *Oslo*

PHILIPPINES
Mandarin Oriental | *Manila*

POLAND
Sheraton | *Warsaw*

PORTUGAL
Four Seasons | *Lisbon*

RUSSIA
Grand/Europe | *St. Petersburg*

SINGAPORE
Conrad Centennial
Four Seasons
Fullerton
Grand Hyatt
Le Méridien
Marina Mandarin
Meritus Mandarin
Raffles The Plaza
Regent
☑ Ritz-Carlton Millenia
Shangri-La
Sheraton Towers
Swissôtel Merchant Ct.
Swissôtel/Stamford

SOUTH AFRICA
Grace in Rosebank | *Johannesburg*
Michelangelo | *Johannesburg*
Table Bay | *Cape Town*

SOUTH KOREA
Westin Chosun | *Seoul*

SPAIN
AC Santo Mauro | *Madrid*
InterContinental | *Madrid*
Villa Magna | *Madrid*
Wellington | *Madrid*
Westin Palace | *Madrid*

SWITZERLAND
Mandarin Oriental | *Geneva*
President Wilson | *Geneva*
Raffles | *Montreux*

TAIWAN
Sherwood | *Taipei*
Westin | *Taipei*

THAILAND
Conrad | *Bangkok*
Dusit Thani | *Bangkok*
Four Seasons | *Bangkok*
Shangri-La | *Bangkok*

UNITED ARAB EMIRATES
Jumeirah Emirates | *Dubai*
Shangri-La | *Dubai*

UNITED KINGDOM – ENGLAND
Four Seasons | *London*
Four Seasons Canary Wharf | *London*

UNITED STATES
☑ Bellagio | *Las Vegas*
Caesars Palace | *Las Vegas*
Ritz-Carlton | *New Orleans*
W Westwood | *Los Angeles*

VIETNAM
Sofitel Metropole | *Hanoi*

CONVENTION

AUSTRALIA
Crowne Plaza | *Sydney*
Sheraton on the Park | *Sydney*
Westin | *Sydney*

BELGIUM
Amigo | *Brussels*

CANADA
Westin | *Calgary*
Westin Bayshore | *Vancouver*

CHILE
Sheraton Miramar | *Santiago*

CHINA
Le Méridien She Shan | *Shanghai*
Shangri-La/Zhongshan | *Hong Kong*

EGYPT
Cairo Marriott | *Cairo*

FRANCE
Le Palais/Mediterranée | *Côte d'Azur*

GERMANY
Ritz-Carlton | *Wolfsburg*

GREECE
Astir Palace | *Athens*
Atheneum InterCont. | *Athens*

GUATEMALA
Westin Camino Real | *Guatemala City*

ITALY
Bauer | *Venice*
Danieli | *Venice*
Gritti Palace | *Venice*
San Domenico | *Sicily*
Westin Europa | *Venice*

JAPAN
Hyatt Regency | *Osaka*

NETHERLANDS
Okura | *Amsterdam*

NEW ZEALAND
InterContinental | *Wellington*

POLAND
Sheraton | *Warsaw*

PORTUGAL
Sheraton Algarve | *Algarve*

SINGAPORE
Swissôtel/Stamford

SPAIN
InterContinental | *Madrid*
Rey Juan Carlos I | *Barcelona*

SWITZERLAND
Mandarin Oriental | *Geneva*
President Wilson | *Geneva*

THAILAND
Royal Orchid | *Bangkok*

UNITED ARAB EMIRATES
Jumeirah Beach | *Dubai*
Jumeirah Emirates | *Dubai*

UNITED KINGDOM – ENGLAND
Four Seasons Canary Wharf | *London*
Sheraton | *London*

UNITED STATES
Biltmore | *Miami*
Fairmont | *Chicago*
Fairmont | *Washington, DC*
🔲 Grand Hyatt | *Hawaii*
Grand Wailea Resort | *Hawaii*
InterContinental | *Atlanta*
JW Marriott | *Las Vegas*
Loews | *Las Vegas*
Loews Santa Monica | *Los Angeles*
🔲 Mandarin Oriental | *New York City*
Mandarin Oriental | *San Francisco*
🔲 Phoenician | *Phoenix/Scottsdale*
Princeville Resort | *Hawaii*
Renaissance | *Chicago*
🔲 Ritz-Carlton | *Orlando*
Ritz-Carlton Buckhead | *Atlanta*
🔲 Ritz-Carlton Kapalua | *Hawaii*
Ritz-Carlton Marina del Rey | *Los Angeles*
Taj Boston | *Boston*
Venetian | *Las Vegas*
Willard InterCont. | *Washington, DC*

URUGUAY
Conrad Resort | *Punta del Este*

COTTAGES/VILLAS

ANGUILLA
Cap Juluca
St. Regis

ANTIGUA
Jumby Bay
St. James's Club

ARGENTINA
NEW Cavas Wine Lodge | *Agrelo*

AUSTRALIA
Bedarra Island | *Great Barrier Reef*
Daintree Eco Lodge | *Great Barrier Reef*
Z Hayman Island | *Great Barrier Reef*
Hyatt Regency | *Sunshine Coast*
Palazzo Versace | *Gold Coast*
Sheraton Mirage | *Gold Coast*
Sheraton Mirage | *Great Barrier Reef*
Voyages Lizard Island | *Great Barrier Reef*

AUSTRIA
Schloss Fuschl | *Salzburg*

BAHAMAS
Four Seasons
Musha Cay
Z One & Only
Pink Sands

BARBADOS
Lone Star
Z Sandy Lane

BELIZE
Blancaneaux | *San Ignacio*
Cayo Espanto | *San Pedro*
Chaa Creek | *San Ignacio*
Turtle Inn | *Placencia*

BERMUDA
Ariel Sands
Cambridge Beaches
Elbow Beach

BHUTAN
Uma Paro | *Paro*

BOTSWANA
Abu Camp | *Okavango Delta*

BRITISH VIRGIN ISLANDS
Bitter End | *Virgin Gorda*
Guana Island | *Virgin Gorda*
Little Dix Bay | *Virgin Gorda*
Long Bay Resort | *Tortola*
Necker Island | *Virgin Gorda*
Peter Island | *Peter Island*
Sugar Mill | *Tortola*

CANADA
Z Hastings House | *Vancouver*
Keltic Lodge | *Cape Breton*

COSTA RICA
Finca Rosa Blanca | *San José*
Punta Islita | *Guanacaste*

DOMINICAN REPUBLIC
Casa de Campo
Punta Cana

FIJI
Shangri-La's Fijian
Turtle Island
Vatulele Island
Wakaya Club

FRANCE
Z Four Seasons Resort | *Provence*
La Réserve/Beaulieu | *Côte d'Azur*
Z Le Château/St-Martin | *Côte d'Azur*
Les Deux Abbesses | *Haute-Loire*

FRENCH POLYNESIA
Bora Bora Lagoon | *Bora Bora*
Le Taha'a | *Taha'a*
NEW St. Regis | *Bora Bora*

GREECE
Z Blue Palace Resort | *Crete*
Santa Marina | *Mykonos*
Vedema Resort | *Santorini*

GRENADINES
Cotton House | *Mustique*
Petit St. Vincent | *Petit St. Vincent*
Raffles Resort | *Canouan Island*

INDIA
Leela Goa | *Goa*
Le Méridien Jaipur | *Rajasthan*
Z Rajvilas Oberoi | *Rajasthan*

INDONESIA
Z Amandari | *Bali*
Banyan Tree | *Bintan*
Z Como Shambala | *Bali*
Z Four Seasons Jimbaran Bay | *Bali*
Four Seasons Sayan | *Bali*
Grand Hyatt | *Bali*
Le Méridien Nirwana | *Bali*
Puri Wulandari | *Bali*

☒ Ritz-Carlton | *Bali*
Viceroy Bali | *Bali*

IRELAND
☒ Adare Manor | *County Limerick*
Sheen Falls Lodge | *County Kerry*

ITALY
Pitrizza | *Sardinia*
San Domenico | *Sicily*
☒ Villa d'Este | *Lake Como Area*

JAMAICA
Half Moon | *Montego Bay*
Jamaica Inn | *Ocho Rios*
Round Hill | *Montego Bay*
Sandals Grande | *Ocho Rios*
Strawberry Hill | *Kingston*
Tryall Club | *Montego Bay*

KENYA
Mount Kenya Safari | *Nanyuki*
Windsor Golf | *Nairobi*

MALAYSIA
☒ Datai | *Langkawi*
Four Seasons | *Langkawi*
Pangkor Laut | *Langkawi*

MALDIVES
Banyan Tree
Four Seasons/Kuda Huraa
NEW Four Seasons/Landaa
  Giraavaru
One & Only
Soneva Fushi
Taj Exotica

MAURITIUS
Le Saint Géran
Le Touessrok
Oberoi
Taj Exotica

MEXICO
☒ Esperanza | *Baja Peninsula*
Hilton Beach | *Cancún*
Hyatt Caribe | *Cancún*
Ikal del Mar | *Playa del Carmen*
NH Krystal | *Puerto Vallarta*
Omni | *Cancún*
Rancho La Puerta | *Baja Peninsula*

NEW ZEALAND
Huka Lodge | *Taupo*
Millbrook | *Queenstown*
☒ Wharekauhau | *Featherston*

PANAMA
Gamboa Rainforest | *Gamboa*

PHILIPPINES
Amanpulo | *Cuyo Islands*

SEYCHELLES
Banyan Tree
Frégate Island
Lémuria Resort
North Island
Taj Denis Island

SOUTH AFRICA
Bay Hotel | *Cape Town*
Cellars-Hohenort | *Cape Town*
Ellerman House | *Cape Town*
Ngala/Game Reserve | *Kruger Area*
Phinda/Game Reserve | *Kruger Area*

SPAIN
Marbella Club | *Costa del Sol*

ST. BARTS
Eden Rock
François Plantation
Isle de France
Le Toiny
Manapany

ST. KITTS & NEVIS
☒ Four Seasons | *Nevis*

ST. LUCIA
Jalousie Plantation
Ladera
Sandals Regency
Windjammer Landing

ST. MAARTEN
Wyndham Sapphire

ST. MARTIN
La Samanna

TANZANIA
Mnemba Island | *Zanzibar*
Zamani Kempinski | *Zanzibar*

THAILAND
- ☑ Amanpuri | *Phuket*
- ☑ Banyan Tree | *Phuket*
- Evason | *Hua Hin*
- Evason | *Phuket*
- **NEW** Four Seasons Resort | *Koh Samui*
- Grand Hyatt Erawan | *Bangkok*
- Le Royal Méridien | *Koh Samui*
- Napasai | *Koh Samui*
- Rayavadee | *Phuket*
- Sheraton Grande | *Phuket*

TURKS & CAICOS
- Grace Bay Club
- Parrot Cay

UNITED ARAB EMIRATES
- Jumeirah Beach | *Dubai*
- ☑ One & Only | *Dubai*

UNITED KINGDOM – ENGLAND
- Cliveden House | *Berkshire*
- ☑ Gidleigh Park | *Devon*
- Lugger | *Cornwall*

UNITED KINGDOM – SCOTLAND
- ☑ Westin Turnberry | *Ayrshire*

UNITED STATES
- ☑ Boulders | *Phoenix/Scottsdale*
- Chateau Marmont | *Los Angeles*
- ☑ Fairmont Kea Lani | *Hawaii*
- Fisher Island | *Miami*
- ☑ Four Seasons/Hualalai | *Hawaii*
- ☑ Peninsula | *Los Angeles*
- ☑ Phoenician | *Phoenix/Scottsdale*
- Ritz-Carlton Huntington | *Los Angeles*
- ☑ Royal Palms | *Phoenix/Scottsdale*
- Soniat House | *New Orleans*

DESTINATION SPA

AUSTRALIA
- Daintree Eco Lodge | *Great Barrier Reef*

COSTA RICA
- Tabacón Grand Spa | *Arenal*

CYPRUS
- Anassa | *Polis*

FRANCE
- Évian Royal Palace | *Haute-Savoie*

GERMANY
- Brenner's Park | *Baden-Baden*
- Nassauer Hof | *Wiesbaden*
- Schloss. Bühlerhöhe | *Baden-Baden*

GREECE
- ☑ Blue Palace Resort | *Crete*

HUNGARY
- Danubius | *Budapest*

INDIA
- Wildflower Hall | *Shimla*

INDONESIA
- ☑ Amandari | *Bali*
- Banyan Tree | *Bintan*
- ☑ Four Seasons Jimbaran Bay | *Bali*
- Mandarin Oriental | *Surabaya*
- Nusa Dua Beach | *Bali*
- Viceroy Bali | *Bali*

IRELAND
- Park Hotel Kenmare | *County Kerry*

ISRAEL
- ☑ Carmel Forest Spa | *Haifa*
- Herods Vitalis Spa | *Eilat*
- Mizpe Hayamim | *Rosh Pinna*

MALAYSIA
- Pangkor Laut | *Langkawi*

MALDIVES
- Taj Exotica

MAURITIUS
- Taj Exotica

MEXICO
- Aventura Spa | *Cancún*
- ☑ Esperanza | *Baja Peninsula*
- ☑ Las Ventanas | *Baja Peninsula*
- Maya Tulum | *Tulum*
- Rancho La Puerta | *Baja Peninsula*

SPAIN
- Son Brull | *Mallorca*

SRI LANKA
- Amangalla

SWITZERLAND
- Kempinski Grand | *St. Moritz*
- Mont Cervin Palace | *Zermatt*

THAILAND
Chedi | *Phuket*
Chiva-Som | *Hua Hin*
Evason | *Hua Hin*

UNITED KINGDOM - ENGLAND
Mandarin Oriental | *London*

UNITED KINGDOM - WALES
St. David's | *Cardiff*

UNITED STATES
🄩 Four Seasons/Hualalai | *Hawaii*
🄩 Four Seasons Wailea | *Hawaii*
Grand Wailea Resort | *Hawaii*
🄩 Phoenician | *Phoenix/Scottsdale*
🄩 Sanctuary/Camelback Mtn. | *Phoenix/Scottsdale*

URUGUAY
🄩 Four Seasons | *Carmelo*

GAME LODGE

AUSTRALIA
Voyages Lizard Island | *Great Barrier Reef*

BELIZE
Blancaneaux | *San Ignacio*
Chaa Creek | *San Ignacio*

BOTSWANA
Abu Camp | *Okavango Delta*
Camp Okavango | *Okavango Delta*
Chief's Camp | *Okavango Delta*
Chobe Chilwero | *Chobe National Park*
Chobe Game Lodge | *Chobe National Park*
Khwai River Lodge | *Okavango Delta*
🄩 Mombo Camp | *Okavango Delta*
Savute Elephant Camp | *Chobe National Park*
Vumbura Plains | *Okavango Delta*

INDIA
Aman-i-Khás | *Rajasthan*

KENYA
Amboseli Serena Safari | *Amboseli Game Reserve*
Governor's Camp | *Masai Mara Game Reserve*
Kichwa Tembo | *Masai Mara Game Reserve*
Little Governor's | *Masai Mara Game Reserve*
Mara Serena | *Masai Mara Game Reserve*
Treetops | *Nairobi*

NAMIBIA
Little Ongava Lodge | *Ongava Game Reserve*

PANAMA
Gamboa Rainforest | *Gamboa*

SOUTH AFRICA
Bushmans Kloof | *Biedouw Valley*
Inyati/Game Lodge | *Kruger Area*
Kwandwe/Game Reserve | *Benmore*
🄩 Londolozi | *Kruger Area*
MalaMala | *Kruger Area*
Ngala/Game Reserve | *Kruger Area*
Phinda/Game Reserve | *Kruger Area*
Sabi Sabi | *Kruger Area*
🄩 Singita | *Kruger Area*
Thornybush | *Kruger Area*
Ulusaba/Game Reserve | *Kruger Area*

TANZANIA
Lake Manyara | *Lake Manyara National Park*
Ngorongoro Crater | *Ngorongoro*
Ngorongoro Serena | *Ngorongoro*
Serengeti Serena Safari | *Serengeti National Park*

ZIMBABWE
Victoria Falls Safari | *Victoria Falls*

GOLF RESORT

ARGENTINA
Llao Llao Hotel | *Patagonia*

ARUBA
Hyatt Regency

AUSTRALIA
Hyatt Regency | *Sunshine Coast*
Sheraton Mirage | *Great Barrier Reef*

BAHAMAS
Atlantis
Four Seasons

☑ One & Only
Westin Our Lucaya

BARBADOS
Cobblers Cove
Coral Reef Club
☑ Sandy Lane

BERMUDA
Fairmont Southampton

CANADA
Fairmont Algonquin | *St. Andrews*
Fairmont Banff Springs | *Canadian Rockies*
Fairmont Empress | *Victoria*
Fairmont/Whistler | *Canadian Rockies*
Le Westin | *Montréal*
Westin | *Canadian Rockies*
🆕 Westin Bear Mtn. | *Victoria*

CAYMAN ISLANDS
Hyatt Regency

COSTA RICA
☑ Four Seasons Resort | *Guanacaste*
Los Sueños Marriott | *Puntarenas*
Paradisus | *Guanacaste*

DOMINICAN REPUBLIC
Casa de Campo
Punta Cana

FIJI
Sheraton
🆕 Westin Denarau

FRANCE
Évian Royal Palace | *Haute-Savoie*
☑ Four Seasons Resort | *Provence*

GRENADINES
Raffles Resort | *Canouan Island*

INDIA
Wildflower Hall | *Shimla*

INDONESIA
Banyan Tree | *Bintan*
Le Méridien Nirwana | *Bali*
☑ Ritz-Carlton | *Bali*

IRELAND
☑ Adare Manor | *County Limerick*

ITALY
☑ Cala di Volpe | *Sardinia*
Pitrizza | *Sardinia*

JAMAICA
Beaches Boscobel | *Ocho Rios*
Half Moon | *Montego Bay*
Ritz-Carlton Golf | *Montego Bay*
Rose Hall Resort | *Montego Bay*
Tryall Club | *Montego Bay*

KENYA
Windsor Golf | *Nairobi*

MALAYSIA
☑ Datai | *Langkawi*
Four Seasons | *Langkawi*

MAURITIUS
Le Prince Maurice

MEXICO
Casa Del Mar | *Baja Peninsula*
Fairmont Pierre | *Acapulco*
Fairmont/Princess | *Acapulco*
Fiesta Americana | *Baja Peninsula*
☑ Four Seasons | *Punta Mita*
Hilton Beach | *Cancún*
Iberostar | *Cancún*
Las Hadas | *Manzanillo*

MOROCCO
Palmeraie Golf | *Marrakech*

NEPAL
Le Méridien | *Kathmandu*

NEW ZEALAND
☑ Kauri Cliffs | *Kerikeri*

PORTUGAL
Penha Longa | *Sintra*
Quinta do Lago | *Algarve*

SEYCHELLES
Lémuria Resort

SOUTH AFRICA
Palace of the Lost City | *Sun City*

ST. KITTS & NEVIS
☑ Four Seasons | *Nevis*

THAILAND
☑ Banyan Tree | *Phuket*
Sheraton Grande | *Phuket*

TURKS & CAICOS
Ocean Club/West

UNITED KINGDOM – SCOTLAND
☒ Gleneagles | *Perthshire*
Old Course | *St. Andrews*
☒ Westin Turnberry | *Ayrshire*

UNITED STATES
☒ Boulders | *Phoenix/Scottsdale*
Disney's Grand | *Orlando*
Fisher Island | *Miami*
☒ Four Seasons | *Dallas/Ft. Worth*
☒ Four Seasons/Hualalai | *Hawaii*
☒ NEW Four Seasons/Lanai | *Hawaii*
☒ Four Seasons Resort | *Phoenix/ Scottsdale*
☒ Grand Hyatt | *Hawaii*
JW Marriott | *Orlando*
Loews | *Las Vegas*
☒ Phoenician | *Phoenix/Scottsdale*
Princeville Resort | *Hawaii*
☒ Ritz-Carlton | *Las Vegas*
☒ Ritz-Carlton | *Orlando*
☒ Ritz-Carlton Kapalua | *Hawaii*

SKI RESORT

ARGENTINA
Llao Llao Hotel | *Patagonia*

CANADA
Fairmont Banff Springs | *Canadian Rockies*
Fairmont/Frontenac | *Québec City*
Fairmont/Lake Louise | *Canadian Rockies*
Fairmont/MacDonald | *Edmonton*
Fairmont/Whistler | *Canadian Rockies*
Le Westin | *Montréal*
NEW Pan Pacific | *Canadian Rockies*
Post Hotel | *Canadian Rockies*
Rimrock | *Canadian Rockies*
Westin | *Canadian Rockies*

CHINA
Banyan Tree | *Yunnan Province*

FRANCE
Évian Royal Palace | *Haute-Savoie*
Les Fermes de Marie | *Haute-Savoie*

IRELAND
Sheen Falls Lodge | *County Kerry*

SWITZERLAND
Kempinski Grand | *St. Moritz*

UNITED STATES
Salish Lodge | *Seattle*

HOTEL TYPES

Special Features

Indexes list the best in each category. Listings are arranged by country and are followed by nearest major city where needed. ▣ indicates places with the highest ratings, popularity and importance.

CASINOS

ANTIGUA
St. James's Club

ARUBA
Aruba Resort
Hyatt Regency
Marriott Resort
Marriott's/Ocean Club
Radisson Resort
Renaissance

BAHAMAS
Atlantis
Four Seasons
Westin Our Lucaya

CHINA
Mandarin Oriental | *Macau*
NEW Shangri-La | *Guangzhou*

COSTA RICA
Los Sueños Marriott | *Puntarenas*
Paradisus | *Guanacaste*

CURAÇAO
▣ Kura Hulanda
Marriott Beach

CZECH REPUBLIC
Grand/Pupp | *Karlovy Vary*

EGYPT
Cairo Marriott | *Cairo*
Conrad | *Cairo*
Four Seasons/First Residence | *Cairo*
InterContinental | *Cairo*
Mena House | *Cairo*
Nile Hilton | *Cairo*

FRANCE
Évian Royal Palace | *Haute-Savoie*
Le Palais/Mediterranée | *Côte d'Azur*
▣ Michel Bras | *Aveyron*

JAMAICA
Couples Swept Away | *Negril*
Rose Hall Resort | *Montego Bay*

MALTA
NEW Le Méridien St. Julians

MAURITIUS
Le Saint Géran

MEXICO
Gran Meliá | *Cancún*

MONACO
▣ de Paris | *Monte Carlo*
Fairmont | *Monte Carlo*

NEPAL
Yak & Yeti | *Kathmandu*

POLAND
Marriott | *Warsaw*

RUSSIA
Baltschug Kempinski | *Moscow*

SOUTH AFRICA
Palace of the Lost City | *Sun City*

SOUTH KOREA
W Seoul-Walkerhill | *Seoul*

SPAIN
Arts | *Barcelona*

SWITZERLAND
Kempinski Grand | *St. Moritz*

UNITED KINGDOM – ENGLAND
Ritz | *London*
Sheraton | *London*

UNITED STATES
▣ Bellagio | *Las Vegas*
Caesars Palace | *Las Vegas*
Green Valley Ranch | *Las Vegas*
JW Marriott | *Las Vegas*
Loews | *Las Vegas*
Mandalay Bay Resort | *Las Vegas*
Venetian | *Las Vegas*
▣ **NEW** Wynn | *Las Vegas*

URUGUAY
Conrad Resort | *Punta del Este*

ZAMBIA
Royal Livingstone | *Livingstone*

CHILDREN NOT RECOMMENDED
(Call to confirm policy)

ANTIGUA
Curtain Bluff
Sandals Resort

ARGENTINA
NEW Cavas Wine Lodge | *Agrelo*

AUSTRALIA
Bedarra Island | *Great Barrier Reef*
Daintree Eco Lodge | *Great Barrier Reef*
Wilson Island | *Great Barrier Reef*

BAHAMAS
Rock House
Sandals Royal

BELIZE
Kanantik Reef | *Dangriga*

BHUTAN
Amankora | *Paro*

BOTSWANA
Abu Camp | *Okavango Delta*
Camp Okavango | *Okavango Delta*
Chief's Camp | *Okavango Delta*
Khwai River Lodge | *Okavango Delta*

BRITISH VIRGIN ISLANDS
Biras Creek Resort | *Virgin Gorda*
Sugar Mill | *Tortola*

CANADA
Dominion 1912 | *Québec City*
Z Hastings House | *Vancouver*

CHINA
Banyan Tree | *Yunnan Province*
JC Mandarin | *Shanghai*

DOMINICAN REPUBLIC
Excellence Punta Cana

FIJI
Vatulele Island

FRANCE
Château/Messardière | *Côte d'Azur*
Costes | *Paris*
Les Deux Abbesses | *Haute-Loire*

GERMANY
25hours | *Hamburg*

GREECE
Katikies | *Santorini*

INDIA
Wildflower Hall | *Shimla*

INDONESIA
Puri Wulandari | *Bali*

ISRAEL
Z Carmel Forest Spa | *Haifa*
Herods Vitalis Spa | *Eilat*

ITALY
Caesar Augustus | *Amalfi Coast*
Certosa di Maggiano | *Siena*
Il Pellicano | *Porto Ercole*
Z Il San Pietro | *Amalfi Coast*
La Scalinatella | *Amalfi Coast*
Le Sirenuse | *Amalfi Coast*
Poseidon | *Amalfi Coast*

JAMAICA
Couples Sans Souci | *Ocho Rios*
Couples Swept Away | *Negril*
Grand Lido | *Negril*
Grand Lido Braco | *Montego Bay*
Jamaica Inn | *Ocho Rios*
Sandals | *Montego Bay*
Sandals Dunn's River | *Ocho Rios*
Sandals Grande | *Ocho Rios*
Sandals Negril Beach | *Negril*

KENYA
Treetops | *Nairobi*

MALDIVES
Taj Exotica

MEXICO
Antigua Villa | *San Miguel de Allende*
Aventura Spa | *Cancún*
Casa/Sierra Nevada | *San Miguel de Allende*
Deseo | *Playa del Carmen*
Z Esperanza | *Baja Peninsula*
NEW Excellence Riviera | *Cancún*
Ikal del Mar | *Playa del Carmen*
Z La Casa Que Canta | *Zihuatanejo*
Maroma | *Cancún*
Rancho La Puerta | *Baja Peninsula*

Royal Hideaway | *Playa del Carmen*
Secreto | *Cancún*
Villa del Sol | *Zihuatanejo*
Villa Rolandi Gourmet | *Cancún*

NEW ZEALAND
Blanket Bay | *Queenstown*

SINGAPORE
Raffles
Regent

SOUTH AFRICA
Bay Hotel | *Cape Town*
Bushmans Kloof | *Biedouw Valley*
Cellars-Hohenort | *Cape Town*
Ellerman House | *Cape Town*
Plettenberg | *Plettenberg Bay*
Singita | *Kruger Area*
Tsala Treetop Lodge | *Plettenberg Bay*

SPAIN
Neri | *Barcelona*

ST. KITTS & NEVIS
Montpelier | *Nevis*

ST. LUCIA
Anse Chastanet
Ladera
Sandals Grande
Sandals Regency

THAILAND
Chiva-Som | *Hua Hin*
Four Seasons Tented | *Golden Triangle*
Le Royal Méridien | *Koh Samui*

UNITED KINGDOM – ENGLAND
Amberley Castle | *West Sussex*
Buckland Manor | *Cotswolds*

UNITED KINGDOM – SCOTLAND
Culloden House | *Inverness*

UNITED KINGDOM – WALES
Bodysgallen Hall | *Llandudno*

UNITED STATES
Grove Isle | *Miami*
Inn at Langley | *Seattle*

Royal Palms | *Phoenix/Scottsdale*
Soniat House | *New Orleans*

ZIMBABWE
Victoria Falls Safari | *Victoria Falls*

DRAMATIC DESIGN

ANGUILLA
Cap Juluca

ANTIGUA
Carlisle Bay

ARGENTINA
NEW Cavas Wine Lodge | *Agrelo*

AUSTRALIA
Daintree Eco Lodge | *Great Barrier Reef*
Palazzo Versace | *Gold Coast*
Park Hyatt | *Sydney*
Sebel Reef House | *Great Barrier Reef*
Westin | *Sydney*

BELGIUM
Amigo | *Brussels*

BELIZE
Blancaneaux | *San Ignacio*
Turtle Inn | *Placencia*

BOTSWANA
Camp Okavango | *Okavango Delta*
Chobe Chilwero | *Chobe National Park*
Mombo Camp | *Okavango Delta*
Savute Elephant Camp | *Chobe National Park*
Vumbura Plains | *Okavango Delta*

BRAZIL
Unique | *São Paulo*

CANADA
NEW Adara | *Canadian Rockies*
Ice Hotel | *Québec City*
Listel | *Vancouver*
Opus | *Vancouver*
SoHo Metropolitan Hotel | *Toronto*
St-Paul Hotel | *Montréal*
W Montreal | *Montréal*

CHILE
Explora En Patagonia | *Patagonia*

CHINA
Banyan Tree | *Yunnan Province*
🅩 Four Seasons | *Hong Kong*
Jia | *Hong Kong*
JW Marriott | *Shanghai*
🅩 Peninsula | *Hong Kong*
Westin | *Shanghai*

COSTA RICA
Paradisus | *Guanacaste*

CZECH REPUBLIC
NEW Mandarin Oriental | *Prague*

DENMARK
NEW Copenhagen Island | *Copenhagen*
Skt. Petri | *Copenhagen*

EGYPT
Oberoi Sahl Hasheesh | *Red Sea*
Sofitel Old Cataract | *Aswan*

ESTONIA
Three Sisters | *Tallinn*

FIJI
Turtle Island
Vatulele Island

FRANCE
du Petit Moulin | *Paris*
Les Deux Abbesses | *Haute-Loire*
Martinez | *Côte d'Azur*
Murano Urban | *Paris*

FRENCH POLYNESIA
Bora Bora | *Bora Bora*
Bora Bora Lagoon | *Bora Bora*
Bora Bora Pearl | *Bora Bora*
Le Méridien | *Bora Bora*
Le Taha'a | *Taha'a*
NEW St. Regis | *Bora Bora*

GERMANY
Park Hyatt | *Hamburg*
Regent | *Berlin*
Ritz-Carlton | *Wolfsburg*
Side | *Hamburg*
Steigenberger Frankfurter | *Frankfurt*

GREECE
🅩 Blue Palace Resort | *Crete*

INDIA
🅩 Oberoi Udaivilas | *Rajasthan*
Taj Lake Palace | *Rajasthan*

INDONESIA
🅩 Amanjiwo | *Borobudur*
🅩 Amankila | *Bali*
🅩 Amanusa | *Bali*
🅩 Como Shambala | *Bali*
🅩 Four Seasons Jimbaran Bay | *Bali*
Four Seasons Sayan | *Bali*
Viceroy Bali | *Bali*

IRELAND
Ashford Castle | *County Mayo*
Merrion | *Dublin*

ISRAEL
Dan Eilat | *Eilat*

ITALY
Bulgari Milan | *Milan*
Ca'Pisani | *Venice*
Capri Palace | *Amalfi Coast*
🅩 Il San Pietro | *Amalfi Coast*
Le Sirenuse | *Amalfi Coast*
Relais Il Falconiere | *Siena*
San Clemente | *Venice*
Santa Caterina | *Amalfi Coast*
Straf | *Milan*
St. Regis | *Rome*

JAPAN
Cerulean Tower | *Tokyo*
Gora Kadan | *Hakone*
Hiiragiya Ryokan | *Kyoto*
🅩 Mandarin Oriental | *Tokyo*
Nikko-Bayside, Hotel | *Osaka*
🅩 Park Hyatt | *Tokyo*

KENYA
Little Governor's | *Masai Mara Game Reserve*

MALDIVES
One & Only
NEW W Retreat & Spa

MEXICO
Camino Real | *Oaxaca*
Deseo | *Playa del Carmen*
Fiesta Americana | *Baja Peninsula*
Gran Meliá | *Cancún*

Habitá | *Mexico City*
Maroma | *Cancún*
Villa del Sol | *Zihuatanejo*
Westin | *Baja Peninsula*
W Mexico City | *Mexico City*

MONACO
Columbus Monaco | *Monte Carlo*

MOROCCO
Dar Loulema | *Essaouira*
Ksar Char-Bagh | *Marrakech*

NETHERLANDS
Le Méridien | *The Hague*

PERU
Monasterio | *Cuzco*

PORTUGAL
Palácio Belmonte | *Lisbon*

QATAR
Four Seasons | *Doha*

SEYCHELLES
North Island

SINGAPORE
Ⓩ Ritz-Carlton Millenia

SOUTH AFRICA
Sabi Sabi | *Kruger Area*
Ⓩ Singita | *Kruger Area*

SOUTH KOREA
W Seoul-Walkerhill | *Seoul*

SPAIN
Alfonso XIII | *Seville*
Arts | *Barcelona*
Barceló La Bobadilla | *Granada*
MiróHotel | *Bilbao*
Puerta America | *Madrid*
Rey Juan Carlos I | *Barcelona*
Westin Palace | *Madrid*

SRI LANKA
Amangalla

ST. LUCIA
Anse Chastanet
Ladera

SWEDEN
ICEHOTEL | *Jukkasjärvi*

SWITZERLAND
Eden au Lac | *Zurich*
Four Seasons | *Geneva*
Park Hyatt | *Zurich*
Widder | *Zurich*

TANZANIA
Mnemba Island | *Zanzibar*
Ngorongoro Crater | *Ngorongoro*

THAILAND
Ⓩ Amanpuri | *Phuket*
Ⓩ Banyan Tree | *Phuket*
Ⓩ Four Seasons | *Chiang Mai*
Ⓩ Oriental | *Bangkok*
Rayavadee | *Phuket*

TURKEY
Marmara | *Bodrum*

TURKS & CAICOS
NEW Amanyara

UNITED ARAB EMIRATES
Ⓩ Burj Al Arab | *Dubai*
Grosvenor House | *Dubai*
Ⓩ One & Only | *Dubai*

UNITED KINGDOM – ENGLAND
Cadogan | *London*
Stoke Park | *London*

UNITED STATES
Ⓩ Bellagio | *Las Vegas*
Biltmore | *Miami*
Burnham | *Chicago*
Crescent Court | *Dallas/Ft. Worth*
Fifteen Beacon | *Boston*
Ⓩ Four Seasons/Hualalai | *Hawaii*
Monaco | *Chicago*
Mondrian | *Los Angeles*
Palomar | *San Francisco*
Ⓩ Park Hyatt | *Chicago*
Raffles L'Ermitage | *Los Angeles*
Ⓩ Ritz-Carlton | *Las Vegas*
Ritz-Carlton | *Philadelphia*
Ritz-Carlton Georgetown | *Washington, DC*
Sofitel | *Chicago*
Ⓩ NEW St. Regis | *San Francisco*
Venetian | *Las Vegas*
Viceroy | *Los Angeles*

Waldorf-Astoria | *New York City*
Z NEW Wynn | *Las Vegas*
Zaza | *Dallas/Ft. Worth*

URUGUAY
Z Four Seasons | *Carmelo*

FISHING

ANGUILLA
Malliouhana
St. Regis

ANTIGUA
Curtain Bluff
Jumby Bay
Sandals Resort

ARGENTINA
Llao Llao Hotel | *Patagonia*

ARUBA
Aruba Resort
Hyatt Regency
Marriott Resort
Marriott's/Ocean Club

AUSTRALIA
Bedarra Island | *Great Barrier Reef*
Dunk Island | *Great Barrier Reef*
Z Hayman Island | *Great Barrier Reef*
Hyatt Regency | *Sunshine Coast*
Palazzo Versace | *Gold Coast*
Voyages Lizard Island | *Great Barrier Reef*

BAHAMAS
Club Med
Four Seasons
Musha Cay
Z One & Only
Pink Sands
Rock House
Sandals Royal
Westin Our Lucaya

BARBADOS
Cobblers Cove
Coral Reef Club
Sandpiper
Z Sandy Lane

BELIZE
Cayo Espanto | *San Pedro*
Kanantik Reef | *Dangriga*
Turtle Inn | *Placencia*

BERMUDA
Cambridge Beaches
Fairmont Hamilton
Fairmont Southampton
Pink Beach Club
Waterloo House

BOTSWANA
Abu Camp | *Okavango Delta*
Camp Okavango | *Okavango Delta*

BRITISH VIRGIN ISLANDS
Biras Creek Resort | *Virgin Gorda*
Bitter End | *Virgin Gorda*
Guana Island | *Virgin Gorda*
Little Dix Bay | *Virgin Gorda*
Necker Island | *Virgin Gorda*
Peter Island | *Peter Island*

CANADA
Aerie | *Victoria*
Delta Victoria | *Victoria*
Fairmont | *Vancouver*
Fairmont Banff Springs | *Canadian Rockies*
Fairmont/Montebello | *Montebello*
Fairmont Empress | *Victoria*
Fairmont Jasper Park | *Canadian Rockies*
Fairmont/Lake Louise | *Canadian Rockies*
Fairmont/MacDonald | *Edmonton*
Fairmont/Whistler | *Canadian Rockies*
Z Four Seasons | *Canadian Rockies*
Z Hastings House | *Vancouver*
Ice Hotel | *Québec City*
Keltic Lodge | *Cape Breton*
Kingsbrae Arms | *St. Andrews*
La Pinsonnière | *Québec City*
Post Hotel | *Canadian Rockies*
Sooke Harbour | *Victoria*
Westin | *Canadian Rockies*

CAYMAN ISLANDS
Hyatt Regency
Z Ritz-Carlton

COSTA RICA

Aguila de Osa | *Osa Peninsula*
▣ Four Seasons Resort | *Guanacaste*
La Paloma Lodge | *Osa Peninsula*
Los Sueños Marriott | *Puntarenas*
Paradisus | *Guanacaste*
Punta Islita | *Guanacaste*
Tabacón Grand Spa | *Arenal*

CYPRUS

Anassa | *Polis*

DOMINICAN REPUBLIC

Casa de Campo
Excellence Punta Cana
Punta Cana

FIJI

Shangri-La's Fijian
Turtle Island
Vatulele Island

FRANCE

Château de Gilly | *Burgundy*
Château de Marçay | *Loire*
Château de Mercuès | *Mercuès*
Château de Noirieux | *Loire*
Château de Noizay | *Loire*
Château d'Esclimont | *Chartres*
Évian Royal Palace | *Haute-Savoie*
Grand Cap-Ferrat | *Côte d'Azur*
La Réserve/Beaulieu | *Côte d'Azur*
Les Deux Abbesses | *Haute-Loire*
Le Vieux Logis | *Dordogne*
▣ Michel Bras | *Aveyron*

FRENCH POLYNESIA

Bora Bora | *Bora Bora*
Bora Bora Lagoon | *Bora Bora*
Bora Bora Pearl | *Bora Bora*
InterContinental | *Moorea*
InterContinental | *Tahiti*
Le Méridien | *Bora Bora*
Le Taha'a | *Taha'a*
NEW St. Regis | *Bora Bora*

GREECE

Astir Palace | *Athens*
Elounda Beach | *Crete*
Vedema Resort | *Santorini*

GRENADINES

Petit St. Vincent | *Petit St. Vincent*

INDIA

Leela Goa | *Goa*

INDONESIA

▣ Amankila | *Bali*
▣ Amanusa | *Bali*
Banyan Tree | *Bintan*
Nusa Dua Beach | *Bali*
▣ Ritz-Carlton | *Bali*

IRELAND

▣ Adare Manor | *County Limerick*
Ashford Castle | *County Mayo*
Dromoland Castle | *County Clare*
K Club | *County Kildare*
▣ Mount Juliet Conrad | *County Kilkenny*
Park Hotel Kenmare | *County Kerry*
Sheen Falls Lodge | *County Kerry*

ITALY

Caesar Augustus | *Amalfi Coast*
▣ Cala di Volpe | *Sardinia*
Capri Palace | *Amalfi Coast*
Eden Roc | *Amalfi Coast*
Grand/Miramare | *Portofino*
Pitrizza | *Sardinia*
Romazzino | *Sardinia*
Splendido | *Portofino*

JAMAICA

Couples Sans Souci | *Ocho Rios*
Couples Swept Away | *Negril*
Grand Lido | *Negril*
Half Moon | *Montego Bay*
Round Hill | *Montego Bay*
Sandals | *Montego Bay*

KENYA

Mount Kenya Safari | *Nanyuki*

MALAYSIA

Four Seasons | *Langkawi*
Pangkor Laut | *Langkawi*

MALDIVES

Banyan Tree
Four Seasons/Kuda Huraa
NEW Four Seasons/Landaa Giraavaru
Soneva Fushi
Taj Exotica
NEW W Retreat & Spa

MAURITIUS
Le Prince Maurice
Le Saint Géran
Le Touessrok
Oberoi
Taj Exotica

MEXICO
Casa Del Mar | *Baja Peninsula*
CasaMagna Marriott | *Puerto Vallarta*
Dreams | *Cancún*
Dreams | *Puerto Vallarta*
☒ Esperanza | *Baja Peninsula*
NEW Excellence Riviera | *Cancún*
Fairmont Pierre | *Acapulco*
☒ Four Seasons | *Punta Mita*
Hyatt Caribe | *Cancún*
JW Marriott | *Cancún*
☒ La Casa Que Canta | *Zihuatanejo*
La Jolla/Mismaloya | *Puerto Vallarta*
Las Alamandas | *Manzanillo*
Las Brisas | *Ixtapa*
Las Hadas | *Manzanillo*
☒ Las Ventanas | *Baja Peninsula*
Maroma | *Cancún*
NH Krystal | *Puerto Vallarta*
Omni | *Cancún*
☒ One & Only | *Baja Peninsula*
☒ Ritz-Carlton | *Cancún*
☒ Royal Hideaway | *Playa del Carmen*
Secreto | *Cancún*
Villa del Sol | *Zihuatanejo*
Villa Rolandi Gourmet | *Cancún*
Westin | *Cancún*
Westin | *Baja Peninsula*

MOROCCO
Amanjena | *Marrakech*

NEW ZEALAND
☒ Blanket Bay | *Queenstown*
Huka Lodge | *Taupo*
☒ Kauri Cliffs | *Kerikeri*

OMAN
Shangri-La | *Muscat*

PALAU
Palau Royal Resort | *Koror*

PANAMA
Gamboa Rainforest | *Gamboa*

PHILIPPINES
Amanpulo | *Cuyo Islands*
Shangri-La | *Cebu*

PORTUGAL
Quinta das Lagrimas | *Coimbra*
Quinta do Lago | *Algarve*
Reid's Palace | *Madeira*

QATAR
NEW Sharq Village & Spa | *Doha*

SEYCHELLES
Frégate Island
Lémuria Resort
North Island
Taj Denis Island

SINGAPORE
Conrad Centennial

SOUTH AFRICA
Inyati/Game Lodge | *Kruger Area*
Palace of the Lost City | *Sun City*
Phinda/Game Reserve | *Kruger Area*

SPAIN
Hostal/Gavina | *Costa Brava*
La Residencia | *Mallorca*
Marbella Club | *Costa del Sol*
Puente Romano | *Costa del Sol*

SRI LANKA
Amangalla

ST. BARTS
Carl Gustaf
Eden Rock
Guanahani & Spa
La Banane

ST. KITTS & NEVIS
Montpelier | *Nevis*

ST. LUCIA
Anse Chastanet
Jalousie Plantation
Windjammer Landing

ST. MAARTEN
Oyster Bay Beach

ST. MARTIN
La Samanna

SWITZERLAND
Bellevue Palace | *Berne*
Gstaad Palace | *Gstaad*
Park Hotel | *Vitznau*
☑ Victoria-Jungfrau | *Interlaken*

TANZANIA
Mnemba Island | *Zanzibar*

THAILAND
☑ Amanpuri | *Phuket*
Evason | *Hua Hin*
☑ Four Seasons Tented | *Golden Triangle*
JW Marriott | *Phuket*
Le Royal Méridien | *Koh Samui*
Napasai | *Koh Samui*
Rayavadee | *Phuket*

TURKS & CAICOS
NEW Amanyara
Grace Bay Club
Ocean Club/West
Parrot Cay

UNITED ARAB EMIRATES
Jumeirah Beach | *Dubai*
Le Royal Méridien | *Dubai*
Park Hyatt | *Dubai*

UNITED KINGDOM - ENGLAND
Bovey Castle | *Devon*
Chewton Glen | *Hampshire*
Four Seasons | *Hampshire*
☑ Gidleigh Park | *Devon*
Sharrow Bay | *Cumbria*

UNITED KINGDOM - SCOTLAND
☑ Gleneagles | *Perthshire*
Inverlochy Castle | *Fort William*
☑ Westin Turnberry | *Ayrshire*

UNITED STATES
Disney's Grand | *Orlando*
Disney's Yacht Club | *Orlando*
☑ Fairmont Kea Lani | *Hawaii*
Fisher Island | *Miami*
☑ Four Seasons/Hualalai | *Hawaii*
☑NEW Four Seasons/Lanai | *Hawaii*
☑ Four Seasons Wailea | *Hawaii*
Grove Isle | *Miami*

Ritz-Carlton | *Orlando*
☑ Ritz-Carlton Key Biscayne | *Miami*
Ritz-Carlton Marina del Rey | *Los Angeles*
Ritz-Carlton South Beach | *Miami*

URUGUAY
Conrad Resort | *Punta del Este*

VIETNAM
Evason Hideaway | *Nha Trang*

ZAMBIA
Royal Livingstone | *Livingstone*

HIKING/WALKING TRAILS

ANGUILLA
Cap Juluca
CuisinArt Resort

ANTIGUA
Jumby Bay
St. James's Club

ARGENTINA
Llao Llao Hotel | *Patagonia*

ARUBA
Hyatt Regency
Renaissance

AUSTRALIA
Bedarra Island | *Great Barrier Reef*
Daintree Eco Lodge | *Great Barrier Reef*
Dunk Island | *Great Barrier Reef*
Hyatt Regency | *Sunshine Coast*
Kewarra Beach Resort | *Great Barrier Reef*
Sails in the Desert | *Ayers Rock*
Sheraton Mirage | *Great Barrier Reef*
Wilson Island | *Great Barrier Reef*

AUSTRIA
Sacher Salzburg | *Salzburg*

BAHAMAS
Atlantis
Club Med
Four Seasons
Musha Cay
Pink Sands

Sandals Royal
Westin Our Lucaya

BELIZE
Blancaneaux | *San Ignacio*
Cayo Espanto | *San Pedro*
Chaa Creek | *San Ignacio*
Kanantik Reef | *Dangriga*

BERMUDA
Cambridge Beaches
Fairmont Hamilton
Fairmont Southampton
Horizons & Cottages

BHUTAN
Amankora | *Paro*
Uma Paro | *Paro*

BOTSWANA
Abu Camp | *Okavango Delta*
Camp Okavango | *Okavango Delta*

BRAZIL
Le Méridien | *Rio de Janeiro*

BRITISH VIRGIN ISLANDS
Biras Creek Resort | *Virgin Gorda*
Bitter End | *Virgin Gorda*
Guana Island | *Virgin Gorda*
Little Dix Bay | *Virgin Gorda*
Long Bay Resort | *Tortola*
Necker Island | *Virgin Gorda*
Peter Island | *Peter Island*

CAMBODIA
◪ Amansara | *Siem Reap*
Raffles Grand | *Siem Reap*

CANADA
Alive Health | *Canadian Rockies*
Fairmont Banff Springs | *Canadian Rockies*
Fairmont/Montebello | *Montebello*
Fairmont Jasper Park | *Canadian Rockies*
Fairmont/Lake Louise | *Canadian Rockies*
Fairmont Waterfront | *Vancouver*
Fairmont/Whistler | *Canadian Rockies*
◪ Four Seasons | *Canadian Rockies*
Grand Pacific | *Victoria*

◪ Hastings House | *Vancouver*
Langdon Hall | *Toronto*
La Pinsonnière | *Québec City*
Le Westin | *Montréal*
Omni | *Montréal*
Opus | *Vancouver*
Pan Pacific | *Vancouver*
NEW Pan Pacific | *Canadian Rockies*
Post Hotel | *Canadian Rockies*
Sooke Harbour | *Victoria*
Westin | *Canadian Rockies*
Westin Bayshore | *Vancouver*
Wickaninnish Inn | *Victoria*

CHILE
Explora En Atacama | *Atacama*
Explora En Patagonia | *Patagonia*
San Cristobal Tower | *Santiago*

CHINA
Banyan Tree | *Yunnan Province*
Kerry Centre | *Beijing*
Le Méridien She Shan | *Shanghai*
NEW Shangri-La | *Guangzhou*

COSTA RICA
Aguila de Osa | *Osa Peninsula*
Finca Rosa Blanca | *San José*
La Mariposa | *Puntarenas*
La Paloma Lodge | *Osa Peninsula*
Paradisus | *Guanacaste*
Tabacón Grand Spa | *Arenal*

CURAÇAO
Marriott Beach

CYPRUS
Anassa | *Polis*

CZECH REPUBLIC
Savoy | *Prague*

ECUADOR
La Mirage Garden | *Quito*

FIJI
Shangri-La's Fijian
Vatulele Island

FRANCE
Château de Bagnols | *Rhône*
Château de Gilly | *Burgundy*
Château de Marçay | *Loire*
Château de Mercuès | *Mercuès*

Château de Noizay | *Loire*
Château d'Esclimont | *Chartres*
Château Eza | *Côte d'Azur*
NEW Cheval Blanc | *Courchevel*
de la Cité | *Carcassonne*
Domaine/Hauts de Loire | *Loire*
☑ du Cap-Eden-Roc | *Côte d'Azur*
Évian Royal Palace | *Haute-Savoie*
☑ Four Seasons Resort | *Provence*
Grand Cap-Ferrat | *Côte d'Azur*
Hostellerie/Crillon | *Provence*
La Bastide/Moustiers | *Provence*
☑ Le Château/St-Martin | *Côte d'Azur*
Le Petit Nice | *Provence*
Les Deux Abbesses | *Haute-Loire*
Les Fermes de Marie | *Haute-Savoie*
Le Vieux Logis | *Dordogne*
☑ Michel Bras | *Aveyron*
Ostapé | *Bidarray*
Oustau Baumanière | *Provence*
Villa Gallici | *Provence*

FRENCH POLYNESIA
Bora Bora Pearl | *Bora Bora*
InterContinental | *Moorea*
InterContinental | *Tahiti*

GERMANY
Eisenhut | *Rothenburg*
Kempinski | *Hamburg*
Ritz-Carlton | *Berlin*
Schloss. Bühlerhöhe | *Baden-Baden*

GREECE
Vedema Resort | *Santorini*

GRENADINES
Petit St. Vincent | *Petit St. Vincent*

GUATEMALA
Atitlán | *Panajachel*

INDIA
Aman-i-Khás | *Rajasthan*
Wildflower Hall | *Shimla*

INDONESIA
☑ Amandari | *Bali*
☑ Amanjiwo | *Borobudur*
☑ Amankila | *Bali*
☑ Como Shambala | *Bali*
Four Seasons Sayan | *Bali*

Grand Hyatt | *Bali*
Laguna Resort | *Bali*
Puri Wulandari | *Bali*
Viceroy Bali | *Bali*

IRELAND
Ashford Castle | *County Mayo*
Dromoland Castle | *County Clare*
K Club | *County Kildare*
☑ Mount Juliet Conrad | *County Kilkenny*
Park Hotel Kenmare | *County Kerry*

ISRAEL
☑ Carmel Forest Spa | *Haifa*

ITALY
Caesar Augustus | *Amalfi Coast*
Capri Palace | *Amalfi Coast*
Eden Roc | *Amalfi Coast*
L'Albereta | *Erbusco*
Le Sirenuse | *Amalfi Coast*
Palumbo | *Amalfi Coast*
Pitrizza | *Sardinia*
Poseidon | *Amalfi Coast*
Relais Borgo Felice | *Siena*
Romazzino | *Sardinia*
Splendido | *Portofino*
Villa Cipriani | *Venice*
Villa San Michele | *Florence*

JAMAICA
Couples Sans Souci | *Ocho Rios*
Couples Swept Away | *Negril*
Grand Lido | *Negril*
Rose Hall Resort | *Montego Bay*
Sandals Dunn's River | *Ocho Rios*
Sandals Grande | *Ocho Rios*
Sandals Negril Beach | *Negril*
Strawberry Hill | *Kingston*

JAPAN
Four Seasons/Chinzan-so | *Tokyo*
☑ Ritz-Carlton | *Osaka*

JORDAN
Mövenpick Resort | *Petra*

KENYA
Giraffe Manor | *Nairobi*
Governor's Camp | *Masai Mara Game Reserve*
Kichwa Tembo | *Masai Mara Game Reserve*

Little Governor's | *Masai Mara Game Reserve*

Mara Serena | *Masai Mara Game Reserve*

Mount Kenya Safari | *Nanyuki*

Windsor Golf | *Nairobi*

MALAYSIA
☒ Datai | *Langkawi*

Four Seasons | *Langkawi*

Mandarin Oriental | *Kuala Lumpur*

Pangkor Laut | *Langkawi*

Tanjong Jara | *Penang*

MALDIVES
One & Only

MEXICO
Aventura Spa | *Cancún*

CasaMagna Marriott | *Puerto Vallarta*

☒ Esperanza | *Baja Peninsula*

Fiesta Americana | *Baja Peninsula*

Fiesta Americana | *Cancún*

☒ Four Seasons | *Punta Mita*

Iberostar | *Cancún*

La Jolla/Mismaloya | *Puerto Vallarta*

Las Alamandas | *Manzanillo*

☒ Las Ventanas | *Baja Peninsula*

Maroma | *Cancún*

Maya Tulum | *Tulum*

☒ One & Only | *Baja Peninsula*

Rancho La Puerta | *Baja Peninsula*

☒ Royal Hideaway | *Playa del Carmen*

Twin Dolphin | *Baja Peninsula*

Westin | *Baja Peninsula*

MONACO
Fairmont | *Monte Carlo*

MOROCCO
Dar Loulema | *Essaouira*

Kasbah du Toubkal | *High Atlas*

Ksar Char-Bagh | *Marrakech*

NEPAL
Le Méridien | *Kathmandu*

NEW ZEALAND
☒ Blanket Bay | *Queenstown*

Huka Lodge | *Taupo*

OMAN
Shangri-La | *Muscat*

PANAMA
Gamboa Rainforest | *Gamboa*

PERU
Machu Picchu Sanctuary | *Cuzco*

PHILIPPINES
Amanpulo | *Cuyo Islands*

PORTUGAL
Penha Longa | *Sintra*

Quinta das Lagrimas | *Coimbra*

Quinta do Lago | *Algarve*

Tivoli Palácio/Seteais | *Sintra*

QATAR
Ritz-Carlton | *Doha*

SEYCHELLES
Frégate Island

Taj Denis Island

SINGAPORE
Pan Pacific

Shangri-La

SOUTH AFRICA
Bushmans Kloof | *Biedouw Valley*

Grande Roche | *Cape Town*

Inyati/Game Lodge | *Kruger Area*

Kwandwe/Game Reserve | *Benmore*

Lanzerac Manor | *Cape Town*

☒ Londolozi | *Kruger Area*

Mount Nelson | *Cape Town*

Ngala/Game Reserve | *Kruger Area*

Palace of the Lost City | *Sun City*

Phinda/Game Reserve | *Kruger Area*

Sabi Sabi | *Kruger Area*

☒ Singita | *Kruger Area*

Tsala Treetop Lodge | *Plettenberg Bay*

Ulusaba/Game Reserve | *Kruger Area*

SOUTH KOREA
Shilla | *Seoul*

W Seoul-Walkerhill | *Seoul*

SPAIN
Arts | *Barcelona*

Kempinski | *Costa del Sol*

La Residencia | *Mallorca*

Rey Juan Carlos I | *Barcelona*

Son Brull | *Mallorca*

SRI LANKA
Amanwella

ST. BARTS

Eden Rock
Guanahani & Spa
Isle de France
Le Toiny

ST. KITTS & NEVIS

☑ Four Seasons | *Nevis*
Montpelier | *Nevis*
Nisbet Plantation | *Nevis*

ST. LUCIA

Anse Chastanet
Jalousie Plantation
Ladera
Sandals Regency
Windjammer Landing

ST. MARTIN

La Samanna
L'Habitation/Lonvilliers

SWITZERLAND

Beau-Rivage Palace | *Lausanne*
Gstaad Palace | *Gstaad*
Mont Cervin Palace | *Zermatt*
Park Hotel | *Vitznau*
☑ Victoria-Jungfrau | *Interlaken*

TANZANIA

Mnemba Island | *Zanzibar*
Ngorongoro Serena | *Ngorongoro*
Serengeti Serena Safari | *Serengeti National Park*
Zamani Kempinski | *Zanzibar*

THAILAND

Anantara Resort | *Golden Triangle*
Evason | *Hua Hin*
☑ Four Seasons Tented | *Golden Triangle*
Le Royal Méridien | *Koh Samui*
Napasai | *Koh Samui*
Rayavadee | *Phuket*
Shangri-La | *Bangkok*
Sheraton Grande | *Phuket*

TURKEY

Kempinski | *Bodrum*

TURKS & CAICOS

Grace Bay Club
Ocean Club/West
Parrot Cay

UNITED KINGDOM - ENGLAND

Bovey Castle | *Devon*
Buckland Manor | *Cotswolds*
Calcot Manor | *Cotswolds*
Chewton Glen | *Hampshire*
Cowley Manor | *Cotswolds*
Four Seasons | *Hampshire*
☑ Gidleigh Park | *Devon*
Gravetye Manor | *West Sussex*
Grove | *Hertfordshire*
Holbeck Ghyll | *Cumbria*
Lower Slaughter | *Cotswolds*
Lucknam Park | *Cotswolds*
Lugger | *Cornwall*
Mandarin Oriental | *London*
Royal Crescent | *Cotswolds*
Sharrow Bay | *Cumbria*
Vineyard at Stockcross | *Berkshire*

UNITED KINGDOM - SCOTLAND

Culloden House | *Inverness*
Inverlochy Castle | *Fort William*
Old Course | *St. Andrews*
☑ Westin Turnberry | *Ayrshire*

UNITED STATES

☑ Boulders | *Phoenix/Scottsdale*
☑ Fairmont Kea Lani | *Hawaii*
Fisher Island | *Miami*
☑ Four Seasons | *Dallas/Ft. Worth*
☑ Four Seasons/Hualalai | *Hawaii*
☑ NEW Four Seasons/Lanai | *Hawaii*
☑ Four Seasons Resort | *Phoenix/ Scottsdale*
☑ Four Seasons Wailea | *Hawaii*
☑ Grand Hyatt | *Hawaii*
Grand Wailea Resort | *Hawaii*
Grove Isle | *Miami*
Loews | *Las Vegas*
Princeville Resort | *Hawaii*
☑ Ritz-Carlton | *Las Vegas*
☑ Ritz-Carlton | *Orlando*
☑ Ritz-Carlton Kapalua | *Hawaii*
Salish Lodge | *Seattle*
☑ Sanctuary/Camelback Mtn. | *Phoenix/Scottsdale*
Willows Lodge | *Seattle*

VENEZUELA
Tamanaco InterCont. | *Caracas*

ZIMBABWE
Victoria Falls Hotel | *Victoria Falls*
Victoria Falls Safari | *Victoria Falls*

ISLAND SETTINGS

ANGUILLA
Cap Juluca
CuisinArt Resort

ANTIGUA
Carlisle Bay
Curtain Bluff
Jumby Bay
Sandals Resort
St. James's Club

ARUBA
Divi Aruba Beach
Hyatt Regency
Marriott's/Ocean Club
Renaissance

AUSTRALIA
Bedarra Island | *Great Barrier Reef*
Dunk Island | *Great Barrier Reef*
Z Hayman Island | *Great Barrier Reef*
Kewarra Beach Resort | *Great Barrier Reef*
Voyages Lizard Island | *Great Barrier Reef*
Wilson Island | *Great Barrier Reef*

BAHAMAS
Atlantis
Club Med
Four Seasons
Musha Cay
Pink Sands
Rock House
Sandals Royal
Westin Our Lucaya

BARBADOS
Coral Reef Club
Sandpiper
Z Sandy Lane

BELIZE
Cayo Espanto | *San Pedro*

BERMUDA
Elbow Beach
Fairmont Hamilton
Fairmont Southampton
Horizons & Cottages
Waterloo House

BOTSWANA
Camp Okavango | *Okavango Delta*

BRITISH VIRGIN ISLANDS
Guana Island | *Virgin Gorda*
Little Dix Bay | *Virgin Gorda*
Necker Island | *Virgin Gorda*
Peter Island | *Peter Island*
Sugar Mill | *Tortola*

CANADA
Fairmont Empress | *Victoria*
Z Hastings House | *Vancouver*

CAYMAN ISLANDS
Z Ritz-Carlton

COSTA RICA
La Mariposa | *Puntarenas*

CURAÇAO
Avila Beach
Marriott Beach

DENMARK
NEW Copenhagen Island | *Copenhagen*

FIJI
Shangri-La's Fijian
Sheraton
Sheraton Denarau Villas
Turtle Island
Vatulele Island
Wakaya Club
NEW Westin Denarau

FRANCE
L'Hotel de Toiras | *Île de Ré*

FRENCH POLYNESIA
Bora Bora | *Bora Bora*
Bora Bora Lagoon | *Bora Bora*
Bora Bora Pearl | *Bora Bora*
InterContinental | *Moorea*
InterContinental | *Tahiti*
Le Méridien | *Bora Bora*

Le Méridien | *Tahiti*
Le Taha'a | *Taha'a*

GREECE
🔢 Blue Palace Resort | *Crete*
Elounda Beach | *Crete*
Katikies | *Santorini*
Vedema Resort | *Santorini*

GRENADINES
Cotton House | *Mustique*
Petit St. Vincent | *Petit St. Vincent*
Raffles Resort | *Canouan Island*

INDONESIA
Banyan Tree | *Bintan*
Laguna Resort | *Bali*
Legian | *Bali*
Puri Wulandari | *Bali*

ITALY
Caesar Augustus | *Amalfi Coast*
🔢 Cala di Volpe | *Sardinia*
Capri Palace | *Amalfi Coast*
Grand/Quisisana | *Amalfi Coast*
La Scalinatella | *Amalfi Coast*
Pitrizza | *Sardinia*
Romazzino | *Sardinia*

JAMAICA
Beaches Boscobel | *Ocho Rios*
Jamaica Inn | *Ocho Rios*
Round Hill | *Montego Bay*
Sandals | *Montego Bay*
Sandals Dunn's River | *Ocho Rios*
Sandals Grande | *Ocho Rios*
Sandals Negril Beach | *Negril*
Tryall Club | *Montego Bay*

MALAYSIA
🔢 Datai | *Langkawi*

MALDIVES
Banyan Tree
Four Seasons/Kuda Huraa
NEW Four Seasons/Landaa
  Giraavaru
One & Only
Soneva Fushi
Taj Exotica

MALTA
NEW Le Méridien St. Julians

MAURITIUS
Le Prince Maurice
Le Touessrok
Oberoi

MEXICO
Secreto | *Cancún*
Villa Rolandi Gourmet | *Cancún*

PORTUGAL
Reid's Palace | *Madeira*

SEYCHELLES
Frégate Island
North Island

SPAIN
La Residencia | *Mallorca*

ST. BARTS
Carl Gustaf
Christopher
François Plantation
La Banane
Le Toiny
Manapany

ST. KITTS & NEVIS
Montpelier | *Nevis*
Nisbet Plantation | *Nevis*

ST. LUCIA
Anse Chastanet
Jalousie Plantation
Ladera
Sandals Grande

ST. MAARTEN
Oyster Bay Beach
Wyndham Sapphire

ST. MARTIN
La Samanna

TANZANIA
Mnemba Island | *Zanzibar*

THAILAND
🔢 Amanpuri | *Phuket*
🔢 Banyan Tree | *Phuket*
Chedi | *Phuket*
Le Royal Méridien | *Koh Samui*
Napasai | *Koh Samui*
Rayavadee | *Phuket*

TURKS & CAICOS
NEW Amanyara
Ocean Club/West
Parrot Cay

UNITED ARAB EMIRATES
Z Burj Al Arab | *Dubai*
Park Hyatt | *Dubai*

UNITED STATES
Z Fairmont Kea Lani | *Hawaii*
Fisher Island | *Miami*
Z Four Seasons/Hualalai | *Hawaii*
Z NEW Four Seasons/Lanai | *Hawaii*
Z Grand Hyatt | *Hawaii*
Grand Wailea Resort | *Hawaii*
Grove Isle | *Miami*
Z Halekulani | *Hawaii*
Inn at Langley | *Seattle*
Z Kahala | *Hawaii*
Princeville Resort | *Hawaii*
Z Ritz-Carlton Kapalua | *Hawaii*
Z Ritz-Carlton Key Biscayne | *Miami*

MOUNTAIN SETTINGS/ VIEWS

ARGENTINA
NEW Cavas Wine Lodge | *Agrelo*
Llao Llao Hotel | *Patagonia*

AUSTRALIA
Hyatt Regency | *Sunshine Coast*
Langham | *Melbourne*
Lilianfels Blue Mtns. | *Blue Mountains*

AUSTRIA
Schloss Fuschl | *Salzburg*

BELIZE
Blancaneaux | *San Ignacio*
Chaa Creek | *San Ignacio*

BHUTAN
Amankora | *Paro*
Uma Paro | *Paro*

CANADA
Aerie | *Victoria*
Fairmont Banff Springs | *Canadian Rockies*

Fairmont Jasper Park | *Canadian Rockies*
Fairmont/Lake Louise | *Canadian Rockies*
Fairmont Tremblant | *Montréal*
Fairmont/Whistler | *Canadian Rockies*
Z Four Seasons | *Canadian Rockies*
Keltic Lodge | *Cape Breton*
Le Westin | *Montréal*
Post Hotel | *Canadian Rockies*
Rimrock | *Canadian Rockies*
Westin | *Canadian Rockies*
NEW Westin Bear Mtn. | *Victoria*

CHILE
Explora En Patagonia | *Patagonia*

CHINA
Banyan Tree | *Yunnan Province*
Le Méridien She Shan | *Shanghai*

COSTA RICA
Finca Rosa Blanca | *San José*
La Paloma Lodge | *Osa Peninsula*
Tabacón Grand Spa | *Arenal*

EGYPT
Oberoi Sahl Hasheesh | *Red Sea*

FRANCE
NEW Cheval Blanc | *Courchevel*
d'Europe | *Provence*
Évian Royal Palace | *Haute-Savoie*
Z Four Seasons Resort | *Provence*
Les Fermes de Marie | *Haute-Savoie*
Z Michel Bras | *Aveyron*

GERMANY
Schloss. Bühlerhöhe | *Baden-Baden*

INDIA
Oberoi Cecil | *Shimla*
Wildflower Hall | *Shimla*

INDONESIA
Z Amandari | *Bali*
Z Amanjiwo | *Borobudur*
Four Seasons Sayan | *Bali*
Puri Wulandari | *Bali*
Viceroy Bali | *Bali*

ISRAEL
Herods Vitalis Spa | *Eilat*

SPECIAL FEATURES

ITALY
Caruso | *Amalfi Coast*
Eden Roc | *Amalfi Coast*
Grand/Timeo | *Sicily*
Il Sole Di Ranco | *Milan*
Relais Borgo Felice | *Siena*

JAMAICA
Strawberry Hill | *Kingston*

JAPAN
Gora Kadan | *Hakone*
🔲 Park Hyatt | *Tokyo*

KENYA
Mount Kenya Safari | *Nanyuki*

MEXICO
Rancho La Puerta | *Baja Peninsula*

MOROCCO
Kasbah du Toubkal | *High Atlas*
Sofitel Palais Jamai | *Fès*

NEW ZEALAND
🔲 Blanket Bay | *Queenstown*

OMAN
Shangri-La | *Muscat*

PERU
Monasterio | *Cuzco*

PORTUGAL
Bussaco Palace | *Bussaco*
Penha Longa | *Sintra*
Quinta das Lagrimas | *Coimbra*
Tivoli Palácio/Seteais | *Sintra*

SOUTH AFRICA
Grande Roche | *Cape Town*
Table Bay | *Cape Town*

SOUTH KOREA
W Seoul-Walkerhill | *Seoul*

SPAIN
Barceló La Bobadilla | *Granada*
Mardavall | *Mallorca*
Parador de Granada | *Granada*
Son Brull | *Mallorca*

ST. LUCIA
Sandals Regency

SWITZERLAND
Badrutt's Palace | *St. Moritz*
Eden au Lac | *Zurich*
Four Seasons | *Geneva*
Grand/Zermatterhof | *Zermatt*
Gstaad Palace | *Gstaad*
Kempinski Grand | *St. Moritz*
Kulm | *St. Moritz*
Mont Cervin Palace | *Zermatt*
Park Hotel | *Vitznau*
Raffles | *Montreux*
🔲 Victoria-Jungfrau | *Interlaken*
Villa Principe Leopoldo | *Lugano*

THAILAND
Anantara Resort | *Golden Triangle*
🔲 Four Seasons | *Chiang Mai*
🔲 Four Seasons Tented | *Golden Triangle*

UNITED KINGDOM – ENGLAND
Sharrow Bay | *Cumbria*

UNITED KINGDOM – WALES
🔲 Bodysgallen Hall | *Llandudno*

UNITED STATES
🔲 Bel-Air | *Los Angeles*
🔲 Boulders | *Phoenix/Scottsdale*
🔲 Four Seasons Resort | *Phoenix/ Scottsdale*
Green Valley Ranch | *Las Vegas*
JW Marriott | *Las Vegas*
Loews | *Las Vegas*
🔲 Phoenician | *Phoenix/Scottsdale*
Salish Lodge | *Seattle*
🔲 Sanctuary/Camelback Mtn. | *Phoenix/Scottsdale*

NOTEWORTHY NEWCOMERS

ARGENTINA
NEW Cavas Wine Lodge | *Agrelo*
NEW Park Hyatt | *Buenos Aires*

CANADA
NEW Adara | *Canadian Rockies*
NEW Pan Pacific | *Canadian Rockies*
SoHo Metropolitan Hotel | *Toronto*
NEW Westin Bear Mtn. | *Victoria*

CHINA
NEW Le Royal Méridien | *Shanghai*
NEW Shangri-La | *Guangzhou*

CZECH REPUBLIC
NEW Mandarin Oriental | *Prague*

DENMARK
NEW Copenhagen Island |
  Copenhagen

FIJI
NEW Westin Denarau

FRANCE
NEW Cheval Blanc | *Courchevel*

FRENCH POLYNESIA
NEW St. Regis | *Bora Bora*

MALDIVES
NEW Four Seasons/Landaa
  Giraavaru
NEW W Retreat & Spa

MALTA
NEW Le Méridien St. Julians

MEXICO
NEW Excellence Riviera | *Cancún*

QATAR
NEW Sharq Village & Spa | *Doha*

RUSSIA
NEW Kempinski/Moika 22 | *St.
  Petersburg*

THAILAND
NEW Four Seasons Resort | *Koh
  Samui*

TURKS & CAICOS
NEW Amanyara

UNITED STATES
NEW Conrad | *Chicago*
Z NEW Four Seasons/Lanai |
  Hawaii
Z NEW St. Regis | *San Francisco*
Z NEW Wynn | *Las Vegas*

VIETNAM
NEW Park Hyatt Saigon | *Ho Chi
  Minh City*

OFFBEAT/FUNKY
_____

ARGENTINA
NEW Cavas Wine Lodge | *Agrelo*

AUSTRALIA
Adelphi | *Melbourne*
Daintree Eco Lodge | *Great Barrier
  Reef*

BELIZE
Turtle Inn | *Placencia*

BOTSWANA
Chief's Camp | *Okavango Delta*
Chobe Chilwero | *Chobe National
  Park*
Khwai River Lodge | *Okavango Delta*
Z Mombo Camp | *Okavango Delta*
Savute Elephant Camp | *Chobe
  National Park*

BRAZIL
Emiliano | *São Paulo*
Unique | *São Paulo*

CANADA
NEW Adara | *Canadian Rockies*
Arc | *Ottawa*
Ice Hotel | *Québec City*
Opus | *Vancouver*
Pacific Palisades | *Vancouver*
SoHo Metropolitan Hotel | *Toronto*

COSTA RICA
Pura Vida Retreat | *San José*

FRANCE
Costes | *Paris*
Cour des Loges | *Rhône*
du Petit Moulin | *Paris*
L'Hotel | *Paris*
Murano Urban | *Paris*
Saint James | *Paris*

FRENCH POLYNESIA
NEW St. Regis | *Bora Bora*

GERMANY
Schloss. im Grunewald | *Berlin*
Side | *Hamburg*
25hours | *Hamburg*

INDONESIA
Banyan Tree | *Bintan*

IRELAND
Fitzwilliam | *Dublin*
Morrison | *Dublin*

ISRAEL
Dan Eilat | *Eilat*

ITALY
Grand/Miramare | *Portofino*

JAPAN
Tawaraya Ryokan | *Kyoto*

KENYA
Treetops | *Nairobi*

MALDIVES
NEW W Retreat & Spa

MEXICO
Camino Real | *Mexico City*
Maya Tulum | *Tulum*

MOROCCO
Ksar Char-Bagh | *Marrakech*

PORTUGAL
Palácio Belmonte | *Lisbon*

RUSSIA
Swissôtel | *Moscow*

SAUDI ARABIA
Al Faisaliah | *Riyadh*

SOUTH AFRICA
Kwandwe/Game Reserve | *Benmore*
Le Quartier Francais | *Franschhoek*

SPAIN
Omm | *Barcelona*
Parador de Granada | *Granada*
Puerta America | *Madrid*

SWEDEN
ICEHOTEL | *Jukkasjärvi*

**UNITED KINGDOM –
ENGLAND**
Charlotte St. | *London*
St. Martins Lane | *London*

UNITED STATES
Chateau Marmont | *Los Angeles*
Library | *New York City*
Mercer | *New York City*
Monaco | *Chicago*
Monaco | *Washington, DC*
Mondrian | *Los Angeles*
Palomar | *San Francisco*
Sofitel | *Washington, DC*
Victor | *Miami*

POWER SCENES
_____

ARGENTINA
Z Alvear Palace | *Buenos Aires*

BRAZIL
Copacabana Palace | *Rio de Janeiro*

CANADA
Four Seasons | *Vancouver*
Loews Hotel Vogue | *Montréal*
SoHo Metropolitan Hotel | *Toronto*
Sutton Place | *Vancouver*
Wedgewood | *Vancouver*
NEW Westin Bear Mtn. | *Victoria*
Windsor Arms | *Toronto*
W Montreal | *Montréal*

CHILE
Ritz-Carlton | *Santiago*

CHINA
Z Four Seasons | *Hong Kong*
Four Seasons | *Shanghai*
Grand Hyatt | *Beijing*
Mandarin Oriental | *Macau*
Mandarin Oriental/Landmark |
   Hong Kong
Peninsula | *Beijing*
Z Peninsula | *Hong Kong*
St. Regis | *Beijing*
Z St. Regis | *Shanghai*

CZECH REPUBLIC
Z Four Seasons | *Prague*
NEW Mandarin Oriental | *Prague*

EGYPT
InterContinental | *Cairo*

FRANCE
Byblos | *Côte d'Azur*
de Crillon | *Paris*
Z Four Seasons George V | *Paris*
Park Hyatt | *Paris*
Z Plaza Athénée | *Paris*
Ritz | *Paris*

GERMANY
Adlon Kempinski | *Berlin*
Steigenberger Frankfurter |
   Frankfurt

INDONESIA
Grand Hyatt | *Jakarta*
Legian | *Bali*
Ritz-Carlton | *Jakarta*

IRELAND
K Club | *County Kildare*

subscribe to zagat.com

ISRAEL
American Colony | *Jerusalem*
Hilton | *Tel Aviv*

ITALY
Ca'Pisani | *Venice*
🇿 Cipriani | *Venice*
🇿 Four Seasons | *Milan*
Gritti Palace | *Venice*
St. Regis | *Rome*

JAPAN
Hyatt Regency | *Osaka*
Imperial | *Tokyo*
🇿 Mandarin Oriental | *Tokyo*
🇿 Park Hyatt | *Tokyo*

MALAYSIA
Mandarin Oriental | *Kuala Lumpur*

MALDIVES
One & Only
Taj Exotica
NEW W Retreat & Spa

MEXICO
🇿 Four Seasons | *Mexico City*

NAMIBIA
Little Ongava Lodge | *Ongava Game Reserve*

NEW ZEALAND
Millbrook | *Queenstown*

OMAN
Shangri-La | *Muscat*

PERU
Monasterio | *Cuzco*

PHILIPPINES
Mandarin Oriental | *Manila*

QATAR
Four Seasons | *Doha*

RUSSIA
Baltschug Kempinski | *Moscow*

SINGAPORE
Raffles
🇿 Ritz-Carlton Millenia

SOUTH AFRICA
Saxon | *Johannesburg*

SPAIN
Ritz | *Madrid*
Villa Magna | *Madrid*
Westin Palace | *Madrid*

SWITZERLAND
Baur au Lac | *Zurich*
Bellevue Palace | *Berne*
Park Hyatt | *Zurich*

TANZANIA
Kilimanjaro/Kempinski | *Dar es Salaam*

THAILAND
Four Seasons | *Bangkok*
🇿 Oriental | *Bangkok*
Sheraton Grande | *Bangkok*

UNITED ARAB EMIRATES
🇿 Burj Al Arab | *Dubai*
Grosvenor House | *Dubai*
Park Hyatt | *Dubai*

UNITED KINGDOM – ENGLAND
Claridge's | *London*

UNITED STATES
Adolphus | *Dallas/Ft. Worth*
🇿 Bel-Air | *Los Angeles*
🇿 Bellagio | *Las Vegas*
Beverly Hills Hotel | *Los Angeles*
Beverly Wilshire | *Los Angeles*
Boston Harbor | *Boston*
Carlyle | *New York City*
Chateau Marmont | *Los Angeles*
Fifteen Beacon | *Boston*
Four Seasons | *Atlanta*
🇿 Four Seasons | *Boston*
🇿 Four Seasons | *Chicago*
Four Seasons | *Houston*
🇿 Four Seasons | *New York City*
🇿 Four Seasons | *San Francisco*
Four Seasons | *Washington, DC*
🇿 Four Seasons Beverly Hills | *Los Angeles*
🇿 Halekulani | *Hawaii*
Hay-Adams | *Washington, DC*
Hilton Checkers | *Los Angeles*
Houstonian | *Houston*
InterContinental | *Atlanta*
Jefferson | *Washington, DC*

🅱 Kahala | *Hawaii*
🅱 Mandarin Oriental | *New York City*
Mandarin Oriental | *San Francisco*
Mansion/Turtle Creek | *Dallas/ Ft. Worth*
Mondrian | *Los Angeles*
New York Palace | *New York City*
🅱 Park Hyatt | *Chicago*
Park Hyatt | *Los Angeles*
Park Hyatt/Bellevue | *Philadelphia*
🅱 Peninsula | *Chicago*
🅱 Peninsula | *Los Angeles*
Peninsula | *New York City*
Raffles L'Ermitage | *Los Angeles*
Rittenhouse | *Philadelphia*
Ritz-Carlton | *Boston*
🅱 Ritz-Carlton | *Chicago*
Ritz-Carlton | *Philadelphia*
🅱 Ritz-Carlton | *San Francisco*
Ritz-Carlton | *Washington, DC*
Ritz-Carlton Battery Park | *New York City*
Ritz-Carlton Buckhead | *Atlanta*
Ritz-Carlton Georgetown | *Washington, DC*
🅱 NEW St. Regis | *San Francisco*
Taj Boston | *Boston*
Trump International | *New York City*
Venetian | *Las Vegas*
Victor | *Miami*
Waldorf-Astoria | *New York City*
Willard InterCont. | *Washington, DC*
🅱 Windsor Court | *New Orleans*
NEW W New Orleans | *New Orleans*
🅱 NEW Wynn | *Las Vegas*

REMOTE

AUSTRALIA
Daintree Eco Lodge | *Great Barrier Reef*
Sails in the Desert | *Ayers Rock*
Wilson Island | *Great Barrier Reef*

BELIZE
Blancaneaux | *San Ignacio*
Chaa Creek | *San Ignacio*

BHUTAN
Amankora | *Paro*
Uma Paro | *Paro*

BOTSWANA
Camp Okavango | *Okavango Delta*
Khwai River Lodge | *Okavango Delta*

BRAZIL
Tropical Manaus | *Amazon*

CAMBODIA
🅱 Amansara | *Siem Reap*
Shinta Mani | *Siem Reap*

CANADA
Alive Health | *Canadian Rockies*
Fairmont Jasper Park | *Canadian Rockies*
Langdon Hall | *Toronto*
🅱 L'Eau a la Bouche | *Montréal*
NEW Pan Pacific | *Canadian Rockies*
Post Hotel | *Canadian Rockies*
Westin | *Canadian Rockies*
Wickaninnish Inn | *Victoria*

CHILE
Explora En Patagonia | *Patagonia*

COSTA RICA
Aguila de Osa | *Osa Peninsula*
🅱 Four Seasons Resort | *Guanacaste*
Paradisus | *Guanacaste*
Tabacón Grand Spa | *Arenal*

FRANCE
Château de Mercuès | *Mercuès*
🅱 Le Château/St-Martin | *Côte d'Azur*

INDIA
Amanbagh | *Rajasthan*
Rambagh Palace | *Rajasthan*

ISRAEL
🅱 Carmel Forest Spa | *Haifa*
Le Méridien | *Dead Sea*
Mizpe Hayamim | *Rosh Pinna*

ITALY
L'Andana | *Castiglione della Pescaia*

JORDAN
Mövenpick Resort | *Petra*

KENYA
Amboseli Serena Safari | *Amboseli Game Reserve*
Kichwa Tembo | *Masai Mara Game Reserve*
Little Governor's | *Masai Mara Game Reserve*

subscribe to zagat.com

Mara Serena | *Masai Mara Game Reserve*
Treetops | *Nairobi*

MALAYSIA
Pangkor Laut | *Langkawi*

MEXICO
☒ Four Seasons | *Punta Mita*

MOROCCO
Kasbah du Toubkal | *High Atlas*

NEPAL
Le Méridien | *Kathmandu*

NEW ZEALAND
☒ Kauri Cliffs | *Kerikeri*
☒ Wharekauhau | *Featherston*

SEYCHELLES
Banyan Tree

SOUTH AFRICA
Bushmans Kloof | *Biedouw Valley*
Kwandwe/Game Reserve | *Benmore*
Lanzerac Manor | *Cape Town*
MalaMala | *Kruger Area*
Plettenberg | *Plettenberg Bay*
Tsala Treetop Lodge | *Plettenberg Bay*

SPAIN
Barceló La Bobadilla | *Granada*

SWEDEN
ICEHOTEL | *Jukkasjärvi*

SWITZERLAND
☒ Victoria-Jungfrau | *Interlaken*

THAILAND
☒ Four Seasons Tented | *Golden Triangle*

UNITED KINGDOM - ENGLAND
Amberley Castle | *West Sussex*

ZIMBABWE
Victoria Falls Safari | *Victoria Falls*

ROMANTIC

ANGUILLA
Cap Juluca
Malliouhana
St. Regis

ANTIGUA
Curtain Bluff
Jumby Bay
Sandals Resort
St. James's Club

ARGENTINA
NEW Cavas Wine Lodge | *Agrelo*
Llao Llao Hotel | *Patagonia*

ARUBA
Aruba Resort
Hyatt Regency
Marriott's/Ocean Club
Radisson Resort
Renaissance

AUSTRALIA
Daintree Eco Lodge | *Great Barrier Reef*
Dunk Island | *Great Barrier Reef*
☒ Hayman Island | *Great Barrier Reef*
Kewarra Beach Resort | *Great Barrier Reef*
Lilianfels Blue Mtns. | *Blue Mountains*
Sebel Reef House | *Great Barrier Reef*
Voyages Lizard Island | *Great Barrier Reef*

AUSTRIA
Goldener Hirsch | *Salzburg*

BAHAMAS
☒ One & Only
Pink Sands
Westin Our Lucaya

BARBADOS
Cobblers Cove
☒ Sandy Lane

BELIZE
Blancaneaux | *San Ignacio*
Cayo Espanto | *San Pedro*
Turtle Inn | *Placencia*

BERMUDA
Ariel Sands
Cambridge Beaches
Elbow Beach
Horizons & Cottages

Pink Beach Club
Reefs

BOTSWANA
⊡ Mombo Camp | *Okavango Delta*

BRITISH VIRGIN ISLANDS
Biras Creek Resort | *Virgin Gorda*
Bitter End | *Virgin Gorda*
Little Dix Bay | *Virgin Gorda*
Necker Island | *Virgin Gorda*
Peter Island | *Peter Island*

CANADA
Aerie | *Victoria*
Dominion 1912 | *Québec City*
Fairmont/Lake Louise | *Canadian Rockies*
⊡ Hastings House | *Vancouver*
Kingsbrae Arms | *St. Andrews*
Langdon Hall | *Toronto*
Le Germain | *Montréal*
Pillar and Post Inn | *Niagara Falls*
Prince of Wales Hotel | *Niagara Falls*
Rimrock | *Canadian Rockies*
Wickaninnish Inn | *Victoria*

CHILE
Explora En Patagonia | *Patagonia*

COLOMBIA
Sofitel Santa Clara | *Cartagena*

COSTA RICA
Punta Islita | *Guanacaste*

CURAÇAO
Avila Beach

DENMARK
Sonderho Kro | *Copenhagen*

DOMINICAN REPUBLIC
Casa de Campo
Excellence Punta Cana

EGYPT
⊡ Four Seasons | *Red Sea*

ESTONIA
Three Sisters | *Tallinn*

FIJI
Turtle Island
Vatulele Island
Wakaya Club

FRANCE
Auberge de Noves | *Provence*
Bernard Loiseau | *Burgundy*
Château/Chèvre D'Or | *Côte d'Azur*
Chateau/Crayeres | *Champagne*
Château de Bagnols | *Rhône*
Château de Gilly | *Burgundy*
Château de Marçay | *Loire*
Château/Messardière | *Côte d'Azur*
Cour des Loges | *Rhône*
d'Europe | *Provence*
Domaine/Hauts de Loire | *Loire*
du Palais | *Biarritz*
du Petit Moulin | *Paris*
⊡ Four Seasons George V | *Paris*
Grand Cap-Ferrat | *Côte d'Azur*
Grand/Lion d'Or | *Loire*
Hostellerie/Crillon | *Provence*
La Bastide/Moustiers | *Provence*
⊡ La Maison Troisgros | *Loire*
La Mirande | *Provence*
La Réserve/Beaulieu | *Côte d'Azur*
La Voile d'Or | *Côte d'Azur*
Le Chateau d'Artigny | *Loire*
Le Prieuré | *Provence*
Le Saint Paul | *Côte d'Azur*
Les Deux Abbesses | *Haute-Loire*
Les Fermes de Marie | *Haute-Savoie*
Saint James | *Paris*
Villa Gallici | *Provence*

FRENCH POLYNESIA
Bora Bora | *Bora Bora*
Bora Bora Lagoon | *Bora Bora*
InterContinental | *Moorea*
Le Méridien | *Bora Bora*
Le Taha'a | *Taha'a*
NEW St. Regis | *Bora Bora*

GREECE
⊡ Blue Palace Resort | *Crete*

GRENADINES
Cotton House | *Mustique*
Petit St. Vincent | *Petit St. Vincent*
Raffles Resort | *Canouan Island*

GUATEMALA
Casa Santo Domingo | *Antigua*

INDIA
⊡ Amarvilas Oberoi | *Agra*
⊡ Rajvilas Oberoi | *Rajasthan*

INDONESIA
- ☒ Amandari | *Bali*
- ☒ Amanusa | *Bali*
- ☒ Como Shambala | *Bali*
- ☒ Four Seasons Jimbaran Bay | *Bali*
- Four Seasons Sayan | *Bali*
- InterContinental | *Bali*
- Le Méridien Nirwana | *Bali*
- Puri Wulandari | *Bali*
- ☒ Ritz-Carlton | *Bali*
- Viceroy Bali | *Bali*

ISRAEL
- ☒ Carmel Forest Spa | *Haifa*
- Eilat Princess | *Eilat*

ITALY
- Certosa di Maggiano | *Siena*
- ☒ Cipriani | *Venice*
- Grand/Villa Serbelloni | *Lake Como Area*
- Gritti Palace | *Venice*
- ☒ Il San Pietro | *Amalfi Coast*
- L'Andana | *Castiglione della Pescaia*
- La Posta Vecchia | *Rome*
- La Scalinatella | *Amalfi Coast*
- Le Sirenuse | *Amalfi Coast*
- Locanda Amorosa | *Siena*
- Monaco | *Venice*
- Palazzo Sasso | *Amalfi Coast*
- Palumbo | *Amalfi Coast*
- Pitrizza | *Sardinia*
- Relais Borgo Felice | *Siena*
- Relais La Suvera | *Siena*
- San Clemente | *Venice*
- Splendido | *Portofino*
- Villa Cipriani | *Venice*
- ☒ Villa d'Este | *Lake Como Area*
- Villa San Michele | *Florence*

JAMAICA
- Half Moon | *Montego Bay*
- Round Hill | *Montego Bay*

JAPAN
- Gora Kadan | *Hakone*

JORDAN
- Mövenpick Resort | *Petra*

KENYA
- Mara Serena | *Masai Mara Game Reserve*
- Mount Kenya Safari | *Nanyuki*

MALAYSIA
- ☒ Datai | *Langkawi*

MALDIVES
- Four Seasons/Kuda Huraa
- One & Only
- Soneva Fushi
- Taj Exotica
- **NEW** W Retreat & Spa

MAURITIUS
- Le Prince Maurice
- Le Saint Géran

MEXICO
- Casa/Sierra Nevada | *San Miguel de Allende*
- Casa Natalia | *Baja Peninsula*
- ☒ Esperanza | *Baja Peninsula*
- ☒ Four Seasons | *Punta Mita*
- Ikal del Mar | *Playa del Carmen*
- ☒ La Casa Que Canta | *Zihuatanejo*
- Las Alamandas | *Manzanillo*
- Las Brisas | *Acapulco*
- Las Hadas | *Manzanillo*
- Las Mañanitas | *Cuernavaca*
- Maroma | *Cancún*
- Maya Tulum | *Tulum*
- ☒ Ritz-Carlton | *Cancún*
- ☒ Royal Hideaway | *Playa del Carmen*
- Secreto | *Cancún*

NEW ZEALAND
- ☒ Blanket Bay | *Queenstown*
- Huka Lodge | *Taupo*

PERU
- Monasterio | *Cuzco*

PORTUGAL
- ☒ Lapa Palace | *Lisbon*
- Palácio Belmonte | *Lisbon*
- Tivoli Palácio/Seteais | *Sintra*

SEYCHELLES
- Banyan Tree
- Frégate Island
- Lémuria Resort
- North Island
- Taj Denis Island

SINGAPORE
- Raffles

SOUTH AFRICA
Kwandwe/Game Reserve | *Benmore*
Le Quartier Francais | *Franschhoek*
Sabi Sabi | *Kruger Area*
🔲 Singita | *Kruger Area*

SPAIN
AC Santo Mauro | *Madrid*
Alfonso XIII | *Seville*
Maria Cristina | *San Sebastián*
Parador de Granada | *Granada*
Puente Romano | *Costa del Sol*
Son Brull | *Mallorca*

SRI LANKA
Amangalla
Amanwella

ST. BARTS
Christopher
Eden Rock
François Plantation
Guanahani & Spa
Isle de France
La Banane
Le Toiny
Manapany

ST. KITTS & NEVIS
🔲 Four Seasons | *Nevis*
Nisbet Plantation | *Nevis*

ST. LUCIA
Anse Chastanet
Jalousie Plantation
Ladera
Sandals Grande

ST. MARTIN
La Samanna

SWITZERLAND
Four Seasons | *Geneva*
Mandarin Oriental | *Geneva*

SYRIA
Four Seasons | *Damascus*

TANZANIA
Mnemba Island | *Zanzibar*
Ngorongoro Crater | *Ngorongoro*

THAILAND
🔲 Amanpuri | *Phuket*
🔲 Banyan Tree | *Phuket*
Chedi | *Phuket*

🔲 Four Seasons | *Chiang Mai*
🔲 Four Seasons Tented | *Golden Triangle*
Le Royal Méridien | *Koh Samui*
🔲 Oriental | *Bangkok*
Rayavadee | *Phuket*

TURKEY
Kempinski | *Bodrum*

TURKS & CAICOS
Grace Bay Club
Parrot Cay

UNITED ARAB EMIRATES
🔲 One & Only | *Dubai*
Ritz-Carlton | *Dubai*

UNITED KINGDOM – ENGLAND
Chewton Glen | *Hampshire*
🔲 Gidleigh Park | *Devon*
Gravetye Manor | *West Sussex*

UNITED KINGDOM – SCOTLAND
Culloden House | *Inverness*

UNITED STATES
🔲 Bel-Air | *Los Angeles*
Beverly Hills Hotel | *Los Angeles*
Carlyle | *New York City*
🔲 Four Seasons/Hualalai | *Hawaii*
🔲 Four Seasons Wailea | *Hawaii*
Grove Isle | *Miami*
Inn at Langley | *Seattle*
🔲 Inn/Little Washington | *Washington, DC*
Lowell | *New York City*
Princeville Resort | *Hawaii*
🔲 Royal Palms | *Phoenix/Scottsdale*
🔲 Sanctuary/Camelback Mtn. | *Phoenix/Scottsdale*
Shutters on the Beach | *Los Angeles*
Soniat House | *New Orleans*
Vitale | *San Francisco*

URUGUAY
🔲 Four Seasons | *Carmelo*

SCUBA/SNORKELING

ANGUILLA
Cap Juluca
CuisinArt Resort

Malliouhana
St. Regis

ANTIGUA
Carlisle Bay
Curtain Bluff
Jumby Bay
Sandals Resort
St. James's Club

ARUBA
Aruba Resort
Divi Aruba Beach
Hyatt Regency
Marriott Resort
Marriott's/Ocean Club
Radisson Resort
Renaissance

AUSTRALIA
Bedarra Island | *Great Barrier Reef*
Daintree Eco Lodge | *Great Barrier Reef*
Dunk Island | *Great Barrier Reef*
☒ Hayman Island | *Great Barrier Reef*
Palazzo Versace | *Gold Coast*
Sheraton Mirage | *Great Barrier Reef*
Voyages Lizard Island | *Great Barrier Reef*
Wilson Island | *Great Barrier Reef*

BAHAMAS
Atlantis
Club Med
Four Seasons
Musha Cay
☒ One & Only
Pink Sands
Rock House
Sandals Royal
Westin Our Lucaya

BARBADOS
Cobblers Cove
Coral Reef Club
Sandpiper
☒ Sandy Lane

BELIZE
Kanantik Reef | *Dangriga*
Turtle Inn | *Placencia*

BERMUDA
Ariel Sands
Cambridge Beaches
Elbow Beach
Fairmont Hamilton
Fairmont Southampton
Horizons & Cottages
Pink Beach Club
Reefs

BRITISH VIRGIN ISLANDS
Biras Creek Resort | *Virgin Gorda*
Bitter End | *Virgin Gorda*
Guana Island | *Virgin Gorda*
Little Dix Bay | *Virgin Gorda*
Long Bay Resort | *Tortola*
Necker Island | *Virgin Gorda*
Peter Island | *Peter Island*
Sugar Mill | *Tortola*

CANADA
Fairmont | *Vancouver*
Fairmont Empress | *Victoria*
Sooke Harbour | *Victoria*

CAYMAN ISLANDS
Hyatt Regency
☒ Ritz-Carlton

COSTA RICA
Aguila de Osa | *Osa Peninsula*
☒ Four Seasons Resort | *Guanacaste*
La Paloma Lodge | *Osa Peninsula*
Los Sueños Marriott | *Puntarenas*
Paradisus | *Guanacaste*

CURAÇAO
Marriott Beach

CYPRUS
Almyra | *Paphos*
Anassa | *Polis*

DOMINICAN REPUBLIC
Casa de Campo
Excellence Punta Cana
Punta Cana

EGYPT
☒ Four Seasons | *Red Sea*
Oberoi Sahl Hasheesh | *Red Sea*

FIJI

Shangri-La's Fijian
Turtle Island
Vatulele Island
Wakaya Club
NEW Westin Denarau

FRANCE

Z du Cap-Eden-Roc | Côte d'Azur
Évian Royal Palace | Haute-Savoie
Grand Cap-Ferrat | Côte d'Azur
InterContinental | Côte d'Azur
La Réserve/Beaulieu | Côte d'Azur
Martinez | Côte d'Azur
Résidence de Pinède | Côte d'Azur

FRENCH POLYNESIA

Bora Bora | Bora Bora
Bora Bora Lagoon | Bora Bora
Bora Bora Pearl | Bora Bora
InterContinental | Moorea
InterContinental | Tahiti
Le Méridien | Bora Bora
Le Méridien | Tahiti
Le Taha'a | Taha'a
NEW St. Regis | Bora Bora

GREECE

Astir Palace | Athens
Z Blue Palace Resort | Crete
Elounda Beach | Crete
Elounda Mare | Crete
Santa Marina | Mykonos
Vedema Resort | Santorini

GRENADINES

Cotton House | Mustique
Petit St. Vincent | Petit St. Vincent
Raffles Resort | Canouan Island

GUATEMALA

Atitlán | Panajachel

INDONESIA

Z Amankila | Bali
Z Amanusa | Bali
Banyan Tree | Bintan
Grand Hyatt | Bali
Laguna Resort | Bali
Nusa Dua Beach | Bali
Z Ritz-Carlton | Bali

ISRAEL

Eilat Princess | Eilat

ITALY

Z Cala di Volpe | Sardinia
Capri Palace | Amalfi Coast
Eden Roc | Amalfi Coast
Excelsior Palace | Portofino
Grand/Miramare | Portofino
Pitrizza | Sardinia
Poseidon | Amalfi Coast
Romazzino | Sardinia
Splendido | Portofino

JAMAICA

Beaches Boscobel | Ocho Rios
Couples Sans Souci | Ocho Rios
Couples Swept Away | Negril
Grand Lido | Negril
Grand Lido Braco | Montego Bay
Half Moon | Montego Bay
Jamaica Inn | Ocho Rios
Ritz-Carlton Golf | Montego Bay
Rose Hall Resort | Montego Bay
Round Hill | Montego Bay
Sandals | Montego Bay
Sandals Dunn's River | Ocho Rios
Sandals Grande | Ocho Rios
Sandals Negril Beach | Negril
Tryall Club | Montego Bay

MALAYSIA

Four Seasons | Langkawi
Tanjong Jara | Penang

MALDIVES

Banyan Tree
Four Seasons/Kuda Huraa
NEW Four Seasons/Landaa
  Giraavaru
Soneva Fushi
Taj Exotica
NEW W Retreat & Spa

MALTA

NEW Le Méridien St. Julians

MAURITIUS

Le Prince Maurice
Le Saint Géran
Le Touessrok
Oberoi
Taj Exotica

MEXICO
Aventura Spa | *Cancún*
Casa Del Mar | *Baja Peninsula*
CasaMagna Marriott | *Cancún*
CasaMagna Marriott | *Puerto Vallarta*
Dreams | *Cancún*
Dreams | *Puerto Vallarta*
Z Esperanza | *Baja Peninsula*
NEW Excellence Riviera | *Cancún*
Fairmont Pierre | *Acapulco*
Fiesta Americana | *Cancún*
Z Four Seasons | *Punta Mita*
Hyatt Caribe | *Cancún*
Iberostar | *Cancún*
Ikal del Mar | *Playa del Carmen*
JW Marriott | *Cancún*
Z La Casa Que Canta | *Zihuatanejo*
La Jolla/Mismaloya | *Puerto Vallarta*
Las Alamandas | *Manzanillo*
Las Brisas | *Acapulco*
Las Brisas | *Ixtapa*
Las Hadas | *Manzanillo*
Z Las Ventanas | *Baja Peninsula*
Maroma | *Cancún*
Maya Tulum | *Tulum*
NH Krystal | *Puerto Vallarta*
Omni | *Cancún*
Z One & Only | *Baja Peninsula*
Z Ritz-Carlton | *Cancún*
Z Royal Hideaway | *Playa del Carmen*
Secreto | *Cancún*
Secrets Capri | *Cancún*
Twin Dolphin | *Baja Peninsula*
Villa del Sol | *Zihuatanejo*
Villa Rolandi Gourmet | *Cancún*
Westin | *Cancún*
Westin | *Baja Peninsula*

NEW ZEALAND
Z Kauri Cliffs | *Kerikeri*

OMAN
Shangri-La | *Muscat*

PALAU
Palau Royal Resort | *Koror*

PHILIPPINES
Amanpulo | *Cuyo Islands*
Shangri-La | *Cebu*

PORTUGAL
Quinta do Lago | *Algarve*
Reid's Palace | *Madeira*
Sheraton Algarve | *Algarve*

SEYCHELLES
Frégate Island
Lémuria Resort
North Island
Taj Denis Island

SOUTH AFRICA
Ngala/Game Reserve | *Kruger Area*
Phinda/Game Reserve | *Kruger Area*

SPAIN
Hostal/Gavina | *Costa Brava*
La Residencia | *Mallorca*
Marbella Club | *Costa del Sol*

SRI LANKA
Amangalla
Amanwella

ST. BARTS
Carl Gustaf
Christopher
Eden Rock
Guanahani & Spa
Isle de France
La Banane
Manapany

ST. KITTS & NEVIS
Z Four Seasons | *Nevis*
Montpelier | *Nevis*
Nisbet Plantation | *Nevis*

ST. LUCIA
Anse Chastanet
Jalousie Plantation
Ladera
Sandals Grande
Sandals Regency
Windjammer Landing

ST. MAARTEN
Oyster Bay Beach
Wyndham Sapphire

ST. MARTIN
La Samanna
L'Habitation/Lonvilliers

SPECIAL FEA

SWITZERLAND
Beau-Rivage | *Geneva*
Park Hotel | *Vitznau*

TANZANIA
Mnemba Island | *Zanzibar*
Zamani Kempinski | *Zanzibar*

THAILAND
☑ Amanpuri | *Phuket*
☑ Banyan Tree | *Phuket*
Chedi | *Phuket*
Evason | *Hua Hin*
Evason | *Phuket*
NEW Four Seasons Resort | *Koh Samui*
JW Marriott | *Phuket*
Le Royal Méridien | *Koh Samui*
Napasai | *Koh Samui*
Rayavadee | *Phuket*
Sheraton Grande | *Phuket*

TURKEY
Kempinski | *Bodrum*

TURKS & CAICOS
NEW Amanyara
Grace Bay Club
Ocean Club/West
Parrot Cay

UNITED ARAB EMIRATES
☑ Burj Al Arab | *Dubai*
Jumeirah Beach | *Dubai*

UNITED STATES
☑ Fairmont Kea Lani | *Hawaii*
Fisher Island | *Miami*
☑ Four Seasons/Hualalai | *Hawaii*
☑ **NEW** Four Seasons/Lanai | *Hawaii*
☑ Four Seasons Wailea | *Hawaii*
☑ Grand Hyatt | *Hawaii*
Grand Wailea Resort | *Hawaii*
Grove Isle | *Miami*
☑ Kahala | *Hawaii*
Princeville Resort | *Hawaii*
☑ Ritz-Carlton Kapalua | *Hawaii*
☑ Ritz-Carlton Key Biscayne | *Miami*
Ritz-Carlton South Beach | *Miami*

VIETNAM
Evason Hideaway | *Nha Trang*

SPA FACILITIES: DIET/NUTRITION

ARGENTINA
Llao Llao Hotel | *Patagonia*

AUSTRALIA
Langham | *Melbourne*
Observatory | *Sydney*
Palazzo Versace | *Gold Coast*
Westin | *Sydney*

BAHAMAS
Atlantis

BHUTAN
Uma Paro | *Paro*

BRAZIL
Grand Hyatt | *São Paulo*

CAMBODIA
☑ Amansara | *Siem Reap*

CANADA
Alive Health | *Canadian Rockies*
Delta Victoria | *Victoria*
Fairmont Empress | *Victoria*
Westin | *Canadian Rockies*
NEW Westin Bear Mtn. | *Victoria*

CHINA
JW Marriott | *Shanghai*
Mandarin Oriental/Landmark | *Hong Kong*
Peninsula | *Beijing*

DENMARK
D'Angleterre | *Copenhagen*

EGYPT
☑ Four Seasons/Nile Plaza | *Cairo*

FIJI
NEW Westin Denarau

FRANCE
Évian Royal Palace | *Haute-Savoie*
☑ Four Seasons Resort | *Provence*
La Réserve/Beaulieu | *Côte d'Azur*
Le Chateau d'Artigny | *Loire*

GERMANY
Bayerischer Hof | *Munich*
Brenner's Park | *Baden-Baden*

GREECE
Grande Bretagne | *Athens*

GRENADINES
Petit St. Vincent | *Petit St. Vincent*

INDIA
Hyatt Regency | *New Delhi*
Taj Lands End | *Mumbai (Bombay)*
Taj Mahal | *New Delhi*

INDONESIA
Banyan Tree | *Bintan*
Mandarin Oriental | *Surabaya*

ISRAEL
⚡ Carmel Forest Spa | *Haifa*
Herods Vitalis Spa | *Eilat*

ITALY
Capri Palace | *Amalfi Coast*
L'Albereta | *Erbusco*

JAPAN
Grand Hyatt | *Tokyo*
Okura | *Tokyo*

MALDIVES
🆕 Four Seasons/Landaa
   Giraavaru
Taj Exotica
🆕 W Retreat & Spa

MAURITIUS
Le Prince Maurice
Taj Exotica

MEXICO
Casa Del Mar | *Baja Peninsula*
Ikal del Mar | *Playa del Carmen*
Maroma | *Cancún*
⚡ One & Only | *Baja Peninsula*
Rancho La Puerta | *Baja Peninsula*
Westin | *Baja Peninsula*

MONACO
⚡ de Paris | *Monte Carlo*
Hermitage | *Monte Carlo*
Metropole | *Monte Carlo*

MOROCCO
Palmeraie Golf | *Marrakech*

NEW ZEALAND
Hyatt Regency | *Auckland*

POLAND
Marriott | *Warsaw*

PORTUGAL
Penha Longa | *Sintra*

QATAR
Four Seasons | *Doha*

SINGAPORE
Four Seasons

SOUTH AFRICA
Ulusaba/Game Reserve | *Kruger
   Area*

SPAIN
Mardavall | *Mallorca*
Omm | *Barcelona*
Ritz | *Madrid*

SRI LANKA
Amangalla

ST. BARTS
Le Toiny

ST. KITTS & NEVIS
⚡ Four Seasons | *Nevis*

ST. MARTIN
La Samanna

SWITZERLAND
Raffles | *Montreux*
⚡ Victoria-Jungfrau | *Interlaken*

THAILAND
Banyan Tree | *Bangkok*
Evason | *Phuket*

UNITED ARAB EMIRATES
Jumeirah Emirates | *Dubai*
Ritz-Carlton | *Dubai*

**UNITED KINGDOM -
ENGLAND**
Chewton Glen | *Hampshire*
Sanderson | *London*

UNITED STATES
Bellevue Club | *Seattle*
Boston Harbor | *Boston*
⚡ Boulders | *Phoenix/Scottsdale*
Crescent Court | *Dallas/Ft. Worth*
Fairmont | *Washington, DC*
⚡ Fairmont Kea Lani | *Hawaii*

Fisher Island | *Miami*

☒ Four Seasons | *San Francisco*

☒ Four Seasons Resort | *Phoenix/ Scottsdale*

☒ Grand Hyatt | *Hawaii*

Grand Wailea Resort | *Hawaii*

Green Valley Ranch | *Las Vegas*

Hilton Checkers | *Los Angeles*

Houstonian | *Houston*

JW Marriott | *Las Vegas*

Le Merigot Beach | *Los Angeles*

Loews Santa Monica | *Los Angeles*

☒ Phoenician | *Phoenix/Scottsdale*

☒ Ritz-Carlton | *Las Vegas*

☒ Ritz-Carlton | *Orlando*

☒ Ritz-Carlton Kapalua | *Hawaii*

☒ Ritz-Carlton Key Biscayne | *Miami*

☒ Royal Palms | *Phoenix/Scottsdale*

☒ Sanctuary/Camelback Mtn. | *Phoenix/Scottsdale*

Venetian | *Las Vegas*

SPA FACILITIES: HYDROTHERAPY

ANGUILLA
CuisinArt Resort

Malliouhana

ANTIGUA
Sandals Resort

ARGENTINA
NEW Cavas Wine Lodge | *Agrelo*

Llao Llao Hotel | *Patagonia*

NEW Park Hyatt | *Buenos Aires*

ARUBA
Hyatt Regency

AUSTRALIA
Daintree Eco Lodge | *Great Barrier Reef*

☒ Hayman Island | *Great Barrier Reef*

Palazzo Versace | *Gold Coast*

Park Hyatt | *Melbourne*

Park Hyatt | *Sydney*

Sebel Reef House | *Great Barrier Reef*

Sheraton Mirage | *Gold Coast*

Sheraton on the Park | *Sydney*

Voyages Lizard Island | *Great Barrier Reef*

Wilson Island | *Great Barrier Reef*

AUSTRIA
Schloss Fuschl | *Salzburg*

BAHAMAS
Atlantis

Four Seasons

Sandals Royal

Westin Our Lucaya

BARBADOS
☒ Sandy Lane

BELIZE
Chaa Creek | *San Ignacio*

BERMUDA
Ariel Sands

Cambridge Beaches

Fairmont Southampton

BHUTAN
Uma Paro | *Paro*

BRAZIL
Sheraton | *Rio de Janeiro*

BRITISH VIRGIN ISLANDS
Necker Island | *Virgin Gorda*

CAMBODIA
Raffles Grand | *Siem Reap*

Shinta Mani | *Siem Reap*

CANADA
Aerie | *Victoria*

Alive Health | *Canadian Rockies*

Delta Victoria | *Victoria*

Fairmont | *Vancouver*

Fairmont Empress | *Victoria*

Fairmont Royal York | *Toronto*

Fairmont Tremblant | *Montréal*

Fairmont/Whistler | *Canadian Rockies*

☒ Four Seasons | *Canadian Rockies*

Langdon Hall | *Toronto*

La Pinsonnière | *Québec City*

Le Westin | *Montréal*

Pan Pacific | *Vancouver*

Park Hyatt | *Toronto*
Post Hotel | *Canadian Rockies*
Westin | *Canadian Rockies*
Westin Harbor Castle | *Toronto*
Wickaninnish Inn | *Victoria*
W Montreal | *Montréal*

CHILE
Explora En Atacama | *Atacama*
San Cristobal Tower | *Santiago*

CHINA
Grand Hyatt | *Hong Kong*
InterContinental | *Hong Kong*
Mandarin Oriental | *Hong Kong*
Mandarin Oriental | *Macau*
Regent | *Shanghai*
St. Regis | *Beijing*
Westin | *Shanghai*

COSTA RICA
Costa Rica Marriott | *San José*
Tabacón Grand Spa | *Arenal*

CYPRUS
Anassa | *Polis*

CZECH REPUBLIC
Hoffmeister | *Prague*
NEW Mandarin Oriental | *Prague*

DENMARK
D'Angleterre | *Copenhagen*

EGYPT
Four Seasons/First Residence |
   Cairo

FIJI
NEW Westin Denarau

FRANCE
du Palais | *Biarritz*
Évian Royal Palace | *Haute-Savoie*
InterContinental | *Paris*
La Réserve/Beaulieu | *Côte d'Azur*
Le Chateau d'Artigny | *Loire*
Les Fermes de Marie | *Haute-Savoie*
Martinez | *Côte d'Azur*
☑ Plaza Athénée | *Paris*
Ritz | *Paris*
Trémoille | *Paris*
Trianon Palace | *Versailles*

GERMANY
Bayerischer Hof | *Munich*
Schloss. Bühlerhöhe | *Baden-Baden*
Schloss. im Grunewald | *Berlin*

GREECE
☑ Blue Palace Resort | *Crete*
Elounda Beach | *Crete*
Elounda Mare | *Crete*
Grande Bretagne | *Athens*
Grecotel | *Mykonos*

HUNGARY
Danubius | *Budapest*

INDIA
Taj Mahal | *New Delhi*

INDONESIA
Dharmawangsa | *Jakarta*
Laguna Resort | *Bali*
Puri Wulandari | *Bali*
☑ Ritz-Carlton | *Bali*

IRELAND
Ashford Castle | *County Mayo*
Dromoland Castle | *County Clare*
Park Hotel Kenmare | *County Kerry*

ISRAEL
☑ Carmel Forest Spa | *Haifa*
Regency | *Jerusalem*

ITALY
Capri Palace | *Amalfi Coast*
de Russie | *Rome*
Excelsior Palace | *Portofino*
Grand/Palace | *Rome*
Grand/Quisisana | *Amalfi Coast*
Grand/Vesuvio | *Naples*
Grand/Villa Serbelloni | *Lake Como
   Area*
Il Pellicano | *Porto Ercole*
L'Albereta | *Erbusco*
Palazzo Sasso | *Amalfi Coast*
Poseidon | *Amalfi Coast*
Relais Borgo Felice | *Siena*
Relais La Suvera | *Siena*
San Clemente | *Venice*
☑ Villa d'Este | *Lake Como Area*

JAMAICA
Beaches Boscobel | *Ocho Rios*
Couples Swept Away | *Negril*

SPECIAL FEATURES

Grand Lido Braco | *Montego Bay*
Half Moon | *Montego Bay*
Jamaica Inn | *Ocho Rios*
Sandals | *Montego Bay*
Sandals Dunn's River | *Ocho Rios*
Sandals Grande | *Ocho Rios*
Sandals Negril Beach | *Negril*
Strawberry Hill | *Kingston*

JAPAN
Gora Kadan | *Hakone*
Grand Hyatt | *Tokyo*
🔲 Mandarin Oriental | *Tokyo*
Nikko-Bayside, Hotel | *Osaka*
Okura | *Tokyo*
🔲 Park Hyatt | *Tokyo*

KENYA
Governor's Camp | *Masai Mara Game Reserve*
Little Governor's | *Masai Mara Game Reserve*

MALAYSIA
Mandarin Oriental | *Kuala Lumpur*
Shangri-La | *Kuala Lumpur*

MALDIVES
One & Only
Taj Exotica

MALTA
NEW Le Méridien St. Julians

MAURITIUS
Le Saint Géran
Le Touessrok
Taj Exotica

MEXICO
Aventura Spa | *Cancún*
Casa Del Mar | *Baja Peninsula*
CasaMagna Marriott | *Cancún*
Dreams Los Cabos | *Baja Peninsula*
Dreams | *Cancún*
🔲 Esperanza | *Baja Peninsula*
NEW Excellence Riviera | *Cancún*
Fairmont/Princess | *Acapulco*
Iberostar | *Cancún*
JW Marriott | *Cancún*
Le Méridien | *Cancún*
🔲 One & Only | *Baja Peninsula*
Rancho La Puerta | *Baja Peninsula*

🔲 Royal Hideaway | *Playa del Carmen*
Secrets Capri | *Cancún*
Westin | *Cancún*
Westin | *Puerto Vallarta*
Westin | *Baja Peninsula*

MONACO
🔲 de Paris | *Monte Carlo*
Hermitage | *Monte Carlo*

MOROCCO
Palmeraie Golf | *Marrakech*

NEW ZEALAND
🔲 Kauri Cliffs | *Kerikeri*
Millbrook | *Queenstown*

PHILIPPINES
Shangri-La | *Cebu*

POLAND
Marriott | *Warsaw*

PORTUGAL
🔲 Lapa Palace | *Lisbon*
Penha Longa | *Sintra*
Quinta do Lago | *Algarve*

QATAR
Four Seasons | *Doha*

RUSSIA
Astoria | *St. Petersburg*

SAUDI ARABIA
Al Faisaliah | *Riyadh*
Four Seasons | *Riyadh*

SINGAPORE
Conrad Centennial
Fullerton
Raffles The Plaza
Shangri-La
Swissôtel Merchant Ct.

SOUTH AFRICA
Bushmans Kloof | *Biedouw Valley*
🔲 Cape Grace | *Cape Town*
Palace of the Lost City | *Sun City*
Park Hyatt | *Johannesburg*
Plettenberg | *Plettenberg Bay*
Sabi Sabi | *Kruger Area*
Table Bay | *Cape Town*

SOUTH KOREA
Westin Chosun | *Seoul*
W Seoul-Walkerhill | *Seoul*

SPAIN
Claris | *Barcelona*
Hostal/Gavina | *Costa Brava*
Kempinski | *Costa del Sol*
Marbella Club | *Costa del Sol*
Mardavall | *Mallorca*
Maria Cristina | *San Sebastián*
Omm | *Barcelona*
Rey Juan Carlos I | *Barcelona*
Son Brull | *Mallorca*

SRI LANKA
Amangalla

ST. KITTS & NEVIS
☑ Four Seasons | *Nevis*

ST. LUCIA
Sandals Grande
Sandals Regency

SWITZERLAND
Badrutt's Palace | *St. Moritz*
Gstaad Palace | *Gstaad*
Kulm | *St. Moritz*
La Réserve | *Geneva*
Lausanne Palace | *Lausanne*
Mont Cervin Palace | *Zermatt*
☑ Victoria-Jungfrau | *Interlaken*

TAIWAN
Sherwood | *Taipei*

THAILAND
☑ Banyan Tree | *Phuket*
Chiva-Som | *Hua Hin*
Conrad | *Bangkok*
Evason | *Phuket*
Metropolitan | *Bangkok*
Napasai | *Koh Samui*
Plaza Athénée | *Bangkok*
Sheraton Grande | *Bangkok*

TURKEY
Çiragan Palace | *Istanbul*
Marmara | *Bodrum*

TURKS & CAICOS
Parrot Cay

UNITED ARAB EMIRATES
☑ Burj Al Arab | *Dubai*
Grosvenor House | *Dubai*
Park Hyatt | *Dubai*
Ritz-Carlton | *Dubai*

UNITED KINGDOM – ENGLAND
Chewton Glen | *Hampshire*
Claridge's | *London*
Dorchester | *London*
Four Seasons Canary Wharf | *London*
Holbeck Ghyll | *Cumbria*
K West | *London*
Royal Crescent | *Cotswolds*
Sanderson | *London*
Stoke Park | *London*
Whatley Manor | *Cotswolds*

UNITED KINGDOM – SCOTLAND
☑ Gleneagles | *Perthshire*
☑ Westin Turnberry | *Ayrshire*

UNITED STATES
☑ Bellagio | *Las Vegas*
Beverly Hills Hotel | *Los Angeles*
Biltmore | *Miami*
Caesars Palace | *Las Vegas*
Crescent Court | *Dallas/Ft. Worth*
Disney's Grand | *Los Angeles*
Disney's Grand | *Orlando*
Fairmont | *Washington, DC*
☑ Fairmont Kea Lani | *Hawaii*
Fairmont Olympic | *Seattle*
Fisher Island | *Miami*
Four Seasons | *Atlanta*
☑ Four Seasons | *Dallas/Ft. Worth*
☑ Four Seasons | *Miami*
☑ Four Seasons Resort | *Phoenix/Scottsdale*
☑ Four Seasons Wailea | *Hawaii*
Grand Wailea Resort | *Hawaii*
Green Valley Ranch | *Las Vegas*
Grove Isle | *Miami*
Hilton Checkers | *Los Angeles*
JW Marriott | *Las Vegas*
JW Marriott | *Orlando*
☑ Kahala | *Hawaii*
☑ Mandarin Oriental | *Miami*

SPECIAL FEATURES

☒ Mandarin Oriental | *New York City*

Mandarin Oriental | *Washington, DC*

Mondrian | *Los Angeles*

New York Palace | *New York City*

☒ Ritz-Carlton | *Las Vegas*

Ritz-Carlton | *New Orleans*

☒ Ritz-Carlton | *Orlando*

☒ Ritz-Carlton | *San Francisco*

Ritz-Carlton | *Washington, DC*

☒ Ritz-Carlton Kapalua | *Hawaii*

☒ Ritz-Carlton Key Biscayne | *Miami*

Ritz-Carlton South Beach | *Miami*

☒ Royal Palms | *Phoenix/Scottsdale*

Salish Lodge | *Seattle*

☒ Sanctuary/Camelback Mtn. | *Phoenix/Scottsdale*

Victor | *Miami*

Waldorf-Astoria | *New York City*

Willows Lodge | *Seattle*

☒ NEW Wynn | *Las Vegas*

URUGUAY
☒ Four Seasons | *Carmelo*

VIETNAM
Evason Hideaway | *Nha Trang*

SPA FACILITIES: MINERAL SPRINGS

CANADA
Fairmont Banff Springs | *Canadian Rockies*

Fairmont Empress | *Victoria*

CHINA
St. Regis | *Beijing*

COSTA RICA
Tabacón Grand Spa | *Arenal*

CZECH REPUBLIC
Grand/Pupp | *Karlovy Vary*

FRANCE
Évian Royal Palace | *Haute-Savoie*

GREECE
Grande Bretagne | *Athens*

INDIA
Taj Lands End | *Mumbai (Bombay)*

ITALY
Principe di Savoia | *Milan*

JAPAN
Four Seasons/Chinzan-so | *Tokyo*

Four Seasons/Marunouchi | *Tokyo*

NEPAL
Le Méridien | *Kathmandu*

POLAND
Marriott | *Warsaw*

PORTUGAL
Penha Longa | *Sintra*

SPAIN
Omm | *Barcelona*

ST. KITTS & NEVIS
☒ Four Seasons | *Nevis*

SWITZERLAND
Kempinski Grand | *St. Moritz*

UNITED KINGDOM – ENGLAND
Bovey Castle | *Devon*

Chewton Glen | *Hampshire*

Royal Crescent | *Cotswolds*

UNITED STATES
Grove Isle | *Miami*

Rittenhouse | *Philadelphia*

SWIMMING POOLS, PRIVATE

ANGUILLA
Cap Juluca

Malliouhana

ANTIGUA
Jumby Bay

AUSTRALIA
Bedarra Island | *Great Barrier Reef*

☒ Hayman Island | *Great Barrier Reef*

Palazzo Versace | *Gold Coast*

Voyages Lizard Island | *Great Barrier Reef*

BAHAMAS
Four Seasons

BARBADOS
Coral Reef Club

Crane

BELIZE
Blancaneaux | *San Ignacio*
Turtle Inn | *Placencia*

BERMUDA
Cambridge Beaches

BOTSWANA
Abu Camp | *Okavango Delta*
Chobe Game Lodge | *Chobe National Park*
Vumbura Plains | *Okavango Delta*

BRITISH VIRGIN ISLANDS
Guana Island | *Virgin Gorda*
Little Dix Bay | *Virgin Gorda*
Peter Island | *Peter Island*

CAYMAN ISLANDS
Hyatt Regency

FRANCE
Château/Chèvre D'Or | *Côte d'Azur*
Château de Marçay | *Loire*
Évian Royal Palace | *Haute-Savoie*
La Réserve/Beaulieu | *Côte d'Azur*
Le Bristol | *Paris*
Le Chateau d'Artigny | *Loire*
Murano Urban | *Paris*

FRENCH POLYNESIA
Bora Bora Lagoon | *Bora Bora*

GREECE
🆉 Blue Palace Resort | *Crete*
Elounda Beach | *Crete*
Elounda Mare | *Crete*
Grecotel | *Mykonos*
Vedema Resort | *Santorini*

GRENADINES
Cotton House | *Mustique*

INDIA
Leela Goa | *Goa*
🆉 Oberoi Udaivilas | *Rajasthan*

INDONESIA
🆉 Amandari | *Bali*
🆉 Amanjiwo | *Borobudur*
🆉 Amankila | *Bali*
🆉 Amanusa | *Bali*
🆉 Como Shambala | *Bali*
🆉 Four Seasons Jimbaran Bay | *Bali*

Four Seasons Sayan | *Bali*
Legian | *Bali*
Puri Wulandari | *Bali*
Viceroy Bali | *Bali*

ITALY
Capri Palace | *Amalfi Coast*
Excelsior Palace | *Portofino*
Il Pellicano | *Porto Ercole*
Principe di Savoia | *Milan*
San Domenico | *Sicily*

JAMAICA
Half Moon | *Montego Bay*
Round Hill | *Montego Bay*
Tryall Club | *Montego Bay*

LUXEMBOURG
Le Royal

MALAYSIA
Pangkor Laut | *Langkawi*

MALDIVES
NEW W Retreat & Spa

MAURITIUS
Le Prince Maurice
Le Saint Géran

MEXICO
Camino Real | *Mexico City*
Casa Del Mar | *Baja Peninsula*
🆉 Esperanza | *Baja Peninsula*
Fiesta Americana | *Baja Peninsula*
Ikal del Mar | *Playa del Carmen*
Las Brisas | *Acapulco*
Las Brisas | *Ixtapa*
Las Hadas | *Manzanillo*
Maroma | *Cancún*
NH Krystal | *Puerto Vallarta*
Villa del Sol | *Zihuatanejo*

MONACO
Metropole | *Monte Carlo*

MOROCCO
Ksar Char-Bagh | *Marrakech*

NAMIBIA
Little Ongava Lodge | *Ongava Game Reserve*

NEW ZEALAND
🆉 Kauri Cliffs | *Kerikeri*

PORTUGAL
Quinta do Lago | *Algarve*
Tivoli Palácio/Seteais | *Sintra*

SEYCHELLES
Banyan Tree
North Island

SOUTH AFRICA
Cellars-Hohenort | *Cape Town*
Kwandwe/Game Reserve | *Benmore*
Le Quartier Francais | *Franschhoek*
🔲 Londolozi | *Kruger Area*
Ngala/Game Reserve | *Kruger Area*
Phinda/Game Reserve | *Kruger Area*
Sabi Sabi | *Kruger Area*
🔲 Singita | *Kruger Area*
Tsala Treetop Lodge | *Plettenberg Bay*

SPAIN
La Residencia | *Mallorca*
Majestic | *Barcelona*
Marbella Club | *Costa del Sol*

SRI LANKA
Amanwella

ST. BARTS
Carl Gustaf
Eden Rock
Guanahani & Spa
Le Toiny

ST. LUCIA
Windjammer Landing

THAILAND
🔲 Amanpuri | *Phuket*

UNITED STATES
Fairmont | *Chicago*
🔲 Fairmont Kea Lani | *Hawaii*
🔲 Four Seasons Resort | *Phoenix/ Scottsdale*
Jefferson | *Washington, DC*
🔲 Ritz-Carlton | *Las Vegas*
Setai | *Miami*

TRENDY PLACES

ANGUILLA
Cap Juluca
Malliouhana
St. Regis

ANTIGUA
Carlisle Bay

ARGENTINA
🔲 Alvear Palace | *Buenos Aires*

AUSTRALIA
Adelphi | *Melbourne*
Palazzo Versace | *Gold Coast*
Park Hyatt | *Sydney*

BAHAMAS
Atlantis

BARBADOS
🔲 Sandy Lane

BELIZE
Blancaneaux | *San Ignacio*
Cayo Espanto | *San Pedro*
Turtle Inn | *Placencia*

BERMUDA
Reefs

BOTSWANA
🔲 Mombo Camp | *Okavango Delta*

BRAZIL
Copacabana Palace | *Rio de Janeiro*
Emiliano | *São Paulo*
Unique | *São Paulo*

CANADA
NEW Adara | *Canadian Rockies*
Arc | *Ottawa*
Loews Hotel Vogue | *Montréal*
Opus | *Vancouver*
SoHo Metropolitan Hotel | *Toronto*
St-Paul Hotel | *Montréal*
Sutton Place | *Vancouver*
Wedgewood | *Vancouver*
NEW Westin Bear Mtn. | *Victoria*
Windsor Arms | *Toronto*
W Montreal | *Montréal*

CHINA
Le Méridien She Shan | *Shanghai*

CZECH REPUBLIC
NEW Mandarin Oriental | *Prague*

DENMARK
Skt. Petri | *Copenhagen*

FRANCE
Byblos | *Côte d'Azur*
Costes | *Paris*
du Petit Moulin | *Paris*
🅩 Four Seasons George V | *Paris*
L'Hotel | *Paris*
Martinez | *Côte d'Azur*
Montalembert | *Paris*
Murano Urban | *Paris*
Park Hyatt | *Paris*

FRENCH POLYNESIA
Le Méridien | *Bora Bora*
NEW St. Regis | *Bora Bora*

GERMANY
Park Hyatt | *Hamburg*
Raffles | *Hamburg*
25hours | *Hamburg*

GRENADINES
Cotton House | *Mustique*

INDONESIA
Four Seasons Sayan | *Bali*

IRELAND
Clarence | *Dublin*
Morrison | *Dublin*

ITALY
Ca'Pisani | *Venice*
🅩 Cipriani | *Venice*
de Russie | *Rome*
Gallery Hotel Art | *Florence*
Grand/Quisisana | *Amalfi Coast*
Savoy | *Florence*
Straf | *Milan*
St. Regis | *Rome*

MALAYSIA
Mandarin Oriental | *Kuala Lumpur*

MALDIVES
Four Seasons/Kuda Huraa
NEW W Retreat & Spa

MEXICO
Deseo | *Playa del Carmen*
🅩 Esperanza | *Baja Peninsula*
🅩 Four Seasons | *Punta Mita*
Habitá | *Mexico City*
W Mexico City | *Mexico City*

MONACO
Columbus Monaco | *Monte Carlo*
Hermitage | *Monte Carlo*

NEW ZEALAND
🅩 Blanket Bay | *Queenstown*

RUSSIA
Baltschug Kempinski | *Moscow*
Park Hyatt Ararat | *Moscow*

SAUDI ARABIA
Al Faisaliah | *Riyadh*

SOUTH AFRICA
Kwandwe/Game Reserve | *Benmore*

SPAIN
AC Santo Mauro | *Madrid*
Casa Camper | *Barcelona*
De Las Letras | *Madrid*
Marbella Club | *Costa del Sol*
Maria Cristina | *San Sebastián*
MiróHotel | *Bilbao*
Omm | *Barcelona*
Puerta America | *Madrid*
Westin Palace | *Madrid*

ST. BARTS
Isle de France
Le Toiny

ST. LUCIA
Ladera

SWEDEN
Berns Hotel | *Stockholm*
Hotel J | *Stockholm*
Rival | *Stockholm*

SWITZERLAND
Badrutt's Palace | *St. Moritz*
Baur au Lac | *Zurich*

TANZANIA
Mnemba Island | *Zanzibar*

THAILAND
Conrad | *Bangkok*
🅩 Four Seasons | *Chiang Mai*
Metropolitan | *Bangkok*

TURKS & CAICOS
Parrot Cay

UNITED ARAB EMIRATES
Grosvenor House | *Dubai*
🅩 One & Only | *Dubai*
Park Hyatt | *Dubai*

SPECIAL FEATURES

UNITED KINGDOM - ENGLAND

Berkeley | *London*
Blakes | *London*
Charlotte St. | *London*
Dorchester | *London*
Metropolitan | *London*
One Aldwych | *London*
Sanderson | *London*
St. Martins Lane | *London*

UNITED STATES

Z Bel-Air | *Los Angeles*
Z Bellagio | *Las Vegas*
Beverly Hills Hotel | *Los Angeles*
Beverly Wilshire | *Los Angeles*
Casa Del Mar | *Los Angeles*
Chambers | *New York City*
Chateau Marmont | *Los Angeles*
Fifteen Beacon | *Boston*
Z Four Seasons | *San Francisco*
Z Halekulani | *Hawaii*
InterContinental | *Atlanta*
Z Kahala | *Hawaii*
Z Mandarin Oriental | *Miami*
Z Mandarin Oriental | *New York City*
Mercer | *New York City*
Monaco | *Chicago*
Monaco | *Washington, DC*
Mondrian | *Los Angeles*
Palomar | *San Francisco*
Z Park Hyatt | *Chicago*
Z Peninsula | *Chicago*
Z Peninsula | *Los Angeles*
Raffles L'Ermitage | *Los Angeles*
Ritz-Carlton Buckhead | *Atlanta*
Shutters on the Beach | *Los Angeles*
Z NEW St. Regis | *San Francisco*
Victor | *Miami*
Vitale | *San Francisco*
Z Windsor Court | *New Orleans*
NEW W New Orleans | *New Orleans*
W Union Square | *New York City*
W Westwood | *Los Angeles*
Z NEW Wynn | *Las Vegas*
Zaza | *Dallas/Ft. Worth*

ALPHABETICAL
PAGE INDEX

Listings followed by (C) are chains. Names are followed by nearest major city and country. ⓩ indicates places with the highest ratings, popularity and importance.

ALPHA INDEX

ALPHA INDEX

ALPHA INDEX

ALPHA INDEX

ALPHA INDEX

ALPHA INDEX

ALPHA INDEX

ALPHA INDEX

ALPHA INDEX

subscribe to zagat.com

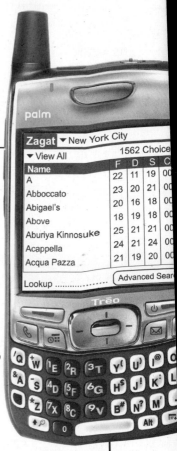